BAKER'S
Student
Encyclopedia
of
Music

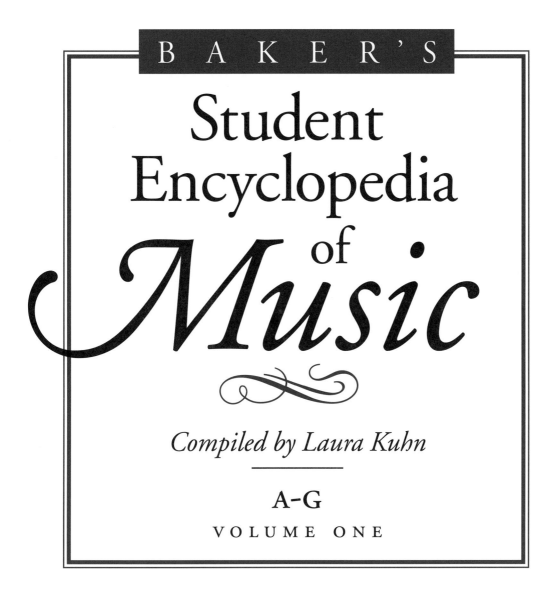

BAKER'S
Student
Encyclopedia
of
Music

Compiled by Laura Kuhn

A–G

VOLUME ONE

SCHIRMER BOOKS

An Imprint of Macmillan Library Reference USA

New York

Copyright © 1999 by Schirmer Books

SCHIRMER BOOKS
An Imprint of Macmillan Library Reference USA
1633 Broadway
New York, NY 10019

Library of Congress Catalog Card Number: 99-31758

Printed in the United States of America

Printing number
1   2   3   4   5   6   7   8   9   10

Library of Congress Cataloging-in-Publication Data
Baker's student encyclopedia of music / edited by Laura Kuhn
    p. cm.
    Includes index.
    ISBN 0-02-865315-7 (all). — ISBN 0-02-865415-3 (vol. 1). — ISBN 0-02-865416-1 (vol. 2). — ISBN 0-02-865421-8 (vol. 3)
1. Music Dictionaries. I. Kuhn, Laura Diane. II. Title: Student encyclopedia of music.
ML100.B26 1999
780′.3—dc21
                                                                99-31758
                                                                CIP

This paper meets the requirements of ANSI/NISO Z39.48-1992 (Permanence of Paper).

Contents

Foreword . . . .*vi*

Introduction to Musical Terminology . . . .*ix*

*Baker's Student Encyclopedia
of Music A–G* *1*

Index *I-1*

Foreword

Compiling a music encyclopedia is always a challenging task, first and foremost for the arduous process involved in the selection of materials to include. The end result should be comprehensive, concise, and informative, and geared appropriately in its selections to the reader it seeks to address. It should also be a balance between what is known and what might be learned, and, in the best of all possible worlds, cast in a form and in language that is a pleasure to read.

Compiling a music encyclopedia for students is particularly challenging, and particularly *now*, for at this point in historical time, youth are remarkably sophisticated when it comes to music, and in ways never dreamed of by their parents.

To be sure, music has long played a critical part of growing up. Friendships can be formed around favorite songs and artists, and attendance at a particular concert can be the focal point of a semester. Entire weekends can be passed listening to music, and participation in music ensembles, as either course requirement or extracurricular activity, can provide a measure of sanity for teens where none otherwise seems to exist. And nothing more than music seems to define a generation, or to distinguish one generation from another. Parents often cannot fathom the musical tastes of their teens, while at the same time they themselves may hear a song, years after the fact, that evokes memories of an entire, long-ago teenage life.

Today's youth are particularly sophisticated when it comes to music in large part because of sheer access. Never before has so much music been available, relatively inexpensively and in so many forms: recorded, online, and live. Students today have easy access not only to classical and popular music, in all of its myriad genres, but to traditional and world musics as well—Indian, African, Indonesian, Japanese—in an amazing array. And composing music has never been easier, through the wide variety of sequencing software currently available for use on home computers and MIDI systems, themselves now commonplace. Students across America are composing music without the customary and often time-consuming intermediate step of learning to read and write traditional notation. This hands-on participation with the actual building blocks of music creates inroads to a kind of understanding of music not easily available to the nonparticipant.

This exposure and participation cause the youth of today to be more sophisticated with respect to music: less hierarchical in their thinking, less privileging of one type of music over another, and also more thoughtful and confident about what they know. As a result, they are also more demanding about the kind of new information they seek and the manner in which it is provided. The present *Baker's Student Encyclopedia of Music*, in three richly illustrated volumes, means to rise to the challenge of that sophistication by presenting its readers with the most accurate, comprehensive, and up-to-date entries on music and musicians across historical time and across stylistic boundaries. Entries on well-known historical figures—John Cage, Claude Debussy, Frédéric Chopin, Sergei Rachmaninoff, among countless others—have been included and brought up to date, of course. But also included are the artists less often included in the standard dictionary format that students want to know more about, ranging from Eric Clapton, Sun Ra, and Marvin Gaye, to Ice Cube, R.E.M., and Public Enemy. Musical styles, genres, and terms, too, have been expanded to include not only those tried and true from the Western European classical past—counterpoint, chromaticism, atonality, and sonata form—but also the latest terms and trends of the contemporaneous present, ranging from rock, jazz, and reggae, to hip-hop, rap, and New Age.

All of this is cast in a language that means to maintain the eloquence and humor that have for nearly 100 years made Nicolas Slonimsky's name and his numerous *Baker's* volumes the music reference of choice. Entries, illustrations, and interesting sidebar facts and anecdotes, all amply cross-referenced throughout, combine in *Baker's Student Encyclopedia of Music* to provide readers of all ages with an easy-to-use reference guide to all things musical.

LAURA KUHN
New York City, March 1999

Introduction to Musical Terminology

ELEMENTS OF NOTATION

Notation is a system of signs used in writing music. The written signs for the time value (length, duration) of musical tones are called *notes*. The written signs for pauses (intervals of silence) between the tones are called *rests*.

NOTES AND RESTS

Whole note ○ Half note ♩ Quarter note ♩

Whole rest ▬ Half rest ▬ Quarter rest ⅊

Eighth note ♪ 16th note ♬ 32nd note ♬ 64th note ♬

Eighth rest ♩ 16th rest ♩ 32nd rest ♩ 64th rest ♩

Whole note ○ = 2 ♩, or 4 ♩, or 8 ♪, or 16 ♪, or 32 ♪, or 64 ♪

Half note ♩ = 2 ♩, or 4 ♪, or 8 ♪, or 16 ♪, or 32 ♪

Quarter note ♩ = 2 ♪, or 4 ♪, or 8 ♪, or 16 ♪

Eighth note ♪ = 2 ♪, or 4 ♪, or 8 ♪

Sixteenth note ♪ = 2 ♪, or 4 ♪

Thirty-second note ♪ = 2 ♪

THE STAFF

The *staff* consists of five parallel horizontal lines. Notes are written on the lines, or in the spaces between. For higher or lower tones, additional short lines are provided, called *leger lines.*

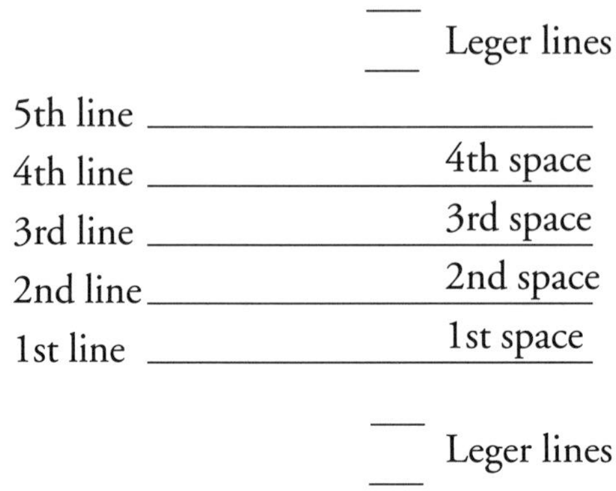

Leger lines

5th line
4th line — 4th space
3rd line — 3rd space
2nd line — 2nd space
1st line — 1st space

Leger lines

THE CLEFS

A *clef* is a sign written at the head (beginning) of the staff to fix the position of one note. The most common clefs are:

the *G* clef (treble clef)  fixing the place of the note g^1

the *F* clef (bass clef)  fixing the place of the note f

the *C* clef, which designates a line on the staff as *c1* (middle C). It acquires a different name according to the line used:

Tenor Clef   Alto Clef    Soprano Clef

THE SCALES

The staff and clefs together fix the pitch of the notes, showing whether they are high or low. A series of eight successive notes on the staff forms what is called a *scale*. To name the notes of the scale, we use the first seven letters of the alphabet, *A B C D E F G*. Scales are named after the notes on which they begin, which is called the *keynote*. The scale of *C*, written in whole notes, in the bass and treble clefs, is as follows:

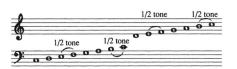

The *C* written on the leger line just below the treble staff and just above the bass staff, is called middle C.

The notes in the same vertical line are of the same pitch and have the same name. For ordinary purposes, any note marked *C (c)* is called simply "*C.*" But, in order to fix the place which any given note occupies among all the others (that is, to fix its "absolute pitch"), the whole range of musical tones is divided into sections of seven notes each, called "octaves," and lettered and named as shown:

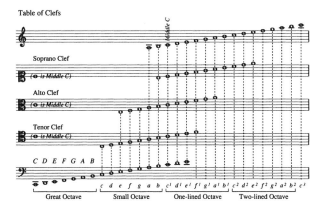

PITCH REGISTERS

In order to indicate the exact location of a note in the total gamut, the following system is used in this encyclopedia:

CHROMATIC SIGNS

The *chromatic signs* are set before notes to raise and lower their pitch.

The *sharp* ♯ raises its note a semitone;

The *flat* ♭ lowers its note a semitone;

The *natural* ♮ restores its note to the natural pitch on the staff (without chromatic signs);

The double sharp × raises its note two semitones;

The double flat ♭♭ lowers its note two semitones;

The sign ♮♯ restores a double sharped note to a sharped note;

The sign ♮♭ restores a double flatted note to a flatted note.

THE INTERVALS

An *interval* is the difference in pitch between two notes. In measuring an interval, it is customary to take the lower note as the basis, and to measure up to the higher note. When the two notes are exchanged and the measurement is made downward, the interval is called "inverted."

DIATONIC INTERVALS OF THE MAJOR SCALE

ALL STANDARD INTERVALS AND THEIR INVERSIONS

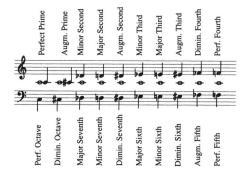

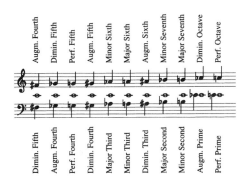

THE KEYS

A *key* is a scale employed harmonically, that is, employed to form chords and successions of chords. On the keynote *C,* or on any other note, two different species of scale or key may be built up:

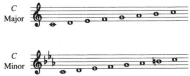

Such a key or scale is called *major* when its third and sixth are major intervals. It is *minor* when its third and sixth are minor intervals. The succession of intervals in every major key is the same as that in *C* major; in every minor key, as in *C* minor. To adjust the intervals properly, chromatic signs are employed, as shown below.

TABLE OF MAJOR KEYS

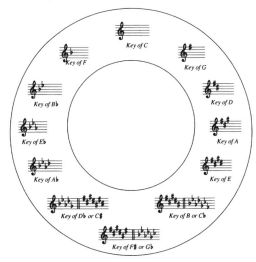

It will be seen, on passing round the circle in either direction, that the keynotes of the successive keys always follow each other at the interval of a perfect fifth; hence, this circle of keys, ending where it began, is called the *circle of fifths*.

CHORDS

A *chord* is formed by a succession of from three to five different tones, built up in intervals of diatonic thirds from a given tone, or *root*. A three-tone chord is a *triad*; a four-tone chord is a *seventh chord* (chord of the *seventh*); a five-tone chord is a *ninth chord* (chord of the *ninth*).

Triads in Major

Triads in Minor

Seventh Chords in Major

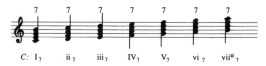

Seventh Chords in Minor

Ninth chords

When the root of the chord is the lowest tone, the chord is in the fundamental position; when some other tone is the lowest, the chord is inverted. Each triad has two inversions; each seventh chord has three.

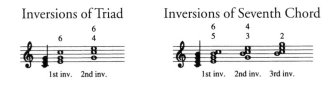

Inversions of Triad

Inversions of Seventh Chord

The first inversion of a triad is called a 6 chord.

The second inversion of a triad is called a $^{6}_{4}$ chord.

The first inversion of a seventh chord is called a $^{6}_{5}$ chord.

The second inversion of a seventh chord is called a $^{4}_{3}$ chord.

The third inversion of a seventh chord is called a 2 chord.

TIME SIGNATURES

The *time signature* appears after the clef, at the beginning of a movement; the lower figure shows the *kind* of notes taken as the unit of measure, while the upper figure shows the number of these notes that can fit a measure, and the groupings of beats.

For instance: $\frac{3}{4}$ (3/4 time) means "three quarter notes to the measure":

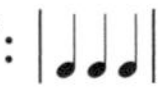

$\frac{12}{16}$ (12/16 time) means "twelve sixteenth notes to the measure":

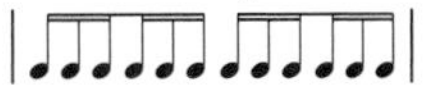

COMPARATIVE TABLE OF TEMPO MARKS

CLASS I

Indicating a Steady Rate of Speed

Largo (broad, stately)
  Largamente
  Larghetto
Grave (heavy, dragging)
Lento (slow)
  Adagissimo
Adagio (slow, tranquil)
  Adagietto
  Andantino

Group I
General signification of terms is SLOW.

Andante (moving, going along)
    Moderato   *Group II*
    Allegretto   General
    Allegramente   signification
Allegro (brisk, lively) [con moto,   of terms is
    vivace] [agitato, appassionato]   FAST.
Presto (rapid) [con fuoco, veloce]
    Prestissimo

CLASS II
Indicating Acceleration

Accelerando	(with increasing rapidity)
Stringendo Affrettando Incalzando	(swiftly accelerating, usually with a crescendo)
Doppio movimento	(twice as fast)
Più mosso Più moto Veloce	(a steady rate of speed, faster than preceding movement)

CLASS III
Indicating a Slackening in Speed

Rallentando Ritardando Allargando Tardando Slentando Strascinando	(gradually growing slower)
Molto meno mosso	($\bullet = \bullet$ del movimento precedente)(half as fast)
Ritenuto Meno mosso Meno moto	(a steady rate of speed, *slower* than preceding movement)

Calando
Deficiendo
Mancando   (growing slower and softer)
Morendo
Sminuendo
Smorzando

DYNAMIC MARKINGS

ITALIAN TERM	ABBREVIATION	MEANING
piano	*p*	soft
pianissimo	*pp*	very soft
mezzo piano	*mp*	moderately soft
mezzo forte	*mf*	moderately loud
forte	*f*	loud
fortissimo	*ff*	very loud
crescendo	*cresc.*	becoming gradually louder
diminuendo *descrescendo*	*dim.* or *dimin.* *descresc.*	becoming gradually softer
forte-piano	*fp*	loud, suddenly followed by soft
forzato *sforzando*	*fz* *sf* or *sfz*	forcing the tone, accenting the note
sforzando-piano	*sfp*	accent, suddenly followed by piano

A composer may increase the number of *f*s or *p*s, i.e. *fff*, extremely loud, or *pppppp* very, very soft.

To many of the above markings, composers often add other modifying words, such as:

ITALIAN TERM	MEANING	EXAMPLE
più	more	*più piano* (more softly)
meno	less	*meno forte* (less loud)
molto	much, very	*crescendo molto* (getting much louder)
non troppo	not too much	*non troppo piano* (not too soft)
subito	suddenly	*subito forte* (suddenly loud)
poco a poco	little by little	*poco a poco ritardando* (slowing little by little)

The following signs are frequently used over a musical passage to indicate crescendo and decrescendo, respectively:

crescendo   decrescendo

<   >

A

A (Eng., Ger., Fr., It., Sp., *la*). 1. The sixth note of the C-major scale. The frequency for A above middle C is 440 cycles (vibrations) per second. 2. In some methods of musical analysis, uppercase *A* stands for the A-major triad, lowercase *a* for the a-minor triad. 3. The note used for tuning an orchestra, usually given out by the oboe because the oboe is the least affected by humidity or other weather conditions of all pitched instruments.

a cappella (It., as in chapel). Performed in the church style; choral singing without instrumental accompaniment. Generally, any unaccompanied vocal performance.

ăh căhp-pel′lăh

A major. A key often associated with springtime. For example, FELIX MENDELSSOHN's *Spring Song,* from the *Songs without Words* (op.62), is in this key. His *Italian* Symphony (No. 4) is in A major, as is PIOTR ILYICH TCHAIKOVSKY's *Italian Capriccio,* because Italy was associated with sun and spirit. LUDWIG VAN BEETHOVEN's most joyful symphony, No. 7, is also in A major.

A minor. The key of resignation. For this reason, few symphonies are set in it. One notable exception is GUSTAV MAHLER's Symphony No. 6, a work of mental depression in which Mahler wrestles with fate.

ABA. A symbolic representation of three-part or TERNARY FORM, in which the first section (A) is repeated after the second (B). Because many classical songs and arias follow this formula, ABA is also known as SONG FORM.

Abbado, Claudio, outstanding Italian conductor; b. Milan, June 26, 1933. Abbado received early music training from

A minor—an introspective and essentially pessimistic key—suits the Russian composer Tchaikovsky perfectly. His Piano Trio opens with a phrase on the cello in A minor, and it comes nearest to the sound of sobbing in music. Tchaikovsky dedicated the work to the memory of his friend NIKOLAI RUBINSTEIN, director of the Moscow Conservatory.

PEOPLE IN MUSIC

1

Claudio Abbado, 1980. (Hulton-Deutsch Collection/ Corbis) ▶

his father, then enrolled in the Milan Conservatory, graduating in 1955 in piano. He made his conducting debut in Trieste, Italy, in 1958 and made his American conducting debut in N.Y. on Apr. 7, 1963. Abbado has subsequently conducted many major orchestras around the world. In 1989 he was named artistic director of the Berlin Philharmonic. Abbado has conducted distinguished performances ranging from the Classical era to the most modern works. His brother Marcello Abbado (b. Milan, Oct. 7, 1926) is a respected pianist and composer.

Abduction from the Seraglio, The (*Die Entführung aus dem Serail*). Opera by WOLFGANG AMADEUS MOZART, 1782. A young woman is captured by a Turkish pasha. A youth in love with her tries to rescue her, but his attempt is foiled by the wily pasha, who yields in the finale to a sudden generous impulse and lets her go with her lover. Mozart cleverly uses "Turkish" tunes and rhythms, along with exotic rhythm instruments, to give the score an "Oriental" feeling.

Abravanel, Maurice, distinguished Greek-born American conductor; b. Salonika, Greece, Jan. 6, 1903. He was taken to Switzerland at the age of 6, then to Berlin, where he studied composition with Kurt Weill. When the Nazis came to power in 1933, Abravanel moved to Paris and conducted ballet, and settled in the U.S. three years later. After conducting at N.Y.'s Metropolitan Opera, for Broadway musicals, and at the Chicago Opera Company, Abravnel became

PEOPLE IN MUSIC

conductor of the Utah Symphony Orchestra in Salt Lake City in 1947. In the 32 years of his tenure, he built it into one of the finest symphony orchestras in the U.S. and introduced many modern works into its repertoire. In 1976 he underwent open-heart surgery; he retired in 1979.

absolute music/abstract music. Musical work that has no program or any other nonmusical subject. "Abstract music" is a 20th-century term for musical works that, like ABSOLUTE music, have no "program." These works are usually short, with quirky rhythms and few recognizable melodies.

Compare PROGRAM MUSIC.

Academic Festival **Overture.** JOHANNES BRAHMS composed this work as a "thank you" for the honorary doctoral degree given to him by the University of Breslau in 1879. The overture is based on student songs, some humorous, some sentimental.

accidental. A note that falls outside the key signature. For example, a C sharp occurring in a melody written in the key of C would be an accidental; however, it would not be an accidental in a melody written in A major. Sharps, flats, naturals, double sharps, and double flats are the accidentals commonly used.

accompaniment. Any part or parts (chords, other harmonic units) that attend or support the voices or instruments that carry the principal part or parts in a composition. For example, in a popular song, the melody is the principal or main part and the chords that accompany it the secondary or supporting one. Accompaniments can be added to a composition by some other person than its original composer. In modern classical music, accompaniment transcends its traditional supporting role and becomes an integral part of the entire composition.

accordion. A musical instrument patented by Cyrillus Demian of Vienna in 1829. The most common accordion today has a piano-style keyboard on one end (on which the

Modern composers are not always strictly logical in their use of accidentals. CHARLES IVES scolded a copyist for trying to correct a seemingly wrong accidental by scribbling in the margin of his manuscript: "Please don't correct the wrong notes. The wrong notes are right." But NIKOLAI RIMSKY-KORSAKOV took offense when his Russian copyist put a question mark over an obviously wrong accidental: "I am not somebody like RICHARD STRAUSS or DEBUSSY, to put in wrong notes deliberately. So fix it!"

MUSICAL INSTRUMENT

Accordian players. (Hulton-Deutsch Collection/Corbis) ▶

Panpipes consist of a group of reeds arranged in a row, and the player blows into the end of a reed to play a note. Using your knowledge of acoustics, which pipe do you think plays a lower note: the short, thin one on the right end or the long, fat one on the left end?

The longer, thicker pipe would sound a lower note because of the shape of the air column.

player plays the melody) and buttons that provide chordal accompaniment on the other. A set of bellows is opened and closed to provide the air power that sets the reeds inside the instrument into vibration, thus producing the musical sound. The accordion is associated with many different styles of music, including Polish polka bands and the Cajun and zydeco bands of Louisiana. *See also* CONCERTINA.

acoustics (Grk., audible). The study of how sound is produced. A note can be produced in many different ways: common among musical instruments are a vibrating string (as on a guitar or violin), the air inside a pipe (the pipe of an organ), a stretched membrane or head (a drum), or a vibrating bar or piece of metal (a bell or vibraphone).

For stringed instruments, the actual note produced depends on the string's overall length and how tightly it is stretched; if the thickness and tautness of a string remain the same, the frequency of vibrations decreases with its length. If a string is set in motion with a greater force so that the amplitude of its vibrations is increased, then the resulting sound becomes louder without changing the pitch.

The length and width of an air column determines the note it produces. For example, a long, fat organ pipe produces a lower pitch or note than a short, thin one.

4

In drums, the smaller and tighter the membrane, the higher the pitch. That's why kettledrums have a deeper tone than tambourines, for example.

In bells, the larger and thicker the bell, the lower the note.

Each string or air column naturally divides itself into component parts to produce overtones, or PARTIALS. Theoretically, each complete vibration produces also two vibrations of ½ that of the sounding body, three vibrations of ½ that of the sounding body, and so on; these partials have the potential to be audible.

Generally, the simpler the fraction produced by the divided string, the more musically pleasing is the interval created by the overtone. When a string is divided into two (½, or 2:1), the note that is heard is one octave higher than the original tone. Other common intervals are the perfect fifth (⅔, or 3:2), the perfect fourth (¾, or 4:3), and the major third (⅘, or 5:4). This theoretically infinite group of intervals comprises the HARMONIC SERIES of intervals.

acoustics, architectural. It is important that a concert hall—or any place where music is performed—be properly designed so that the music can be heard in proper balance, no matter where an audience member is sitting. Everything from the curtains in the room to the floor of the stage, the height of the ceiling, the number of lights and baffles, etc., can contribute to the total balance of sound.

act (It. *atto;* Ger. *Aufzug*). A primary division of an opera or scenic cantata. In opera, each act may be subdivided into several scenes or tableaux.

action. In keyboard instruments, the mechanism set in motion by the fingers, or by the feet (organ pedals). In the harp, the "action" (a set of pedals) does not directly produce the sound, but changes the key by shortening the strings by a semitone or whole tone.

action song. A children's song in which bodily movements depict the action of the words, such as folding the hands and closing the eyes to represent sleep, fluttering the fingers

The range of audible sounds for the human ear is between 16 and 25,000 cycles per second (cps), a cycle being one complete vibration of an oscillating string. Dogs hear sounds far above the human range; high-pitched whistles, inaudible to humans, are used by handlers to summon them.

For more than 2,000 years theorists have wrestled with this problem: 12 perfect fifths on the keyboard of the piano (or any instrument built on the tempered scale) is supposed to be identical to seven octaves. But this is an impossible equation, because two to the seventh power does not equal 3:2 to the 12th! Therefore, the acoustic perfection of the perfect fifth was sacrificed in order to fit twelve 3:2s into the compass of seven octaves; a similar adjustment was made in other intervals.

When the piano tuner tunes a "perfect fifth," it is actually slightly narrower (flatter) than a "pure" 3:2. Violinists and players of other string instruments, however, tune their strings in nontempered perfect fifths. If a violinist plays a fifth on the open strings and the piano accompanist plays the same fifth, a disagreeable discrepancy results.

It was not until the late CLASSIC period that acousticians finally abandoned all hope of reconciling the pure harmonic series with practical instruments, and EQUAL TEMPERAMENT became generally accepted.

PEOPLE IN MUSIC

downward to represent rain, crossing the arms in a circular movement to represent the sun, flapping the hands to imitate a bird in flight, etc. An example of this genre is *The Itsy Bitsy Spider.*

Acuff, Roy (Claxton), American country music singer, guitarist, and songwriter; b. Maynardville, Tenn., Sept. 15, 1903; d. Nashville, Dec. 23, 1992. Acuff was raised in the Tennessee mountains and originally hoped to be a professional baseball player. However, a bad case of sunstroke as a teenager left him bedridden; during his recovery he began to play the fiddle and later appeared as a singer and guitarist. Acuff formed a band in the early 1930s and began touring and appearing on radio. He made his first recordings in 1936 and two years later became a featured artist on Nashville's GRAND OLE OPRY radio program. Acuff became famous with his renditions of *The Great Speckled Bird, Wabash Cannonball,* and *Wreck on the Highway.* He also composed *Precious Jewel* and was active as a music publisher. In 1962 he became the first living musician to be elected to the Country Music Hall of Fame. In 1988 he celebrated his 50th anniversary at the Grand Ole Opry.

ăhd lĭ′bi-tŭm

ad libitum (Lat., at will; abbr. *ad. lib.;* Ger. *Nachgefallen*). 1. Employ the tempo or expression freely. 2. An indication that a vocal or instrumental part may be left out. *Cadenza ad libitum,* a cadenza that may be performed or not, or may have another substituted for it or improvised, at the performer's will.

Adagio for Strings. A 1938 transcription of the slow movement of SAMUEL BARBER's String Quartet (1930). It has become Barber's best-known piece and probably the most frequently played short work by any American. Because of its somber harmonies, it is often performed at funerals, including the services for President Franklin Delano Roosevelt in April 1945 as well as Barber's own funeral in January 1981.

PEOPLE IN MUSIC

Adam, Adolphe (-Charles), celebrated French opera and ballet composer; b. Paris, July 24, 1803; d. there, May 3,

1856. He studied piano, then attended the Paris Conservatory. Adam was a prolific composer of operas, writing two or more a season, with a total of 53 in all, many of which have been forgotten. However, Adam ranks with DANIEL-FRANÇOIS-ESPRIT AUBER as one of the creators of French opera, and he wrote expressive melodies that contributed to the dramatic development of his works. *Le Postillon de Longjumeau* (1836) and the comic opera *Si j'étais roi* (1852) are the best remembered. Despite his fame as an opera composer, Adam's most durable work is probably the ballet *Giselle* (1841), a perennial favorite to this day. The song *Cantique de Noël* (*O Holy Night*) also became popular. Unfortunately, Adam was a poor businessman; in 1847 he ventured into the field of management with the Opéra-National, which failed miserably and brought him to the brink of financial ruin. In 1849 he was appointed professor at the Paris Conservatory; he also traveled widely in Europe, visiting London, Berlin, and St. Petersburg.

Adam (Adan) **de la Halle** (Hale), called "Le Bossu d'Arras" (Hunchback of Arras); b. Arras, c. 1237; d. Naples, c. 1287. Adam was a famous trouvère, many of whose works have been preserved. The most interesting is a dramatic pastoral, *Le Jeu de Robin et de Marion* (1285), written for the Anjou court at Naples and resembling an OPÉRA COMIQUE in its plan. He was gifted in the dual capacity of poet and composer. Both simple melodies and harmonized works that he wrote have survived to today.

PEOPLE IN MUSIC

Adams, John (Coolidge), prominent American composer; b. Worcester, Mass., Feb. 15, 1947. Adams was raised in Vermont and New Hampshire. His father taught him clarinet, and he later took lessons with Felix Viscuglia, a member of the Boston Symphony Orchestra. He then entered Harvard College (B.A., 1969; M.A., 1971), where his principal teachers were DAVID DEL TREDICI and ROGER SESSIONS. Adams conducted the Bach Society Orchestra and was a substitute clarinetist with the Boston Symphony Orchestra and the Boston Opera Company. In 1969 he played the solo part in WALTER PISTON's Clarinet Concerto at Carnegie Hall in N.Y.

PEOPLE IN MUSIC

In 1971 Adams moved to San Francisco, where he worked as a composer and conductor. He was head of the composition department at the San Francisco Conservatory from 1971 to 1981, and in 1978 he became new music advisor to the San Francisco Symphony. From 1981 to 1985 he was also its composer-in-residence. In 1982 he was awarded a Guggenheim fellowship. From 1988 to 1990 he held the title of creative advisor to the St. Paul (Minnesota) Chamber Orchestra.

In his compositions Adams is a MINIMALIST, using spare harmonies and simple melodies and repeating short melodic MOTIVES. He is best known for his topical opera *Nixon in China* (1987), which brought him international attention. Several of its movements, e.g., *The Chairman Dances,* have become popular concert pieces. He followed it with another opera based on contemporary history, *The Death of Klinghofer* (1991). In 1995 he received the Grawemeyer Award of the University of Louisville for his Violin Concerto (1993).

Adams, John Luther, gifted American composer; b. Meridian, Miss., Jan. 23, 1953. He was influenced by the experimental practices of FRANK ZAPPA, EDGARD VARÈSE, MORTON FELDMAN, HENRY COWELL, and ANTON WEBERN. After studies with Leonard Stein and James Tenney at the California Institute for the Arts in Valencia, he moved to Alaska in 1975, where he played timpani in the Fairbanks Symphony Orchestra from 1982 to 1992.

Adams is also a devoted environmentalist and outdoorsman, and many of his works evoke the placid beauty of the Alaskan terrain. Among his most notable compositions are *Dream in White on White* for string quartet, harp, and string

PEOPLE IN MUSIC

John Adams. (Photo © Dennis Weeley) ▶

orchestra, in "white note" tonality (1992); *Earth and the Great Weather* (1993), a plotless opera that includes recorded sounds from nature and a recitation of Eskimo place-names; and *Clouds of Forgetting, Clouds of Unknowing* for orchestra (1990–95).

added seventh. A minor or major seventh added to the major triad. In jazz, the minor seventh (e.g., in the chord C, E, G, B♭) is one of the BLUE NOTES (along with the minor third). Depending on the context, the major seventh can be more or less pleasing when added to a closing tonic major triad.

added sixth. A sixth added to the major tonic triad, often at the end of a phrase, and treated as a consonance. First used by CLAUDE DEBUSSY and others early in the 20th century, the added-sixth chord (e.g., C, E, G, A) became extremely popular in JAZZ piano playing.

Adderley, "Cannonball" (Julian Edwin), African-American jazz alto saxophone player; b. Tampa, Fla., Sept. 15, 1928; d. Gary, Ind., Aug. 8, 1975. Adderley was one of the best-known jazz saxophonists of the 1950s and '60s, equally famous for his own bands and his work with trumpeter MILES DAVIS. He got his nickname from a mispronunciation of "cannibal," a reference to his large appetite. In 1956 he formed a group with his brother Nat (b. Tampa, Nov. 25, 1931), a cornetist. Cannonball was also featured on Miles Davis's famous *Kind of Blue* album in 1957. However, unlike Davis, whose music was an acquired taste, Adderley's own music drew on gospel-like melodies that were easy to remember and had foot-tapping beats. Among his best-known recordings were *African Waltz; Dis Here; Sermonette; Work Song; Jive Samba; Mercy, Mercy, Mercy; Walk Tall;* and *Suite Cannon.* Many of these pieces were hits on the pop and R&B charts, an unusual achievement for a jazz musician. Adderley's popularity diminished in the 1970s. In 1975 he suffered a stroke during a concert engagement and subsequently died.

PEOPLE IN MUSIC

Adeste Fideles (*O Come All Ye Faithful*). A popular hymn now sung at Christmastime. The Latin words are usually attributed to St. Bonaventura (13th cent.). The musical setting is dated much later and is variously ascribed to various composers. The English text was first published in London in 1760.

Adieux, Les. LUDWIG VAN BEETHOVEN's Piano Sonata in E♭ Major, op.81a. The full title is *Les Adieux, l'absence et le retour.* The French titles were given by Beethoven himself, who even added an alternative title, *Sonate caractéristique.* The title refers to a vacation taken by Archduke Rudolph, a friend of Beethoven. The opening theme imitates the notes of a coach horn (a descending three-note scale harmonized in "horn fifths": major third, perfect fifth, and minor sixth), the sound that would be heard before a trip. The second movement leads into the third without pause.

PEOPLE IN MUSIC

Adler, Kurt Herbert, notable Austrian-American conductor and operatic administrator; b. Vienna, April 2, 1905; d. Ross, Calif., Feb. 9, 1988. He studied at the Vienna Academy of Music and the University of Vienna. He made his debut as a conductor at the Max Reinhardt Theater in Vienna in 1925 and subsequently conducted at the Volksoper there, as well as in Germany, Italy, and Czechoslovakia. He served as assistant to ARTURO TOSCANINI at the Salzburg Festival in 1936. As the dark cloud of Nazism descended upon Central Europe, Adler moved to the U.S. and from 1938 to 1943 was on the staff of the Chicago Opera. He subse-

Kurt Adler, 1978. (Ira Nowinski/© Corbis)

▶

quently was appointed choirmaster (1943), artistic director (1953), and general director (1956) of the San Francisco Opera. After his retirement in 1981, he was made general director emeritus. Under his direction the San Francisco Opera prospered greatly, advancing to the foremost ranks of American opera theaters. In 1980 he was awarded an honorary knighthood by Queen Elizabeth II of England.

Adorno (born Wiesengrund), **Theodor,** significant German musician and philosopher; b. Frankfurt am Main, Sept. 11, 1903; d. Visp, Switzerland, Aug. 6, 1969. Adorno was one of the most influential 20th-century critics of music. Educated in Vienna, he became a professor at the University of Frankfurt in the 1920s. Later in the decade he returned to Vienna, where he edited an important journal on new music, *Anbruch* (1928–31). When the Nazis came to power, he left Germany, emigrating first to England and then the U.S., where he taught at Princeton University (1938–41) and then lived in California. He returned to Frankfurt in 1949 and became director of the Institut für Sozialforschung; that same year he published his best-known book, *Philosophy of the New Music.* He introduced ideas from Sigmund Freud's writings about human behavior and Karl Marx's about society into his studies of music.

PEOPLE IN MUSIC

Adriana Lecouvreur. FRANCESCO CILÈA's most famous opera, 1902, dealing with a historical figure, Adrienne Lecouvreur, an 18th-century Parisian actress who is involved in a love triangle. She is poisoned by a bouquet of lethal violets sent to her by a jealous lover.

aeolian harp or **lyre** (from Grk. *Aeolus,* god of wind). A stringed instrument sounded by the wind. It is a narrow wooden box with low bridges at either end, across which are stretched a number of gut strings. The harp is placed in an open window where a draft of air will sweep the strings. Modern wind chimes are another type of wind-driven instrument.

MUSICAL INSTRUMENT

Aeolian mode. *See* AUTHENTIC MODE(S).

aerophones (Grk., *aeros* + *phonos,* air sound). A classification of musical instruments that produce their sound by the vibration of air, including the accordion, pipe and reed organ families, flutes, brasses, and mouth-blown reed instruments.

Affects, Doctrine of. The relationship between music and human emotions. This theory dates back to Greek antiquity, when the relationship between music and soul was accepted as scientific fact.

During the RENAISSANCE (1550–1600), musical thinkers expanded this idea to include tempo (fast-slow), registers (high-low), and dynamics (loud-soft). For instance, faster pieces were linked to happier emotions, while slower pieces were more appropriate for funeral marches or other expressions of grief or sadness.

The major and minor keys have similar associations, major keys being "happier" than minor ones. One cannot imagine ROBERT SCHUMANN's *The Happy Farmer* in a minor key, or FRÉDÉRIC CHOPIN's *Funeral March* (from the op.35 Sonata) in a major key.

JOHANN SEBASTIAN BACH used these ideas in his compositions. In one piece, he set the words "Get up, Get up!" to an ascending group of notes; the climbing notes express the idea of rising. Similarly, the phrase "Follow me" is illustrated by a long ascending scale passage, and the fall into hell is punctuated by a drop of the diminished seventh.

A-flat major. A key of joyous celebration and human devotion. While easily played on the piano, it is more difficult for stringed instruments, and therefore is rarely if ever selected as the principal key for a large orchestral work. A♭ major describes a festive mood in ROBERT SCHUMANN's *Carnaval,* and it is used for a romantic theme in FRANZ LISZT's *Liebestraum.*

Africaine, L'. GIACOMO MEYERBEER's last opera, premiered posthumously, in 1865. The African of the title is Selika, the Malagasy whom Vasco da Gama brings back to his native Portugal from his African adventures. Becoming aware of the racial barrier, she sacrifices her life so that Vasco can marry his former white mistress. The opera takes nearly six hours to

The Greek word for *affect* is "pathos," which conveys the meaning of deep emotion. In medieval Latin treatises, the term *musica pathetica* was attached to music that represents emotions. The adjective *pathétique* still retains that meaning, as used in the subtitle of PIOTR ILYICH TCHAIKOVSKY's Symphony No. 6.

During the BAROQUE period (1600–1750), some musical philosophers actually drew comparative tables between states of mind and corresponding intervals, chords, tempos, and the like. One famous 18th-century music critic stated that "it is possible to give a perfect representation of the nobility of soul, love, and jealousy with simple chords and their progressions."

At the beginning of Shakespeare's play *Twelfth Night,* the lovesick Duke of Illyria states, "If music be the food of love, play on." The idea that love could be inspired by a musical theme draws directly from the doctrine of musical affect.

perform, but it attained tremendous popularity with sentimental audiences of the last third of the 19th century.

African music. Africa is a huge continent with many hundreds of peoples, with various cultures and traditions. The most clear separation occurs between the peoples who live north of the Sahara, who belong to Arabic cultures, and those who live in the sub-Saharan region, primarily of black heritage. Usually, the term *African music* is used to refer to the sub-Saharan regions. Even with that limitation, the term embraces many different cultures that perform music in a wide variety of styles. Nevertheless, some similarities can be drawn across the many different regions and cultures.

A common stereotype is that African music is primarily played on drums; and indeed, rhythm is a key part of African music. Unlike European compositions, which tend to have melody and harmony follow the same rhythm, African pieces often feature two or more rhythms played at the same time (called polyrhythm). These interlocking rhythms create much of the excitement and interest in the performance.

African melodies are generally short, repeated phrases. Again, two or more melodic parts may be performed at the same time, but the effect is not of harmony but of a shifting relationship. Africans favor a pentatonic (or five-note) scale. However, the singing is highly ornamented, with many microtones—or notes that fall between the usual scale steps—used to embellish the music. Many nonmusical sounds—grunts, groans, shouts, and other vocalizations—may also be heard.

Song texts are invocations to the gods of the village, laments when disaster strikes, and celebrations for important local events, marriages, or the inauguration of a new chief. There are hundreds of dialects among African tribes, and the language itself serves as a dynamic means of communication. Thus the unique clicks of the Bushmen and others may serve to mark the ending of a musical phrase. Intonation is of prime significance; a slight rise or drop in pitch may change the meaning of the phrase.

The most common African ensemble contains drums of various sizes, gourds with rattling beads attached as shakers,

At the end of the 20th century, Africa has become the source of a new musical art with great influence upon European and American musicians. Earlier in the century, Cuban avant-garde composers such as Alejandro García Caturla and Amadeo Roldán borrowed extensively from African music, as did Brazilians such as HEITOR VILLA-LOBOS and Marlos Nobre. Western musicians now go to Africa to learn their music. STEVE REICH took a summer course in African percussion techniques at the University of Ghana, and upon his return to the U.S. wrote a piece for voices and drums entitled *Drumming*. Conversely, African popular music has flourished with distinctive national and group-associated styles, incorporating a large dose of Western popular music and contributing significantly to world music.

metal bells, slit log drums, and various manufactured products. Characteristic instruments include the TALKING DRUM, the MBIRA, and the KORA with 21 strings. Animal horns are the most prominent AEROPHONES.

Afro-Pop Music. The wedding of traditional African vocal, instrumental, and composition styles with Western pop styles, particularly the electric instruments of rock and roll. Sometimes called "Afrobeat."

Age of Anxiety, The. Symphony No. 2 by LEONARD BERNSTEIN, for piano and orchestra, its title borrowed from a poem by W. H. Auden. The work portrays the unquiet mid-20th century by using a variety of techniques and styles, all enlivened by pungent rhythms. The work was first performed by the Boston Symphony Orchestra on Apr. 8, 1949, with Bernstein as piano soloist.

Agnus Dei. The fifth and usually last section of the Catholic High Mass ORDINARY, divided into two parts: *Agnus Dei* (Lamb of God) and *Dona nobis pacem* (Give us peace).

agogic (Grk., to lead). A slight deviation from the main rhythm in order to accentuate a note. This may allow melodically important notes to linger without disruption of the musical phrase. RUBATO is an agogical practice. In musical rhetoric, it is opposed to the concept of DYNAMICS, which provides accentuation by varying the degree of loudness.

Agon (Grk., competition). Ballet by IGOR STRAVINSKY, with choreography by George Balanchine, 1957. An abstract contest between groups of players matches the sharply delineated choreography.

aguinaldo. Spiritual Spanish song glorifying Jesus and the saints, almost invariably in TERNARY (THREE-PART) FORM. Also called an *adoración*.

Aida. Opera by GIUSEPPE VERDI, 1871, one of the most melodramatic of all time, written to the most tragic and most implausible of all libretti (scripts) ever contrived. Radames, commander of the ancient Egyptian army, falls in love with a captive Ethiopian princess, Aida. He inadvertently reveals a crucial military secret to her while her father, the king of Ethiopia, also captured anonymously, listens from behind the bushes. Amneris, the Egyptian king's daughter, who is affianced to Radames, discovers the treachery but is willing to save Radames if he relinquishes Aida. Radames refuses and, joined by Aida, is buried alive in a stone crypt.

Aida was commissioned for the inauguration of the Cairo Opera House. The outbreak of the Franco-Prussian War delayed the delivery of the costumes from Paris, however, and the production was postponed until Christmas Eve 1871. The premiere was spectacular, with shiploads of notables and music critics converging on Cairo; but the ever unsocial Verdi declined the invitation to attend. Egyptian scholars regarded *Aida* as quite inauthentic in its story and music, and it didn't enter the repertoire of the Cairo Opera House. Nevertheless, it has since become a worldwide favorite opera.

Aida trumpet. A long trumpet specially constructed for use in GIUSEPPE VERDI's opera *AIDA*. The original, manufactured in France, was called *trompette thébaine,* or "trumpet of Thebes." It produced only four notes: A♭, B♭, B♮, and C.

Air on the G String. Nickname of the Air from JOHANN SEBASTIAN BACH's Orchestral Suite No. 3, BWV 1068.

al fresco (It., in the open air). A description of outdoor concerts, operatic performances, and other events, usually free of charge.

alba (Prov., light of dawn). A Provençal morning song, popular with the TROUBADOURS, that corresponds to the serenade, or evening song. *See also* ALBORADA, AUBADE.

Albéniz, Isaac (Manuel Francisco), eminent Spanish composer; b. Camprodon, May 29, 1860; d. Cambo-les-Bains (Pyrenees), May 18, 1909. Albéniz was a child prodigy on

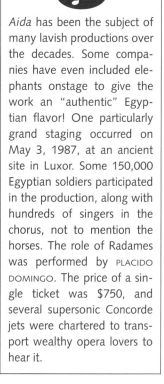

Aida has been the subject of many lavish productions over the decades. Some companies have even included elephants onstage to give the work an "authentic" Egyptian flavor! One particularly grand staging occurred on May 3, 1987, at an ancient site in Luxor. Some 150,000 Egyptian soldiers participated in the production, along with hundreds of singers in the chorus, not to mention the horses. The role of Radames was performed by PLACIDO DOMINGO. The price of a single ticket was $750, and several supersonic Concorde jets were chartered to transport wealthy opera lovers to hear it.

PEOPLE IN MUSIC

the piano. At age seven, after several years of studying at home in Spain, he was taken to Paris, where he studied with the famous teacher of GEORGES BIZET and CLAUDE DEBUSSY, Antoine-François Marmontel. Returning to Spain, he studied at the Madrid Conservatory during his teen years. Possessed by the spirit of adventure, Albéniz stowed away on a ship bound for Puerto Rico and eventually made his way to the southern U.S., where he earned a living by playing at places of entertainment.

Albéniz returned to Spain in the late 1870s and began several years of travel in Europe as a performing pianist; in 1880 he met FRANZ LISZT in Budapest. After a trip to South America he settled in Barcelona in 1883. Influenced by Liszt, who was a champion of his own country's music, he began to explore the national music of Spain. Almost all of his works are for piano, and all are inspired by Spanish folklore. He established the modern school of Spanish piano composition by drawing on native rhythms and melodies rather than by imitating French and Russian composers. His piano suite *Iberia* (1906–9) is a brilliant display of piano virtuosity.

In later life Albéniz stopped performing to focus on composition. Although strongly Spanish in spirit, at various times he lived in London, Paris, and Barcelona. In 1903 he moved to Nice. He later went to Cambo-les-Bains, where he died.

MUSICAL INSTRUMENT

Alberti bass. A type of harmonic accompaniment in an even tempo, traditionally for the left hand on the keyboard. Usually, the chords are played in sequence as a series of individual notes (i.e., as ARPEGGIOS). Popularized (if not invented) by the Italian singer, harpsichordist, and composer Domenico Alberti (b. Venice, 1710; d. Formio [or Rome], c. 1740). in the 18th century it was used extensively by FRANZ JOSEPH HAYDN, WOLFGANG AMADEUS MOZART, and LUDWIG VAN BEETHOVEN, among others.

PEOPLE IN MUSIC

Albinoni, Tomaso (Giovanni), Italian violinist and composer; b. Venice, June 8, 1671; d. there, Jan. 17, 1751. Between 1694 and 1740 he produced 53 operas, mostly in Venice, but his historical significance lies with his concertos, sonatas, and trio sonatas. JOHANN SEBASTIAN BACH admired Albinoni's music and made arrangements of two fugues taken from his trio sonatas. However, the famous Adagio for strings and organ is almost totally the work of Remo Giazotto, a 20th-century Italian musicologist.

albisifono (It.) Bass flute, an octave plus the pedal B below the standard flute, invented by Albisi, 1910. *See also* BASS FLUTE.

alborada (Sp.). Spanish morning song, originally performed on a primitive oboe with drum accompaniment as a morning serenade. *See* ALBA, AUBADE.

Alceste. Opera by Wilhelm Archibald GLUCK, based on the tragedy of Euripides, 1767. The mythological story deals with Alcestis, who volunteers to enter Hades in place of her dead husband; she is subsequently saved from the nether region by Hercules. Both JEAN-BAPTISTE LULLY and GEORGE FRIDERIC HANDEL wrote operas on the same story, but Gluck's remains the most important historically. In his preface to the published score, Gluck criticizes the emphasis that was then given to performers, scenery, and costumes in contemporary operatic productions. He believed that the dramatic and poetic content should be the most important consideration in any artistic stage work. Gluck's approach resulted in "reform opera," or a return to an emphasis on the music and story rather than grand productions.

aleatory music (from Lat. *alea,* a dice game). Composing or playing music by "chance." The composer or performer uses some random method of deciding which notes to play. Usually this is done by randomly selecting a series of numbers, either by throwing dice or using a computer program or some other method. These numbers then are assigned musical values (pitch, duration, rests, etc.), and a piece of music is created.

This random/chance method can be extended to the performance itself. The player may be given multiple options of phrases to play—or how long, how many times, or how loudly or softly they should be played.

MUSICAL INSTRUMENT

ăhl-bŏ-răh′dăh

Chance music is nothing new, having been practiced as early as the 18th century. WOLFGANG AMADEUS MOZART amused himself by writing a piece with numbered bars that could be assembled in a random order by throwing dice. Aleatoric music in modern times, however, is a more serious business, especially as cultivated by JOHN CAGE, who often used numbers derived from the Chinese *I Ching*. His classic aleatoric works include *Music of Changes* for piano. KARLHEINZ STOCKHAUSEN wrote numerous aleatoric pieces for piano and chamber ensemble, as did his many disciples in Europe and Japan.

Human or animal phenomena may also serve as primary data for chance composition. Configurations of fly specks on paper, curves and parabolas produced by geometry and trigonometry, flight patterns of birds over a specific location, etc., are all possible materials for aleatoric music. Mauricio Kagel made use of partially exposed photographic film for aleatoric composition.

See also PROBABILITY, INFORMATION THEORY, STOCHASTIC COMPOSITION, CYBERNETICS, EXPERIMENTAL MUSIC, COMPUTER MUSIC, EMPIRICAL MUSIC, and INDETERMINACY.

Alexander Nevsky. Cantata by SERGEI PROKOFIEV, first performed in Moscow on May 17, 1939. The score is based on the music Prokofiev wrote for a Sergei Eisenstein film depicting the Russian hero who routed German invaders in 1242.

Alexander's Feast, or The Power of Music. Oratorio by GEORGE FRIDERIC HANDEL, 1736, with a text derived from John Dryden's famous ode. The oratorio would have been forgotten were it not for Handel's decision to add the Concerto Grosso in C Major to the score, which became known as *The Celebrated Concerto from Alexander's Feast.*

Alexander's Ragtime Band. Song by IRVING BERLIN, 1910. The piece is not in ragtime but is a march, and there was no bandleader named Alexander. (However, "Alexander" was a common slang word at that time used to refer to a person of African-American descent.) Nonetheless, it popularized RAGTIME as a musical genre, particularly by introducing syncopated rhythms into popular song.

alleluia. The Latin form of the Hebrew *Hallelujah* (Praise the Lord!), an acclamation found throughout the Roman Catholic liturgy. In the High MASS the alleluia chant follows the GRADUAL. It is in three-part form, with a verse in the middle. When joy is not called for (e.g., in the REQUIEM MASS), the alleluia is replaced by the TRACT.

ăhl-lĕh-mähn′dăh   **allemanda** (It.), **allemande** (Fr.). 1. In the RENAISSANCE a German dance in $\frac{2}{4}$ time . 2. In the CLASSIC period a German dance in $\frac{3}{4}$ time, similar to the LÄNDLER. 3. A movement in the BAROQUE suite (usually the first or following a prelude) in $\frac{4}{4}$ time and moderate tempo (*andantino*). It is as much French in style as German.

Allison, Mose, American jazz singer, songwriter, and pianist; b. Tippo, Miss., Nov. 11, 1927. After serving in the U.S. Army he formed his own trio, then played with saxophonists STAN GETZ and GERRY MULLIGAN. His early songs were heavily blues-influenced. His mature songs were often satirical or cynical, and have been performed by Van Morrison, the Who, John Mayall, Georgie Fame, and Bonnie Raitt. Some of his best-known songs include *Seventh Son* (a hit for Johnny Rivers), *One of These Days, Parchman Farm, Tell Me Something, I Don't Want Much,* and *Perfect Moment.*

Almeida, Laurindo, Brazilian pop-jazz guitarist; b. São Paulo, Sept. 2, 1917; d. Van Nuys, Calif., July 26, 1995. Almeida brought Brazilian dance rhythms into jazz, preparing the way for its burst of popularity in the 1960s. He is best remembered for his performances with jazz saxophonist STAN KENTON in the 1950s, and for his solo recordings with small jazz-influenced ensembles.

Aloha oe. Song by Liliuokalani, the princess regent of Hawaii, 1878, while she was imprisoned by the Republican government of the island. The melody of the refrain is taken from an 1847 GEORGE F. ROOT ballad, *There's Music in the Air.*

alphorn (Ger. *Holztrompete*). A long wooden natural horn able to produce up to the 12th partial, used by shepherds in the Alps to call the sheep back home at sunset.

Alpine **Symphony.** A panoramic work by RICHARD STRAUSS, 1915. It depicts the ascent of an Alpine peak and a fearful thunderstorm near the summit. The thunder is depicted by chords containing all seven notes of the diatonic scale. Thunder and wind machines are included in the huge score for realistic effect.

PEOPLE IN MUSIC

PEOPLE IN MUSIC

JOHANNES BRAHMS notated an Alpine horn tune on a postcard he sent to CLARA SCHUMANN in 1868 with the words, "Hoch auf'm Berg, tief im Tal, grüss'ich dich viel tausendmal!" (High on the mountain, deep in the valley, I greet you many thousand times). Eight years later he made use of it in the famous horn solo in the last movement of his Symphony No. 1, which contains an approximation (F♯, 3½ octaves above the fundamental C) of the 11th partial.

Also sprach Zarathustra (Thus Spake Zarathustra). Symphonic poem by RICHARD STRAUSS, 1896, inspired by the philosophical poem by Nietzsche. Nietzsche's high-flown philosophy concerning religion, science, human emotions, and other lofty ideas is portrayed musically in this multipart work. Although damned by critics as chaotic in its early history, the work gained renown when its opening theme was used as a melodic signature for the celebrated Stanley Kubrick film *2001: A Space Odyssey* (1968).

alteration. A generic term for raising or lowering a note's pitch by means of an ACCIDENTAL.

altered chords. Chords containing chromatic alterations of harmonies normally expected within the tonality of the music; also called chromatic chords.

MUSICAL INSTRUMENT

---

althorn (U.S. Eng., Ger.). The B♭ alto saxhorn, patented by ADOLPHE SAX in 1845 and perfected by the Bohemian maker Václav Nervenv in 1859. Its original French name was *saxhorn ténor.*

alti naturali (It., naturally high ones). In the Middle Ages, male FALSETTO singers, as opposed to *voci artificiali,* the CASTRATI.

ăhl′tōh

alto (It., from Lat., *altus,* high). 1. The deeper of the two main divisions of women's or boys' voices, the SOPRANO being the higher; the standard alto range is from g to c^2; in voices of great range, down to d and up to f^2 or higher. Alto singers possess resonant chest voices. In opera, the parts of young swains who unsuccessfully court the heroine are often given to altos (TROUSER ROLES, e.g., Siebel in GOUNOD's *FAUST*). Also called *contralto.* 2. An instrument of similar compass, such as the alto saxhorn, alto saxophone, alto recorder, alto flute, and alto clarinet (basset horn). 3. The countertenor voice. 4. (Fr.) The viola; tenor violin.

Amahl and the Night Visitors. Opera by GIAN CARLO MENOTTI to his own libretto, broadcast on Christmas Eve 1951 by NBC Television. This is the first operatic work written for television, and its success was such that for several years it became an annual Christmas presentation. Suggested by Bosch's painting *The Adoration of the Magi,* the story deals with the crippled boy Amahl, who is miraculously healed when he gives his crutches to the visiting Wise Men as a gift for the Christ child.

amateur (It. *dilettante*). An art lover who, while possessing an understanding for and a certain practical knowledge of it, does not pursue it as a profession. It has come to mean persons who dabble in the arts without requisite skill or understanding. In the 18th century the word had a complimentary meaning. A flourishing society in Paris was called the Concerts des Amateurs. Composers dedicated their works to persons described as amateurs. Such publications could also be directed at a specific market; C. P. E. BACH entitled a set of clavier sonatas "à l'usage des dames" (for the use of ladies).

Chess players love music. The 18th-century composer FRANÇOIS-ANDRÉ DANICAN PHILIDOR earned a place in chess history by his opening known as Philidor's Defense. Sergei Prokofiev reached the rank of a top chess player in Russia, and JOHN CAGE, who was taught by Marcel Duchamp, reached a remarkable level of proficiency.

Painters, too, are often musical. The famous French artist Ingres loved to play the violin, even though he could never quite master it. Hence, the expression *violon d'Ingres* is applied to a passionate but inefficient amateur. Conversely, many musicians show a respectable talent for painting; ARNOLD SCHOENBERG, GEORGE GERSHWIN, and Cage had public exhibitions of their art. CARL RUGGLES devoted himself entirely to painting and stopped writing music during the last 40 years of his very long life. DANE RUDHYAR painted hundreds of pictures symbolic of his mystical beliefs.

Some statesmen were accomplished music amateurs. Many royal personages were amateurs in the best sense of the word, among them Frederick the Great of Prussia (who performed regularly with C. P. E. Bach and JOHANN JOACHIM QUANTZ) and Albert, Prince Consort of England. Francis Hopkinson, a signer of the Declaration of Independence, claimed the distinction of being the first American to produce a musical composition. Thomas Jefferson played the harpsichord, violin, and recorder; Benjamin Franklin

Of all professions, medical doctors are probably the most enthusiastic amateurs of music. There are doctors' symphony orchestras in several major cities of the U.S. and in other countries. A story is told about a famous pianist who played a concerto with a doctors' orchestra. Shortly afterward he suffered an attack of appendicitis; several surgeons from the orchestra volunteered to operate on him, but he declined. "I prefer to have my appendix removed by a member of the N.Y. Philharmonic," he declared in all solemnity.

perfected the glass harmonica. Presidents Truman and Nixon played the piano, but their repertory was limited; Bill Clinton is the finest presidential saxophonist in U.S. history. On the other hand, the great Polish patriot IGNACY PADEREWSKI was a pianist first, a statesman second. It is said that, when he met the French prime minister Clemenceau at the Versailles Peace Conference following World War I, Clemenceau exclaimed, "So you are the famous pianist, and now you are prime minister! What a comedown!" Even GIUSEPPE VERDI was a member of the first Italian parliament.

Amati. Renowned Italian family of violin makers working at Cremona. (1) Andrea (b. between 1500 and 1505; d. before 1580) was the first violin maker of the family. He established the modern violin design, which has since been used in all instruments. His sons were (2) Antonio (b. c. 1538; d. c. 1595), who built violins of varying sizes, and (3) Girolamo (b. c.1561; d. Nov. 2, 1630), who continued the tradition established by his father, working together with his brother. (4) Nicola (Niccolò) (b. Dec. 3, 1596; d. Apr. 12, 1684), the most illustrious of the family, was the son of (3) Girolamo. He built some of the "grand Amatis," large violins of powerful tone surpassing in clarity and purity those made by his father and grandfather. In Nicola's workshop both GUARNERI and STRADIVARI received their training. (5) Girolamo (b. Feb. 26, 1649; d. Feb. 21, 1740), son of Nicola and the last of the family, produced violins inferior to those of his predecessors. He departed from the family tradition in many respects, seemingly influenced by Stradivari's method without equaling his superb workmanship.

ambitus. 1. The range of notes comprising a given mode. The determination of the ambitus can depend on the mode's being AUTHENTIC, PLAGAL, or mixed. 2. The range of a voice, instrument, or piece.

Ambrosian chant. A system of PLAINCHANT associated with the fourth-century bishop of Milan, St. Ambrose (b. Trier [Treves], c. 333; d. Milan, Apr. 4, 397). It preceded by two centuries the establishment of GREGORIAN CHANT. There are many theories concerning Ambrosian chant. Some musicologists see it primarily as an unformed predecessor of Gregorian chant, while others consider it a style refreshingly free from the stricter Gregorian doctrine. Still others view it as an extension of Eastern liturgical sources. The last interpretation is supported by its use of florid quasi-exotic melismas (embellishments), sometimes including more than 100 notes, that adorn its melodies and move freely between modes. Perhaps the most convincing theory about the historical place of Ambrosian chant is that it represents a Milanese branch of the liturgical ritual, the other main branches being the Gregorian of Rome, the Gallican of France, and the Mozarabic of Moorish Spain. This division corresponds with the emergence of Romance languages from their common Latin source.

ambulation. The indicated movement of performers while playing a piece. In an ambulatory composition, the players may be instructed to make their entrances or exits while playing their instruments; they may be suspended from the flies or rise from beneath the stage; they may move about the concert hall in random or specified directions; or they may "interact" with each other, with varying degrees of improvisatory freedom. Percussionists may have more than one set-up on stage and be required to move between them, sometimes quite rapidly.

Amen (Heb. lit. "may it be so"). The concluding word in a Jewish or Christian prayer, as an expression of faith. Sometimes an Amen section in an oratorio, as in Handel's *Messiah,* is extended so as to become a concluding chorus of considerable length.

America. Patriotic song to words written by Samuel Francis Smith in 1832. Commissioned to write a chorus for children, he selected a German song with the first line, "Heil, dir im Siegerkranz." Smith's version, which began with "My country, 'tis of Thee," became widely popular. It was not chosen as the American national anthem because its tune is identical to that of England's GOD SAVE THE KING. *America* was first performed by a children's choir at the Park Street Church, Boston, on July 4, 1832.

America the Beautiful. Patriotic song to words by Katherine Lee Bates, professor of English at Wellesley College, inspired by the view from Pikes Peak, Colorado. Her poem was published to great acclaim on July 4, 1895; songwriters vied to set the words to music, but no one could create a sufficiently powerful melody. Finally, an unknown performer set the words to *O Mother Dear Jerusalem* (*Materna*) by Samuel Augustus Ward (1882), and the hymn became an obligatory effusion at patriotic gatherings. Bates lived long enough (until 1929) to see her work enshrined as an American classic.

American Festival Overture. Concert overture by WILLIAM SCHUMAN, 1939. The work incorporates the calls of American children at play.

In the film *An American in Paris,* inspired by this orchestral work, Gene Kelly performs a ballet set to portions of the music.

American in Paris, An. Symphonic poem by GEORGE GERSHWIN, 1928, in which he introduces realistic sounds such as taxi horns and Parisian popular songs of the time.

American Quartet. A nickname for ANTONÍN DVOŘÁK's String Quartet in F major, op.96, written during his sojourn in the U.S. Dvořák uses syncopated rhythms in this work, inspired by his admiration for traditional African-American spirituals, as well as PENTATONIC melodies reminiscent of American Indian music.

Amériques. Symphonic poem by EDGARD VARÈSE, 1926, composed in the U.S. (1918 – 22). The score, a panorama of North and South America, abounds in resonant discords and is built on a gargantuan scale of instrumental sonorities. It was received with typical critical incomprehension.

Amico Fritz, L'. Opera by PIETRO MASCAGNI, 1891, in which a wealthy bachelor landowner succumbs to the charms of the daughter of one of his tenants.

Amirkhanian, Charles (Benjamin), American avant-garde composer and influential radio producer of Armenian extraction; b. Fresno, Calif., Jan. 19, 1945. In his early percussion compositions, Amirkhanian experimented with various

PEOPLE IN MUSIC

sounds not usually heard in musical compositions. For example, his 1965 *Symphony I* is scored for 12 players and 200-odd objects ranging from pitch pipes to pitch forks. With painter Ted Greer he also developed a radical notation system based on visual images that were transformed by performers into sound events. Amirkhanian is perhaps best known for his developments in text-sound composition, featuring a voice percussively intoning and articulating

◀ *Charles Amirkhanian. (Photo © Mark Estes)*

words and phrases; an especially rewarding example is *Dutiful Ducks* (1977). Since the early 1980s his works have used sampled ambient sounds manipulated by a SYNCLAVIER, as in *Metropolis San Francisco* (1985 – 86), *Pas de Voix* ("Portrait of Samuel Beckett," 1987), and *Im Frühling* (1990). From 1969 to 1992 he was music director of the Bay Area radio station KPFA-FM, and from 1992 to 1997 executive director of the Djerassi Resident Artists Program in Woodside, California. He is also program director of San Francisco's Other Minds festival.

Amor brujo, El (Love, the Magician). Ballet by MANUEL DE FALLA, 1915, from which a successful symphonic suite was drawn. The romantic scenario deals with a jealous, but dead, gypsy lover who insists that his surviving beloved not yield to any living human. But a new lover conquers the ghostly prohibition.

amplifier. Electronic device used in all reproducing sound systems to control and heighten volume.

amplitude. The widest disturbance in a vibration. Amplitude is the scientific correlate to the sensation of loudness.

amplitude modulation (AM). A change made to the amplitude of a sound wave that converts it into an electromagnetic wave. This electromagnetic wave can then be "broadcast," or delivered through the air to a remote location, such as in AM radio.

ăn-ŭ-kroo′sĭs   **anacrusis** (Grk., upbeat). In music, the weak beat, or weak part of a measure, with which a piece or phrase may begin.

analysis. The study of musical FORM. Attempting to describe a musical composition in words raises some interesting problems. Critics have come up with various solutions: to paint a word picture with poetic metaphors; to confine themselves to describing the nuts and bolts of a composition, i.e., its melodic phrases, rhythmic terms, harmonic progressions, contrapuntal combinations, and formal designs; to develop an overarching theory that explains a composer's use of melodies, harmonies, or rhythms; or to apply a theory from the study of human behavior or society, such as Freudianism or Marxism. Often, criticism combines two or more of these methods to describe a composition.

anapest (Grk.). A metrical foot of three syllables, two short (unstressed) and one long (stressed). In music, anapest corresponds to an upbeat of two quick notes followed by a long note in $\frac{4}{8}$ time.

Anchors Aweigh. A 1907 marching song of the U.S. Navy, composed by Charles Zimmerman, music director of the Naval Academy at Annapolis (although Alfred H. Miles is sometimes credited with joint authorship).

Anderson, Laurie, composer, violinist, and performance artist; b. Chicago, June 5, 1947. One of the earliest and most popular of the "performance artists," Anderson combines her own movement, speech, singing, and musical virtuosity into a single "composition." Her first popular success was the minimalist *O Superman* (1977), built on a repeating

PEOPLE IN MUSIC

phrase. In 1983 she produced the large-scale collage epic *United States* on themes of travel, politics, money, and love. Anderson often performs in front of screens on which are projected images, including images of herself. She uses a variety of instruments, including a homemade violin activated by a luminous bow made of electronic tape. She also alters her natural voice electronically, making use of vocal glissandi, crooning, panting, and heavy aspiration.

Anderson, Marian, celebrated black American contralto; b. Philadelphia, Feb. 17, 1897; d. Portland, Oreg., Apr. 8, 1993. Born into impoverished circumstances, Anderson sang in the choir of the Union Baptist Church in South Philadelphia, where her talents were first recognized. In 1923 she won first prize at a Philadelphia singing contest, and two years later received top honors at a contest held by the N.Y. Philharmonic, winning a solo appearance. In 1929 she gave a recital at Carnegie Hall and made her first European appearance in London a year later. Anderson subsequently toured Europe and the Soviet Union, where her singing of traditional spirituals produced a sensation.

In Feb. 1939 Anderson gained national attention when the Daughters of the American Revolution (DAR) refused to let her appear at their Constitution Hall in Washington, D.C., citing the organization's policy of racial segregation. The resulting publicity led to Eleanor Roosevelt's resigning from the DAR and an invitation to Anderson to sing at the Lincoln Memorial on Easter Sunday, Apr. 9, 1939: a huge audience attended, and the concert was nationally broadcast. Another landmark occurred when Anderson sang the role of Ulrica in *Un ballo in maschera* at N.Y.'s Metropolitan Opera on Jan. 7, 1955, the first black singer to appear there. Her remaining years were filled with a seemingly unending list of honors. Her nephew is the greatly talented conductor James DePreist (b. Philadelphia, Nov. 21, 1936).

Andrea Chénier. Opera by UMBERTO GIORDANO, 1896. The libretto by Luigi Illica deals with the historical fate of a poet condemned to the guillotine by the French revolutionary tribunal in 1793. His beloved tries to incriminate herself in his revolutionary plot in order to die with him.

PEOPLE IN MUSIC

Andrews, Julie (born Julia Elizabeth Wells), English actress and singer of popular music; b. Walton-on-Thames, Oct. 1, 1935. Andrews's mother was a pianist, and her stepfather, whose surname she adopted, was a music-hall singer. Andrews began performing on the radio in England when she was a teenager, as well as performing in London's music halls. She was first heard in the U.S. in the Broadway musical *The Boy Friend* (1954), impressing the critics and audiences with her considerable vocal range and technique. Her portrayal of Eliza Doolittle in *My Fair Lady* (1956–60) won her the N.Y. Drama Critics Award. She subsequently co-starred with Richard Burton in *Camelot* (1960–62), a show created to highlight her talents.

Turning her attention to films, Andrews appeared in the whimsical *Mary Poppins* (1964), for which she won an Academy Award for best actress, and *The Sound of Music* (1966). In later years she appeared in several films directed by her husband, Blake Edwards, by which she hoped to alter her squeaky clean image. Their biggest success was *Victor, Victoria,* a farce on gender role-playing, made into a Broadway musical (1995) with Andrews in the lead.

Andrews Sisters. Popular American singing group. (Members: LaVerne [b. Minneapolis, July 6, 1915; d. Brentwood, Calif., May 8, 1967]; Maxene [b. Minneapolis, Jan. 3, 1918]; and Patricia [Patti] [b. Minneapolis, Feb. 16, 1920].) The group was discovered by the famous music manager Lou Levy (who later married Maxene), who helped them get their first recording contract with Decca. Among their most popular songs were *Bei Mir Bist Du Schoen* (1937), *Rum and Coca*

*The Andrews Sisters, 1948.
(Hulton-Deutsch Collection/
Corbis)*

Cola (1944), and *Winter Wonderland* (1947). They were excellent at BOOGIE-WOOGIE renditions, performing in close three-part harmony. Their songs included *Beat Me, Daddy, Eight to the Bar* and *Boogie Woogie Bugle Boy;* the latter was reinterpreted by BETTE MIDLER in 1973 (with Midler doing all three vocal parts), setting off a resurgence of interest in their music.

Anglican chant. Liturgical singing generally adopted in English-speaking Protestant liturgy, usually harmonized with simple chords.

Animals and animal music. Because birds are the primordial music makers of the animal world, it is not surprising that composers have for centuries imitated bird calls in their works. The cuckoo has the most immediately identifiable call, a falling major or minor third. LUDWIG VAN BEETHOVEN immortalized it, along with the trilling nightingale and the repetitive quail, in his *Pastoral Symphony.* The 18th-century French composer Louis-Claude Daquin wrote a harpsichord piece entitled *The Cuckoo,* which became a universal favorite. OLIVIER MESSIAEN expanded the musical aviary by filling his compositions with painstakingly notated exotic bird calls. The rooster is glorified in NIKOLAI RIMSKY-KORSAKOV's opera *Le Coq d'or,* sounding his call on the muted trumpet. HEITOR VILLA-LOBOS reproduces the piercing cry of the araponga on high B♭ in one of his *Bachianas brasileiras.*

Non-avian creatures are represented as well. Buzzing insects provide an obvious source of animal onomatopoeia. Rimsky-Korsakov's *Flight of the Bumble Bee* is a famous example; another is Béla Bartók's *Diary of a Fly* from his *Mikrokosmos.* In the score of his opera *L'Enfant et les sortilèges,* MAURICE RAVEL includes a couple of meowing amorous cats. The bleating of sheep is imitated by a cacophonous ensemble of wind instruments in RICHARD STRAUSS's *Don Quixote.* In the *Duet for Two Cats* traditionally attributed to GIOACCHINO ROSSINI, two sopranos sing their parts to the most familiar phrase associated with felines. CAMILLE SAINT-SAËNS portrays an entire menagerie in his *Carnival of the Animals.*

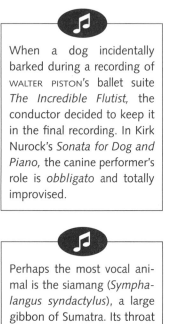

When a dog incidentally barked during a recording of WALTER PISTON's ballet suite *The Incredible Flutist,* the conductor decided to keep it in the final recording. In Kirk Nurock's *Sonata for Dog and Piano,* the canine performer's role is *obbligato* and totally improvised.

Perhaps the most vocal animal is the siamang (*Symphalangus syndactylus*), a large gibbon of Sumatra. Its throat sac swells like a red balloon during vocalization, and it has the loudest voice among primates, not excluding sopranos.

Sometimes instruments are invented to imitate animal sounds, such as the toy cuckoo used in LEOPOLD MOZART's *Toy* Symphony. Actual reproductions of animal noises on phonograph, disc, or tape are used in some modern scores; OTTORINO RESPIGHI introduced a recording of a nightingale in his symphonic poem *The Pines of Rome.*

GEORGE CRUMB and ALAN HOVHANESS have used recorded sounds of humpback whales. These giant marine animals have no vocal cords but are capable of producing tones covering the entire human range; furthermore, the whale voice has a tremendous endurance and can carry a tone as long as 18 minutes. In the late 1960s an entire album of the songs of the humpback whales was released and for a while was very popular.

Are animals themselves sensitive to music in any selective way? Experiments conducted on dairy farms in New Zealand in 1947 seemed to show that cows produce more milk when jazz is played. On a New Jersey farm, 2,500 pigs that were exposed to a constant flood of jazz in 1950 put on weight faster than pigs not so favored. A farmer in Surrey, England, wrote to the British Broadcasting Corporation that his cows gave their highest milk yield when Haydn's string quartets were played for them. The curator of reptiles at Chicago's Brookfield Zoo noted that the alligator mating calls approximated the pitch of B♭ below middle C. He hired four French horn players and instructed them to play B♭ in unison, but no visible mating ensued. These and numerous other attempts to connect music with physiological processes in animals have failed in the end, proving, as if proof were needed, that animals lack talent for music appreciation.

Anna Magdalena Book. A common name for JOHANN SEBASTIAN BACH's *Clavierbüchlein* (Little clavier book), a collection of keyboard music composed for his young second wife.

Années de pèlerinage (Years of wandering). Three series of piano works by FRANZ LISZT, begun in 1837 (1855, 1858, 1883), each bearing a descriptive title, including *Sposalizio,* inspired by Raphael's painting of the wedding of Joseph and

Mary; *Il Pensieroso,* inspired by Michelangelo's monuments to Lorenzo de' Medici in Florence; *Après une lecture de Dante* (Upon reading Dante); *Au bord d'une source* (By the bank of a brook); three *Sonnets of Petrarch; Venezia e Napoli; Les Jeux d'eau à la Villa d'Este* (Fountains at the Villa d'Este); and *Aux cyprès de la Villa d'Este* (Cypresses at the Villa d'Este).

Annie Get Your Gun. Musical with songs by IRVING BERLIN about Annie Oakley and Buffalo Bill Cody, 1946, starring Ethel Merman. Includes *There's No Business Like Show Business; Anything You Can Do, I Can Do Better;* and *Doin' What Comes Natur'lly.* This was Berlin's last great Broadway success.

Annie Laurie. A Scottish song composed by Lady John Scott in 1835. Annie Laurie may have been a real person whose unhappy romance with a member of a rival Scottish clan was the subject of the poem reputedly written by her lover.

Anon. Abbreviation for *Anonymous,* used in the attribution of religious music of the Middle Ages, traditional music, and many other pieces. Most ecclesiastical chants are anonymous.

answer. In a FUGUE, the second voice or part (COMES), which takes up (starting at a different pitch) the subject (DUX, fugal theme) given in the first voice or part. A *real answer* is derived from the subject by transposing it exactly to the dominant (a fifth above the tonic or original key). A *tonal answer* requires a modification, replacing the tonic with the supertonic (the second scale step), to fulfill certain harmonic requirements.

antecedent (Ger. *Vordersatz*). The theme or subject of a CANON or FUGUE, as stated in its first part; the DUX. Also, any theme or motive that is imitated later in a piece.

Antheil, George (Georg Johann Carl), American modern composer; b. Trenton, N.J., July 8, 1900; d. N.Y., Feb. 12, 1959. Antheil was famous in his day for composing music

PEOPLE IN MUSIC

that glorified the age of the machine. He went to Europe in 1922 and gave several concerts featuring his compositions as well as Impressionist music. Antheil spent a year in Berlin, then went to Paris, where he lived for several years. He was one of the first American students of the legendary French theorist NADIA BOULANGER. In Paris he made contact with James Joyce and Ezra Pound, two influential writers; Pound quickly championed Antheil's music as representing the best of the new.

In celebration of the world of the modern machine, Antheil composed the *BALLET MÉCANIQUE* with the avowed intention to *épater les bourgeoisie* (startle the middle class), and collaborated with French artist Fernand Léger on a film to be synchronized with the music, which was never completed. He returned to America, staging a spectacular production of the *Ballet mécanique* in N.Y. on Apr. 10, 1927, employing airplane propellers, eight pianos, and a large percussion battery, creating an uproar in the audience and much publicity in the newspapers.

His subsequent works were less successful. Antheil moved to Hollywood (1936), where he wrote some film music and ran a syndicated lonelyhearts column. He continued to write symphonies, operas, and other works, none of which were much performed until recently. Nevertheless, he remains a herald of the avant-garde of yesterday.

anthem (*antem,* Mid. Eng.). A liturgical song performed by a chorus, with or without accompaniment, of moderate length, developed primarily in the Lutheran and Anglican (Protestant) churches. Anthem singing arose in the Reformation (during the mid-1600s), when these churches were first being formed. Many anthem texts are based on Scripture, but others are newly composed. The form corresponds to the Roman Catholic MOTET. More widely, the term came to signify any solemn song performed by a community. *National anthems* are the patriotic extensions of the prayerful religious anthems.

antiphonal. In music, alternating or responding parts. *See* CALL-AND-RESPONSE.

antiphon(e) (from Grk., *anti* + *phōnē* countersound) 1. Originally, a responsive system of singing by two choirs (or divided choir), an early feature in the Catholic service of song, where the same phrase would be repeated an octave higher by a second chorus composed of women and boys. 2. Responsive or alternate singing, chanting, or intonation in general, as practiced in the Greek, Roman, Anglican, and Lutheran churches. 3. A choral response after the singing of a psalm, usually sung in a plain syllabic manner. 4. A short sentence, generally from Holy Scripture, sung before and after the psalms for the day.

antique cymbals. Small hollow-sphere brass cymbals, originally used in accompanying dances in ancient Greece. They are used in modern scores for special effects. Also called *krotala* (Grk.) or *crotales* (Fr., from Lat., *crotalum*).

MUSICAL
INSTRUMENT

Antony and Cleopatra. Opera by SAMUEL BARBER, based on Shakespeare's play, 1966, commissioned by the Metropolitan Opera for the inauguration of its new house at N.Y.'s Lincoln Center. The work was not well received on its initial performance, and Barber revised the score in 1975.

anvil (Fr. *enclume;* It. *incudine*). A metal bar struck by a hammer, first used in DANIEL-FRANÇOIS-ESPRIT AUBER's *Le Maçon,* 1825, and made famous in the so-called Anvil Chorus in GIUSEPPE VERDI's *Il trovatore,* 1853. In *Das Rheingold* RICHARD WAGNER introduces 18 anvils to illustrate the forging of the ring of the Nibelung. The anvil is also used by EDGARD VARÈSE (*Ionisation,* 1931) and CARL ORFF (*Antigonae,* 1949).

MUSICAL
INSTRUMENT

Anvil Chorus. Popular name of the scene in Act II of GIUSEPPE VERDI's *Il trovatore,* in which gypsy-camp blacksmiths strike anvils in time with the chorus. Nowhere in Verdi's manuscript does the name "Anvil Chorus" appear, however. It is one of the most celebrated single passages in all opera; during the celebration of the Peace Jubilee in Boston in 1872, 100 city firemen beat anvils during a performance of this number.

Anything Goes. Musical by COLE PORTER, concerning the denizens of a transatlantic boat journey, 1934. It includes several hits, including the title song, *Blow Gabriel Blow, You're the Top,* and *I Get a Kick Out of You.* The show has often been revived, although rarely with its original book or song selection.

***Apocalyptic* Symphony.** The nickname of ANTON BRUCKNER's Symphony No. 8 in C Minor, to point out its religious depth and expectations of eternity. It was premiered in 1892; a newly edited version premiered in 1973.

Apollon musagète (Apollo, leader of the Muses). Ballet with string orchestra by IGOR STRAVINSKY, first performed in Washington, D.C., 1928. This work was noteworthy as among the first that Stravinsky wrote in the neoclassical style, showing his renewed interest in the classical rules of composition and a turning away from the dissonant harmonies and folk rhythms of his earlier work.

Appalachian Spring. Ballet by AARON COPLAND, with choreography by Martha Graham, first performed in Washington, D.C., 1944. The title is from a poem by Hart Crane, although the music is only peripherally related to the text. There are eight sections, all descriptive of a wedding celebration on a farm in the Appalachian hills. As with most of his ballet scores, Copland drew an orchestral suite from it, first performed in N.Y., 1945.

***Appassionata* Sonata.** The title given by LUDWIG VAN BEETHOVEN's publisher to his Piano Sonata in F Minor, op.57. Beethoven entitled it simply *Grande sonate pour piano.* There is certainly enough passion in the work—somber and unpredictable in the first movement, stormy and unrestrained in the third, with a lyrical second in between—to justify the nickname.

applause. A seemingly instinctive reaction to an excellent artistic performance. Shouts of "Bravo!" often join the applause (from Lat., *plaudere,* clap hands); outside Italy, "Bravo!" is shouted equally at men and women performers, although the proper form for a female artist is "Brava!" (Kudos addressed to more than one performer take the form "Bravi!") In Islamic countries, audiences cry out "Allah, Allah!" to commend a singer; in Spain it is "Olé, olé!"

At the opera, applause often greets the entrance of a favorite singer. When there is an orchestral coda after a particularly successful aria, it is often drowned out by the applause, as in the case of the soft instrumental conclusion to the famous tenor's aria in RUGGERO LEONCAVALLO's *PAGLIACCI*. A tug-of-war can ensue when the conductor makes a serious effort to proceed with the music while the singer is eager to prolong the applause. In the heyday of opera, a singer, dying at the end of an aria, might have been forced to rise again and bow to the public. Cries of "Bis!" (twice, encore) can bring a repetition of the aria.

A peculiar type of responsorial applause emerged in Russia toward the middle of the 20th century, when the artists themselves applauded the audience, usually in a rhythmic measure of one long and two short claps. The origin of this custom can be traced to the practice of political leaders returning the applause of an enthusiastic audience.

Whistling, an expression of passionate pleasure at a performance in England and America, is equivalent to hissing or booing in France and Russia. Shortly after the conclusion of World War II, American soldiers greeted the Russian dancers in Berlin with whistling; the performers were in tears, believing that they had been roundly dismissed. The so-called Bronx cheer, produced by sticking out the tongue between closed lips and exhaling vigorously, is the most emphatic American way of expressing displeasure at the quality of a performance, short of physical violence.

In commercial musical programs on radio and television, for which timing is essential, the amount and the loudness of applause is precisely proportioned by signs passed in front of the audience; an even safer practice is "canned applause," the time and volume of which can be controlled by studio engineers. However, unrestrained outbursts of adulation are usually preferred by highly paid popular performers.

April in Paris. VERNON DUKE's most famous song, to words by E. Y. "YIP" HARBURG, first heard in the musical *Walk a*

It was once common practice among opera singers, especially in the 19th century, to hire people to applaud them. The hired group was known as a CLAQUE.

Little Faster, 1932. The phrase was supposedly taken from a remark made by Dorothy Parker during a bleak and cold N.Y. December: "I wish I were in April in Paris." It is said that a N.Y. dandy, inspired by the song, went to Paris in April, found it damp and chilly, and reported his disillusion to Duke, who said, "Okay, so Paris is miserable in April. It is lovely in May, but I needed a word with two syllables for the rhythm."

Arab music. The traditional music of Arab nations of the Mediterranean and Persian Gulf basins, along with all of the Arab peoples who live north of the Sahara in the African continent.

Arab musical meters and rhythms lack the regularity of their Western counterparts, and Arab melodies are not based on the Western tempered scale. The melodic range is narrow, and the development of the principal theme consists in florid melodic variations and embellishments. The melodies themselves register to a Western-trained ear as progressions of quarter tones, semitones, and other divisions of the whole tone.

The 12 basic modes (each called *maqām*) in Arab music tend to emphasize the minor third. Harmonization and polyphony in the Western sense of the words are nonexistent. When a musical instrument accompanies the singing voice, generally it follows the same melody line; however, occasionally the instrument may perform a complementary part, creating a kind of heterophony (more than one melody being performed at the same time).

Notation of Arab chants and rhythmic modes usually gives the hand positions on indigenous instruments, which have undergone practically no changes in their construction and tuning throughout the centuries. In addition to the Arab lute ('ūd), musicians typically use a variety of vertical flute (nāy), one-string fiddle (rabāb), vase-shaped drum (darabukka), and tambourine (tār).

Arabella. Opera by RICHARD STRAUSS to a Hugo Hofmannsthal libretto, 1923. This is a Viennese version of a daughter's true love triumphing over a father's mercenary motives.

Production score for Arabella *by Strauss. (Ira Nowinski/© Corbis)*

arabesque. A type of character piece for piano, featuring ornamental passages accompanying or varying a melody, usually in a pronounced rhythmic manner in $\frac{2}{4}$ time. The term is derived from Western ideas of what Arab music sounds like, notions that have little to do with real Arab music. ROBERT SCHUMANN, PIOTR ILYICH TCHAIKOVSKY, CLAUDE DEBUSSY, and others wrote arabesques.

***Archduke* Trio.** LUDWIG VAN BEETHOVEN's last piano trio, in B♭ major, op.97 (1811). Its name comes from its dedication to the composer's pupil and patron, Archduke Rudolph of Austria.

Argento, Dominick, greatly talented American composer excelling in opera; b. York, Pa., Oct. 27, 1927. Argento's operas are noteworthy for their tuneful scores and memorable songs. Although there are occasional touches of unusual harmonies and vocal embellishments, Argento's work is far more traditional than that of most modern composers.

Argento has long been associated with the Minnesota Opera, which he helped to found, and most of his works have premiered there. Among his many operas are *Christopher Sly,* a scene from Shakespeare's *The Taming of the Shrew* (1963); *Postcard from Morocco* (1971); *The Voyage of Edgar Allan Poe,* which achieved great critical acclaim (1976); *Miss*

PEOPLE IN MUSIC

Havisham's Fire, after Dickens (1979); *Casanova's Homecoming,* a comic opera (1985); and *The Aspern Papers* (1988).

aria (It.; from Lat., *aer;* plural *arie;* Ger. *Arie*). An air, song, tune, or melody. The term is most commonly applied to a solo song in OPERA.

In 17th-century England the spelling *ayre* designated a wide variety of songs, whether serious or popular. BAROQUE instrumental pieces of a songful character were often called arias.

aria da capo (It., to the head). An aria in symmetric THREE-PART (TERNARY) FORM, with the third part being the exact repetition (ABA) or slight variation (ABA¹) of the first part. This type, also called a *da capo aria,* was popularized by composers of the Neapolitan school in the second half of the 17th century. It became the most common form of the operatic aria, especially among Italian and Italianate composers of the 18th and 19th centuries.

In ROMANTIC opera, this type evolved into the *grand aria* (or *aria grande*), divided into (1) the main theme, fully developed; (2) a more peaceful and richly harmonized second section; and (3) a repetition *da capo* of the first, with heavier ornamentation.

Specialized categories of aria came to be used in Italian opera, including *aria buffa,* comic or burlesque aria; *aria cantabile,* "songful" aria, expressing sorrow or yearning; ARIA DA CAPO; *aria da chiesa,* church aria, as opposed to secular; *aria da concerto,* aria for concert singing; *aria d'entrata,* aria sung by any operatic character upon his or her first entrance; *aria di bravura,* rapid, virtuosic song expressing violent passion; and *aria parlante,* "talking aria," in a spoken manner.

Ariadne auf Naxos. Opera by RICHARD STRAUSS to a libretto by Hugo Hofmannsthal. The first version, 1912, was a single act, but the

Scene from Ariadne and Naxos. *(Robbie Jack/Corbis)* ▶

work was expanded into a full opera in 1916. The plot is very complicated, involving a production of a serious opera that is interrupted by a troupe of comic players. The opera centers on the mythical Ariadne, abandoned on the island of Naxos, praying for death to release her; she is often interrupted by the comedians. Bacchus arrives opportunely and takes Ariadne with him to the heavens, to the approval of the onstage spectators.

arietta (It.). A short aria, lacking the da capo repeat; similar to the CAVATINA found in BAROQUE Italian OPERA.

ariette (Fr.). A short aria or song; usually an insertion into a French DIVERTISSEMENT rather than an OPERA.

arioso. In vocal music, descriptive of a style between full ARIA and lyric RECITATIVE, or a short melodious strain interrupted by or ending in a recitative. This song form was invented by the Florentine opera pioneers, who called it *recitativo arioso.* It also occasionally refers to an impressive, dramatic style suitable for the *aria grande;* hence, a vocal piece in that style. In instrumental music, the same as CANTABILE.

Arkansas Traveler. An American dancing song of 1847. Its composer is unknown; the attribution to Colonel Sanford D. Faulkner of Arkansas is highly dubious. *Arkansas Traveler* is also an American square dance of unknown origin that achieved popularity in the mid-19th century.

Arlen, Harold (born Hyman Arluck), American composer of popular songs, Broadway musicals, and Hollywood film scores; b. Buffalo, Feb. 15, 1905; d. N.Y., Apr. 23, 1986. Arlen was the son of a Jewish immigrant who worked as a cantor directing the choir in a synagogue in Buffalo, N.Y., where the family had settled. Arlen's early musical training came from his father. He first found professional work as a teenager as a pianist and vocalist, working on steamboats on Lake Erie, which featured live entertainment, and in nightclubs. In the late 1920s, he moved to N.Y. City, where he worked as a vocalist, performer, and arranger.

A comic dialogue between a city dweller and a country farmer has long been associated with *Arkansas Traveler.* The city traveler is supposedly lost in rural Arkansas, and can't find his way home. He stops to ask a farmer for help. City Fella: "Say, farmer, does this road go to Little Rock?" Farmer: "That road hain't moved since I've been living here!" City Fella: "Say, you're pretty dumb." Farmer: "Well, I hain't lost."

ăh-rē-oh′sōh

PEOPLE IN MUSIC

Arlen first found success as a songwriter by composing the music for Harlem's popular Cotton Club Revues between 1930 and 1934; among the songs that he created were *Get Happy, Between the Devil and the Deep Blue Sea, I Love a Parade, I Gotta Right to Sing the Blues,* and *Stormy Weather,* all with lyrics by Ted Koehler. He then partnered with lyricist E. Y. "YIP" HARBURG for a series of musicals and films, most memorably *The Wizard of Oz* (1939), including the revered *Over the Rainbow,* originally sung by Judy Garland. Arlen and Harburg also composed dozens of popular songs such as *It's Only a Paper Moon* and *Happiness Is a Thing Called Joe* (used in the film *Cabin in the Sky,* 1943).

During the later 1940s and 1950s Arlen worked with many collaborators, including Ira Gershwin (the 1954 film *A Star Is Born,* including the song *The Man Who Got Away*), Johnny Mercer (the musicals *St. Louis Woman,* 1946, and *Saratoga,* 1959; several films, among them 1944's *Here Come the Waves,* including *Ac-cen-tchu-ate the Positive*), and Truman Capote (the 1954 musical *House of Flowers*).

Arlen was less active in the final three decades of his life, when he virtually retired from the music business.

PEOPLE IN MUSIC

Armatrading, Joan, West Indies–born English singer and songwriter; b. St. Kitts, Dec. 9, 1950. Armatrading's family moved to Birmingham, England, in 1956, and Armatrading moved to London in the early 1970s, where she paired up with another singer-songwriter Pam Nestor. They produced two moderately successful albums, *Whatever's for Us* (1974) and *Back to the Night* (1975). She gained widespread popularity with her first solo album, *Joan Armatrading* (1976), which was a hit both in England and the U.S. With lessening interest in the singer-songwriter style in the 1980s, Armatrading's popularity declined. Armatrading has maintained a core of fans, however, and many of her songs, with their acoustic sound, jazz-styled vocals, and mature, often feminist lyrics, have had lasting appeal.

Armide. Opera by CHRISTOPH WILLIBALD GLUCK, 1777, based on Tasso's *Gerusalemme liberata.* A medieval crusader is bewitched by a magic love garden and its owner; after a lengthy dalliance, he abandons her for other conquests, leaving her to destroy the garden with its memories of love. This plot is shared by JEAN-BAPTISTE LULLY's *Armide et Renaud* and many other operas.

Armstrong, Louis, famous black American jazz trumpeter, cornetist, singer, bandleader, and entertainer, familiarly known as Satchmo, Satchelmouth, Dippermouth, and Pops; b. New Orleans, Aug. 4, 1901; d. N.Y., July 6, 1971. Armstrong grew up in Storyville, New Orleans's "red-light" district, known for its bars, gambling dens, and "houses of ill repute." Raised by a single mother, Armstrong was placed in the Home for Colored Waifs after being arrested for firing a gun on a public street. As luck would have it, the home had an excellent brass band, and Armstrong was trained on the cornet and learned its repertoire of marches, rags, and songs. After his release he worked at a number of low-level jobs while he learned jazz style in blues bands in local honky-tonks and played in trombonist "KID" ORY's band (1918–19).

PEOPLE IN MUSIC

In 1922 Armstrong was invited to Chicago to play in KING OLIVER's Creole Jazz Band. Oliver was a well-known cornet player, and his band was one of the most celebrated in the country. Armstrong played second cornet in the group, and made his first recordings with it in 1923. His playing

◄

Louis Armstrong, c. 1950.
(Corbis-Bettmann)

created an immediate sensation, and he was invited to join Fletcher Henderson's well-known dance band in N.Y. in 1924–25. Returning to Chicago, he organized his own jazz combo, the Hot Five, in 1925, and made a series of now historic recordings with it, the Hot Seven, and other groups he led until 1928; from about 1926 the trumpet was his principal instrument. He married pianist Lil Hardin (b. Memphis, Tenn., Feb. 3, 1898; d. Chicago, Aug. 27, 1971), who had played in Oliver's band and also Armstrong's Hot Five and Seven, and who had encouraged Armstrong to be a bandleader.

In 1929 he returned to N.Y. and became notably successful through appearances on Broadway, in films, and on radio. He led his own big band, which toured extensively through the U.S. and the world from 1935 to 1947. After World War II, big bands fell out of favor, and there was a renewed interest in New Orleans jazz. Armstrong organized his All Stars ensemble in 1947 to play what was then called DIXIELAND jazz, recalling his earlier recordings. In succeeding years he made innumerable tours of the U.S. and abroad. Armstrong became enormously successful as an entertainer and made many television appearances and hit recordings, including his celebrated version of *Hello, Dolly* (1964). Although he suffered a severe heart attack in 1959, he made appearances until his death.

Armstrong was one of the greatest figures in the history of jazz and one of the most popular entertainers of his time. His revolutionary "hot" style of improvisation moved jazz away from the New Orleans ensemble style in the 1920s. His unique gravel-voiced scat singing and song renditions became as celebrated as his trumpet virtuosity.

PEOPLE IN MUSIC

Arne, Thomas Augustine, famous English dramatic composer; b. London, March 12, 1710; d. there, March 5, 1778. Arne attended Eton, the famous British private school. He then spent three years apprenticed to a lawyer, while studying music and acquiring considerable skill on the violin. He began to write musical settings "after the Italian manner" for various plays. His most important work was *Comus* (1738). In 1740 he produced the masque *Alfred;* the finale contains the celebrated song *Rule Britannia,* which became a patriotic song of Britons everywhere. In 1737 he married Cecilia Young, a singer who performed with his company until 1754.

In addition to nearly 100 dramatic works, Arne contributed separate numbers to 28 theatrical productions and composed two oratorios, many secular vocal pieces, and miscellaneous instrumental music. His sister was the celebrated actress Mrs. Cibber; his natural son, Michael (b. c.1740; d. Lambeth, Jan. 14, 1786), wrote dramatic works and songs.

arpeggio (It.; plural *arpeggi*) Playing the tones of a chord in rapid, even succession; playing broken chords. Hence, a chord so played; a broken or spread chord, or chord passage.

ar-ped′jōh

arrangement. The adaptation, transcription, or reduction of a composition for performance on an instrument, or by any vocal or instrumental combination, for which it was not originally written. Also, any composition so adapted or arranged.

In the 19th century, symphonic scores were "reduced" for a single pianist or for piano four hands. In this way, in the days before radio and audio recordings, people could "hear" symphonies at home. With the advent of the phonograph this practice declined.

A special form of reduction was the so-called theater arrangement, adaptations of symphonic works for small amateur productions. Theater arrangements usually contained indications for optional substitutions of one instrument by another, with the piano part filling in as needed.

Piano works that are labeled "transcriptions" tend to be grander and freer than a straightforward arrangement. Paraphrases may be said to be even freer, more inspired by than translating their models, such as Franz Liszt's many lied and operatic paraphrases.

An arrangement can also be any reworking of a popular melody. For example, the popular song "Tonight We Love" was drawn from PIOTR ILYICH TCHAIKOVSKY'S Piano Concerto No. 1. Similarly, FRÉDÉRIC CHOPIN's Prelude in C Minor provided the melody for Barry Manilow's 1975 hit "Could It Be Magic."

Arrau, Claudio, eminent Chilean-born American pianist; b. Chillán, Feb. 6, 1903; d. Mürzzuschlag, Austria, June 9, 1991. Arrau received early training from his mother and as a child played publicly in Santiago. In 1910 he was sent to Berlin and gave piano recitals in Germany and Scandinavia (1914–15), attracting attention by his talent. In 1921 he returned to Chile and three years later made his first American tour as a concerto soloist. He was then appointed to the faculty of the Stern Conservatory, in Berlin. Over the next decade and a half he toured the world several times as a performer.

PEOPLE IN MUSIC

In 1941 Arrau settled permanently in N.Y. and continued performing, teaching, and touring. From 1962 to 1969 he recorded the complete Beethoven piano sonatas and supervised a scholarly edition of them. In 1978 he gave up his Chilean citizenship in protest against the repressive Pinochet regime, becoming a U.S. citizen in 1979. Nevertheless, Arrau remained a revered figure in Chile and was awarded the Chilean National Arts Prize (1983), touring the country in 1984, after an absence of 17 years.

ars antiqua (Lat., old art) A designation applied by music historians to describe the music of the 12th and early 13th centuries that had two or more simultaneous parts. Ars antiqua had its inception in France, with its great early representatives being the masters of the Notre Dame or Paris school. There were two basic styles: ORGANUM and DESCANT.

ahrz ăn-tē′kwŭ

LEONINUS was called *optimus organista,* "best composer of the organum," two-part music with a slow-moving lower voice set against a highly embellished upper voice with chantlike rhythm. The younger PEROTINUS was described as *optimus discantor,* "best composer of discant," a style that used more similar lower and upper voices, producing a somewhat note-against-note effect. An intermediate system between organum and descant was COPULA.

The organum eventually gave birth to the CLAUSULA, a brief melodic interlude. When a liturgical text in Latin was added to the upper voice of the clausula, it evolved into the MOTET. When this process was applied to secular music, many different texts, in French as well as Latin, were added to the upper voices, and the cantus firmus voice became an instrumental part.

Of the two basic rhythms in the ars antiqua, the more common was the tempus perfectum (based on three-note groupings), while considered less desirable was the TEMPUS IMPERFECTUM (based on two-note groupings). In medieval times, triple rhythms represented the Holy Trinity, so the preference for tempus perfectum had a religious significance. Franco of Cologne, active in the 13th century, in his treatise *Ars cantus mensurabilis,* described the basic music theory of this style.

ars musica (Lat., the art of music). In medieval universities, music was regarded as one of the *septem artes* (seven liberal arts), taught, like most subjects, in the Latin language. It was a part of the *quadrivium: arithmetica, geometria, musica,* and *astronomia.* The remaining *trivium* of the *septem artes* included *grammatica, rhetorica,* and *dialectica* (logic). In medieval Latin, *ars* fell below the elevated concept of *scientia* (science) and above the common category of *usus* (use).

In the 11th century, when Guido d'Arezzo introduced *neumes* (or notes), first without lines (*neumae usuales*) and later with lines (*neumae regulares,* from *regula,* line), he elevated the *ars musica* to the point of *scientia canendi,* the science of singing. This marked the beginning of musical notation, which was first described in the treatise *Ars nova,* compiled c.1320 by PHILIPPE DE VITRY and subtitled *Ars nova notandi* (The new art of notating music). As this "scientific" aspect of music began developing further in medieval universities, it was divided into branches, such as *ars cantus plani,* the art of plainchant, and *ars componendi,* the art of composing. JOHANN SEBASTIAN BACH subtitled his *Musikalisches Opfer* "*ars canonica,*" or the art of writing canons.

ars nova (Lat., new art). In the fourteenth century, a group of musical theorists and composers challenged the older style of composing known as ARS ANTIQUA. They developed modern ideas of notating music, preferring BINARY (two-part) rhythmic patterns over the earlier TERNARY (three-part) patterns. They favored simpler and more clearly stated melodies, along with more modern sounding harmonies for them. Later in the ars nova period, this emphasis on simplicity gave way to more complex works, emphasizing COUNTERPOINT (setting one melody against another), which led directly to the heyday of the FUGUE.

ahrz nō′vŭ

The term *ars nova* stems from the treatise of the same name written by PHILIPPE DE VITRY, c.1320, and from a work by Johannes de Muris, *Ars novae musicae,* dating from 1321. Actually, the new art originally had modest goals, as the subtitle of de Vitry's book suggests: to serve as a new method of notating music (*Ars nova notandi*).

The two theorists expanded music notation to include smaller note values, down to the quarter note. They also

The "novelties" proposed by the followers of ars nova angered the musicians who still practiced the *ars antiqua*. Jacques de Liège, in his treatise *Speculum musicae* (Mirror of Music, early fourteenth century) declared ruefully, "Regnat nova ars, exulat antiqua" (New art reigns, old art is exiled). He scorned the ars nova's rhythms and harmonies as "unnatural."

The final fugue in the work is based on a melody of four notes, B–A–C–B♭. In German, B♭ is commonly referred to by the letter H, so that this theme spells out the name Bach. In the score of the work, Bach's son wrote on the page following this final fugue: "During the composition of this fugue the author died."

proposed the binary division of the measure, which medieval composers had avoided. The ars nova also introduced the acceptance of thirds and sixths, along with fourths and fifths, in harmonies.

The most important representatives of the ars nova were Guillaume de Machaut (c.1300–1377), a French poet and composer, and the Italian composer Francesco Landini (c.1325–97). Machaut incorporated the rhythms and melodies of popular dances and songs, including ballades, rondeaux, and virelais, into his compositions. The flowing works of Landini were notated in a manner strikingly close to modern notation; he is known for the LANDINI CADENCE, which, however, he did not invent.

Jean Ciconia (c.1335–1411), a Flemish composer active in Italy at the end of the fourteenth century, developed a new direction for ars nova. He favored richly developed counterpoint, in which a melody stated by one voice was set against another melodic line stated by a second part. He was a forerunner of the great Netherlandish contrapuntal school that reached its height in the Renaissance (the 16th century). In this way, ars nova, which began as a movement of simplification in music, was transformed into something far more complex. This, in turn, inspired another return to simpler forms, the Florentine school of c.1600.

To modern ears, the music of the ars antiqua sounds more familiar than that of the ars nova, because of the use of rhythms and harmonies that have continued to be used by classical composers to today.

Art of Fugue, The (*Die Kunst der Fuge*). The last great work of JOHANN SEBASTIAN BACH, which remained unfinished. It was edited and published by Bach's son Wilhelm Friedemann, who also named the work. Bach's original was set simply as a collection of *contrapuncti*, canonic and fugal examples all based on the same subject or theme, written in D minor. It seems more a manual of composition than a work for performance. The pianist GLENN GOULD was famous for his emotional interpretation of this work.

articulation. 1. How individual notes are joined one to another by the performer; a principal component of PHRASING.

2. The art of clear pronounciation in singing and precise rhythmic accentuation in instrumental playing.

artificial harmonics. Harmonics produced on a stopped string rather than on an open string (as on the violin). Two fingers of the left hand are required to perform these notes: the finger nearer the neck presses the string (establishing the FUNDAMENTAL), and the finger nearer the bridge lightly touches the string to produce the HARMONIC relative to the fundamental. For example, touching the spot a perfect fourth above the stopped fundamental produces a note two octaves higher than that fundamental.

ASCAP (American Society of Composers, Authors, and Publishers). Organization for collecting copyright fees. At the turn of the 20th century, composers and publishers profited by selling sheet music and recordings of songs, but were unable to control public performances of their works, such as in a nightclub or on stage. A group of American composers, including IRVING BERLIN and VICTOR HERBERT, formed ASCAP as a means of protecting their compositions from unauthorized performances. In a number of lawsuits, ASCAP argued successfully that, because nightclubs and theatrical events charge an admission, they are profiting from the music that is performed, and therefore the composers and publishers deserve a portion of that profit. ASCAP collects royalties for its members for any public performance of a musical work.

Radio station owners, particularly resistant to paying fees for use of ASCAP-controlled music, in the 1940s formed an alternative organization, Broadcast Music International (BMI). This opened the door to composers who wrote in styles that ASCAP found less acceptable, such as country music and blues. In time, both BMI and ASCAP came to accept as members composers across all musical genres.

As Time Goes By. Song by Herman Hupfeld, 1931, for the musical *Everybody's Welcome.* Its popularity was boosted when it was used in the 1942 movie *Casablanca.* In the film, the song reminds barroom owner Rick (Humphrey Bogart) of his love affair with Ilse (Ingrid Bergman) that occurred several years previously in Paris. Ever since, he has forbidden his pianist Sam (portrayed by popular vocalist Dooley Wilson) to play it, and is thus startled when he hears it being performed. Ilse has arrived in Casablanca with her new husband, the revolutionary Victor Laslow, and requests the song when she sees Sam in the bar.

PEOPLE IN MUSIC

Ashkenazy, Vladimir (Davidovich), greatly gifted Russian pianist and conductor; b. Gorki, July 6, 1937. Ashkenazy's parents were professional pianists who taught him at an early age. He subsequently took lessons at the Central Music School and the Moscow Conservatory, winning second prize at the International Chopin Competition in Warsaw in 1955. A turning point in his career occurred when, in 1956, he won first prize in the Queen Elisabeth of Belgium International Competition, Brussels, which led to his first U.S. tour two years later. In 1962 he shared the first prize in the Tchaikovsky International Competition in Moscow.

In 1961 Ashkenazy married a young Icelandic pianist, Sofia Johannsdottir. They moved to England in 1963, then settled in Reykjavík in 1968; Ashkenazy became a citizen of Iceland in 1972.

As a piano virtuoso Ashkenazy gained an international reputation for his mastery of the entire range of keyboard works, from FRANZ JOSEPH HAYDN to early 20th-century composers. He is particularly known for his superb performances of SERGEI RACHMANINOFF's piano concertos. As a conductor, he is best known for his interpretation of 19th- and 20th-century works. Ashkenazy prepared and conducted his own effective orchestration of MODEST MUSSORGSKY's *Pictures at an Exhibition.*

PEOPLE IN MUSIC

Ashley, Robert (Reynolds), avant-garde American composer; b. Ann Arbor, Mich., Mar. 28, 1930. Ashley is a composer who creates works that combine theater, performance art, and music. He studied music at the University of Michigan in the early 1950s, and then did graduate work in Manhattan. Returning to Michigan, he continued his musical studies but also became interested in the study of acoustics and speech. He became involved with a number of avant-garde theater companies and festivals in Michigan, including the ONCE Festival and ONCE Group (1958–69) and the Sonic Arts Union (1966–76), touring with them in the U.S. and Europe. He directed the Center for Contemporary Music at Mills College in Oakland, California. (1969–81).

Ashley has produced numerous music and music-theater works for live performance as well as audio and video recordings and for television, which have been performed throughout the world. His scores often combine vernacular speech and song, sometimes with several different parts occurring at once. Often, the plot or story line is fragmented into several brief episodes, and striking visual images—including sets, costumes, and projected images—are used to underscore the plot.

Some of Ashley's better-known works include *Music with Roots in the Aether* (1976), *Perfect Lives (Private Parts)* (1978–80), *Atalanta (Acts of God)* (1982), and the four-part *Now Eleanor's Idea*, comprised of *I: Improvement* (*Don Leaves Linda*) (1984–85), *II: Foreign Experiences* (1994), *III: eL/Aficionado* (1987), and *IV: Now Eleanor's Idea* (1993).

Astaire, Fred (born Frederick Austerlitz), charismatic American dancer, choreographer, singer, and actor; b. Omaha, May 10, 1899; d. Los Angeles, June 22, 1987. With his sister Adele (b. Omaha, Sept. 10, 1897; d. Phoenix, Jan. 25, 1981), Astaire appeared in dance and comedy routines from the age of seven. They worked on the vaudeville circuit, then starred in revues and musicals. Following his sister's retirement, he went to Hollywood and teamed up with dancing actress Ginger Rogers. Astaire gained renown through such films as *The Gay Divorcée* (1934), *Roberta* (1935), *Top Hat* (1935), *Swing Time* (1936), and *Shall We Dance* (1937).

In addition to his dancing skills, Astaire was a talented drummer and a singer. While his voice was somewhat thin, he had a good feeling for popular song phrasing, and many songs were written to suit his half-spoken style. In the 1950s he achieved success as a recording artist, usually performing material associated with his films.

PEOPLE IN MUSIC

The Hungarian composer Béla Bartók introduced many compound meters into 20th-century classical music. He discovered these rhythms thanks to his interest in the folk music of Eastern Europe. As a young man, he spent several years collecting and studying this music.

asymmetry. A departure from the customary BINARY (two-part) or TERNARY (three-part) rhythm. Asymmetry is common outside Western European and related music. COMPOUND METERS are intrinsically asymmetric, as are the subdivisions of binary and ternary meters into unequal groups, as are typical of Serbian, Croatian, Bulgarian, Macedonian, and Romanian folk music.

athematic, athematic composition. Without theme, or lacking a subject or melody. Athematic compositions have no overarching form and appear to be randomly composed. Usually, the athematic composer tries to avoid repeating any melodic material, because repetition would give one theme more importance over all others.

In the 20th century, many composers have deliberately tried to downplay, if not eliminate, a recognizable melody. Different composers have come up with different ways to achieve this. The German electronic-music composer KARL-HEINZ STOCKHAUSEN (*Klavierstück XI*) and others organize some works in segments (MOBILE FORM) playable in any order whatsoever, with the stipulation that when a performer, accidentally or intentionally, arrives at an already performed segment, the piece ends.

Others, like the American composer JOHN CAGE, have written nonmelodic pieces for percussion instruments or altered melody instruments. Cage put bits of metal, rubber, and other material inside a grand piano (calling his revised instrument a PREPARED PIANO) in order to dull the tones to a series of thuds and pings rather than recognizable melodic notes.

A-Tisket, A-Tasket. Pop hit by ELLA FITZGERALD and Al Feldman, 1938, based on the children's nursery rhyme.

Atkins, Chet (Chester Burton), American country guitarist and producer; b. Luttrell, Tenn., June 20, 1924. Atkins taught himself guitar as a child. He began performing on the radio in the late 1940s, including on Nashville's famous GRAND OLE OPRY program, and also recorded as a solo musician and backed up other artists. In 1957 he became an executive for RCA Victor, managing its recording studio in Nashville.

PEOPLE IN MUSIC

Atkins became a leader in the movement toward popular country-western music (known as the "Nashville sound"), using electric instruments, vocal choruses, and jazz-flavored arrangements, and downplaying traditional musical instruments like banjo and fiddle. A versatile guitarist, he felt at ease in many popular genres and has toured Europe, the Far East, and Africa. He was elected to the Country Music Hall of Fame in 1973.

Although officially "retired" since the early 1970s, Atkins continues to record and perform. Among those who admire his guitar playing and have recorded with him are jazz guitarist Les Paul, rock guitarist Mark Knopfler, and country singer Suzy Bogguss.

atonality. The absence of tonality, avoiding the established relationships between the notes of the major and minor scales. Traditional tonal structures are abandoned, as is the key signature. Instead, the composer freely uses all 12 scale tones, avoiding any sequence of pitches that would imply a specific key.

The term *atonality* became current among progressive musicians in Vienna at the turn of the century. Although ARNOLD SCHOENBERG denied credit (or blame) for the invention of atonal composition, he certainly was among the first to create a theory of atonal music and to practice it in his writing. Around 1924 he created the 12-tone technique (DODECAPHONY), in which all semitones are related to each other without reference to a tonal center or key.

Atonal composers avoid the repetition of a particular tone to avoid implying a TONIC note. Atonal melodies usually feature wide leaps between notes, to avoid a series of small scale steps. Although individual phrases in atonal music are usually short, the entire "melody" appears long and sustained. Usually, there is balance in an atonal melody, so that high notes are balanced by lower ones, with a solid "center" representing the majority of essential notes.

In order to avoid implying any key, atonal harmonies tend to be dissonant. The perfect fifth and octave are usually avoided, replaced by the TRITONE (the interval of three whole tones) and the major seventh. The tritone, which divides the octave in half, is in a sense neutral.

Like many other musical terms (such as *jazz*), the term *atonal* was first negatively used by critics to deride the new musical form. Schoenberg and his leading pupil, Alban Berg, disliked the use of the term *atonality*. Berg concluded a 1930 radio talk on the subject with these words: "Antichrist himself could not have thought up a more diabolical appellation than atonal!"

ōh-băhd

aubade (from Fr. *aube,* dawn; Ger. *Morgenlied;* It. *mattinata*). Morning music, as contrasted with SERENADE, evening music. Aubades were popular in the 17th and 18th centuries, when they were played by military and municipal ensembles on special occasions. The aubade corresponds to the Spanish ALBORADA. Several 20th-century composers have written aubades as a nostalgic evocation of the past. *See also* ALBA.

PEOPLE IN MUSIC

Auber, Daniel-François-Esprit, prolific French composer of comic operas; b. Caen, Normandy, Jan. 29, 1782; d. Paris, May 12, 1871. His father, a Parisian art dealer, sent him to London to learn the family business; instead, Auber studied music and wrote songs for social entertainment there. Political tension between France and England forced his return to Paris (1803), and afterward he devoted himself exclusively to music.

Auber's first opera to be given a public performance in Paris was *Le Séjour militaire* (1813); *La Bergère châtelaine* (1820) was his first success. From then on, hardly a year elapsed without the production of a new Auber opera; 45 operas were staged professionally in Paris between 1813 and 1869. He was fortunate in his collaboration with the best French librettist of the time, Eugène Scribe, who wrote (alone, or with others) no fewer than 37 librettos for him. Auber's greatest success was *Masaniello, ou La Muette de Portici* (1828); historically, it laid the foundation of French grand opera along with GIACOMO MEYERBEER's *Robert le diable* and GIOACCHINO ROSSINI's *Guillaume Tell.* Its vivid portrayal of nationalist fury stirred French and Belgian audiences; anti-Dutch riots followed its performance in Brussels (1830). Another popular success was *Fra Diavolo* (1830), which became a repertory standard.

Despite his successes with grand opera, Auber is best seen as a founder of later French *opéra comique;* Rossini and RICHARD WAGNER valued his music. He lived most of his life in Paris, even during the Franco-Prussian war and the German siege; he died during the days of the Paris Commune. Among his other operas are *Le Cheval de bronze* (1835), *Le Domino noir* (1837), and *Manon Lescaut* (1856).

Aucassin et Nicolette. A French CHANSON DE GESTE of the 13th century, illustrating the tale of a young Provençal prince who falls in love with a slave girl captured by the Saracens. The lovers are united after overcoming many trials, when Nicolette is revealed to be of noble blood. Several modern composers have used this subject to evoke the medieval period.

audiences. At one time, there was little separation between audience and performers; in fact, everyone was a "performer" who participated in some way in the music making, if only by stamping his or her feet. As classical music has grown—and music making has become limited primarily to concert halls—the primary role for the audience is to respond to a performance.

Most audiences follow unwritten rules of comportment. At a classical concert, applause occurs only at the conclusion of a complete work; at a jazz performance, however, it is customary to applaud following a solo. At classical events, latecomers are seated only during the pauses between movements of a work or between pieces; coughing or sneezing is allowed during these pauses, but not during the performance; and so on.

The response of an audience to a new work or to an artist's debut is of crucial significance to public success. Yet there are numerous cases in which the first performance of a famous work was a fiasco: THE BARBER OF SEVILLE, *Tosca, Pelléas et Mélisande,* and *Tannhäuser.* On the other hand, wild applause has greeted many an artistic failure.

Generally speaking, audiences in England, America, and Germany are restrained in their vocal expression of disapproval; in France, audience reaction, particularly to opera, is more pronounced; most exuberant and uninhibited of all are the audiences of Italy. Because Italian operagoers often know the music as well as or better than the singers themselves, they often shout encouragement or condemnation.

Enthusiasm for popular pianists, violinists, and especially singers often carries the audience away to extremes. At the height of the golden age of opera, admirers were known to unharness the horse from the prima donna's carriage and

When a tenor sang flat at a Naples performance, a listener pointed his index finger upward and shouted: "Su! Su!" (higher, higher).

When in a scene of romantic discovery the weighty leader of thieves warned his followers not to attack the svelte lady of the castle, whom he recognized as his half-sister, by saying, "Desist! On the same milk were we nurtured!," a member of the audience shouted, "You must have lapped up all the cream!"

In the opposite situation, when the male singer was slight and the prima donna ample, and the scenario required him to carry her off the stage, someone in the audience suggested, "Make it in two trips!"

pull her and it to her home or hotel. In the 1890s young girls with scissors invaded the stage after a concert by Polish pianist IGNACY PADEREWSKI, intent on cutting off a lock of his flowing hair.

The adulation for serious artists in Russia was extraordinary. Music lovers stood in line all night to get a ticket for a recital by the legendary bass singer FEODOR CHALIAPIN, and were known as Chaliapinists. One crooked entrepreneur in Leningrad collected a considerable number of rubles in the 1920s by selling tickets for a recital by the renowned Polish pianist JOSEF HOFMANN that never occurred!

None of these expressions of enthusiasm can approach the frenzy of rock concert fans. Fans have been known to literally follow their favorite band; such were the Deadheads, who traveled with their beloved GRATEFUL DEAD band until its demise. Punk rock fans have been known to form mosh pits, where excited audience members can dance. Audience members will sometimes dress like their favorite stars—the teenaged girls who were fans of Madonna in the early 1980s were called "Madonna-Wannabes" because of their close mimicking of her makeup and clothing; and Spice Girls clones in the late 1990s became rampant. When lead singer Kurt Cobain of the group Nirvana committed suicide, there was a mass public expression of grief.

When the folksinger BOB DYLAN decided to perform with an electric backup band in 1965, many of his fans were outraged. At a famous concert held in Manchester, England, one audience member was so angry that when the electrified portion of the concert began, he shouted "Judas!" (to indicate he believed that Dylan was "betraying" folk music).

audition. A performance test given to an aspiring actor, singer, instrumentalist, or symphony conductor before the offer of a place in a conservatory or professional company.

In the commercial world, the fate of a trembling hopeful performer usually lies in the hands of an all-powerful manager, casting director, or talent scout. In more "humane" classical auditions, a jury of professional musicians, usually consisting of retired concert players or opera singers, is engaged to sit in judgment. The greatest nightmare for an auditioning performer is to be suddenly interrupted, while playing, by a jury member who exercises his or her temporary power with a curt "thank you." It is comforting to realize that many budding celebrities were originally cast aside in their first auditions, only later to rise to the heights as critically acclaimed artists and commercially successful stars.

Auer, Leopold, celebrated Hungarian violinist and peda-gogue, great-uncle of György (Sándor) Ligeti; b. Veszprém, June 7, 1845; d. Loschwitz, near Dresden, July 15, 1930. He studied with Ridley Kohne at the Budapest Conserva-tory. After making his debut in the MENDELSSOHN Concerto in Budapest, he continued his training with Jacob Dont in Vienna and then with Joseph Joachim in Hannover (1861–63). He was concertmaster in Dusseldorf (1864–66) and Hamburg (1866–68). In 1868 he was called to St. Petersburg as soloist in the Imperial Orchestra and as professor of violin at the newly founded Conserva-tory. He became one of the most famous violin teachers in Russia, numbering among his pupils Mischa Elman, Efrem Zimbalist, and JASCHA HEIFETZ. PIOTR ILYICH TCHAIKOVSKY originally dedi-cated his Violin Concerto to him but, offended when Auer sug-gested some revi-sions, changed the dedication to Adolf Brodsky. Nevertheless, the concerto became one of Auer's fa-vorite works, and he made it a *pièce de résistance* for all of his pupils. In 1918 he settled permanently in the U.S. He pub-lished the manu-als *Violin Playing as I Teach It* (N.Y., 1921) and *Violin Master Works and Their Interpreta-tion* (1925), as well as an autobiography, *My Long Life in Music* (1923). His performances were marked by an assured technique, exemplary taste, and nobility of expression.

Leopold Auer. (Hulton-Deutsch Collection/Corbis)

Aufstieg und Fall der Stadt Mahagonny (The rise and fall of the city of Mahagonny). Opera by KURT WEILL, to Bertolt Brecht's libretto, 1930. Weill and Brecht were famous for their operas with social messages, and this work was no exception. In it, four honest workers are living in a city where the law is weighted toward the owners of property and goods. Murder and rape are punished lightly, but crimes against property are penalized by execution. The score is influenced by American popular song and JAZZ, particularly in the *Alabama-Song.* The first production was accompanied by shouts from the audience, "Es stinkt!" (This stinks!) and "Schweinerei" (What a mess!).

In his C-minor fugue in book 2 of THE WELL-TEMPERED CLA-VIER, Bach combines the original theme with itself at half the speed.

augmentation (Ger. *Vergrösserung*). Doubling (or otherwise multiplying) the duration of the notes of a melody, so that it is presented at half speed. This simple arithmetical device is commonly used in composing FUGUES; in JOHANN SEBASTIAN BACH's fugues, augmentation is employed to illustrate one of the basic techniques of COUNTERPOINT.

In organ works, augmentation can be used impressively in the bass register of the pedals. The reciprocal (opposite) device is called DIMINUTION.

augmented interval. Any interval enlarged by an enharmonic semitone (half step). For example, in the C-major scale, a normal fourth would be the interval from C to F, while an augmented fourth is from C to F♯. The augmented triad consists of two major thirds, as in C, E, G♯.

Auld Lang Syne. (Scot., old long since). A famous celebratory song with words by the Scottish poet Robert Burns. The composer of the melody is unknown. The song is traditionally sung on New Year's Eve as a means of remembering the year past.

MUSICAL INSTRUMENT

aulos (Grk., reed, pipe). Ancient Greek wind instrument. It usually had two connected pipes, branching out in the shape of the letter V. The player blew into a single, bulbous mouthpiece, which often contained a DOUBLE REED. The aulos could be made of reed, wood, ivory, or bone; both pipes had an equal number of symmetrically placed holes. While fingers of both hands could play either pipe, it seems possible that one of the pipes functioned as a DRONE. The aulos is associated with the dances that celebrated the god Dionysus, as opposed to the music of the KITHARA (harp), which was dedicated to the god Apollo.

Auric, Georges, notable French composer; b. Lodève, Hérault, Feb. 15, 1899; d. Paris, July 23, 1983. Auric studied music at the Montpellier Conservatory, then went to Paris, where he studied at the Conservatory and at the Schola Cantorum (church singing school). By age 20 he had composed around 300 songs and piano pieces, a ballet, and a comic opera.

PEOPLE IN MUSIC

In the aftermath of World War I, Auric and many other members of his generation were disillusioned with their government and the ideals of the middle class. Traditional Romantic ideals of beauty were replaced with new ideas, emphasizing DISSONANCE over harmony and ugliness over beauty. Auric joined a revolutionary group of five composers of his generation, which was first described as Les Nouveaux Jeunes (The New Youth), and later LES SIX (the others were DARIUS MILHAUD, ARTHUR HONEGGER, FRANCIS POULENC, LOUIS DUREY, and GERMAINE TAILLEFERRE). Les Six became famous for their championing of new musical styles that threw out the old ideas of melody, harmony, and rhythm.

Auric achieved his first successes composing for Sergei Diaghilev's famous Ballets Russes, which was then resident in Paris. Particularly successful were his scores for *Les Facheux* (1924) and *Les Matelots* (1925). He also wrote music for numerous films, among them *Le Sang d'un poète* (1930), *A nous la liberté* (1932), *La Belle et la Bête* (1946), *Orphée* (1949), and *Lola Montes* (1955). His theatrical experience earned him important administrative posts, and he acted as general administrator of both the Paris Opéra and the Opéra-Comique (1962–68). In later life Auric served as president of the French Union of Composers and Authors (1954–77) and was elected to the Académie (1962).

Aus Italien. Early symphonic fantasy by RICHARD STRAUSS, 1887. The score contains the tune *Funiculì, Funiculà,* which

Strauss believed to be a Neapolitan folk song; it was actually composed by Luigi Denza.

authentic mode(s). In GREGORIAN CHANT, the four MODES whose scales range from the lower tonic (final) to the upper tonic: DORIAN (D to D), PHRYGIAN (E to E), LYDIAN (F to F), and MIXOLYDIAN (G to G). The complements of the authentic modes are the *plagal modes,* whose scales range from the lower dominant, a fourth below the tonic final, to the upper dominant; the prefix *hypo,* as in *Hypodorian,* indicates that it lies "below" the corresponding authentic mode. In the 16th century, four more modes were introduced—Aeolian (A to A), Hypoaeolian, Ionian (C to C), and Hypoionian—for a total of 12 church modes.

MUSICAL
INSTRUMENT

autoharp. A 19th-century ZITHER, invented by Charles Zimmerman, with devices for playing preset chords. It is used to demonstrate harmonic progressions and to accompany simple songs. The instrument has special harmony buttons that dampen all strings except those needed for the desired chord, so that the player can strum arpeggios freely with the fingers or a pick. The autoharp is also used in U.S. Appalachian traditional music.

automatic composition. The use of a computer (or other electronic machine) to compose compositions, either by random number generation or by programming it to work with musical information. The first such work was the *ILLIAC Suite* for string quartet (1955–56), generated by a computer at the University of Illinois under the supervision of Lejaren Hiller.

avant-garde (Fr., *vanguard,* in advance). A term, dating from 1910, referring to radical or incomprehensible art as viewed in its own time. Generally, yesterday's avant-garde becomes today's commonplace. The term *avant-garde* is the heir to a long series of terms used to describe progressive art: modern, ultramodern, new, modernistic, experimental, empiric. *See* EXPERIMENTAL MUSIC.

Ave Maria. One of the most celebrated religious songs, adapted by CHARLES GOUNOD to the C-major prelude of JO-

HANN SEBASTIAN BACH's *WELL-TEMPERED CLAVIER,* book 1. Its original version (1853) was an instrumental *Méditation;* the version with words was published in 1859.

Ax, Emanuel, outstanding Polish-born American pianist; b. Lwów, Poland, June 8, 1949. Ax began playing the violin at age six, while he also studied piano with his father. His family moved to Warsaw when he was eight, and to Winnipeg when he was 10. In 1961 Ax's family settled in N.Y., and he was enrolled at the Juilliard School of Music. He toured South America in 1969 and became a U.S. citizen in 1970.

In 1973 Ax made his N.Y. concert debut, subsequently touring the world as a highly acclaimed performer. In addition to his fine interpretations of the standard repertoire, he also distinguished himself as a champion of contemporary music.

ayre. An English court song of the 16th and 17th centuries, usually accompanied on the lute. The word is an old English spelling of *air.*

Aznavour (born Aznavurian), **Charles,** French ballad singer and songwriter; b. Paris, May 22, 1924. A son of an Armenian baritone from Tiflis, Aznavour received his early musical training at home. He acted in Paris variety shows at age five and subsequently learned to play guitar. His songs became popular in the 1940s, championed by popular French vocalists including MAURICE CHEVALIER and EDITH PIAF. He made several American tours as a nightclub entertainer and also acted in several films.

Aznavour composed a great number of songs, mostly ballads on the subject of lost or frustrated love. His best-known songs in translation include *Yesterday When I Was Young, All the Pretty Girls, The Old-Fashioned Way,* and *She.* His operetta *Monsieur Carnaval* was produced in Paris in 1965. Aznavour has appeared in several one-man shows on Broadway and returned to the N.Y. stage in the autumn of 1998.

PEOPLE IN MUSIC

PEOPLE IN MUSIC

B

PIOTR ILYICH TCHAIKOVSKY'S *Pathétique Symphony,* one of the most melancholy pieces ever written, is in B minor, as are FELIX MENDELSSOHN'S overture *Fingal's Cave* (suggesting aloofness and remoteness) and the bassoon solo in the second movement of NIKOLAI RIMSKY-KORSAKOV'S *Scheherazade.* The first movement of FRANZ SCHUBERT'S *Unfinished* Symphony expresses deep sadness; not surprisingly, it is written in B minor.

B (Ger. *H;* Fr., It., Rus., Sp., *si*). 1. The seventh tone and degree in the diatonic scale of C major. 2. In music theory, uppercase *B* designates the B-major triad, while lowercase *b* indicates the b-minor triad. 3. In German, B♭. This unique usage makes it possible to render JOHANN SEBASTIAN BACH'S name in musical notes, since the German *H* corresponds to B♮ (see B–A–C–H). 4. (Abbr.) BASS, basso; *c.B., col Basso; B.C.,* BASSO CONTINUO).

B major. A key of velvety warmth, rich in texture and emotion. The scale of B major, numbering all five black keys (F♯, C♯, G♯, D♯, A♯) and two white keys (B, E), is well-suited to the piano but not suited for orchestral works, because only the SUBDOMINANT of B major (E) is represented by an open string on the violin and double bass. As for brass instruments, they are easier to play in flat keys, which B major certainly is not. Its ENHARMONIC EQUIVALENT, C-flat major, with seven flats, has a certain affinity with the standard tuning of transposing wind instruments. IGOR STRAVINSKY'S *The Firebird* has a section in C-flat major, a rarity in orchestral music.

B minor. As described by the French composer and organist GUSTAVE CHARPENTIER, a *solitaire et mélancolique* (solitary and melancholy) key.

Babbitt, Milton (Byron), prominent American composer, teacher, and theorist; b. Philadelphia, May 10, 1916. Raised in Jackson, Mississippi, Babbitt showed a flair for music and mathematics from an early age, beginning violin studies at age four and later learning saxophone and clarinet. He entered the University of Pennsylvania at age 15, then transferred to N.Y. University to pursue his interest in music. He began studying modern music theory with composer/ teacher Roger Sessions, who hired him to be his assistant at Princeton University, where he would teach from 1948 to his retirement in 1984. Beginning in 1973, he also taught at the Juilliard School in N.Y.

Milton Babbitt, 1965. (Oscar White/Corbis)

Babbitt was a pioneer in using a synthesizer to create music. In the late 1950s he established, along with the composer VLADIMIR USSACHEVSKY, a Center for Electronic Music that was cofunded by Princeton and Columbia universities. The center had the largest and most powerful synthesizer then available. Many of Babbitt's pieces from the 1960s were composed for this instrument.

Babbitt has also contributed to 20th-century music theory, building on the theories of one of his mentors, ARNOLD SCHOENBERG. His mathematically based theories have profoundly influenced the musical thinking of younger American composers. In 1982 he won a special citation of the Pulitzer Committee for "his life's work as a distinguished and seminal American composer."

Babes in Arms. Musical by RICHARD RODGERS and LORENZ HART, 1937. The plot involves young actors who are stranded on Long Island and a transatlantic aviator who rescues them. Includes the well-known songs *My Funny Valentine* and *The Lady Is a Tramp.*

baccheta di legno (It.). Wooden drumstick used for a dry (nonresonant) beat. *Baccheta di tamburo,* a larger drumstick. *Bacchetto, a* smaller drumstick. *Bacchetta,* conductor's baton.

B–A–C–H. The letters of BACH's name, which in German pitch nomenclature correspond to the notes B♭, A, C, and B♮. JOHANN SEBASTIAN BACH used this chromatic theme in the unfinished last fugue of *THE ART OF THE FUGUE*, and many composers have since paid tribute by writing pieces based on the same four notes.

PEOPLE IN MUSIC

Bach, Carl Philipp Emanuel, the "Berlin" or "Hamburg" Bach, third son of JOHANN SEBASTIAN BACH; b. Weimar, Mar. 8, 1714; d. Hamburg, Dec. 14, 1788. Carl studied with his father at the Thomasschule, Leipzig, and then studied jurisprudence at the universities of Leipzig and Frankfurt-an-der-Oder. In 1738 he went to Berlin, where, two years later, he became chamber musician to Frederick the Great of Prussia. In 1768 he became cantor at the Johanneum, Hamburg, and directed the music for the city's five major churches. He held these posts until his death.

Abandoning the strict polyphonic style of composition of his father, C. P. E. Bach became a leader of the new school of writing called EMPFINDSAMKEIT, a highly ornamented, emotional style similar to the French ROCOCO. His *Essay on the True Art of Playing the Clavier* (2 parts, 1753–62) was influential and gives insights into the musical practices of his time.

PEOPLE IN MUSIC

Bach, Johann (John) **Christian,** the "London" Bach, noted German composer, 11th son of JOHANN SEBASTIAN BACH; b. Leipzig, Sept. 5, 1735; d. London, Jan. 1, 1782. Johann Christian studied with his father and, after 1750, with his stepbrother C. P. E. Bach in Berlin. In 1754 he went to Italy, where he studied with Padre Martini. He remained in Italy through 1762, traveling widely and composing several successful operas there. In his final years in the country, Johann Christian converted to Catholicism in order to hold the post of organist at Milan's Cathedral.

In 1762 Johann Christian moved to London, where his opera *Orione, ossia Diana vendicata* was premiered a year later. Its success led to his appointment as music master to the queen in 1764. Bach remained in London for the rest of his life and became a highly celebrated composer and performer. When young WOLFGANG AMADEUS MOZART came to London in 1764, Bach took an interest in him and improvised with him at the keyboard. Mozart retained a lifelong affection for him and used three of Bach's keyboard sonatas as models for his earliest piano concertos.

In addition to his operas, Johann Christian Bach wrote many instrumental works in different styles, including 49 symphonies, several keyboard concertos, chamber music, violin sonatas, and numerous piano sonatas. His music was based on the GALLANT STYLE of the second half of the 18th century, highly ornamented, with parts specifically written to display the instrumentalist's virtuosity. In this way, he totally departed from his father's ideals, and his music became an important influence on the Classical era.

Bach, Johann Sebastian, supreme arbiter and lawgiver of music, a master comparable in greatness of stature with Aristotle in philosophy and Leonardo da Vinci in art; b. Eisenach, Mar. 21 (baptized Mar. 23), 1685; d. Leipzig, July 28, 1750. Bach was born to an illustrious family of musicians who were active in various capacities as performing artists, composers, and teachers. He attended the Latin school in Eisenach and apparently was a good student. His mother died in 1694; his father remarried but died soon afterward. Bach was then adopted by his brother Johann Christoph (1671–1721), who supported his musical studies. In 1695 he began attending the Lyceum, Ohrdruf, and five years later, was admitted to the Mettenchor (choir) of the Michaeliskirche (St. Michael's Church), Lüneburg (1700).

Bach's first professional position came in 1703 when he was hired as the organist at the Neukirche (New Church) in Arnstadt. In 1705 he obtained a leave of absence to travel to Lübeck to hear the famous organist DIETRICH BUXTEHUDE (c.1637–1707). Buxtehude was famous for his highly ornamented style of playing the organ, and Bach would be inspired by hearing him play to add more ornamentation to his work.

In 1707 Bach became organist at the Blasiuskirche in Mühlhausen and also married his cousin Maria Barbara

PEOPLE IN MUSIC

Bach time line

1685	Born
1695–1702	School years
1703	First professional job, as church organist in Arnstadt
1705	Takes leave of absence to study organ with Dietrich Buxtehude in Lübeck
1707	Hired as church organist in Mühlhausen; weds first wife, also his cousin, Maria Barbara Bach
1708	First published work, the choral *Gott ist mein König* (God is my King)

63

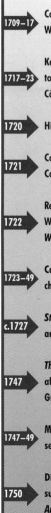

1709–17	Court organist to the duke of Weimar
1717–23	Kapellmeister and music director to Prince Leopold of Anhalt in Cöthen
1720	His first wife dies
1721	Composes the *Brandenburg Concertos*
1722	Remarries, Anna Magdalena Wilcken, and composes *The Well-Tempered Clavier*
1723–49	Cantor of Leipzig; directs church choirs and choir school
c.1727	*St. Matthew Passion* composed and performed
1747	*The Musical Offering* composed after a visit to Frederick the Great of Prussia
1747–49	Mass in B Minor assembled from several earlier choral works
1750	Dies following failed cataract surgery, leaving unfinished *The Art of the Fugue*

For many years the story was told that Bach made the journey to Lübeck on foot, supposedly indicating his strong devotion to learning more about organ playing. However, it is physically impossible for him to have walked that far in the time allotted. He may have hired himself out as a valet to a coach passenger, a not un-

(1684–1720). In 1708 Bach presented his first published work, his cantata *Gott ist mein König* (God is my King; BWV 71), for the installation of a new Mühlhausen town council. Although his employment in Mühlhausen was satisfactory, he resigned that summer after receiving the better-paid post of court organist to Duke Wilhelm Ernst of Weimar. In 1714 the duke gave Bach the position of *Konzertmeister* (concert master), at a time when Bach considered taking a position in Halle. Three years later Bach accepted the position of Kapellmeister and music director to Prince Leopold of Anhalt in Cöthen (1717), but his request for release was at first refused by Wilhelm Ernst, who imprisoned Bach for a month in late 1717 before allowing him to leave.

The Cöthen period was one of the most productive and least troubled in Bach's life. During this time he composed much of his great instrumental music: the set of six BRANDENBURG concertos, *Clavierbüchlein [Clavier Book] für Wilhelm Friedemann Bach*, book 1 of *Das Wohltemperierte Clavier* (THE WELL-TEMPERED CLAVIER), and the solo violin and cello works. In 1720 Bach accompanied Prince Leopold to Karlsbad; while he was away, his wife Maria Barbara took ill and died, leaving Bach to care for their seven children. He remained a widower for nearly a year and a half before he married Anna Magdalena Wilcken (1701–60), the daughter of a Weissenfels court trumpeter. They had thirteen children during their happy marital life.

In 1721 Bach completed his *Brandenburg* Concertos. It was also in the early 1720s that Prince Leopold married a woman who had no interest in music; Bach was thus ready to consider a job change. When Johann Kuhnau, the cantor of Leipzig, died in 1722, Bach applied for the post and was officially hired in 1723. As director of church music, Bach supervised musicians in four churches, provided music for performance at two of them, and taught at the Thomasschule, a school for training young choirboys. There were more mundane obligations that Bach was expected to discharge (for example, gathering firewood for the Thomasschule), about which Bach had many disputes with the rector. In Leipzig Bach created his greatest sacred works: the ST. MATTHEW PASSION (BWV 244), *St. John Passion* (BWV 245), the B Minor Mass (BWV 232), *Magnificat* (BWV 243), the holiday oratorios, and most of the church cantatas. In 1729 he organized the famous Collegium Musicum, made up of professional musicians and university students with whom he gave regular weekly concerts, leading this group until 1737 and again from 1739 to 1741. He made several visits to Dresden, where his son Wilhelm Friedemann was organist at the Sophienkirche.

In the late 1740s Bach's health began to fail. He suffered from a cataract that was gradually darkening his vision. An operation in 1749, performed with the crude tools of the time, left him almost totally blind. It is said that his vision suddenly returned in mid-1750, but he then suffered a cerebral hemorrhage, and a few days later he was dead. Bach's final work, *Die Kunst der Fuge* (The Art of Fugue), designed to show the range and depth of counterpoint, remained unfinished.

Bach made many contributions to music history. His collection *The Well-Tempered Clavier* (in 2 books, 1722, 1742), often referred to as "the 48," contains 48 preludes

common practice among young men of the time, in order to pay for his trip.

Another reason for Bach's trip was presumably his hope of obtaining Buxtehude's position as organist upon his retirement, but there was a catch: having five unmarried daughters, Buxtehude expected his successor to marry the eldest. Unwilling to accept this condition, Bach returned to Arnstadt.

Bach's father, Johann Ambrosius, had a twin brother. They so closely resembled each other that, according to Carl Philipp Emanuel Bach, their own wives had difficulty telling them apart. To avoid confusion, they wore vests of different colors.

◄

J. S. Bach. (Courtesy The Free Library of Philadelphia)

Perhaps Bach's greatest achievement in counterpoint is *Das Musikalische Opfer* (The musical offering, BWV 1079), composed for Frederick the Great of Prussia. Carl Philipp Emanuel Bach, who was serving Frederick, arranged for his father to visit Frederick's palace in Potsdam in 1747. The King, who liked to show off his musical skills, gave Bach a melody (that he supposedly composed himself) and asked him to improvise a fugue upon it. Upon his return to Leipzig, Bach composed a set of pieces based on the King's theme. The work is divided into 13 sections, including a puzzle canon in two parts, marked "quaerendo invenietis" ("you will find it by seeking"). Bach had the score engraved and sent it to the king.

and 48 fugues in all major and minor keys arranged in chromatic order, alternating in major and minor keys. It showed the importance of tuning keyboard instruments in EQUAL TEMPERAMENT, then a new concept, in order to play in a wide range of keys without producing unpleasant or out-of-tune notes.

Bach was one of the great masters of VARIATION, or creating different versions of the same melody. A superb example is his set known as the GOLDBERG VARIATIONS (BWV 988), so named because it was commissioned by the Russian diplomat Keyserling through Bach's pupil J. G. Goldberg (1727–56), who was in Keyserling's service as a harpsichordist.

A different type of Bach's great musical compositions is his *Concerts à plusieurs instruments,* better known as the *Brandenburg* Concertos (BWV 1046–51) because of their dedication to Christian Ludwig, margrave of Brandenburg (possibly because Bach was seeking to win a position from him). They represent the crowning achievement of BAROQUE orchestral music; Nos. 2, 4, and 5 are examples of CONCERTO GROSSO, in which a group of solo instruments (CONCERTINO) is contrasted with the accompanying string orchestra (RIPIENO).

Die Kunst der Fuge (The Art of Fugue; BWV 1080), Bach's last composition (begun in 1749), is an encyclopedia of fugues, CANONS, and COUNTERPOINT based on the same theme, using various methods of composition including INVERSION, canon, AUGMENTATION, DIMINUTION, DOUBLE FUGUE, and TRIPLE FUGUE.

Of Bach's 20 children, 10 reached maturity. His sons WILHELM FRIEDEMANN, CARL PHILIPP EMANUEL, Johann Christoph Friedrich, and JOHANN (JOHN) CHRISTIAN made their mark as independent composers. Contrary to conventional wisdom, Bach was not unappreciated by his contemporaries. His sons kept his legacy alive for a generation after Bach's death, however much their own styles might have differed. WOLFGANG AMADEUS MOZART, LUDWIG VAN BEETHOVEN, and FRÉDÉRIC CHOPIN studied Bach's preludes and fugues. While FELIX MENDELSSOHN's Berlin revival of the *St. Matthew Passion* (1829) was an important event, Bach's works were never really forgotten. They remain a core part of the classical repertory to today.

The standard Bach thematic catalogue is W. Schmieder's *Thematisch-systematisches Verzeichnis der musikalischen Werke von J. S. B. (Bach-Werke-Verzeichnis* or *BWV)* (Leipzig, 1950; 3d ed., 1961).

Bach, P. D. Q. *See* SCHICKELE, PETER.

Bach, Wilhelm Friedemann, the "Halle" Bach, eldest son of JOHANN SEBASTIAN BACH; b. Weimar, Nov. 22, 1710; d. Berlin, July 1, 1784. He studied with his father at the Thomasschule (1723–29) and violin with J. G. Graun in Merseburg (1726). In 1729 he enrolled at the University of Leipzig in mathematics, philosophy, and law. Between 1733 and 1770 he held several positions as organist and choir master in various cities, eventually settling in Berlin in 1774, where he spent the final decade of his life. He also became involved in unfortunate business dealings and died in poverty.

PEOPLE IN MUSIC

Wilhelm was a highly gifted composer, alternating between his father's style and the more emotional music favored by CARL PHILIPP EMANUEL. Wilhelm also blackened his own reputation when he claimed some of his father's music for his own, and, conversely, forged the older Bach's signature on at least one of his own pieces.

Bacharach, Burt, American composer of popular songs; b. Kansas City, May 12, 1928. Bacharach began his career as a jazz pianist working in nightclubs while attending McGill University in Montreal. After graduation he took courses with modern composers DARIUS MILHAUD and HENRY COWELL at N.Y.'s New School for Social Research. Between 1958 and 1961, he toured with Marlene Dietrich as her accompanist.

PEOPLE IN MUSIC

In 1962 he joined forces with lyricist Hal David, and together they wrote such classic songs as *Reach Out for Me, Make It Easy on Yourself, Walk on By, What the World Needs Now Is Love, Do You Know the Way to San Jose?, The Look of Love,* and *I'll Never Fall in Love Again,* as well as the successful Broadway musical *Promises, Promises* in 1968. Many of their individual songs were recorded by vocalist Dionne Warwick (b. 1941), who was closely associated with their work through the 1960s.

Bacharach also wrote songs for the films *What's New Pussycat?*, *Wives and Lovers*, *Alfie*, *Promise Her Anything*, and *Butch Cassidy and the Sundance Kid*. After many years of relative inactivity, Bacharach returned to writing pop songs in the 1990s, collaborating on an album with British songwriter ELVIS COSTELLO in 1998.

Bachianas Brasileiras. Nine pieces for various instrumental combinations by HEITOR VILLA-LOBOS, written between 1930 and 1945. The works, which combine Brazilian folk rhythms with classical COUNTERPOINT, are scored for orchestra, piano, chorus, and woodwinds. Two feature cello ensembles, including the engaging No. 5, with soprano (1938 – 45).

Baez, Joan (Chandos), politically active American folksinger, guitarist, and songwriter of English, Irish, and Mexican descent; b. Staten Island, N.Y., Jan. 9, 1941. Baez learned guitar by ear. While studying drama at Boston University she began appearing at a local coffeehouse, becoming popular for her interpretations of traditional folk songs and ballads. She made her first important appearance at the Newport Folk Festival in 1959. She subsequently recorded a number of best-selling albums and was one of the earliest supporters of the music of BOB DYLAN, introducing him as a special guest in many of her concerts.

In 1965 Baez founded the Institute for the Study of Non-Violence. She joined the anti–Vietnam War movement

PEOPLE IN MUSIC

Joan Baez. (Courtesy Vanguard Records) ▶

and supported the organizing fight of the United Farm Workers' Union, giving many benefit concerts for those organizations. Baez had her biggest commercial success in 1971 when she had a No. 1 hit with *The Night They Drove Old Dixie Down,* written by Robbie Robertson of the Band. In 1975–76 she performed as part of Bob Dylan's Rolling Thunder tours.

Baez continued to record and perform through the 1990s, to varying degrees of success.

bagatelle (Fr., trifle). A short, light piece without specific form, usually for keyboard. The term was first used by FRANÇOIS COUPERIN for a RONDEAU (*Les Bagatelles,* 1717). LUDWIG VAN BEETHOVEN wrote three sets for piano (opp. 33, 119, 126), many of which are far from trifling. Many other composers have used this term through the modern era.

bagpipe(s). An ancient wind instrument of Eastern origin, still popular in Great Britain, Ireland, and many European cultures. Basically, the instrument consists of an air-holding bag and pipes. The Scottish highland bagpipe is typical with its four pipes: three drone pipes, single- or double-reed pipes tuned to a tone, its fifth, and its octave; and one chanter (melody pipe), a single- or double-reed pipe with six or eight holes. The bag is a leather sack. Held upright, it is filled with wind either from the mouth (through a blowpipe) or from small bellows worked by the player's arm; the sounding pipes are inserted in and receive wind from the bag. The most familiar Irish pipe is the union or uilleann pipe, which is smaller, bellows-blown, and lap-held and adds regulator pipes, whose keys are played with the heel of the hand, permitting chords to be played.

Although the bagpipe is the national instrument of Scotland and Ireland, many similar instruments are found in Europe: Northumbrian small-pipe (England); *musette, cornemuse,* and *biniou* (France); *gaita* and *zampoña* (Spain, Portugal); *Dudelsack* (Germany); *zampogna* and *cornamusa* (Italy); *gajde* (Yugoslavia, Macedonia, Bulgaria); *duda* (Hungary, Belarus); *cimpoi* (Romania); *dudy* (Czech Republic); *gajdy* (Slovakia); *dudy* and *koziol* (Poland); and *mashq* (India). The *bag-hornpipe* is a family of instruments found from

FRANZ LISZT's *Bagatelle ohne Tonart,* written c.1880 and published after his death, is remarkable in that it lacks a key signature and also cultivates augmented fourths (TRITONES), major sevenths, and other dissonant intervals, forecasting 20th-century works.

MUSICAL INSTRUMENT

Crete and Turkey to the Caucasus and Volga regions and in northern Africa; these lack drones, and have double-chanter (or melody) pipes.

Baiser de la fée, Le (The fairy's kiss). Allegorical ballet by IGOR STRAVINSKY, 1928, based on melodies of PIOTR ILYICH TCHAIKOVSKY, with choreography by Ida Rubinstein; the premiere was conducted by the composer. The scenario, adapted from Hans Christian Andersen's *The Snow Maiden,* involves a fairy who kisses a stolen baby boy, then leaves him to be found by villagers. When he grows up and plans to wed, she disguises herself as his fiancée and reclaims him, sealing their union with another kiss.

PEOPLE IN MUSIC

Baker, Dame Janet (Abbott), celebrated English mezzo-soprano; b. Hatfield, Yorkshire, Aug. 21, 1933. Baker began singing lessons in London as a teenager. When she was 21 she attended classes at the Mozarteum, in Salzburg, Austria. In 1966 Baker made her American debut with the San Francisco Symphony in GUSTAV MAHLER's *Das Lied von der Erde* and presented a solo recital in N.Y., both gaining excellent reviews. Her career was given a substantial boost when she joined BENJAMIN BRITTEN's English Opera Group; in 1971 she created the role of Kate Julian in Britten's television opera *Owen Wingrave.* Through the 1970s Baker toured extensively around the world, becoming known as one of her day's greatest opera and LIEDER singers. In 1976 Queen Elizabeth II made her a Dame Commander of the Order of the British Empire. She gave her operatic farewell performance in 1982.

Baker was an outstanding artist, her extensive operatic repertoire ranging from CLAUDIO MONTEVERDI and GEORGE FRIDERIC HANDEL to RICHARD STRAUSS and Britten. She was also one of the great lieder artists of her day, excelling in songs by FRANZ SCHUBERT and ROBERT SCHUMANN.

PEOPLE IN MUSIC

Baker, Josephine, African-American-born French dancer, singer, and actress; b. St. Louis, June 3, 1906; d. Paris, Apr. 12, 1979. Baker was a street musician and dancer by age 13. She toured on the vaudeville circuit and gained recognition in the show *Chocolate Dandies* (1924). Making her way to

Paris in 1925, she starred in *La Revue nègre,* then the famous nightclub, the Folies-Bergère. Baker was an immediate hit in Paris, thanks to her talents as a singer and dancer and her exotic, revealing costumes, the most famous of which consisted of a string of bananas tied around her waist.

Baker remained a major star in Paris through the 1940s. In the 1930s she was featured in a number of films and starred in a revival of JACQUES OFFENBACH's *La Créole* in 1934. During World War II, Baker entertained troops and assisted in the French Resistance during the Nazi occupation of France. After the war she turned to humanitarian causes, adopting orphans from various countries. She was also active in the U.S. civil rights movement.

Balakirev, Mily (Alexeievich), significant Russian composer, leader of the Russian national school, member of the "Mighty Five"; b. Nizhny-Novgorod, Jan. 2, 1837 (new style; Dec. 21, 1836, old style); d. St. Petersburg, May 29, 1910. Balakirev went to Moscow as a teenager to pursue his musical studies. One of this teachers introduced him to an author and owner of an estate in his hometown, where Balakirev played piano in private musical evenings.

In 1853–54 Balakirev attended the University of Kazan to study mathematics, but in 1855, while visiting St. Petersburg, he met Russian composer MIKHAIL GLINKA who encouraged him to pursue his musical interests. In 1856, he made his compositional debut there, playing the solo part in the first movement of his Piano Concerto. Three years later his *Overture on the Theme of Three Russian Songs* was performed in Moscow, as well as his *Overture to King Lear* in St. Petersburg.

In 1863, while living in St. Petersburg, Balakirev organized a group known as the Balakirev Circle, to promote Russian national music and to oppose the influence of classical German compositions, which were very popular in Russia at that time. He also founded the Free Music School and gave concerts of Russian and German compositions. At the same time, other patriotic Russian writers and artists were promoting home-grown art.

In 1867 Balakirev organized a concert at his Free Music School of Russian and Czech music that included pieces by

PEOPLE IN MUSIC

In 1860 Balakirev took a boat ride down the Volga River from Nizhny-Novgorod to the Caspian Sea delta. While he was traveling, he collected, notated, and harmonized Russian folk songs. His 1866 collection included the ever-popular *Song of the Volga Boatmen,* also known as *Song of the Burlaks* (peasants who pulled large grain boats upstream on the Volga).

ALEXANDER BORODIN, CESAR CUI, MODEST MUSSORGSKY, NIKOLAI RIMSKY-KORSAKOV, and himself. A critic who attended this event called this group the "Mighty Five," and the name has become associated in music history with a return to Russian national melodies and rhythms. The Mighty Five were also influenced by Islamic and Asian musical styles. Balakirev became fascinated with the quasi-oriental melodies and rhythms of the Caucasus during several trips there. In 1869 he wrote a brilliant oriental fantasy for piano entitled *Islamey;* its technical difficulties rival FRANZ LISZT's études.

In the early 1870s Balakirev began to slow down in his work as a composer, conductor, and teacher. He consistently had trouble completing his scores. In 1872 he discontinued his concerts at the Free Music School. Instead, he took a job with the national railroad and subsequently became an administrator in two women's educational institutions in St. Petersburg.

In 1881 Balakirev returned to musical activities. In 1882 he conducted the premiere of the Symphony No. 1 by the 16-year-old composer ALEXANDER GLAZUNOV. He also revised and completed his earlier scores, including the *Second Overture on Russian Themes,* renamed *Russia* (1864 – 82), the symphonic poem *Tamara* (1867 – 82), and the Symphony No. 1 in C Major (1864 – 97). Balakirev retired from teaching in 1894 and spent his remaining years composing. He composed his Symphony No. 2 in D Minor in 1909 and took up the Second Piano Concerto, which he had begun in 1861, but left it unfinished.

Meanwhile, Balakirev had a falling out with many of his old friends, including Rimsky-Korsakov. From 1890 they would no longer greet each other in public, such was the anger between the two men. However, Rimsky-Korsakov continued to perform Balakirev's music at his concerts.

Balakirev made a tremendous impact on Russian music, particularly because of his conviction that Russia could rival Germany and other nations in the art of music. If his output seems relatively small, it can be attributed to illnesses, among them encephalitis (an inflammation of the brain) and severe depression. Nonetheless, he left powerful and exotically colored works.

balalaika (Rus.). Popular Russian instrument similar to the guitar, with a triangular body, long neck, and normally three strings. It became popular in the 18th century. Toward the end of the 19th century, serious Russian musicians became interested in constructing different sized balalaikas and combining them with the more ancient DOMRA in ensembles.

ballad (from Lat. *ballare,* to dance). 1. Originally a song intended for dance accompaniment; the melody of such a song. 2. In modern usage a simple narrative poem, often sentimental or dramatic, generally meant to be sung. The ballad has been especially popular in English-speaking countries, often taking mysterious legends or horror stories as subject matter. 3. Originally a short, simple vocal melody, set to one or more symmetrical stanzas, with a light instrumental accompaniment; the term now includes instrumental melodies of a similar character. 4. A composition for single instruments or orchestra, embodying the idea of a narrative. 5. In the U.S., any folk song, regardless of content.

ballad opera. A musical stage work primarily made up of folk songs or their tunes. Unlike most classical opera, there is also spoken dialogue.

Ballad operas were popular in 18th-century England and its northern colonies and are related to the French VAUDEVILLE. The work that popularized the style was *THE BEGGAR'S OPERA,* 1728, by JOHN GAY, with music arranged by John Christopher Pepusch (1667–1752). Subsequent English ballad operas drew freely on arias and choruses of past composers. The genre exhausted itself toward the end of the 18th century. More than a century later, the ballad opera was revived in Germany by KURT WEILL and Bertolt Brecht.

ballade (Fr., from Lat. *ballare,* dance). A term of widely ranging meanings. It first applied to trouvère songs and vocal compositions of ARS NOVA. Among the most significant ballades in a POLYPHONIC (multipart) vocal form are those by GUILLAUME DE MACHAUT; later development of the French genre were BERGERETTES and pastoral songs of the 18th century.

MUSICAL INSTRUMENT

băhl-lăhd′

In the Romantic period the ballade had become either a balladlike art song or an instrumental solo piece, as applied by German-speaking composers. FRANZ SCHUBERT and ROBERT SCHUMANN set many popular poems by Goethe, Schiller, and other current poets, in which all stanzas were sung to the same music. A more elaborate type of ballade was *durchkomponiert* (THROUGH-COMPOSED), in which each stanza could be set to different music.

Instrumental ballades were designed as wordless narratives, with FRÉDÉRIC CHOPIN's ballades for piano the greatest examples. Piano ballades were also written by FRANZ LISZT, JOHANNES BRAHMS, and EDVARD GRIEG.

The Russian pianist-composer Nicolai Medtner introduced a combined sonata-ballade for piano. Orchestra ballades were also composed, e.g., ALEXANDER GLAZUNOV's *Concerto Ballata* for cello and orchestra (op.108, 1931).

băhl-lah′tăh

ballata (It.). The most popular song form of the early Italian Renaissance, close in function and spirit to the French VIRELAI and the Spanish VILLANCICO. It has several stanzas, each followed by a *ripresa* (refrain). While the word may be derived from the Lat. *ballare* (dance), no dance-related ballates have been found. In the Trecento (14th century), many composers produced masterpieces in this genre, particularly Francesco Landini (c.1325 – 97).

băl-lay′

ballet (Eng., Fr.; It. *balletto;* Ger. *Ballett*). 1. An integral dance work, or dance introduced in an opera or other stage work. 2. A pantomime, with music and dances setting forth the plot of the story.

ballet de cour (Fr.). A court dance of French royalty, from Henry III to Louis XIV, with court members, including the king, participating in the performance. Subject matter included mythology, non-Christian "primitives and savages," and the glory of the royal state. Stylistically, the genre borrowed from the Italian MASCHERATA and INTERMEDIO and French courtly pantomimes and *fêtes;* it was similar to the English MASQUE. Louis XIV danced from 1651 (at age 13) until 1670; thereafter, the genre began a decline that, excepting a brief revival under Louis XV, saw its extinction by the mid-18th century. Most major French composers of the period wrote music for these performances.

Ballet mécanique. Quasi-symphonic poem by American composer GEORGE ANTHEIL, a celebrated work for a percussion ensemble that shocked Paris at its first performance in 1926. It shocked the American public even more the following year in N.Y., where Antheil added airplane propellers, buzz saws, and loud drums to the orchestra.

Several revivals of *Ballet mécanique* have occurred over the years, but it has become a period piece; the only shock that present-day audiences experience is from the knowledge that this music ever shocked anyone at all.

It is said that at the N.Y. premiere performance the propellers were so powerful that several men in the audience had their hairpieces blown off.

ballo (It.). 1. A dance. 2. A short theatrical work with dance. 3. A dramatic musical work with dance, e.g., CLAUDIO MONTEVERDI's *Il ballo delle ingrate*.

băhl′lōh

Ballo in maschera, Un (A masked ball). Opera by GIUSEPPE VERDI, 1859, adapted from the true story of the assassination of King Gustavus III of Sweden in 1792. Killing a king was not regarded as appropriate by the stage censors when Verdi's opera was premiered in Rome, so the locale was changed to America and the victim of the plot to the "governor of Boston," a nonexistent title (therefore a safe choice). The governor consults a fortune-teller for a reading of his future, and she tells him that he will be murdered. Operatic fortune-tellers are never wrong, and the unfortunate governor is stabbed to death at a masked ball by his male secretary. (The secretary was angry because the governor had been secretly sleeping with his wife.)

In 20th-century productions, when the assassination of royal personages was no longer banned on the operatic stage, attempts have been made to restore the original libretto, but they are rarely successful. Opera audiences prefer romantic invention to historic truth.

band. 1. An instrumental ensemble consisting of brass, woodwind, and percussion instruments, to the exclusion of string instruments. The term is used for such groups as MILITARY BANDS, jazz bands, dance bands, and BRASS BANDS. In jazz, a stylistic distinction exists between big bands (orchestra) and small bands (combos, groups). 2. A company of musicians playing military or sports-oriented music. 3. A section of the orchestra playing instruments of the same family (brass band, STRING BAND, WIND BAND, WOOD BAND). *See also* BIG BAND.

Band Played On, The. BALLAD in waltz time by John E. Palmer, 1895. The song's copyright was bought by the vaudevillian Charles R. Ward, to Palmer's subsequent and great regret.

band, brass. 1. Large ensemble consisting of brass instruments. Mostly used for military and sports displays or municipal entertainments, brass bands sometimes present concerts of classical music or specially commissioned works by modern composers. 2. The brass section of the orchestra.

band, military. A large, mobile ensemble designed to accompany military activities.

Military bands, dominated by brass and percussion, arose in Europe during the Middle Ages; Frederick the Great added other melody instruments such as oboes and clarinets. In the latter 18th century the instrumentation of military bands included the sound of JANISSARY MUSIC, with drums, cymbals, and bells. About the middle of the 19th century, inventor ADOLPHE SAX enriched the sonority of French military bands with instruments later known as saxophones.

As a rule, each branch of the military has its own band. In the U.S. the bands of the marines, army, navy, and air force maintain a high professional standard. In Great Britain there are several excellent military bands, notably that of the Scots Guard Royal Artillery, with its signature bagpipes. In France the Garde Républicaine still presents regular concerts.

band, string. 1. Traditional Appalachian music ensemble that evolved in the 19th century from black minstrelsy, work songs, and Anglo-Irish balladry. The instrumentation generally includes banjo, fiddle, and guitar. 2. The string section of the orchestra.

band, symphonic. Usually, an ensemble modeled on the MILITARY BAND that plays more "serious" music than the marches and patriotic tunes often associated with this type of ensemble. An American university, college, or high school

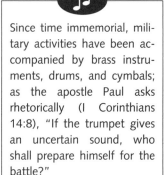

Since time immemorial, military activities have been accompanied by brass instruments, drums, and cymbals; as the apostle Paul asks rhetorically (I Corinthians 14:8), "If the trumpet gives an uncertain sound, who shall prepare himself for the battle?"

band includes more wind instruments than a regular symphony orchestra; a large symphonic band may have up to two dozen clarinets, numerous brass and saxophones, and an impressive contingent of percussion; double basses may also be included.

Many works have been written for symphonic band, beginning with the *Harmoniemusik* that JOSEF HAYDN wrote for Prussian regimental bands. Many 20th-century composers have also written pieces for symphonic bands. The number of active American symphonic bands (also called concert bands or wind orchestras) is one of the music world's best-kept secrets.

band, wind. 1. MILITARY or SYMPHONIC BAND. 2. The wind section of the orchestra.

banda (It.). 1. MILITARY BAND. 2. The brass instruments and percussion in the orchestra. 3. An ensemble playing onstage in an opera.

băhn′dăh

bandmaster. Conductor of a MILITARY BAND.

bandola (*pandura;* Sp.). 1. A Latin American relative of the Spanish BANDURRIA, with a teardrop shape and concave back. 2. *Bandolón,* a larger bandurria, with six sets of three or four strings.

băhn-doh′lăh

MUSICAL INSTRUMENT

MUSICAL INSTRUMENT

bandoneon (Sp., from Ger. *Bandoneon, Bandonion*). A large square accordionlike instrument with single or double action, invented by the German instrument manufacturer Heinrich Band in the 1840s. The instrument has become a staple of South American tango music, widely popularized by the virile and virtuosic ASTOR PIAZZOLLA.

bandoura (*bandura;* Ukr.). 1. A large-bodied Ukrainian LUTE. 2. A hybrid Ukrainian psaltery with an unfretted neck, tuned chromatically and played with a plectrum. Large groups of bandoura players sometimes perform together as an instrumental ensemble.

MUSICAL INSTRUMENT

MUSICAL INSTRUMENT

bandurria (*pandurria;* Sp.). A flat-backed member of the LUTE family from Spain, with six pairs of steel or gut strings and fretted short neck, and played in TREMOLO style with a plectrum). It is similar to the MANDOLIN. *See* BANDOLA.

banjo. An instrument with African roots that developed in the American South. It features a guitarlike neck attached to a round, wooden rim; across the rim is stretched an animal hide (more recently, a plastic head). Instruments with different

MUSICAL
INSTRUMENT

Five-string banjo player. (Courtesy Smithsonian Institution) ▶

ent numbers of strings were made through the early 1800s; around 1830 it was standardized with five strings. The fifth string is a shorter string that serves as a DRONE, while the other four are fretted to play notes and chords. In the later 1800s a second type of banjo, called the tenor or tango banjo, was introduced with only four strings, designed to be played with a pick.

The first written references to a banjo forerunner, designated as *strum-strum* or *banza,* occur in the 17th century; later names include *banjer* and *banjar.* A nearly identical instrument called the *ramkie* was in use in southern Africa by the early 18th century. Undoubtedly similar instruments existed long before these. In the U.S. the banjo was first popularized by blackface minstrels, such as J. W. Sweeney and DAN EMMETT, who played the instrument as part of their stage act.

Appalachian and southern old-time STRING BAND musicians play the banjo in a strummed style called variously "frailing," "rapping," or "knocking." More recently, BLUEGRASS banjo style, developed first by North Carolina-born player EARL SCRUGGS, in which the player picks the strings with three fingers, has become more popular.

The banjo was featured in the 1973 movie *Deliverance.* The piece played on the sound track, *Dueling Banjos* (actually a banjo and a guitar) became a No. 1 pop hit that year.

bar, barline (It. *stanghetta;* Ger. *Taktstrich*). 1. A vertical line dividing MEASURES on the STAFF, indicating where the strong

DOWNBEAT falls. The first regular usage of the bar occurs in 15th-century TABLATURES, although the downbeat and up-beat were not consistently notated until the BAROQUE period (mid-1600s). 2. An American name for measure; thus, the notes and rests contained between two barlines.

Barber of Seville, The (*Il barbiere di Siviglia*). Opera by GIOACCHINO ROSSINI, 1816, based on Beaumarchais's play *Le Barbier de Séville,* originally titled *Almaviva, ossia L'Inutile precauzione* (Almaviva, or The futile precaution). Count Almaviva is in love with Rosina, ward of Doctor Bartolo, who plans to marry her. The clever barber Figaro arranges various disguises for Almaviva to help him pursue his quest. After much intrigue, the lovers are united by Bartolo's own notary. Rossini's setting was preceded by that of Giovanni Paisiello (1740–1816), which enjoyed considerable success (1782).

Barber, Samuel, Gifted American composer; b. West Chester, Pa., Mar. 9, 1910; d. N.Y., Jan. 23, 1981. His aunt was the esteemed operatic contralto Louise Homer (b. Shadyside, near Pittsburgh, Apr. 30, 1871; d. Winter Park, Fla., May 6, 1947), her husband the composer Sidney Homer (b. Boston, Dec. 9, 1864; d. Winter Park, Fla., July 10, 1953). Barber began composing at age seven and played piano at school functions and organ in church. He enrolled at age 14 in the newly founded Curtis Institute of Music in Philadelphia. A baritone, he sang successfully in public; however, composition became his main interest.

Unlike many other 20th-century composers, Barber adopted a lyrical and ROMANTIC idiom, creating distinctly original melodies and harmonies. His early successes included 1933's Overture to *The School for Scandal,* based on the play by Thomas Sheridan, and *Dover Beach* for baritone and string quartet, after the poem by Matthew Arnold. *Music for a Scene from Shelley* followed in 1935, and the one-movement Symphony No. 1 two years later. In 1938 the First Essay for Orchestra and Adagio for Strings (arranged from his 1936 String Quartet) were performed by famous conductor Arturo Toscanini; the passionately serene *Adagio* became one of the most popular American works.

An American hit song of the BOOGIE-WOOGIE era called *Beat Me, Daddy, Eight to the Bar* plays off the double meanings of "beat" and "bar."

PEOPLE IN MUSIC

Between 1939 and 1942 Barber taught intermittently at the Curtis Institute, then joined the army air force, which commissioned him to write his second symphony. The original score, with an electronic instrument imitating the sound of radio signals, was premiered in 1944. After the war, Barber eliminated these sound effects for a new version premiered in 1948. Still dissatisfied, he discarded the work except for the second movement, which was revised as 1964's *Night Flight.* (The complete work was rediscovered and revived after his death.) Barber was discharged in 1945, and settled in Mount Kisco, N.Y., in a house (named "Capricorn") that he shared with the noted Italian opera librettist and composer GIAN CARLO MENOTTI.

Barber was always devoted to the theater. He wrote a ballet, *Medea (The Serpent Heart),* for Martha Graham in 1946, which was revised and danced by her group as *Cave of the Heart* a year later. Barber used some of the same music for an orchestra suite, also composed in 1947, and for the 1956 work *Medea's Meditation and Dance of Vengeance.*

Barber next turned his attention to opera. To prepare himself for writing a full-scale work, he produced a light operatic sketch, *A Hand of Bridge,* to a Menotti libretto (composed 1953; revised 1959); it is a staple of the opera workshop repertory. Then, in 1957, he wrote his first full opera, *Vanessa,* to a romantic libretto by Menotti. It was successfully produced by N.Y.'s Metropolitan Opera in 1958 and earned Barber his first Pulitzer Prize in music. Twenty years later he revised the opera for a performance at the Spoleto Festival in South Carolina.

A more ambitious opera, commissioned by the Metropolitan, was *Antony and Cleopatra,* based on Shakespeare's play. It was the first production at the opening of the new Metropolitan Opera House in 1966. Unfortunately, the production was haunted by mechanical mishaps: a revolving stage did not rotate properly, the acoustics were bad, and the annoyed newspaper critics damned the music along with the staging. In 1975 Barber revised the libretto and music, and this new version received a more positive response.

In addition to his operas, Barber wrote many fine instrumental works. He composed many works for piano, including the witty suite *Excursions,* written in 1945; his Piano

Sonata, which was premiered by noted pianist VLADIMIR HOROWITZ in 1949; and the Piano Concerto of 1962, a striking work in an original modern style, which won him his second Pulitzer Prize. Barber wrote many well-known vocal works with memorable and beautiful melodies, among them *Knoxville: Summer of 1915,* composed in 1948; 1953's *Hermit Songs; Andromache's Farewell* from 1963; and numerous songs and song cycles.

Barber combined the best of traditional classical composition with modern ideas. He was a master of COUNTERPOINT, writing CANONS and FUGUES in a style that recalled the BAROQUE masters. He primarily used traditional TONAL harmonies, but was also able to draw on more modern CHROMATIC techniques. His ORCHESTRATIONS are full and dramatic without being overdone. His writings for solo instruments draw on each instrument's unique personality and demand great virtuosity.

barbershop harmony. A CAPPELLA close harmony singing, usually in four parts. It developed in the late 19th century when men waiting for haircuts crooned favorite songs. Most of the repertoire is drawn from popular songs of decades ago, such as *Sweet Adeline* and *I'm Looking Over a Four Leaf Clover.* Professional and amateur groups were very popular in the first quarter of the 20th century. Groups continue to be popular today, often wearing period costumes (striped shirts and straw hats). On university campuses, glee clubs like Princeton's Tigertones continue the barbershop tradition. There are also serious female practitioners.

Barbirolli, Sir John (actually, Giovanni Battista), eminent English conductor of Italian-French descent; b. London, Dec. 2, 1899; d. there, July 29, 1970. He studied cello on scholarship in London at Trinity College of Music (1910) and the Royal Academy of Music (graduated in 1916), making his first appearance as a cellist at the age of 12. In 1916 he became a member of the Queen's Hall Orchestra in London, and in 1923 joined the International String Quartet. In 1924 he organized a chamber orchestra in Chelsea. He was also a conductor with the British National Opera Company from 1926 to 1929. He gained recognition on Dec. 12,

PEOPLE IN MUSIC

Sir John Barbirolli, c. 1970. (Hulton-Deutsch Collection/ Corbis)

1927, when he successfully substituted for THOMAS BEECHAM at a concert of the London Symphony Orchestra. In 1928 he was a guest conductor at London's Covent Garden, serving as a regular conductor there from 1929 to 1933. In 1933 he was named conductor of both the Scottish Orchestra in Glasgow and the Leeds Symphony Orchestra. He made his American debut with the N.Y. Philharmonic on Nov. 5, 1936, and was engaged as its permanent conductor in 1937. He failed to impress the N.Y. critics, however, and in 1943 returned to England, where he was named conductor of the Hallé Orchestra of Manchester. Renewing his American career, he served as conductor of the Houston Symphony Orchestra from 1961 to 1967, while continuing his tenancy of the Hallé Orchestra, from which he finally retired in 1968 with the title of Conductor Laureate for Life. He was knighted in 1949 and made a Companion of Honour in 1969. A commemorative postage stamp with his portrait was issued by the Post Office of Great Britain on Sept. 1, 1980.

Barbirolli was distinguished primarily in the ROMANTIC repertoire, his interpretations marked by nobility, expressive power, and brilliance. He had a fine pragmatic sense of shaping music according to its inward style, without projecting his own personality unduly upon it. However, this very objectivity tempered his success with American audiences, accustomed to charismatic flamboyance. He had a special affinity for English music and performed many works of ED-WARD ELGAR, FREDERICK DELIUS, and BENJAMIN BRITTEN. He conducted the first performances of the Seventh and Eighth Symphonies of RALPH VAUGHAN WILLIAMS. He also made transcriptions for string orchestra and horns of five pieces from the Fitzwilliam Virginal Book. For his second wife, oboist Lady Evelyn Barbirolli (b. Wallingford, Jan. 24, 1911), he composed an Oboe Concerto on themes by GIO-VANNI BATTISTA PERGOLESI.

barcarolle (*barcarole;* Fr., from It. *barce + rollo,* bark rower; It. *barcarola, barcarole;* Ger. *Gondellied, Barcarole*). 1. A song of the Venetian gondoliers (or boatmen). The genre is inseparably associated with the taxi-boaters who entertained and delighted tourists in the 19th century. The barcarolle is usually set in $\frac{6}{8}$ or $\frac{12}{8}$ time, suggesting the lulling motion of the waters in the Venetian canals. The most famous operatic barcarolle is in JACQUES OFFENBACH's *TALES OF HOFFMANN.* GILBERT AND SULLIVAN turned the gondoliers into sentimental lovers in their operetta *The Gondoliers.* Also called *gondoliera.* 2. A vocal, instrumental, or concerted piece imitating the Venetian gondoliers' songs.

bard. A name given to Celtic epic poets and musicians. The activities of the bards were first described in ancient Greek and Roman sources, but the tradition dates to the pre-Christian British Isles, when they were dominated by Celtic peoples. By the later Middle Ages bards were included in a caste system. The use of an elaborate metric system and classical Gaelic, the ancient Celtic language, persisted into the 17th century in Ireland and the 18th century in Scotland (where *bard* still means "poet" in Scots Gaelic). Bards were accompanied by (or accompanied themselves on) the Irish harp or the CRWTH (Welsh lyre). The medieval Welsh bards established an annual festival, the *Eisteddfod,* which was revived in 1880 as a choral festival.

Barenboim, Daniel, greatly talented Israeli pianist and conductor; b. Buenos Aires, Argentina, Nov. 15, 1942. Barenboim studied and played piano publicly in Buenos Aires un-

bar-kăh-roh'lĕ

FRÉDÉRIC CHOPIN wrote a poetic barcarolle for piano (op.60, 1845) in which the accompaniment maintains a constant movement from the tonic to the dominant while the melody engages in artful *fioritures* (ornamental turns or embellishments). FELIX MENDELSSOHN has three gondola pieces in his *Songs without Words.*

PEOPLE IN MUSIC

til 1952, when the family moved to Israel. During the summers of 1954–56 Barenboim studied piano in Salzburg, Paris (with NADIA BOULANGER), and Siena, Italy. In these years he made his first public performances in Paris and London, then made his N.Y. solo premiere in 1958. In 1960 Barenboim played all 32 BEETHOVEN sonatas in a concert series in Tel Aviv, an unusual achievement, and repeated the cycle in N.Y. In 1967 he married cellist JACQUELINE DUPRÉ, with whom he appeared in numerous sonata programs until she was stricken in 1972 with multiple sclerosis and abandoned her career.

While pursuing his career as a pianist, Barenboim also made his conducting debut in Haifa, Israel, in 1957. A decade later he toured with the Israel Philharmonic in the U.S. He made his debut as an opera conductor at the Edinburgh Festival in 1973. In 1988 Barenboim was named artistic director of the new Bastille Opéra in Paris, although disagreements over artistic policy led to his abrupt dismissal a year later. However, he immediately was appointed music director of the Chicago Symphony Orchestra, following the tenure of SIR GEORG SOLTI.

As a pianist Barenboim sometimes emphasized ROMANTIC flexibility over CLASSIC balance of form and thematic content. As a conductor he favored the Romantic masterpieces and particularly focused on the music of PIOTR ILYICH TCHAIKOVSKY, EDWARD ELGAR, and ANTON BRUCKNER.

barform (Ger.). A medieval German STROPHIC structure, with each stanza divided into two sections, a *Stollen* or *Aufgesang* (on song), followed by an *Abgesang* (off song). In musical settings, the first section is repeated before moving to the second (which is not repeated); thus, the formal model is AAB. The term would have been long forgotten if it were not revived in the 19th century by opera master RICHARD WAGNER.

Baritones are rarely given leading operatic roles, usually the property of tenors; yet WOLFGANG AMADEUS MO-

baritone (Grk., deep sound). 1. The medium-range male voice, lower than the tenor and higher than the bass, with a compass from A to about f^1. An ideal baritone voice possesses the character of lyric masculinity.

2. A valved brass instrument in B♭, with the range of the TROMBONE and a narrower bore than the EUPHONIUM. The baritone serves to fill harmony rather than play solo. The distinction between baritone and euphonium is maintained in the U.K., France, and Germany (*Tenorhorn* and *Bariton,* respectively); in the U.S. the name *baritone* tends to be used for either instrument.

Baroque music. The classical music developed between 1600 and 1750. Although the term *Baroque* (from Port. *barroco,* irregularly shaped pearl) originally implied a bizarre and even crude quality, it has acquired the opposite meaning of dignity and precise craftsmanship.

The term originated with French critics and was used in a negative sense. In the 18th and early 19th centuries the expression *goût baroque* came to mean having a taste for fanciful design in architecture and painting. A change of attitude came about in 19th-century Germany, when the term took on a more positive meaning. Curt Sachs applied the term to music in 1919; despite some disagreement, it came to refer to the era of the greatest flowering of COUNTERPOINT in instrumental and vocal music.

The Baroque period coincided with the birth of OPERA, a genre that originally challenged the highly intricate POLYPHONY of the late Renaissance. In the early 1600s a group of Italian composers based in Florence developed a new, simple style of theatrical vocal music where the melody was kept simple to emphasize the words of the text. By the mid-18th century, however, talented singers had begun introducing vocal embellishments into their performances, and highly ornamented melodies became the norm. Unstaged religious operas called ORATORIOS were written to avoid the church's ban on theatrical presentations during Lent. In other vocal music, the medieval MADRIGAL or partsong grew into the more elaborate CANTATA, with group vocal parts interspersed with solos and duets, and with elaborate instrumental accompaniments.

Even more dramatic developments occurred in instrumental music, which developed an independent identity from the vocal music it had mostly accompanied. In addition to the solo keyboards, brass ensembles, and string con-

ZART entrusted the role of Don Giovanni to a baritone. Character baritones range from villains to saints, from the tricky Scarpia in *TOSCA* to saintly Amfortas in *Parsifal.* The most famous dramatic baritone part is the toreador Escamillo in *CARMEN.* Baritones are often given comic parts, such as Mr. Lavender-Gas, a professor of literature in GIAN CARLO MENOTTI'S *Help! Help! The Globolinks!*

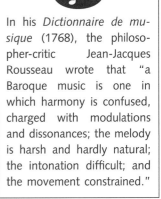

In his *Dictionnaire de musique* (1768), the philosopher-critic Jean-Jacques Rousseau wrote that "a Baroque music is one in which harmony is confused, charged with modulations and dissonances; the melody is harsh and hardly natural; the intonation difficult; and the movement constrained."

sorts that had existed before 1600, the orchestra and mixed chamber ensembles became extremely popular. Important instrumental genres that developed during this period included the SONATA, CONCERTO, SUITE, PRELUDE and FUGUE, THEME AND VARIATIONS, and SINFONIA.

Another major development was the BASSO CONTINUO, a performance practice by which figures (numbers) were added to instrumental bass lines to indicate the basic harmonies. By that time German composers had revitalized the polyphonic style with the fugue, within or without the basso continuo framework. The Baroque period also established the modern ideas of KEY SIGNATURES and TONAL harmony.

The excesses of the Baroque period—its heavy reliance on flourishes and embellishments and its great emotional force—would be addressed in turn by younger composers, such as WOLFGANG AMADEUS MOZART and FRANZ JOSEPH HAYDN, who would introduce a new era, the CLASSICAL period.

MUSICAL
INSTRUMENT

Baroque organ. A highly developed Gothic organ with several MANUALS (keyboards) and a variety of STOPS, as used by JOHANN SEBASTIAN BACH.

Baroque suite. *See* SUITE.

MUSICAL
INSTRUMENT

barrel organ. A type of mechanical organ in which a

Barrel organ players, London, 1908. (Hulton-Deutsch Collection/Corbis)

wooden cylinder (or barrel), covered with small pins, is rotated with a hand crank. The pins on the cylinder's body trigger the desired notes. The wind required to produce the sound is generated by a bellows operated by the same hand crank.

Although originally used in the church, the instrument became most famous when street musicians began using it to accompany themselves in the 19th century. The popular stereotype of the barrel organ player was that he traveled with a monkey on a string, who would dance to the music produced by the mechanical instrument. Related instruments include the ORCHESTRION and Maelzel's PANHARMONICON.

barrelhouse. A style of piano playing related to BOOGIE-WOOGIE, using ragtime, stomping, or walking basses, $\frac{4}{4}$ meter, and blues-based melodies. Barrelhouse was in vogue in the 1920s and 1930s, beginning in the South and then moving north.

Barrett, "Syd" (Roger). *See* PINK FLOYD.

Bartered Bride, The (*Prodaná nevěsta,* The bride who is sold). Opera by BEDŘICH SMETANA, written in 1866. In early 19th-century Bohemia, the parents of a young woman intend to give her in marriage to a rich man's son, but she loves another. The marriage broker attempts to bribe the woman's lover, but he refuses to trade love for money. All ends well when the lover reveals that he is himself wealthy, a prodigal son of the village headmaster.

Bartók, Béla, great Hungarian composer; b. Nagyszentmiklós (now Sinnicolau Mare, Romania), Mar. 25, 1881; d. N.Y., Sept. 26, 1945. Bartók's mother gave him his first piano lessons. After his father's death in 1888, the family moved from place to place, finally settling in Pozsony, where he continued his musical studies. In 1899 he enrolled at the Budapest Academy of Music. In his early career he was best known as a pianist. His early compositions reveal the influences of ROMANTIC composers like FRANZ LISZT, JOHANNES BRAHMS, and RICHARD STRAUSS. His first public success was with the symphonic poem *Kossuth* (1903).

PEOPLE IN MUSIC

PEOPLE IN MUSIC

Béla Bartók. (Courtesy New York Public Library) ▶

In 1904, Bartók became interested in the traditional music of his native Transylvania, including Hungarian, Romanian, Slovak, and other ethnic folk music. Along with fellow Hungarian composer and musicologist ZOLTÁN KODÁLY, Bartók traveled throughout Hungary collecting folk songs, publishing the results in *Magyar népdalok* in 1906. From then on Bartók journeyed all over Hungary, doing fieldwork and making recordings. In the 1930s Bartók completed his long-planned *Corpus musicae popularis Hungaricae* (Collection of the popular music of Hungary), cataloguing 13,000 Hungarian and 2,500 Romanian items, among the greatest collections of traditional music ever assembled.

In 1907 Bartók became the director of the Academy of Music in Budapest, a position he held until 1934. A brilliant pianist, he limited his recitals primarily to his own compositions. Bartók regularly toured throughout Europe, often giving two-piano concerts with his second wife, Ditta Pásztory (b. Rimaszombat, Oct. 31, 1903; d. Budapest, Nov. 21, 1982), whom he married in 1923. Bartók's first international recognition as a composer came following the success of his ballet *The Wooden Prince,* which premiered in 1917, and his opera *BLUEBEARD'S CASTLE,* from the following year.

In the years 1927–28 Bartók toured as a pianist in the U.S., and in the following year toured the Soviet Union. The shadow of Nazism gradually made life intolerable for Bartók in Hungary, even as he composed some of his most important works. The Nazis were not sympathetic to modern composers and their music, and the state-controlled newspapers attacked Bartók and his works as radical. Consequently, Bartók ceased performing and waited for an opportunity to leave the country. After his mother's death in 1939 and the outbreak of war, he had no reason to stay in Hungary and so fled to the United States.

Bartók was not immediately successful on his arrival in America. His health was failing, and his duo-piano recitals with his wife were poorly received. The musical society ASCAP helped support the Bartóks in his last years. One of his last works, the *Concerto for Orchestra* (1944), commissioned by the Boston Symphony conductor SERGE KOUSSEVITZKY, proved to be his most popular work (and last completed score). A year later, Bartók died after years of poor health.

At the time of his death, Bartók's Third Piano Concerto was virtually complete except for the last seventeen bars, but his Viola Concerto was just a sketch. His pupil Tibor Serly finished the first and realized the second. Ironically but typically, performances and recordings of Bartók's music increased enormously after his death. Forty-three years after his death, his remains were taken to Budapest (as he had requested) for a state funeral in 1988.

Bartók was an ardent student of folkways, seeking the roots of classical music in the songs and dances of the people. Indeed, he regarded his analytical studies of popular melodies as his most important contribution to music. He was similarly interested in the natural musical expression of children, firmly believing them capable of absorbing modern melodies and rhythms with greater ease than adults trained in the rigid disciplines of established music schools. His remarkable collection of piano pieces, *Mikrokosmos* (Small studies; 6 volumes, 1940), was intended as a method to initiate beginners into the world of modern music. These pieces are still popular today for training young pianists.

For adult listeners and performers, Bartók left a considerable legacy. In his piano works he exploited the extreme REGISTERS of the keyboard, often in the form of TONE CLUSTERS (several notes played at once) to simulate pitchless drumbeats (as in his *Allegro Barbaro,* 1911). He made use of the unusual rhythms of Hungarian folk music, often in time signatures like $\frac{7}{8}$, giving his music a definite "foreign" feeling.

Many composers have had bad reviews of their works; modern composers have particularly struggled with critics. A critic for the *Musical Quarterly* writing in 1915 described Bartók's piano music as "consist[ing] of unmeaning bunches of notes, apparently representing the composer promenading the keyboard in his boots. Some can be played with the elbows, others with the flat of the hand. None require fingers to perform nor ears to listen to."

His use of folk melodies, scales, and harmonies enhanced this sense of the exotic.

In addition to his well-known piano music, Bartók composed in nearly all forms, including stage works, choral music (both a cappella and accompanied), songs, instrumental works, including the powerful *Music for Strings, Percussion, and Celesta* (1937), and chamber music, featuring several violin and piano works, the Sonata for Solo Violin (1944), and the quirky *Contrasts* (1938), written for Hungarian-born violinist JOSEPH SZIGETI and jazz clarinetist BENNY GOODMAN. His best-known chamber works are the six string quartets, composed between 1908 and 1939. In their breadth and depth, these are the most important works in this style since LUDWIG VAN BEETHOVEN, and one wishes that Bartók had lived to write his planned seventh.

MUSICAL INSTRUMENT

FRANZ JOSEPH HAYDN wrote around 175 chamber works for baryton because his patron, Count Nikolaus Esterházy, was an avid amateur player of the instrument.

PEOPLE IN MUSIC

baryton (It. *viola di bordone,* drone viol). A now-archaic string instrument. It is about the size of the VIOLA DA GAMBA, with six or seven gut strings that are fretted and bowed, and up to twenty wire SYMPATHETIC strings that are plucked. Somewhat popular in the 18th century, the instrument sank into oblivion thereafter.

Basie, "Count" (William), eminent African-American jazz pianist and bandleader in the BIG-BAND era; b. Red Bank, N.J., Aug. 21, 1904; d. Hollywood, Fla., April 26, 1984. After studying with his mother, Basie traveled to N.Y. and learned from important stride pianists James P. Johnson and "Fats" Waller. From 1923 to 1926, he toured on the vaudeville circuit, performing with several N.Y.-based jazz bands. In 1927 he was stranded in Kansas City and began playing with Bennie Moten's Kansas City Orchestra, a pioneering swing band. After Moten's death in 1935, Basie took over as the band's leader. In a few years, it had gained fame, recording contracts, and a new name: the Count Basie Orchestra.

Basie attracted attention by his peculiar piano technique, emphasizing passages played by a single finger while directing his band with a glance or a movement of the eyebrow. He developed a powerful, swinging style, emphasized by the entire rhythm section of the band. He also nurtured many important jazz musicians, including saxophonist Lester Young.

Basie's band remained popular through the 1930s and '40s, although its activity was curtailed following the outbreak of World War II. After the war, big band music was no longer as popular, and big bands became difficult and expensive to keep together. From 1950 to 1951 Basie reduced his band's membership to eight pieces. However, he soon organized a new big band, which toured Europe successfully several times, playing a command performance for the queen of England in 1957.

Basie was one of the few big band leaders who managed to keep his group together through the 1960s and '70s without changing his original sound or style. In 1976 he suffered a heart attack and was less active from that point until his death in 1984, although the band continued to perform. Basie received the Kennedy Center Award in 1981 and the Medal of Freedom, awarded posthumously, in 1985. Among his greatest hits were *One O'Clock Jump* (which became his theme song), *Jumpin' at the Woodside, Goin' to Chicago, Lester Leaps In, Broadway, April in Paris,* and *L'il Darlin'.*

bass (Eng., Ger.; It. *basso*). 1. The lowest male voice, with an ordinary compass from F to e^1; its extreme compass ranges from C to f^1. Bass parts in opera are usually assigned to the roles of sinners or devils, e.g., Mephistopheles in CHARLES GOUNOD's *FAUST,* the villainous Boris Godunov in MODEST MUSSORGSKY's opera of the same name, and the treacherous but victimized Hunding in RICHARD WAGNER's *DIE WALKÜRE.* 2. A singer having such a voice. There have been exceptional bass singers, particularly Russian, who could go well below the normal range. Some speculate that the vast expanse of the Russian landscape somehow contributes to the formation of powerful chest cavities, whereas the warm waters of the Bay of Naples favor the development of the lyric tenor voice in Italy. 3. The lowest tone in a chord, or the lowest part in a composition. 4. The DOUBLE BASS or ELECTRIC BASS. 5. The bass VIOLA DA GAMBA. 6. A family of organ stops on the pedals, e.g., GEMSHORNBASS. 7. A valved brass instrument used in BRASS and MILITARY BANDS with a range similar to that of the TUBA.

In his drama *The Sea Gull,* the Russian playwright Anton Chekhov tells of an Italian bass singer who sang at the Imperial Opera in St. Petersburg, rousing the audience to admiring frenzy when he reached low C, whereupon a choir bass singer in the audience shouted "Bravo!" an octave lower (C^1).

MUSICAL INSTRUMENT

The bass drum entered the classical orchestra in the work of WOLFGANG AMADEUS MOZART, and LUDWIG VAN BEETHOVEN introduced it in the finale of his Symphony No. 9. The often ominous sound of the bass drum was used dramatically by RICHARD STRAUSS and GUSTAV MAHLER, who punctuated his symphonies with single drum strokes. In RUGGERO LEONCAVALLO'S *PAGLIACCI*, the bass drum is one of the props used by the clown who is tormented by jealousy. In French composer Henry Litolff's overture *Robespierre*, it illustrates a beheading.

bass clarinet. A B♭ instrument an octave below the standard (soprano) clarinet. Like other members of the clarinet family, it evolved from the now obsolete CHALUMEAU. The first extant instruments date from the end of the 18th century; the modern form was patented by instrument designer ADOLPHE SAX (who also invented the saxophone) in 1838. The bass clarinet has been popular among 20th-century composers.

bass drum (It. *tamburo, cassa grosso;* Fr. *grosse caisse*). A large cylindrical drum of indefinite pitch with heads on both sides; the orchestra instrument is at least 32 inches in diameter. The instrument is commonly found in MILITARY BANDS.

bass flute. The lowest member of the flute family, with a wide cylinder and wound tubing. The range starts at C, an octave below the standard (soprano) flute. The bass flute requires considerable lung power and good lip technique. Although the instrument is reported in the 16th century, a truly usable version did not appear until early in the 20th century (*see* ALBISIFONO).

bass guitar. Tuned like the DOUBLE BASS, the bass guitar has a guitar-shaped body, four strings, and is held against the body like the GUITAR. Most electric basses are solid bodied, like electric guitars. It is used to provide rhythmic and harmonic underpinnings in a standard ROCK band.

bass line. Since the RENAISSANCE, the lowest voice; since the BAROQUE, the basis of the melody and essential factor in the harmony. The bass line is often and incorrectly regarded as a subsidiary component of a musical work, but each of its notes serve as the lowest pitch in a series of progressive harmonies, determining the position of each chord.

bass-baritone (Eng.; It. *basso cantante*). High BASS voice.

basse danse (Fr., flat or low dance; It. *bassadanza*). The principal court dance of the late Middle Ages and RENAISSANCE. The word *basse* describes the nature of the dance, in which partners move with striding steps without leaving the

băhs dăns

floor. The basse danse was usually accompanied by wind instruments, with a $\frac{3}{2}$ meter and a slow and stately tempo. Although the dance was first cited by a TROUBADOUR in 1340, the earliest extant choreography dates from the late 15th century.

basset horn (Fr., *cor de basset;* Ger. *Bassetthorn;* It. *corno di bassetto*). A relative of the CLARINET and CHALUMEAU, now pitched in F, with a bent or curved tube and a mellow, somber timbre. The range has varied, with a present compass from F to c^3; this later instrument, with its larger bore, makes it virtually identical with the 19th-century alto clarinet.

The original basset horn in G, with a narrow bore, was developed in the late 18th century and was favored by WOLFGANG AMADEUS MOZART. LUDWIG VAN BEETHOVEN, FELIX MENDELSSOHN, and RICHARD STRAUSS also composed for this CLASSIC-period instrument.

basso buffo (It.). A comic bass, such as the music master Don Basilio in GIOACCHINO ROSSINI's opera *The Barber of Seville.*

băhs′sōh boof′fōh

basso continuo (It., *continuous bass;* Eng. *figured bass, thoroughbass;* Fr. *basse continue, chifrée, figurée;* Ger. *Generalbass, bezifferter Bass;* abbr. *continuo*). In BAROQUE ensemble music, the part played by two instruments: a keyboard or fretted string instrument (harpsichord, organ, lute) and a low-pitched instrument (cello, viola da gamba, bassoon); also, the notational system used for it. Only the bass line is given; the numerical figures located above or below it indicate the intervals above it to be played, thus spelling out the harmony. The number of notes, or the position of the voices, is not specifically marked.

băhs′sōh kōhn-tē′noo-ōh

Historically, the basso continuo developed as an aid to improvisation and as an indicator of the main harmony in the keyboard part, which supplied the accompaniment. Thus $\frac{6}{4}$ under the bass D in the key of A major would indicate the notes D, E, G♯, and B, without indicating in which octave each note should be played. Ornamentation and contrapuntal writing could be included in the improvisation,

> MUSICAL
> INSTRUMENT

depending on the ability and taste of the player. This method was widely used in the educational system in Baroque music and retained in musical training through the 19th century.

bȧhs′sōh ōhb-blē-gah′tōh

basso obbligato (It.). An indispensable bass part or accompaniment.

bȧhs′sōh ōh-stē-nah′tōh

basso ostinato (It., obstinate bass). A bass line consisting of a repeated THEME or PHRASE that serves as the foundation for variations in the upper voices. A basso ostinato can be greatly diversified as a composition, or it can also approach the more static quality of the English GROUND BASS. The PASSACAGLIA and CHACONNE are musical forms that use a basso ostinato.

bȧhs′sōh prō-fōhn-dōh

basso profondo (It., profound bass). The lowest bass voice. It is often misspelled *basso profundo*.

MUSICAL INSTRUMENT

The Italian name *fagotto* and the German name *Fagott* mean "a bundle of sticks," a description of the bassoon's shape.

bassoon (It., *bassone, fagotto;* Fr. *basson;* Ger. *Fagott*). A low-pitched woodwind instrument of the oboe family. Its double reed is attached by means of a curved metal mouthpiece to the conical double bore, which consists of four joints wrapped vertically, ending in a slightly flared bell. The normal range is from $B\flat^1$ to f^2, sometimes higher. The bassoon's tone is soft and mellow, with the nasal quality associated with double-reed instruments.

The bassoon developed from the curtal in the mid-1600s, with gradual expansions of range and keys until the 19th century, when two schools of bassoon making—French and German—were distinct. At first used for BASSO CONTINUO, the bassoon was given independent parts from the mid-18th century on, as well as concertos (WOLFGANG AMADEUS MOZART, K. 191, 1774). The opening of IGOR STRAVINSKY's *The Rite of Spring* (1913) gives the bassoon a solo in its upper register, producing an unusual but memorable effect. *See also* CONTRABASSOON, OBOE.

Bastien und Bastienne. SINGSPIEL (light opera) by WOLFGANG AMADEUS MOZART, 1768, with a simple tale of young love for a plot. It was produced in Vienna when Mozart was only twelve years old, at the home of Dr. Franz Mesmer, who was famous for treating his patients by hypnotizing them (hence the word *mesmerized*).

baton (Fr. *bâton,* stick, roll; Fr. *baguette;* Ger. *Taktstock*). 1. A conductor's stick. Batons were in common use by the mid-18th century, although they had several predecessors. 2. In the U.S. the term is also used for the twirling stick of a drum major or majorette in a marching band.

battaglia (It., battle; Eng. *battle piece*). In musical usage, compositions featuring imitations of trumpet flourishes, fanfares, drum rolls, and similar explosions of sound. The genre evolved in the 14th century. Battle pieces were invariably set in march time, with a typical rhythmic figure consisting of a half note followed by two quarter notes. During the BAROQUE period, battaglias were favored in operas and oratorios.

Of later works, perhaps the most famous battaglia is PIOTR ILYICH TCHAIKOVSKY's *Overture: 1812,* commemorating the Russian victory over Napoleon with a full complement of cannon shots and other militaristic sound effects. One of the best operatic battaglias is the orchestral interlude in NIKOLAI RIMSKY-KORSAKOV's *The Legend of the Invisible City of Kitezh,* describing the battle between Russians and Mongols.

battery (Fr., *batterie*). 1. A group of percussion instruments. 2. A drum roll. 3. An 18th-century term for ARPEGGIATED figures; also, the RASGUEADO. 4. A SONNERIE.

Battle Cry of Freedom, The. A Civil War ballad composed by GEORGE FREDERICK ROOT in 1863, which became a rallying song in the Union (Northern) camp. President Lincoln wrote to Root saying that his song had done more for the cause of the Union than 100 generals and 1,000 orators.

Battle Hymn of the Republic, The. A song with words written by Julia Ward Howe (1862), to the well-known tune of *Glory, Glory, Hallelujah!* The composer of the music is unknown. Another set of words to the same tune is *John*

A characteristic piece of Renaissance battle music is *La Guerre de Marignan* (1528), a four-part chanson by Clément Janequin. A famous battaglia for keyboard is the representation of the combat between David and Goliath in the first sonata of the *Biblische Historien* (1700) by the German organist Johann Kuhnau.

Brown's Body Lies A-Mouldering in the Grave, referring to the martyred abolitionist. Both were popular in the Civil War era and remain well-known folk songs.

Battle, Kathleen, outstanding African-American soprano; b. Portsmouth, Ohio, Aug. 13, 1948. Battle studied with Franklin Bens and made her debut at the Spoleto Festival singing the BRAHMS Requiem in 1972. Subsequently, she sang with the N.Y. Philharmonic, Cleveland Orchestra, Los Angeles Philharmonic, and other leading American orchestras.

Battle made her debut at N.Y.'s Metropolitan Opera as the Shepherd in RICHARD WAGNER's *TANNHÄUSER* in 1978, remaining a member of the company until January 1993 when a disagreement with the company's management led to her departure. In 1985 she appeared for the first time at Covent Garden, London, as Zerbinetta in RICHARD STRAUSS's *Ariadne auf Naxos.* Noted conductor Herbert von Karajan chose her as soloist for the New Year's Day concert of the Vienna Philharmonic in 1987, telecast throughout the world.

Battle excels in the light, lyric soprano repertoire. Besides appearing with major opera companies, she has also established a concert and recital career.

Bax, (Sir) Arnold (Edward Trevor), outstanding English composer; b. London, Nov. 8, 1883; d. Cork, Ireland, Oct. 3, 1953. Bax studied at London's Royal Academy of Music. In 1905 he traveled to Ireland and became profoundly interested in ancient Irish folklore after reading Irish poet-playwright William Butler Yeats. Bax wrote poetry and prose under the pseudonym Dermot O'Byrne and found inspiration for his musical compositions in Celtic legends.

In 1910 Bax returned to England. Also that year he visited Russia, composing a series of piano pieces in a pseudo-Russian style and writing music for J. M. Barrie's skit *The Truth about the Russian Dancers.* The rest of his career was spent in Britain, with visits to Ireland. By the 1930s he was receiving frequent official acknowledgments (he was knighted in 1937 and made Master of the King's Musick in 1941); but the days of his greatest creativity were over, and he also suffered from periods of depression.

Bax's style is rooted in neo-ROMANTICISM, but IMPRESSIONISTIC elements are much in evidence in his instrumental compositions. His harmony is elaborate and rich, his COUNTERPOINT free and emphasizing complete independence of the component melodies. In his many settings of folk songs, Bax adapted simple melodies to effective modern accompaniments. In addition to seven symphonies, concert overtures, and many chamber and piano works, Bax composed many orchestra works with Celtic inspiration, among them *In the Faery Hills* (1909), *Spring Fire* (1913), *The Garden of Fand* (1916), *November Woods* (1917), *Tintagel* (1919), *The Happy Forest* (1921), *Winter Legends* (1930), and *A Legend* (1944). He was an excellent pianist but a reluctant public performer; he never appeared as a conductor of his own works. He published a candid autobiography, *Farewell, My Youth* (London, 1943).

Beach, Amy Marcy Cheney (Mrs. H. H. A.), eminent American composer; b. Henniker, N.H., Sept. 5, 1867; d. N.Y., Dec. 27, 1944. Like many women of her day, Beach studied piano as a child, showing great skill. She subsequently studied with some of the best teachers of the day and made her debut in Boston on Oct. 24, 1883. In 1885 she married Dr. H. H. A. Beach, a Boston surgeon, who was a quarter of a century older than she was. The marriage was a happy one, and she used as her professional name Mrs. H. H. A. Beach.

Beach began to compose modestly, mostly for piano, but then, in 1892, completed a Mass in E♭, performed by the Handel and Haydn Society in Boston. In 1896 her *Gaelic* Symphony, based on Irish folk tunes, was performed by the Boston Symphony with exceptional success. This was probably the first performance of a female composer's symphony in the U.S. In 1897 she premiered her Violin Sonata with the well-known violinist FRANZ KNEISEL taking the solo part and, three years later, appeared as soloist with the Boston Symphony in the first performance of her Piano Concerto in C♯ Minor. She also wrote a great many songs in a ROMANTIC style.

After her husband died in 1910, Beach traveled to Europe, playing her works in Berlin, Leipzig, and Hamburg,

PEOPLE IN MUSIC

Germany. She attracted considerable attention as the first American woman to compose music at a European level of excellence. She returned to the U.S. in 1914 and lived in N.Y. Among later works, her opera *Cabildo* (1932) has received attention in recent years.

PEOPLE IN MUSIC

GOOD VIBRATIONS took months to record and was said to cost a million dollars in studio time to create. Incidentally, it was one of the first pop songs to make use of the THEREMIN, an early electronic musical instrument.

Beach Boys, The. (Leader/bass/vocal: Brian Wilson, b. Hawthorne, Calif., June 20, 1942; Guitar/vocal: Carl Wilson, b. Hawthorne, Calif., Dec. 21, 1946, d. Feb. 6, 1998; Drums/vocal: Dennis Wilson, b. Hawthorne, Calif., Dec. 4, 1944, d. Dec. 28, 1983; Guitar/vocal: Al Jardine, b. Los Angeles, Sept. 3, 1942; Lead vocal: Mike Love, b. Los Angeles, Mar. 15, 1941.) Surf-and-sun harmony group of the 1960s. Formed around the musical Wilson family, the group was led by the talented, although troubled, teenager Brian Wilson, who wrote and arranged most of their material.

The group first scored hits with surf-oriented material, then expanded into general California teen lifestyle subjects (*Surfer Girl, Fun Fun Fun, California Girls*). Wilson's studio skills grew to such an extent that he was able to create dense arrangements, both vocal and instrumental, influenced by producer PHIL SPECTOR. He reached the zenith of his creativity with the 1966 album *Pet Sounds* and the hit song *Good Vibrations* from a year later.

Increasing drug use, mental problems, and tensions within the group led Brian to withdraw from performing and composing after this time, and the quality of the group's work diminished. The group suffered further blows when Dennis Wilson died in an accidental drowning in 1983, and Carl Wilson died of cancer in 1998. The Beach Boys have since survived primarily as a nostalgia band, although occasionally Brian has returned to recording, writing, and performing, both with the group and as a solo artist, with mixed results. The band was inducted into the Rock and Roll Hall of Fame in 1988.

beam(s). Horizontal line(s) connecting adjacent notes.

Bear, The (*L'ours*). Symphony No. 82 in C Major by FRANZ JOSEPH HAYDN, 1786. The nickname may derive from the imitation bagpipe passage, because circus bears were often made to dance to the accompaniment of bagpipes. The symphony is one of the six "Paris" symphonies written for performances there, thus the frequent listing under its French nickname.

beat (It. *ribattuta,* back stroke; Ger. *Takt*). 1. A division or unit of musical time in a MEASURE. 2. A movement of the hand in marking ("beating") time. 3. In a TRILL, the pulsation of two consecutive tones. 4. An *appoggiatura.* 5. A throbbing or pulsing sound caused by the interfering waves of two tones of slightly different pitch. Beats are used to tune instruments correctly.

Beatles, The. (Leader/guitar/vocal: John [Winston] Lennon, b. Liverpool, Oct. 9, 1940; d. N.Y., Dec. 8, 1980; Vocal/bass/piano: [John] Paul McCartney, b. Liverpool, June 18, 1942; Lead guitar/vocal: George Harrison, b. Liverpool, Feb. 25, 1943; Drums/vocal: Ringo Starr [Richard Starkey], b. Liverpool, July 7, 1940.) Original, innovative, and highly influential rock band of the 1960s.

John Lennon formed his first band with art school friends when he was a teenager. Named for their school, the Quarry Men first played in 1957 at church bazaars and local events. Paul McCartney joined the band originally as a guitarist and brought on board a younger school friend, George Harrison, to play lead guitar. Lennon brought his friend Stu

PEOPLE IN MUSIC

◀

The Beatles, 1965. (UPI/Corbis-Bettmann)

Inspired by BUDDY HOLLY and the Crickets, Lennon hit upon the Beatles' name, which played on the meaning of the word, crossing *beat* with the insect name *beetle*.

The Beatles were so popular that Beatles dolls, wigs, posters, boots, lunch boxes, and just about every other type of souvenir were marketed and quickly sold out when they first arrived in America.

Sutcliffe, an art student who tried (not too successfully) to play the bass. The group was known first as the Silver Beatles, and then simply the Beatles. The Beatles opened at the pseudo-exotic Casbah Club in Liverpool in 1959 and soon moved to the more prestigious Cavern Club in 1961, where Pete Best joined as drummer.

In 1960 the group made their first trip to Hamburg, Germany, where they played at the Star Club, attracting many fans and taking on a new, leather-clad look. Back in England, the Beatles crept on to fame. In 1961 Brian Epstein, who owned a local record shop, heard the band and decided to become their manager. With contacts in the music industry from his experience selling records, he began promoting the group and remaking their image. Meanwhile, Sutcliffe died of a brain hemorrhage in 1962, and McCartney took up the role of bass player. Best, forced out of the group after their first audition tapes were made for the British Decca label, was replaced by local drummer Richard Starkey, a.k.a. Ringo Starr.

The quartet opened at the London Palladium in 1963 and drove the youthful audience to a frenzy. The strong reaction of teenage fans to their music and performances led journalists to coin the word *Beatlemania.* In 1964 Beatlemania came to America. The group made a famous appearance on the Ed Sullivan Show, at the time the most important variety program on television. Their records immediately hit No. 1 and were much imitated, both by other British groups and dozens of new American groups. Their early songs were fairly simple, emphasizing sunny harmonies, upbeat rhythms, and teenage subject matter. Early hits included *I Want to Hold Your Hand, She Loves You,* and *Can't Buy Me Love.*

Proving themselves to be more than one-hit wonders, the Beatles made two successful films, the semi-autobiographical *A Hard Day's Night* (1964) and the farce *Help!* (1965). Meanwhile, their music continued to mature. Under the influence of BOB DYLAN, Lennon began writing more introspective songs. In 1966 they decided to abandon touring and devote themselves to recording, a highly unusual move for a pop group. Their subsequent records reflected both the drug-influenced "psychedelic" sound of the day and their increased musical sophistication. Songs like *Strawberry Fields Forever* and the album *Sgt. Pepper's Lonely Hearts Club Band* showed their considerable range.

In 1967 Brian Epstein died and was never replaced. The band itself began to fall apart as well, as different interests pulled the individual members in different directions. In 1968 the group made a much-publicized trip to India to study with the leader of the Transcendental Meditation movement. Following this trip, they recorded the so-called *White Album* (it featured a blank white cover with the name "The Beatles" embossed on it), which was more like a series of solo tracks by Lennon, McCartney, and Harrison, rather than a group effort. It was followed by the disastrous sessions for what would become the *Let It Be* album and film, which showed how the group was disintegrating in painful detail. Before releasing these unsuccessful recordings to the public, the group came together one last time to record the beautiful, elegiac *Abbey Road* album, featuring some of their most accomplished harmony singing and heartfelt playing.

Lennon became enamored of the experimental artist Yoko Ono in 1968; she attended many of the Beatles' last sessions, further alienating the other group members. But despite his unhappiness, Lennon did not officially quit the band until after Paul McCartney announced, in April 1970, that he was leaving. Subsequent bitter attacks and counterattacks among the four members, and many lawsuits, led to their failure to work together again until the mid-1990s. At that time, a decade and a half after Lennon's death, the remaining band members released many previously unreleased recordings and temporarily reunited to record two new songs based on home recordings left behind by Lennon. A six-hour television documentary was released along with six CDs, and the group became one of the best-selling (nonexisting) bands of the 1990s.

For their post-Beatles careers, *see also* JOHN LENNON and PAUL MCCARTNEY.

Beautiful Dreamer. STEPHEN FOSTER's last song, 1864. Unlike his earlier songs, which presented stereotyped images of happy slaves working "down on de old plantation," this was a sentimental ballad.

When recording *Abbey Road*, Paul McCartney hit on the idea of stringing together a number of songs to make a single, unified composition. This took up most of the second side of the album. Lennon, who at this time was against any artistic ambitions, insisted that the first side of the album be devoted to simple recordings of rock and roll songs, culminating in his own riff-driven song *I Want You (She's So Heavy)*, whose title is practically its entire lyric.

bebop. A type of JAZZ that emerged in America in the 1940s, associated most strongly with saxophonist CHARLIE PARKER, trumpeter DIZZY GILLESPIE, and pianists THELONIOUS MONK and BUD POWELL. The name derives from the nonsense syllables (*bebop, rebop, bop*) sung by SCAT singers to jazz melodies. The invention of the term and the technique is generally attributed to Dizzy Gillespie.

The most striking characteristic of bebop is its high speed. Boppers sometimes play 20 notes a second with clear articulation and a strong off-beat stress. Bebop is marked by irregular SYNCOPATION, a widely ranging melody line, and an accompaniment in rapidly changing modernistic harmonies, making use of unresolved DISSONANCES and POLYTONAL combinations.

The boppers were famous for taking standard chord progressions from popular songs of the day and improvising new melodies over them. In this way, a rhythm section could play along without knowing in advance anything about the melody, simply following the preset harmonic pattern of a well-known number.

Initially, older jazz musicians like LOUIS ARMSTRONG resisted bop, considering it noise, not music. Today, bebop music is accepted as an important part of the jazz tradition. In fact, many current avant-garde musicians view bebop as conservative and old-fashioned—just as beboppers viewed earlier jazz styles in their day.

In the mid-1950s, the Beat generation of authors, including Jack Kerouac and Allen Ginsberg, made the bebop musicians their heroes, emulating the way they spoke, dressed, and acted.

PEOPLE IN MUSIC

Bechet, Sidney (Joseph), famous Creole-American jazz clarinetist and soprano saxophonist; b. New Orleans, May 14, 1897; d. Garches, France, May 14, 1959. Bechet learned to play blues and rags on clarinet in honky-tonks in Storyville, the brothel district of New Orleans. He subsequently played with leading jazz musicians in New Orleans, Chicago, and on tour. He purchased a soprano saxophone in London around 1919 and was among the first jazz musicians to play the instrument.

In addition to making frequent trips to Europe throughout the 1920s, he worked with LOUIS ARMSTRONG (as part of Clarence Williams's Blue Five and the Red Onion Jazz Babies), DUKE ELLINGTON, Noble Sissle, Johnny Hodges, Tommy Ladnier, and Zutty Singleton. The 1930s saw a decline in his fortunes, but the Dixieland revival brought him to the forefront once more. During the 1940s he led his own jazz groups in N.Y., and also made recordings with Mezz Mezzrow. Bechet settled in Paris in 1951, remaining there until his death eight years later.

Bechet was one of the most important jazz musicians of his era, unchallenged on the soprano saxophone and admired for his passionate playing and unbridled freedom of expression. His autobiography, *Treat It Gentle,* was published posthumously (N.Y., 1960).

Beecham, (Sir) Thomas, celebrated English conductor; b. St. Helens, near Liverpool, Apr. 29, 1879; d. London, Mar. 8, 1961. Beecham's father was a man of great wealth, derived from the manufacture of the once-famous Beecham pills, which were supposed to cure anemia. Thanks to this, young Thomas could pursue an interest in the arts without worrying about supporting himself.

PEOPLE IN MUSIC

Beecham enjoyed a long career as an orchestra organizer and leader and opera and theater producer and conductor. He first came to London in 1905 and by the decade's end had already organized the first of many symphony orchestras. In 1910 he began a three-year engagement as a producer of operas, bringing the radical German composer RICHARD STRAUSS to London to conduct his own works.

By the midteens Beecham had established himself as a favorite of audiences and critics alike; in recognition of his contributions to English music, he was knighted in 1916. Beecham had squandered much of his fortune on his career, however, and in 1919 was forced to declare bankruptcy. He was able to pull himself quickly out of debt and soon continued his work in the arts.

The 1920s saw Beecham establish himself as a world figure in classical music. In 1928 he made his American debut conducting the N.Y. Philharmonic. He continued to promote the work of modern composers, organizing a festival of the music of the British IMPRESSIONIST composer FREDERICK DELIUS in London in 1929. The 1930s saw Beecham adopting a more conservative tone, however. He became an outspoken supporter of the Nazi regime in Germany, taking the London Philharmonic to Berlin for a concert attended personally by Hitler in 1936.

Never supporting the British war effort, he went to the U.S. in 1940 and toured Australia. In the early 1940s he was engaged as music director and conductor of the Seattle Symphony Orchestra and filled guest engagements at N.Y.'s Metropolitan Opera. He was much criticized in America for his high-handed treatment of his orchestras, and also for his continued criticism of the Allied effort to defeat Germany.

After World War II Beecham returned to England and founded yet another orchestra, the Royal Philharmonic, in 1946. In 1951 he resumed his post as conductor at Covent Garden. In 1957, despite his previous criticism of Britain during the war, Queen Elizabeth II made him a Companion of Honour. He died four years later.

Beer, Jacob Liebmann. *See* MEYERBEER, GIACOMO.

PEOPLE IN MUSIC

Beethoven, Ludwig van, great German composer whose unsurpassed genius, expressed with supreme mastery in his symphonies, chamber music, concertos, and piano sonatas, revealed an extraordinary power of invention and marked a historic turn in the art of composition; b. Bonn, Dec. 15 or 16 (baptized, Dec. 17), 1770; d. Vienna, Mar. 26, 1827. (Beethoven himself maintained that he was born in 1772, and that the 1770 date referred to an older brother, deceased in infancy, whose name was also Ludwig, but who in fact was born in 1769.)

The family was of Dutch extraction (the name means "beet garden"). Beethoven's grandfather, also named Ludwig van Beethoven (b. Malines, Belgium, Jan. 5, 1712; d. Bonn, Dec. 24, 1773), was a choral director and singer who settled in Bonn in the early 1730s, where he married Maria Poll in 1733. The couple's only surviving child was Johann van Beethoven (b. Bonn, c.1740; d., Bonn, Dec. 18, 1792), who worked for the elector of Bonn as a musician from 1752. Johann married a young widow, Maria Magdalena Leym, in 1767; they were the composer's parents.

Beethoven received basic instruction in music from his father and other local musicians. His first important composition teacher was Christian Gottlob Neefe (1748–98), a thorough musician who understood his young pupil's great potential. Neefe guided Beethoven through the study of JOHANN SEBASTIAN BACH and keyboard improvisation.

Beethoven published his first work in 1783, his *Nine Variations for Piano on a March of Dressler.* Recognizing his talents, the Bonn elector Maximilian Franz appointed him to the post of deputy court organist, a post he held from 1784 until 1792. At the same time, Beethoven also served as a violist in theater orchestras. In 1787 the elector sent him to Vienna, where he stayed briefly and may have met WOLFGANG AMADEUS MOZART. When he returned to Bonn, he discovered his mother was dying of tuberculosis. His father had become a heavy drinker, so it fell to Beethoven to provide for his two younger brothers. He successfully petitioned the elector for half of his father's salary in 1789 and he supplemented his income by giving piano lessons. Several wealthy patrons provided him with gifts and Beethoven continued to compose.

In 1790 FRANZ JOSEPH HAYDN was honored in Bonn by the elector on his way to London. It is likely that Beethoven was introduced to him and that Haydn encouraged him to come to Vienna to study with him. Beethoven went to Vienna in November 1792 and began his studies with Haydn. It is said that the two did not get along well, however, and when Haydn went to London again in early 1794, Beethoven began formal COUNTERPOINT study with Johann

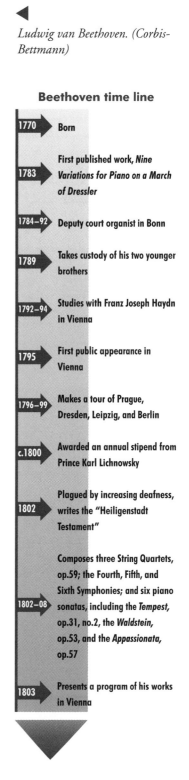

Beethoven time line

1770	Born
1783	First published work, *Nine Variations for Piano on a March of Dressler*
1784–92	Deputy court organist in Bonn
1789	Takes custody of his two younger brothers
1792–94	Studies with Franz Joseph Haydn in Vienna
1795	First public appearance in Vienna
1796–99	Makes a tour of Prague, Dresden, Leipzig, and Berlin
c.1800	Awarded an annual stipend from Prince Karl Lichnowsky
1802	Plagued by increasing deafness, writes the "Heiligenstadt Testament"
1802–08	Composes three String Quartets, op.59; the Fourth, Fifth, and Sixth Symphonies; and six piano sonatas, including the *Tempest,* op.31, no.2, the *Waldstein,* op.53, and the *Appassionata,* op.57
1803	Presents a program of his works in Vienna

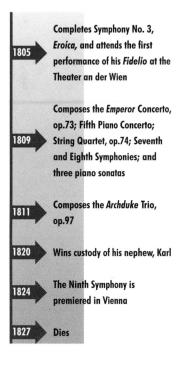

1805 Completes Symphony No. 3, *Eroica*, and attends the first performance of his *Fidelio* at the Theater an der Wien

1809 Composes the *Emperor* Concerto, op.73; Fifth Piano Concerto; String Quartet, op.74; Seventh and Eighth Symphonies; and three piano sonatas

1811 Composes the *Archduke* Trio, op.97

1820 Wins custody of his nephew, Karl

1824 The Ninth Symphony is premiered in Vienna

1827 Dies

There is a story that when Beethoven was in Vienna in 1787, Mozart heard him play and pronounced him a genius. Like many such stories, this was probably manufactured by an early biographer to enhance Beethoven's reputation.

Georg Albrechtsberger (1736–1809), a learned musician and knowledgeable teacher. These studies continued for about a year, until 1795. Beethoven also took lessons in vocal composition with Antonio Salieri, the imperial kapellmeister at the Austrian court.

Beethoven made his first public appearance in Vienna on Mar. 29, 1795, as soloist in one of his piano concertos (probably the B♭ Major Concerto, op.19). Over the next few years he played in Prague, Dresden, Leipzig, and Berlin. Around 1800 Beethoven found a generous patron, Prince Karl Lichnowsky, who awarded him an annual stipend. Beethoven was quite prolific during this period, composing his first two symphonies, five piano sonatas (including the famous *Moonlight*), six string quartets, and many other works.

Beethoven enjoyed a successful career in Vienna. He was popular not only as a virtuoso pianist and composer but also as a social figure welcome in aristocratic circles. His students included society ladies and even royal personages, such as Archduke Rudolf of Austria, to whom Beethoven dedicated the so-called ARCHDUKE trio (1811, op.97). But Beethoven's life was fatefully affected by a mysteriously growing deafness, which reached a crisis in 1802. Beethoven increasingly suffered from tinnitus (a constant buzzing in the ears), which made it painful for him even to listen to music.

Remarkably, Beethoven continued his creative work with his usual energy. There were few periods of interruption in the chronology of his works, and similarly there was no apparent influence of his health or moods of depression on the content of his music. Tragic and joyful musical passages had equal shares in his inexhaustible flow of varied works.

During 1803–05, Beethoven composed his great Symphony No. 3 in E♭ Major, op.55, the EROICA, originally dedicated to Napoleon Bonaparte. According to Beethoven's student Ferdinand Ries, Beethoven tore off the title page of the manuscript of the score after learning that Napoleon had proclaimed himself emperor of France in 1804; Beethoven supposedly exclaimed, "So he is a tyrant like all the others after all!" However, Ries's account comes from 34 years after the piece was written, and as late as 1804 Beethoven was still referring to the work as his "Bonaparte" symphony. In October 1806, when the first edition of the orchestra parts was published in Vienna, the symphony received the title *Sinfonia eroica composta per festeggiare il souvenire d'un grand' uomo* (Heroic symphony composed to celebrate the memory of a great man). But who was the great man whose memory was being celebrated in Beethoven's masterpiece? Napoleon was very much alive and leading his Grande Armée to new conquests (his forces entered Vienna in 1805). Yet the famous funeral march (second movement) expresses a sense of loss and mourning. Is the tribute now a generalized one? Or is Beethoven mourning the passing of Napoleon, First Consul? The mystery remains.

In 1803 Beethoven began work on his only opera, based on J. N. Bouilly's play *Leonore, ou L'Amour conjugal.* The completed opera was named *Fidelio, oder Die eheliche Liebe,* known now simply as FIDELIO. It was given at the Theater an der Wien in late 1805 under difficult circumstances, a few days after the French army entered Vienna. There were only three performances before the opera was rescheduled for the spring of 1806; a final and greatly revised version was produced in 1814. Beethoven wrote three overtures for the earlier versions (now known as *Leonore* 1, 2, and 3); for the final version, he wrote a fourth overture, now known as *Fidelio.*

An extraordinary profusion of creative masterpieces marked the years 1802–8. He brought out the three String Quartets, op.59, dedicated to Count Razumovsky; the Fourth, Fifth, and Sixth Symphonies; six piano sonatas, including the *Tempest* (D minor, op.31/2), the *Waldstein* (C major, op.53), and the *Appassionata* (F minor, op.57); and many other works.

The famous *da-da-da-duh* figure that opens the Fifth Symphony is perhaps the most familiar melody in all of classical music. Beethoven specifically denied that the famous introductory call represented the knock of Fate at his door, but the symbolic association was too powerful to be removed from the legend. CARL CZERNY, Beethoven's student and friend, claimed that Beethoven derived the theme from the cry of a songbird, which was piercing enough to penetrate Beethoven's increasing deafness as he took one of his frequent walks in the Vienna woods. However it may be, the

In October 1802 Beethoven wrote a poignant document known as the "Heiligenstadt Testament," after the village in which he resided at the time. The document, discovered after Beethoven's death, voiced his despair at the realization that his sense of hearing was failing. To the end of his life, Beethoven hoped to find a remedy for his deafness among the latest "scientific" medications, including experimenting with treatments of "sulfur vapor," mercury, and a vibration machine.

The four-note theme of Beethoven's Fifth Symphony was used as a victory call by the Allies in World War II. Coincidentally, three short beats followed by one long spelled V for *Victory* in Morse code. German citizens who opposed the war effort took to humming the tune on the streets. The Nazis could not very well jail people for whistling a Beethoven tune, so they took it over themselves as representing the first letter of the archaic German word *Viktoria,* and trumpeted it over their radios.

four-note motif became associated with the voice of doom for enemies and the triumph of the victor in battle.

Between 1809 and 1812 Beethoven wrote his Fifth Piano Concerto, the String Quartet in E♭ Major, op.74 (nicknamed the *Harp*), the Seventh and Eighth Symphonies, and three piano sonatas, including the E♭ Major, op.81a, whimsically subtitled *Das Lebewohl, Abwesenheit, und Wiedersehn,* also known by its French subtitle, *Les Adieux, l'absence, et le retour.* Another famous work by Beethoven was the *Emperor* Concerto, op.73. He wrote it in 1809, when Napoleon was still highly regarded as a freedom fighter. Some critics believe the work was a tribute to the French emperor. Francis I, emperor of Austria, could also have been intended, however, because the work was dedicated to his brother, Archduke Rudolf.

Personal misfortunes, chronic ailments, and quarrels with friends and relatives preoccupied Beethoven's entire life. He ardently called for peace among nations, but he never achieved peace with himself. He was overly suspicious of other people's motives, and he exaggerated his poverty. He was untidy in personal habits, often using preliminary drafts of his compositions to cover a pan of soup on the stove or his chamber pots, leaving telltale circles on the manuscripts! He was also superstitious, studying the winning numbers of the Austrian government lottery, hoping to find a clue to a fortune for himself.

Beethoven had many devoted friends and admirers in Vienna, but he spent most of his life in solitude. He never married, and apparently what few attachments he had were unsuccessful. Deprived of the pleasures of family life, Beethoven sought to find a surrogate in his nephew, Karl, son of his brother Caspar Carl, who died in 1815. Beethoven, regarding his sister-in-law Johanna as an unfit mother, went to court to gain sole guardianship over the boy, implying that she was engaged in prostitution. In 1820 he won custody. He proceeded to make his nephew's life difficult, particularly by banning visits to his mother. In 1826 Karl attempted suicide because of Beethoven's smothering attention. Thankfully, Karl survived, went into the army, was the sole inheritor of his uncle's estate, and enjoyed a normal life.

That Beethoven dreamed of an ideal life companion is clear from his candid letters to friends, in which he often asked them to find him a suitable bride. But he never kept company with any particular woman in Vienna. Beethoven lacked social graces; he could not dance; he was unable to carry on a light conversation; and behind it all was the dreadful reality of his deafness. There were several objects of his secret passions among his pupils or the society ladies to whom he dedicated his works. But he either didn't propose marriage or chose unsuitable women; most married less hesitant or more conventional suitors. In his famous undated letter addressed to an "unsterbliche Geliebte" (Immortal Beloved), Beethoven movingly expressed his longing for a happy relationship. The letter was never mailed, however, and was discovered in the secret compartment of Beethoven's writing desk after his death.

The so-called third or mature style of Beethoven is generally assigned to the last ten or fifteen years of his life. It included the composition of his monumental Ninth Symphony, first performed in Vienna in 1824 on a program that also included excerpts from the *Missa solemnis,* op.123, and *Die Weihe des Hauses* (The consecration of the house, 1815). It is reported that Caroline Unger, the alto soloist in the *Missa solemnis,* had to pull Beethoven by the sleeve at the end of the second movement so he would see and thus acknowledge the applause he could not hear. With the Ninth Symphony, Beethoven completed the evolution of the symphonic form as he envisioned it. The choral finale, with its reminiscences of the previous three movements, was his manifesto addressed to the world at large, using as its text the German poet Friedrich von Schiller's ode *An die Freude* (To joy). In it, Beethoven, through Schiller, appealed to all humanity to unite in universal love.

Beethoven's last five string quartets (opp. 127, 130, 131, 132, and 135) served as counterparts to his Ninth Symphony in their striking innovations, dramatic pauses, and novel instrumental TONE COLORS. Other works of importance were the 10th Violin Sonata, op.96; the six late piano sonatas (as original as the string quartets); the monumental *33 Variations on a Waltz by Diabelli,* op.120; two sets of bagatelles, opp. 119 and 126; and numerous English-language folk song arrangements.

In December 1826, on his way back to Vienna from a visit in Gneixendorf, Beethoven was stricken with a fever. His condition rapidly deteriorated, and he died on the afternoon of Mar. 26, 1827. It was widely reported that an electric storm struck Vienna as Beethoven lay dying, a fact confirmed by the contemporaneous Viennese weather bureau. But the story that he raised his clenched fist aloft as a gesture of defiance to an overbearing Heaven is probably untrue. The funeral of Beethoven was held in all solemnity, and his life and work has since been honored on many occasions and in many ways.

Beethoven's music marks a division between the CLASSICAL period of the 18th century and the great works of Wolfgang Amadeus Mozart and Franz Joseph Haydn, and the new spirit of ROMANTIC music that characterized the entire course of the 19th century.

Music in the 18th century was composed in prodigious quantities, suggesting mass production. The accepted number of Haydn's symphonies, according to his own count, is 104; Mozart wrote about 45. Haydn's symphonies were constructed according to an easily defined formal structure; while Mozart's last symphonies show greater depth of penetration, they do not depart from the Classical convention. Besides, both Haydn and Mozart wrote other multimovement instrumental works variously entitled cassations, serenades, divertimentos, and suites.

On the other hand, Beethoven's symphonies were few in number and all different. The First and Second may still be classified as Classical, but with the Third he entered a new world of music: it was on a grander scale than previous symphonies, contained the intense contrast of a funeral march movement, and merged the scherzo with the finale. Although the Fifth Symphony had no designated PROGRAM, its thematic unity was unprecedented. And the addition of the choral finale to the Ninth Symphony, with its clearly stated message of hope and faith, elevated symphonic writing to the realm of great philosophy.

Similarly novel were Beethoven's string quartets; a great depth separated his last string quartets from his early essays.

Trios, violin sonatas, cello sonatas, and the 32 great piano sonatas also represent changing ideas about composition. Although Beethoven did not break the classic rules of harmony, contemporary critics found some of his practices repugnant, going so far as to describe Beethoven as an eccentric bent on destroying music. Equally strange were pregnant pauses and sudden key changes in his instrumental works.

Beethoven was not a master of the fugue, as Johann Sebastian Bach and the other Classical composers were. However, he substituted his lack of skill at counterpoint with a strong imagination and an ability to offer many different variations on a single theme.

The basic works catalogues are those by G. Kinsky and H. Halm, *Beethoven's Works: Thematic-bibliographical Catalogue of His Collected Completed Compositions* (Munich, 1955), and W. Hess, *Catalogue of Works Missing from the Gesamtausgabe of Ludwig van Beethoven's Published Compositions* (Wiesbaden, 1957).

Beggar's Opera, The. A satirical BALLAD OPERA to a text by JOHN GAY, with music collated by the German-born composer John Christopher Pepusch.

The performance was usually introduced by an actor dressed as a beggar announcing the wedding of two popular ballad singers. The musical score mixed popular tunes with French airs, while the text contained direct references to contemporary politicians and criminals.

The first production took place in London on Jan. 29, 1728, in a theater frequented by the poor rather than the aristocracy that patronized performances of Italian opera. Its tremendous success brought forth countless imitations and established the popularity of the ballad opera genre in Britain.

The idea of mixing rogues and politicians in a play accompanied by light music was attractive in the 20th century as well as the 18th. The German composer KURT WEILL, in collaboration with the radical dramatist Bertolt Brecht, adapted *The Begger's Opera* to a satire on the world conditions in 1928, under the title *Die Dreigroschenoper.* The American playwright MARC BLIZTSTEIN made an adapation

The music historian Sir John Hawkins very seriously wrote, "Rapine and violence have been gradually increasing ever since the first representation of *The Begger's Opera.*" The famous author and dictionary compiler Samuel Johnson stated that there was in the work "such a labefactation [weakening] of all principles as might be injurious to morality."

of the opera, entitled *The Three-Penny Opera.* It remains one of the most popular works of our time.

beguine. A Latin American dance in a lively syncopated rhythm. COLE PORTER made a brilliant play on words in his song title *Begin the Beguine* (from *Jubilee,* 1935), a song imitative of Latin rhythms. He composed it after hearing the beguine during a cruise in the West Indies.

Beiderbecke, (Leon) **Bix,** American jazz cornet player; b. Davenport, Iowa, Mar. 10, 1903; d. N.Y., Aug. 6, 1931. Beiderbecke began to play music as a small child, developing a flair for ragtime and jazz. Sent to a private high school, Beiderbecke sneaked away after hours to play his cornet in small clubs in Chicago and St. Louis. His clear, bell-like tone set him apart from other players, along with his unusual sense of harmony.

Along with a group of other young white players, including saxophonist Frank Trumbauer, Beiderbecke formed a number of successful recording and performing bands in the mid-1920s. He was so popular that he was invited to join PAUL WHITEMAN's successful jazz orchestra in N.Y. in 1927. However, by the late 1920s he had become an alcoholic, and he succumbed to the disease in 1931.

Beiderbecke was one of the first white jazz musicians to be admired by black performers. After his death, a cult was formed around him and his small legacy of recorded performances. In addition to his cornet playing, he also com-

PEOPLE IN MUSIC

Bix Beiderbecke, c. 1927. ▶

posed a few IMPRESSIONISTIC piano pieces, most notably *In a Mist.*

bel canto (It., beautiful song). 1. The art of lyrical and virtuosic performance that was developed by the finest Italian singers of the 18th and 19th centuries. The term represents the once-glorious tradition of vocal perfection for beauty's sake. The secret of bel canto was exclusively the property of Italian singing teachers, who spread the technique to Russia, England, and America. It was, above all, applied to lyric singing, particularly in OPERA. The art of bel canto is still being taught in conservatories and music schools as training for an operatic career. 2. The operatic repertoire composed to highlight bel canto singers, notably late BAROQUE and early ROMANTIC Italian opera. This repertoire was revived after World War II, when singers such as MARIA CALLAS, JOAN SUTHERLAND, and BEVERLY SILLS brought new life to the works of VINCENZO BELLINI, GAETANO DONIZETTI, GEORGE FRIDERIC HANDEL, and others.

bel kăn'tōh

bell (Fr. *pavillon;* It. *campana*). 1. A hollow metallic percussion instrument sounded by a clapper hanging inside of it or by a hammer outside. See BELLS. 2. The flaring, open end of wind instruments such as the trumpet, trombone, or French horn. The instruction "bells up" signifies that the player should hold the instrument upward for a louder sound.

MUSICAL INSTRUMENT

Bell Song. The memorable aria for coloratura soprano in LÉO DELIBES's opera *Lakmé,* in which the heroine, a daughter of a Brahman priest but unhappily in love with a British officer in colonial India, sings to the resonant accompaniment of temple bells.

Bellini, Vincenzo, famous Italian opera composer and master of operatic BEL CANTO; b. Catania, Sicily, Nov. 3, 1801; d. Puteaux, near Paris, Sept. 23, 1835. Bellini's grandfather and father were *maestri di cappella* (masters of the chapel, or choir directors) in Catania. After studying with them, Bellini entered the Real Collegio di Musica di San Sebastiano in Naples.

PEOPLE IN MUSIC

In 1824 Bellini published his first compositions, and a year later, his first opera, *Adelson e Salvini,* was given at the Collegio. In 1827 he went to Milan, where he wrote his first OPERA SERIA, *Il pirata,* for the Teatro alla Scala. In 1831 he composed his two best-known works, *La sonnambula* and *Norma. La sonnambula* premiered in Milan with the celebrated soprano Giuditta Pasta as Amina. She also appeared in the title role of *Norma,* produced at La Scala, which gradually established Bellini's reputation as a master of the Italian operatic bel canto style.

Vincenzo Bellini. (Hulton-Deutsch Collection/Corbis)

After an unsuccessful production in 1833, Bellini traveled to London and Paris. In 1835 he produced in Paris his last opera, *I puritani,* which was a great success, thanks in part to its superb cast (featuring Giulia Grisi, Giovanni Battista Rubini, Antonio Tamburini, and Luigi Lablache). Bellini was planning future productions and marriage when he was stricken with an infection and died six weeks before his 34th birthday. His remains were removed to his native Catania in 1876.

Bellini's music represents the Italian operatic school at its most melodious, truly representative of BEL CANTO. In his compositions, words, rhythm, melody, harmony, and instrumental accompaniment unite in mutual perfection. The lyric flow and dramatic expressiveness of his music provide a natural medium for singers in the Italian language. His greatest masterpieces, *La sonnambula* and *Norma,* remain in the active repertoire of opera houses throughout the world.

bells (Fr. *cloche*). A generic name for church bells, carillons, tubular chimes, etc. In the case of church bells, the collective name is a *ring*, and the sound they make together is a *peal;* thus, "the peal of a ring of five bells" is a typical phrase. Church bells are rarely used in musical scores, although their sounds are often produced by imitation.

Some other types of bells include the following:

Tubular bells (also called tubular chimes or simply chimes) are suspended from a horizontal bar and struck with a hammer. Mike Oldfield, a British pop composer, had a major hit with his 1973 album of music for tubular bells.

Sleighbells, such as are attached to the harness of a horse-drawn sleigh, are included in scores by WOLFGANG AMADEUS MOZART, GUSTAV MAHLER, and EDGARD VARÈSE. Brian Wilson of the BEACH BOYS often used sleighbells in his arrangements.

Cowbells, heavier bells with a clapper, are found in a few classical scores and are very common in popular music. The opening measures of the ROLLING STONES' *Jumpin' Jack Flash* features a memorable rhythm played on a cowbell.

MUSICAL INSTRUMENT

The largest church bell was the Czar's Bell, which was cast in Moscow in 1733 but fell and cracked. It weighed nearly 500,000 pounds and was about 20 feet in diameter. The Liberty Bell in Philadelphia is far smaller, and also cracked, but is famous because it was rung when the Declaration of Independence was signed on July 4, 1776.

◀

Forging bells. (G. E. Kidder-Smith/© Corbis)

Domestic handbells are used for special effects in some operas, while *handbell orchestras,* consisting of a number of handbells of varying pitches, are popular in churches in the U.K. and U.S. In the U.K. they are played using the CHANGE-RINGING system.

Glockenspiel is a set of bells in the form of metal bars (the XYLOPHONE is a similar instrument featuring wooden bars).

Carillon is a tower of stationary bells (inside or outside a church), which are played by means of a large keyboard. John Cage composed numerous works for carillon (1952–67) in GRAPHIC NOTATION.

The science of making and playing bells is *campanology.*

Bells Are Ringing. Musical comedy with music by JULE STYNE and lyrics by Betty Comden and Adolph Green, 1956. It tells the story of a telephone answering service operator who helps men in distress and foils an illegal betting ring. Includes the hit songs *Just in Time, Drop That Name,* and *The Party's Over.*

Benedictus (Lat., blessed). The concluding portion of the SANCTUS in the Roman Catholic MASS. In choral settings it often appears as a separate movement.

Benjamin, George, gifted English composer, pianist, and conductor; b. London, Jan. 31, 1960. He was seven when he began piano study and nine when he commenced composition lessons. He pursued training at the Paris Conservatory (1976–78) with OLIVIER MESSIAEN (composition) and Yvonne Loriod (piano), then continued composition studies with Alexander Goehr at King's College, Cambridge (1978–82) and with Robin Holloway. From 1984 to 1987 he conducted research in electronic music at IRCAM in Paris. In 1979 he made his debut in London as a pi-

PEOPLE IN MUSIC

George Benjamin. (© Sisi Burn)

▶

anist and in 1980 became the youngest composer ever to have a work performed at the London Proms when his *Ringed by the Flat Horizon* (1979–80) was given there. He was a visiting professor at the Royal College of Music in London (from 1988) and principal guest artist of the Hallé Orchestra in Manchester (from 1993). In 1998 he became artistic consultant to BBC Radio 3's "Sounding the Century," an ambitious three-year broadcast festival of 20th-century music. In his works Benjamin avails himself of a wide variety of compositional resources. His *Antara,* a complex synthesis of panpipe sonorities re-created in concert form with IRCAM's famous 4X computer, was the subject of a 1987 BBC documentary. Recent works include *Three Inventions* for chamber orchestra (1995), *Sometime Voices* for baritone, chorus, and orchestra (1996), and *Viola, Viola* for viola duo (1997).

Berberian, Cathy, versatile American mezzo-soprano; b. Attleboro, Mass., July 4, 1925; d. Rome, Mar. 6, 1983. Berberian studied singing, dancing, and pantomime in her native Massachusetts. After college she traveled to Italy, where she attracted wide attention in 1958 when she performed *Aria* (with the electronic *Fontana Mix*) by JOHN CAGE, which demanded a fantastic variety of sound effects. Her vocal range extended to three octaves, causing one bewildered music critic to remark that she could sing both Tristan and Isolde.

Thanks to her ability to reproduce a variety of animal noises, guttural sounds, grunts, growls, squeals, squeaks, squawks, clicks, clucks, shrieks, screeches, hisses, hoots, and hollers, she instantly became the darling of inventive composers of the avant-garde, who eagerly dedicated to her their nearly unperformable works. She married the modern Italian composer LUCIANO BERIO in 1950, and he wrote *Circles, Epifanie, Visage, Sequenza, Recital I (for Cathy),* and *Folk Songs* for her before they were separated in 1966 (divorced two years later). She could also perform earlier music, making a well-received recording of vocal works by CLAUDIO MONTEVERDI. Among her own compositions are the multimedia *Stripsody,* an arresting combination of unusual vocal sounds, and a piano piece, *Morsicat(h)y.*

PEOPLE IN MUSIC

bâr-söz'

berceuse (Fr., *berceau,* cradle; Ger. *Schlummerlied,* slumber song, *Wiegenlied*). A cradle song or lullaby, usually set in $\frac{6}{8}$ time, suggesting the rocking of a cradle. FRÉDÉRIC CHOPIN's famous Berceuse, op.57, for piano has a cleverly varied melody set against a steady accompaniment on a PEDAL POINT (repeated bass note). Composers such as MILY BALAKIREV, CLAUDE DEBUSSY, MAURICE RAVEL, FERRUCCIO BUSONI, and IGOR STRAVINSKY wrote berceuses.

PEOPLE IN MUSIC

Berg, Alban (Maria Johannes), greatly significant Austrian composer, celebrated pupil of ARNOLD SCHOENBERG, whose music combined classical clarity of design and highly original melodic and harmonic techniques; b. Vienna, Feb. 9, 1885; d. there, Dec. 24, 1935. Berg played piano and composed songs without formal training as a young man. In 1904 he met Arnold Schoenberg, who became his teacher, mentor, and close friend. ANTON WEBERN was a fellow classmate, and the three initiated the radical movement known as the Second Viennese School. In 1918 Berg assisted Schoenberg in organizing Vienna's Society for Private Musical Performances with the purpose of performing works unacceptable to the musical establishment for a small, private audience; the group produced concerts for four years. In 1925 Berg joined the newly created ISCM, which continued the promotion of fresh musical ideas for public audiences.

One particularly critical review of the original production of *Wozzeck* read: "As I left the State Opera last night I had a sensation not of coming out of a public institution, but out of an insane asylum. ... In Berg's music there is not a trace of melody. There are only scraps, shreds, spasms, and burps. ... I regard Alban Berg as a musical swindler and a musician dangerous to the community."

In 1917 Berg began work on his opera *WOZZECK* (based on Georg Büchner's fragmentary play). The score combines forms drawn from classical music with composition techniques drawn from modern theory. It is organized in three acts, each with five scenes, each with a unique musical accompaniment. Its first production at the Berlin State Opera in 1925 inspired a storm of protests and negative press reviews. It was equally criticized when it was premiered a year later in Prague. Undismayed, Berg and his friends responded by publishing a brochure incorporating these bad reviews. Conductor LEOPOLD STOKOWSKI gave the first American performance in Philadelphia in 1931, where it was very well received. Thereafter, performances multiplied in Europe and in Russia, and in due time *Wozzeck* became recognized as a modern masterpiece.

Berg then wrote the *Lyric Suite* for string quartet in six movements, which was premiered in Vienna by the Kolisch Quartet in 1927. This celebrated work was written to secretly express his love for a woman to whom he was not married. Many years later, the original score was discovered with a vocal finale, a setting of a poem by Charles Baudelaire. In this form, it was performed for the first time in N.Y. in 1979.

Berg's second opera, *Lulu* (1928–35), to a libretto derived from two plays by Wedekind, was left unfinished at Berg's death. The two completed acts were performed posthumously in Zurich in 1937. The third act of the work was finally reconstructed from various manuscripts and notes by the Austrian composer Friedrich Cerha, at the request of Berg's music publishers. The premiere of the complete opera was given in 1979 at the Paris Opéra, with TERESA STRATAS as Lulu and PIERRE BOULEZ conducting, and the first American performance followed in Santa Fe later that year. As in *Wozzeck,* Berg drew on classical forms, but incorporated modern tonalities based on Schoenberg's theory of TWELVE-TONE composition.

Berg's last completed work was the Violin Concerto, commissioned by the American violinist Louis Krasner, who gave its first performance at the 1936 ISCM Festival in Barcelona. The score bears the inscription "Dem Andenken eines Engels" (To the memory of an angel), a reference to Manon, the daughter of Alma Mahler and Walter Gropius, who had just died of consumption at an early age. The work is based on the 12-tone technique, with quotations from a Carinthian folk song and the JOHANN SEBASTIAN BACH chorale *Es ist genug* (from *O Ewigkeit, du Donnerwort,* BWV 60).

bergerette (Fr., *berger,* shepherd). 1. A pastoral or rustic song popular in 18th-century France, and the poetry associated with it. 2. An instrumental dance of the 16th century.

bâr-zhâr-et′

Berio, Luciano, outstanding Italian composer of extreme musicoscientific tendencies; b. Oneglia, Oct. 24, 1925.

He studied music with his father and subsequently in conservatories in Italy and the U.S. In 1950 he married CATHY BERBERIAN who sang his most difficult soprano parts;

PEOPLE IN MUSIC

they were divorced in 1968, but she continued to perform his music. In the early 1950s Berio returned to Italy and joined the staff of the Italian Radio. He founded the Studio di Fonologia Musicale in 1955 for experimental work on acoustics, and between 1956 and 1960 edited the progressive magazine *Incontri musicali.*

Returning once again to the U.S., Berio joined the faculty of N.Y.'s Juilliard School of Music, where he taught between 1965 and 1972, providing an alternative to its traditionally conservative atmosphere. He went to Paris in the mid-1970s to join the Institut de Recherche et de Coordination Acoustique/Musique (IRCAM), an institute founded by composer-conductor PIERRE BOULEZ to encourage new music. In 1976 Berio returned to Italy to become the director of the Accademia Filarmonica Romana. In 1989 he was awarded Germany's Siemens Prize for his contributions to contemporary music and in 1996 Japan's prestigious Premium Imperiale.

Perhaps the most unusual characteristic of Berio's creative philosophy is his impartial eclecticism, by which he permits himself to use the widest variety of resources, from Croatian folk songs to *objets trouvés.* He is equally liberal in his use of GRAPHIC NOTATION, and some of his scores look like Expressionist drawings. He is one of the few contemporary composers who can touch the nerve endings of sensitive listeners and music critics, one of whom described his *Sinfonia* (1968–69, his best-known work) with ultimate brevity: "It stinks." (The last traceable use of the word was in Eduard Hanslick's 1881 response to PIOTR ILYICH TCHAIKOVSKY's Violin Concerto.) But if *Sinfonia* stank, then, by implication, so did the ample quotes from GUSTAV MAHLER, MAURICE RAVEL, and RICHARD STRAUSS incorporated in the score. Apart from "pure" music, many of Berio's works use all manner of artifacts and artifices of popular pageants, including mimodrama, choreodrama, concrete noises, acrobats, and organ grinders. Other important compositions include the *Sequenza* series for various solo instruments (1958–88); *Passaggio,* a *messa in scena* for soprano, two choruses, and orchestra (1961–62); *Opera* for 10 actors, two sopranos, tenor, baritone, vocal ensemble, orchestra, and tape (1969–70);

Voci for viola and two instrumental groups (1984); and *Formazioni festum* for orchestra (1989). He also composed numerous keyboard pieces and electronic scores, including *Schubert-Berio: Rendering* for orchestra (1989), a restoration of fragments from a Schubert symphony.

Berlin, Irving (born Israel Balin), fabulously popular Russian-born American composer of hundreds of songs that became the musical conscience of the U.S.; b. Mogilev, Russia, May 11, 1888; d. N.Y., Sept. 22, 1989, at the incredible age of 101. Berlin's family emigrated to the U.S. from Russia when he was five years old and landed in N.Y. His father was a synagogue cantor, and while in his teens, Irving worked as a newsboy, a busboy, and a singing waiter. He improvised on the bar piano and wrote the lyrics to a song, *Marie from Sunny Italy;* when the song was published (1907), his name appeared as Berlin instead of Balin.

Berlin worked as a song plugger and performer of his own songs. His first big hit was ALEXANDER'S RAGTIME BAND (1911). His first wife died of typhoid fever, contracted during their honeymoon in Havana in 1912. Berlin wrote his first ballad in her memory, *When I Lost You,* which sold a million copies. His first complete score was written in 1914 for *Watch Your Step,* a musical comedy featuring the well-known dance team of Vernon and Irene Castle.

Berlin was drafted into the U.S. Army in 1917 but did not serve in military action. Instead he wrote a revue, *Yip, Yip, Yaphank,* in which he starred and performed along with an all-army cast. The show included the hit song *O! How I Hate to Get Up in the Morning* and originally included GOD BLESS AMERICA. The song was omitted from the show, but Berlin revised it for singer Kate Smith in 1938 and it became an unofficial American anthem.

After the war ended, Berlin opened his own Broadway theater, the Music Box, producing a series of hit revues there between 1921–25. In 1925 he met Ellin Mackay, daughter of the millionaire head of the Postal Telegraph Cable Co., and proposed to her. She accepted; however, her father threatened to disinherit her if she married a Jewish immigrant. The story was widely covered in the tabloid press of

PEOPLE IN MUSIC

Berlin never learned to read or write music, and played only on the black keys of the piano. He had a special hand clutch built into his piano so the entire keyboard could be shifted, enabling him to play in any key. This piano is now on display at the Smithsonian Institution, Washington, D.C.

the day. The two eventually married in a civil ceremony. The marriage proved to be happy, lasting 62 years until Ellin's death in 1988.

In 1935 Berlin turned his attention to films and musicals. His most successful films were *Top Hat,* with FRED ASTAIRE and Ginger Rogers (1935); *Follow the Fleet* (1936); *On the Avenue* (1937); *Holiday Inn,* with BING CROSBY singing the hit song *White Christmas* (1942); and *Easter Parade* (1948).

His first Broadway musical was *Louisiana Purchase* (1940); the most successful were ANNIE GET YOUR GUN (1946) and *Call Me Madam* (1950). He ended his career with *Mr. President* (1962), which was a resounding flop. His lack of success in the last decades of his life haunted him, and Berlin became a recluse, talking on the phone to old friends but rarely seeing anyone.

Berlin was a talented lyricist, capturing the rhythms of ordinary American speech. He also was able to craft his songs to fit the popular styles of the day. He began writing typical character songs that appealed to the immigrant population of N.Y. He then introduced RAGTIME and JAZZ elements into his music as the 1920s saw a new interest in African-American melodies and rhythms. In the 1930s he wrote more sophisticated ballads, influenced by his contemporaries JEROME KERN and COLE PORTER. Then, in the late 1940s and '50s, he showed himself to be the match of Broadway composers like RICHARD RODGERS and OSCAR HAMMERSTEIN in his score for *Annie Get Your Gun.* Berlin enjoyed the longest success of any American composer and produced more hits than any other composer in popular song.

Berlioz, (Louis-) **Hector,** great French composer and master of orchestration; b. La Côte-Saint-André, Isère, Dec. 11, 1803; d. Paris, Mar. 8, 1869. Berlioz played the flute and guitar as a youth. In 1822 he went to Paris and entered the école de Médecine, but at the same time studied composition. Two years later he abandoned his medical studies to compose, producing his first important work, a *Messe solennelle* in 1825. In 1828 he presented the first complete concert of his works at the Paris Conservatory. In 1828–29 he wrote *Huit scènes de Faust,* after the play by Goethe, which

PEOPLE IN MUSIC

was eventually revised and produced as *La Damnation de Faust* (1845 – 46). In 1830 he won the Prix de Rome, after three unsuccessful tries, for his CANTATA *La Mort de Sardanapale.* During his sojourn in Italy that was funded by the prize, Berlioz produced the overtures *Le Roi Lear* and *Rob Roy* (both 1831).

Berlioz's home in Paris. (Gianni Dagli Orti/Corbis)

Meanwhile, in 1827 Berlioz became hopelessly infatuated with the Irish actress Harriet Smithson after seeing her portray Ophelia in Shakespeare's *Hamlet* in Paris. Berlioz knew no English and Miss Smithson knew no French, and thus he made no effort to speak directly with her. Instead, he began to write his most ambitious and enduring work, the *Symphonie fantastique,* which was to be an offering of adoration and devotion to Miss Smithson.

In the five-movement work, the object of the hero's passion haunts him. This is expressed through a repeated melodic motif (an IDÉE FIXE). His lover appears first as an entrancing but unattainable vision, next as an enticing dancer at a ball, and then as a nymph. He penetrates her disguise and kills her, a crime for which he is led to the gallows. At the end she reveals herself as a wicked witch at a Sabbath orgy.

The *Symphonie fantastique's* unflagging popularity for a century and a half since its composition testifies to its power. The work was first performed at the Paris Conservatory in 1830, with considerable success. However, Miss Smithson herself did not grace the occasion with her presence.

Berlioz followed the *Symphonie fantastique* with a sequel, *Lélio, ou Le Retour à la vie,* supposedly signaling the hero's renunciation of his obsessive love. Both works were performed at a single concert in Paris in 1832, with Miss Smithson in attendance. Music proved to be the food of love, and the two soon became emotionally involved. They were married in 1833, but their marriage proved happy for no more than six years. They had one son, Louis, but throughout their life together she was beset by debilitating illnesses. Berlioz found a more convenient companion, the singer Marie Recio, whom he married shortly after Smithson's death in 1854. Berlioz survived his second wife, too, who died in 1862.

Berlioz's next important work was *Harold en Italie* (1834) for solo viola with orchestra, based on Byron's *Childe Harold.* Commissioned by the famous string player NICCOLÒ PAGANINI, it had too little solo viola writing to satisfy him and he returned it to Berlioz, letting the composer keep the fee. Berlioz followed it with an opera, *Benvenuto Cellini* (1834–37), which had its first performance at the Paris Opéra in 1838. It was not successful, and Berlioz subsequently revised the score; the new version had its first performance in Weimar, conducted by FRANZ LISZT, in 1852. In the mid-1830s Berlioz expanded his musical activities to include conducting and writing music criticism.

Now a celebrated member of the Parisian cultural world, Berlioz composed the *Grande messe des morts* (Requiem; 1837), which called for a huge chorus divided into smaller groups spread throughout the hall. In late 1838 he conducted a successful concert of his works; legend has it that Paganini came forth after the concert, knelt in homage to Berlioz, and (if Berlioz is to be trusted) subsequently gave Berlioz 20,000 francs. In 1839 Berlioz conducted the first performance of his dramatic symphony *Roméo et Juliette,* based on Shakespeare's play. The work is one of the most moving and lyrical envocations of Shakespeare's tragedy, rich in melodic invention and instrumental interplay. In 1840 Berlioz premiered the *Grande symphonie funèbre et triomphale,* commemorating the soldiers fallen in the fight for Algeria. In it he exploits the MILITARY BAND to the fullest.

In the 1840s Berlioz conducted and composed for increasingly large ensembles. For his 1855 orchestral work *L'Impériale* he had 1,200 performers, augmented by huge

According to contemporary witnesses, Berlioz conducted the *Grande symphonie funèbre et triomphale* with a drawn sword instead of a baton. He led his orchestra through the streets of Paris, accompanying the ashes of the military heroes who lost their lives in Algeria to their interment in the Bastille column.

choruses and a military band. To coordinate this massive group, he hired five assistant conductors and, to keep them in time, activated an "electric metronome" with his left hand while holding the conducting baton in his right.

As a critic and composer Berlioz had a great influence on his contemporaries, among them RICHARD WAGNER, FRANZ LISZT, and the Russian school of composers. In 1843 he published his *Grand traité d'instrumentation et d'orchestration modernes* (Grand treatise on modern instrumentation and orchestration), which became a standard text. In the mid-1840s he composed a series of successful works for more modest-sized ensembles, including the revision of his earlier Faust work as an oratoriolike "dramatic legend," *La Damnation de Faust*. The score included an arrangement of the *Rákóczy* March, a melody closely associated with Hungarian nationalism, which became extremely popular as a concert piece.

Between 1847 and 1848 Berlioz undertook successful tours of Russia and England. In 1849 he composed his grand Te Deum, which was premiered six years later. In 1852 he traveled to Weimar at the invitation of Liszt, who organized a festival of Berlioz's music (including the revised *Benvenuto Cellini*).

Despite past failures with operatic productions, Berlioz returned to composing for the stage in the mid-1850s. He chose the *Aeneid* of Virgil as his text, selecting episodes concerning the Trojan War and Aeneas's visit to Carthage. He titled this grand opera *Les Troyens* (1856–60). Berlioz, never able to produce the work in its entirety, divided the score into two parts: *La Prise de Troie* and *Les Troyens à Carthage*. Only the second part was produced in his lifetime, at Paris's Théâtre-Lyrique in 1863. The opera's success made it possible for Berlioz to abandon his occupation as a music critic. His next operatic project was *Béatrice et Bénédict,* after Shakespeare's play *Much Ado about Nothing*. Berlioz conducted its first performance in Baden-Baden in 1862.

Despite frail health and a state of depression generated by his belief that he was a failure as a composer and conductor, Berlioz achieved a series of successes abroad. He conducted *La Damnation de Faust* in Vienna in 1866, then traveled to Russia during the 1867–68 season. He was received enthusiastically by the Russian musicians, who welcomed him as a true prophet of the new era in music. But the 1867 death of his beloved son, Louis, who was serving in the military, was a final blow to his well-being. He died two years later.

Posthumous recognition came slowly to Berlioz. Long after his death some conservative critics still referred to his music as bizarre and dissonant. No cult comparable to the ones around the names of Wagner and Liszt was formed to glorify Berlioz's legacy. Only the overtures, the *Symphonie fantastique,* and the songs (particularly the beautiful *Les nuits d'été,* 1841) entered the repertory. Performances of his operas were extremely rare. Because he did not write solo works for any instrument, concert recitals could not include his name in the program. Writings about and recordings of his works nevertheless mushroomed after World War II, particularly in the English language and by British artists. These have now secured his rightful place in music history.

PEOPLE IN MUSIC

Bernstein, Elmer, talented American composer of film music; b. N.Y., Apr. 4, 1922. Bernstein studied classical composition with modern composers Roger Sessions and Stefan Wolpe. He served in the U.S. Air Force during World War II, then settled in Hollywood, where he became a highly successful and versatile composer of film scores. Of these, the most effective were *The Man with the Golden Arm* (1955), *The Ten Commandments* (1956), *Desire under the Elms* (1958), *The Magnificent Seven* (1960), *Walk on the Wild Side* (1962), *To Kill a Mockingbird* (1963), *The Great Escape* (1963), *Hawaii* (1966), *True Grit* (1969), *The Shootist* (1976), *Airplane!* (1980), and *Ghostbusters* (1984). He also composed chamber music, the musical *How Now Dow Jones* (1967), three orchestral suites, chamber music, and songs.

PEOPLE IN MUSIC

Bernstein, Leonard (born Louis), prodigiously gifted American conductor and composer, equally successful in writing symphonic music and Broadway shows, and a charismatic performer; b. Lawrence, Mass., Aug. 25, 1918, of a family of Russian Jewish immigrants; d. N.Y., Oct. 14, 1990. Bernstein studied piano as a youth, and then at Har-

◀

Leonard Bernstein and family, 1957. (UPI/Corbis-Bettmann)

vard University, where he enrolled in 1935. Four years later he moved to Philadelphia to continue his studies. In 1940–41, he attended the summer music festival at Tanglewood, Mass., where he worked with SERGE KOUSSEVITZKY, then conductor of the Boston Symphony.

In 1943 he became assistant conductor to Artur Rodzinski, director of the N.Y. Philharmonic. Bernstein's break came on Nov. 14, 1943, when, in true Hollywood fashion, he was called on at the last minute to take up the baton. The critics and audience were impressed, and a career was born. He became the Philharmonic's first American-born music director in 1958 and over the next several years toured with the orchestra in South America, Russia, and 16 other European and Near Eastern countries, Japan, Alaska, and Canada. In 1969 he resigned his directorship of the Philharmonic to devote more time to composition and other projects. The orchestra bestowed upon him the unprecedented title of "laureate conductor." In 1976 he took the orchestra on a Bicentennial tour of 11 European cities, giving 13 concerts in 17 days.

Bernstein was also a talented educator. From 1951 to 1955 he taught at Brandeis University and also, during the summers, at Tanglewood. In 1958 he initiated a televised series of Young People's Concerts, which became popular with audiences of all ages. He also arranged a series of educational music programs for television. In 1973 Bernstein was invited to give the prestigious Charles Eliot Norton lectures at Harvard University.

As an interpreter and program maker Bernstein showed a unique affinity with the music of GUSTAV MAHLER, whose symphonies he repeatedly performed in special cycles. In late 1989 he conducted celebratory performances of LUDWIG VAN BEETHOVEN's Ninth Symphony on both sides of the Berlin Wall, to celebrate its fall. The orchestra was made up of members from the Bavarian Radio Symphony Orchestra, Munich, augmented by players from N.Y., London, Paris, Dresden, and Leningrad.

Musical history knows of a number of composers who were also excellent conductors, but few professional conductors who were also significant composers. Bernstein seemed uniquely and equally talented as a symphonic and operatic conductor as well as a composer of complex musical works and original and enormously popular stage productions. In his WEST SIDE STORY (1957) he created a significant social drama, filled with memorable tunes. His other successful shows were *On the Town* (1944) and *Candide* (1956). In his second symphony, THE AGE OF ANXIETY (1949; rev. 1965), he reflected the turbulence of modern life. Among his choral works is a devout choral symphony, *Kaddish* (1963; rev. 1977) and the semidramatic *Mass* (1971).

In 1990 Bernstein finally succumbed to a long battle with emphysema and heart disease. Although he was a heavy smoker and was very ill for the last years of his life, he remained active as a conductor onstage until literally weeks before his death.

Berry, Chuck (Charles Edward Anderson), African-American rock singer, guitarist, and songwriter; b. San Jose, Calif., Jan. 15, 1926. Berry sang as a member of the Antioch Baptist Church's choir as a youth in St. Louis. At the same time, he learned to play guitar and improvised tunes in a jazz manner. In 1955 he went to Chicago and recorded his song *Maybellene* for the Chess record company. It quickly climbed the charts in all three major categories—rhythm and blues, country-western, and popular—an unheard of achievement.

Hit songs from *West Side Story*, with lyrics by STEPHEN SONDHEIM, include *Maria*, *America*, and *There's a Place for Us*.

PEOPLE IN MUSIC

He scored many more hits with his own compositions through the late 1950s, including *Brown-Eyed Handsome Man, Roll Over Beethoven, Rock and Roll Music, Johnny B. Goode, Sweet Little Sixteen,* and *Memphis, Tennessee.*

Around this time Berry opened the Chuck Berry Club Bandstand in St. Louis. It prospered, but he ran into trouble when a 14-year-old hatcheck girl employed in the club brought charges that he had transported her across state lines for "immoral purposes." He was found guilty of violating the Mann Act and served two years in the federal penitentiary in Terre Haute (1961–63). Jail made him bitter, but on his release he continued to perform and had hits through the 1960s, including *Nadine, No Particular Place to Go,* and *My Ding-a-Ling,* his last big hit in the early 1970s. Other than a tax-evasion conviction that put him back in prison briefly in 1979, he maintained an active career as a lively oldie-but-goodie performer, still doing his patented "duckwalk" across the stage.

Berry's guitar style was based on rapid rhythm-and-blues riffs, showing also country influences. He exploited the electric guitar's potential for highly rhythmic chording (perhaps the most distinctive feature of his playing) and ringing overtones. His songs were primarily of the blues type, with strong emphasis on "a backbeat [so that] you can't lose it/ Any old time you use it." He was extremely influential on later musicians.

Bethune, "Blind Tom" (Thomas Greene), African-American pianist and composer; b. Columbus, Ga., May 25, 1849; d. Hoboken, N.J., June 13, 1908. Born blind and into slavery, Tom was purchased, along with his parents, Charity and Mingo Wiggins, by James N. Bethune in 1850. He was taught to play piano by Bethune's daughter, who recognized his talent.

Taking advantage of Tom's musical ability, his master began "exhibiting" him throughout Georgia in 1857. He then "leased" him for three years to Perry Oliver, a Savannah planter, who arranged concert appearances for him throughout the southern states as well as in Washington, D.C. With the outbreak of the Civil War, Bethune took full charge of Tom's career, touring around the Confederacy to raise

PEOPLE IN MUSIC

money for the war cause. In 1865 he obtained legal custody and a major part of Tom's earnings.

Tom spent the rest of his career playing in Europe and North America. He was never able to escape the grip of the Bethune family. A court upheld their "guardianship" in 1887. By the end of his public performing days, he was working the vaudeville circuit.

Tom Bethune was an excellent pianist. His programs usually included classical works by JOHANN SEBASTIAN BACH, LUDWIG VAN BEETHOVEN, FRANZ LISZT, FRÉDÉRIC CHOPIN, and LOUIS MOREAU GOTTSCHALK, as well as his own compositions, mostly improvised character pieces. These were arranged, published, and supplied with appropriate titles by his managers, e.g., *Rainstorm* (1865), *The Battle of Manassas* (1866), *Wellenlänge* (Wavelength, 1882), and *Imitation of the Sewing Machine* (1889). He also improvised on themes supplied by members of his audiences.

> ♫
>
> Most modern machines—such as electric motors, fans, and washing machines—buzz, whir, and hum on the 60-cycle B♭, corresponding to the lowest note of the bassoon.

B-flat major (Ger. *B dur*). If any key can claim to be the key of the universe, it is B♭ major. The transposing instruments of the orchestra, particularly trumpets and clarinets, are most often in B♭. This tuning enables them to be played in the key of B♭ major with the same ease that pianists play in C major.

Because natural trumpets are tuned to B♭ major, it is the key of fanfares and of festival and military marches. The march of the soldiers in CHARLES GOUNOD's *FAUST*, the return of Radames from the conquest of Ethiopia in GIUSEPPE VERDI's *AIDA*, the march of the children and the signal call summoning Don José back to the barracks in GEORGES BIZET's *CARMEN*, and the dramatic trumpet call in LUDWIG VAN BEETHOVEN's *FIDELIO*, announcing the arrival of the governor, are all in B♭ major.

Standard arrangements of national anthems, including *The Star-Spangled Banner* and the *Marseillaise*, are in B♭ major. GEORGE M. COHAN's song *Over There*, imitating the bugle calls of the doughboys of World War I, is in B♭ major, as is the bugle call that announces the opening of horse races. And then there is that gloriously uninhibited upward sweep of the clarinet (a B♭ clarinet, of course) that opens GEORGE GERSHWIN's *Rhapsody in Blue*.

B-flat minor (Ger. *B moll*). The key of B♭ minor is favored by pianists because it is the parallel key of B♭ major, both scales having five flats in the key signature. PIOTR ILYICH TCHAIKOVSKY's famous Piano Concerto No. 1 is nominally in the key of B♭ minor, but after a few measures in the principal key, it explodes into action with the famous optimistic D♭ major theme. FRÉDÉRIC CHOPIN wrote a scherzo (op.31) and a piano sonata (op.35) in this key; the sonata's slow movement is the well-known *Marche funèbre.*

It is difficult to find any symphonic works unambiguously set in B♭ minor. A good example is the *ALPINE SYMPHONY* by RICHARD STRAUSS, in which the ascent and the descent to and from the summit are illustrated by the correspondingly ascending and descending scales of B♭ minor. The Russian composer Nikolai Miaskovsky assigned the key of B♭ minor to his Symphony No. 11, but then he wrote symphonies in virtually every key.

Biber, Heinrich (Ignaz Franz von), famous Bohemian violinist and composer; b. Wartenberg, Bohemia, Aug. 12, 1644; d. Salzburg, May 3, 1704. After employment in smaller cities, Biber became a member of the royal chapel at Salzburg in 1670. Nine years later he was appointed vice-kapellmeister (chapel or choir master) and finally kapellmeister in 1684. He was in the service of the Emperor Leopold I, who ennobled him in 1690.

Biber's best-known collections are his so-called *Mystery* Sonatas and Passacaglia for Violin (c. 1676; published 1905) and the trios published as *Harmonia artificiosa* (1712). He composed three operas, only one of which, *Chi la dura la vince* (1687), survived. He also wrote sacred music, including a Mass and Requiem, and chamber music.

Biches, Les (The does or, colloquially, The little darlings). Ballet by FRANCIS POULENC, 1924, with chorus, originally written for DIAGHILEV's Ballets Russes. The work satirizes the young *nouveau-riche* of the '20s. Poulenc also wrote one section satirizing the musical excesses of RICHARD WAGNER.

bicinium (Lat., double song). A 16th-century term for a composition for two voices or instruments. The first

PEOPLE IN MUSIC

Biber was a founder of the German school of violin playing and was among the first to employ SCORDATURA, the practice of retuning the violin to make it easier to play certain sections of a composition.

significant collection was *Bicinia gallica, latina, germanica,* published by Georg Rhau in 1545. The popularity of bicinia rose primarily in reaction to the complicated, multipart compositions of the Flemish school of the Renaissance. Bicinia also served as teaching devices in theoretical textbooks. The genre remained popular until the early BAROQUE, with ORLANDO DI LASSUS the greatest practitioner. A revival took place in the early 20th century, when BÉLA BARTÓK and PAUL HINDEMITH composed pieces of this type, using dissonant harmony.

Bicycle Built for Two, A. Song by Harry Dacre, 1892, originally titled *Daisy Bell.* It has a continuing nostalgic cachet and serves as the last verbal emission of the computer HAL in *2001: A Space Odyssey.*

big band. The primary ensemble of the SWING era of American jazz and popular music of the 1930s and '40s. Big band music is scored for multiple trumpets, trombones, clarinets, and saxophones (melody group), while small groups usually employ at most one of each instrument. Usually the sections of the band perform alternately, in CALL-AND-RESPONSE style. That is to say, the saxophones play (call) a riff, and then the trumpets respond. In both big and small bands, the rhythm section is piano and/or guitar, drum kit, and double bass.

PEOPLE IN MUSIC

Bigard, "Barney" (Alban Leon), African-American jazz clarinetist; b. New Orleans, Mar. 3, 1906; d. Culver City, Calif., June 27, 1980. Bigard originally played E♭ clarinet, then switched to tenor saxophone in local New Orleans bands. He went to Chicago, where he worked with famous cornetist–band leader KING OLIVER between 1925 and 1927. While in Chicago, he recorded with all the major New Orleans jazzmen, including LOUIS ARMSTRONG, JELLY ROLL MORTON, and JOHNNY DODDS, and began playing clarinet again.

In 1927 he joined DUKE ELLINGTON's band, with which he played until 1942. He collaborated on such well-known Ellington compositions as *Clarinet Lament, Mood Indigo, Ducky Wucky,* and *Saturday Night Function.* He later formed small bands of his own, working mostly in Los Angeles and N.Y. After World War II Bigard played intermittently with Armstrong's small Dixieland jazz revival group, the All Stars, between 1947 and 1961.

Bigard was regarded as one of the best jazz clarinet players. He was known for his warm tone and a capacity for smooth GLISSANDOS and CHROMATIC runs.

Biggs, E(dward George) **Power,** eminent English-born American concert organist; b. Westcliff, Mar. 29, 1906; d. Boston, Mar. 10, 1977. After studies and performances in his native Britain, Biggs came to the U.S. in 1930, becoming a naturalized citizen in 1937. His first employment was as an organist in Newport, R.I., between 1930 and 1931. He made his N.Y. debut at the Wanamaker Auditorium in 1932.

PEOPLE IN MUSIC

After his stint in Rhode Island he moved to Cambridge, Mass., serving as organist at Cambridge's Christ Church and as music director of the Harvard Church, Brookline. During the 1930s he toured Europe, surveying old church organs throughout Europe in search of the type of organ that JO-HANN SEBASTIAN BACH and GEORGE FRIDERIC HANDEL played. His repertoire consisted mostly of the BAROQUE masters, but he also commissioned works from contemporary American composers (WALTER PISTON, ROY HARRIS, HOWARD HANSON, QUINCY PORTER), as well as the British composer BENJAMIN BRITTEN. His precise and clean style of performance was inspired by the Baroque school of organ playing.

Biggs became well known to American music lovers through his weekly organ recitals broadcast over the CBS network between 1942 and 1958. He gave live performances until arthritis forced him to reduce his concert activities during the 1960s but continued recording organ music and editing organ works for publication. Biggs refused to perform on electronic instruments, which in his opinion vulgarized and distorted the classical organ sound.

Bill Bailey, Won't You Please Come Home? RAGTIME song by Hughie Cannon, 1902. Bailey was a real person, a vaudevillian, but the text concerned a fictional story of his being locked out of his house for a night by his wife.

PEOPLE IN MUSIC

Billings had a good sense of humor. He harmonized the piece *Jargon* entirely in DIS-SONANCES, dedicating the work to the Goddess of Discord. Another work, *Modern Music,* opens with these lyrics: "We are met for a concert of modern invention/To tickle the ear is our present intention."

Billings, William, pioneer American composer of hymns and anthems and popularizer of FUGING TUNES; b. Boston, Oct. 7, 1746; d. there, Sept. 26, 1800. A tanner's apprentice, Billings learned musical rudiments by reading the writings and studying the works of British hymn writers. He compensated for his lack of training by a wealth of original ideas and a determination to put them into practice.

His first collection of choral music, *The New England Psalm Singer* (Boston, 1770), contained what he later described as "fuging pieces . . . more than 20 times as powerful as the old slow tunes." By "fuging pieces," Billings meant he used COUNTERPOINT in writing for several voices, but tried to give each voice equal weight so that, in his words, "each part [could] striv[e] for mastery and victory." A prolific composer, he published many other collections of choral music between 1778 and 1794. Several of his religious songs became popular, particularly *Chester* and *The Rose of Sharon.* An interesting work historically is his *Lamentation over Boston,* written in Watertown while Boston was occupied by the British during the Revolutionary War.

Despite his skill, Billings could not earn a living by his music or as a singing master (music teacher). His physical handicaps limited his opportunities, although he held various minor municipal positions. Billings attempted to raise funds from several patrons but was unsuccessful, and he died in poverty.

Billings's combination of deep religious belief with humor makes his songs unique in the history of American music, inspiring many modern American musicians. The 20th century composer HENRY COWELL wrote a series of "fuging tunes" in Billings's style, and WILLIAM SCHUMAN's *New England Triptych* is based on three Billings tunes. JOHN CAGE's *Apartment House 1776,* written to commemorate the bicentennial of the American Revolution, is comprised of 44 "rewritten" four-part choral works by Billings and other American composers.

Billy Budd. Opera by BENJAMIN BRITTEN, 1951, based on Melville's novella. It describes a mutiny on the British warship *Nore* in 1797, during which the young sailor Billy Budd kills his brutal superior officer and is hanged for it. The work is unique as a large-scale opera written exclusively for men's voices.

Billy the Kid. Ballet by AARON COPLAND, 1938, with choreography by Eugene Loring. It traces the brief career of the famous Western outlaw while incorporating several cowboy songs. Copland derived a popular orchestral suite from it in 1940.

Billy Budd, *San Francisco Opera production, 1978. (Ira Nowinski/© Corbis)*

binary. Dual; two-part; in music, two-part form or rhythm. *Binary form* is a structural form founded on two principal THEMES (*see* SONATA FORM), or divided into two distinct or contrasted sections.

The harmonic plan in binary composition is symmetrical (or balanced). The first section proceeds from the TONIC to the DOMINANT, and the second section begins on the dominant and ends on the tonic. The ALLEMANDE is typical. Although a large number of compositions are set in TERNARY forms, the basis is always binary, with the third section being the repetition of the first part. This repetition is either literal, as in DA CAPO ARIAS, or oblique, as in the sonata form, where the RECAPITULATION differs in tonality and sometimes in structure from the EXPOSITION.

Binary measure refers to COMMON TIME, where the first of every two components takes the ACCENT (regular and equal alternation between DOWNBEAT and UPBEAT). Binary rhythms may contain two subdivisions per beat. In medieval music, binary division in metrical time was called *tempus*

> In discussing binary forms, musicologists refer to the first theme as "A" and the second theme as "B." A common ternary form is thus ABA, where the third part is a repetition of the first.

imperfectum, "incomplete rhythm," the ternary division being *tempus perfectum,* "complete rhythm."

PEOPLE IN MUSIC

Binchois (Binch, Binche), **Gilles (de),** important Franco-Flemish composer; b. probably in Mons, Hainaut, c. 1400; d. Soignies, near Mons, Sept. 20, 1460. After training as a chorister (choral singer), Binchois was made an "honorably chivalrous soldier," probably in the service of the earl of Suffolk, who was among the English occupying France in 1424. Binchois joined the Burgundian court by 1427, where he advanced from fifth chaplain in 1436 to second, retaining the latter position until his death. During this period he met his great contemporary, the composer GUILLAUME DUFAY.

Binchois greatly distinguished himself as a composer of both sacred (religious) and secular works. He was noted for writing balanced melodies following the accepted rhythmic rules of his day. In writing COUNTERPOINT he created strong, independent melodies. His style is considered traditional when compared to Dufay's.

PEOPLE IN MUSIC

Bing, Sir Rudolf (Franz Joseph), Austrian-born English opera producer; b. Vienna, Jan. 9, 1902; d. N.Y., Sept. 2, 1997. Bing studied at the University of Vienna, taking singing lessons on the side. He worked for opera houses in Darmstadt, Germany, between 1928 and 1930 and in Berlin from 1930 to 1933. After the Nazis came to power, he went to England in 1934 and became general manager of the famous Glyndebourne Opera Festival, a position he held from 1936 to 1949. Bing became a British subject in 1946. A year later he helped organize the Edinburgh Festival, an annual, week-long festival of theater and music, serving as its artistic director from 1947 to 1950.

In 1950 Bing was appointed general manager of N.Y.'s Metropolitan Opera, which began one of the most eventful and at times turbulent periods in its history. Bing ran the company with a strong hand and had little interest in catering to the sometimes large egos of the stars who performed there. In 1971 Queen Elizabeth II of England conferred on him the title of Knight Commander of the Order of the British Empire, and he resigned from the Metropolitan a year later. He published two volumes of memoirs, *5,000 Nights at the Opera* (N.Y., 1972) and *A Knight at the Opera* (N.Y., 1981). Bing suffered from Alzheimer's disease during the last years of his life.

Bingen, Hildegard von. *See* HILDEGARD VON BINGEN.

bitonality. The composition of a work so that each part (melody and accompaniment or TREBLE and BASS) are in different keys. This is often termed POLYTONALITY, but bitonality is a more accurate description.

Bitonality is a well-established practice in 20th-century music. The most effective type is the combination of two major triads whose TONICS form the interval of a TRITONE. The combination of C-major and F♯-major triads forms the harmonic foundation of IGOR STRAVINSKY's *Petrushka,* and is often called the "Petrushka chord."

There are many other ways to compose bitonal music. In NEOCLASSICAL music, a MODAL type of bitonality has come into existence. For example, when C major and D major are combined, the resulting music falls within the Lydian mode. Another type of bitonality is a combination of two major or minor triads with a tone in common; for instance, C major combined with E major or E♭ major. This type of bitonal composition is favored particularly by composers exploring traditional or folk music, among them the British composer RALPH VAUGHAN WILLIAMS and the American ROY HARRIS.

Stravinsky used a radical bitonality in his early works, playing one part in C major and the other in C minor (C-E-G vs. C-E♭-G). It makes for a friction point between the major and the minor third, creating melodies that are almost atonal. In his variations on the tune *America,* reportedly written in 1891, CHARLES IVES combines F major with A♭ major. In order to bring out the bitonal nature, he marked one of the tonalities *pianissimo* and the other *fortissimo*.

biwa. A Japanese plucked, flat-backed LUTE. It usually has four strings and is played upright in a sitting position. The Chinese equivalent is the PIP'A.

Before the 20th century, playing in two different keys at the same time was regarded only as a joke. WOLFGANG AMADEUS MOZART's *Ein musikalischer Spass* (A musical joke, K. 522) uses bitonal writing. The subtitle of the piece, *Dorfmusikanten* (Village musicians), reveals his real purpose: to ridicule the inability of untrained players to perform music correctly.

MUSICAL INSTRUMENT

Bizet, Georges (Alexandre-César-Léopold), great French opera composer; b. Paris, Oct. 25, 1838; d. Bougival, June 3, 1875. Bizet's father was a singing teacher and composer, and his mother was an excellent pianist. At age nine Bizet entered the Paris Conservatory, studying with many famous French teachers and composers, including Fromental Halévy, whose daughter, Geneviève, he married in 1869.

In 1857 Bizet both won the Grand Prix de Rome and shared a prize offered by noted composer JACQUES OFFENBACH for the best one-act OPÉRA COMIQUE, *Le Docteur Miracle*. While in Rome, Bizet composed a two-act Italian opera buffa, *Don Procopio* (composed 1858–59 but not premiered until 1906), and another one-act opera, *La Guzla de l'Émir*, which was accepted for production but withdrawn by the composer.

Returning to Paris, over the next decade Bizet produced a series of grand and one-act operas, as well as incidental music for plays, none of which were successful at the time. In 1875 he produced the work that would make his reputation, CARMEN, based on an 1845 novel by Prosper Mérimée. On its initial performance the public was not enthusiastic, however, and several critics attacked the storyline for its lurid subject matter and the music for supposedly drawing too closely on the style of RICHARD WAGNER. Although attendance was not high, there were 37 performances before the end of the season.

Bizet, unhappy at the initial reception of his masterpiece, suddenly died of a heart attack following its 33rd performance. Some historians have claimed that his death was a direct result of the harsh criticism the work received. However, the composer had been in poor health for years.

Following its initial performance, *Carmen* soon became a triumphant success all over the world, receiving stagings in London (in Italian), St. Petersburg, Vienna, Brussels, Naples, Florence, Mainz, and N.Y. The Metropolitan Opera first produced *Carmen* in Italian in 1884, then in French, in 1893.

Bizet also wrote or planned several other stage works, composed a few notable orchestral works (Symphony in C Major, *Roma, Patrie*), piano music (including the fine suite *Jeux d'enfants* for piano duet), choral works (notably *Vasco da Gama,* an "ode-symphony"), and songs.

Björling, Jussi (Johan Jonatan), eminent Swedish tenor; b. Stora Tuna, Feb. 5, 1911; d. Siaro, near Stockholm, Sept. 9, 1960. Björling studied singing with his father and joined the family's vocal male quartet between 1916 and 1921, during which time they made a tour of the U.S. In the late 1920s he studied vocal technique in Stockholm and made his operatic debut at the Royal Swedish Opera there as the Lamplighter in GIACOMO PUCCINI's *MANON LESCAUT* (1930). He remained a company member until 1938, while also singing with the Vienna State Opera, the Dresden State Opera, and at the Salzburg Festival.

Björling made his professional American debut in a concert broadcast from Carnegie Hall, N.Y., in 1937. He made his first appearance with N.Y.'s Metropolitan Opera as Rodolfo in LA BOHÈME (1938); he continued to sing there until 1941, subsequently returning to the company for several extended engagements (1945–54, 1956–57, and 1959). In early 1960 he suffered a heart attack as he was preparing to sing at London's Covent Garden and appeared for the last time in a Stockholm concert later that year. He died that September.

Björling was highly regarded for his fine vocal technique. His vocal quality was even throughout his entire range. He showed great restraint in his interpretation and knowledge of the style appropriate to each composer or work. He excelled in the works of Puccini, GIUSEPPE VERDI, and CHARLES GOUNOD, and also attempted some Russian operas.

Black Crook, The. A musical extravaganza put together from miscellaneous popular numbers, first produced in N.Y. on Sept. 12, 1866. The incredible storyline served as an excuse to show off what were for the time advanced special theatrical effects, as well as to parade before the audience a collection of young, scantily clad female dancers. It remained popular for decades, despite many clergymen and critics who denounced it.

Blackbirds of 1928. An African-American revue, 1928, with music by Jimmy McHugh and lyrics by Dorothy Fields. Successfully produced in N.Y., the revue is a series of topical skits. The score includes the famous song *I Can't Give You Anything but Love, Baby.*

Blades, Rubén, Panamanian singer and songwriter; b. Panama City, July 16, 1948. Blades was self-taught in

PEOPLE IN MUSIC

music. Despite receiving a law degree at the Univ. Nacional de Panamá in 1974, he went to work for Fania Records in N.Y. Discovered by bandleader Ray Barretto, he made his singing debut at Madison Square Garden. Blades collaborated with well-known percussionist Willie Colon and gained a reputation as a fine performer and songwriter. Many of his songs had specific social or political messages.

Organizing his own band, Seis del Solar, Blades produced the successful album *Buscando América* in 1984. He also wrote the score for and starred in the film *Crossover Dreams* (1985), and also acted in Spike Lee's *Mo' Better Blues* (1990). In 1998 he appeared on Broadway as the lead in PAUL SIMON's unsuccessful musical *The Capeman.*

Blake, Eubie (James Herbert), African-American jazz piano player, dancer, vaudevillian, and composer of popular music; b. Baltimore, Feb. 7, 1883; d. N.Y., Feb. 12, 1983, five days after his 100th birthday. Blake was a naturally talented pianist, with enormous hands (his long fingers could reach across an octave and a half on the keyboard). He had some training on organ as a child, but would play RAGTIME and popular music when his parents and teachers weren't around. As a teenager, he snuck out of his house after supposedly going to bed to play in the local bordellos, where he earned good money from tips.

Blake was also an inventive composer. In 1899 he wrote his *Charleston Rag,* which became a hit. It was one of the first published pieces with a BOOGIE-WOOGIE-style bass. In 1915 he joined with vocalist-lyricist Noble Sissle, and they appeared on the vaudeville circuit together, advertised as the Dixie Duo. In 1921 they composed the landmark musical *Shuffle Along,* the first all-black musical on Broadway. The score included *I'm Just Wild about Harry,* which became a hit. Another hit song was *Memories of You,* which Blake wrote for the musical *Blackbirds of 1930.*

After World War II, Blake enrolled at N.Y. University to study modern composition techniques. He was "rediscovered" in 1969 when he recorded the album *The 86 Years of Eubie Blake,* which launched a revival of interest in his music and himself as a musical performer. In 1972 he formed his own record company. In the late 1970s a Broadway revue

PEOPLE IN MUSIC

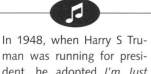

In 1948, when Harry S Truman was running for president, he adopted *I'm Just Wild about Harry* as his campaign theme song.

billed simply *Eubie!* was produced with resounding success. In 1981 he received the Medal of Freedom from President Reagan. He made his last public appearance at the age of 99, at N.Y.'s Lincoln Center, on June 19, 1982.

During his career Blake composed musicals, rags, études, boogies, novelties, waltzes, and a plethora of miscellaneous popular numbers. Among other songs were *Love Will Find a Way, That Charleston Dance, Roll Jordan, Harlem Moon,* and *Ain't We Got Love.*

Blakey, Art (called Abdullah Ibn Buhaina), African-American jazz drummer and bandleader; b. Pittsburgh, Oct. 11, 1919; d. N.Y., Oct. 16, 1990. Blakey first studied piano, then turned to drums. He went to N.Y. City in the early 1940s and initially played with pianist MARY LOU WILLIAMS in 1942, then joined big bands led by FLETCHER HENDERSON (1942–43) and Billy Eckstine (1944–47), as well as Buddy de Franco's quartet (1952–53).

In 1947 he formed the Jazz Messengers to play modern, bebop-influenced music, which went through several transformations. The group became a full-time unit when pianist HORACE SILVER joined in 1954, although he only stayed two years. Numerous important musicians jumped from the Blakey springboard into the spotlight, including WYNTON MARSALIS. Blakey participated in the Giants of Jazz tour with DIZZY GILLESPIE and THELONIOUS MONK 1971–72, and in a memorable drum battle with MAX ROACH and BUDDY RICH at the 1974 Newport Jazz Festival. In 1984 the Jazz Messengers won a Grammy Award for their album *New York Scene.*

Blakey's driving, freewheeling style was quintessential in the hard-bop period of jazz. In addition to performing with various groups and his work as a bandleader, he was a popular session musician in the 1950s and '60s, playing with numerous leading jazz musicians.

Bliss, Sir Arthur (Drummond), eminent English composer; b. London, Aug. 2, 1891; d. there, Mar. 27, 1975. He studied COUNTERPOINT with Charles Wood at Cambridge University (Mus.B., 1913), then pursued training with CHARLES STANFORD, RALPH VAUGHAN WILLIAMS, and GUSTAVE HOLST at the Royal College of Music in London

PEOPLE IN MUSIC

PEOPLE IN MUSIC

(1913–14). While serving in the British Army during World War I, he was wounded in 1916 and gassed in 1918. After the Armistice, he gained recognition as something of an *enfant terrible* with his *Madame Noy* for soprano and seven instruments (1918) and *Rout* for soprano and 10 instruments (1920). With such fine scores as *A Colour Symphony* (1921–22), the Introduction and Allegro for orchestra (1926), the Oboe Quintet (1927), and the Clarinet Quintet (1932), he rose to prominence as a composer of great distinction. His music for H. G. Wells's film *Things to Come* (1934–35) and the *Music for strings* (1935) added luster to his reputation, which was further enhanced by his outstanding ballets *Checkmate* (1937), *Miracle in the Gorbals* (1944), and *Adam Zero* (1946). After a sojourn as a teacher in Berkeley, Calif. (1939–41), Bliss served as director of music for the BBC in London (1942–44). In 1950 he was knighted, in 1953 was made a Knight Commander of the Royal Victorian Order, and in 1971 was made a Companion of Honour.

Sir Arthur Bliss, c. 1941. (Hulton-Deutsch Collection/Corbis)

Blitzstein, Marc, important American composer of theater music; b. Philadelphia, March 2, 1905; d. Fort-de-France, Martinique, Jan. 22, 1964. Blitzstein played piano as a child, then enrolled at Philadelphia's Curtis Institute of Music to further his studies. In 1926 he went to Europe to study with many leading 20th-century composers and teachers, including ARNOLD SCHOENBERG and NADIA BOULANGER. While in Berlin he heard the new theatrical works of KURT WEILL and Bertolt Brecht that combined social and political

PEOPLE IN MUSIC

messages with JAZZ-influenced music. Returning to the U.S., Blitzstein devoted himself to this new musical form.

Blitzstein's best-known work was THE CRADLE WILL ROCK, a one-act opera produced in 1937. It was originally sponsored by the Federal Theatre Project, a Depression-era government program dedicated to funding new works of art. However, because of its subject matter—the growth of the steel unions—the government withdrew its support. The work was produced in a workshop production by Orson Welles's Mercury Theater in N.Y., with Blitzstein playing the piano.

In 1940 Blitzstein received a Guggenheim fellowship. During World War II he was stationed in England with the U.S. Armed Forces, where he composed the *Airborne* Symphony for narrator and orchestra, which premiered in N.Y. in 1946. In 1952 he translated and adapted Brecht and Weill's *Der Dreigroschenoper* into THE THREEPENNY OPERA, which was an enormous success on Broadway and subsequently revived many times.

The most successful of Blitzstein's own works after World War II were the opera *Regina*, based on Lillian Hellman's play *The Little Foxes* (1949), and two musicals: *Reuben Reuben* (1955) and *Juno*, after Irish playwright Sean O'Casey's *Juno and the Paycock* (1959). Unfortunately, an opera commissioned by the Ford Foundation on the lives of Sacco and Vanzetti was never finished.

Bloch, Ernest, remarkable Swiss-born American composer and teacher of Jewish ancestry; b. Geneva, July 24, 1880; d. Portland, Oreg., July 15, 1959. Between 1894 and 1899 Bloch studied music in Geneva and Brussels. In 1900 he went to Munich to continue his studies, and began the composition of his first symphony, in C♯ minor (1910), in four movements, each originally intended to portray a different mood. In 1902 he spent a year in Paris, where he met CLAUDE DEBUSSY; his first published work, the song cycle *Historiettes au crépuscule* (1903), shows Debussy's influence.

In 1904 Bloch returned to Geneva, where he began work on his only opera, *Macbeth* (premiered in 1910), based on Shakespeare's play. As a tribute to his homeland he outlined the orchestra work *Helvetia*, based on Swiss motifs, as

The song MACK THE KNIFE from Blitzstein's *Threepenny Opera* was a major pop hit in the late 1950s for Bobby Darin and LOUIS ARMSTRONG.

PEOPLE IN MUSIC

early as 1900, but the full score was not completed until 1928. During World War I Bloch began to express his Jewish heritage in such musical works as *3 Jewish Poems; Israel* for soloists, chorus, and orchestra; and *Schelomo,* a "Hebrew rhapsody" for cello and orchestra. Long after his death, *Schelomo* retains its popularity.

In 1916 Bloch toured the U.S. as conductor, then a year later returned to teach at the Mannes School of Music in N.Y., where he remained until 1920. He subsequently directed Cleveland's Institute of Music from 1920 to 1925, and then the San Francisco Conservatory until 1930. He became an American citizen in 1924. In his various teaching positions, Bloch had many devoted students who went on to be important composers, including ROGER SESSIONS, GEORGE ANTHEIL, DOUGLAS MOORE, VIRGIL THOMSON, QUINCY PORTER, and LEON KIRCHNER.

In 1927 Bloch won first prize in a *Musical America* competition for his epic rhapsody *America.* The work was performed with a great outpouring of publicity in five cities, but as happens often with prizewinning works, it has since been forgotten. Bloch returned to Switzerland during the 1930s but then resettled in the U.S. and taught at the University of California, Berkeley, from 1940 until his retirement in 1952. His daughter, Suzanne Bloch (b. Geneva, Aug. 7, 1907), was a well-known lutenist and harpsichordist.

PEOPLE IN MUSIC

Blow, John, great English composer and organist; b. Newark-on-Trent, Nottinghamshire (baptized), Feb. 23, 1649 (1648, Julian calendar); d. Westminster (London), Oct. 1, 1708. In 1660–61 Blow was a member of the choir at the Chapel Royal. He subsequently studied organ with Christopher Gibbons and was appointed organist of Westminster Abbey in 1668. In 1679 he left this post; HENRY PURCELL, who had been Blow's student, succeeded him. After Purcell's untimely death, Blow was reappointed in 1695 and remained at Westminster Abbey until his death. Blow held several positions at the Chapel Royal directing the children's choir there, and from 1687 to 1703 he was also master of the choristers (choral director) at London's St. Paul's Cathedral.

While still a young chorister of the Chapel Royal, Blow began to compose church music. He eventually composed music for Anglican services, secular part-songs, CATCHES (or rounds), and organ and instrumental music. He wrote odes for many occasions, among them one for New Year's Day 1682, *Great Sir, the Joy of All Our Hearts,* and *Ode on the Death of Purcell* (1696), and numerous anthems, including two for the coronation of James II. Blow's collection of 50 songs *Amphion Anglicus* was published in 1700. His best-known work was the MASQUE *Venus and Adonis* (c.1685). While this is his only complete score for the stage, he contributed separate songs for numerous dramatic plays.

Henry Purcell regarded Blow as "one of the greatest [music] masters in the world."

blue note. In the BLUES, singers and instrumentalists typically alter the pitch of the third and seventh notes of the major scale. For example, in C major, E and B will be sung as closer in pitch to E♭ and B♭. These are known as "blue notes," because of their strong association with JAZZ and the blues.

Bluebeard's Castle. Opera by BÉLA BARTÓK, produced in Budapest on May 24, 1918. The justly infamous Bluebeard (possibly a historic character) lets his last bride open seven secret doors of his castle that conceal torture chambers and the dead bodies of his previous wives. As Bluebeard proclaims love for his last bride, she joins the dead wives behind the last door. Bartók's dissonant music matches the melodramatic storyline.

bluegrass. A musical style pioneered by mandolinist Bill Monroe with his famous group the Blue Grass Boys (named for his home state of Kentucky). Monroe's rapid-fire mandolin playing, high vocal harmonies, and bluesy compositions all became standard ingredients for the bluegrass style. The instrumentation of his most successful band—guitar, mandolin, banjo, fiddle, and bass—became the model for the standard bluegrass lineup. Two key musicians in Monroe's 1945–48 group, LESTER FLATT and EARL SCRUGGS, separated from the master and formed their own successful band, most notably providing the music for the 1967 film *Bonnie and Clyde,* which did much to popularize the style.

Bluegrass band. L to r: Todd Phillips, J. D. Crowen, Doyle Lawson, Tony Rice, Bobby Hicks. (Courtesy Rounder Records) ▶

More recent bluegrass (known as "newgrass") exhibits the influence of other styles, including JAZZ and progressive ROCK.

blues. A traditional black American BALLAD style. It is in $\frac{4}{4}$ time, with a melody characterized by lowered third and seventh (BLUE NOTES), and has developed into a stereotyped, 12-measure harmonic pattern: I (×4)—IV (×2)—I (×2)—V (×1)—IV (×1)—I (×2). The colloquialism "blues" (sadness) dates back to at least the early 19th century, but the musical form evolved from spirituals, work songs, field hollers, and ballads, both Anglo- and African-American.

The country blues style seems to have existed by the 1890s, performed by a singer accompanying himself on banjo, piano, or guitar. The style was associated with the southern states as far west as Texas. The country genre was popularized first by traveling performers on the medicine show circuit or by street singers.

At the same time, bandleader and composer W. C. HANDY claimed to be the "discoverer" of the blues. He published two of the most successful blues songs of the time, *Memphis Blues* (1911) and *St. Louis Blues* (1914), which were aimed at city audiences. Female singers like Ma Rainey, Mamie Smith, Alberta Hunter, Ida Cox, and the great BESSIE SMITH began performing Handy's and other composed blues songs, both on vaudeville stages and on recordings.

The popularity of urban blues on record ironically led recording labels to seek out older performers in the country blues styles. Artists like Charley Patton, Blind Lemon Jefferson, Son House, Blind Boy Fuller, Bukka White, Texas Alexander, Bo Carter, Blind Willie McTell, Memphis Minnie, and the last great traditional blues musician, Robert Johnson, were all recorded from the mid-1920s through the mid-1930s. After World War II John Lee Hooker, Lightnin' Hopkins, Fred McDowell, Sonny Terry and Brownie McGhee, and Mance Lipscomb contributed to the style. A blues revival in the 1960s (paralleling the folk revival) led to the rediscovery of long-unrecorded musicians, including House, White, Sleepy John Estes, and Mississippi John Hurt.

In the late 1930s, the center of the blues scene shifted to Chicago, where artists like Tampa Red, BIG BILL BROONZY, Washboard Sam, and the first Sonny Boy Williamson began performing a new style of blues. After World War II the electrification of the guitar led to the development of small blues combos, featuring guitar, bass, harmonica, piano, and drums. The electric blues known as Chicago style was originated by performers like Muddy Waters, Howlin' Wolf, James Cotton, Otis Spann, Little Walter, and the second Sonny Boy Williamson. This style also became popular among white musicians, including Mike Bloomfield and Paul Butterfield, as well as influencing English musicians like ERIC CLAPTON and many others.

Blues has enjoyed continuing popularity in all of its many styles. There are performers of classic country blues, 1920s-style jazz blues, and more recent Chicago blues. Performers like B. B. KING have helped keep the blues tradition alive for a new millennium.

Although many blues express sad feelings, there are also happy blues songs. Blues can also comment on current events or problems in the community, as well as being about love gone wrong.

BMI (Broadcast Music Incorporated). A music licensing organization founded in N.Y. in 1940 as an alternative collecting agency to ASCAP. In the 1930s radio stations were becoming increasingly frustrated with paying the high fees ASCAP charged for the music it represented. This situation was made worse by an ASCAP strike where the agency refused to allow any of its music to be played on the air. In response, a group of radio executives formed Broadcast Music International, or BMI.

BMI attracted African-American, country, and other popular song composers whom ASCAP had turned down in the past. In this way, it opened the music industry to many new influences and helped many minority or specialized composers earn a living from their music.

boat song. *See* BARCAROLE.

Boccherini, (Ridolfo) **Luigi,** famous Italian composer and cellist; b. Lucca, Feb. 19, 1743; d. Madrid, May 28, 1805. Boccherini was raised in a musical family and studied cello as a child. In 1757 he was hired as a cellist in the orchestra of the Court Theater, Vienna. From 1761 to 1766 he was in Lucca; he then undertook a concert tour with the violinist Filippo Manfredi, arriving in Paris in 1768. In France he became exceedingly popular as a performer and composer.

In 1769 Boccherini became chamber composer to the Infante Luis at Madrid; after the latter's death in 1785 he remained in Spain and received a pension. In 1786 he was appointed court composer *in absentia* to Friedrich Wilhelm II of Prussia, remaining in this position until the king's death in 1797. From 1800 to 1801 he enjoyed the patronage of Napoleon's brother, Lucien Bonaparte, who served as French ambassador to Madrid. For some reason, however, Boccherini lost his appeal to his patrons and to the public. He supposedly died in poverty in 1805. In a belated tribute to a native son, the authorities in Lucca had his remains transferred there and reburied with great solemnity in 1927.

Boccherini had profound admiration for FRANZ JOSEPH HAYDN; indeed, so close was Boccherini's style to Haydn's that this affinity gave rise to the saying, "Boccherini is the wife of Haydn." He was an exceptionally prolific composer, specializing almost exclusively in chamber music. He also wrote secular and sacred vocal music, including a Christmas cantata. One of Boccherini's works became the unwitting star of the 1955 film *The Ladykillers* (from England's famed Ealing Studios) starring Alec Guinness as the slightly demented leader of a group of thieves who are planning a heist in a boardinghouse while pretending to be a string quartet.

Bock, Jerry (Jerrold Lewis), American songwriter of popular music; b. New Haven, Conn., Nov. 23, 1928. Bock studied

PEOPLE IN MUSIC

PEOPLE IN MUSIC

at the University of Wisconsin, then settled in N.Y. after graduation. He composed songs for revues (*Catch a Star!*, 1955) and television's *Your Show of Shows.* He gained wide recognition with his Broadway musicals, the best known of which was *Fiddler on the Roof* (1964), also made into a movie.

bodhran (Gael.). Traditional Irish drum with a goat hide stretched over a circular shallow frame, played with a two-headed beater. Used in uptempo dance pieces, the bodhran sets a steady fast beat. The player is able to change the drum's TIMBRE by changing the amount of tension on the head.

Boehm system. A key system making the flute easier to play than its open-holed predecessor. This new design was named after its inventor, Theobald Boehm (1794–1881). Boehm, a flute player, fixed the position and size of the holes so as to obtain purity of INTONATION and fullness of TONE; all holes were covered by keys, whereby prompt and accurate "speaking" was assured. The bore (or width of the instrument) was modified, rendering the tone much fuller and mellower.

Boethius (Anicius Manlius Torquatus Severinus Boetius), Roman philosopher and mathematician; b. Rome, A.D. c.480; d. 524. Boetius's treatise in five books *De Institutione Musica,* became the chief theoretical source for the music theory of the Middle Ages. His treatise was published in most major cities in various languages, first in Venice and then through most of Northern Europe, during the 16th century. The so-called Boethian notation system, which uses Latin numbers to indicate the individual notes, may or may not have been his invention. Boethius was executed on suspicion of treason by the Emperor Theodoric, whose counselor he had been for many years.

Boeuf sur le toit, Le (The bull on the roof). Pantomime by DARIUS MILHAUD, 1920, with music derived mainly from Brazilian dances (Milhaud served as an attaché to the French Embassy in Rio de Janeiro during World War I). Originally scored to accompany a film, Milhaud later transformed the work into an orchestra ballet.

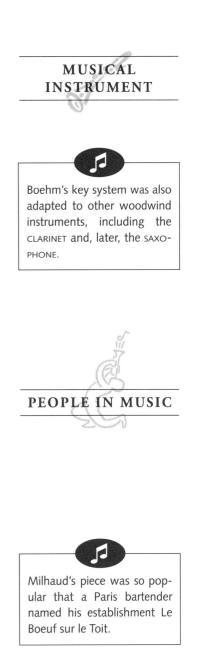

MUSICAL INSTRUMENT

Boehm's key system was also adapted to other woodwind instruments, including the CLARINET and, later, the SAXOPHONE.

PEOPLE IN MUSIC

Milhaud's piece was so popular that a Paris bartender named his establishment Le Boeuf sur le Toit.

The story of *La Bohème* was adapted to modern times in the hit Broadway musical *Rent* (1997). In this version, the two artists live on N.Y.'s Lower East Side, with the lover's consumption replaced by AIDS.

PEOPLE IN MUSIC

Bohème, La. Opera by GIACOMO PUCCINI, 1896. It depicts the life of four impoverished Parisian artists, one of whom befriends a neighboring girl. They fall in love, but are separated first by poverty and then by her death from consumption (tuberculosis). The realism of the subject and the relative modernity of the score made *La Bohème* a scandalous landmark in opera. A year later, the Italian opera composer RUGGERO LEONCAVALLO produced an opera on the same subject with the same French title in Venice. However, it never equaled the popularity of Puccini's masterpiece.

Bohemian Girl, The. Opera (1843) by the Irish composer Michael William Balfe (1808–70) on a subject derived from *La gitanella* by Miguel de Cervantes. A young girl, abducted by gypsies from her father, is finally restored to him and allowed to marry her Polish lover. The opera was first produced in London; it was by far Balfe's greatest success and has been popular in England ever since. It includes the nostalgic aria *I Dreamt That I Dwelt in Marble Halls.*

Böhm, Karl, Austrian conductor of great renown; b. Graz, Aug. 28, 1894; d. Salzburg, Aug. 14, 1981. Böhm originally studied law, earning his degree in 1919, but then enrolled at the Vienna Conservatory to study music. After service in the Austrian army during World War I, he held positions as conductor or director of opera companies in Graz, Munich, and Darmstadt through 1931. Böhm already showed an interest in all parts of the operatic repertoire, conducting both the classics and new works, including ALBAN BERG's controversial opera WOZZECK in a 1931 production that particularly pleased its composer.

From the early 1930s through World War II, Böhm's career continued to flourish. He worked in Hamburg and Dresden—where he gave the first performances of two operas by RICHARD STRAUSS: *Die Schweigsame Frau* (1935) and *Daphne* (1938), which Strauss dedicated to him—and finally, from 1943 to 1945, at the Vienna State Opera.

After the war Böhm went to Buenos Aires, where he organized and conducted German opera seasons until 1953. He returned to the Vienna State Opera in 1954, conducting

LUDWIG VAN BEETHOVEN's *FIDELIO* at the opening of the re-constructed Vienna State Opera House a year later. He made his first U.S. appearance with the Chicago Symphony Orchestra in 1956 and a year later gave his debut at N.Y.'s Metropolitan Opera, where he continued to conduct occasional performances until 1974. Meanwhile, he continued to conduct in Berlin and Vienna, leading major tours, including the Berlin Philharmonic's tours of the U.S. and Japan in the early 1960s and the Vienna State Opera's first U.S. tour in 1979. He also conducted radio and television performances.

While Böhm conducted operas from the CLASSICAL, ROMANTIC, and modern periods, he was always true to the style of each work. Thus, when conducting works by WOLFGANG AMADEUS MOZART, he never introduced any elements that would be inappropriate to the Classical period.

Boieldieu, François-Adrien, celebrated French opera composer; b. Rouen, Dec. 16, 1775; d. Jarcy, near Grosbois, Oct. 8, 1834. Boieldieu's father worked for the church in Rouen, and his mother ran a sewing shop. After showing talent for music as a youth, Boieldieu was apprenticed to the local organist-composer Charles Broche, who made him an assistant organist at St. André's church in Rouen. His first two operas were produced in Rouen in 1793 and 1795, bringing him to the attention of major Italian and French composers. Among other early works were several collections of popular songs, which were printed in Paris in 16 volumes between 1794 and 1811, and nine piano sonatas, composed between 1795 and 1800.

But opera was Boieldieu's true love; he produced one opera after another and had no difficulties getting them Parisian performances. One particularly successful work was the OPÉRA-COMIQUE *Le Calife de Bagdad* (1800), which appealed to the public because of its exotic subject and pseudo-oriental arias.

In 1802 Boieldieu married the dancer Clotilde Mafleurai but separated from her the following year. He was then invited to write operas for the imperial theaters in St. Petersburg, Russia, and produced at least one opera annually through 1811. Despite a salary increase and a comfortable

PEOPLE IN MUSIC

life, Boieldieu decided to leave Russia in 1811 and return to Paris. His estranged wife died in 1826, and he married the singer Jenny Phillis-Bertin the following year.

True to his custom, Boieldieu resumed composing operas for the Paris theaters. He was appointed professor of composition at the Paris Conservatory, a position he held from 1817 to 1826, and was also named a Chevalier of the Legion of Honor in 1821. After a number of insignificant productions, he achieved his greatest success in 1825 with his opéra-comique *La Dame blanche,* based on a story by Walter Scott. The suspenseful story and the effective, atmospheric musical setting strongly appealed to public tastes at the time.

In 1833 Boieldieu received a grant of 6,000 francs from the French government and retired to his country house at Jarcy, where he died. During the last years of his life he became interested in painting, showing a modest talent in landscapes. He was also successful as a teacher.

Boieldieu's natural son, Adrien-Louis-Victor Boieldieu (1815–1883), was also a composer. His mother was Thérèse Louise Antoinette Regnault, a singer at the Paris Opéra. He wrote ten operas, including *Marguerite,* sketched by his father but left incomplete, and *L'Aïeule.*

Boieldieu composed about 40 operas, many written in collaboration with other major French composers of the time. Boieldieu's significance in the history of French opera is great, even though the hopes of the French music critics and others that he would rival GIACOMO ROSSINI (whom he admired) did not materialize. He simply lacked the tremendous power of invention, both in dramatic and comic aspects, that made Rossini a magician of 19th-century opera.

Bolcom, William (Elden), American pianist and composer; b. Seattle, May 26, 1938. Bolcom is an eclectic composer and teacher whose work has ranged from popular recordings of RAGTIME and sentimental songs to serious modern compositions. After study with a number of modern composers, including John Verrall, DARIUS MILHAUD, and Leland Smith, Bolcom taught musicology at a number of universities beginning in 1965. He joined the faculty of the music depart-

PEOPLE IN MUSIC

ment at the University of Michigan in 1973, where he continues to teach.

In his compositions, Bolcom has experimented with many different techniques, including SERIAL composition, musical collage and quotation, and ELECTRONIC MUSIC. His compositions include five symphonies, the actors' opera *Dynamite Tonight* (1963), *Commedia* for chamber orchestra (1971), *Frescoes* for 2 keyboardists (1971), the secular oratorio *Songs of Innocence and of Experience* (1981), the theater piece *Casino Paradise* (1990), and the opera *McTeague* (1992). In 1988 Bolcom won the Pulitzer Prize in music for his *12 New Etudes* for piano.

Bolcom has also been active as a pianist, recording and giving recitals of ragtime piano. With his wife, the singer Joan Morris, he has given concerts of popular American songs of the 19th and early 20th centuries.

Bolden, "Buddy" (Charles Joseph), African-American jazz cornetist; b. New Orleans, Sept. 6, 1877; d. Jackson, La., Nov. 4, 1931. Bolden was a pioneering figure in early JAZZ, active in New Orleans at the turn of the century. By 1901 he was leading a six-piece band, playing in honky-tonks and dives of Storyville. Bolden's career ended suddenly when he began showing symptoms of mental illness, perhaps brought on by alcoholism. He was confined to a state hospital in 1906, where he lingered for many years before dying in 1931, a totally forgotten figure.

Because Bolden never recorded, it is impossible to describe accurately either how he played or the sound or style of the bands he led. From contemporary accounts given by LOUIS ARMSTRONG and others, however, Bolden had a powerful sound that carried well. From the one surviving photograph of his band, it appears to be a transitional group from the violin-led dance bands of the 1880s and '90s to the brass-led jazz groups of the 1910s and '20s.

bolero (Sp.). 1. A Spanish national dance in syncopated $\frac{3}{4}$ time and lively tempo (*allegretto*), the dancers accompanying their steps with castanets. It evolved from either the FANDANGO or SEGUIDILLA and resembles the Andalusian *cachu-*

PEOPLE IN MUSIC

Louis Armstrong recalled one concert where Bolden was playing in a New Orleans park. He could hear Bolden's cornet flourishes from several blocks away, testifying to Bolden's extraordinary power as a player.

bōh-leh′rōh

cha. 2. A Cuban dance in $\frac{2}{4}$ time, closer to the HABANERA. 3. A composition in bolero style, such as FRÉDÉRIC CHOPIN's piano piece (op.19) and MAURICE RAVEL's famous orchestral work.

Boléro. Celebrated ballet by MAURICE RAVEL, 1928, inspired by the popular Spanish dance and written for the dancer Ida Rubinstein. Two alternating sections repeat several times, but the insistent rhythm, melody, and harmony never change. An extraordinary variety and buildup is created by different instrumentation and colorful DYNAMICS. With the exception of a brief E major section before the CODA, the entire piece is written in C major, an unusual feat. Ravel grew to despise the piece because it became so popular and overplayed. It was the last original orchestral work he was to compose, save the two piano concertos.

bomba. A traditional dance of Puerto Rico. Also, its music, a significant predecessor of SALSA.

MUSICAL INSTRUMENT

bombard (Eng., Ger.; It. *bombardo;* Fr. *bombarde*). A low-pitched member of the SHAWM family, used during the 14th to 16th centuries, now obsolete. *See also* POSAUNE.

Bombo. Musical extravaganza, 1921, featuring AL JOLSON in blackface in a farce about Christopher Columbus. Includes Jolson's theme song, *My Mammy,* as well as other hits: *April Showers, Yoo Hoo,* and *California Here I Come.*

MUSICAL INSTRUMENT

bones. A primitive rhythm instrument of two bones or pieces of wood that are clicked together by the fingers of one hand. Bones have been used in Irish traditional music, American blackface MINSTRELSY, and old-time Appalachian music.

MUSICAL INSTRUMENT

bongos. Paired, knee-held Cuban drums, struck by the fingertips. They furnish a distinct sound that stands out in percussive ensembles. Bongos have also been adopted by many symphonic composers.

boogie-woogie. A piano-based JAZZ style that developed in the late 1920s, beginning in Chicago and quickly spreading to N.Y. and elsewhere. Its characteristic features are found in the bass accompaniment: rapid EIGHTH NOTES (often played as ♪♪) in broken OCTAVES, following the WALKING BASS pattern; or the so-called doubled blues bass, following the standard blues harmonic pattern (*see* BLUES).

In the late 1930s a boogie-woogie craze swept the U.S., and as a result, many important pianists enjoyed brief popularity: Albert Ammons, Meade "Lux" Lewis, Pete Johnson, Jimmy Yancey, and "Cripple" Clarence Lofton. The style was adopted or transmogrified by swing bands and songs, most notably in the hit song *Boogie Woogie Bugle Boy* by the ANDREWS SISTERS (1941). After World War II boogie-woogie was incorporated into the blues, particularly as practiced by Chicago pianists.

bop. *See* BEBOP.

bore. The shape of the body of WOODWIND and BRASS INSTRUMENTS, beginning with the diameter of the cylinder.

Borge, Victor (born Borge Rosenbaum), talented Danish pianist and musical comedian; b. Copenhagen, Jan. 3, 1909. Borge was born to a Russian-Jewish family who had emigrated to Denmark so that his father could avoid being drafted into the Russian army. Borge showed talent as a pianist from a young age. He took theory courses at the Copenhagen Conservatory, then went to Berlin. Borge's plans for a Swedish concert tour in the late 1930s were prevented by the Nazi invasion of Denmark. He emigrated to the U.S. in 1940 and became a U.S. citizen eight years later.

After attempting to establish himself as a serious classical pianist, Borge appeared in the highly successful one-man Broadway show, *Comedy in Music,* in 1953, giving a total of 849 performances, a record at that time for a solo show. This lay the basis for a four-decade career as a musical humorist. He traveled throughout the world giving concerts that combined bad puns, slapstick, and some piano playing.

Boris Godunov. Opera in four acts by MODEST MUSSORGSKY, originally composed in 1868–69 and revised in

The Dutch painter Piet Mondrian, who lived in N.Y. from the 1930s on, painted a number of pictures inspired by boogie-woogie. A famous example is *Broadway Boogie-Woogie,* an abstract painting in which straight lines, interrupted by blank spaces, cross at right angles another set of broken straight lines.

PEOPLE IN MUSIC

1871–72 and again in 1874, in which year it was finally premiered. Based on the historical tragedy by Russian poet Aleksandr Pushkin, the action takes place in 15th-century Russia. After his coronation as czar, Boris is tormented by the murder of the young czarevich Dmitri, lawful heir to the Russian throne, perpetrated on his behalf by assassins. A young monk, Gregory, decides to pretend that he is the "true Dmitri," miraculously saved from Boris's assassins. The Polish government backs the claim and leads its army to Moscow with Gregory as the pretender to the throne. Boris begins to go mad and demands proof from his henchmen that it was the child Dmitri who was actually slain. The opera ends with Boris's death (after placing his young son Fyodor on the throne), while Gregory and his troops are about to enter Moscow.

In its original form, *Boris Godunov* had seven scenes and no act subdivisons. In the four-act revised version, Mussorgsky eliminated one scene, added three new scenes, and altered others. After his death it was radically revised by his friend, fellow composer NIKOLAI RIMSKY-KORSAKOV, who worked on his version between 1891 and 1906. It was in this version that the opera became internationally famous.

From the late 1920s various attempts to restore Mussorgsky's version began, sometimes in a mixture with the Rimsky-Korsakov adaptation. The original score was republished in 1928 and 1975. Some recent performances have combined the two Mussorgsky versions into one gigantic work.

Borodin, Alexander (Porfirievich), celebrated Russian composer; b. St. Petersburg, Nov. 12, 1833; d. there, Feb. 27, 1887. The illegitimate son of a Russian prince, Borodin received an excellent education. As a youngster he learned several foreign languages and learned to play the piano and the flute. At age 14 he wrote a piece for flute and piano and a string trio on themes from GIACOMO MEYERBEER's *Robert le Diable.* However, Borodin soon developed other interests beyond composing and performing. He entered the Academy of Medicine in St. Petersburg in 1850, where he developed a great interest in chemistry. He subsequently graduated with honors and joined the academy's staff as assistant

PEOPLE IN MUSIC

professor in 1856. Borodin contributed important scientific papers to the Russian Academy of Sciences' bulletin and traveled in Europe to continue studies during 1859 – 62.

Although mainly preoccupied with scientific pursuits, Borodin continued to compose. In 1863 he married Ekaterina Protopopova, an accomplished pianist who shared her appreciation of FRÉDÉRIC CHOPIN, FRANZ LISZT, and ROBERT SCHUMANN with him. In 1862 Borodin met MILY BALAKIREV, and subsequently met MODEST MUSSORGSKY and other musicians of the Russian national school. Influenced by their interest in Russian folk music and rhythms, Borodin began composing in a new style, excelling in a type of Russian orientalism that had a great attraction for Russian musicians at the time. Although he never became a consummate craftsman like his compatriot NIKOLAI RIMSKY-KORSAKOV, his feeling for rhythm and orchestral color was extraordinary. His ability to paint exotic scenes in his orchestral works and in his masterpiece, the opera *Prince Igor* (1869 – 87; premiered 1890), was superb.

Composition was a slow process for Borodin. Several of his works, including *Prince Igor,* remained incomplete and were edited after his death by Rimsky-Korsakov and ALEXANDER GLAZUNOV. Borodin also composed two symphonies (and part of a third), the symphonic poem *In Central Asia,* two string quartets and a piano quintet, *Petite Suite* for piano, several songs, and a large number of unfinished and fragmentary chamber works.

bossa nova (Port., new beat). Popular Brazilian song and dance music in SYNCOPATED $\frac{2}{4}$ time, derived from SAMBA and influenced by JAZZ. In its purest form, the vocal part is largely improvised to rhythmic accompaniment. Bossa nova became internationally popular in the late 1950s and '60s, thanks largely to ANTONIO CARLOS JOBIM—who had a hit with his composition *Desafinado* in 1959—STAN GETZ, ASTRUD GILBERTO, and others.

Boston (*Valse Boston*). *See* HESITATION WALTZ.

bouffe (Fr.). Comic, burlesque. *Opéra bouffe,* comic opera.

bouffon (Fr., jester, comedian). Mime-dancers who performed exotic dances at French courts in the 16th century. The famous war between the fans of Italian versus French opera in mid-18th-century Paris became known as the GUERRE DES BOUffons (war of the bouffons).

PEOPLE IN MUSIC

Boulanger, Nadia (Juliette), illustrious French composition teacher; b. Paris, Sept. 16, 1887; d. there, Oct. 22, 1979. Boulanger's grandmother, father, and mother were all professional musicians, and her mother was her first teacher. She studied further at the Paris Conservatory and in 1908 received the second Prix de Rome for her cantata *La Sirène*. She then collaborated with Raoul Pugno and completed his opera *La Ville morte* after his death.

Although she composed other works, Boulanger devoted herself to teaching, beginning in 1909 at the Paris Conservatory and continuing for four decades, where she found her greatest fame. Besides her faculty positions, Boulanger also had a large class of private pupils from all parts of the world. So many well-known composers studied with her—including AARON COPLAND, ROY HARRIS, WALTER PISTON, VIRGIL THOMSON, and PHILIP GLASS—that she became recognized as one of the most important music teachers in the world. Not all of her students were enthusiastic about her methods, however. Some of them complained about the strict discipline she imposed, but all benefited by her insistence on perfection of form and accuracy of technique.

Boulanger visited the U.S. several times. She played the organ part in Copland's *Organ* Symphony (which she advised him to compose) with the N.Y. Symphony Orchestra in 1925. She was also a fine conductor and led the premiere of IGOR STRAVINSKY's *Dumbarton Oaks* Concerto. She was the first woman to conduct subscription concerts of the Boston Symphony Orchestra (1938), any concert of the N.Y. Philharmonic (1939), and any London orchestra (Royal Philharmonic Society, 1937).

Because of the German occupation of Paris during World War II, Boulanger remained in America, teaching at several colleges. She returned to Paris in 1946, where she continued her private teaching for three decades. Her 90th birthday was celebrated in 1977, with tributes from her many students in Europe and America. She died two years later.

Her sister, Lili (Juliette Marie Olga) Boulanger (b. Paris, Aug. 21, 1893; d. Mezy, Seine-et-Oise, Mar. 15, 1918), was a talented French composer.

Boulez, Pierre, celebrated French composer and conductor; b. Montbrison, Mar. 26, 1925. Boulez studied composition with composer-teachers OLIVIER MESSIAEN and René Leibowitz, who introduced him to the procedures of SERIAL music. In 1948 he became a theater conductor in Paris and four years later made a tour of the U.S. with a French ballet troupe. In 1954 he organized in Paris a series of concerts, Domaine Musical, devoted mainly to avant-garde music. Boulez next went to Germany, where he gave courses at the International Festivals for New Music in Darmstadt in 1958.

◀

Pierre Boulez, 1975. (Hulton-Deutsch Collection/Corbis)

Boulez delivered a course of lectures on music at Harvard University in 1963 and made his American debut as a conductor in N.Y. a year later. In 1971 he was engaged as music director of the N.Y. Philharmonic, a choice that surprised many and delighted many more. Still, his decision to program many modern works annoyed the Philharmonic's conservative audience, and he left his post six years later.

While attending to his duties at the helm of the N.Y. Philharmonic, Boulez also accepted outside obligations.

From 1971 to 1975 he served as chief conductor of the BBC Symphony Orchestra in London. He also gave exemplary performances of RICHARD WAGNER's operas in Germany and elsewhere. It was in Germany that he had originally gained experience as a conductor of opera. He was one of the few Frenchmen to conduct Wagner's *PARSIFAL,* and was engaged to conduct the *Ring* cycle in Bayreuth (1976). The quality of his leadership and his knowledge of the score produced a profound impression on both audience and critics.

In the early 1970s Boulez established his residence in Paris, where he had founded the Institut de Recherche et Coordination Acoustique/Musique (IRCAM). This institute, dedicated to the composition of new music using ELEC-TRONIC techniques, including DIGITAL SYNTHESIZERS and computers, was well funded by the French government. The institute continues to be active to the present day, and many composers have worked there.

Boulez's music—including *Domaines* for solo clarinet and 21 instruments (1968), *Notations* for orchestra (1980), and *Répons* for chamber orchestra and six solo instruments (1981)—is fiendishly difficult to perform and even more difficult to describe.

PEOPLE IN MUSIC

Boult, Sir Adrian (Cedric), eminent English conductor; b. Chester, Apr. 18, 1889; d. London, Feb. 22, 1983. His mother, a professional writer on music, gave him early piano lessons. At 19 he entered Christ Church, Oxford, and sang in the Oxford Bach Choir. He then studied with Hans Sitt at the Leipzig Conservatory (1912–13), attended rehearsals and concerts in Leipzig of the Gewandhaus Orchestra under Arthur Nikisch, and sang in the Gewandhaus Choir. Upon his return to England he took his D.Mus. at Oxford and joined the staff of London's Covent Garden in 1914. In 1916 he appeared as guest conductor with the Liverpool Philharmonic and in 1918 with the London Symphony Orchestra. During the autumn season of 1919 he was principal conductor of DIAGHILEV's Ballets Russes in London and from 1919 to 1924 conductor of the British Symphony Orchestra, an ensemble made up of former British army soldiers. In 1919 he also became a conducting teacher at the Royal College of Music in London, a post he retained until

◀

Sir Adrian Boult, 1935. Hulton-Deutsch Collection/ Corbis)

1930. From 1924 to 1930 he was music director of the City of Birmingham Orchestra, and from 1928 to 1931 of the Bach Choir.

In 1930 Boult was appointed director of music for the BBC in London, retaining this position until 1942. He was also charged with organizing the BBC Symphony Orchestra, which he conducted in its first concert on Oct. 22, 1930. Under his discerning guidance it became one of the principal radio orchestras in the world. He led it on several tours abroad, including a notably successful one to Paris, Vienna, Zurich, and Budapest in 1936. During these years he also appeared as guest conductor with the Vienna Philharmonic (1933), Boston Symphony Orchestra (1935), NBC Symphony Orchestra in N.Y. (1938), N.Y. Philharmonic (leading it in the premieres of Arnold Bax's Seventh Symphony and Arthur Bliss's Piano Concerto at the 1939 World's Fair), Chicago Symphony Orchestra (1939), and the Concertgebouw Orchestra of Amsterdam (1945). From 1942 to 1950 he was associate conductor of the Henry Wood Promenade Concerts in London. He was music director of the London Philharmonic from 1950 to 1957 and led it on a major tour of the Soviet Union in 1956. In 1959–60 he was again music director of the City of Birmingham Symphony Orchestra and from 1962 to 1966 once more taught conducting at the Royal College of Music. In 1937 he was knighted and in

1969 was made a Companion of Honour. In 1944 he was awarded the Gold Medal of the Royal Philharmonic Society. He was conductor at the coronations of King George VI in 1937 and Queen Elizabeth II in 1953.

Boult's style of conducting was devoid of glamorous self-assertion. His ideal was, rather, to serve music with a minimum of display, and for this he was greatly respected by the musicians he led. Throughout his long and distinguished career he championed the cause of British music. He was particularly esteemed for his performances of the works of RALPH VAUGHAN WILLIAMS, whose *Pastoral* Symphony (Jan. 26, 1922), Fourth Symphony (Apr. 10, 1935), and Sixth Symphony (Apr. 21, 1948) he premiered in London.

bourrée (Fr.). 1. A dance of French or Spanish origin, in rapid tempo, having two sections of eight measures each, in $\frac{2}{4}$ or $\frac{4}{4}$ time. 2. An optional movement in the BAROQUE instrumental SUITE, in *alla breve* (cut) time.

boo-rā′

bow (Fr. *archet;* Ger. *Bogen;* Sp., It. *arco*). 1. A long, slender piece of flexible wood strung with a length of horsehair, used to play string instruments. Originally the bow was curved like an archery bow. The modern type of bow was standardized early in the 19th century; earlier bows were shorter and had a greater distance between the bow itself and the hair. CELLO and DOUBLE-BASS bows are usually heavier and shorter than VIOLIN and VIOLA bows. Also called *fiddle-bow* or *fiddlestick*. 2. Play a note with a bow. Mark a piece of music with signs indicating the bowing. *See also* BOWING.

bowed instrument. Any instrument, e.g., the VIOLIN, VIOLA, CELLO, etc., played with a bow.

Bowie, David (born David Jones), British ROCK musician; b. South London, Jan. 8, 1947. Bowie studied art while performing his own original songs in London's clubs in the late 1960s. With guitarist Mick Ronson and drummer Woody Woodmansey, he formed his first important band around 1970. Along with Ronson, he wrote songs about a fictional rock star named Ziggy Stardust in 1972. Performing as Ziggy, Bowie wore outrageous costumes and garish makeup.

MUSICAL INSTRUMENT

Some unusual bowed instruments include the *bowed guitar,* a kind of violin with a guitar-shaped body; *bowed zither,* a heart-shaped, three-stringed instrument developed in Bavaria around 1823 (another type, the 4-stringed, viol-shaped *Breitoline,* was developed about 30 years later in Moravia and fingered like a viol); *bowed piano.*

PEOPLE IN MUSIC

Through the 1970s Bowie's stage shows grew more elaborate, and critics named this style of performance "glitter" or "glam" (for "glamorous") rock, based on the showy costumes and magnificent sets that Bowie used.

Bowie also pursued an acting career, starring in the space fantasy *The Man Who Fell to Earth* (1976), in which he (quite appropriately) portrayed an alien. In 1980 he took the title role in the stage play *Elephant Man* and two years later appeared in Bertolt Brecht's *Baal.* His other important film roles include *Christian F., Merry Christmas, Mr. Lawrence, Absolute Beginners,* and the role of Andy Warhol in Julian Schnabel's *Basquiat,* released in 1998.

From the late 1970s on, Bowie has continued to change his musical style—and his stage appearance—although he has only occasionally had a pop hit. His most significant music in the last two decades includes three moody SYNTHESIZER albums made with avant-garde composer BRIAN ENO between 1977 and 1979.

Bowie, Lester, American jazz trumpeter and avant-garde composer; b. Frederick, Md., Oct. 11, 1941. Bowie began playing in St. Louis, originally performing in the rhythm and blues bands of Albert King and Little Milton. In 1965 he moved to Chicago, where he helped found the Association for the Advancement of Creative Musicians (AACM), an organization composed of young, avant-garde black jazz players. In 1969 he became a founding member of the Art Ensemble of Chicago, which became one of the most important groups in contemporary jazz. His most popular recordings include *Fast Last* (1974), *The Fifth Power* (1978), and *All the Magic* (1982). His *23 Facts in Two Acts* for musicians, dancers, chorus, and actors was premiered at the Brooklyn Academy of Music in 1989.

bowing. The art of playing with the bow on string instruments. Because a bow is of finite length, a melody must be played alternately with up- and downbows. Upbows move against gravity, therefore more effort must be applied than to a downbow, which follows the direction of gravity.

When a composer wishes to produce a series of strong sounds, down-bows are indicated by a sign that looks like a

PEOPLE IN MUSIC

square bracket turned 90 degrees to the right ⌐. A succession of upbows, used to produce lighter sounds, is indicated by a capital letter V above the note.

When several notes are used in the same stroke of a bow, the first and last notes are connected by a curved line. Apart from LEGATO, which in theory should not have any interruption of the sound, the most common stroke is STACCATO, Italian for "detached." For special effects, the player is instructed to bow *sul ponticello,* close to the bridge, *sul tasto,* on the fingerboard, or *col legno,* with the wooden part of the bow.

PEOPLE IN MUSIC

Bowles, Paul (Frederic), American composer and novelist; b. Jamaica, N.Y., Dec. 30, 1910. As a youth, Bowles became fascinated with visual art and poetry. After a sojourn in Paris, he returned to N.Y., where he worked as a bookshop clerk and composed. He impressed AARON COPLAND by his early vocal pieces and studied with him privately.

In the early 1930s Bowles returned to Paris, where he befriended American composer VIRGIL THOMSON and studied with the famed teacher NADIA BOULANGER. In 1936 he returned once more to the U.S. and wrote his first stage work, the ballet *Yankee Clipper* in 1937. He also wrote incidental music for theatrical productions as well as a short opera, *The Wind Remains,* to a text by Spanish poet Federico García Lorca, produced in N.Y. with Leonard Bernstein conducting in 1943.

The N.Y. scene failed to satisfy his psychological attraction to exotic lands, however, and Bowles soon set off for Tangier. A total change in artistic orientation occurred in 1949 when he published the novel *The Sheltering Sky,* the first of his many bone-chilling novels, short stories, and translations of Moroccan literature. He completed his third opera, *Yerma,* based on the García Lorca play, in 1959. He settled permanently in Tangier in 1959.

While his writings are dark, even grim, Bowles's musical works recall those of the French NEOCLASSICAL school, with a fair amount of nostalgia, wit, and hints of jazz, Mexican, and Moroccan traditional music. In addition to his other works, he composed 16 film scores, chamber and piano music, and the genteel *A Picnic Cantata* for women's voices, two pianos, and percussion, which was premiered in N.Y. in 1954. Bowles was intermittently united in marriage to Jane (Auer) Bowles, a fine novelist; she died in 1973.

boy (boys') choir. Especially in the Anglican church, a group of young males singing SOPRANO parts, with the ALTO parts sung by COUNTERTENORS or older boys.

boy soprano. A young male singing in the upper register. In religious settings that banned females, such as chapel choirs, the boy soprano was an essential performer. Many RENAISSANCE, BAROQUE, and early CLASSIC composers started their careers in this capacity, losing their jobs when their voices broke.

Boyce, William, significant English organist and composer; b. London (baptized), Sept. 11, 1711; d. Kensington, Feb. 7, 1779. As a youth, Boyce was a chorister in St. Paul's Cathedral. He studied with Maurice Greene, the cathedral organist, and subsequently was hired as organist at the Earl of Oxford's chapel (1734–36), and then at St. Michael's church in Cornhill (1736–68).

In 1736 Boyce was named composer to the Chapel Royal. His main task consisted in providing sacred music for the chapel, but he also contributed incidental music to theatrical productions. In 1757 he became Master of the King's Musick, but increasing deafness forced him to abandon active musical duties after 1769.

In his last years, Boyce compiled the remarkable collection *Cathedral Music* (3 volumes, 1760, 1768, and 1773). This anthology comprises morning and evening services, anthems, and other church music by a number of important British composers from the early RENAISSANCE to Boyce's day. His compositions were nearly all vocal music, but it is his remarkable instrumental works that maintain his reputation: 12 sonatas for two violins and bass (London, 1747), eight symphonies (London, 1760), 12 overtures (London, 1770), and 10 organ or harpsichord solos (London, 1779).

PEOPLE IN MUSIC

Boys from Syracuse, The. Musical by RICHARD RODGERS and Lorenz Hart, 1938, based on Shakespeare's *A Comedy of*

Errors, which itself presents the age-old plot of confused identities. Includes *Falling in Love with Love.*

brace. 1. The sign ({) that connects two or more STAVES, indicating that the parts are to be played simultaneously. 2. The group of staves so connected, as the *upper brace.*

Brahms, Johannes, great German composer; b. Hamburg, May 7, 1833; d. Vienna, Apr. 3, 1897. Brahms's father, a double bassist in the Hamburg Philharmonic Society, taught Brahms the rudiments of music. On his own, Brahms eked out his subsistence by playing piano in taverns, restaurants, and other establishments.

In 1848 Brahms gave a solo concert in Hamburg under an assumed name. While there, he met the Hungarian violinist Eduard Reményi (born Hoffmann), who taught him the fine points of the traditional Gypsy style, and with whom he made a successful concert tour in 1853. During that tour, Brahms formed a friendship with the Hungarian violinist/composer JOSEPH JOACHIM, who gave him an introduction to FRANZ LISZT in Weimar. Of greater significance was his meeting with ROBERT and CLARA SCHUMANN in Düsseldorf, also in 1853. Later that year, the important music publishers Breitkopf und Härtel issued Brahms's two piano sonatas and his op.3 songs.

Schumann's death in 1856, after years of agonizing mental illness, deeply affected Brahms. He remained a devoted friend of Schumann's family; his correspondence with Clara (14 years his senior) reveals a deep affection and intimacy. Although Brahms had several relationships with eligible

PEOPLE IN MUSIC

Johannes Brahms. (Courtesy New York Public Library) ▶

Brahms time line

1833	Born
1853	Meets Robert and Clara Schumann in Düsseldorf
1857–59	Court pianist, chamber musician, and choir director in Detmold
1859–62	Forms and leads a women's chorus in Hamburg
1863–64	Conductor of the Viennese Singakademie
1865	Mother dies
1868	Completes *German Requiem*
1872–75	Artistic director of the concerts of Vienna's Gesellschaft der Musikfreunde

women and considered marriage, like LUDWIG VAN BEE-
THOVEN, he never surrendered his bachelorhood.

From 1857 to 1859 Brahms was employed in Detmold,
Germany, as court pianist, chamber musician, and choir director. In 1859 he completed and performed his First Piano
Concerto in Hanover, with Joachim as conductor. Returning to Hamburg, Brahms formed a women's chorus, which
he led from 1859 to 1862. Other important works of the
period were the two orchestra serenades and the First String
Sextet. Brahms hoped to be named conductor of the Hamburg Philharmonic Society, but he was passed over. Instead,
he became conductor of the Viennese Singakademie between 1863 and 1864. For financial reasons, he focused on
composing A CAPPELLA works, giving him the opportunity to
study BAROQUE music.

As early as 1857 Brahms began work on his choral masterpiece *Ein deutsches Requiem* (German Requiem). Deeply
saddened by his mother's death in 1865, he now concentrated on and completed the score three years later. The first
performance of the final version was given in Leipzig in
1869. Brahms composed prolifically during this period, producing many other important vocal and chamber works. He
also published two volumes of Hungarian Dances for piano
in 1869 and 1880, which were extremely successful.

In 1872 Brahms was named artistic director of the concerts of Vienna's famed Gesellschaft der Musikfreunde, a position he held for three years. During this time, he composed
the Variations on a Theme by Joseph Haydn, op.56a (1873).
Although this theme was drawn from a MILITARY BAND work
by HAYDN, it is not Haydn's own—the composer is unknown.

For many years, friends and admirers of Brahms urged
him to write a symphony. As early as 1855 he began work
on a full-fledged symphony, but it was not until 1862 that
he nearly completed the first movement of what was to be
his First Symphony. The famous horn solo in its finale was
jotted down by Brahms on a picture postcard he wrote to
Clara Schumann in 1868 from his summer place in the Ty-
rol; he heard the tune played by a shepherd on an ALPHORN.
Yet it would be eight years before Brahms finally completed
the great C-minor Symphony, op.68.

1873	Composes the Variations on a Theme by Joseph Haydn, op.56a
1876	Completes his Symphony No. 1, op.68, in C Minor
1877–85	Completes his Symphony No. 2, op.73 (1877); Symphony No. 3, op.90 (1883); and Symphony No. 4, op.98 (1885)
1879	His Violin Concerto, op.77, is premiered by the Gewandhaus Orchestra
1879	Receives an honorary Ph.D. from the University of Breslau, for which he composes his *Academic Festival Overture*, performed there in 1882
1881	Soloist at the premiere of his Second Piano Concerto, op.83, in Budapest
1896	Composes *Four Serious Songs*, op.121
1897	Dies

Robert Schumann's early
praise of Brahms's music
helped launch the younger
composer's career. He called
Brahms a "young eagle,"
and reiterated his positive
appraisal in his famous article
"Neue Bahnen" (New
Paths), which appeared in
the *Neue Zeitschrift für
Musik* in 1853. In it he described young Brahms as
having "come into life as

Minerva sprang in full armor from the brow of Jupiter." (Schumann was referring to the Roman myth that told how Jupiter's daughter was born. She leapt out from her father's brow, already mature and dressed for battle.)

The title "German Requiem" does not mean that this work was drawn from German music or explores German themes. It simply indicates that the text is in German rather than the more usual Latin and that the texts are drawn from Luther's Bible rather than the Latin (Catholic) text.

HANS VON BÜLOW, the great German conductor, called Brahms's First Symphony "the 10th," thus placing Brahms on a direct line from Beethoven. Brahms was both aware of his debt to the older composer and, like many of his contemporaries, haunted by it.

Brahms would compose three more symphonies between 1877 and 1885. He made fewer departures from the classic symphonic plan than BEETHOVEN, and never introduced any material that broke the general line. Brahms was a true classicist, a quality that endeared him to the critics who were repelled by RICHARD WAGNER's "music of the future." On the other hand, those critics who were in search of something new found Brahms's works hopelessly old-fashioned.

Brahms's chamber music possesses similar symphonic qualities. Like his symphonies, Brahms's string quartets follow the classic models and, within these well-defined limits, achieve the height of perfection. His three violin sonatas and op.8 Piano Trio (1854, rev. 1889) have long been recognized as permanent treasures of musical classicism.

Pianists have always kept Brahms's rhapsodies, intermezzos, and other character pieces in their repertoire. He was able to impart sheer delight in his Hungarian rhapsodies and waltzes. His song cycles continued the evolution of the art of the LIED (or art song), a natural continuation of the works of FRANZ SCHUBERT and Robert Schumann, culminating in the starkly beautiful *Four Serious Songs* (op.121, 1896).

Brahms was sociable and made friends easily. He traveled to Italy and liked to spend his summers in the solitude of the Austrian Alps. But he was essentially reserved, unsentimental, at times even insensitive, someone who needed privacy. Even Clara Schumann wrote in 1880 that she considered him "as much a riddle—I might almost say as much a stranger—as he was 25 years ago." But he was also a selfless family member who tried to save his parents' marriage and helped support his stepmother and stepbrother after his father's death. He was always ready and willing to help others, especially young composers (his earnest efforts on behalf of ANTONÍN DVOŘÁK were notable).

At first Brahms was reluctant to appear as a center of attention, turning down the honorary degree of Mus.D. from Cambridge University in 1876, but then accepted the Gold Medal of the Philharmonic Society in London a year later. Two years later he received an honorary Ph.D. from the University of Breslau. As a gesture of appreciation and gratitude he wrote his famous *ACADEMIC FESTIVAL OVERTURE* in 1881.

Brahms was extremely neat in his working habits (his manuscripts were clean and legible), but he avoided formal dress, preferring a loosely fitting flannel shirt and a detachable white collar, but no tie. He liked to dine in simple restaurants, and he drank a great deal of beer. He lived a good life but nonetheless died a painful death of liver cancer.

From the perspective of over a century, Brahms appears the greatest master of COUNTERPOINT after JOHANN SEBASTIAN BACH. He excelled in variation forms; his Variations on a Theme of PAGANINI are among the most difficult piano works of the 19th century. His symphonic works remain an important part of the repertoires of all the world's great orchestras.

Branca, Glenn, art rock composer and performer; b. Harrisburg, Pa., Oct. 6, 1948. After drama studies Branca moved to N.Y. in 1976, where he cofounded the experimental musical group Theoretical Girls. Later in the decade Branca began composing works for large groups of electric guitars, later adding brass, percussion, and other electric instruments.

PEOPLE IN MUSIC

Most of his works are called symphonies, in the original sense of "masses of sound." His music is generally extremely loud and works best in a live setting. Stylistically, the symphonies can evoke EDGARD VARÈSE, the FUTURISTS, 1930s percussion pieces, instrumental art rock, and the second MINIMALIST school, but Branca's music is totally distinctive. He received considerable publicity in 1982 when JOHN CAGE responded to a Branca performance by calling his work "fascist."

Brandenburg **Concertos.** The popular name of a set of 6 concertos by JOHANN SEBASTIAN BACH (BWV 1046–51), for various instrumental combinations. These works were gathered in 1721 and dedicated to the margrave of Brandenburg. Perhaps Bach was seeking employment from the Margrave, although, if this was the case, he was unsuccessful. Strictly speaking, only three of the pieces belong to the category of the CONCERTO GROSSO. The concertos remain among Bach's most popular works.

brahn′l′

branle, bransle (Fr.; Eng. *brangle,* brawl). Popular 16th-century French dance in which several persons joined hands and took the lead in turn. There were several varieties, in both BINARY and TERNARY forms. The MINUET grew out of the ternary branle.

Brant, Henry, Canadian-born American ultramodern composer and pioneer of spatial music; b. Montreal (of American parents), Sept. 15, 1913. Brant learned the basics of music from his father. In 1929 he moved to N.Y., where he studied with the modern composers WALLINGFORD RIEGGER, GEORGE ANTHEIL, and Fritz Mahler (Gustav's nephew). He taught at Columbia University, the Juilliard School, and Bennington College, and then settled in Santa Barbara, Calif. in 1982.

Brant was a pioneer in the field of SPATIAL MUSIC, almost all of his works since the early 1950s exploring SPATIAL DISTRIBUTION, that is to say, music in which the singers and instrumentalists are placed (distributed) in different parts of the hall. In conducting these works, Brandt developed a unique method of turning to face the various instrumentalists. He also gave cues by actually imitating the appearance of the entering instruments, miming the violin bow, a trombone valve, a piccolo, or a drum by the movement of his body or by facial movements.

Brant wrote for a wide variety of instruments and also objects not traditionally considered musical instruments, such as kitchen utensils and tin cans. He also used non-Western musical instruments and ensembles, including Javanese, African, and Indian groups, and incorporated JAZZ groups into his orchestral works.

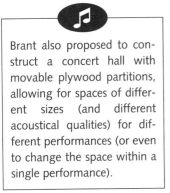

PEOPLE IN MUSIC

Brant also proposed to construct a concert hall with movable plywood partitions, allowing for spaces of different sizes (and different acoustical qualities) for different performances (or even to change the space within a single performance).

MUSICAL INSTRUMENT

brass instruments (Fr. *cuivre;* Ger. *Blechinstrumente;* It. *ottoni*). Wind instruments made of metal, forming one of the Western orchestral instrument families.

The four orchestral brass instruments are the FRENCH HORN, TRUMPET, TROMBONE (the only modern unvalved brass instrument), and TUBA. Most other brass instruments are or were found in brass, military, and wind bands: COR-NET, BUGLE, TENOR HORN, FLUGELHORN, BARITONE, EUPHO-NIUM, BOMBARDON, SAXHORN, OPHICLEIDE, and SERPENT.

A refinement of the definition of brass instruments involves the size of the mouthpiece and shape of the bore. Thus the saxophone, found in most bands, is technically a woodwind made of metal, while the serpent, popular in bands until the early 19th century, is a "brass" instrument that was actually made of wood.

bravura (It., Eng.; Ger. *Bravour;* Fr. *bravoure*). Boldness, spirit, dash, brilliancy; a resounding display of technical virtuosity. *Bravourstück,* a vocal or instrumental piece of a brilliant and difficult character; *valse de bravoure,* an instrumental waltz in brilliant, showy style. *See also* ARIA DI BRAVURA.

brǎh-voo′rǎh

Braxton, Anthony, African-American jazz alto saxophonist, contrabass clarinetist, and composer; b. Chicago, June 4, 1945. After early studies in both jazz and classical music, Braxton joined the Association for the Advancement of Creative Musicians (AACM) in 1966 and a year later formed his own avant-garde group, the Creative Construction Co., with Leroy Jenkins and Wadada Leo Smith. In the late 1960s he moved to N.Y., where he played in the improvisation ensemble Musica Elettronica Viva (1970) and CHICK COREA's free-jazz quartet Circle (1970–71).

PEOPLE IN MUSIC

Although Braxton's activities and influence have been most visible in avant-garde jazz improvisation, his output in the 1970s included more traditional compositions for band and piano. His album *For Alto* (1968) was the first recording for unaccompanied saxophone.

break (1). A short and lively improvised instrumental solo in JAZZ that momentarily disrupts the full band's performance of a tune. Breaks can be of various lengths, can be improvised by one instrumentalist or by several solo instruments, and can result in extremely clever and even complex COUNTERPOINT (two melodies played at once).

break (2). 1. The point where one register of a voice or instrument passes over into another. In the voice, the junction of the head and chest registers; in the clarinet, between the three registers. 2. A false or imperfect tone produced by incorrect lipping of a horn or trumpet; or by some difficulty with the reed of the clarinet (called "the goose"). 3. In an organ stop, when playing up the scale, the sudden return to the lower octave (caused by an incomplete set of pipes); in compound stops, any point in their scale where the relative pitch of the pipes changes. 4. A change in the voice that occurs when a boy passes through adolescence, usually resulting in a drop in the pitch of his voice.

breakdown. A lively American traditional dance in $\frac{4}{4}$ time, associated with the old-time FIDDLE and BANJO style, dating from the late 19th century. In BLUEGRASS, the breakdown became the genre for friendly rapid-finger competition between players.

PEOPLE IN MUSIC

Bream, Julian (Alexander), noted English guitarist and lutenist; b. London, July 15, 1933. Bream was educated at the Royal College of Music in London and made his concert debut at the age of 17. Through his numerous concerts and recordings he has helped to revive interest in Elizabethan LUTE music. He was named an Officer of the Order of the British Empire in 1964 and a Commander of the Order of the British Empire in 1985. Several works have been written for him.

PEOPLE IN MUSIC

Brel, Jacques, Belgian-born French singer and songwriter; b. Brussels, Apr. 8, 1929; d. Paris, Oct. 9, 1978. Brel rose to fame in France in the 1950s as a singer and writer of popular songs that emphasized such themes as unrequited love, loneliness, death, and war. In 1967 he quit the concert stage and turned to the theater as a producer, director, and actor. In 1968 the composer Mort Shuman brought Brel's songs to New York in his musical *Jacques Brel Is Alive and Well and Living in Paris.* The title proved ironic; stricken with cancer, Brel abandoned his career in 1974 and made his home in the Marquesas Islands. In 1977 he returned to Paris to record his final album, *Brel.*

Brendel, Alfred, eminent Austrian pianist; b. Wiesenberg, Moravia, Jan. 5, 1931. After study under several eminent teachers, Brendel made his concert debut in Graz, Austria, in 1948, which launched a successful career in Europe. In 1963 he made his first tours of North and South America, Japan, and Australia. He is a particularly distinguished interpreter of the CLASSIC piano repertoire, but he also included in his active repertoire ARNOLD SCHOENBERG's difficult Piano Concerto. In 1983 he presented in N.Y. a cycle of seven concerts of the complete piano sonatas of LUDWIG VAN BEETHOVEN. In 1989 he was knighted by Queen Elizabeth II of England.

Brice, Fanny (born Fannie Borach), American comedienne and singer; b. N.Y., Oct. 29, 1891; d. Los Angeles, May 29, 1951. After singing in her parents' tavern, Brice toured the burlesque circuit. She was discovered by the famous revue producer Florenz Ziegfeld, who featured her in his 1910 *Follies*. Subsequently she appeared in other editions of the *Follies* and in Broadway musicals. In the *Ziegfeld Follies of 1934* she created the role of Baby Snooks, a character she continued to portray on radio from 1938 until her death. She played herself in the 1936 film *The Great Ziegfeld*. Her third husband was the producer and songwriter Billy Rose (married, 1929; divorced, 1938).

Brico, Antonia, Dutch-born American pianist, teacher, and conductor; b. Rotterdam, June 26, 1902; d. Denver, Aug. 3, 1989. Brico's family moved to California in 1906. She took courses at the University of California, Berkeley, graduating in 1923. She then went to Berlin, where she took conducting lessons and studied piano at the State Academy of Music.

In the late 1920s Brico played piano recitals in Europe, but her main interest was conducting. At the time it was unusual for a woman to be an orchestral conductor, so Brico had to raise funds to conduct a special concert with the Berlin Philharmonic in 1930. She then received a conducting engagement in Finland, where her talents were recognized by the renowned composer JEAN SIBELIUS. She later became associated with Albert Schweitzer, visiting his hospi-

PEOPLE IN MUSIC

PEOPLE IN MUSIC

Brice's career was the subject of the 1964 Broadway musical *Funny Girl*, later made into a film starring BARBRA STREISAND (1968).

PEOPLE IN MUSIC

tal in South Africa and receiving from him suggestions for performing the works of JOHANN SEBASTIAN BACH.

In 1974 Brico was the subject of a film documentary, *Antonia,* in which she eloquently pleaded the feminist cause in music. On its strength she obtained some engagements, among them an appearance at the Hollywood Bowl in a program of common favorites. She settled in Denver, where she maintained a studio as a piano teacher.

MUSICAL INSTRUMENT

bridge (It. *ponticello;* Ger. *Steg*). 1. In bowed instruments, a thin, arching piece of wood set upright on the belly to raise and stretch the strings above the sound box, to which the bridge communicates the vibrations of the strings. 2. In the piano and other stringed instruments, a rail of wood or steel over which the strings are stretched. 3. In popular song, the contrasting melody that serves as a link between the verse and the chorus.

Brigadoon. Musical by ALAN LERNER and Frederick Loewe, 1947, telling the story of a supernatural Scottish town that is visible for only one day per century. A visiting American tourist must choose between staying with the woman he loves in Brigadoon or returning to the natural world. Includes the title tune, *Come to Me Bend to Me, The Heather on the Hill,* and *Almost Like Being in Love.*

brēn′dē-zē   **brindisi** (It., from Ger. *bring′ dir′s,* I bring it to you; Ger. *Trinklied*). A salutatory drinking song or toast, not connected to the Italian city of Brindisi. The earliest known operatic brindisi is in GAETANO DONIZETTI's *Lucrezia Borgia,* while the best known is in GIUSEPPE VERDI's *La traviata* (*Labiamo!*).

PEOPLE IN MUSIC

Britten, (Edward) **Benjamin,** Lord Britten of Aldeburgh, one of the most remarkable composers of England; b. Lowestoft, Suffolk, Nov. 22, 1913; d. Aldeburgh, Dec. 4, 1976. Britten was raised in a middle-class household. His father was an orthodontist and his mother an amateur singer.

As a child Britten played the piano (and later viola) and improvised simple tunes, some of which, many years later, he used in his *Simple Symphony.* At the age of 13 he was accepted as a composition pupil of the British composer Frank Bridge, whose influence was decisive. In 1930 Britten entered the Royal College of Music in London, where he studied piano and composition.

Britten progressed rapidly. Even his earliest works showed a mature mastery of technique and a fine lyrical sense. He became associated with the theater and began composing background music for films. He was in the U.S. at the outbreak of World War II. He returned to England in the spring of 1942 but was exempted from military service as a conscientious objector. After the war he organized the English Opera Group in 1947 and cofounded the Aldeburgh Festival, devoted mainly to the production of short operas by English composers. The festival became an important cultural institution, and many of Britten's own works were performed for the first time there, often under his own direction.

◀

Benjamin Britten with collaborator Peter Pears. (Hulton-Deutsch Collection/Corbis)

Because the Aldeburgh Festival was not richly endowed, Britten scored many of his operas for an orchestra of 12 players, with the piano filling out the texture. Despite this economy, which placed his works within the reach of small opera groups and university workshops, Britten created a rich spectrum of instrumental colors in an idiom ranging from simple classic progressions to dissonant modern harmonies.

A characteristic feature in Britten's operas is the inclusion of orchestral interludes, which act as independent symphonic poems loosely related to the dramatic action. The cries of seagulls in Britten's most popular and musically most striking opera, PETER GRIMES (1945), create a fantastic quasi-surrealistic imagery. Britten was equally successful in treating tragic subjects, as in BILLY BUDD (1951); comic subjects, exemplified by ALBERT HERRING (1947); mystical subjects, as in THE TURN OF THE SCREW (1954); and patriotic subjects, as in *Gloriana* (1953), composed for the coronation of Queen Elizabeth II. He possessed a flair for writing music for children, in which he presented a degree of sophistication and artistic simplicity.

Britten was an adaptable composer who could perform a given task according to the specific requirements of the occasion. Besides a realization of JOHN GAY's THE BEGGAR'S OPERA (1948), he also wrote modern parables for church performance and produced a contemporary counterpart of the medieval English miracle play *Noye's Fludde* (1958). Among his other works, perhaps the most remarkable is the *War Requiem* (1962), a profound tribute to those who have died in battle, mixing the Latin Requiem with Wilfred Owen's poetry.

Britten won many awards and honors in his lifetime. In 1952 he was made a Companion of Honour, and in 1965 he received the Order of Merit. In June 1976 he was created a life peer of Great Britain by Queen Elizabeth II, the first composer to be so honored.

Broonzy, "Big Bill" (born William Lee Conley), African-American BLUES singer; b. Scott, Miss., June 26, 1893; d. Chicago, Aug. 14, 1958. Broonzy was raised in Mississippi, where he learned to play the fiddle. After making his way to Chicago in 1920, he learned to play the guitar and subsequently began his career as a blues singer. Initially, he recorded in a traditional country blues style, then began absorbing more contemporary sounds. In the early 1950s he was "discovered" during the first folk revival and became popular in both Europe and the U.S., making tours in 1951, 1955, and 1957. He added to his repertoire American folk songs as well as traditional blues in order to appeal to this new audience.

Broschi, Carlo or **Riccardo.** *See* FARINELLI.

PEOPLE IN MUSIC

Brown, Clifford ("Brownie"), African-American JAZZ trumpeter; b. Wilmington, Del., Oct. 30, 1930; d. June 26, 1956. He studied at Delaware State College and Maryland State College, gaining experience playing in college jazz bands. Brown made his first professional appearance with TADD DAMERON's group. He toured Europe in 1953 with LIONEL HAMPTON's orchestra, and then returned to the U.S. working with drummer ART BLAKEY. He subsequently formed the Brown-Roach Quintet with drummer MAX ROACH. Brown recorded prolifically in the 1950s as a sideman and group leader. His career was cut short when he died in an automobile accident while on tour in 1956.

Brown, Earle (Appleton, Jr.), experimental American composer; b. Lunenburg, Mass., Dec. 26, 1926. Brown played trumpet in school bands, then enrolled at Northeastern University, Boston, to study engineering. He played trumpet in the U.S. Army Air Force Band during World War II and also served as a substitute trumpet player with the San Antonio Symphony.

Returning to Boston, he studied modern music theory and soon adopted the most advanced types of techniques in composition, experimenting with SERIAL methods as well as with ALEATORIC IMPROVISATION. Influenced by abstract expressionism in painting and mobile sculptures, he developed the idea of OPEN (MUSICAL) FORMS, using GRAPHIC NOTATION.

Brown, James, African-American GOSPEL-SOUL singer, dancer, and composer; b. Barnwell, Ga., May 3, 1928. Brown originally played keyboards, drums, and string bass, in addition to singing. In the early 1950s, he formed a group, the Famous Flames, and in 1956 released his first hit, *Please, Please, Please,* which hit the top of the charts. Other big hits through the mid-1960s include *Try Me, Prisoner of Love, It's a Man's World, Out of Sight,* and *Papa's Got a Brand New Bag.* In the late 1960s, Brown's songs acquired a political flavor, such as his militant proclamation *Black Is Beautiful; Say It Loud, I'm Black and I'm Proud;* and *Living in America.*

At the height of his fame as a soul singer, Brown was nicknamed "Soul Brother Number One," "Godfather of

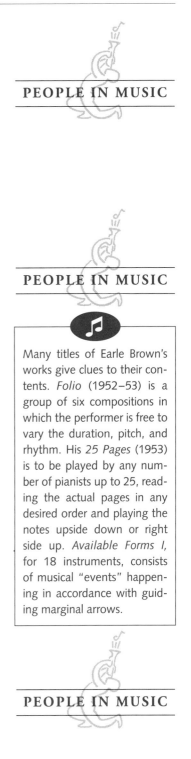

PEOPLE IN MUSIC

PEOPLE IN MUSIC

Many titles of Earle Brown's works give clues to their contents. *Folio* (1952–53) is a group of six compositions in which the performer is free to vary the duration, pitch, and rhythm. His *25 Pages* (1953) is to be played by any number of pianists up to 25, reading the actual pages in any desired order and playing the notes upside down or right side up. *Available Forms I,* for 18 instruments, consists of musical "events" happening in accordance with guiding marginal arrows.

PEOPLE IN MUSIC

Soul," and "King of Soul." Despite several run-ins with the law and advancing age, Brown continues to perform and tour.

PEOPLE IN MUSIC

Brubeck, Dave (David Warren), prominent American JAZZ pianist, bandleader, and composer; b. Concord, Calif., Dec. 6, 1920. Brubeck received classical piano training from his mother and played in local jazz groups from age 13. He also studied music at the College of the Pacific in Stockton, Calif. between 1941 and 1942, and received instruction in composition from DARIUS MILHAUD at Mills College in Oakland and from ARNOLD SCHOENBERG in Los Angeles.

During military service in World War II, Brubeck led a band in Europe. He then founded his own octet and trio in 1949. Subsequently, in 1951 he organized the Dave Brubeck Quartet, which acquired a reputation as one of the leading jazz groups of the era. Along with saxophonist PAUL DESMOND, Brubeck created some of the 1950s' most popular jazz compositions, including the often-covered *Take Five* (written in $\frac{5}{4}$ time) and *Blue Rondo à la Turk*.

After the original Brubeck quartet broke up in the late 1960s, Brubeck formed a new group that featured his sons Darius (b. San Francisco, June 14, 1947), a keyboard player, Chris (b. Los Angeles, March 19, 1953), a bass guitar and bass trombone player, and Danny (b. Oakland, May 5, 1955), a drummer. This group played more contemporary jazz-rock, and achieved some popular success through the mid-1980s. Although Brubeck has continued to record and perform, his activity has slowed over the past decade.

Besides jazz compositions, Brubeck has written classical pieces that include jazz elements, including two ballets, a musical, *The Real Ambassador* (1962), two ORATORIOS and three CANTATAS, and many piano pieces. But he is best regarded as a jazz performer.

Brubeck's brother, Howard R(engstorff) (b. Concord, Calif., July 11, 1916), is a composer who served as chairman of the music department at Palomar Junior College in San Marcos, Calif. (1953–78).

PEOPLE IN MUSIC

Bruch, Max, celebrated German composer; b. Cologne, Jan. 6, 1838; d. Friedenau, near Berlin, Oct. 2, 1920. Bruch's mother, a professional singer, was his first teacher. He afterward studied theory in Bonn, and in 1852 won a student scholarship of the Mozart Foundation in Frankfurt for four years. At the age of 14 his First Symphony was performed in Cologne, and at 20 he produced his first stage work there. Between 1858 and 1861 he taught in Cologne. In 1863 Bruch was in Mannheim, where he produced his first full-fledged opera, *Die Loreley* (1863). About the same time he wrote an effective choral work, *Frithjof,* presented with great success in various German towns and in Vienna.

From 1865 to 1867 Bruch was music director of a concert organization in Koblenz, where he wrote his First Violin Concerto in G Minor, which became a great favorite among violinists. He next was hired as court kapellmeister (chapel master) in Sonderhausen. In 1870 he went to Berlin, where his last opera, *Hermione,* based on Shakespeare's *The Winter's Tale,* was produced in 1872.

In 1880 Bruch accepted the post of conductor of the Liverpool Philharmonic, remaining in England for three years. In 1883 he visited the U.S. and conducted his choral work *Arminius* in Boston. From 1883 to 1890 he was music director of an orchestra society in Breslau; in 1891 he became a professor of composition in Berlin, retiring in 1910. Bruch was married to the singer Clara Tuczek (d. 1919).

Bruch was a master of HARMONY, COUNTERPOINT, and INSTRUMENTATION; he was equally adept at handling vocal masses. He contributed a great deal to the development of the secular ORATORIO through his compositions *Odysseus, Arminius, Das Lied von der Glocke,* and *Achilleus.* Among his instrumental works, the *Scottish Fantasy* for violin and orchestra (1880) was extremely successful when Spanish violinist PABLO SARASATE (to whom it was dedicated) performed it all over Europe.

The most popular of all Bruch's work is *Kol Nidrei,* for cello and orchestra, composed for the Jewish community of Liverpool in 1880. Its success led to the erroneous assumption that Bruch himself was Jewish (he was, in fact, of a clerical Protestant family). His Concerto for Two Pianos and Orchestra was commissioned by the American duo-piano team Ottilie and Rose Sutro; when they performed it for the first time in Philadelphia in 1916, they drastically revised

PEOPLE IN MUSIC

Bruckner time line

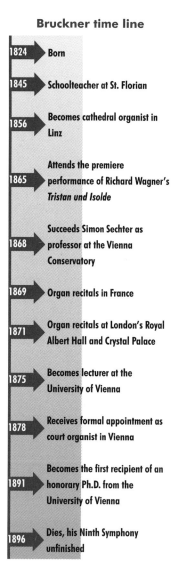

1824	Born
1845	Schoolteacher at St. Florian
1856	Becomes cathedral organist in Linz
1865	Attends the premiere performance of Richard Wagner's *Tristan und Isolde*
1868	Succeeds Simon Sechter as professor at the Vienna Conservatory
1869	Organ recitals in France
1871	Organ recitals at London's Royal Albert Hall and Crystal Palace
1875	Becomes lecturer at the University of Vienna
1878	Receives formal appointment as court organist in Vienna
1891	Becomes the first recipient of an honorary Ph.D. from the University of Vienna
1896	Dies, his Ninth Symphony unfinished

the original. The authentic version, discovered in Berlin in 1971, was given its first performance by Nathan Twining and Mer Berkofsky with the London Symphony in 1974.

Bruckner, (Josef) **Anton,** inspired Austrian composer; b. Ansfelden, Sept. 4, 1824; d. Vienna, Oct. 11, 1896. Bruckner studied music with his father, a village schoolmaster and church organist, and also took music lessons with his cousin, Johann Baptist Weiss. After his father's death in 1837, Bruckner enrolled as a chorister at St. Florian, where he attended classes in organ, piano, violin, and theory. In 1840–41 he entered the special school for educational training in Linz and studied music theory in Enns.

While in his early youth, Bruckner held teaching positions in elementary public schools in Windhaag (1841–43) and Kronstorf (1843–45). In 1845 he was hired as a schoolteacher at St. Florian, where he remained for a decade, while also holding the title of provisional organist there between 1848 and 1851. At the age of 31 Bruckner went to Vienna to study harmony and counterpoint with the renowned pedagogue Simon Sechter. Bruckner continued his studies with him off and on until 1861.

In 1856 Bruckner became cathedral organist in Linz. Determined to acquire still more technical knowledge, he took lessons in orchestration with Otto Kitzler, first cellist of the Linz municipal theater, between 1861 and 1863. He also took it upon himself to study the masters of Italian and German COUNTERPOINT, including particularly the works of JOHANN SEBASTIAN BACH. These tasks preoccupied him so completely that he did not engage in composition until he was nearly 40 years old.

At that time, Bruckner fell under the powerful influence of RICHARD WAGNER's music. In 1865 he attended the premiere of *TRISTAN UND ISOLDE* in Munich and met the master himself. Although he greatly admired Wagner's music, he continued to compose in the classic German style. Whereas Wagner strove toward the ideal union of drama, text, and music in a new type of operatic production, Bruckner kept away from the musical theater, confining himself to symphonic and choral music. Even in his harmonic techniques,

Bruckner seldom followed Wagner, and he never tried to emulate the passionate rise and fall of Wagnerian "endless" melody.

The personal differences between Wagner and Bruckner could not be more striking. Wagner was a man of the world who devoted his life to the promotion of his art, while Bruckner was unsure of his abilities and desperately sought recognition. Coming from a humble peasant background, Bruckner was unable to secure the respect and honor that he craved. One proof of his lack of self-confidence was his willingness to revise his works repeatedly, not always to their betterment, taking advice from conductors and well-wishers.

Bruckner also suffered from periodic attacks of depression. His entire life seems to have been a study in unhappiness, most particularly in his numerous attempts to find a wife. In his desperation, he made halfhearted proposals of marriage to women beneath his class. The older he grew, the younger were the objects of his misguided affections. A notorious episode was his proposal to a chambermaid at a hotel in Berlin. Bruckner died a virgin.

Bruckner was a devout Catholic. To him the faith and the sacraments of the Roman Catholic Church were not mere rituals but profound experiences. Following the practice of FRANZ JOSEPH HAYDN, he signed most of his works with the words "Omnia ad majorem Dei gloriam"; indeed, he must have felt that every piece of music he composed redounded "to the greater glory of God." From reports of his friends and contemporaries, it appears that he regarded each happy event of his life as a gift of God and each disaster as an act of divine wrath.

Bruckner was a poor conductor but a master organist. In 1869 he appeared in recitals in France, and in 1871 he visited London. He was also esteemed as a teacher. In 1868 he succeeded Simon Sechter as professor of harmony, counterpoint, and organ at the Vienna Conservatory, and he was also named provisional court organist, an appointment formally confirmed in 1878.

In failing health, Bruckner retired from the Vienna Conservatory in 1891, the same year he gratefully accepted an honorary Ph.D. from the University of Vienna, the first mu-

Bruckner's adulation of Wagner was extreme. The dedication of his Third Symphony reads: "To the eminent Excellency Richard Wagner the Unattainable, World-Famous, and Exalted Master of Poetry and Music, in Deepest Reverence Dedicated by Anton Bruckner."

sician to be so honored. The remaining years of his life were devoted to the composition of his Ninth Symphony, which, however, remained unfinished at his death.

Bruckner's symphonies (1865–96), original and with a deep spiritual content, are a monumental achievement. His choral works share similar qualities. Bruckner is usually paired with GUSTAV MAHLER, who was a generation younger but whose music had a similar grand quality. Accordingly, Bruckner and Mahler societies sprouted in several countries, with the express purpose of promoting their music.

Because Bruckner made many revisions of his scores, conflicting versions of his symphonies have been published. With the founding of the International Bruckner Society, a movement was begun to publish the original versions of his manuscripts, the majority of which he bequeathed to the Hofbibliothek in Vienna. A complete edition of Bruckner's works, under the supervision of Robert Haas and Alfred Orel, began to appear in 1930; in 1945 Leopold Nowak was named its editor-in-chief.

bruitism (Fr., *bruitisme; bruit* = noise). A term, originally used negatively, denoting the use of noise as a compositional element. The pioneer work of bruitism was *Arte dei rumori* by the Italian FUTURIST LUIGI RUSSOLO. He produced special instruments called noise producers (*intonarumori*) specifically for this composition. EDGARD VARÈSE used noise as the basis of his famous work, *Ionisation* (1929–31).

brunette (Fr., dark-haired woman). French song genre of the 17th and 18th centuries, similar to the BERGERETTE. It was based on traditional and street ballad melodies. JEAN-BAPTISTE LULLY and JEAN-PHILIPPE RAMEAU wrote brunettes into their operas.

Bryars, Gavin, English composer and teacher; b. Goole, Yorkshire, Jan. 16, 1943. Bryars studied philosophy at Sheffield University while also studying composition. He began his career as a bassist, turning in 1966 to composition and quickly emerging as one of England's most influential experimental composers. His compositions, INDETERMINATE

PEOPLE IN MUSIC

and filled with repeated melodies and rhythms, often use electronic instruments.

Bryars has collaborated with a number of well-known musicians, including BRIAN ENO, STEVE REICH, and CORNELIUS CARDEW. A number of his pieces have been choreographed by American modern dancer Lucinda Childs, and in 1999 he embarked on a collaborative project with the celebrated American choreographer MERCE CUNNINGHAM. In 1984 his opera *Medea,* in collaboration with Robert Wilson, was premiered at the Opéra de Lyon.

Bryars's warmth and humor is shown in his *The Sinking of the Titanic* (1969), a multimedia work that includes a collage of excerpts from pieces the drowning orchestra might have been playing.

buccina. Ancient Roman semicircular metal horn used during festivals, usually adorned with a metal ornament in the shape of an animal horn. Similar to a shepherd's horn.

MUSICAL INSTRUMENT

Buchla, Donald (Frederick), American electronic-instrument designer and builder, composer, and performer; b. Southgate, Calif., Apr. 17, 1937. After studying physics at the University of California, Berkeley, Buchla was active with the San Francisco Tape Music Center, where in 1966 he installed the first Buchla SYNTHESIZER. That same year he founded Buchla Associates in Berkeley for the manufacture of synthesizers. In addition to designing and manufacturing electronic instruments, he also installed electronic music studios at the Royal Academy of Music, Stockholm, and at IRCAM, Paris, among other institutions.

PEOPLE IN MUSIC

In 1975 Buchla cofounded the Electric Weasel Ensemble, a live electronic music group. In 1978 he was awarded a Guggenheim fellowship and was appointed codirector of the Artists' Research Collective in Berkeley.

buffa (It.). Comic, burlesque. *See also* ARIA BUFFA, OPERA BUFFA. *Buffo* (from *buffone,* jester), a comic actor or operatic singer.

boof-fäh

Buffalo Springfield. (Leader/guitar/vocal: Stephen Stills, b. Dallas, Jan. 3, 1945; Lead guitar/vocal: Neil Young, b. Toronto, Nov. 12, 1945; Rhythm guitar/vocal: Richie Furay, b. Yellow Springs, Ohio, May 9, 1944; Bass: Bruce Palmer, b. Liverpool, Ont., 1946; Drums: Dewey Martin,

PEOPLE IN MUSIC

b. Chesterville, Ont., Sept. 30, 1942. Jim Messina, b. Maywood, Calif., Dec. 5, 1947, replaced Palmer in late 1967.) Buffalo Springfield was a popular rock band of the 1960s that took its name from a brand of tractor. The original band was short-lived (c.1965–68), with one enduring hit, Stills's social protest song *For What It's Worth*. The band combined various influences, from folk and country to progressive rock. Stills went on to form the "supergroup" Crosby, Stills, and Nash. Young performed with them for a time (Crosby, Stills, Nash, and Young) and also undertook a solo career. Furay and Messina formed the country-rock group Poco, with Messina subsequently moving on to partner with Kenny Loggins (b. Everett, Wash., Jan. 7, 1948) to form the popular duo Loggins and Messina.

bugaku. Japanese masked dances, derived from Chinese and Korean court traditions. The musical accompaniment is slow and stately, emphasizing woodwinds and drums.

MUSICAL INSTRUMENT

bugle. 1. A wind instrument of brass or copper, with cupped mouthpiece, used for military calls and infantry signals; a trumpet without keys. 2. The keyed-bugle, with six keys and a compass of over two octaves. 3. The valve bugle; *See* SAXHORN.

PEOPLE IN MUSIC

Bull, John, famous English organist and composer; b. probably in Old Radnor, Radnorshire, c.1562; d. Antwerp, Mar. 12, 1628. Bull studied music at the Chapel Royal and received his music degree from Oxford in 1586. He was sworn in as a Gentleman of the Chapel Royal in 1586, becoming its organist in 1591.

In 1596, on Queen Elizabeth's recommendation, Bull was appointed professor of music at Gresham College and in 1597 was elected first public lecturer there. Bull got into difficulties with Gresham College when he had a child out of wedlock with Elizabeth Walter, and he was forced to resign in 1607. The couple were married two days later. In 1610 he entered the service of Prince Henry but in 1613 was charged with adultery and had to flee England.

In September 1615 Bull became assistant organist at the Antwerp Cathedral in Belgium and was named its principal organist in 1617. In the Netherlands he became acquainted with the organist and composer JAN SWEELINCK. They both had great influence on the development of keyboard music of the time. Bull also composed many CANONS and ANTHEMS.

bull-roarer. A musical instrument consisting of a small, usually notched, piece of wood, bone, or stone to which a string is attached. When spun above the player's head, it produces a low, dull roar, from which comes its name.

Bülow, Hans (Guido) **von,** celebrated German pianist and conductor; b. Dresden, Jan. 8, 1830; d. Cairo, Feb. 12, 1894. At the age of nine, Bülow began to study piano and theory. He then went to Leipzig, where he studied law at the university, although he continued his music studies on the side.

From 1846 to 1848 Bülow lived in Stuttgart, where he made his debut as a pianist. In 1849 he attended the University of Berlin, where he joined radical social groups. Shortly afterward, he went to Zurich and met RICHARD WAGNER, who was living there in exile. After a year in Switzerland, where he conducted theater music, Bülow proceeded to Weimar, where he studied with FRANZ LISZT. In 1853 he made a tour through Germany and Austria as a pianist. In 1855 he was appointed head of the piano department at the Stern Conservatory in Berlin, retaining this post until 1864. He married Liszt's daughter, Cosima, in 1857.

In 1864 he was called by Ludwig II to Munich as court pianist and conductor. The king, who was a great admirer of Wagner, also summoned Wagner to Munich, and Bülow himself became Wagner's ardent champion. On June 10, 1865, he conducted at the Court Opera in Munich the first performance of *TRISTAN UND ISOLDE,* and on June 21, 1868, the premiere of *DIE MEISTERSINGER VON NÜRNBERG.* It was about this time that Wagner fell in love with Cosima. After her divorce from Bülow she married Wagner, in 1870. Despite this betrayal, Bülow continued to conduct Wagner's music.

In 1872 Bülow lived in Florence. He then resumed his career as a pianist, winning triumphant successes in England and Russia. During his American tour in 1875–76 he gave 139 concerts, and he revisited America in 1889 and 1890.

MUSICAL INSTRUMENT

PEOPLE IN MUSIC

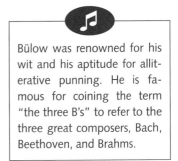

Bülow was renowned for his wit and his aptitude for alliterative punning. He is famous for coining the term "the three B's" to refer to the three great composers, Bach, Beethoven, and Brahms.

An important chapter in his career was his conductorship in Meiningen from 1880–85. In 1882 he married a Meiningen actress, Marie Schanzer. He was conductor of the Berlin Philharmonic from 1887 to 1893, when a lung ailment forced him to seek a cure in Egypt. He died shortly after his arrival in Cairo.

As a conductor, Bülow was an uncompromising disciplinarian. He insisted on perfection of detail and was also able to project considerable emotional power. He was one of the first conductors to dispense with the score. His memory was fabulous; it was said that he could memorize a piano concerto by simply reading the score, sometimes while riding a train. The mainstay of his repertoire was CLASSIC and ROMANTIC music, but he was also receptive toward composers of the new school.

When PIOTR ILYICH TCHAIKOVSKY, unable to secure a performance of his First Piano Concerto in Russia, offered the score to Bülow, he accepted it and gave its world premiere as soloist with a pickup orchestra in Boston in 1875. The music was too new and strange to American ears of the time, however, and the critical reactions were hostile. Bülow also encouraged the young RICHARD STRAUSS, and gave him his first position as conductor.

Bülow was a composer himself, but his works were only competent and well structured, devoid of originality. He made masterly transcriptions and annotated and edited LUDWIG VAN BEETHOVEN's piano sonatas. These editions were widely used by piano teachers, even though criticism was voiced against his occasional alterations of Beethoven's original to enhance the resonance.

Bumbry, Grace (Melzia Ann), greatly talented African-American mezzo-soprano; b. St. Louis, Jan. 4, 1937. Bumbry sang in church choirs as a child. In 1955 she studied voice at Northwestern University with the celebrated German-born soprano Lotte Lehmann, continuing lessons with her at the Music Academy of the West in Santa Barbara, Calif.

Bumbry made her professional debut in a concert in London in 1959, then made a spectacular operatic appearance as Amneris in GIUSEPPE VERDI's *AIDA* at the Paris Opéra

PEOPLE IN MUSIC

in 1960. In a stroke of luck, Wieland Wagner engaged her to sing Venus in RICHARD WAGNER's *TANNHÄUSER* at the Bayreuth Festival on July 23, 1961. She was the first African-American to be featured in the role of a goddess. This event brought her immediate attention, and she was invited by Jacqueline Kennedy to sing at the White House in 1961. She then undertook a grand tour in the U.S. In 1963 she performed the role of Venus again at the Chicago Lyric Opera and also sang it at Lyons, France.

In 1965 Bumbry made her N.Y. Metropolitan Opera debut as Princess Eboli in VERDI's *DON CARLOS.* In 1966 she sang GEORGES BIZET's *CARMEN* at the Salzburg Festival under the direction of HERBERT VON KARAJAN, a role she repeated at the Metropolitan with extraordinary success. In 1970 she sang STRAUSS's *SALOME* at Covent Garden, London, and again, in German, at the Metropolitan Opera in 1973. She proved her ability to perform mezzo-soprano and soprano roles with equal brilliance by singing both Aida and Amneris, and both Venus and Elisabeth. In 1963 she married the Polish tenor Erwin Jaeckel, who also became her business manager.

Burgundian school. The ill-defined name of the 15th-century school of composition that formed a natural transition from the ARS NOVA, in which the MOTET was the crowning achievement, to the great FLEMISH SCHOOL, creators of lush POLYPHONY, which achieved its flowering during the late Renaissance.

Most of the musicians who created this transitional style served at the various courts in the large area ruled by the dukes of Burgundy—Philip the Good and Charles the Bold—which included much of the Netherlands and Belgium, as well as Burgundy proper in central France. Although not one of the masters of the Burgundian school was born in Burgundy, the name *Burgundian school,* despite various alternatives, is the most common for this style.

The greatest masters of this period were GUILLAUME DUFAY and GILLES BINCHOIS. Dufay was known as "cantor illustrissimi ducis burgundie" (court musician of the illustrious duke of Burgundy), although his term of tenure at the duchy was relatively short.

The Burgundian school helped establish THIRDS and SIXTHS as CONSONANT (or pleasing) intervals; previously, they had been avoided in church harmony. The TONIC and DOMINANT TRIADS became the mainstays of harmonic texture, particularly in CADENCES. The MAJOR KEY, shunned just a century before, now was frequently used, particularly in secular music.

Generally speaking, the Burgundian school contributed to the relaxation of the rigid rules that were previously developed by the church and that hampered the natural development of musical composition. This cleared the way for the advent of the new musical art of the Netherlands in the Renaissance.

boor-les′kah

burlesca (It., jest). A short piece, usually for keyboard, in a light mood. Johann Sebastian Bach was among the first to write one.

burlesque. A popular type of theatrical entertainment that flourished in the 18th century parallel to the BALLAD OPERA. It usually included comic dialogue and songs with original texts set to preexisting popular tunes. In the 19th century the genre became a dignified instrumental or vocal form. RICHARD STRAUSS wrote a *Burleske* for piano and orchestra, as did BÉLA BARTÓK. IGOR STRAVINSKY's *PETRUSHKA* is subtitled *Scènes burlesques.*

In the late 19th and 20th centuries the stage burlesque devolved into the *burlesque show,* a popular type of entertainment that became the staple of American musical theater in the second half of the 19th century. Imported from England, the first true burlesque show was an exhibition called *British Blondes.* The burlesque presented scantily clad young women (hence the name "girlie show"). The burlesque had much in common with the musicals of the period, which were more like REVUES and featured chorus lines.

Striptease was added to the burlesque in the 20th century. One famous club was the subject of a film, *The Night They Raided Minsky's.* Today the closest thing to a burlesque show is the lavish Las Vegas revue or floor show, which includes dance numbers featuring chorus lines interspersed with comedy and song.

Burney, Charles, celebrated English music historian; b. Shrewsbury, Apr. 7, 1726; d. Chelsea, Apr. 12, 1814. Burney was a pupil of Edmund Baker, the organist of Chester Cathedral; of his eldest half brother, James; and, from 1744 to 1747, of noted composer THOMAS ARNE in London. Bur-

PEOPLE IN MUSIC

ney worked as an organist at several churches between 1749 and 1760. He returned to London in 1760, when he began writing his masterwork, *A General History of Music.* Work on this book took him to France, Switzerland, and Italy in 1770 and Germany, the Netherlands, and Austria in 1772, consulting libraries, attending concerts of sacred and secular music, and forming contacts with leading musicians and scholars. Two volumes entitled *The Present State of Music* (1771, 1773) resulted.

A General History of Music appeared in four volumes between 1776 and 1789. It remains one of the most important documents of 18th century music, and a model of early music criticism.

Burns, Robert, great Scottish poet and songwriter, b. Alloway, Jan. 25, 1759; d. Dumfries, July 21, 1796. In addition to writing some of the greatest Scottish poetry, Burns had a lifelong interest in traditional Scottish ballads and songs. He collected traditional songs, completed fragmentary songs, and wrote lyrics in traditional style, matching them to folk melodies. His major publication, *The Scots Musical Museum* (6 vols., 1787–1803), remains one of the great collections of Scottish traditional music and song.

PEOPLE IN MUSIC

Busoni, Ferruccio (Dante Michelangiolo Benvenuto), influential Italian-German composer, greatly admired pianist, and writer on modern aesthetics; b. Empoli, near Florence, Apr. 1, 1866; d. Berlin, July 27, 1924. Busoni's father played the clarinet, and his mother, Anna Weiss, was an amateur pianist. Busoni grew up in an artistic atmosphere and learned to play the piano as a child. At eight he played in public in Trieste, Italy. He gave a piano recital in Vienna when he was 10 and included in his program some of his own compositions.

In 1877 the family moved to Graz, where Busoni continued his piano lessons. He conducted his *Stabat Mater* there at the age of 12. At 15 he was accepted as a member of the Accademia Filarmonica in Bologna, where he performed his ORATORIO *Il sabato del villaggio* in 1883. In 1886 he went to Leipzig, where he undertook a profound study of JOHANN SEBASTIAN BACH's music. In 1889 he was appointed a profes-

PEOPLE IN MUSIC

sor of piano at the Helsingfors Conservatory in Sweden, where among his students was JEAN SIBELIUS (who was actually a few months older than his teacher). At that time Busoni married Gerda Sjostrand, whose father was a celebrated Swedish sculptor. They had two sons, both of whom became well-known artists.

In 1890 Busoni participated in the Rubinstein Competition in St. Petersburg, winning first prize with his *Konzertstück* for Piano and Orchestra. On the strength of this achievement he was engaged to teach piano at the Moscow Conservatory for a year. In 1891 he accepted the post of professor at the New England Conservatory of Music in Boston, where he remained for three years. At the same time he made several European tours, maintaining his principal residence in Berlin. During the 1912–13 season he made a triumphant tour of Russia and in 1913 was appointed director of the Liceo Musicale in Bologna. The outbreak of the war in 1914 forced him to move to neutral Switzerland, where he remained until 1923. He then went to Paris before returning to Berlin, remaining there until his death.

Busoni was a philosopher of music who wrote several influential books that continue to be studied by serious students of modern music. He believed that CLASSICAL ideals of composition should be incorporated into modern music. He also sought to establish a link between architecture and composition, for example, by creating drawings illustrating the architectonic plan of Bach's fugues. Busoni also advanced the use of over 100 different MODES and suggested the possibility of writing music in subchromatic intervals (intervals smaller than the half-step in the Western scale, such as the QUARTER TONE). In addition to his writing, Busoni taught piano and composition in various cities at various times. He influenced the musical theories and compositions of the important modern composer EDGARD VARÈSE, who was living in Berlin when Busoni was there.

Busoni was also a celebrated pianist. The few recordings that survive suggest the grandeur and quasi-orchestral sonority of his playing.

PEOPLE IN MUSIC

Buxtehude, Dietrich (Didericus), significant Danish-born German organist and composer; b. probably in Helsingborg, c.1637; d. Lübeck, May 9, 1707. His father, Johannes Buxtehude (1601–74), an organist of German extraction, was active in Holstein, which was under Danish rule. After receiving a thorough education, in all probability from his father, Dietrich held several positions as organist in his native country before being appointed organist and WERKMEISTER at St. Mary's church in Lübeck in 1668. To take this position, Buxtehude was required to marry his predecessor's daughter, Anna Margaretha; he did so, later that year. He continued the *Abendmusiken,* concerts consisting of organ music and pieces for chorus and orchestra, held annually in Lübeck in late afternoon on five of the six Sundays immediately preceding Christmas.

In 1705 JOHANN SEBASTIAN BACH made a pilgrimage allegedly to hear the *Abendmusik,* to study with Buxtehude, and possibly to investigate the possibility of taking Buxtehude's position as church organist. Although the details of Bach's trip are unknown, there can be no doubt that Buxtehude exercised a profound influence on Bach as both organist and composer. Buxtehude died in 1707, and his successor, Johann Christian Schieferdecker, dutifully married Buxtehude's eldest daughter.

Buxtehude exerted a major influence on succeeding organists. Though little of his music exists in manuscript, many composers were known to have made copies of his works for their own study. His major student was Nicolaus Bruhns.

Bye Bye Birdie. Musical by Charles Strouse, 1960, satirizing the first generation of rock 'n' roll groupies. It includes the hit song *Put On a Happy Face.*

Byrd, Henry Roeland ("Professor Longhair"), American BLUES pianist; b. Bogalusa, La., Dec. 19, 1918; d. New Orleans, Jan. 30, 1980. Byrd received rudimentary instruction in music from his mother. He subsequently developed an individual style that combined blues, New Orleans, and Caribbean elements. He made recordings in the 1950s that were locally successful, then made further recordings upon his "rediscovery" in the 1970s. His nickname came from the admiration other musicians had for his technique; a "profes-

Buxtehude appears prominently in the painting *Domestic Music Scene* (1674) by Johannes Voorhout.

PEOPLE IN MUSIC

sor" is a pianist of great skills, while the term *longhair* once denoted a person of refined artistic tastes. FATS DOMINO, Huey Smith, and Allen Toussaint made his style popular outside New Orleans.

PEOPLE IN MUSIC

Byrd (Byrde, Bird), **William,** great English composer and organist; b. probably in Lincoln, 1543; d. Stondon Massey, Essex, July 4, 1623. There are indications that Byrd studied with the English organist and composer THOMAS TALLIS. In 1563 Byrd was appointed organist of Lincoln Cathedral, and in 1570 he was sworn in as a Gentleman of the Chapel Royal. Two years later he was appointed organist at the Chapel Royal, a position he shared with Tallis.

William Byrd. (Courtesy New York Public Library) ▶

In 1575 Byrd and Tallis were granted a patent by Queen Elizabeth I for the exclusive privilege of printing music and selling music paper for a term of 21 years. In 1585, after the death of Tallis, the license passed wholly into Byrd's hands. Their earliest publication was the first set of *Cantiones sacrae* for five to eight voices, published in 1575 and dedicated to the queen.

Byrd was unsurpassed in his time as a versatile composer. His masterly technique is revealed in his religious works, instrumental music, MADRIGALS, and solo songs. Many of Byrd's keyboard pieces appeared in the manuscript collection *My Ladye Nevells Booke* (1591) and in Francis Tregian's collection, the *Fitzwilliam Virginal Book* (c.1612–19), among others.

During the winter of 1592–93 Byrd moved to a small town outside of London. He subsequently was involved in various lawsuits and disputes concerning the ownership of the property. Between 1592 and 1595 he published three masses and between 1605 and 1607 two volumes of songs sung at mass. His last collection, *Psalmes, Songs and Sonnets,* was published in 1611.

Byrds, The. (Leader/guitar/vocal: Jim [later Roger] McGuinn, b. Chicago, July 13, 1942; Guitar/vocal: David Crosby, b. Los Angeles, Aug. 14, 1941; Guitar/vocal: Gene Clark, b. Tipton, Mo., Nov. 17 1941; d. Sherman Oaks, Calif., May 24, 1991; Bass/vocal: Chris Hillman, b. Los Angeles, Dec. 4, 1942; Drums: Mike Clarke, b. N.Y., June 3, 1944; d. Treasure Island, Fla., Dec. 19, 1993.) Harmonious American folk-rock group of the 1960s. They first scored hits with their sunny harmonies on folk/social protest songs like BOB DYLAN's *Mr. Tambourine Man* (1965), introduced by McGuinn's jangly electric 12-string guitar, and PETE SEEGER's *Turn Turn Turn.* They next introduced IMPROVISATION and electronic effects in songs like *Eight Miles High* (1966), thought to refer to a drug experience (although McGuinn claimed it had to do with an airplane flight). The group dropped to a quartet when Clark left, and then a trio when Crosby bailed out.

In 1968, McGuinn formed a new Byrds, recording the influential country-rock album *Sweetheart of the Rodeo* (a commercial failure at the time). This new group lasted through 1973, with various lineups. In 1975 the "original" Byrds reunited for one album, and in the mid-1980s McGuinn, Hillman, and Clark performed as a trio. The original group reunited for recording only when a boxed set of their original records was issued in the early 1990s.

Byrne, David, Scottish-born American musician; b. Dumbarton, Scotland, May 14, 1952. Byrne's family moved to the U.S. when he was a youngster. He entered the Rhode Island School of Design, where he developed the belief that dance, song, instrumental music, drama, and film were parts of a total art. While there he formed a trio called TALKING HEADS in 1975 with fellow students Chris Frantz and Tina Weymouth. They began playing at local clubs and soon after

PEOPLE IN MUSIC

PEOPLE IN MUSIC

were booked at N.Y.'s influential punk rock club CBGBs. Guitarist Jerry Harrison completed the band's lineup in 1977, when they were signed to a major record contract.

The group centered on Byrne's stage presence. He effected a wild-eyed stare, giving himself a slightly geeky appearance, and jerked his arms and legs in spasms to the music. This was enhanced by the lyrics to his songs, particularly the band's first hit, *Psycho Killer,* describing a deranged murderer. Byrne also affected a hiccupy vocal style, something like the sound of BUDDY HOLLY, that contributed to his overall nervous appearance.

In 1978 the band began working with avant-garde composer and producer BRIAN ENO, who added many electronic sound effects to their music and introduced them to world music, particularly African rhythms.

In the early 1980s, while continuing to work with the band, Byrne embarked on a few solo projects. He composed the music for *The Catherine Wheel* (1981), choreographed by the modern dancer Twyla Tharp. This score combines the widely differing ingredients of new-wave rock and spiritual soul music. He also wrote scores for several films and theater pieces.

Meanwhile, the Talking Heads continued to score hits, achieving their biggest chart success with 1983's *Burning Down the House.* A year later, the film maker Jonathan Demme made a feature film, *Stop Making Sense,* recording their unique concert performances. The group made their last recording together in 1988, although they did not officially disband until 1991.

Byrne embarked on a solo career of some success. His 1989 album *Rei Momo* consists of songs that, backed by a 16-piece band, combine Latin and pop styles. He followed with more conventional rock-style albums but never achieved the success he experienced with the Talking Heads.

Byzantine chant. The church system of MODES as established in the Byzantine Empire of Constantine the Great in A.D. 330 and continuing until the fall of Constantinople to the Turks in 1453. Byzantine hymnody is similar to GREGORIAN CHANT in its use of a single melody line, without any

MODULATION or change in key, broken into sections of different length without any single, overall rhythm scheme.

The development of Byzantine chant can be traced through the emergence of various types of hymns: *kontakion* in the sixth century, *troparion* in the seventh century, and *kanon* in the eighth century. The essentially syllabic chant (one syllable sung to each note) began to be adorned with flowery melodic elaborations as the style matured.

Byzantine music masters outlined a system of modes, or *echoi,* that paralleled the system of modes in the Western church. The language of Byzantine chant from its inception to its decline remained Greek, but there is no relation between the Byzantine echoi and the ancient Greek modes.

C

C (Eng., Ger.; Fr. *ut;* It. *do*). 1. The first tone and degree of the C-major or C-minor scale. The TONIC of the first scale in the cycle of scales, with neither sharps nor flats in the key signature. 2. In music theory, uppercase *C* designates the C-major triad, lowercase *c* represents the c-minor triad. 3. *Middle C* is the note c1 on the piano keyboard.

C major (Ger. *C dur*). This is the key of exultant joy, triumphant jubilation, and communal celebration.

It is natural that pianists should be addicted to C major, because it is the first scale they practice when they begin lessons, being free from the bothersome black keys. And naturally, pianists who become composers often make full use of their familiar white keys.

C minor (Ger. *C moll*). The key of concentration and solemnity, a key of introspection, quite different from its major relative, C MAJOR. But the two keys are intimately related, not through the traditional cycle of scales, but by the virtue of the PICARDY THIRD, in which the minor third of a minor triad is replaced by a major third. Thus, no matter how dark or ominous an opening C minor can be, there is always a promise of C major in the FINALE.

cabaletta (It., rhythmic verse). In 18th-century Italian opera, a short song (like a CAVATINA). Later, the term took the meaning of the concluding section of an ARIA or duet, forming a summary in rapid tempo and with heightened intensity.

kăh-băh-let′tah

Caballé, Montserrat, celebrated Spanish soprano; b. Barcelona, Apr. 12, 1933. Caballé learned to sing at a convent that she attended as a child. At age eight she was accepted at the Conservatorio del Liceo in Barcelona. She graduated in 1953, then went to Italy, where she sang minor roles.

After a successful appearance as Mimi in LA BOHÈME at the Basel Opera, Caballé advanced rapidly, singing many standard operatic roles. She also mastered such difficult modern parts as Salome, Elektra, and Marie in ALBAN BERG's *WOZZECK*. She filled guest engagements at the Vienna State Opera, then made a grand tour through Germany. In 1964 she sang Manon in Mexico City and married Bernabé Marti, a Spanish tenor, with whom she subsequently appeared in joint recitals.

Caballé made a triumphant American debut in 1965, when she was summoned to substitute for MARILYN HORNE in the title role of DONIZETTI's *Lucrezia Borgia*. The usually restrained N.Y. critics praised her without reservation for the beauty of her voice and expressiveness of her dramatic interpretation. Several other American appearances followed, all highly successful. She made her debut at N.Y.'s Metropolitan Opera as Marguerite in 1965, subsequently appearing there in a wide variety of roles. In 1989 she created the role of Queen Isabella in Leonardo Balada's *Cristobal Colón* in Barcelona.

cabaret. A form of nightclub entertainment dating from c.1880 – 1930s, especially popular in Paris and Berlin. The French cabaret featured witty and slyly ironic songs, performed by artists such as Yvette Guilbert (1885 – 1944), who inspired a

Well-known pieces in C minor include:

Ludwig van Beethoven's Fifth Symphony (its finale is in C major). Also, Beethoven's *Pathétique* Sonata.

FRANZ SCHUBERT's Fourth Symphony, which bears the designation *Tragic*.

Anton Bruckner's First, Second, and Eighth Symphonies.

Gustav Mahler's tragic Second Symphony, which concludes with a choral finale that proclaims the dubious promise, "You must die to live."

Alexander Scriabin's Second and Third Symphonies, both ending in redeeming C major.

The most frequently performed of Camille Saint-Saëns's symphonies, his Third, with organ. It also has a C-major finale, with the organ literally pulling out all the stops.

The most popular piano concerto of modern times, the Second by Sergei Rachmaninoff, with its overwhelming C-major finale.

Tod und Verklärung by Richard Strauss. C minor represents here the corruption of death, but the work concludes in triumphant C major, depicting the triumph of the soul over death.

◀

Montserrat Caballe taking a curtain call, 1978. (Ira Nowinski/ © Corbis)

host of 20th-century *CHANTEURS* and *chanteuses.* The Berlin cabaret world continued until the Nazi succession in the 1930s, having inspired the political music of KURT WEILL, HANS EISLER, and PAUL DESSAU.

Cabaret. Musical by JOHN KANDER and Fred Ebb, 1966, based on Christopher Isherwood's *Berlin Stories.* It relates the story of an American writer who records the murky and ominous atmosphere in pre-Hitler Berlin, especially the denizens of a Berlin cabaret. Includes the title song, *Willkommen, Don't Tell Mama, Two Ladies, If You Could See Her through My Eyes,* and the hauntingly prophetic *Tomorrow Belongs to Me.*

Cabin in the Sky. Musical fantasy by VERNON DUKE, 1940. It uses an all-black cast to retell the story of the devil and the Lord battling over a soul. Includes the title song and *Taking a Chance on Love.*

căht′chăh   caccia (It., chase, hunt). Italian medieval musical form originating in Florence in the 14th century. Initially the caccia used words concerned with hunting and therefore was often arranged in the form of a CANON (or ROUND) in which one voice "chased" another. It was often combined with a MADRIGAL, with such compound forms becoming known as canonic madrigals. MOTETS containing canonic imitation were called *caccia motets. Alla caccia,* in hunting style, thus accompanied by HORNS. ANTONIO VIVALDI's Violin Concerto in B-flat Major (c.1725), op.8/10, is called *La caccia.*

Caccini, Francesca "La Cecchina," (b. Florence, Sept. 18, 1587; d. Florence, c. 1640), daughter of GUILUIO CACCINI, was probably the first woman composer of operas. Caccini wrote a *Ballo delle zingare* (Florence, 1615) in which she acted as one of the gypsies. Her sacred drama *Il martirio di Sant'Agata* was produced in Florence in 1622. Her opera-ballet *La liberazione di Ruggiero dall'isola d'Alcina* was produced at a palace near Florence in 1625, and a book of songs from it was published that same year.

PEOPLE IN MUSIC

PEOPLE IN MUSIC

Caccini, Giulio "Romano," important Italian composer of MONODY, an originator of opera and teacher, father of

Francesca Caccini; b. probably in Tivoli, Oct. 8, 1551; d. Florence (buried), Dec. 10, 1618. Caccini was a pupil of Scipione delle Palla in singing and lute playing. His first compositions were MADRIGALS in the traditional POLYPHONIC style. Influenced by the new ideas coming out of Florence, however, Caccini began to write vocal works in RECITATIVE form (then termed *musica in stile rappresentativo*), which he sang with consummate skill to his own accompaniment on the THEORBO.

These first compositions in a dramatic idiom were followed by his settings of separate scenes written by Giovanni de' Bardi, including *Il combattimento d'Apolline col serpente* (Apollo's battle with a serpent). Next came two collaborations, *Euridice* (libretto by Rinuccini, 1600) and *Il rapimento di Cefalo* (libretto by Chiabrera, 1600). In 1602 he composed the opera *Euridice* as his own.

Caccini is best known for two volumes of *Le nuove musiche,* sets of madrigals for solo voice with bass, which were published in Florence in 1601 and 1614. The song *Amarilli mia bella* from volume 1 remains popular. From the mid-1560s Caccini lived in Florence as a singer at the Tuscan court. Angelo Grillo called him "the father of a new style of music," and Bardi said of him that he had "attained the goal of perfect music."

cacophony (Grk., bad sound). 1. Noise; many sounds at once, so that the overall impression is one of ear-splitting noise. 2. Term used by critics to describe music they can't understand. Thus, an English writer reviewing FRÉDÉRIC CHOPIN's recital in London in 1842 described his music as "excruciating cacophony."

cadence (Lat., *cadere,* fall; Ger. *Kadenz*). A generic term denoting the conclusion of a MELODY or MOVEMENT or the close or ending of a PHRASE, SECTION, or movement. The purpose of a cadence is to establish the terminal KEY of a musical composition.

A cadence consisting of a DOMINANT triad followed by the TONIC triad (V–I) is called an *AUTHENTIC CADENCE.* A cadence consisting of a SUBDOMINANT triad leading to a tonic triad (IV–I) is called a *PLAGAL CADENCE* (also called *amen* or *oblique*). In order to outline the tonality more fully, three chords are often used: the subdominant, the dominant, and the concluding tonic triad. This *full authentic cadence* (*complete, perfect*), includes all seven notes of the scale, thus outlining the key unambiguously.

Cadences that do not end on the tonic are an important feature of tonal music. The most common is the *half cadence* (*imperfect*), where the harmonic progression ends on the dominant chord, approached from any number of chords. An important type of irregular cadence is the *deceptive cadence* (*evaded, interrupted*), in which the dominant seventh chord leads into the SUBMEDIANT triad instead of the tonic triad, thus "deceiving" the expectations of the ear. In major keys, such a deceptive submediant is a minor triad (e.g., in C major, the A-minor chord), while in minor keys the submediant triad is major (e.g., in C minor, A-flat major).

In this *Landini cadence,* named after the ARS NOVA composer FRANCESCO LANDINI, the leading tone in the melody is diverted to the submediant, a degree below, before resolving into the tonic (7–6–8). To modern ears, this melodic twist creates a momentary impression of a plagal cadence.

Cadences can be endlessly ornamented, and the final resolution to the tonic chord endlessly delayed, creating harmonic suspense. The concluding tonic chord may then be repeated several times, in varying rhythmic figures and harmonic positions, so that the melody may traverse through the third or the fifth note of the tonic triad before arriving at the fundamental.

In modern compositions cadences are apt to be abrupt. SERGEI PROKOFIEV's March from his *Love for 3 Oranges* ends in a single C-major chord preceded by the briefest appearance of the dominant. While in CLASSICAL and ROMANTIC music the final chord cannot possibly consist of more than three notes of the tonic harmony, 20th-century composers have introduced a type of a cadence in which the tonic triad is supplemented, so that the C-major triad blossoms out into a chord of C–E–G–A, C–E–G–B, or C–G–E–A–D, or other combinations of those ingredients, comprising every degree of the scale except the subdominant. JAZZ musicians popularized harmonies with "added notes," culminating in final chords with added sixths, sevenths (natural or flatted),

There can be numerous repetitions of the tonic chord at the end of a composition. In the resonant C-major coda of Ludwig van Beethoven's Fifth Symphony, the tonic chord is repeated, after alternating with the dominant triad, 15 times. At the end of his Eighth Symphony, it is repeated 24 times.

ninths, 11ths (usually sharped), and 13ths. These chords are all technically classified as DISSONANCES, but they all sound more satisfying in a jazz context than undiluted, old-fashioned tonic harmony.

cadenza (It., cadence; from Lat., *cadere,* fall; Ger. *Kadenz*). 1. In an aria or other accompanied vocal piece, a brilliant improvisatory passage for the soloist in free time, usually performed near the end of the piece. During the "golden age" of opera (18th and early 19th centuries) COLORATURA singers were expected to perform a formidable line of TRILLS and ARPEGGIOS. But composers began to rebel against this sometimes indulgent artistic license, and composers such as HECTOR BERLIOZ, RICHARD WAGNER, and GIUSEPPE VERDI did everything they could to prohibit such improvisation. By the 20th century the vocal cadenza was extinct per se, used only at the specific direction of the composer. 2. An elaborate passage or FANTASIA at the end of the first or last movement of a CONCERTO, played by the solo instrument. In its original conception, *cadenza* signified an improvisatory interpolation in an instrumental or vocal work, mainly intended to demonstrate the technical brilliance of the virtuoso performer. Solo cadenzas in CLASSICAL concertos were rarely written out by the composer, but were contributed by performers.

   Most 20th-century composers have abandoned the cadenza as a virtuoso exercise. As a working rule, a competently written cadenza should incorporate the main themes of the original. In ROMANTIC concertos, the device of continued sequences and MODULATIONS into RELATIVE KEYS are common.

cæsura. *See* CESURA.

café chantant (Fr., singing café). A predecessor of the CABARET that flourished in Paris between 1852 and 1870. The repertoire usually consisted of sentimental ballads. It eventually evolved into larger places of entertainment of which the most celebrated was the Folies-Bergère (follies of the Bergère district). The shows became more sexually explicit as well, featuring scantily clad young ladies. When the

Beethoven wrote his own cadenzas in his piano concertos, as did Robert Schumann and Johannes Brahms. Frédéric Chopin and Franz Liszt avoided long cadenzas in their concertos, preferring brief fiorituras or embellishments.

café chantant was transferred to England it assumed the name MUSIC HALL but was scorned by Victorian society as a center of low-class entertainment.

Cage, John (Milton, Jr.), outstanding American composer, writer, philosopher, and visual artist; b. Los Angeles, Sept. 5, 1912; d. N.Y., Aug. 12, 1992. His father, John Milton Cage,

Sr., was an inventor, and his mother was active as a club-woman in California. As a young man, Cage studied piano in Los Angeles and in Paris. Returning to the U.S., he studied composition in California with ARNOLD SCHOENBERG and in N.Y. with Henry Cowell.

In 1938–39 Cage was employed as a dance accompanist at the Cornish School in Seattle, where he also organized a percussion group. There he met the dancer MERCE CUNNINGHAM, with whom he would collaborate for most of the rest of his life. Cage developed Cowell's piano idiom, making use of TONE CLUSTERS and playing directly on the strings. He also developed the PREPARED PIANO, for which he composed the magnum opus *Sonatas and Interludes* (1946–48).

Cage taught for a season at the School of Design in Chicago in 1941–42, then moved to N.Y., where he was re-united with Cunningham. He served as musical advisor to the Merce Cunningham Dance Company until 1987. An-

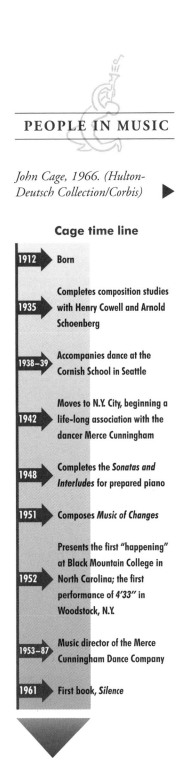

PEOPLE IN MUSIC

John Cage, 1966. (Hulton-Deutsch Collection/Corbis) ▶

Cage time line

1912	Born
1935	Completes composition studies with Henry Cowell and Arnold Schoenberg
1938–39	Accompanies dance at the Cornish School in Seattle
1942	Moves to N.Y. City, beginning a life-long association with the dancer Merce Cunningham
1948	Completes the *Sonatas and Interludes* for prepared piano
1951	Composes *Music of Changes*
1952	Presents the first "happening" at Black Mountain College in North Carolina; the first performance of *4'33"* in Woodstock, N.Y.
1953–87	Music director of the Merce Cunningham Dance Company
1961	First book, *Silence*

other important association was his collaboration with the pianist DAVID TUDOR, who became one of Cage's best interpreters. In 1952, at Black Mountain College in North Carolina, Cage presented a theatrical event historically marked as the earliest musical HAPPENING.

With the passing years, Cage ceased using precise musical notation and definite ways of performance, electing instead to mark his creative intentions in GRAPHIC NOTATION. He established the principle of INDETERMINACY in musical composition, producing works any two performances of which can never be identical.

In 1952 he produced one of his most famous works, a piece entitled *4'33"*, in three movements, during which no sounds are intentionally produced. It was performed in Woodstock, N.Y., by Tudor, who sat at the piano playing nothing for the length of time stipulated in the title. This was followed by another "silent" piece, *0'00"*, which is "to be played in any way by anyone." It was presented for the first time in Tokyo in 1962. Any sounds, noises, coughs, chuckles, groans, or growls produced by the listeners are automatically regarded as integral to the piece itself.

In order to eliminate the subjective element in composition, Cage developed a method of selecting the components of his pieces by dice throwing, suggested by an ancient Chinese classic, the *I Ching*. The length, pitch, loudness or softness, tempo, and placement of each note could be chosen by a throw of a die or the toss of a coin. Cage used this method first in his *Music of Changes* for piano (1951) and, later, to compose his stage work EUROPERAS 1 and 2, which he wrote, designed, staged, and directed in 1987. Different excerpts from well-known operas, along with stage sets, costumes, and other elements, are selected at random to be performed. A computer program, named by Cage IC (in homage to the *I Ching*), was used to make the random choices.

Cage was also a brilliant writer, much influenced by the manner, grammar, and style of Gertrude Stein. Among his works are *Silence* (1961), *A Year from Monday* (1967), *M* (1973), *Empty Words* (1979), and *X* (1983). He developed a style of poetry called "mesostic," which uses an anchoring string of letters down the center of the page that spell a name, a word, or a line of text relating (or not) to the subject

1968 Elected to the American Academy of Arts and Letters

1978 Makes the first of annual visits to Crown Point Press in California to make visual art works

1982 Named Commander of the Order of Arts and Letters by the French minister of culture

1987 *Europeras* 1 and 2 performed in Frankfurt

1988–89 Charles Eliot Norton Professor at Harvard University

1989 Travels to Russia to oversee performances in Leningrad and Moscow, and then to Japan, receiving the Kyoto Prize

1992 Dies

Cage once said of his writing: "I have nothing to say and I'm saying it—and that is poetry."

of the poem. Mesostic poems may be composed by computer, the "source material" pulverized and later enhanced by Cage into a semicoherent, highly evocative poetic text. His most substantial writing in this form was his set of six lectures published as *I–VI*, delivered by him as holder of the Charles Eliot Norton Chair in Poetry at Harvard University during the 1988–89 academic year.

His scores have been exhibited in galleries and museums, but Cage was also an accomplished visual artist. Beginning in 1978 he returned annually to Crown Point Press in San Francisco to make etchings. A series of 52 paintings, the *New River Watercolors,* executed from 1988 to 1990 at the Miles C. Horton Center at the Virginia Polytechnic Institute and State University, were shown at the Phillips Collection in Washington, D.C., in 1990. In 1992, shortly after his death, an exhibition of his works was given at the Venice Biennale.

Cage received numerous awards and honors throughout his life, including the prestigious (and lucrative) Kyoto Prize in 1989. He suffered a massive stoke in his N.Y. apartment in August 1992 dying the next day at St. Luke's Hospital, without regaining consciousness. His cremated remains, along with those of Tudor, were scattered in 1997 within the community in which both once lived, the Gatehill Co-op, in Stony Point, N.Y.

PEOPLE IN MUSIC

Cahn (Kahn), **Sammy** (born Samuel Cohen), American song lyricist; b. N.Y., June 18, 1913. Cahn played violin in variety shows and organized a dance band while still a teenager. In 1940 he went to Hollywood and wrote songs with JULE STYNE for several films, including *Youth on Parade* (1942), *Carolina Blues* (1944), *Anchors Aweigh* (1945), *It Happened in Brooklyn* (1947), and *Romance on the High Seas* (1948). In 1955 he started a music publishing company. Among his best-known songs are *Bei Mir Bist Du Schoen, I Should Care, Three Coins in a Fountain, I'll Never Stop Loving You, The Tender Trap,* and *High Hopes* (which became John F. Kennedy's 1960 campaign song). He published *The Songwriter's Rhyming Dictionary* in 1983.

Caissons Go Rolling Along, The. Song composed by Edmund Gruber, 1907, for the Fifth U.S. Artillery in the

Philippine Islands. JOHN PHILIP SOUSA arranged it for band. Eventually the song became a semi-official march for the artillery.

cakewalk. An African-American dance in quick $\frac{2}{4}$ time which became popular in blackface MINSTRELSY in the latter part of the 19th century. Its vogue soon spread all over the world. The cakewalk was used in the walk-around finale in the minstrel show and, later, VAUDEVILLE and BURLESQUE. Its syncopated rhythm is essentially that of RAGTIME. It was called a cakewalk because the best performer would "take the cake" (i.e., win the grand prize, a freshly baked cake).

Cale, John. *See* VELVET UNDERGROUND.

California Girls. Ode to sun-fun-and-surf by Brian Wilson of the BEACH BOYS, a major hit in 1965.

call and response. 1. A synonym for antiphony, used in English-speaking religious contexts. 2. The style of singing of African-American workers, in which the leader sings one line (the call) and the group replies with another (the response). *See* ANTIPHONAL.

Call Me Madam. Musical by IRVING BERLIN, 1950. In this satire written for ETHEL MERMAN, a Washington hostess is chosen as American ambassador to "Lichtenburg." It includes the hits *The Best Thing for You, It's a Lovely Day Today, Marrying for Love,* and *You're Just in Love.*

Callas, Maria (born Maria Anna Sofia Cecilia Kalogeropoulos), celebrated American soprano; b. N.Y., Dec. 3, 1923; d. Paris, Sept. 16, 1977. Callas's father was a Greek immigrant to the U.S. The family returned to Greece when she was 13. She studied voice at the Royal Academy of Music in Athens with the Spanish soprano Elvira de Hidalgo and made her debut in a school production of MASCAGNI's *CAVALLERIA RUSTICANA* in 1938. Her first professional appearance was in a minor role at the Royal Opera in Athens when she was 16. She sang her first major role, Tosca, there in 1942.

CLAUDE DEBUSSY included *Golliwog's Cakewalk* in his piano suite *Children's Corner.*

PEOPLE IN MUSIC

Callas returned in 1945 to N.Y., where she auditioned for the Metropolitan Opera Company. She was offered a contract but decided to go to Italy, where she made her operatic debut in the title role in *LA GIOCONDA* in Verona in 1947.

Callas was encouraged in her career by the famous conductor TULLIO SERAFIN, who engaged her to sing at various Italian productions. In 1951 she became a member of the famous opera company LA SCALA in Milan. She was handicapped by her excessive weight, but by a supreme effort of will she slimmed down from 210 to 135 pounds. With her now trim physique, coupled with her classic Greek profile and penetrating eyes, she made a striking impression on the stage. In the tragic role of Medea in CHERUBINI's opera, she mesmerized the audience by her dramatic representation of pity and terror. Some critics faulted her vocal technique, but her power of interpretation was such that she was soon acknowledged as one of the greatest dramatic singers of the century.

Callas's professional and personal life was as tempestuous as that of any PRIMA DONNA of the bygone era. In 1949 she married the Italian industrialist G. B. Meneghini (d. 1981), who became her manager, but they separated 10 years later. Her romance with the Greek shipping magnate Aristotle Onassis was a recurrent topic of sensational gossip. Given to outbursts of temper, she regularly made newspaper headlines when she walked off the stage following some disagreement or failed to appear altogether at scheduled performances. Yet her eventual return to the stage would be all the more eagerly welcomed by her legion of admirers.

Perhaps the peak of Callas's success came with her brilliant debut at the Metropolitan Opera in N.Y. as Norma in 1956. Following a well-publicized disagreement with its management, she quit the company only to reach an uneasy truce with it to return as Violetta in LA TRAVIATA in 1958. That same year she left the company again, returning only in 1965 to sing Tosca before abandoning the operatic stage altogether. In 1971 she gave a seminar on opera at the Juilliard School of Music that was enthusiastically attended by students. This seminar was fictionalized in the play *Master Class,* a hit on Broadway in 1996. In 1974 she went on a concert tour with the tenor Giuseppe di Stefano, but there was no possibility of a comeback.

Callas retired to Europe and died suddenly of a heart attack in her Paris apartment in 1977. Her body was cremated, and her ashes (after being stolen from the famed Paris cemetery Père Lachaise and later recovered) were scattered on the Aegean Sea.

calliope. A circus pipe organ with very loud whistles activated by steam, sometimes called steam organ. It was named for the Greek goddess Calliope, the muse of eloquence.

Calloway, Cab(ell), noted African-American JAZZ singer and bandleader; b. Rochester, N.Y., Dec. 25, 1907; d. Cokebury Village, Del., Nov. 8, 1994. After making his way to Chicago, Calloway began his career as a singer and dancer. He led the jazz band the Alabamians in 1928–29, and then took over the leadership of the Missourians, with which he established himself in N.Y. in 1929–30. Calloway also appeared in the Broadway revue *Hot Chocolates* in 1929.

In the 1930s Calloway led the band at Harlem's famous Cotton Club. This led to a career in films. Calloway had a bold personality, commanding the stage with his large physique and expressive face. He preferred comic songs to ballads

Cab Calloway, 1955. (Hulton-Deutsch Collection/Corbis)

and often added SCAT SINGING to his work. He was known as the "Hi-de-ho Man," after the scat chorus of his biggest and most enduring hit, 1931's *Minnie the Moocher.*

Calloway's popularity faded after World War II, but he continued to perform into the late 1980s. He was featured in the popular 1980 comic film *The Blues Brothers.*

calypso. Popular music of the West Indies, originating in Trinidad in the 1920s. Much influenced by American JAZZ, its meter is $\frac{4}{4}$ with sharp SYNCOPATIONS. The mostly English lyrics often reflect topical subjects. Accompaniment may include drums, maracas, kitchen utensils, and bottles. Calypso is the wellspring from which many Caribbean dance and song genres have arisen.

Camelot. Musical by ALAN JAY LERNER and Frederick Loewe, 1960. The plot is derived from the legend of King Arthur, Queen Guinevere, and her youthful lover Sir Lancelot. The play's success in the early years of the Kennedy administration led to comparisons of the Kennedys with the mythical court of King Arthur. Includes the title song, *The Lusty Month of May, If Ever I Would Leave You, How to Handle a Woman,* and *What Do the Simple Folk Do?*

kah'měh-răh   **camera** (It.). Chamber, room, small hall. *Alla camera,* in the style of CHAMBER MUSIC; *musica da camera,* chamber music.

Camerata. Florentine intellectual and artistic group organized by Giovanni de' Bardi (c.1573–87), including aristocratic poets, philosophers, and music lovers. Besides functioning as a musical salon, its aim was to reinstate a "pure" singing manner with minimal accompaniment as it was believed to have been practiced in ancient Greek drama. Renouncing the high Renaissance practice of writing rich and florid POLYPHONY, the Camerata cultivated lyric melody and simple accompaniments, the basis for the imminent birth of OPERA.

Campanella, La. Brilliant piano composition by FRANZ LISZT, 1832, arranged by him from the Violin Concerto No. 2 by NICCOLÒ PAGANINI. Liszt expanded the tune into a veritable feast of upper-register notes.

MUSICAL INSTRUMENT

campanology. The science of bell making and ringing. *See* BELLS.

Camptown Races. The popular name for a dialect song by STEPHEN FOSTER, 1850, originally titled *Gwine to Run All*

Night. It was one of many songs he composed in the style of African-American folk songs, for which Foster became famous.

canary (Fr. *carnarie;* Sp. *canario*). A European dance, popular in the 16th and 17th centuries, derived from an old dance of the Canary Islands. Most composers expressed the rhythm in triple ($\frac{3}{8}$, $\frac{3}{4}$) or compound ($\frac{6}{4}$, $\frac{6}{8}$) meters, but there are examples in duple meter. The music resembles that of the SARABANDE or passamezzo moderno.

Johann Joachim Quantz distinguished the canary from the gigue by noting that "the Gigue is played with a short and light bow, but in the Canarie, which consists always of dotted notes, the bowing is short and sharp."

cancan. A lively dance that arrived in Paris from Algeria about 1830, set in rapid $\frac{2}{4}$ time, musically similar to a GALOP. At the height of its popularity under the Second Empire, the cancan, as danced by young women on the VAUDEVILLE stage, shocked the sensitivities of conservative French audiences because the beskirted choristers used to kick their legs above their waists in time with the music and perform leg splits. It is still performed as a show dance.

cancel. The natural sign (♮). The term was current in American schools in the second half of the 19th century.

canción (Sp.). Song, applied specifically to the poetic type of 15th-century Spanish popular ballad. It is considered more dignified than the rustic Spanish song, the villancico. The verse is usually strophic, and the musical setting strictly symmetrical. *Cancionero,* a gathered or published collection of Spanish-language songs. Many cancioneros of Spanish Renaissance secular music are preserved in Spanish archives. There are also numerous collections of sacred music surviving in Mexico.

kăhn-sē-ōn′

Candide. Musical by LEONARD BERNSTEIN, 1956, with text by, among others, Lillian Hellman, Richard Wilbur, and Dorothy Parker. It is derived from Voltaire's famous story of a youth learning the sordid side of the *Best of All Possible Worlds.* Also includes the songs *It Must Be So, Glitter and Be Gay, You Were Dead You Know, I Am Easily Assimilated,* and *Make Our Garden Grow.* Bernstein's later "opera-house version" was produced in N.Y. in 1982.

canon. 1. A composition of two or more voices in which a SUBJECT (theme) introduced by one of the voices is strictly imitated by another, while the first voice continues with a suitable part.

The most common type of canon, called *canon at the (in) unison,* is imitation on the same pitch or an octave higher. A more difficult imitation is the *canon at the fifth,* which gave rise to the FUGUE. In a classical fugue, the imitating voice is in the key of the DOMINANT, entering either a fifth higher or a fourth lower than the initial subject.

The most popular canons are in two voices, but the earliest canon ever written, *Sumer is icumen in,* is in four. Examples are known of canons in 8, 16, 32, and even more voices, but the subjects of such canons are inevitably reduced to a series of broken tonic triads, with few auxiliary notes, and so contribute little to the essence of the form. There are also canons in which the subject is imitated by AUGMENTATION or by DIMINUTION.

In *canon by inversion* the imitating voice inverts the melodic INTERVALS of the subject. Canons by inversion are also called "mirror canons" because they form the mirror image of the subject. The most ingenious, artificial, and difficult to compose canon is the *canon cancrizans,* that is, crab-walking canon, in which the melody is imitated by playing it backward. (Actually, crabs walk not backwards, but sideways; the old canon writers were apparently not acquainted with the walking modes of crabs.) If the crab-walking voice is inverted, the result is *imitation by retrograde inversion* (or, by inverted retrograde). Most canons are furnished with an ending by way of an AUTHENTIC CADENCE.

Canons that return to the beginning, called *perpetual canons* or ROUNDS, are popular group songs. The best known of this type is likely *Row, Row, Row Your Boat.* There is also the *circular canon,* which closes in the key a semitone above that in which it began. Twelve repetitions of the theme would thus carry the musicians through the "circle" of all twelve keys.

Composers of the BAROQUE period found pleasure in asking the performer or the person to whom the canon is dedicated to decide at what particular beat the imitating voice should enter, with a suitable Latin quotation, such as "seek and ye shall find." JOHANN SEBASTIAN BACH's *Musikalisches Opfer* (MUSICAL OFFERING), which he wrote for Frederick the Great of Prussia, is full of such verbal riddles, e.g. "Ascenden teque modulatione ascendat gloria regis" (With an ascending modulation, let the king's glory ascend also), meaning that the canon must modulate by ascending degrees. This type of canon is fittingly called a *riddle canon.* The masters of the Baroque developed fantastic ingenuity in writing canons in all conceivable forms.

2. The established repertoire for a particular genre.

Canonical Hours. The Divine Office, which established times for daily prayer within the Roman Catholic Church. Beginning in the morning, the present cycle (adopted in 1971) comprises *lauds, terce, sext, nones, vespers,* and COM-PLINE. The old night Office, *matins/vigils,* is now an *office of readings,* which may be said at any time.

cantabile (It.). In a songful manner. This Italian term came into widespread use in the 18th century when it was used positively to describe a melodic work. As applied to vocal compositions, *cantabile* appears redundant, for it is obvious that a singer ought to sing singingly, but it was used as an expression mark in instrumental writing.

    Often the term *cantabile* is part of the name of the movement itself, as in WOLFGANG AMADEUS MOZART's *Andante cantabile con espressione* in his A-minor Piano Sonata, K.310, and in LUDWIG VAN BEETHOVEN's *Adagio cantabile* in his Second Violin Sonata, op.12/2. ROMANTIC composers made use of the term with increasing frequency, as PIOTR ILYICH TCHAIKOVSKY did in the *Andante cantabile* of his First String Quartet, op.11. In the piano music of FRÉDÉRIC CHOPIN, ROBERT SCHUMANN, and other Romantic composers, *cantabile* has the same meaning as LEGATO.

cantata (It., work to be sung; Ger. *Kantate*). A vocal work with instrumental accompaniment, often scored for solo voices (singing RECITATIVES, ARIAS, DUETS, etc.), chorus, and instruments. It developed at the same time as the emergence of OPERA and ORATORIO in the early 17th century. Cantata is distinguished from SONATA, "a work to be sounded, or played."

kăhn-tah′bē-lĕh

In contrast to the oratorio, of religious origin, the cantata appeared first as a secular composition, as a series of vocal stanzas in strophic form. Only later, growing out of German 17th-century SACRED CONCERTOS through the works of JOHANN SEBASTIAN BACH, did the cantata become primarily a medium of religious composition.

A cantata is usually of shorter duration than an oratorio. Its form is flexible, admitting both lyrical and dramatic elements. It can be shaped as a series of extended arias or as an operatic scene with recitatives. Bach's cantatas contributed to the standardization of the form. In his hands, the cantata grew to dimensions of fervent religious devotion and dramatic grandeur within a POLYPHONIC framework of incomparable mastery. Bach was not averse to writing cantatas of a topical nature, such as his justly celebrated *Coffee Cantata.*

Beginning early in the 19th century, the composition of secular cantatas was mandatory in order to obtain the Prix de Rome at the Paris Conservatory. Because practically all French composers competed for this honor, the number of prize-winning and prize-losing French cantatas reached the tens of thousands.

In the 20th century the borderline between oratorio and cantata became more difficult to trace. SERGEI PROKOFIEV's suite for the patriotic film *Alexander Nevsky* resembles both the oratorio in the solemnity of its invocation and the cantata in the brevity of its individual numbers. Generally, modern composers have resorted to the writing of cantatas when festive occasion demands. BENJAMIN BRITTEN wrote two particularly memorable cantatas: *Cantata Accademica* (1960), based on the *Carmen basiliense,* and *Cantata Misericordium* (1963), commemorating the centennial of the International Red Cross. BÉLA BARTÓK's *Cantata Profana* (*The Nine Enchanted Stags,* 1934) is a choral work with orchestra, with text and musical themes borrowed from Romanian folklore. Alberto Ginastera wrote an effective cantata, *Cantata para América Mágica* (1961), to pseudo-Indian texts and based on traditional South American melodies.

canti carnascialeschi (It., carnival songs). 15th-century Italian songs performed at Florentine festivals. The songs combine two or more melodic parts performed at once. They are

PETER SCHICKLE, the 20th-century creator of P. D. Q. Bach, the supposed youngest son of J. S. Bach, wrote a piece called the *Sanka Cantata,* a satire of Bach's *Coffee Cantata.*

historically important because they drew on traditional work songs, such as those of tailors, scribes, and perfume makers, preserving them for future generations. They are similar in form to the FROTTOLA.

canticle (Lat., canticum, song). Christian HYMNS whose texts are in the nature of PSALMS, taken from the Bible, but not from the Book of Psalms itself. The term is sometimes extended to include nonscriptural texts and certain psalms. Canticles are called major when they are taken from the New Testament, minor when from the Old Testament. Texts from the Song of Solomon are often set.

Canticum sacrum ad honorem Sancti Marci nominis. Sacred CANTATA by IGOR STRAVINSKY, 1956. The text is Latin, the form drawn from GREGORIAN CHANT. Stravinsky conducted its premiere in the Basilica of San Marco, Venice. This is the first work in which he adapted ARNOLD SCHOENBERG's 12-TONE system of composition.

cantiga. A medieval Spanish or Portuguese song to vernacular texts. Secular cantigas were subdivided into several categories according to content, such as *cantigas de amor* (sung by a woman), *cantigas de amigo, cantigas de escarnio* (satires), and *cantigas de gesta* (narrative and epic songs). Religious cantigas were most often sung in praise of the Virgin Mary.

At first it was believed that cantigas were of Arabic origin and brought to Spain by the Moors. However, most probably they are varieties of the Spanish choral songs called VILLANCICOS, with some influence from French and Provençal singers.

Only two sets of cantigas have survived, the six secular love songs by the Galician Martín Codax (c.1230) and the voluminous *Cantigas de Santa Maria* (c.1250–80). The latter includes more than 400 religious songs collected and illustated by employees of King Alfonso X ("el Sabio," the Wise) of Castile and León.

cantilena (It., little song; Ger. *Cantilene;* Fr. *cantilène*). 1. Originally, PLAINCHANT (a single melody line, sung in unison by a large group). 2. Medieval secular MONOPHONY (unaccompanied vocal music). 3. An English song genre of the late 13th and 14th centuries, featuring two melody lines in COUNTERPOINT. 4. From the 19th century, a flowing, songlike passage on an instrument.

kăhn-tē-lâ′năh

cantillation (Lat. *cantillare,* to sing softly). Religious chanting in the Jewish synagogue service, usually a RECITATIVE with a text from the Jewish liturgy. Cantillation is performed in an emotional manner and is often set in the style of a lamentation. Its rhythm follows the natural accents of its text.

kähn′tōh **canto** (It.). 1. A melody, song, or CHANT. 2. The SOPRANO, i.e., highest vocal or instrumental part. *Canto a cappella,* sacred song performed without accompaniment; *canto fermo, see* CANTUS FIRMUS; *canto figurato,* florid POLYPHONIC writing rich in melodic embellishment.

cantor (Lat., *cantare,* sing). 1. In the Roman Catholic Church, the soloist in the liturgical CHANTS, while the chorus is called *schola.* 2. In Lutheran liturgy, the music director (as JOHANN SEBASTIAN BACH was in Leipzig). 3. In the Jewish synagogue, the soloist who sings the CANTILLATION.

cantus firmus (firm song). A fixed or given melody that serves as the primary part of a composition, to which other melodic parts are then added. Historically it was the term for the main musical subject in medieval and RENAISSANCE POLYPHONIC music, traditionally a PLAINCHANT melody.

The practice dates back to the ORGANUM of the Parisian Notre Dame school in the 12th century and continued to appear in the religious music of the Renaissance. In 14th-century masses, the melody of the cantus firmus was often taken from secular popular songs, such as *L'homme armé.*

In the middle ages the cantus firmus was called the TENOR and consisted of long notes of even values. However, later Renaissance composers used the cantus firmus as thematic material (one example is Flemish composer JOSQUIN DES PREZ's *Missa Pange lingua*). In the BAROQUE period the cantus firmus was often placed in the bass, as in organ CHORALES, where it is played on the pedals.

Other modified examples of cantus include *cantus ambrosianus,* AMBROSIAN CHANT; *cantus choralis* or *planus,* GREGORIAN CHANT performed as notes of equal length; *cantus fractus,* chant with subdivisions of long notes, thus a chant consisting of notes of different metrical value, as distinct from *cantus planus; cantus gemellus* (twin song; Eng., *gymel*), a type of two-part writing in parallel thirds or sixths; *cantus gregorianus,* Gregorian chant; *cantus mensuratus* (measured song), chant consisting of precisely measured notes, usually of equal duration.

canzona (It.; Fr. *chanson*). 1. A (vocal) song or folk song. In Dante's time, a lyrical poem consisting of several stanzas. Also, the name of the settings of such poems.

During the RENAISSANCE the canzona acquired traits of folk melody, with a simple harmonic accompaniment. Such a canzona became known as a *canzona alla napoletana,* a designation applied to a lyric BALLAD. The term was frequently applied to a MADRIGAL-style part-song.

2. An instrumental piece. The term was first used for LUTE or keyboard works. During the Renaissance the instrumental canzona developed into the *canzona francese* (*canzona alla francese*), in which each section was performed in a different style, TEMPO, or METER. An instrumental canzona for ensemble was called *canzona da sonar,* that is, a canzona to be played, rather than sung.

As canzonas became more complex, they developed into a composition featuring a single theme followed by FREE VARIATIONS. In this way, they shared similarities with the instrumental RICERCAR. In fact, during the BAROQUE period almost any instrumental work could be called a canzona, further confusing what was already becoming a fairly loose term.

The plural of *canzona* is *canzone,* but *canzone* is also used as a singular noun, in which case the plural is *canzoni.*

Canzonet (*canzonetta,* little canzona), a solo song or part-song, or a brief instrumental piece.

With the advent of neoclassicism (the revival of classical music models) in the second quarter of the 20th century, composers once again began writing canzonas, in a style derived from the Baroque period.

Capeman, The. Musical by PAUL SIMON, with a book and lyrics co-written with Derek Walcott, 1998. Its story is based on the troubled and troublesome life of the teenage Puerto Rican gang leader Salvador "the Capeman" Agron. Agron was convicted in 1959 of the merciless killing of two rival gang members and was sentenced to death at the age of 16 (but subsequently pardoned, in 1979, and died seven years later). The musical, costing some $11 million, may constitute Broadway's biggest financial flop in history; it closed after only 68 performances. The score merges DOO-WOP, GOSPEL, SALSA, and ROCK 'N' ROLL.

Capitán, El. Comic opera by JOHN PHILIP SOUSA, 1896, his most successful in this style. The Viceroy of Peru hears of a conspiracy to overthrow him. He disguises himself as El Capitán, a legendary bandit, and infiltrates the rebel forces. When he reveals his real identity, the plot against him collapses. The popular MARCH of the same name is a MEDLEY of tunes from the opera.

kah′pōh **capo** (It.). Chief, head, beginning.

Da capo, from the beginning.

Capo tasto (*capotasto, capo,* head FRET). 1. A wood, ivory, or metal bar placed on the fingerboard of GUITARS or LUTES to shorten the length of all strings and thus raise their pitch. This enables a player to transpose to other keys without changing the fingering. 2. The NUT of stringed instruments having a fingerboard.

kăhp-pel′lăh **cappella** (Lat., It., chapel). A CHORUS, an ORCHESTRA, or a court or CHAPEL ensemble. Through the centuries, the word was used in two senses: as the place of worship, and as persons participating in the church service.

A (or *alla*) *cappella* (as in chapel), without instrumental accompaniment. Beginning in the RENAISSANCE, this term described music, mostly POLYPHONIC choral works, composed and performed according to the practice of the chapel.

kăh-prit′chōh **capriccio** (It., from Lat. CAPER, goat). A light-hearted, whimsical composition; a caprice, a musical caper. The capriccio originated in the RENAISSANCE as a lively instrumental composition that was freely improvised by the performer. The term itself was interchangeably used for such varied forms as RICERCAR, CANZONA, or TOCCATA. In the 19th century the capriccio reasserted its capricious character.

With the revival of interest in CLASSICAL music forms in the 20th century, the term *capriccio* regained its original meaning as an instrumental piece in the manner of a ricercar. IGOR STRAVINSKY's 1929 Capriccio for Piano and Orchestra is an example.

The proper Italian plural of *capriccio* is *capricci.*

Capriccio brillante. Concert piece by FELIX MENDELSSOHN for piano and orchestra, first performed in 1835. The soloist

Most of the major classical and romantic composers wrote instrumental capriccios. The violin virtuoso NIC-COLÒ PAGANINI composed 24 capriccios for solo violin, arranged by other composers for various instruments. JO-HANN SEBASTIAN BACH entitled one of his few pieces frankly expressing a sentiment *Capriccio on the Departure of His Beloved Brother.* LUD-WIG VAN BEETHOVEN notated

was Clara Wieck, ROBERT SCHUMANN's future wife. The adjective *brillante* describes the nature of the work, but the noun *capriccio* does not necessarily imply freedom in the music. On the contrary, the piece is highly organized in a balanced formal fashion.

Capriccio Espagnol. Symphonic suite on Spanish themes by NIKOLAI RIMSKY-KORSAKOV, 1887. The themes and harmonies are borrowed from a collection of authentic Spanish songs, but orchestrated for various combinations of instruments.

Capriccio Italien. Symphonic fantasy by PIOTR ILYICH TCHAIKOVSKY, 1880, based on authentic Italian songs that Tchaikovsky heard during a visit to Italy. There is a BOLERO, a Neapolitan BALLAD, and a TARANTELLA.

Capricorn Concerto. CONCERTO GROSSO by SAMUEL BARBER, 1944, with flute, oboe, and trumpet as the CONCERTANTE instruments. It is in three sections, alternately thoughtful and playful. Barber named it after the home he co-owned in Mt. Kisco, N.Y., with his great friend and fellow composer GIAN CARLO MENOTTI.

Cardew, Cornelius, English experimental composer; b. Winchcombe, Gloucester, May 7, 1936; d. London, Dec. 13, 1981. Cardew sang in the chorus at Canterbury Cathedral until puberty, then studied composition with Howard Ferguson at the Royal Academy of Music in London between 1953 and 1957. In 1957 he went to Cologne and worked at the electronic studio there as an assistant to KARLHEINZ STOCKHAUSEN.

Returning to England in 1960, he organized concerts of experimental music. In 1967 he was appointed to the faculty of the Royal Academy of Music in London. In 1969, together with Michael Parsons and Howard Skempton, he organized the Scratch Orchestra, a group dedicated to performances of new music.

Under the influence of the teachings of the Chinese communist leader Mao Tse Tung, Cardew renounced modern music and subsequently attacked his former associate in

his Rondo, op.129, nicknamed *Rage Over a Lost Penny,* "quasi un capriccio."

The free form of capriccio makes it especially suitable for works of national colors. PIOTR ILYICH TCHAIKOVSKY wrote a *Capriccio Italien,* NIKOLAI RIMSKY-KORSAKOV A *Capriccio Espagnol,* and CAMILLE SAINT-SAËNS A *Capriccio Arabe.* RICHARD STRAUSS's 1942 opera *Capriccio* is an 18th-century musical play within a play on the evergreen operatic question of the relative importance of words and music.

PEOPLE IN MUSIC

a book ominously entitled *Stockhausen Serves Imperialism* (London, 1974). He also repudiated his own magnum opus, *The Great Learning*, originally performed at the 1968 Cheltenham Festival. It was scored for a nonsinging chorus to the words of Ezra Pound's translation of Confucius. In performing the work, the chorus was instructed to bang on stones, to whistle and shriek, but never to stoop to vocalizing. In the revised version of the work he appended to the title the slogan, "Apply Marxism–Leninism–Mao Zedong Thought in a living way to the problems of the present." This version was first performed by the Scratch Orchestra in a Promenade concert in London in 1972.

Cardew's other works include *Volo Solo* for any handy musical instrument (1965) and *Three Winter Potatoes* for piano and various assorted concrete sounds, as well as for newspapers, balloons, noise, and people working (Focus Opera Groups, London, 1968). In addition, he compiled an important description of his musical beliefs, *Scratch Music* (London, 1970).

kăh-rē-yŏhn′

MUSICAL INSTRUMENT

Tuning a carillon. (Hulton-Deutsch Collection/Corbis) ▶

carillon (Fr.; Ger. *Glockenspiel*). 1. A set of church BELLS suspended from a beam in the belfry (church tower), operated either by swinging or from a keyboard, with the keys connected to the clappers of the bells. Modern carillons may

have as many as 50 bells and are capable of playing rapid scales, complete harmonies, and trills. 2. A tune played on this instrument; an instrumental piece imitating its effect.

carioca. Brazilian dance in a fast $\frac{4}{4}$ time. It is derived from the rhythm of the SAMBA, originating in the vicinity of Rio de Janeiro (*carioca* is colloquial for the inhabitants of a Rio neighborhood).

Carlos, Wendy (born Walter), American organist, composer, and electronics virtuoso; b. Pawtucket, R.I., Nov. 14, 1939. Carlos played piano as a child, then studied music

PEOPLE IN MUSIC

Wendy Carlos at the synthesizer, 1972. (UPI/Corbis-Bettmann)

and physics at Brown and Columbia universities, where he took courses with electronic composer VLADIMIR US-SACHEVSKY. At the same time he began working with Robert Moog in perfecting the MOOG SYNTHESIZER.

Moog and Carlos collaborated on one of the most successful albums of electronic music ever released, *Switched-on Bach* (1968). Selling over a million copies, it featured famous works by JOHANN SEBASTIAN BACH performed on the synthesizer. This was followed in 1969 by *The Well-Tempered Synthesizer,* engineered entirely by Carlos.

At the age of 32 he underwent a sex-change operation and, on St. Valentine's Day 1979, he officially changed his first name from Walter to Wendy. She produced the film scores for *A Clockwork Orange, The Shining,* and *TRON.*

Carmen. Opera by GEORGES BIZET, 1875. The action takes place in Seville around 1820. Don José, a soldier, falls in love at first sight with a gypsy cigarette girl, Carmen. He deserts the army to marry her, but in vain, because Carmen abandons him for a bullfighter. Distraught, Don José stabs her to death.

The most famous arias in *Carmen* are the bullfighter's victory song, *Toreador* (from the Sp. *torero*), and Carmen's song, *Habanera* (often misspelled Habañera), borrowed unintentionally by Bizet from a song by the Cuban composer Sebastian Yradier. Just how a Cuban song got into an opera with the action taking place in Seville remains a mystery.

The oft-repeated story that *Carmen* was a disaster on its first performance, and that Bizet expired of chagrin over it, is untrue. Bizet died on the night of its 33d performance, three months after its premiere, surely a very satisfactory run. With CHARLES GOUNOD's *FAUST* and GIUSEPPE VERDI's *AIDA, Carmen* became one of the most successful operas in the repertory, continually produced all over the world.

Carmen Jones. Musical play, 1943, with a text by OSCAR HAMMERSTEIN and a score preserved almost intact from GEORGES BIZET's *CARMEN.* In his modern version, Hammerstein shifts the scene from Seville to a southern American town during World War II. Carmen is a worker in a parachute factory, Don José is a black corporal, and the toreador is a prizefighter. Don José kills Carmen outside a Chicago arena during her lover's fight for the heavyweight championship.

PEOPLE IN MUSIC

Carmichael, Hoagy (Hoagland Howard), American pianist and composer of popular music; b. Bloomington, Ind., Nov. 22, 1899; d. Rancho Mirage, Calif., Dec. 27, 1981. Carmichael's ambition as a youth was to become a lawyer. In fact, he graduated from the Indiana University law school and initially played the piano only as a hobby. He was soon playing in Chicago-area clubs, however, and became friendly with such players as BIX BEIDERBECKE and other young, white musicians who were interested in the new musical style JAZZ.

In 1929 Carmichael went to Hollywood but failed to obtain work as a musician. He nonetheless organized a SWING band and composed songs for it. Although unable to notate music, he revealed a natural gift for melody, and soon made a success with such songs as *Riverboat Shuffle* and *Washboard Blues*. He made a hit with his song STARDUST, which became the foundation of his fame and fortune. Among other popular tunes were GEORGIA ON MY MIND (brought to the height of its popularity by RAY CHARLES), *Ivy, I Get Along without You Very Well, Heart and Soul,* and *In the Cool, Cool, Cool of the Evening,* which won an Academy Award in 1951. He was also active as an actor in films and on television.

Carmina Burana. Scenic cantata by CARL ORFF, 1937, first performed in Frankfurt. The texts, in rhymed verse in Latin, French, and Provençal, date from the 12th and 13th centuries. They were discovered in the Benediktenbeuren Cloister in Bavaria, and the collection became known under the Latin name *Burana Sancti Benedicti.* Despite the difficulty posed by the text being sung in so many different languages, *Carmina Burana* became extremely popular. Orff later combined this work with his *Catulli Carmina* (1943) and *Trionfi d'Afrodite* (1953) to form the trilogy *Trionfi.*

Carnaval. Piano cycle by ROBERT SCHUMANN, op.9 (1835), subtitled *Scènes mignonnes sur quatre notes.* One of Schumann's most popular compositions.

It is mind-boggling that this complex composition is based on a four-note theme. Schumann chose these notes to spell the name of the town (Asch) where he had a girlfriend.

Schumann weaves a colorful tapestry out of these letter-notes, creating 21 sections that include musical portraits of FRÉDÉRIC CHOPIN, NICCOLÒ PAGANINI, and Schumann's future wife, CLARA. There is also a "silent" section entitled *Sphinxes,* which notates the "riddle" of the piece.

In order to spell A–S–C–H, using the German musical alphabet, Schumann chose these notes: A, S (*Es,* German for E♭), C, and H (German for B♭). The same town can also be spelled in three letter notes, AS (*As,* or A♭), C, and H.

Carnegie Hall. The most famous concert hall in the U.S. It opened in N.Y. in 1891, built with funds provided by the wealthy Scottish-born magnate Andrew Carnegie (1835–1919), who built an immense fortune from success-

ANDREW CARNEGIE, L.L.D. (lavish library distributor), who believes it a great disgrace to die rich. This sentiment is, however, not taken seriously by his old associates who are earnestly striving to be disgraced.

Andrew Carnegie, 1902. (Corbis-Bettmann)

Perhaps the most famous joke in all of music is:
Q. How do you get to Carnegie Hall?
A. Practice!

Many composers have written pieces glorifying the Carnival season:

Hector Berlioz's orchestral Roman Carnival Overture

Franz Liszt's Ninth Hungarian Rhapsody, subtitled *Carnaval de Pest*

Camille Saint-Saëns's clever suite *The Carnival of the Animals*

ROBERT SCHUMANN'S PIANO SUITE, *CARNAVAL*, SUBTITLED *SCENES MIGNONNES SUR QUATRE NOTES.*

ful investments in steel and oil. Carnegie believed that wealthy people had a responsibility to support education and the arts. In addition to Carnegie Hall, he endowed many libraries and other cultural institutions.

Carnegie Hall is beloved by concert performers for its remarkable acoustics, although recent changes to the hall have been controversial. In the subculture of movies and rock, the name Carnegie Hall has assumed a magical aura as a passport to greatness in music.

Carnival. Musical by Bob Merrill, 1961, based on the motion picture *Lily*. It tells the story of an orphan who runs away to join the circus. Includes *Love Makes the World Go Round* and *Mira*.

Carnival (from Lat. *carne*, meat; + *vale*, from Lat. *levare*, abandon). Carnival is the occasion for eating meat for the last time before Lent.

Carnival songs, a generic description of festive songs that mark Mardi Gras celebrations in Europe and South America. For the Florentine variety, *see* CANTI CARNASCIALESCHI.

Carnival of the Animals, The (*Le Carnaval des animaux*). A "grand zoological fantasy" by CAMILLE SAINT-SAËNS, 1886 (premiered posthumously, 1922). Marvelously witty and musically enchanting, this work is scored for two pianos and orchestra.

The 14 pieces imitate various animals. The cello solo that constitutes the 13th piece, *The Swan,* was adapted as the accompaniment for Anna Pavlova's famous dance solo *The Dying Swan* and has become a celebrated concert piece. Although he completed the score in 1886, Saint-Saëns did not allow it to be performed publicly or even be published during his lifetime.

carol. A joyous Christmas song. The name may be derived from the French medieval *carole,* a round dance often accompanied by singing. The most common type, established in the 19th century, is in four-part harmony, balanced in structure, and in a major key.

Carousel. Musical play by RICHARD RODGERS and OSCAR HAMMERSTEIN, 1945. A young man turns to crime, is killed, goes to purgatory, and returns to earth for a day to be redeemed by love. Includes *June Is Bustin' Out All Over, If I Loved You,* and *You'll Never Walk Alone.*

Carpenter, John Alden, American composer; b. Park Ridge, Ill., Feb. 28, 1876; d. Chicago, Apr. 26, 1951. Carpenter received his B.A. degree from Harvard University in 1897, where he also studied music. He entered his father's shipping supply business and from 1909 to 1936 was its vice-president. During his early years in business he continued his music studies in Rome and Chicago. His compositions in the 1910s and '20s were widely admired, and he was awarded several degrees and honors. After his retirement from business in 1936 he devoted himself entirely to composing. In 1947 he was awarded the Gold Medal of the National Institute of Arts and Letters.

Carpenter's music combined ideas he derived from modern European composers with American urban subjects, adding the resources of JAZZ rhythms. His first well-known work was the orchestral suite *Adventures in a Perambulator* (1915). His "jazz pantomime" *Krazy Kat,* inspired by the well-known comic strip, premiered in 1921. He then wrote a large-scale musical panorama, *Skyscrapers* (1926), which

PEOPLE IN MUSIC

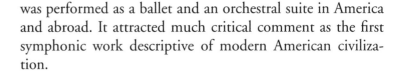

was performed as a ballet and an orchestral suite in America and abroad. It attracted much critical comment as the first symphonic work descriptive of modern American civilization.

PEOPLE IN MUSIC

Carreño, (Maria) **Teresa,** famous Venezuelan pianist, singer, and composer; b. Caracas, Dec. 22, 1853; d. N.Y., June 12, 1917. As a child, Carreño studied with her father, an excellent pianist. Driven from home by a revolution, the family settled in N.Y. in 1862, where she studied with pianist and composer LOUIS GOTTSCHALK. At the age of eight she gave a public recital in N.Y.

Carreño moved to Paris to continue her keyboard studies, beginning her performing career there from 1866 to 1870. Moving to London, she developed a singing voice, surprising her critics and fans by appearing in Edinburgh as the Queen in GIACOMO MEYERBEER's opera *Les Huguenots* in 1872. She was again in the U.S. in 1876, where she studied singing in Boston.

Invited in 1885 to appear at the 100th anniversary of the revolution of Simon Bolivar in her home town of Caracas, she appeared as singer, pianist, and composer of the festival hymn, written at the request of the Venezuelan government. While there, she once again demonstrated her versatility when for the last three weeks of the season she conducted the opera company managed by her husband, the baritone Giovanni Tagliapietra.

After these musical experiments, Carreño resumed her career as a pianist, making her German debut in Berlin in 1889. In 1907 she toured Australia. Her last appearance with an orchestra was with the N.Y. Philharmonic in 1916, and her last recital took place in Havana in 1917.

Carreño was married four times: to the violinist Emile Sauret (1873), baritone Giovanni Tagliapietra (1876), composer Eugene d'Albert (1892–95), and Arturo Tagliapietra, Giovanni's younger brother (1902). Early in her career she wrote a number of compositions, some of which were published. Her waltz *Mi Teresita* enjoyed considerable popularity. She was one of the first pianists to play EDWARD MACDOWELL's compositions in public (MacDowell took lessons from her in N.Y.).

Carreño was greatly venerated in Venezuela. In 1938, long after her death in N.Y., her remains were solemnly transferred to Caracas.

Carreras, José (Maria), prominent Spanish TENOR; b. Barcelona, Dec. 5, 1946. Carreras was a pupil of Jaime Francesco Puig at the Barcelona Conservatory. In 1970 he made his performing debut in Barcelona. During the 1970s and '80s he was much in demand at all the major opera houses in the world, performing with the N.Y. City Opera from 1972 to 1975, as well as debuting at the Metropolitan in 1974.

Carreras's career was endangered in 1987 when he was stricken with acute leukemia. After exhaustive medical treatment, Carreras appeared at a special Barcelona outdoor concert in 1988 that drew an audience of some 150,000 admirers. That same year he founded the José Carreras Leukemia Foundation. In 1989 he sang in recital in Seattle and N.Y. and also returned to the operatic stage.

In addition to his many performances in opera and recitals, Carreras joined with PLACIDO DOMINGO and LUCIANO PAVAROTTI to perform as the "Three Tenors." These concerts, among the most successful recitals in the history of vocal performance, have elevated all three to the level of superstars.

Carry Me Back to Old Virginny. Song by James A. Bland (1854–1911), 1878. Influenced by Negro SPIRITUALS, it was until recently the official song of the state of Virginia.

The African-American songwriter-performer Bland learned to play BANJO and joined a MINSTREL troupe in his early twenties. From 1881 to 1901 he lived in England, enjoying great success, including a command performance for Queen Victoria. However, he squandered his savings and died in poverty. Ironically, although written by an African-American, the song has been attacked for its racial stereotypes and offensive language.

Carter, Benny (Bennett Lester), outstanding African-American JAZZ instrumentalist, bandleader, arranger, and composer; b. N.Y., Aug. 8, 1907. After learning to play pi-

PEOPLE IN MUSIC

PEOPLE IN MUSIC

ano as a child, Carter took up trumpet and alto saxophone. From 1923 to 1928 he worked with various bands before gaining wide recognition as a talented arranger.

Carter led his own band from 1932 to 1934, then went to London, where he was an arranger for the BBC dance orchestra from 1936 to 1938. Upon his return to the U.S. in 1938, he led his own orchestra in N.Y. until 1940. He then organized a big band and settled in Los Angeles in 1942. After 1946 he devoted himself mainly to composing and arranging scores for films and television, and also worked as an arranger for major jazz singers.

Carter made occasional appearances as an instrumentalist in later years, including tours abroad, and also made a number of recordings. He also assumed a new role as a teacher, giving lectures at various universities and colleges. One of the outstanding jazz alto saxophonists of his day, Carter also shone as a trumpeter, trombonist, clarinetist, and pianist. In 1974 he was awarded an honorary doctorate from Princeton University.

Carter, Elliott (Cook, Jr.), highly respected and innovative American composer; b. N.Y., Dec. 11, 1908. After graduating from the Horace Mann High School in 1926, Carter entered Harvard University, majoring in literature and languages. At the same time he studied piano at the Longy School of Music in Cambridge, Mass.

In 1930 Carter devoted himself exclusively to music. He obtained his M.A. in 1932, then went to Paris, where he studied with NADIA BOULANGER. In the interim he also learned mathematics, Latin, and Greek.

In 1935, Carter returned to America. He held a series of jobs teaching music at a number of universities, while his own compositions were increasingly recognized as among the best modern American works. Carter's works evolved through three stylistic periods. Early in his career he was influenced by the NEOCLASSIC movement and emulated the formal structures of the CLASSICAL period. He then began experimenting with the 12-TONE composition system of ARNOLD SCHOENBERG. Finally, he expanded Schoenberg's ideas to include all the elements of an individual composition, including intervals, metric divisions, rhythm, counterpoint, harmony, and instrumentation. He coined the term METRIC MODULATION to describe his theory of changing the rhythm of a work just as you might vary the melody or harmony.

Carter has received numerous awards and honors. He was awarded two Guggenheim fellowships (1945, 1950) and the American Prix de Rome (1953). His string quartets have been particularly honored, the Second (1960) and Third (1973) both earning him a Pulitzer Prize in music. In 1985 he was awarded the National Medal of Arts by President Reagan.

Carter Family, The. (Guitar/autoharp/vocal: "Mother" Maybelle [Addington]; b. Nickelsville, Va., May 10, 1909; d. Nashville, Oct. 23, 1978; Vocal: A[lvin] P[leasant] Delaney Carter, b. Maces Spring, Va., Apr. 15, 1891; d. there, Nov. 7, 1960; Autoharp/vocal: Sara Dougherty Carter, b. Flat Woods, Va., July 21, 1898; d. Lodi, Calif., Jan. 8, 1979.) Well-known country singing group, formed in 1927 by A. P. Carter, his wife, and his wife's cousin. Through recordings and radio broadcasts (1927–1943) they led the way to the widespread popularity of mountain folk and COUNTRY MUSIC. Among their greatest successes were their versions of *Wildwood Flower, It Takes a Worried Man to Sing a Worried Song, Will the Circle Be Unbroken, Wabash Cannonball,* and *Amazing Grace.*

In later years Maybelle appeared with her three daughters at the GRAND OLE OPRY in Nashville, where she displayed talents as a guitarist, autoharpist, and songwriter. She also made appearances with her son-in-law, JOHNNY CASH.

PEOPLE IN MUSIC

Carter, Ron (ald Levin), African-American jazz double bass player; b. Ferndale, Mich., May 4, 1937. Carter took up cello at 10 and double bass at 17. He continued his studies at the Eastman School of Music in Rochester, N.Y., where he earned his bachelor's degree in music in 1959. He earned a master's degree at the Manhattan School of Music in N.Y. two years later.

While playing in CLASSICAL orchestras, Carter also became interested in performing jazz. After playing in saxophonist Chico Hamilton's quintet, he did stints with "CAN-

PEOPLE IN MUSIC

NONBALL" ADDERLEY, THELONIUS MONK, and others. From 1963 to 1968 he was a member of MILES DAVIS's influential quintet. In subsequent years he worked with the N.Y. Jazz Quartet and led his own quartet.

Carter has been innovative in jazz by championing the bass as a lead melodic instrument, rather than just an accompanying one. He has led a quartet including his own piccolo bass (a smaller-bodied, higher-pitched instrument tuned like a standard bass). He has also introduced a wide variety of playing techniques, both plucked and bowed.

PEOPLE IN MUSIC

Caruso, Enrico (Errico), legendary Italian TENOR; b. Naples, Feb. 25, 1873; d. there, Aug. 2, 1921. Caruso taught himself to sing, performing Neapolitan BALLADS by ear. As a youth he auditioned for a part at the Teatro Fondo in Naples but was unable to follow the orchestra at the rehearsal and had to be replaced by another singer.

Caruso's first serious vocal study was with Guglielmo Vergine from 1891 to 1894. His operatic debut took place at the Teatro Nuovo in Naples in 1894, in *L'amico francesco,* by an amateur composer, Mario Morelli. In 1895 he appeared at the Teatro Fondo in *LA TRAVIATA, LA FAVORITE,* and *RIGOLETTO.* During the following few seasons he added *AIDA, FAUST, CARMEN, LA BOHÈME,* and *TOSCA* to his repertoire.

The decisive turn in his career came when Caruso was chosen to appear as leading tenor in the first performance of UMBERTO GIORDANO's *FEDORA,* given in Milan in 1898, in which he made a great impression. Several important engagements followed. In 1899 and 1900 he sang in St. Petersburg and Moscow. Between 1899 and 1903 he appeared in four summer seasons in Buenos Aires. His early career reached a high point when he was given the opportunity to sing at Milan's famous opera house LA SCALA. In 1900 he appeared in *La Bohème* there, and, in 1901, in the first performance of PIETRO MASCAGNI's *Le maschere.*

The year 1902 saw several important engagements. Caruso's first appearance in Monte Carlo was so successful that he was immediately signed to appear for the next three seasons. He made his London debut as the Duke in *Rigoletto* (Covent Garden, 1902) and was an immediate sensation with the British public and press. In the 1902–03 season Caruso sang in Rome and Lisbon, and during the summer of 1903 he was in South America.

Finally, in 1903, he made his American debut at N.Y.'s Metropolitan Opera in *Rigoletto.* After that memorable occasion, Caruso was connected with the Metro-

Enrico Caruso portraying Canio in Pagliacci. *(Corbis-Bettmann)*

politan to the end of his life. He achieved his most spectacular successes in America, attended by enormous publicity. He traveled with various American opera companies from coast to coast. He happened to be performing in San Francisco when the 1906 earthquake nearly destroyed the city. In 1907 Caruso also sang in Germany (Leipzig, Hamburg, Berlin) and in Vienna, to great acclaim.

Caruso's fees soared from $2 as a boy in Italy in 1891 to the fabulous sum of $15,000 for a single performance in Mexico City in 1920. He made recordings in the U.S. as early as 1902, and his annual income from this source alone netted him $115,000 at the peak of his career. He excelled in realistic Italian and French operas, but the German repertoire remained completely alien to him. His only appearances in Wagnerian roles were three performances of LOHENGRIN in Buenos Aires in 1901.

Caruso's voice possessed such natural warmth and great strength in the middle register that as a youth he was believed to be a BARITONE. His ability to sustain, or hold, a note was exceptional and enabled him to give superb interpretations of LYRIC parts. For dramatic effect, he often resorted to the "coup de glotte" (which became known as the "Caruso sob"), where the singing gave way to a dramatic crying sound. While Caruso was criticized from a musical standpoint for adding these effects to his performances, his characterizations on the stage were overwhelmingly impressive.

Although of robust health, Caruso abused it by maintaining a breakneck schedule. He was stricken with a throat hemorrhage during a performance at the Brooklyn Academy of Music in 1920 but was able to sing in N.Y. one last time later that year. Several operations were performed in an effort to save his health. Caruso was taken to Italy, but succumbed to the illness after several months of remission.

Caruso's private life was turbulent. An affair with the singer Ada Giachetti, by whom he had two sons, led to a court battle in 1912, creating much bad publicity. There were also suits brought against him by two American women. In 1906 the celebrated "monkey-house case" (in which Caruso was accused of improper behavior toward a lady while viewing the animals in Central Park) threatened for a while his continued success in America. In 1918 he married Dorothy Park Benjamin of N.Y., over the strong opposition of her father, a rich industrialist.

Caruso received numerous decorations from European governments, among them the Order of Commendatore of the Crown of Italy, France's Légion d'Honneur, and the Order of the Crown Eagle of Prussia.

Casals, Pablo (Pau Carlos Salvador Defilló), outstanding Catalan cellist and conductor; b. Vendrell, Catalonia, Dec. 29, 1876; d. San Juan, Puerto Rico, Oct. 22, 1973. Casals was the second of 11 children, seven of whom died at birth. Legend has it that Casals barely escaped the same fate when the umbilical cord became entangled around his neck and nearly choked him to death.

His father, a parish organist and choirmaster in Vendrell, gave Casals instruction in piano, violin, and organ. When Casals was 11 he first heard the cello performed by a group of traveling musicians and decided to study the instrument. In 1888 his mother took him to Barcelona, where he enrolled in the Escuela Municipal de Música. There he studied cello, theory, and piano. He excelled at the cello, giving a

Caruso was known as a lover of fine food (a brand of pasta was named after him). He possessed a gift for caricature, and a collection of his drawings was published in N.Y. in 1922.

PEOPLE IN MUSIC

solo recital in Barcelona at the age of 14, in 1891, and graduating with honors in 1893.

Following his graduation, the composer ISAAC ALBÉNIZ, who heard him play in a café trio, gave him a letter of introduction to Count Morphy, private secretary to Maria Cristina, Queen Regent, in Madrid. Casals was asked to play at informal concerts in the palace and was granted a royal stipend for study in composition with Tomás Bretón.

In 1893 Casals entered the Conservatory de Música y Declamación in Madrid. In 1895 he went to Paris and, deprived of his stipend from Spain, earned a living by playing second cello in a club orchestra. He decided to return to Spain, where he received, in 1896, an appointment to the faculty of the Escuela Municipal de Música in Barcelona. In 1897 he appeared as soloist with the Madrid Symphony Orchestra, and was awarded the Order of Carlos III from the Queen. His career as a cello virtuoso was assured.

In 1899 Casals played at the Crystal Palace in London and was later given the honor of playing for Queen Victoria. He also appeared as soloist at a prestigious Lamoureux Concert in Paris and played with the well-known conductor and violinist Charles Lamoureux again later that year, attaining exceptional success with both public and press. He then embarked on a series of tours, including his first tour of the U.S. in 1901–02 and a grand tour of South America in 1903. In 1904 he was invited to play at the White House for President Theodore Roosevelt.

In 1906, Casals became associated with the talented young Portuguese cellist Guilhermina Suggia, who studied with him. She began to appear in concerts billed as "Mrs. P. Casals-Suggia," although they were not legally married. Their relationship ended in 1912, and in 1914 Casals married the American socialite and singer Susan Metcalfe. They separated in 1928 but were not divorced until 1957.

Continuing his brilliant career, Casals organized, in Paris, a concert trio with the pianist ALFRED CORTOT and the violinist JACQUES THIBAUD. They played concerts together until 1937. Casals also became interested in conducting and in 1919 organized, in Barcelona, the Orquesta Pau Casals, leading its first concert in 1920. With the outbreak of the Spanish Civil War in 1936, it ceased its activities.

Another legend (supported by Casals himself) is that he was conceived when JOHANNES BRAHMS began to compose his B♭-Major Quartet, op.67 (of which Casals owned the original manuscript), and that he was born when Brahms completed its composition. (This is impossible because the quartet in question was completed and performed before Casals was even born.)

Casals was an ardent supporter of the Spanish Republican government, and after its defeat by the fascists led by Francisco Franco, he vowed not to return to Spain until democracy was restored. He settled in the French village of Prades, on the Spanish frontier. So fierce was his opposition to the Franco regime in Spain that he even declined to appear in countries that recognized the totalitarian Spanish government, making an exception when he took part in a concert of chamber music in the White House in 1961, at the invitation of President Kennedy, whom he admired.

In June 1950 Casals resumed his career as conductor and cellist at the Prades Festival, which he organized and led until 1966. In 1956 he settled in San Juan, Puerto Rico (his mother was born there when the island was still under Spanish rule), and a year later, an annual Festival Casals was inaugurated there. Beginning in the 1950s, Casals gave master classes throughout the world, some of which were televised, establishing his reputation as an excellent teacher. In 1957, at the age of 80, Casals married his young pupil Marta Montañez. Following his death, she married the pianist Eugene Istomin in 1975.

Casals was also a composer. Perhaps his most effective work is *La sardana* (1926), for an ensemble of cellos. His oratorio *El pessebre* (The manger) was performed for the first time in Acapulco in 1960. One of his last compositions was the *Himno a las Naciones Unidas* (Hymn of the United Nations), which he first conducted in a special concert at the U.N. in 1971, two months before his 95th birthday.

Casals did not live to see the liberation of Spain from the Franco dictatorship. However, he was posthumously honored by the Spanish government of King Juan Carlos I, which issued a commemorative postage stamp in honor of his 100th birthday.

Casey Jones. An American railroad BALLAD, composed sometime after 1900. It is based on an actual event that occurred in 1900 in which John Luther "Casey" Jones (1864–1900), a daring railroad engineer on the Cannonball Limited, bravely stayed with his train, allowing his crew to escape a head-on collision. In the collision, he was either crushed or scalded to death. The song was popular in the

VAUDEVILLE circuit. Various songwriters claimed to be its composer.

Cash, Johnny, popular American COUNTRY singer, guitarist, and songwriter of partly Indian descent (one-quarter Chero-

kee); b. in a railroad shack near Kingsland, Ark., Feb. 26, 1932. Cash worked as a child for a local farmer's family. He sang Baptist HYMNS in church and at age 17 won five dollars at a local amateur talent contest. In 1950 he enlisted in the U.S. Air Force and served in Germany, returning to the U.S. in 1954. He learned to play guitar while in

Johnny Cash, 1977. (Corbis-Bettmann)

the service. In 1955 he began a series of appearances on the radio and various country circuits, and while he never learned to read music, he soon began to compose songs, both lyrics and tunes.

The subjects of Cash's songs include the miseries of common folks as well as prison life. His most popular recordings include FOLSOM PRISON BLUES (inspired by his imprisonment overnight in El Paso on the charge of smuggling tranquilizer tablets from Mexico), *Ring of Fire, I Walk the Line, A Boy Named Sue,* and *Understand Your Man.* In 1968 he married the well-known country music singer June Carter Cash (b. Maces Spring, Va., June 23, 1929). His daughter by an earlier marriage, Rosanne Cash (b. Memphis, May 24, 1955), is a new-country singer and composer.

Cash enjoyed renewed popularity in the 1990s when he became associated with producer Rick Rubin, better known for working with contemporary RAP acts than country ones. Cash was inducted into the Rock and Roll Hall of Fame in 1995 for his early recordings in a ROCK style. Sadly, however, he soon after retired from performing, announcing that he was suffering from a degenerative nerve disease.

cassation. An 18th-century instrumental form that combines elements of a SERENADE, SUITE, DIVERTIMENTO, and SINFONIA. There are many theories regarding the origins of the term: some say it came from the Italian *cassare,* to dismiss, release; others from the French *casser,* to break; while still others propose the German *gassatim gehen,* to perform in the streets (18th century). The multimovement cassation had an extremely brief currency, limited to the latter 18th century.

MUSICAL INSTRUMENT

castanets (Sp. *castaña,* chestnut). A pair of small concave pieces of wood or ivory, attached by a cord to a dancer's thumb and forefinger, and struck together in time with the music. Of Spanish origin, the name refers to the chestnut wood (*castaña*) traditionally used for the instrument. In their orchestral version, the small concave pieces are attached to a central piece of wood ending in a handle, by which they are held and shaken or struck against the palm.

PEOPLE IN MUSIC

Castelnuovo-Tedesco, Mario, significant Italian-born American composer; b. Florence, Apr. 3, 1895; d. Los Angeles, Mar. 16, 1968. Castelnuovo-Tedesco began to compose at an early age. His first organized composition, *Cielo di settembre* for piano, showed the influence of IMPRESSIONISM. He wrote a patriotic song, *Fuori i barbari,* during World War I. He attained considerable eminence in Italy between the two world wars, and his music was often heard at European festivals.

The rise of the fascist government of Mussolini forced him to leave Italy. In 1939 Castelnuovo-Tedesco settled in the U.S., becoming a naturalized citizen in 1946. He became active as a composer for films in Hollywood but continued to write orchestral and chamber music. A creator of memorable melodies, he was an adaptable composer who created fine music suited to the particular assignment.

Castor et Pollux. *Tragédie en musique* (musical tragedy) by JEAN-PHILIPPE RAMEAU, 1737. It tells the story of the mythical twins, brothers of Helen and Clytemnestra, who ended their days as a constellation.

castrato (It.; plur. *castratos, castrati*). A castrated adult male singer with SOPRANO or ALTO voice.

Young males were castrated at puberty to inhibit their maturation, thereby preserving their high voices. This barbarous practice originated in the 16th century, not long before the development of opera and the demand for "angelic" voices in certain mythological roles such as that of Orpheus.

After 1750 the production of castrato singers became an increasingly hidden affair. It was finally completely forbidden in the latter 19th century. The last castrato singer was Alessandro Moreschi (1858–1922), known as the "Angelo di Roma" because of his celestially pure voice. There are recordings of Moreschi's singing made in 1903.

catcalls. Derogatory hissing at a performance. The term is unfair to cats, who meow only in happiness.

catch. A popular type of English social song, for three or more male parts and in the form of a CANON or ROUND. The term is derived from the need for each singer to "catch" or take up his part at the right instant. The word *catch* itself is probably derived from the Italian CACCIA, or chase, because one voice "chases" another as in a canon.

Catches were favorite songs in the aristocratic clubs of London in the late 16th, 17th, and 18th centuries, along with the GLEE. These clubs often commissioned celebrated composers to write catches for them, which were usually collected and published in anthologies. HENRY PURCELL, JOHN BLOW, and GEORGE FRIDERIC HANDEL were among the many who composed catches.

The texts often contained humorous references to topical events and puns. Among the earliest catches was *Three Blind Mice.* Another begins with the famous line, "Catch that catch can."

In the 18th century the castrati became so famous that they could command large fees to sing in opera houses. GEORGE FRIDERIC HANDEL wrote special parts for the famous castratos Senesino and Nicolini. Perhaps the most celebrated castrato singer was Carlo Broschi, better known as Farinelli, who was engaged by the court of Philip II of Spain. Farinelli sang for Philip, who suffered from depression, the same four songs every night for 25 years. A lavish film, entitled simply *Farinelli*, was released in 1995.

In his singing ballet *L'Enfant et les sortilèges,* Maurice Ravel introduces an amorous baritone tomcat and a nubile mezzo-soprano kitten singing a fine atonal duet. In a modern piece, *Anatomy of Melancholy,* an anonymous composer has a part for cat solo. The cat "player" is instructed to pull the animal's tail at climactic moments.

PEOPLE IN MUSIC

catgut. Common but misleading name for gut strings, which are generally made from lamb intestines.

cats. 1. *Katzenmusik* (German, cat music) was a term used by critics to describe music they found unlistenable. Cat lovers were alienated by such comparisons.

2. *Cats* is also a 20th-century Americanism for musicians in popular bands and by extension can be applied to any human, mostly of the masculine gender. The term carries a bantering, friendly, and even affectionate connotation.

Cats. ANDREW LLOYD WEBBER's most spectacular theatrical production, inspired by T. S. Eliot's *Old Possum's Book of Practical Cats.* It was first produced in London (1981), then in N.Y. (1982), with fantastic success. It is currently the longest-running show on Broadway.

Cat's Fugue. Harpsichord piece in G minor by DOMENICO SCARLATTI, with a theme based on curiously unrelated rising intervals. According to a common but unverifiable story, this theme was inspired by a domestic cat walking up Scarlatti's keyboard. The British professor Edward Dent tried to coax his cat to repeat this feat, but failed.

Caturla, Alejandro García, Cuban composer and government official; b. Remedios, Mar. 7, 1906; assassinated there, Nov. 12, 1940. Caturla studied with Pedro Sanjuán in Havana, then with NADIA BOULANGER in Paris in 1928. In 1932 he became founder and conductor of the Orquesta de Conciertos de Caibarién in Cuba. He also served as district judge in Remedios.

Caturla's compositions combine Afro-Cuban rhythms and themes with modern composition techniques. Some of his better-known works include the *Suite of Three Cuban Dances* (1928); *Bembé* for 14 instruments (1929); *Dos poemas Afro-Cubanos* for voice and piano (1929; also for orchestra); *Yambo-O,* Afro-Cuban oratorio (1931); *Rumba for Orchestra* (1931); *Primera suite cubana* for piano and eight wind instruments (1930); and *Manita en el Suelo,* "mitologia bufa Afro-Cubana" for narrator, marionettes, and chamber orchestra, to a text by Alejo Carpentier (1934).

Cavalleria rusticana. Opera by PIETRO MASCAGNI, 1890, the title translating as "rustic chivalry." The drama takes place in Sicily and is based on an actual event. A young villager is emotionally torn between his attachment to a local girl and his passion for a married woman. The unfortunate lover is confronted by the husband, a duel ensues, and he is killed.

Cavalleria rusticana launched the vogue of operatic VERISMO after its first production in Rome. Because *Cavalleria rusticana* is unusually short, it is often programmatically paired with RUGGERO LEONCAVALLO's *PAGLIACCI.* In America, the two works are affectionately referred to as *Cav* and *Pag.*

Cavalli (Caletti), **Pier Francesco,** historically significant Italian opera composer; b. Crema, Feb. 14, 1602; d. Venice, Jan. 14, 1676. His father, Giovanni Battista Caletti (known also as Bruni), *maestro di cappella* (choir master) at the Cathedral in Crema, gave him his first music instruction. As a youth Pier Francesco sang under his father's direction in the cathedral choir. The Venetian nobleman Federico Cavalli, who was also mayor of Crema, took him to Venice for further training, and as was the custom, he adopted his sponsor's surname.

In December 1616, Cavalli entered the choir of S. Marco in Venice, beginning a life-long association with that institution. He sang there when CLAUDIO MONTEVERDI was directing the choir, and also served as an organist at Ss. Giovanni e Paolo (Saints John and Paul) from 1620 to 1630. In 1638 he turned his attention to the new art form of OPERA and helped to organize an opera company at the Teatro S. Cassiano. His first opera, *Le nozze di Teti e di Peleo,* was performed there in 1639, and nine more followed within the next decade.

In 1639 Cavalli successfully competed against three others for the post of Second organist at S. Marco. In 1660 Cardinal Mazarin invited him to Paris, where he presented a special version of his opera *Serse* for the marriage festivities of Louis XIV and Maria Theresa. While there he also composed the opera *Ercole amante,* which was given at the Tuileries in 1662. He returned to Venice in 1662, and in 1665 he was officially appointed first organist at S. Marco. Three years later he was named *maestro di cappella* there.

PEOPLE IN MUSIC

After Monteverdi, Cavalli stands as one of the most important Venetian composers of opera in the mid-17th century. He also composed much sacred music, with several works available in modern editions.

cavata (It., extraction). An operatic melody expressing the sentiment of a scene, placed at the end of a RECITATIVE (*recitativo con cavata*). It eventually evolved into the CAVATINA.

kăh-văh′ta

cavatina (It.; Ger. *Kavatine*). A short song; an operatic ARIA without a second section or DA CAPO. It is often preceded by an instrumental introduction and concludes with a CABALETTA.

kăh-văh-tē′năh

CD. *See* COMPACT DISC.

CD-ROM (COMPACT DISC–Read Only Memory). A system of data storage that preserves an impressive amount of aural, written, and/or visual information on a CD-sized disk in digital format.

Cecilianism (after St. Cecilia, patron saint of music). A reform movement in Roman Catholic church music, intended to restore Roman Catholic choral POLYPHONY in all its purity, as opposed to the ROMANTIC treatment of religious themes. The Cecilian movement began in Germany in the 19th century, where numerous choral organizations were founded. Later in the century, Cecilianism spread to the U.S., where it was cultivated mostly by German emigré societies and their publications.

PIOTR ILYICH TCHAIKOVSKY discovered the celesta during a visit to Paris. He was so enchanted with its sound that he warned his music publisher not to tell any composers about its existence, specifically naming NIKOLAI RIMSKY-KORSAKOV and ALEXANDER GLAZUNOV as those who might use it before him. Tchaikovsky included a part for celesta in the *Dance of the Sugar Plum Fairy* in THE NUTCRACKER.

celesta (Fr. *céleste,* heavenly). A keyboard instrument built on the principle of a GLOCKENSPIEL. Its keys activate hammers that strike steel bars, thus setting them into vibration. Its keyboard, once limited to four octaves, has been expanded to five. The celesta has a soft, ingratiating, "celestial" sound, which explains the name given it by its Parisian inventor, Auguste Mustel, in 1886.

Another type of celesta is the *dulcitone,* probably dating from the 1860s, which uses tuning forks instead of steel bars to produce sound.

cell. A small group of notes, indicative of PITCH or RHYTHM, serving as the basic elements of a composition. The term is usually applied to ATONAL or 12-TONE music.

cello (It.; plur. *cellos, celli*). Abbreviation of VIOLONCELLO.

cembalo (It.). Harpsichord; pianoforte, clavier; formerly, dulcimer. The term was often used interchangeably with BASSO CONTINUO.

cencerros (Sp., lead-mule bell). Cuban COWBELLS, heard often in Latin American dance music.

Cenerentola, La, o la bontà in trionfo (Cinderella, or the Triumph of goodness). Opera by GIACOMO ROSSINI, 1817, based on the classic fairy tale.

Ceremony of Carols, A. Choral cantata by BENJAMIN BRITTEN, 1942, for treble voices and harp. There are nine carols (including *Deo Gratias*), a harp solo, and a "recession," a repetition of the opening "procession." The melodies all come from medieval CHANTS.

cesura (*caesura;* from Lat. *caedere,* cut). The dividing line between two melodic and rhythmic phrases. It is called *masculine* or *feminine* depending upon whether it occurs after a strong or weak beat.

Chabrier, (Alexis-)**Emmanuel,** famous French composer; b. Ambert, Puy de Dome, Jan. 18, 1841; d. Paris, Sept. 13, 1894. Chabrier studied law in Paris from 1858 to 1861, as well as composition, piano, and violin. He served in the government from 1861, at the same time continuing to pursue his interest in music.

With the composers HENRI DUPARC, VINCENT D'INDY, and others he formed a private group of music lovers and was an enthusiastic admirer of RICHARD WAGNER. He began to compose in earnest in the late 1870s and produced two light operas, *L'Étoile* (1877) and *Une éducation manquée* (1879).

In 1879 Chabrier went to Germany with Duparc to hear Wagner's operas. Returning to Paris, he published some pi-

MUSICAL
INSTRUMENT

chel′ōh

chĕm′bäh-lōh

MUSICAL
INSTRUMENT

MUSICAL
INSTRUMENT

PEOPLE IN MUSIC

ano pieces. He then traveled to Spain, the fruit of this journey being his most famous work, the rhapsody *España* (1883), which produced a sensation when performed by the conductor Charles Lamoureux in 1884. Another work of Spanish inspiration was the *Habanera* for piano (1885).

In the meantime he served as chorus master for Lamoureux. This experience developed his knowledge of vocal writing, evidenced by his brief CANTATA for mezzo-soprano and women's chorus *La Sulamite* (1885) and his operas *Gwendoline* (1886), *Le Roi malgré lui* (1887), and *Briséïs* (concert performance, 1897; stage performance, 1899).

In his operas Chabrier attempted a grand style, combining Wagner's passion with a more conventional type of French stage music. Although his operas enjoyed critical success, they never became popular. Instead, Chabrier's place in music history is secured exclusively by his *España* and piano pieces such as *Bourrée fantasque* (1891). His *Joyeuse Marche* for orchestra (originally entitled *Marche française*, 1888) is also popular.

cha-cha. Latin American dance in an insistent binary rhythm, a variant of the MAMBO. It is sometimes called more emphatically cha-cha-cha. It had a wave of popularity in Europe and the U.S. in the 1950s.

shăh-kŏhn´

chaconne (Fr.; Sp. *chacona;* It. *ciaccona*). 1. A Spanish dance in triple meter, imported from Latin America in the early 17th century. 2. An instrumental piece derived from the dance of the same name, consisting of a series of variations above a ground bass not over eight measures in length, in $\frac{3}{4}$ time and slow tempo. The chaconne is close in structure to and often difficult to distinguish from the PASSACAGLIA.

Chaliapin, Feodor (Ivanovich), celebrated Russian BASS; b. Kazan, Feb. 13, 1873; d. Paris, Apr. 12, 1938. Chaliapin was of humble origin and at the age of 10 was apprenticed to a shoemaker. At 14 he got a job singing in a chorus in a traveling opera company.

Chaliapin's wanderings brought him to Tiflis, in the Caucasus, where he was introduced to the singing teacher Dimitri Usatov (1847–1913), who immediately recognized

PEOPLE IN MUSIC

his extraordinary gifts and taught him free of charge, helping him besides with food and lodging.

In 1894 Chaliapin received employment in a summer opera company in St. Petersburg and shortly afterward was accepted at the Imperial Opera during the regular season. In 1896 he sang in Moscow with a private opera company and produced a great impression by his dramatic interpretation of the bass parts in Russian operas. He also gave numerous solo concerts, which were sold out almost immediately. Young music lovers were willing to stand in line all night to obtain tickets.

Chaliapin's first engagement outside Russia was in 1901, at LA SCALA in Milan. He returned to La Scala in 1904 and again in 1908. In 1907 he made his American debut at N.Y.'s Metropolitan Opera, returning in 1908 for a second season. He did not return to America until 1921, when he sang one of his greatest roles, Boris Godunov. He continued to appear at the Metropolitan until 1929.

Chaliapin returned to Russia in 1914 and remained there during World War I and the Revolution. He was given the rank of People's Artist by the Soviet government, but this title was withdrawn after Chaliapin emigrated in 1922 to Paris, where he remained until his death, except for appearances in England and America.

Chaliapin was indeed one of the greatest singing actors of all time. He dominated every scene in which he appeared, and to the last he never failed to move audiences, even though his vocal powers declined considerably. He was especially famed for his interpretation of the role of Boris Godunov. He was equally great as Méphistophélès and in the BUFFO roles of Don Basilio and Leporello. He also played the title role in a film version of *Don Quixote*. His last American recital took place in N.Y. in 1935.

Another member of this traveling opera company was the famous writer Maxim Gorky, who also sang in the chorus. Together, Gorky and Chaliapin made their way through the Russian provinces, often walking the railroad tracks when they could not afford the fare.

chalumeau. 1. A single-reed, cylindrical-bore woodwind instrument, related to the CLARINET. The chalumeau was developed in the 17th century, originally with no keys. Keys were added in the 18th century. While many view the chalumeau as the ancestor of the clarinet, the two instruments coexisted in the 18th century. The chalumeau was stronger in the lowest register than the clarinet. By the end

shăl-u-moh′

MUSICAL
INSTRUMENT

of the century, the chalumeau had fallen out of use, but not before influencing the construction of the bass clarinet. 2. The lowest register of the clarinet.

chamber music. Vocal or instrumental music suitable for performance in a room or small hall, e.g., QUARTETS and similar concerted pieces for solo instrument ensembles.

chamber orchestra. A small ORCHESTRA, with a much reduced STRING section and fewer winds and PERCUSSION than a full orchestra.

chamber opera. An opera suitable for performance in a small hall, with a limited number of performers and accompanied by a CHAMBER ORCHESTRA.

chamber symphony. A symphony for a small ORCHESTRA, usually of lesser musical scale.

champagne aria. Don Giovanni's aria in Act 1 of WOLFGANG AMADEUS MOZART's opera, in which he orders Leporello to make preparations for his masked ball. Giovanni probably drank sherry, however.

chance music. *See* CHANCE OPERATIONS; ALEATORY.

chance operations. The systematic practice, highly developed by JOHN CAGE, of composing music by chance means (throwing dice, consulting the *I Ching*, making use of random number generators, etc.). The idea was to create music that would be uninfluenced by the composer's personal taste or bias.

Chandos Anthems. Anthems by GEORGE FRIDERIC HANDEL, 1717–18, written for the duke of Chandos.

change. 1. In harmony, MODULATION (the progression from KEY to key). 2. In the voice, MUTATION (moving from one REGISTER to another). 3. Any melodic phrase or figure played on a chime of BELLS. *Change-ringing,* the art and practice of ringing a peal of bells in varying and systematic order.

chanson. (Fr.). 1. Song. It is used as a generic term for songs of any description, but specifically to describe the type cultivated during the 15th and 16th centuries in France and the Netherlands. Such chansons were usually STROPHIC in structure, with the same melody repeated for different stanzas. 2. A French equivalent to the LIED, also called *mélodie.* 3. French popular song genres from the 17th century on.

Chansonette, a song of a light nature, popular in France in the 19th century in CAFÉS CHANTANTS, often containing off-color lyrics.

chanson de geste (Fr., heroic song). A medieval lyric genre, of which the *Chanson de Roland* is the most famous example. Such poems are fantastically long, sometimes numbering more than 20,000 lines in an unchanging meter. They were usually sung to monotonous melodic phrases by professional minstrels. Improvisation was apparently an integral feature. Some of these melodies are preserved through quotations in the *Jeu de Robin et Marion* by ADAM DE LA HALLE and in the 13th-century *Aucassin et Nicolette.*

Chansons de Bilitis. Song cycle by CLAUDE DEBUSSY, 1897, set to the poems by the French poet Pierre Louÿs, in imitation of Greek lyric poetry. Debussy wrote these songs using neo-Grecian MODES. Another work of the same title by Debussy dating from 1901 is a MELODRAMA for reciting voice and small ensemble.

chant. 1. A sacred song. 2. An Anglican song, adapted to the CANTICLES and PSALMS, consisting of seven measures, harmonized. The time value of the single note constituting the first and fourth measures are lengthened or shortened to fit the words, whereas the others are sung in strict time. Each of its two divisions (of three and four measures, respectively) begins on a RECITING NOTE and ends with a FINAL. 3. A Gregorian song, with a melody repeated with the several verses of biblical prose text. It has five divisions: (1) intonation, (2) first dominant, or reciting note, (3) mediation, (4) sec-

shăn-sōhn′

Buddhist monks chanting. (Hulton-Deutsch Collection/ Corbis)

ond dominant, or reciting note, and (5) final. 4. (Fr.) Song; singing; melody; tune. 5. The vocal part, as distinguished from its accompaniment.

Chant de rossignol, Le (The song of the nightingale). SYMPHONIC POEM by IGOR STRAVINSKY, 1917, based on his OPERA *Le Rossignol.*

MUSICAL INSTRUMENT

chanter. The melody pipe of the BAGPIPE.

chanteur (Fr.). Singer (male); *chanteuse,* singer (female).

chantey (chanty). *See* SHANTY.

Chantilly Lace. A 1958 hit by J. P. Richardson, a.k.a. "The Big Bopper," who died in the same airplane crash that took the lives of BUDDY HOLLY and RITCHIE VALENS.

chapel (Fr. *chapelle*). 1. A church building or assembly room where congregants worship. 2. A company of musicians attached to the establishment of any distinguished personage, as in the Chapel Royal of England.

character piece (Ger. *Charakterstück*). A musical genre cultivated in the 19th century, usually applied to piano pieces and furnished with titles suggesting a mood, impression, scene, event, landscape, or pictorial subject. Among typical titles are BAGATELLES, IMPROMPTUS, *moments musicaux, Lieder ohne Worte,* and *Albumblätter.*

Modern composers abandoned the German model of character pieces but were not averse to using imaginative titles, as illustrated by SERGEI PROKOFIEV's *Visions fugitives.* ALEXANDER SCRIABIN appended titles of a mystical nature to some of his short piano pieces, as in *Flammes sombres, Desir,* and even *Poème satanique.*

charango (Sp.). Peruvian GUITAR, usually with ten strings, many tuned to the same note for greater sonority.

charivari. A raucous and noisy SERENADE calculated to ridicule or upset a pompous official or a honeymooning couple. This type of entertainment arose in France in medieval times. The word is pronounced *shivaree.*

Charles, Ray (born Ray Charles Robinson), outstanding African-American RHYTHM AND BLUES and SOUL singer, pianist, arranger, and songwriter; b. Albany, Ga., Sept. 23, 1930. Born to impoverished parents, Charles was stricken with glaucoma and became totally blind at the age of six. Nevertheless, he began playing piano and was sent to the St. Augustine (Florida) School for the Deaf and Blind, where he received instruction in composition and learned to com-

ROBERT SCHUMANN composed a number of character pieces under the titles *Fantasiestücke, Nachtstücke, Kinderszenen, Waldszenen,* and *Carnaval.* The genre was anticipated by FRANÇOIS COUPERIN and JEAN-PHILIPPE RAMEAU, who used such descriptive titles as *Les langueurs-tendres, La triomphante,* etc. Character pieces are usually short, symmetrically constructed, and not difficult to perform.

PEOPLE IN MUSIC

◀

Ray Charles, 1981, feeling his star on the Hollywood Walk of Fame. (UPI/Corbis-Bettmann)

pose in Braille. He also learned to play trumpet, alto saxophone, clarinet, and organ.

Charles quit school at 15 and formed his own combo. He settled in Seattle, where he acquired a popular following. Shortening his name to Ray Charles to avoid confusion with the boxer Sugar Ray Robinson, he scored his first hit recording with *Baby Let Me Hold Your Hand* (1951). It was followed by *I've Got a Woman* (1955), *Hallelujah, I Love Her So* (1956), *The Right Time* (1959), *What'd I Say* (1959), *Hit the Road, Jack* (1961), *One Mint Julep* (1961), and *I Can't Stop Loving You* (1962). Among his notable albums were *The Genius of Charles* (1960) and *Modern Sounds in Country and Western Music* (1962). He also toured widely and frequently performed on radio and television.

Charles has rarely had a hit record over the last few decades but nonetheless continues to record and perform. He remains one of the best known and easily recognized of all performers in popular music.

Charleston (named after the city in South Carolina). 1. A SYNCOPATED dance tune by JAMES P. JOHNSON, 1923. The song was originally introduced in the all-black revue *Runnin' Wild* (1923), which launched one of the most widespread dance fads in American history. 2. The dance associated with the tune; it involves twisting knees and heels while hands and arms follow in alternation.

PEOPLE IN MUSIC

Charpentier, Gustave, famous French opera composer; b. Dieuze, Lorraine, June 25, 1860; d. Paris, Feb. 18, 1956. Charpentier studied at the Paris Conservatory from 1881 to 1887. He received the Grand Prix de Rome in 1887 for the CANTATA *Didon.*

Charpentier owes his fame to one amazingly successful opera, *LOUISE,* to his own LIBRETTO. The opera is partially autobiographical; his mistress at the time was also named Louise and, like the heroine of his opera, was employed in a dressmaking shop. It was produced at the Opéra-Comique in Paris in 1900. The score includes such realistic touches as the street cries of Paris vendors. Its success was immediate, and it entered the repertoire of opera houses all over the

Gustave Charpentier, c. 1929. (Hulton-Deutsch Collection/ Corbis)

world. Its first American production, at the Metropolitan Opera, N.Y., took place in 1921.

Encouraged by this success, Charpentier wrote a sequel under the title *Julien* (1913), but it failed to arouse comparable interest.

Charpentier, Marc-Antoine, significant French composer; b. Paris, c.1645–50; d. there, Feb. 24, 1704. Charpentier studied with the well-known composer Giacomo Carissimi in Italy. After returning to Paris, he became active as a composer for the noted playwright Jean-Baptiste Moliere's acting troupe.

Charpentier had several important appointments to the nobility as well. He served Marie de Lorraine, the Duchess of Guise, working as her *maître de musique* (music master or director) until her death in 1688. Louis XIV granted him a pension in 1683, and he subsequently served as music teacher to Philippe, Duke of Chartres, was *maître de musique* to the Jesuit church of St. Louis, and finally held that post at Sainte-Chapelle from 1698 to 1704.

Charpentier was one of the leading French composers of his era, distinguishing himself in both sacred and secular works. His extensive output of sacred music includes 11 MASSES, 10 MAGNIFICATS, 4 TE DEUMS, 37 ANTIPHONS, 19 HYMNS, 84 PSALMS, and over 200 MOTETS, many akin to OR-

PEOPLE IN MUSIC

ATORIOS. He also composed sacred instrumental works, secular instrumental pieces, and dances for strings.

Among his 30-odd stage works are the *tragédies lyriques* (lyric tragedies) *David et Jonathas* (1688) and *Medée* (1693), CANTATAS, OVERTURES, BALLET airs, PASTORALS, incidental pieces, *airs serieux* (serious songs), *airs à boire* (drinking songs), and so forth.

Chattanooga Choo Choo. Song by HARRY WARREN, 1941, from the film *Sun Valley Serenade.* It was made famous by Glenn Miller's band.

Chávez (y Ramirez), **Carlos** (Antonio de Padua), distinguished Mexican composer and conductor; b. Calzada de Tacube, near Mexico City, June 13, 1899; d. Mexico City,

PEOPLE IN MUSIC

Aug. 2, 1978. Chávez studied piano as a child with Pedro Luis Ogazón and also harmony. He began to compose early in life, producing a symphony at 16. He made effective piano arrangements of popular Mexican songs and also wrote many piano pieces of his own.

Chávez's first important work was a BALLET on an Aztec subject, *El fuego nuevo* (1921), commissioned by the Secretariat of Public Education of Mexico. He continued to draw on historical and national Mexican subject matter in most of his works. However, he rarely directly used Mexican folk melodies and rhythms; instead, he incorporated their

Carlos Chavez. (Library of Congress/Corbis)

flavor into his own work, creating a unique blend of CLASSICAL and traditional elements.

In 1922–23 Chávez traveled in France, Austria, and Germany and was exposed to modern developments in composition. The influence of this period is reflected in the abstract titles of his piano works, such as *Aspectos, Energía,* and *Unidad.* Returning to Mexico, he organized and conducted a series of concerts of new music, giving the first Mexican performances of works by IGOR STRAVINSKY, ARNOLD SCHOENBERG, ERIK SATIE, DARIUS MILHAUD, and EDGARD VARÈSE. From 1926 to 1928 he lived in N.Y.

On his return to Mexico in the summer of 1928 Chávez organized the Orquesta Sinfónica de México, of which he remained the principal conductor until 1949. Works of modern music occupied an important part in the program of this orchestra, including 82 first performances of works by Mexican composers, many of them commissioned by Chávez. SILVESTRE REVUELTAS was among those encouraged by Chávez.

During his tenure as conductor Chávez engaged a number of famous foreign musicians as guest conductors, as well as numerous soloists. In 1948 the orchestra was renamed Orquesta Sinfónica Nacional, and it remains to the present day a vital institution. Chávez served as director of the Conservatory Nacional de Música from 1928 to 1933 and again in 1934. He was general director of the Institute Nacional de Bellas Artes from 1946 to 1952.

Beginning in 1936, Chávez conducted a great number of concerts with major American orchestras, and also conducted concerts in Europe and South America. Culturally, he maintained a close connection with progressive artists and authors of Mexico, particularly the painter Diego Rivera. His *Sinfonía proletaria* for chorus and orchestra reflects his political commitment. In 1958–59 Chávez was Charles Eliot Norton Lecturer in Poetry at Harvard University. His lectures were published as *Musical Thought* (Cambridge, Mass., 1960). He also published a book of essays, *Toward a New Music* (N.Y., 1937).

Chávez is best known for his ballets—*El fuego nuevo, Los cuatro soles, Caballos de Vapor/HP, Antígona, La hija de*

Cólquide, and *Pirámide*–and his symphonies, including the *Sinfonía india,* No. 2 (1935), and the *Sinfonía romántica,* No. 4 (1952).

Checker, Chubby (born Ernest Evans), African-American ROCK 'N' ROLL singer and dancer; b. Philadelphia, Oct. 3, 1941. Chubby Checker was "discovered" by American Bandstand host and record producer Dick Clark in the late 1950s. Checker was given his new name by Clark's wife as a takeoff on FATS DOMINO. Clark was looking for someone to cover Hank Ballard's dance song *The Twist,* which he felt had the potential to be a hit. True enough, Checker's 1960 version topped the charts. He then toured the U.S. to exploit the new dance craze. The song then became a hit again in 1962, the only time a pop song has reached No. 1 in two different years.

Checker also issued a number of other twist songs, and the dance became so popular that there were reports that then-first lady Jacqueline Kennedy was seen twisting at a party at the White House. However, with the arrival of the BEATLES in 1964 in America, Checker's career ended. In later years his performances were relegated to the U.S. nostalgia circuit.

Checkmate. Ballet by ARTHUR BLISS, 1937. The ballet tells of a match between love and death in which love loses. It was choreographed by Ninette de Valois.

cheironomy (Grk., law of the hand). An ancient system of leading the CHOIR with the aid of sign language, in which movements of the fingers indicate TEMPO, INTERVALS, and RHYTHM. There is evidence in ancient art works that cheironomy was used in ancient Egypt (among Coptic Christians), in India, in Israel, and in Byzantine and Roman CHANT.

cheng. *See* ZHENG.

Cherry, Don(ald), African-American JAZZ cornetist, trumpeter, and pianist; b. Oklahoma City, Nov. 18, 1936; d. Malaga, Spain, Oct. 19, 1995. Cherry studied trumpet and harmony while attending high school in Los Angeles. He began his performing career in 1951, appearing with Red Mitchell, DEXTER GORDON, and other jazz musicians.

In the late 1950s, Cherry went to N.Y., where he worked and recorded with saxophonist ORNETTE COLEMAN. Together, they pioneered FREE JAZZ. After 1963 he left Coleman and toured extensively in Europe and Africa.

Cherry continued to perform through the 1980s and early '90s. In his later years he performed a more conventional music, although he also began experimenting with adding African instruments to the standard jazz lineup.

His stepdaughter, Neneh (b. Stockholm, Sweden, Mar. 10, 1964), enjoyed brief success with 1989's dance hit *Buffalo Stance*.

Cherubini, (Maria) **Luigi** (Carlo Zenobio Salvatore), famous Italian composer and teacher; b. Florence, Sept. 14, 1760; d. Paris, Mar. 15, 1842. Cherubini first studied with his father, the *maestro al cembalo* (keyboard player) at the Teatro della Pergola in Florence, and then composition with several Florentine masters. In 1778 he received a grant from the Grand Duke Leopold of Tuscany, which enabled him to continue his studies in Milan. By this time he had composed a number of works for the church and also several stage INTERMEZZI. His first operatic success came with *Armida abbandonata* in 1782.

In the autumn of 1784 Cherubini set out for London, where he was commissioned to write an OPERA for the King's Theatre. *La finta principessa* was produced there in 1785, followed by *Il Giulio Sabino* in 1786, which brought him public acceptance and the admiration of the Prince of Wales. In the summer of 1785 he made his first visit to Paris, where he was introduced to Marie Antoinette by her court musician, and in the spring of 1786 he made Paris his home. He made one last visit to Italy to oversee the production of his opera *Ifigenia in Aulide* in 1788. Cherubini's first opera for Paris, *Démophon* (1788), was a failure, owing largely to J. F. Marmontel's inept libretto and Cherubini's less than total command of French prosody.

In 1789 two of the queen's musicians obtained a license to establish an Italian opera company at the Tuileries, and

PEOPLE IN MUSIC

Cherubini became its music director and conductor. He produced his opera *Lodoïska* there in 1791, with notable success. With this score he effectively developed a new dramatic style, destined to have profound impact on the course of French opera. The increased breadth and force of its ensemble numbers, its novel and rich orchestral combinations, and its generally heightened dramatic effect inspired French composers to follow his lead.

With the French Revolution in full swing, the Italian Opera was disbanded in 1792. Cherubini then went to Normandy, but returned to Paris in 1793 to become an instructor at the new Institute National de Musique (National Institute of Music, later called the Paris Conservatory). His opera *Medée* (1797), noteworthy for the mastery of its ORCHESTRATION, proved a major step in his development as a dramatic composer. With *Les Deux Journées, ou Le Porteur d'eau* (1800), he scored his greatest triumph with the public as a composer for the theater. This opera was soon performed throughout Europe to much acclaim.

In 1805 Cherubini received an invitation to visit Vienna, where he was honored at the court. He also met the foremost musicians of the day, including FRANZ JOSEPH HAYDN and LUDWIG VAN BEETHOVEN. He composed the opera *Faniska* there, which was successfully premiered in 1806. After Napoleon captured Vienna, Cherubini was extended royal favor by the French emperor, who expressed his desire that Cherubini return to Paris. When Cherubini's 1809 opera *Pimmalione* failed to please the Parisians, he retired to the chateau of the prince of Chimay, occupying himself with gardening and painting.

At the request to compose a MASS for the church of Chimay, he produced the celebrated three-part Mass in F Major. He subsequently devoted much time to composing sacred music. In 1815 he was commissioned by the Philharmonic Society of London to compose a SYMPHONY, a CANTATA, and an OVERTURE, and he visited London that summer for their performances.

In 1816 Cherubini was appointed co-superintendent of France's Royal Chapel, and in 1822 director of the Paris Conservatory, a position he held until a month before his death. During the last years of his life he composed six fine string quartets. In 1814 he was made a member of the Institute and a Chevalier of the Legion d'Honneur, and in 1841 a Commander of the Legion d'Honneur, the first musician to be so honored. He was accorded a state funeral, during which ceremony his Requiem in D Minor (1836) was performed.

Cherubini was an important figure in the transitional period from the CLASSIC to the ROMANTIC eras in music. His influence on the development of French opera was of great historical significance. Although his operas have not found a permanent place in the repertoire, several have been revived in modern times. His Symphony in D Major (1815) is still performed by enterprising conductors. He also played a major role in music education in France during his long directorship of the Paris Conservatory. His influence extended beyond the borders of his adoptive homeland through his valuable treatise *Cours de contrepoint et de fugue* (Course in COUNTERPOINT and FUGUE), written with the noted French composer and teacher FROMENTAL HALÉVY (Paris, 1835; English translation, 1837).

chest register. The lower register of the male or female voice, the tones of which produce SYMPATHETIC VIBRATION in the chest.

Chest tone (*voice*): 1. Vocal quality of the chest register. 2. A manner of voice PRODUCTION recommended by Italian teachers for TENORS and BASSES, which feels as if it were traveling into the chest from the larynx. The corresponding expansion of the lungs produces a richer tone.

Chester. American Revolutionary song by WILLIAM BILLINGS, 1778. Although the tune is hymnlike, it was adapted to the ringing revolutionary words, "Let tyrants shake their iron rod." It serves as the basis for a movement in WILLIAM SCHUMAN's *New England Triptych*.

Chevalier, Maurice, popular French singer; b. Paris, Sept. 12, 1888; d. there, Jan. 1, 1972. Chevalier began his career as a singer in Parisian cafés and music halls, then acted in films. In 1929 he went to Hollywood and soon established himself as one of the foremost musical comedy stars. His

As the all-powerful director of the Paris Conservatory, Cherubini established an authoritarian regimen. He rejected any changes from strict form, harmony, counterpoint, or orchestration. He regarded Ludwig van Beethoven's Ninth Symphony as the composer's greatest mistake. He rejected descriptive music and refused to attend rehearsals or performances of the *Symphonie fantastique* by Hector Berlioz, then a student at the conservatory. But his insistence on the letter of the musical law was nonetheless a positive factor, and his treatise on counterpoint remained for many years an important textbook.

PEOPLE IN MUSIC

early films included *The Innocents of Paris* (1929), *Love Me Tonight* (1932), and *The Merry Widow* (1934). Chevalier established a man-of-the-world personality, and his French accent and straw hat became symbols for Americans of continental style.

Chevalier remained in France during the German occupation and gave shows for French prisoners of war in Germany. He returned to Hollywood to resume his career after the war. His later films included *Gigi* (1958), *Can-Can* (1960), and *Fanny* (1961). A special Academy Award was presented to him in 1958 in appreciation of his contributions to popular entertainment.

chiave (It., diminutive plur., *chiavette*). CLEFS commonly used in the 16th and 17th centuries to change the range of the standard clef in order to avoid the use of extra lines above or below the STAFF. The baritone clef, like the bass clef but with the F on the third line instead of the fourth, is an example. The C clefs placed on different lines of the staff are standard, however, and are therefore not considered CHIAVETTE.

kee-eh′sah

chiesa (It.). Church. *Sonata da chiesa,* an instrumental piece suitable for church performance.

Child of Our Time, A. Oratorio by MICHAEL TIPPETT, 1944, to his own text. It was inspired by a tragic episode when a young Jew killed a Nazi diplomat in Paris shortly before World War II. To underline its theme of the terrors of racism, Tippett included several quotations from African-American spirituals. The work was first performed in London. During the war, Tippett himself served a brief prison term as a conscientious objector.

child prodigy. A child who possesses unusual musical talents. In many cases, the prodigy is shamelessly promoted by adults in order to profit from his or her talents. However, only about 10 percent of child prodigies become adult VIRTUOSOS.

While child violinists and pianists are not uncommon in the musical prodigy market, child composers are relatively

The files of early music magazines are filled with stories of musical prodigies. The *Musical Courier* of June 4, 1884, published this item: "A Boston Musical Wonder, Master Herbert Bitswell, is only 5 years old and yet has excited great astonishment by his remarkable performance of a Bach gavotte. He is considered a prodigy." Where is Master Bitswell now?

rare, since it takes more ability and mature concentration to compose an organized piece of music than to play through a piano sonata or a violin concerto. However, there are some famous exceptions: WOLFGANG AMADEUS MOZART's music composed at 15 shows unmistakable genius, and FRANZ SCHUBERT wrote some of his greatest songs at 17.

Child conductors enjoyed a vogue in the 1940s. Among them only one continued a career in music: LORIN MAAZEL, who made several appearances with the N.Y. Philharmonic Orchestra when he was just 11 years old. The newspaper *PM,* in its issue of July 6, 1941, described the event in this colorful headline: "11-Year-Old Wrings Zing out of Toscanini's Band." Maazel has had a distinguished career in conducting, but his story is unusual in the world of prodigies, most of whom never mature into concert artists.

Among piano prodigies, Josef Hofmann was undoubtedly the greatest. His American tour in 1887–88 was sensational. His parents also ran into trouble with the Society for the Prevention of Cruelty to Children, who objected to his heavy concert schedule. As a result of this, Josef's tours were interrupted for a period of several years, and he was given full opportunity to study and relax. He returned to America as an adult virtuoso at the age of 22.

Child, Francis, BALLAD collector and scholar; b. Boston, Feb. 1, 1825; d. there, Sept. 16, 1896. Child was a professor of literature at Harvard University who became interested in traditional British ballads. He is remembered for his *English and Scottish Popular Ballads* (1882), in which he collected the words to more than 300 songs, including different texts for the same song. He numbered his songs, and these "Child numbers" are still used today in referring to these ballads.

Francis Child.

children's chorus. A choir of boys and girls, all singing TREBLE parts, often called for in opera (e.g., *CARMEN*) and less often in symphonic works.

Children's Corner. Suite of piano pieces by CLAUDE DE-
BUSSY, 1908, written for his little daughter. The English title
is explained by the fact that she had an English governess.
There are six movements: the first, *Doctor Gradus ad Parnassum,* parodies Italian composer MUZIO CLEMENTI's famous
piano studies; the last, *Golliwog's Cakewalk,* is a rollicking
pseudo-American RAGTIME, with a quotation from RICHARD
WAGNER's *TRISTAN UND ISOLDE* thrown in.

MUSICAL
INSTRUMENT

chimes. 1. A set of between five and 12 BELLS tuned to a
SCALE. Also, a tune so played. 2. A set of bells and hammers
played by a keyboard; a CARILLON. 3. Tubular bells.

ch'in. *See* QIN.

MUSICAL
INSTRUMENT

chinese blocks (Ger. *Holzblöcke*). Hollowed out polished
boxes of resonant wood. When struck with a drumstick or
mallet, they produce a XYLOPHONE-like tone. Chinese
blocks, which are actually Caribbean in origin, are popular
in JAZZ and popular percussion, and can also be arranged in
a set approximating a SCALE. Also called Chinese temple
blocks, temple blocks, woodblocks, or clog boxes.

MUSICAL
INSTRUMENT

chocalho (*kocalho;* Port.) Brazilian tube rattle in the form of
a long cylinder filled with seeds or buckshot, held sideways
between the fingers of both hands and shaken rhythmically.
The sound is similar to that of MARACAS. The chocalho accompanies the SAMBA and other Brazilian dances.

choir. 1. A company of singers, especially in a church. 2. A
choral society. 3. In the Anglican church, the singers of the
daily choral service who sit divided on the *decani* and *can-
toris* sides of the chancel. 4. A subdivision of a CHORUS; for
example, the first and second choirs in eight-part music.
5. Instrumental groups, such as a brass choir.
    Choirmaster, leader of a choir.

PEOPLE IN MUSIC

Chopin, Frédéric (-François) (Fryderyk Franciszek), incomparable Polish composer and genius of the piano who created a unique ROMANTIC style of keyboard music; b. Zela-
zowa Wola, near Warsaw, probably Mar. 1, 1810 (his

Plaque on Chopin's London home. (Adam Woolfitt/Corbis)

Chopin time line

1810	Born
1818	Public recital in Gyrowetz
1825	First published work, Rondo for Piano, op.1
1829	Gives two successful concerts in Vienna
1830	First public performance of his Piano Concerto in F Minor, op.21, and Piano Concerto in E minor, op.11, in Warsaw
1831	Meets many celebrated musicians in Paris, including Franz Liszt
1832	First Paris concert
1835	Completes the Ballade No. 1 in G Minor, op.23
1836	Begins a tempestuous liaison with Amandine Aurore Lucie Dupin Dudevant, a.k.a. George Sand
1839	Composes the Piano Sonata No. 2 in B-flat Major, op.35
1841	Composes the Fantasie in F Minor/A-flat Major, op.49
1847	Chopin and Sand part company
1848	Final concerts in Paris and London
1849	Dies

certificate of baptism gives the date Feb. 22, 1810); d. Paris, Oct. 17, 1849. Chopin's father, Nicolas Chopin, was a native of Marainville, France, who went to Warsaw to work as a teacher of French. His mother, Tekla-Justyna Krzyzanowska, was Polish.

Chopin's talent was manifested in early childhood. At the age of eight he played a piano concerto in public, and he had already begun to compose POLONAISES, MAZURKAS, and WALTZES. He received primary instruction from the Bohemian pianist Adalbert Zywny, who resided in Warsaw at the time. A much more important teacher was Józef Elsner, director of the Warsaw School of Music, who instructed him in theory and form.

Chopin was 15 years old when his Rondo for Piano, op.1, was published in Warsaw. In the summer of 1829 he set out for Vienna, where he gave two highly successful concerts. While in Vienna he made arrangements to have his variations on WOLFGANG AMADEUS MOZART's *Là ci darem la mano* (from *DON GIOVANNI*) for piano and orchestra published (op.2).

Returning to Warsaw, Chopin gave the first public performance of his Piano Concerto in F Minor, op.21, in 1830. Later that year, he was soloist in his Piano Concerto in E Minor, op.11. He spent the winter of 1830–31 in Vienna.

The Polish rebellion against Russian rule, which ended in defeat, saddened Chopin. He decided to settle in Paris, visiting Linz, Salzburg, Dresden, and Stuttgart on the way.

Chopin's Variations on *Là ci darem la mano* attracted the attention of ROBERT SCHUMANN, who, although several months younger than the Polish composer, was already writing music criticism. Schumann saluted Chopin in a famous article written in late 1831, in which Schumann exclaims, "Hats off, gentlemen! A genius!"

Chopin and Sand's entire affair is captured in the delightful 1990 film *Impromptu*, in which Judy Davis portrays the sassy, obsessive Sand and Hugh Grant the brilliant but sickly Chopin. Others of note include Mandy Patinkin as the poet Alfred de Musset (Sand's discarded and bitter lover), Bernadette Peters as the perpetually pouting Countess d'Agoult, and Julian Sands as Franz Liszt.

He arrived in Paris in 1831 and was introduced to most of the leading composers and musicians of the day; he became particularly friendly with FRANZ LISZT. Many other Polish artists had already settled in Paris, and Chopin maintained his contacts with the Polish circle there. He presented his first Paris concert in early 1832 and also taught piano. During this period he also visited Germany and London.

In 1836 Chopin met the famous novelist Amandine Aurore Lucie Dupin Dudevant, who published her works under the English name George Sand. They became lovers, even though they had quite different personalities. Sand was involved in social affairs and held radical views, while Chopin was a poet who cared little about the events of the world. In the winter of 1838–39 Chopin accompanied Sand to the island of Majorca, where she attended to him with total devotion. After many difficult years together, they parted in 1847, by which time he was quite ill with tuberculosis.

Chopin gave his last concert in Paris in early 1848 and his last concert in London, a benefit for Polish émigrés, in late 1848. He died the following year. Mozart's Requiem was performed at Chopin's funeral, performed by the orchestra and chorus of the Paris Conservatory. He was buried at the famous Père-Lachaise cemetery between the graves of LUIGI CHERUBINI and VINCENZO BELLINI. At his own request, however, his heart was sent to Warsaw for burial in his homeland.

Chopin was the first great piano soloist. He composed with the piano's strengths and limitations in mind, rather than trying to copy the orchestra's sound on the keyboard. The poetry of his pianism, its depth of feeling, the overwhelming sadness in his NOCTURNES and BALLADES, and the bounding energy of his SCHERZOS and ÉTUDES were never equaled. Among his many great solo piano works are the Ballade No. 1 in G Minor, op.23 (1831–35); Sonata No. 2 in B-flat Minor, op.35, the *Funeral March* (1839); Fantasie in F Minor/A-flat Major, op.49 (1841); and Polonaise in A-flat Major, op.53, the *Heroic* (1842).

Chopsticks. A celebrated children's piano exercise played by two hands, each using a single finger, or else with both hands turned sideways imitating the chopping of wood, which explains the origin of the name.

The piece was first published in England in 1877 under the title *The Celebrated Chop Waltz*, without an inkling of the composer's name. Subsequent research has failed to determine who wrote it. It was known in Germany as *Koteletten Walzer*, and in France as *Cotelettes*, that is, "cutlets." Several Russian composers published a set of variations on *Chopsticks*, and FRANZ LISZT added one of his own.

choral. Relating or pertaining to a CHORUS, or to vocal concerted music. *Choral notes*, square notes used for writing PLAINSONG; *choral service*, church service with music by the CHOIR.

Choral Symphony. The popular name for LUDWIG VAN BEETHOVEN's mighty Ninth Symphony in D Minor, op.125, with a final chorus based on Schiller's *Ode to Joy*. Beethoven worked on this symphony for nearly 10 years and completed it barely in time for the scheduled first performance in Vienna, 1824.

It is easy to call the work a masterpiece over a century and a half after its creation, but at the time it appeared as a challenge to an established tradition. A choral ending seemed unfit for an instrumental work. And what an ending! Beethoven forced the singers into the upper region of their ranges with a massive accompaniment of the orchestra. There is another departure from tradition: Beethoven places the SCHERZO as the second, instead of the third, movement, as in his previous symphonies. There follows the slow movement, leading to the choral finale, which opens with a horrendously DISSONANT chord containing all seven notes of the D HARMONIC MINOR SCALE.

chorale (from Lat. *choralis*, of the chorus). Generic term for religious choral compositions employed in German Protestant churches.

The historical development of the chorale within the German Protestant service is intimately connected with the activities of Martin Luther, the founder of the Protestant church. Luther had the Latin hymns of the Roman Catholic

Many contemporary critics failed to appreciate Beethoven's Ninth. Even the well-known composer and conductor LOUIS SPOHR was repelled, saying: "The fourth movement [i.e., the famous ODE TO JOY] is so ugly, in such bad taste, and in the conception of Schiller's Ode so cheap that I cannot even now understand how such a genius as Beethoven could write it down."

An anonymous critic writing in Providence, R.I., in 1868, said: "[The choral part] opened with eight bars of a commonplace theme, very much like *Yankee Doodle*. … I regret to say that it appeared to be made up of the strange, the ludicrous, the abrupt, the ferocious, and the screechy…. what all the noise was about, it was hard to form any idea. The general impression it left on me is that of a concert made up of Indian war whoops and angry wildcats."

kōh-rahl′

Church translated into German, making it possible for the congregation to take part in the singing. Most of these texts were direct translations from Latin, so that *Te deum laudamus* became *Herr Gott, Dich loben wir,* and the Credo opening became *Wir glauben all' an einen Gott.* But the Lutheran church also boldly borrowed the melodies from secular songs. One of the most popular was *Durch Adams Fall ist ganz verderbt* (Through Adam's fall we sinned all).

Collections of Lutheran chorales were published in Germany as early as 1524, when the Protestant movement was still fighting the stigma of heresy. Soon these chorales became the sources for multivoiced instrumental compositions, thus making a link between chorale and instrumental music.

The chorale reached its peak in the works of JOHANN SEBASTIAN BACH, who harmonized hundreds of known chorale melodies and composed many more.

Thus the purely practical movement of the Protestant chorale, begun in the early 16th century with the purpose of forming a repertory of songs in the German tongue in order to bring sacred music closer to the people, grew into a great art, embracing all genres of sacred and secular music.

Chorale cantata, one in which harmonized chorales are used in some or all sections of a CANTATA; *chorale prelude,* an organ composition based on a chorale or HYMN tune that serves as a PRELUDE to Protestant church services; in Roman Catholic usage, this genre corresponds to the organ hymn; *chorale variations,* a common term for VARIATIONS on a chorale tune, particularly in the 17th and 18th centuries, in the form of keyboard compositions.

chord. 1. Any tonal combination containing three or more different notes. The major triad (three-note chord) is colloquially described as a common chord, but this does not mean that other chords are uncommon. In CLASSICAL music theory, any chord containing more than three different notes was regarded as a DISSONANCE, requiring resolution into a CONSONANCE according to traditional academic rules. Discrimination against unrestricted use of dissonant chords has been abolished in the music of the 20th century. 2. A HAR-

MONY of from three to seven tones, forming an ascending series of DIATONIC THIRDS.

Block, flat, or *solid chord,* one whose notes are played simultaneously; *broken* or *rolled chord,* one where the notes are played in series; an ARPEGGIO.

chord organ. An electronic keyboard instrument invented by the Hammond organ company in 1950 that allows harmonies to be produced by pressing appropriate buttons.

chordophones (Grk., string sound). Instruments that produce their sound by means of vibrating strings, such as a violin or guitar. Part of a classification system invented by the German musicologists Erich von Hornbostel and Curt Sachs.

choree (Grk.; Lat. *chorea*). In Greek verse, a foot of two syllables in which the first is accented. It is also called trochee. Modern examples include the POLKA and GALOP.

choreography (Grk. choreo + Fr. *graphie*). 1. The composition and arrangement of dances, particularly ballet and modern types. 2. Notation of such a composition, indicating the position and movement of the dancer(s).

choro. A generic term used in Brazil to describe urban instrumental music, beginning in the 1870s. The music performed is played by an ensemble with a soloist. All kinds of music have been performed by choro groups: POLKA, WALTZ, modinha, SAMBA, maxixe, and the Brazilian TANGO.

chôro. Music written in a Brazilian style. The term is most closely associated with the composer HEITOR VILLA-LOBOS, who wrote 14 chôros for various instrumental groups under this name. The most engaging is Chôro No. 5 for Piano (1926), subtitled *Alma brasileira* (Brazilian soul).

chorus (Eng.; Fr. *coeur*). 1. Ensemble of voices, consisting of SOPRANOS, ALTOS, TENORS, and BASSES, abbreviated SATB. A female or boys' chorus consists of sopranos (or TREBLES) and

MUSICAL
INSTRUMENT

MUSICAL
INSTRUMENT

altos, while a male chorus consists of tenors, baritones, and basses. A double chorus often involves a spatially separated ensemble. In any case, there are usually several singers to a part. 2. A REFRAIN in traditional music, popular songs, show tunes, JAZZ, and similar music.

cr̄es′tā ā-lā′ē-sohn

Christe eleison (Grk., Christ, have mercy). Part of the KYRIE. *See* MASS.

PEOPLE IN MUSIC

Christian, Charlie, African-American JAZZ guitarist; b. Bonham, Tex., July 29, 1916; d. N.Y., Mar. 2, 1942. Christian's parents and four brothers were musicians. As a child he played in the family band, and at maturity he began playing an ELECTRIC GUITAR in order to be heard when he was playing in a band.

Christian was "discovered" by jazz producer John Hammond, who heard him playing in a club. Hammond urged his client BENNY GOODMAN to hire Christian for his band, thus breaking the "color line" then in force (Goodman was white, Christian black). From 1939 to 1941 Christian played in Goodman's band and smaller sextet, playing single-string solos on an electric guitar, then a great novelty.

In the early 1940s Christian worked with DIZZY GILLESPIE and THELONIUS MONK, who were then developing the new BEBOP style. Sadly, because of a recording ban then in place, there exist only amateur recordings made in clubs of their work together. Christian's career was tragically cut short when he was stricken with tuberculosis and died at the young age of 25.

Christmas Oratorio. A cycle of six cantatas by JOHANN SEBASTIAN BACH, 1734–35, for performance on six separate days after Christmas Day (BWV 248).

PEOPLE IN MUSIC

Christoff, Boris (Kirilov), celebrated Bulgarian BASS; b. Plovdiv, May 18, 1914; d. Rome, June 28, 1993. Christoff sang in the Gusla Choir in Sofia, where he was heard by Bulgaria's King Boris, who made it possible for him to go to Rome to study. He made his concert and OPERA debuts in Rome in 1946. He subsequently appeared at La Scala, Milan, in

1947; at Covent Garden, London in 1949; and in his U.S. debut as Boris Godunov with the San Francisco Opera in 1956.

During his distinguished career, Christoff appeared at leading opera houses, singing most of the principal bass roles in the VERDI operas. He was most renowned for his dramatic portrayal of MODEST MUSSORGSKY's Boris Godunov, which recalled the interpretation of FEODOR CHALIAPIN. His brother-in-law was the famous Italian baritone Tito Gobbi (1913–84).

Christophe Colomb. Opera by DARIUS MILHAUD, 1930, to a text by the French poet Paul Claudel. It is a two-act extravaganza containing 27 scenes, drawing on diverse musical styles.

chromatic (Grk. *chroma,* color). 1. A progression of NOTES by half-steps. 2. Tones foreign to a given DIATONIC SCALE or HARMONY.

Chromatic signs, see ACCIDENTALS.

chromaticism. A consistent and frequent use of HALF-STEPS in a melodic progression. Also the regular insertion of intermediary NOTES between two DIATONIC degrees (or WHOLE STEPS).

In the key of C major, every sharp and every flat constitutes a chromatic note, which is a SEMITONE apart from the preceding or succeeding diatonic degree. However, a distinction is made between a chromatic and a diatonic semitone. The interval from E to F is a diatonic semitone, but the interval between F and F♯ is a chromatic one, because the two notes share the same letter name. In the progression F–F♯–G, the F♯ constitutes a chromatic passing note.

Chromatic MELODY and HARMONY achieved their ultimate development in the 12-tone method of composition formulated by Arnold Schoenberg.

Chronochromie (Color of time). Orchestral work by OLIVIER MESSIAEN, 1960. Instrumental sounds represent the different colors, and rhythms represent time.

Christophe Colomb is full of playful imagery. At one point a flock of doves is released onstage. The word for "dove" in French is *colomb.*

Chung, Kyung-Wha, brilliant Korean violinist, sister of MYUNG-WHA CHUNG and MYUNG-WHUN CHUNG; b. Seoul, Mar. 26, 1948. Kyung-Wha began violin study as a small child, making her orchestral debut in Seoul at the age of nine, playing the MENDELSSOHN Concerto. In 1961 she went to the U.S., where she studied at the Juilliard School of Music, N.Y.

In 1967 Kyung-Wha shared first prize with PINCHAS ZUKERMAN in the Leventritt Competition. In 1968 she appeared as soloist with the N.Y. Philharmonic and made her European debut two years later with the London Symphony Orchestra. She then embarked upon a far-flung concert tour in Europe and Asia. She gave numerous trio concerts with her sister and brother and also appeared as a soloist with her brother acting as conductor.

Chung, Myung-Wha, Korean-born American cellist, sister of KYUNG-WHA CHUNG and MYUNG-WHUN CHUNG; b. Seoul, Mar. 19, 1944. Myung-Wha studied cello in Seoul, making her orchestral debut there in 1957. In 1961 she went to the U.S., where she studied at the Juilliard School of Music, N.Y. She made her U.S. debut in San Francisco in 1967 and her European debut in Spoleto two years later. She won first prize in the Geneva Competition (1971), the same year she became a naturalized U.S. citizen. She appeared as soloist with orchestras in Europe and America and also played trio concerts with her siblings.

Chung, Myung-Whun, Korean-born American pianist and conductor, brother of MYUNG-WHA CHUNG and KYUNG-WHA CHUNG; b. Seoul, Jan. 22, 1953. Myung-Whun played piano as a child, making his debut as soloist with the Seoul Philharmonic when he was seven. He then went to the U.S., where he studied at the Mannes College of Music in N.Y. and at the Juilliard School (diplomas in piano and conducting, 1974).

Myung-Whun made his conducting debut in Seoul in 1971, subsequently winning second prize in piano at the Tchaikovsky Competition in Moscow in 1974. He became a naturalized U.S. citizen in 1973. He pursued a dual career as a pianist and conductor and gave trio concerts with his sisters. He was assistant conductor of the Los Angeles Philharmonic (1978 – 81) and chief conductor of the Saarland Radio Symphony Orchestra, Saarbrucken (1984 – 90).

In 1986 Myung-Whun made his Metropolitan Opera debut in N.Y. conducting GIUSEPPE VERDI's *Simon Boccanegra.* In 1989 he became music director designate and in 1990 was confirmed in the prestigious position of music director of Paris's new Bastille Opéra. This appointment, considering his relative youth and lack of experience, created a sensation among opera fans and the press.

church modes. The SCALES employed in MEDIEVAL and RENAISSANCE church music. *See* AUTHENTIC MODES, PLAGAL MODES.

church sonata. *See* SONATA DA CHIESA.

Cielito lindo (Sp., beautiful little heaven). Popular Latin American song, stylistically Mexican, possibly written by Quirino Mendoza.

Cilèa, Francesco, Italian composer; b. Palmi, Calabria, July 23, 1866; d. Varazze, Nov. 20, 1950. Cilèa studied piano and composition at the Naples Conservatory between 1881 and 1889. He then taught piano there (1894 – 96) and also harmony at the Istituto Musicale in Florence (1896 – 1904). From 1913 to 1916 he was head of the Palermo Conservatory, then from 1916 to 1935 director of the Conservatory di San Pietro a Majella in Naples.

PEOPLE IN MUSIC

Cilèa wrote relatively few works, most of them operas. His most famous work is *ADRIANA LECOUVREUR,* which debuted in Milan in 1902 and remains in the opera repertoire.

Cimarosa, Domenico, famous Italian composer; b. Aversa, near Naples, Dec. 17, 1749; d. Venice, Jan. 11, 1801. Cimarosa was the son of a stonemason. After his father's death, his mother placed him in the monastery school in Naples, where he began his musical training with the monastery organist. He then enrolled at the Conservatory di San Maria di Loreto in 1761, where he studied voice, violin,

PEOPLE IN MUSIC

and keyboard. His first OPERA, *Le stravaganze del conte,* was staged in Naples in 1772.

From 1776 on, Cimarosa composed operas at a prolific rate, producing about 65 works for the major Italian opera centers as well as those abroad. In the early 1780s he also served as one of the organists at the Royal Chapel in Naples, and as maestro of the Ospedaletto, a conservatory for girls in Venice.

In 1787 Cimarosa was given the post of *maestro di cappella* (choir master) to the court of Catherine the Great in St. Petersburg. During his Russian years he wrote three operas and various other works for the court and the nobility. The court cut back on its funding of music, however, and Cimarosa's contract ended in 1791.

Cimarosa proceeded to Vienna, where Emperor Leopold II appointed him *kapellmeister* (court conductor). He then composed his masterpiece, *Il matrimonio segreto,* which was premiered with great acclaim on Feb. 7, 1792. The emperor was so taken by the opera that he ordered that it be repeated that evening, undoubtedly the most unusual encore in the history of opera. The opera's fame spread throughout Europe, and Cimarosa returned to Italy in 1793 as one of the most celebrated musicians of the age.

In 1796 Cimarosa was appointed first organist of the Royal Chapel in Naples.

In 1800 Cimarosa went to Venice, where he died while working on his opera *Artemisia.* It was rumored abroad that he had been poisoned by order of Queen Caroline of Naples. The rumor was so persistent, and popular feelings so pronounced, that the pope's personal physician was sent to Venice to make an examination. According to his sworn statement, Cimarosa died of an infected abdominal tumor.

Cimarosa was an outstanding composer of Italian OPERA BUFFA in his day. His melodic inventiveness, command of form, superb vocal writing, and masterly orchestration were unexcelled until GIACOMO ROSSINI arrived upon the scene.

In 1799 Cimarosa got into trouble when he supported the citizens of Naples who wished to overthrow the monarchy. Their movement was briefly successful, and Cimarosa celebrated by composing a patriotic hymn for the burning of the royal flag. The monarchy was restored later that year, however, and Cimarosa was arrested in December 1799 and sent to prison for four months. He was released only after several people with ties to the royal court begged for his pardon.

MUSICAL INSTRUMENT

cimbalom (Ger. *Zimbalo[n]*). A large DULCIMER, played in Hungarian and other GYPSY bands, with a range of four octaves (E to e^3). The body is shaped like a trapezoid. The player strikes the strings with two mallets or small hammers.

A type with a chromatic scale and damper pedal was developed in the 1870s.

Cinderella. Ballet by SERGEI PROKOFIEV, 1945, based on the classic fairy tale.

Cinq Doigts, Les (The five fingers). A group of eight PIANO pieces by IGOR STRAVINSKY, 1921. Ostensibly written for children, the pieces are DISSONANT and rhythmically difficult to play. The object is that once the five fingers are set on five keys of the piano, they don't have to be moved. The pieces illustrate Stravinsky's desire at the time to create a new simplicity in music without sacrificing content.

cipher. 1. The practice of basing a composition on pitches that are tonal equivalents to letters of the alphabet, e.g., B–A–C–H. 2. On the ORGAN, a note that, owing to some mechanical problem, continues in sounding.

circle (cycle) of fifths (Ger. *Quintenzirkel*). 1. A series of fifths tuned (as on the piano) in EQUAL TEMPERAMENT, so that the 12th fifth in the series has the same letter name as the first note. 2. A chart showing the 12 major and 12 minor keys, arranged by ascending fifths and represented graphically by the face of a clock beginning at 12 o'clock with C major and A minor, each having no sharps or flats. The direction of sharp keys is clockwise, the direction of flat keys counterclockwise.

circular breathing. A performance technique used primarily by vocalists and wind players to play a long, uninterrupted tone. This is achieved by the performer inhaling through the nose while simultaneously exhaling through the mouth. No break in the sound occurs, as would in normal performance, where the player would have to stop to take a breath.

circus music. A type of BAND music associated with circuses. The INSTRUMENTATION is that of a MILITARY BAND, sometimes supplemented by unusual instruments such as the CALLIOPE.

ZOLTÁN KODÁLY uses the cimbalom in his *HÁRY JÁNOS*, and IGOR STRAVINSKY employs it in his *Renard* and in a provisional version of *LES NOCES*. FRANZ LISZT imitates the sound of the cimbalom in his Hungarian Rhapsody No. 11 for piano, specifically indicating the passage as *quasi-Zimbalo* (like a cimbalom).

Circus Polka. Orchestral sketch by IGOR STRAVINSKY originally written for piano. It was commissioned by the Ringling Brothers' Circus to accompany the entrance of the elephants. Stravinsky conducted its first performance for symphony orchestra in 1944.

MUSICAL INSTRUMENT

citole (Ger. *Citole, Zitole;* It. *cetula*). A MEDIEVAL and early RENAISSANCE fretted string instrument with a one-piece body (i.e., it does not have a separate NECK). The instrument generally had four strings, which were plucked with a quill (or feather).

sit′tern

MUSICAL INSTRUMENT

cittern (*cithern, cithren;* Fr. *cistrel;* Ger. *Cister, Cither, Zitter*). A fretted string instrument used in the 16th and 17th centuries. It had a pear-shaped body and was strung with wire and played with a PLECTRUM. The most common had four to six paired strings.

Clair de lune. see SUITE BERGAMASQUE.

MUSICAL INSTRUMENT

clappers. A pair of wooden or metal disks or sticks held between the fingers and struck together to mark the beat in a dance. This is a rudimentary type of CASTANETS, perhaps the most ancient PERCUSSION instrument.

PEOPLE IN MUSIC

Clapton, Eric (Patrick), also called "Slowhand," prominent English electric BLUES and ROCK guitarist; b. Ripley, Surrey, Mar. 30, 1945. Clapton played guitar as a youth, and at 18 joined the Metropolitan Blues Quartet, later known as the Yardbirds. Clapton played with it for a short time, but was turned off by its turn toward commercialism. In 1965 he joined John Mayall's Bluesbreakers, to return to performing traditional blues.

A year later, however, Clapton left to form a trio named Cream, with bassist Jack Bruce and drummer Ginger Baker. This group turned the rock world upside down by introducing long improvised jams. The group was also the first "power trio" in rock, influencing the original Jimi Hendrix Experience.

After Cream disbanded in 1968, Clapton organized a "supergroup" called Blind Faith, with Baker, Steve Winwood, and Rick Grech. However, the conflicting egos of the band's members led the group to fold almost as quickly as it formed.

After a brief period backing the duo Delaney and Bonnie, Clapton formed Derek and the Dominoes, which received a certified Gold Award in 1971 with its album *Layla*. This song, telling of Clapton's love affair with his friend GEORGE HARRISON's then wife, is perhaps his most famous composition, featuring a memorable guitar HOOK that is immediately recognized by fans.

The group disbanded in 1972, and Clapton withdrew from performing as he became addicted to cocaine. He finally kicked his habit by the late 1970s and returned as a solo performer. After a period of scoring motion pictures and recording albums of varying quality, Clapton returned to the charts in the early 1990s with his ode *Tears in Heaven*, inspired by the death of his son, who died after falling out of an open window. He also enjoyed success thanks to his appearance on MTV's popular *Unplugged* (acoustic performance) series.

claque (Fr., clapping). A group of people in the audience who loudly applaud a performer in return for pay.

The practice of engaging a claque began in the early 19th century in Italy among opera stars, then rapidly spread into France, England, and America. Occasionally, an ambitious opera star would engage an anticlaque to drown out a rival's claque.

Claques were officially banned at the Metropolitan Opera House in N.Y. in 1935 but apparently still prospered as late as 1960, at the cost of up to $100 for a group of young males on Saturday afternoons.

clarinet (It. *clarinetto, clarino;* from Lat. *claro,* clear; Ger. *Klarinette;* Fr. *clarinette*). A SINGLE-REED WOODWIND instrument derived from the 18th-century CHALUMEAU, and a standard member of the Classical orchestra since the latter part of the 18th century. The instrument is first mentioned in 1710.

The clarinet has a cylindrical tube of African blackwood, pierced by 18 holes, 13 being closed by keys. Its compass

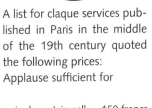

A list for claque services published in Paris in the middle of the 19th century quoted the following prices: Applause sufficient for

a single curtain call	150 francs
Overwhelming applause	225 francs
Hissing a rival singer	250 francs
Ovation after the last act, serenading before the window of the artist's home	price by special arrangement

MUSICAL INSTRUMENT

comprises three octaves in four different registers: low (chalumeau), medium (throat), high (clarion), and and extreme (altissimo).

The clarinet is a vertical pipe with a beak (or MOUTH-PIECE) at one end and a bell-shaped aperture at the other. The player blows into the mouthpiece and, by opening and closing holes along the instrument's length, is able to effect changes of pitch.

The modern clarinet is a rather late addition to the family of woodwind instruments. As an orchestral instrument it did not come into usage until the middle of the 18th century. The Bohemian composer JOHANN STAMITZ was the first to include a clarinet part in an orchestral score: in 1755 he wrote a "symphony with a clarinet and double basses."

The written range of the clarinet is from E below the treble clef to the high G or beyond above the treble clef (i.e., $e-g^3$). It is a transposing instrument, which means that the written note sounds at a different pitch. The most commonly used clarinet is the soprano in B♭, for which the written note C sounds B♭ (for the A clarinet, the written C sounds A, etc.). A clarinet in C was formerly much in use but is now rare.

As with other transposing instruments, the key signatures are affected. For example, if a work is written in the key signature of five flats, the clarinet in B♭ needs only three. That is why in orchestral scores key signatures in the clarinet parts differ from those in the strings.

The clarinet family includes two small (sopranino) clarinets, tuned in D and E♭, which transpose, respectively, a major second and a minor third up. The most striking example of the clarinet in D appears in the score of *Till Eulenspiegel* by RICHARD STRAUSS, where it portrays the famous prankster of the title. Parts for the small clarinet in D are often played on the more common clarinet in E♭.

The clarinet in F transposing down a fifth is called the BASSET HORN. An alto clarinet in E♭, transposing down a major sixth, is used in BANDS but appears rarely in orchestral scores. The bass clarinet in B♭ transposes an octave below the common clarinet, and the contrabass clarinet transposes two octaves lower than the common B♭ instrument or one octave

Some modern composers prefer to write orchestral clarinet parts in the conductor's score without transposition, while writing the individual clarinet parts in B♭. This saves the conductor the trouble of figuring out the proper transposition but still provides the correct transpositions to clarinet players themselves.

below the alto clarinet (in E♭). Playing the contrabass requires exceptionally strong lungs.

A large repertory of music written for the clarinet exists. JOHANN STAMITZ was only one of the Mannheim composers to write for the new instrument. WOLFGANG AMADEUS MOZART bemoaned the absence of clarinets at Salzburg in 1778. He soon had two fine clarinetists (the Stadler brothers), for whom he wrote the first significant corpus of clarinet music. Among popular clarinet concertos are those by Mozart, CARL MARIA VON WEBER, LOUIS SPOHR, CARL NIELSEN, CLAUDE DEBUSSY (*Première rapsodie*), PAUL HINDEMITH, AARON COPLAND, and THEA MUSGRAVE. GEORGE GERSHWIN's *RHAPSODY IN BLUE* is practically a double concerto for clarinet and piano. Its opening clarinet solo reaches a high B♭, approached by a GLISSANDO, a virtuoso effect.

clarino. 1. The high register of the TRUMPET, where it is possible to produce a complete DIATONIC scale in natural HARMONICS. 2. The long-tubed BAROQUE trumpet, capable of fast tempo and clear ARTICULATION, made obsolete by the modern trumpet.

Clarke, Rebecca (Thacher), English-born American composer and violist; b. Harrow, Aug. 27, 1886; d. N.Y., Oct. 13, 1979. Clarke studied violin at the Royal Academy of Music from 1902 to 1904, and composition at the Royal College of Music in London from 1904 to 1910. She then switched to the viola, taking a few private lessons and becoming the first female member of Henry Wood's Queen Hall Orchestra in 1912. In 1928 she formed the English Ensemble, with which she played until 1929. She married James Friskin in 1944 and then lived in N.Y.

Clarke's fine music, all chamber works, is quite advanced. While firmly rooted in English IMPRESSIONISM, she employed techniques that forecast 20th-century ATONALISM. For some of her compositions she used the name Anthony Trent, probably to overcome the prejudice many in the classical world had against a woman composer.

Her greatest fame came from tying for first place with ERNEST BLOCH for the 1919 Coolidge Competition with her

The clarinet was an essential instrument in jazz ensembles through the Dixieland/New Orleans, Chicago/"hot," and swing/big band eras. One of the first great jazz clarinet players was Johnny Dodds, a New Orleans-born musician who played with both King Oliver and LOUIS ARMSTRONG. IGOR STRAVINSKY wrote his *EBONY CONCERTO* for jazz orchestra leader WOODY HERMAN. Its title refers to the slang term for clarinet, *ebony stick.*

PEOPLE IN MUSIC

Viola Sonata. The award eventually went to Bloch, owing in large part to the sponsor's discomfort with the notion of a woman composer being equal to any man.

Classic era (from Lat. *classicus,* of the highest rank). The classical music style dating c.1750–1825. It was preceded by the ornate BAROQUE style and ended with the expansion of the ROMANTIC period of composition.

Stylistically, Classic music is distinguished by: (1) symmetry of form, set in either BINARY (two-part) or TERNARY (three-part) structures; (2) movement from key to key (MODULATION) governed by strict rules; (3) relatively simple rhythms; (4) well-developed COUNTERPOINT (two or more melodies played at once); and (5) harmonies that followed set rules to be "pleasing to the ear." Instrumental technique in the Classic era was conservative. Virtuosity was encouraged as long as it served the dignified formality of the general design. Because the formulas of Classic HARMONY, MELODY, and RHYTHM were standardized to a considerable degree, composers of the period were able to turn out hundreds of SYMPHONIES, CONCERTOS, and SONATAS, and dozens of OPERAS, CANTATAS, and other works, all tailored to a fairly uniform model, no matter how different their stylistic contents.

The term *classical music* does not apply only to the period of FRANZ JOSEPH HAYDN, WOLFGANG AMADEUS MOZART, and LUDWIG VAN BEETHOVEN, which in this dictionary is called the CLASSIC PERIOD.

classical music. Any highly evolved music that is written down or NOTATED in some form, as opposed to popular or folk music, whose survival has depended on some form of ORAL TRADITION (passing from player to player, with no formal written score). For better or worse, classical music is also called *serious music, highbrow music, cultivated music,* or *art music.* See also CLASSICISM.

***Classical* Symphony.** Symphony No. 1 in D Major by SERGEI PROKOFIEV, 1917. It was one of the first 20th-century works in the NEOCLASSICAL style (a revival of classical rules of composition and forms).

classicism. Art that emphasizes purity of design, perfection of form, and the meeting of the highest standards. These qualities were connected in the minds of RENAISSANCE historians with the ancient civilizations of Greece and Rome. For them, classicism meant a return to what they believed were the standards of Greek and Roman art.

For example, the emergence of OPERA at the beginning of the 17th century was the outgrowth of an attempt to revive the performing style of ancient Greek drama. A group of artists and historians in Florence, Italy, believed that the text of these Greek plays was chanted or recited by the actors to simple melodies. Therefore, their original operas consisted of simple chanted melodies in an attempt to revive what was believed to be the ancient Greek style.

clausula (Lat., *claudere,* conclude). A formal ending to a ME-DIEVAL vocal composition sung in POLYPHONY (with more than one melodic part at once). A clausula was usually sung to a single vowel or syllable. The singing of a clausula signaled the end of a work, and thus served a definite function in performance.

Similar to a CADENCE, except a cadence is used to end a single melody accompanied by a harmony part. In the REN-AISSANCE, some writers used the two terms interchangeably.

clavecin (Fr.; It. *clavicembalo*). *see* HARPSICHORD, VIRGINAL.

klăh-v'săn

claves (Sp.). A pair of sticks made of resonant polished hardwood, struck one against the other, producing a sharp sound. Claves are used in much Latin American popular music.

MUSICAL
INSTRUMENT

clavichord (Lat. *clavis,* key + Grk. *chorda,* string). A KEY-BOARD instrument popular during the RENAISSANCE and BAROQUE periods, particularly in Germany, where it was the favored domestic instrument.

MUSICAL
INSTRUMENT

A forebear of the pianoforte, it differs from the latter in having, instead of hammers, upright brass wedges called TANGENTS on the rear end of the keys. Upon pressing a key, the tangent strikes the string and remains pressed against it until the finger is lifted, causing only one section of the string to vibrate. It thus differs in construction from the HARPSICHORD and the VIRGINAL, in that the strings are not

During the Baroque era, composers designated strung keyboard music as being "for clavier," but in some cases they may have meant either harpsichord or clavichord. Further, this wording may have been added by the music's publisher in order to attract the widest possible audience.

Baroque composers made use of various C clefs even in their keyboard compositions. Johann Sebastian Bach's Two-Part Invention No. 15 in F Major (BWV 786) is notated in the soprano clef (middle C on the first line) for the right hand and in the tenor clef for the left. This notation is apt to startle a piano-minded clef reader who happens to come upon Bach's Inventions in the facsimile edition.

PEOPLE IN MUSIC

plucked but struck. It is therefore closer to the sound production of a modern piano.

The clavichord has a delicate, intimate sound, much softer than that of the harpsichord. A talented player can create an unusual VIBRATO or wavering sound by varying the pressure on the keys after they are depressed. Its range was between three and five octaves.

clavier (Ger.). 1. The KEYBOARD or manual of any keyboard instrument, used in this way from the early 16th century. 2. In the late 17th and 18th centuries, any strung keyboard instrument; in the 19th century, the piano. In 20th-century Germany the spelling was changed to *Klavier.*

clef(s) (Ger. *Schlüssel*). A character set in the STAFF at the beginning of a composition to fix the PITCH or position of one note, and thus of the rest.

Two clefs are used in piano music, the treble clef (𝄞), indicating the position of the note G above middle C on the second line, and the bass clef (𝄢), indicating the position of the note F below middle C on the fourth line. The present shape of the G clef evolved from the Gothic capital letter (𝕲). The F clef was first indicated as a red line and later evolved from the capital letter F.

A group of clefs called C clefs indicate the position of middle C on the staff. Its visual form varies, but a shape suggestive of a Gothic letter *K* is now customary. The most common C clefs are the alto clef, also called viola clef, placing middle C on the third line, and the tenor clef, placing middle C on the fourth line. The alto clef is used in viola and occasionally trombone parts, while the tenor clef is used in cello, bassoon, and trombone parts to notate passages that lie above the bass register.

Tenor vocal parts, formerly written in tenor clefs, are now written in treble clef, sounding an octave below written pitch. This TRANSPOSITION is sometimes indicated by a double treble clef or a hybrid superimposition of the C clef onto the treble clef.

Clementi, Muzio (baptized Mutius Philippus Vincentius Franciscus Xaverius), celebrated Italian pianist and composer; b. Rome, Jan. 23, 1752; d. Evesham, Worcestershire, England, Mar. 10, 1832. Clementi began organ studies at age seven and later studied voice. By January 1766 he was organist of the parish San Lorenzo in Damaso. About this time Peter Beckford, cousin of the English novelist William Beckford, visited Rome and was struck by Clementi's youthful talent. With the permission of Clementi's father, he took the boy to England. For the next seven years Clementi lived, performed, and studied at Beckford's estate.

During the winter of 1774–75 Clementi settled in London, making his first appearance as a harpsichordist in a benefit concert in 1775. For the next several years he appears to have spent most of his time as harpsichordist at the King's Theatre, where he conducted operatic performances. In 1779 his Six Sonatas, op.2, were published, bringing him his first public success both in England and on the Continent. In 1780 he embarked on a tour of the Continent, giving a series of piano concerts in Paris. In 1781 he continued his tour with appearances in Strasbourg, Munich, and Vienna.

In 1786 several of Clementi's symphonies were performed in London, only to be outdone by the great symphonies of FRANZ JOSEPH HAYDN. In 1790 he retired from public performances as a pianist but continued to conduct orchestral concerts from the keyboard. After 1796 he appears to have withdrawn from all public performances and devoted himself to teaching, collecting large fees.

Clementi lost part of his fortune through the bankruptcy of his publishers in 1798. He formed a partnership on the ruins of the old company, however, and became highly successful as a music publisher and piano manufacturer. Clementi remained a successful businessman over the next three decades.

From 1802 to 1810 Clementi traveled extensively on the Continent, pursuing business interests, teaching, composing, and giving private concerts. While in Vienna in 1807 he met LUDWIG VAN BEETHOVEN and arranged to become his major English publisher. He returned to England in 1810 and in 1813 helped organize the Philharmonic Society of London, with which he appeared as conductor. In 1816–17 he conducted his symphonies in Paris, followed by engage-

It was during Clementi's stay in Vienna in 1781 that the famous piano contest with WOLFGANG AMADEUS MOZART took place at court before Emperor Joseph II. There are conflicting reports of who "won" the battle.

ments in Frankfurt in 1817–18. He again visited Paris in 1821 and was in Munich in 1821–22.

Returning to England, Clementi made several more conducting appearances with the Philharmonic Society until 1824. However, his symphonies were soon dropped from the repertoire as Beethoven's masterpieces eclipsed his own efforts. In 1830 he retired from his mercantile ventures and eventually made his home at Evesham, Worcestershire. As a teacher, Clementi had many distinguished pupils.

Clementine. A sentimental American song of uncertain authorship, originally published as *Oh My Darling, Clementine.*

Clemenza di Tito, La. Opera seria by WOLFGANG AMADEUS MOZART, his last, 1791. The libretto by Metastasio deals with the generous pardon granted by the Roman emperor Titus to those who plotted against him. The same libretto was set to music by numerous composers, before and after Mozart.

PEOPLE IN MUSIC

Cleveland, James, African-American GOSPEL singer and composer; b. Chicago, Dec. 5, 1931; d. Los Angeles, Feb. 9, 1991. Cleveland was encouraged to develop his natural talent for music by the pianist and gospel performer Roberta Martin, a family friend. He was a pianist and singer with the Caravans and then formed his own Gospel Chimes in 1959. He also became a licensed minister of the Church of God in Christ. His song *Grace Is Sufficient* (1948) became a gospel standard, and his album *Peace Be Still* (1963) added further to his renown. In 1970 he founded the Cornerstone Institutional Baptist Church, which he also served as pastor.

PEOPLE IN MUSIC

Cliburn, Van (Harvey Lavan, Jr.), brilliant American pianist; b. Shreveport, La., July 12, 1934. His mother, Rildia Bee Cliburn, was a pupil of the well-known German pianist Arthur Friedheim, who himself studied with FRANZ LISZT. She was Van's only teacher until 1951, when he entered the Juilliard School of Music in N.Y., graduating in 1954.

Van Cliburn was four when he made his first appearance in public in Shreveport. After the family's move to Kilgore, Texas, he won the Texas State Prize in 1947 and appeared as soloist with the Houston Symphony Orchestra. In 1948 he won the National Music Festival Award, in 1952 the Dealy Award and the Kosciuszko Foundation Chopin prize, in 1953 the Juilliard School of Music concerto competition, and in 1954 the Roeder Award and the Leventritt competition in N.Y. That same year he appeared as a soloist with the N.Y. Philharmonic.

In subsequent years Cliburn toured extensively, appearing as a soloist with leading orchestras and as a recitalist. In 1978 he withdrew from public performances but appeared again in 1987 as a recitalist in a concert for President Reagan and Soviet general secretary Gorbachev at the White House in Washington, D.C. In 1989 he appeared as soloist in concertos by FRANZ LISZT and PIOTR ILYICH TCHAIKOVSKY with the Philadelphia Orchestra, and also traveled to Moscow on Gorbachev's invitation.

Cliburn's playing combines technique with genuine depth of feeling. He is particularly effective as an interpreter of the music of Tchaikovsky and SERGEI RACHMANINOFF. The Van Cliburn International Piano Competition was organized in 1962 and is held every four years in Fort Worth, Texas, the home of the Van Cliburn Foundation.

In 1958 Cliburn captured first prize at the Tchaikovsky Competition in Moscow, the first American to achieve this feat. It was the height of the cold war, and Cliburn's success was widely viewed as an American triumph over communism. Upon his return to N.Y., he received a hero's welcome in a ticker tape parade.

Cline, Patsy (born Virginia Patterson Hensley), American COUNTRY MUSIC singer; b. Winchester, Va., Sept. 8, 1932; d. in an airplane crash, Camden, Tenn., Mar. 5, 1963.

Cline was raised in rural Virginia. Her father was a farmer with two daughters from a previous marriage when he married her mother, Hilda. Cline was born when Hilda was 16. Cline learned to tap dance at the age of four and started to teach herself piano when she was seven. She also listened regularly to the GRAND OLE OPRY radio program out of Nashville, where she first heard country music.

At the age of 14 Patsy began performing with local radio personality "Joltin'" Jim McCoy as a singer in his band, the Melody Boys. When country star Wally Fowler was passing through Winchester in 1948, he heard Patsy sing and imme-

PEOPLE IN MUSIC

diately recommended her to the Grand Ole Opry. However, her initial audition for the Opry was unsuccessful.

In 1952 Patsy met another local performer-promoter, Bill Peer. She began touring the South as the vocalist with his band. He arranged for her first recordings to be made in the fall of 1954, with the small Four Star label. Her first sessions failed to produce a hit, but she finally scored in late 1956 with her recording of *Walking after Midnight*. In 1957 she won national recognition on Arthur Godfrey's *Talent Scouts* television program with her rendition of the song.

Cline failed to score a follow-up hit between 1958 and 1960. She then returned to the charts strongly with *I Fall to Pieces*. She followed with her hit 1961 recording of WILLIE NELSON's song *Crazy*. She was at the peak of her popularity in early 1963 when she met her untimely death in an airplane crash that also took the lives of country singers Hawkshaw Hawkins and Cowboy Copas. Her recording of *Sweet Dreams* was a massive hit after her death. In 1973 she was elected to the Country Music Hall of Fame.

Cline was among the first country singers to gain a pop audience as well. She also was the first to wear formal clothing on stage, rather than the cowgirl outfits of boots and frilly jackets that were the normal stage attire for female singers. Her strong voice inspired countless other singers, including a young LORETTA LYNN, whom she befriended, and the Canadian singer k.d. lang, who named her band the *Re-Clines* in Cline's memory.

Clock, The (*Die Uhr*). Symphony No. 101 in D Major by FRANZ JOSEPH HAYDN, 1794, written for his London tours. The nickname comes from the pendulumlike accompanying figure in the slow movement.

Clooney, Rosemary, American singer of popular music; b. Maysville, Ky., May 23, 1928. Both Rosemary and her sister, Betty, were talented singers as youngsters, performing at family gatherings and for local functions. The duo made their professional debut on the radio in Cincinnati, where the family had moved when Rosemary was 13. In 1945 the pair auditioned successfully for bandleader Tony Pastor and

PEOPLE IN MUSIC

toured with him for four years. After Betty quit the band, Rosemary continued as a soloist.

Clooney made her first solo recording in 1946, but scored her first hit in 1951 with *Come On-A My House.* She scored a number of pop hits over the next five years, as well as appearing on her own television program. In 1953 she began a film career; her best-remembered role is as the female lead in the Bing Crosby film *White Christmas,* in 1954.

Clooney's career went quickly downhill in the 1960s. A long-standing dependence on drugs resulted in a mental collapse in 1968. However, she resumed her career in 1976. From that point to today, she has primarily performed at nightclubs, drawing on a repertoire of jazz standards. She has established herself as one of the great interpreters of American popular song.

cluster. *See* TONE CLUSTER.

***Cockaigne* Overture** ("In London Town"). Concert overture by EDWARD ELGAR, 1901. It depicts a mythical paradise in the north, associated with London, the "city of Cockneys."

Coco. Musical by ANDRÉ PREVIN, 1969. It is based on the life of the Parisian designer Gabrielle "Coco" Chanel. The show's success was due in part to Katharine Hepburn's playing the lead.

coda (It., tail; Ger. *Anhang*). A closing passage after the formal structure of a movement has been fulfilled.

Codas usually are announced by one or more of the following: (1) a strong statement of the DOMINANT harmony (V) in the bass; (2) a rapid acceleration followed by a pronounced RETARD; and (3) a pronounced increase in volume (CRESCENDO) or, conversely, a decrease in volume (DIMINUENDO).

Coffee Cantata. Secular CANTATA by JOHANN SEBASTIAN BACH, 1732. It is unique among his works in being a vocal composition in a style of OPERA BUFFA (comic opera).

When it was written, coffee was still regarded, along with tobacco, as a dangerous product. The cantata deals

In the *Coffee Cantata*, the serious style of Bach's music humorously contradicts the lightness of the subject. It is rare to find musical humor like this in the work of Bach.

with an attempt of the father of a willful young woman to persuade her to abandon her addiction. As a reward he promises to find her a handsome husband and actually produces a candidate. She likes his looks, but she likes drinking coffee even more.

PEOPLE IN MUSIC

Cohan, George M(ichael), celebrated American composer of musicals and popular songs; b. Providence, R.I., July 3 (not, as Cohan believed, July 4), 1878; d. N.Y., Nov. 5, 1942. Cohan was raised in a performing family and took to the stage naturally. Along with his parents and sister Josephine, he performed as a part of the "Four Cohans" on the vaudeville stage. He wrote dramatic sketches for the family to perform. His first song, *Why Did Nellie Leave Home?*, was published when he was 16.

George M. Cohan, c. 1905. (UPI/Corbis-Bettmann) ▶

Cohan married another singer-performer, Ethel Levey, in 1899, and the act was expanded to suit her talents. Two years later he wrote his first Broadway show for the family, *The Governor's Son,* writing both text and music. It was only a modest success, however.

Cohan finally hit pay dirt in 1904 with his show *Little Johnny Jones.* The patriotic story of an American jockey who is accused of taking a bribe to purposely lose the English Derby had immediate audience appeal. The show also produced many hit songs, including *Yankee Doodle Boy* and the standard *GIVE MY REGARDS TO BROADWAY.*

Over the next decade and a half Cohan had a hit a year on Broadway, most following the formula of his first show. All produced popular songs, including *You're a Grand Old Flag, Harrigan,* and the 1917 World War I anthem *Over There,* which earned him a congressional medal.

In the 1920s and '30s Cohan's hit-making days on Broadway slowed. He continued to produce plays and appeared in dramatic parts. He also made a few film appearances, but his appeal did not transfer well to the screen.

The film *Yankee Doodle Dandy* (1942) and the Broadway musical *George M!* (1968) were both based on his life.

Cole, "Cozy" (William Randolph), African-American JAZZ drummer; b. East Orange, N.J., Oct. 17, 1906; d. Columbus, Ohio, Jan. 29, 1981. After taking up the DRUMS while young, Cole began his career in 1928. He played with JELLY ROLL MORTON, Stuff Smith, and others before joining CAB CALLOWAY's band in 1938.

PEOPLE IN MUSIC

Cole appeared on Broadway in 1943 in the musical *CARMEN JONES,* displaying his expertise in the number *Beat Out Dat Rhythm on a Drum.* He also appeared in the 1945 production of *The Seven Lively Arts* with BENNY GOODMAN's Quintet. He later played with LOUIS ARMSTRONG and then formed his own band, which toured Africa in 1962. From 1969 to 1976 he was also a member of the Jonah Jones Quintet. In the later 1970s he was artist-in-residence at Capital University in Columbus, Ohio.

Cole, Nat "King" (born Nathaniel Adams Coles), beloved African-American pianist and singer; b. Montgomery, Ala., Mar. 17, 1917; d. Santa Monica, Calif., Feb. 15, 1965. Cole's father was a minister in the First Baptist Church of Montgomery, and his mother served as choir director and pianist there. The family moved in 1921 to Chicago, where Cole's mother taught him to play the piano. He also had the chance to hear many local JAZZ pianists.

PEOPLE IN MUSIC

Cole's first professional job came as a pianist with a revival touring company of *Shuffle Along.* The company ran out of money in Los Angeles, where Cole landed a club job. In 1939 he formed his first trio, which featured piano, guitar, and bass, but no drums—an innovation for a small jazz group at that time.

Cole's first hit came in 1943 with his humorous vocal on *Straighten Up and Fly Right.* However, it was his 1946 recording of *The Christmas Song* ("Chestnuts roasting on an open fire . . .") that established him on the pop charts.

Cole combined an easy-to-listen-to vocal style with a subdued jazz feeling, the perfect combination for the conservative 1950s. He began the decade with a massive hit, *Mona Lisa,* and followed through the years with many more popular hits in a similar style. He also became a regular performer on radio and television, an unusual accomplishment for an African-American singer at the time, and made a few movie appearances.

Cole died of lung cancer in 1965. His daughter, Natalie (b. Los Angeles, Calif., Feb. 6, 1950), established a career as a popular singer in the 1980s and '90s.

PEOPLE IN MUSIC

Coleman, Cy (born Seymour Kaufman), American composer of popular music; b. N.Y., June 14, 1929. Coleman studied at the N.Y. College of Music and began his career as a composer for radio and television. With the lyricist Joseph A. McCarthy he composed the songs *I'm Gonna Laugh You out of My Life* and *Why Try to Change Me Now?* To the words of Carolyn Leigh he wrote the song *Witchcraft,* which became a hit for FRANK SINATRA.

Coleman is primarily known for a long-running career as a Broadway composer. He wrote the MUSICAL *Wildcat* (1960), best remembered for the song *Hey, Look Me Over; Little Me* followed in 1962. He achieved further success with *Sweet Charity,* composed in 1966, to the lyrics of Dorothy Fields. Fields and Coleman again collaborated for the hit musical *Seesaw* (1973). Among his later works were *I Love My Wife* (1977), *On the Twentieth Century* (1978), *Barnum* (1980), and *City of Angels* (1989).

PEOPLE IN MUSIC

Coleman, Ornette, African-American JAZZ alto saxophonist and composer, innovator of a radically new free-style form of IMPROVISATION; b. Fort Worth, Tex., Mar. 9, 1930. Coleman was largely self-taught, serving his apprenticeship playing in carnival and RHYTHM AND BLUES bands.

In the later 1950s Coleman, then living in Los Angeles, began experimenting with a new form of jazz along with trumpeter DON CHERRY. In 1958 the quartet was hired to play a two-week engagement at N.Y.'s famous jazz club, the Five Spot. The group was so controversial that it ended up staying at the club for over four years. It also led to the land-mark recording *Free Jazz,* a name that would be given to Coleman's new style. The quartet entered the studio with no arrangements; even the HARMONY was left up to chance. In-stead, they freely improvised, listening to each other play and developing complementary parts based on what they heard.

In the mid-1960s Coleman went into semi-retirement as a performer, turning his attention to writing concert pieces and film scores. He continued to record with a variety of players. Coleman returned to performing in the mid-1970s with a jazz-rock FUSION band called Prime Time, featuring ELECTRIC GUITARS and a ROCK rhythm section. Coleman has continued to perform with various bands using this name through the 1990s.

Coleman has developed his own unique and complex music theory, which he calls "harmolodics." He has also written concert music in a modern style. Among his works are *Forms and Sounds* for woodwind quintet (1965), *Skies of America* for orchestra (1972), and *Sex Spy* (1977).

Coleridge-Taylor, Samuel, esteemed English composer of African descent (his father was a native of Sierra Leone, his mother English); b. London, Aug. 15, 1875; d. Croydon, Sept. 1, 1912. Coleridge-Taylor studied violin at the Royal College of Music in 1890, then won a composition scholar-ship in 1893. In 1903 he formed a successful amateur string orchestra, later adding professional woodwind and brass. In 1898 he was appointed a violin teacher at the Royal Acad-emy of Music. In 1903 he became a professor of composi-tion at Trinity College in London and in 1910 at the Guild-hall School. From 1904 to 1912 he was conductor of the London Handel Society.

Coleridge-Taylor made three concert tours of the U.S. in 1904, 1906, and 1910, conducting his own works. From the beginning his compositions showed an individuality that

PEOPLE IN MUSIC

rapidly won them recognition, and his short career was watched with interest. His most successful work was the trilogy *The Song of Hiawatha,* including *Hiawatha's Wedding Feast* (1898), *The Death of Minnehaha* (1899), and *Hiawatha's Departure* (1900), which was given its first complete performance in Washington, D.C., in 1904.

collage. *See* MUSIQUE-CONCRÈTE

collective composition. The practice of assigning the composition of an OPERA or another large work to several composers.

Collective composition is frequently used by writers of popular MUSICAL COMEDIES. Sometimes several names are given as composer of a successful song.

During the early years of the communist government in Russia, the idea of musical collectivism fascinated student composers at the Moscow Conservatory. They formed the Productive Collective of Student Composers of the Moscow Conservatory (PROCOLL). Its announced aim was to represent the collectivism of the masses. Chinese musicians have also contributed to musical collectivism. The *Yellow River* Concerto for Piano and Orchestra, produced by the Beijing Opera Troupe in Shanghai, was purportedly written by a committee. Several Chinese revolutionary operas have been produced without giving credit to their composers. *See also* PASTICCIO.

Collegium musicum (Lat.). A group organized to make music for pleasure. The first collegium musicum was formed in 1616 in Prague. A similar group was organized by Bach in Leipzig. A contemporary description of the collegium musicum in Frankfurt in 1718 stated that its purpose was "to quicken the spirit after a day of work by providing innocent pastime." At such gatherings, amateur musicians were given an opportunity to play instrumental music and discuss musical matters.

The practice was revived in colleges and universities in Europe and America in the 20th century, primarily with the purpose of studying and reviving EARLY MUSIC.

The composers GEORGE FRIDERIC HANDEL, Giovanni Bononcini, and Filippo Amadei wrote one act each for the opera *Muzio Scevola* for a London performance in 1721. It served as a test of excellence, which Handel apparently won. The brothers Paul and Lucien Hillemacher collaborated on a number of operas and even adopted a joint signature, P. L. Hillemacher.

colophane. ROSIN applied to the hair of string instrument BOWS to make them more sticky.

colophon. Inscription at the end of a manuscript giving information regarding its production.

color. 1. TIMBRE. 2. In 14th- and 15th-century ISORHYTHMIC music, a repeated pitch pattern.

color hearing. A supposed natural relationship between sound and color. For centuries, scientists and musicians have claimed that certain sounds are associated with certain colors. The first scientific (or pseudo-scientific) treatment of this supposed association was given by the English rationalist philosopher John Locke in *An Essay Concerning Human Understanding* (1690). An English ophthalmologist, Theodore Woolhouse, drew an arbitrary table of sounds and colors, asserting, for instance, that the sound of a trumpet is red. The magic number seven determined both the number of degrees in the diatonic scale and the number of colors of the spectrum as outlined by Isaac Newton.

If a true correspondence existed between tones and sounds, then the chromatic scale should follow the spectrum from red to violet, from low to high frequency of vibrations, which apparently is not the case.

Alexander Scriabin inserted a part for a color organ in the score of his last orchestral work, *Promethée*. It would fill the concert hall with changing colors corresponding to the pitches in the score.

coloratura (It.). 1. An ornamental passage in opera consisting of rapid runs and TRILLS, often applied in CADENZAS and occurring in the highest register. Coloratura is intended to show off the brilliance of a composition and the singer's skill. A coloratura SOPRANO is a soprano singer capable of performing these virtuoso passages.

Famous examples are in the aria of the Queen of the Night in WOLFGANG AMADEUS MOZART'S *THE MAGIC FLUTE,* and in GIUSEPPE VERDI'S *RIGOLETTO.* NIKOLAI RIMSKY-KORSAKOV wrote a highly chromatic coloratura part for the Queen of Shemaha in *LE COQ D'OR.* Tenor roles may also fall into this category.

2. A similar passage in instrumental music.

kōh-lōh-răh-too′răh

Colour Symphony, A. Orchestral work by SIR ARTHUR BLISS, 1922. The colors of the movements are heraldic, not instrumental: *Purple, Red, Blue,* and *Green.*

Coltrane, John (William), remarkable African-American JAZZ musician, a virtuoso on the tenor saxophone; b. Hamlet, N.C, Sept. 23, 1926; d. Huntington, Long Island, N.Y., July 17, 1967. Coltrane was raised by his maternal grandfather, who was a minister. He began clarinet lessons in grade school; his school bandleader recommended that he switch to the alto saxophone. When Coltrane's grandfather died, he went to Philadelphia to live with his mother and studied classical clarinet briefly at local conservatories.

PEOPLE IN MUSIC

John Coltrane. (Courtesy New York Public Library) ▶

After serving in the Navy in World War II, Coltrane began playing with various jazz bands, landing a job with DIZZY GILLESPIE's band in 1949. It was while playing with Gillespie that he was exposed to BEBOP music and switched to tenor saxophone.

Coltrane came into his own in the 1950s. In 1955 he played briefly with MILES DAVIS, establishing himself, along with SONNY ROLLINS, as the leading saxophonist of his generation. He then worked briefly with the eccentric pianist THELONIOUS MONK. In 1957 he returned to Philadelphia and put together the first of his own quartets.

The group had its first success with the album *Giant Steps,* recorded in 1960 and featuring Coltrane's incredible, high-speed soloing. Coltrane also made waves by recording an unusual version of the pop song *My Favorite Things,* which became a minor hit for him.

In the mid-1960s, Coltrane began showing an interest in African and Asian traditional music, along with an interest in Eastern philosophy. He recorded the more improvisational albums *A Love Supreme* and *Ascension* during this period. In 1966 he also married the keyboardist Alice McLeod, who would continue his musical legacy after his death.

Since Coltrane's death in 1967, his recorded legacy has continued to be influential on jazz and ROCK musicians.

Columbia, the Gem of the Ocean. Song of uncertain ancestry, dating from the mid-19th century. It is known in England under the title *Britannia, the Pride of the Ocean.* However, several early editions were published under the title *Red, White and Blue,* which are, of course, the colors of both the American and British flags. The American composer CHARLES IVES often quoted this melody in his music.

Combattimento di Tancredi e Clorinda, Il (The combat between Tancredi and Clorinda). Dramatic "MADRIGAL of war" by CLAUDIO MONTEVERDI, 1624. It is based on the episode from the Italian poet Tasso's *Gerusalemme liberata,* in which a Christian crusader unintentionally kills his Persian lover.

combination tones. Tones that are generated when two notes are played simultaneously very loudly. Such PARASITE tones are of two types: DIFFERENTIAL and SUMMATION tones. If the two sounding pitches have frequencies of 440 Hz and 300 Hz, for instance, the differential tone would have a frequency of 130 Hz, or the difference between the two original tones, while the summation tone would have a frequency of 740 Hz, or the sum of the two tones.

The differential tone was first noticed by the Italian violin virtuoso GUISEPPE TARTINI, who called it a "wolf" tone.

Comden and Green (Duo: Betty Comden, American musician, lyricist, and dramatist, b. N.Y., May 3, 1915; and Adolph Green, American musician, playwright, and lyricist, b. N.Y., Dec. 2, 1915.)

PEOPLE IN MUSIC

Both Comden and Green were struggling actors when they met in N.Y. City in the mid-1930s. To find work, they formed a trio with another then-unknown performer, Judy Holliday, and began performing comic songs and sketches. Comden and Green first collaborated on material for their group, which they called the Revuers.

The composer LEONARD BERNSTEIN heard them perform and invited them to help him adapt his ballet score FANCY FREE into a stage MUSICAL. The result was the hit 1944 Broadway show *On the Town* (which was also made into a movie). This success led to many other Broadway shows, including BELLS ARE RINGING (1956), which reunited them with Holliday.

Comden and Green also established a career in Hollywood, beginning with the wonderful score for the Gene Kelly film *Singing in the Rain* (1952). The duo had a few more Broadway successes in the last decades, including 1970's *Applause, On the Twentieth Century* from 1978, and 1991's *The Will Rogers Follies*. They have also performed together as a nightclub act.

Come Home, Father. A tear-jerking ballad by HENRY CLAY WORK, 1864. A dying child begs his dad to come home from an extended drinking bout. It was featured in the melodrama *Ten Nights in a Barroom*.

comédie-ballet. A type of dramatic performance developed by the composer JEAN-BAPTISTE LULLY and the playwright Molière for the court of Louis XIV. Two of their works in this style were *Les plaisirs de l'île enchantée* (1664) and *Le bourgeois gentilhomme* (1670). The comédie-ballet included, besides the dialogue and BALLET, ARIAS and choral pieces.

coh′mās **comes** (Lat., from *companion*). Answer to the SUBJECT (DUX) in a FUGUE or CANON. It is also known as *riposta*.

comic opera. Opera with a comic subject. In its original usage, the term simply applied to any stage work dealing with human (as opposed to divine) subjects. However, in contemporary usage, comic operas must necessarily include elements of comedy. The comic operas of GILBERT AND SULLIVAN are typical in this respect.

Historically, comic opera was the opposite of OPERA SERIA. However, composers through the centuries were not consistent in attaching the description of comic opera or opera seria to their works. Even such an unquestionably tragic opera as WOLFGANG AMADEUS MOZART'S *DON GIOVANNI* bore the description *dramma giocoso* (jocose drama).

Comin' thro the Rye. A Scottish song with a text by ROBERT BURNS. The song was the source for the title of J. D. Salinger's novel *The Catcher in the Rye.*

comma. The Greek term for the tiny difference between corresponding PITCHES generated by contrasting tuning schemes. For instance, in PYTHAGOREAN tuning the last of 12 PERFECT FIFTHS above C (i.e., B♯) differs from the seventh OCTAVE above C (i.e., another C) by a minute INTERVAL less than one-fourth of a SEMITONE. EQUAL TEMPERAMENT was devised to circumvent this discrepancy.

commedia dell'arte (It., artistic play). An Italian genre of theatrical performance that emerged during the RENAISSANCE. It incorporated elements of pantomime, acrobatics, masks, music, and dance. Most of the action was improvised, but the main characters were almost always the same.

Some composers have used these characters in their own OPERAS and BALLETS, e.g., RUGGERO LEONCAVALLO with *PAGLIACCI,* and IGOR STRAVINSKY with *PETRUSHKA* and *PULCINELLA.*

commedia per music (It., play with music). An early designation for OPERA, not necessary comic.

commercials, singing. Short melodic phrases used in the marketing of consumer products.

common time. A duple or quadruple METER in which one MEASURE contains of two HALF NOTES or four QUARTER NOTES. The TIME SIGNATURE may be represented by a capital

As used by French composers, comic operas are any operas with spoken dialogue. Thus, BIZET'S *CARMEN,* a tragic story, is called a comic opera because of the presence of dialogue along with the singing.

After a while, the stock characters in the commedia dell'arte were given standard names. They were Pantalone, a difficult old man; Columbine, his beautiful daughter; Harlequin, her lover, usually a handsome young man whom Pantalone despises; Punchinello, a grotesque clown with a big nose; and Scaramouche, a pompous soldier.

Nicolas Slonimsky, the famous Russian composer and musicologist, claimed to have written some of the earliest singing commercials in 1925. He took his texts from advertisements in the

C, derived from the semicircle that served as the medieval symbol for duple time.

compact disc (abbrev., CD, disc). Developed in the early 1980s, the CD has replaced the LP (long-playing record) as the most popular recording medium. The CD stores recorded music in digital format.

Company. Musical by STEPHEN SONDHEIM, 1970. A bachelor confronts both the marital woes of his friends and his ambivalent feeling towards bachelorhood. Includes the title song, *Side by Side by Side, What Would We Do without You?, Ladies Who Lunch, Being Alive,* and *I'm Not Getting Married.*

comparative musicology (Ger. *vergleichende Musikwissenschaft*). The original term for ETHNOMUSICOLOGY.

compass. The range of a voice or instrument, i.e., the SCALE of all the tones it can produce, from the lowest to the highest.

complement (complementary interval). Two INTERVALS that, when added together, make up an OCTAVE. A PERFECT FOURTH is the complement of a PERFECT FIFTH, a MINOR THIRD of a MAJOR SIXTH, and so forth.

complin(e) (from Lat., *completorium*, completion). A short, early evening service, one of the CANONICAL HOURS of the Roman Catholic liturgy.

Tinctoris, the author of the first dictionary of music, describes the composer as a writer of a new melody. Later theorists drew the distinction between *compositio*, a conscious act of composing, and *sortisatio*, a random improvisation.

composer (from Lat., *componere*, put things together; Ger. *Komponist*). A person who writes music and transmits it by written or oral means. The musical sense of the term is at least 1,000 years old. GUIDO D'AREZZO includes it in his Latin treatise *Micrologus,* establishing the necessary properties for a melody to be well "put together" (*componenda*). The medieval Latin term for "composer" was *compositor,* the word that is now reserved in English for typesetters. However, the designation *compositor* is preserved in Spanish in its original Latin sense.

Although the rules for composition have varied enormously through the centuries, these differences have not altered the basic definition of a composer as a person who puts notes together in a more or less logical and coherent manner.

composition (Ger. *Tonkunst, Tonsatz*). The broadest term for writing music in any form for any instruments or voices. Also, the music so written.

compound meters. 1. Any TIME SIGNATURE that combines two SIMPLE meters. For example, $\frac{5}{4}$ is the sum of $\frac{2}{4}$ plus $\frac{3}{4}$; $\frac{7}{4}$ equals $\frac{4}{4}$ plus $\frac{3}{4}$, and so forth. 2. A meter with a triple pulse within each of its BEATS; e.g., $\frac{6}{8}$ and $\frac{12}{8}$.

computer. A programmable electronic device that stores, retrieves, and processes data in digital form. Computers can be used by composers and theorists to calculate details of compositions, store information for subsequent use, or generate new sounds (or transform existing ones).

computer music. Music generated by COMPUTER, whether directly, through interaction with live instruments, or as the product of precompositional data.

For many centuries theorists and composers cherished the notion that beautiful melodies and harmonies could be produced by mathematical means. It was only natural that when digital computers were perfected in the middle of the 20th century, musicians began to explore using them to create new musical resources.

Digital computers and other electronic devices could not produce any output more valuable than the input fed into the computer by human programmers. Programming a computer by a series of numbers is no different from the process of writing notes on paper. In one of the earliest computerized compositions, with a relatively primitive computer called Illiac, two programmers (including LEJAREN HILLER) produced an *Illiac Suite,* which ended with a lengthy coda in C major.

More recently, the composer David Cope has developed a sophisticated computer program that can imitate the styles of well-known composers such as JOHANN SEBASTIAN BACH or WOLFGANG AMADEUS MOZART. Listeners have been unable to distinguish some of these pieces from "real" compositions by those composers.

Computers have many other uses for the student of music. Typesetting programs enable SCORES and TABLATURE to be produced quickly and economically. Analysis of musical scores can be done so that common themes can be identified and patterns of notes or rhythms isolated. And special software can be used to ORCHESTRATE original compositions.

Comte Ory, Le (Count Ory). Opera by GIOACCHINO ROSSINI, 1828, produced in Paris. This was the first of Rossini's two operas to French texts. The story deals with an evil count's attempt to seduce a woman whose husband is out on a Crusade.

concert. A musical performance in the presence of an AUDIENCE.

Public concerts were first organized in Italy in the early 17th century. Solo performances and chamber ensemble concerts were popular in London in the 18th century. In France a series of concerts was organized in 1725 under the name Concert Spirituel. In the 19th century concerts became part of cultural life in every part of the world.

The word *recital* for a solo concert came into vogue in the middle of the 19th century, invented by FRANZ LISZT's London manager. Regular SYMPHONY concerts were organized in Paris in 1828, later spreading to England, Russia, and throughout Europe.

concert overture. An OVERTURE for full ORCHESTRA, performed as an independent composition at a SYMPHONY concert.

concert pitch. The actual sound produced by an instrument, as distinct from a written note in transposing instruments. Thus, for the B♭ clarinet, the written note C sounds B♭.

As for the pitch itself, the 440 Hz frequency for a^1 (A above MIDDLE C) now considered standard has not always been the standard. Pitch has been consistently on the rise for more than a century. As recently as the 1930s, concert pitch was not standardized, and competing orchestras would be unable to play together.

If WOLFGANG AMADEUS MOZART were to come back to life and hear his C-major *Jupiter* Symphony, to his ear it would sound like it was in D♭.

Concert Spirituel. A famous series of concerts in Paris, 1725. The concerts, given on religious holidays when the opera house was closed, featured both secular and sacred music.

concertante (It.). 1. A concert piece. 2. A composition or section of a composition for two or more solo voices or instruments with accompaniment by orchestra or organ. Each soloist is given a prominent section to perform in turn. 3. A composition for two or more unaccompanied solo instruments in orchestral music, often called a SINFONIE CONCERTANTE.

Concertante style, a style admitting of a brilliant display of skill on the soloist's part.

köhn-chär-tähn′těh

concerted music. Music written in parts for several instruments or voices, i.e., TRIOS, QUARTETS, etc.

concertina. A FREE-REED instrument with two hexagonal or octagonal (eight-sided) ends, each with a button keyboard and handle, connected by expandable bellows. The instrument was patented by Charles Wheatstone in 1829 and 1844.

Two basic types of concertina have been popular. In the fully chromatic English system, each button produces the same note on the extension and compression of the bellows. In the German-Anglo system, each button produces one pitch on the extension and a different pitch on the compression on a principle similar to the HARMONICA.

Concertinas come in registers ranging from soprano to double bass. Its repertory has included classical, light classical, novelty, and traditional music.

MUSICAL INSTRUMENT

concertino (It.; Ger. *Konzertstück*). 1. A small CONCERTO, scored for a small ensemble. 2. The group of soloists in a CONCERTO GROSSO.

concertmaster (from Ger. *Konzertmeister;* U.K. *leader;* Fr. *premiere violon, chef d'attaque;* It. *violino primo;* Sp. *concertino*). The first VIOLIN player in an ORCHESTRA.

kŏhn-châr'tōh

The history of the term *concerto* is subject to debate. The most logical origin is from the Latin verb *concertare* (to compete, to contend with one another). Another conjecture is that *concerto* comes from the Latin verb *conserere* (to come together). In fact, the spelling *conserto* is found in some 17th-century Italian manuscripts.

A special type of piano concerto is written for left hand alone. Many of these works were commissioned by the noted concert pianist Paul Wittgenstein, who lost his right arm on the Russian front in World War I. MAURICE RAVEL, RICHARD STRAUSS, SERGEI PROKOFIEV, and several other composers obliged him with one-armed works.

concerto (It.). An extended composition for a solo instrument (or instruments) and orchestra, frequently in a (modified) SONATA form. A concerto for orchestra with a group of soloists is called CONCERTO GROSSO.

The form of the classical concerto is similar to that of a sonata. Most concertos are in three movements, most commonly fast-slow-fast. The chief characteristic of a concerto is *antiphony*, with the soloist and the orchestra presenting the main themes in alternation.

Many concerti open with some type of introduction stated by the entire ensemble, though piano concerti sometimes open with a solo passage. A striking example is LUDWIG VAN BEETHOVEN's Fourth Piano Concerto in G Major. SERGEI RACHMANINOFF's Second Piano Concerto opens with a short prelude in the solo part, letting the orchestra present the main theme.

Numerically, piano concertos are in the majority. Composers who are pianists themselves naturally give preference to their own instrument. Modern piano concertos tend to be more compact than their ROMANTIC predecessors. Following the example of FRANZ LISZT's concertos, they are often compressed into a single MOVEMENT subdivided into several sections that allow changes of TEMPO and character.

The number of violin concertos is almost as large as that of piano concertos. Antonio Vivaldi and other BAROQUE composers wrote hundreds of them. Among cello concertos of the CLASSIC period, those by Franz Joseph Haydn and Luigi Boccherini are well established. The viola is the orphan of the string family, because few composers have been charitable enough to write concertos for the instrument. In modern times, however, PAUL HINDEMITH and WILLIAM WALTON contributed viola concertos, and BÉLA BARTÓK was working on one at the time of his death. Conductor SERGE KOUSSEVITZKY wrote a concerto for double bass, an instrument on which he was a virtuoso.

In the woodwind department there are concertos for practically every instrument. JOHANN JOACHIM QUANTZ, court flutist for FREDERICK THE GREAT, wrote dozens of flute concertos for himself and for his patron to play. There is an oboe concerto by Leon Goossens that he wrote for his brother, an oboe virtuoso, and one by RICHARD STRAUSS, written in his later years. Clarinet concertos are not lacking in quantity. There are some by WOLFGANG AMADEUS MOZART, CARL MARIA VON WEBER, and CARL NIELSEN, and one by THEA MUSGRAVE, written in an ultramodern idiom. IGOR STRAVINSKY composed an *Ebony Concerto* for clarinet and jazz ensemble. There are several bassoon concertos available for ambitious performers, beginning in the Baroque period. ALEXANDER GLAZUNOV composed a saxophone concerto. FRANZ JOSEPH HAYDN's Trumpet Concerto is a brilliant virtuoso piece, recently recorded by the classical and jazz virtuoso WYNTON MARSALIS. Richard Strauss wrote two concertos for horn and orchestra (his father was a renowned horn player). There are a few scattered trombone concertos. And RALPH VAUGHAN WILLIAMS wrote a concerto for tuba.

Concertos for harp and orchestra are not numerous, but MAURICE RAVEL's *INTRODUCTION AND ALLEGRO* for harp and six other instruments is in effect a harp concerto. CARLOS SALZEDO wrote a harp concerto accompanied by wind instruments. Guitar concertos have been written by the Latin composers MANUEL PONCE, MARIO CASTELNUOVO-TEDESCO, and JOAQUIN RODRIGO. The Russian composer REINHOLD GLIÈRE wrote a concerto for voice and orchestra.

Double concertos are those in which two instruments are soloists on equal standing. The Concerto for Violin, Cello, and Orchestra by JOHANNES BRAHMS is an example. Béla Bartók orchestrated his Sonata for two pianos and percussion into a Concerto for Two Pianos and Orchestra. The category of triple concerto is represented by JOHANN SEBASTIAN BACH's mighty Concerto for Three Harpsichords and Orchestra, and by Ludwig van Beethoven's Concerto for Violin, Cello, Piano and Orchestra.

LOUIS SPOHR wrote a quadruple concerto for string quartet and orchestra. However, such multiple concertos effectively cross the line between solo concertos and the CONCERTO GROSSO.

concerto, sacred. *See* SACRED CONCERTO.

concerto for orchestra. A symphonic work in which the orchestral instruments play the role of soloists in free rotation. The pioneering work of this type is BÉLA BARTÓK's, from 1943.

Of the many exotic concerti written, perhaps none are more unusual than HENRY COWELL's concerto for the Japanese koto. There is even a concerto for kazoo, by the American composer Mark Bucci.

kŏhn-châr′tōh grô′sōh

concerto grosso (It., grand concerto). An instrumental composition employing a small group of solo instruments (CONCERTINO, "little group") within a larger group or full ORCHESTRA (RIPIENO, "filling up"). This essentially BAROQUE genre differs from a solo CONCERTO because of the nature of the concertino, functioning as a multiple soloist, alternating with the ripieno, also designated by the Italian term TUTTI (all, every instrument). The concertino usually has two violins and a cello, with the harpsichord furnishing the BASS harmony. The tutti consist of a fairly large ensemble of strings supplemented by trumpets, flutes, oboes, and horns.

The earliest works in this genre were ARCANGELO CORELLI's *Concerti Grossi con duoi violini e violoncello di concertino obbligati e duoi altri violini, e viola, e basso di concerto grosso ad arbitrio,* probably composed in 1680 but not published until much later. GIUSEPPE TORELLI, another early Italian violinist, wrote a group of concerti grossi about 1690.

The concerto grosso was further developed by ANTONIO VIVALDI. It consisted of three movements: *Allegro, Adagio, Allegro.* JOHANN SEBASTIAN BACH's *Brandenburg* Concertos are basically of the concerto grosso type, but Bach often added a wider variety of instruments to the concertino parts in the manner of a solo concerto. GEORGE FRIDERIC HANDEL's concerti grossi observe the Corellian model more strictly than the concertos of Bach.

In the second half of the 18th century, with the growing tendency toward classical symphonic forms, the concerto grosso evolved into the SYMPHONIE CONCERTANTE and eventually into a full-fledged SYMPHONY without individual solo groups. In the 19th century the concerto grosso was virtually obsolete, and it was left to the 20th century to revive the concerto grosso in the original Baroque form. A typical example is Max Reger's *Konzert im alten Stil* (Concerto in the old style), in which the Baroque structure is tinted with Romantic colors. ERNEST BLOCH's Concerto Grosso No. 1 for strings and piano obbligato (1924 – 25) has enjoyed periods of favor.

Concerto in F. Piano CONCERTO by GEORGE GERSHWIN, 1925, in three movements, full of JAZZ rhythms and harmonies.

concord. Euphony; HARMONY; CONSONANCE.

Concord **Sonata.** The second multimovement piano sonata by CHARLES IVES, 1915, subtitled *Concord, Mass.: 1840–60.* Its four movements, *Emerson, Hawthorne, The Alcotts,* and *Thoreau,* are named after writers who lived in or near Concord.

Ives published the *Concord* Sonata at his own expense in 1920. The difficulties of the music were insurmountable to ordinary piano virtuosi, and it took the stamina and perseverance of John Kirkpatrick to give its first complete performance in N.Y. in 1939. Eventually the work became a standard, performed by a number of pianists in America and Europe.

As with many Ives works, there is no definitive edition of the *Concord* Sonata. Kirkpatrick had hoped to create one, but he died before he could complete the project.

concrete music. *See* MUSIQUE CONCRÈTE.

conducting. The art of rehearsing and directing a large EN-SEMBLE.

When a number of singers or instrumentalists perform together, it is convenient to have a leader whose function is to give the signal to begin the music and to indicate the TEMPO. In BAROQUE practice, it was usually up to the *maestro al cembalo* (master at the keyboard) to perform this job. When performing groups evolved into multimusical bodies, the first violinist usually initiated the proceedings with a motion of his violin BOW.

An alternative was for the composer-conductor to beat time on the desk with a small stick or a roll of paper, occasionally emphasizing the beat by stamping his foot on the floor, or by using a long cane to accomplish the same effect.

The present tradition of conducting with a wooden BA-TON originated early in the 19th century. FELIX MENDELSSOHN mentions in one of his letters that he conducted an ORCHESTRA in London "with a white stick." Although the baton is the emblem of the art of conducting, some conductors found it convenient to dispense with it and lead an orchestra with their bare hands. The Russian conductor Wass-

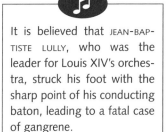

It is believed that JEAN-BAP-TISTE LULLY, who was the leader for Louis XIV's orchestra, struck his foot with the sharp point of his conducting baton, leading to a fatal case of gangrene.

ily Safonoff was the first to become batonless, and he said that in abandoning the baton, he acquired ten batons with his fingers. LEOPOLD STOKOWSKI did away with the baton during his entire U.S. career and made an eloquent use of his aristocratic fingers.

In the early days of professional conducting, it was not unusual for conductors to face the audience rather than the orchestra, and indeed it would have been regarded as impolite to turn one's back to the public. But since this made it virtually impossible for the conductor to control his players, the orchestral leaders gradually decided to "face the music." Yet as late as 1925 Walter Damrosch would turn toward the public for the grand finale in LUDWIG VAN BEETHOVEN'S FIFTH SYMPHONY.

As with many branches of music, it was in Germany that the art of conducting was formalized. A whole generation of conductors set the tradition of "dictators of the baton," commanding their players in the manner of a feudal lord ordering about his slaves. HANS VON BÜLOW was famous for his Prussian brutality toward the players. A typical anecdote deals with his dislike of two members of his orchestra named Schultz and Schmidt. One day the manager announced to him that Schmidt had died. "And Schultz?" von Bülow asked coldly. Another time he remarked to his soprano soloist that she was not pretty enough to sing so badly out of tune.

When major symphony orchestras were organized by unions, the orchestra men began to assert their rights. ARTURO TOSCANINI was probably the last conductor who could afford to hurl insulting words at his orchestra members. At the last rehearsal for his last concert, he shouted at his men: "Imbecili! Tutto è scritto. La più bella musica del mondo!" ("You imbeciles! It's all written in the score! The most beautiful music in the world!")

The art of conducting is the most elusive of musical professions. Ideally, it requires a total mastery of the musical SCORE and an ability to coordinate the players and singers so that they create a harmonious ensemble. The tempo must be established with a wave of the hand that is clear without being obtrusive. The subtlest nuances must be communicated to the players with a gentle motion of the fingers or a suitable facial expression. A common gesture (often immortalized on professional photographs) is to put the index finger of the left hand on the lips to indicate PIANISSIMO. An imperious thrust of the right hand toward the brass section indicates FORTISSIMO.

While a pianist or violinist must practice for years to build even a passable technique, a conductor may begin his career without any preparation, for his instrument is an orchestra on which he cannot practice at home. The basic technique of conducting can be learned in a few lessons. As traditionally established, conductors must give the downbeat on the first beat of the measure, and an upbeat on the second, when the meter is $\frac{2}{4}$. In $\frac{3}{4}$ the stick must describe a triangle. In $\frac{4}{4}$, after the mandatory downbeat, the hand moves northwest, then across to northeast, then at an angle to north, and down south for the next downbeat. Other meters combine these fundamental motions.

Whatever the technique used by a professional conductor, his or her prime duty is to translate the written notes in an orchestral score into an effective panorama of sound, faithfully rendering the composer's creative designs.

Paradoxically, composers are rarely the best interpreters of their own works. Perhaps only RICHARD WAGNER, HECTOR BERLIOZ, GUSTAV MAHLER, and LEONARD BERNSTEIN, all excellent conductors in their own right, gave full justice to their own masterpieces. PIOTR ILYICH TCHAIKOVSKY conducted his passionate music in a singularly pedestrian manner. NIKOLAI RIMSKY-KORSAKOV never knew how to bring out the brilliant sounds of his operatic suites in actual performance. CLAUDE DEBUSSY lacked the sensitivity required to project the impressionistic colors of his scores when he was called upon to act as composer-conductor. MAURICE RAVEL was so uncertain on the podium that he was content with just managing to finish beating time when the orchestra played the last bar of his score. No wonder then that composers must have their interpreters, much as presidents must have their speechwriters. It is in this sense that one talks about "Toscanini's Beethoven," "Walter's Mozart," or "Furtwängler's Brahms."

In the 19th century the majority of conductors were Germans. They filled the ranks not only in Germany and Central Europe but also in Scandinavia, Russia, England, and the U.S. When Major Henry Lee Higginson decided to finance the Boston Symphony Orchestra in 1881, he stipulated that conductors must be German by origin. It was many years before members of other nationalities—let alone women or members of other ethnic groups—were able to enter the conducting profession. One striking symbol of this change came in the 1970s when two major U.S. orchestras—the N.Y. Philharmonic and the Boston Symphony Orchestra—were led by ZUBIN MEHTA, of Indian background, and SEIJI OZAWA, of Japanese parentage, respectively.

299

conductus (Lat., from *conducere,* to escort). A song genre of the ARS NOVA period; the text is usually sacred and in Latin. Conductus may be MONOPHONIC or POLYPHONIC; when the latter is based on a pre-existing melody, that line is called the TENOR, regardless of range.

As their name indicates, conductus were associated with processions, whether the movements of characters in liturgical drama or the carrying of scripture to the lectern prior to the reading during the MASS.

confinalis. The secondary final tone, usually the DOMINANT, in ecclesiastical MODES. The confinalis of the Dorian mode is particularly important because it corresponds to A, which in the 16th century became the primary tone of the alphabetical SCALE.

conga. An Afro-Cuban ballroom dance in duple time, with a rhythmic anticipation at every second beat.

MUSICAL
INSTRUMENT

conga drum. A long, tapered, barrel-shaped drum with a single head. It is based on African models, but it was developed in Cuba. The drum is played with fingers and palms of the hands. The drums are usually featured in pairs, with the head tightened by a metal rim.

MUSICAL
INSTRUMENT

conical mouthpiece. The deeper, cone-shaped form of mouthpiece for BRASS wind instruments, as opposed to the shallower cupped mouthpiece.

conical tube. An instrument tube that tapers gradually; as opposed to the CYLINDRICAL TUBE, which does not taper.

conjunct degree. The nearest degree in the SCALE (CHROMATIC or DIATONIC) to a given degree. Thus, in the chromatic scale, C♯ is the conjunct degree of C.

Conjunct motion, progression by conjunct degrees or INTERVALS.

Connecticut Yankee, A. Musical by RICHARD RODGERS and LORENZ HART, 1927, a reworking of Mark Twain's social satire about a time traveler ending up in King Arthur's Camelot. Includes *Thou Swell* and *My Heart Stood Still.*

Connotations. Orchestral work by AARON COPLAND, 1962, written for the opening of Philharmonic Hall at Lincoln Center for the Performing Arts in N.Y. This was Copland's first work in which he used 12-TONE COMPOSITION.

consecutive intervals. The progression of two VOICES moving in the same direction at the distance of a perfect FIFTH, strictly forbidden in conventional HARMONY. The progression of consecutive FOURTHS was also not allowed in most cases in two-part COUNTERPOINT. Likewise, consecutive OCTAVES, particularly between the two outer voices, was strictly prohibited, with the exception of course if two voices are mere duplications of one another.

By the early 20th century, the prohibition of these consecutive intervals in free composition had been quietly dropped. Indeed, they were a major component of the IMPRESSIONIST styles.

consequent. In a CANON, the COMES (follower). The part imitating the ANTECEDENT or DUX (LEADER).

conservatoire (Fr.); **conservatorium** (L.); **conservatory** (Eng., abbrev. cons.). A public or private institution for providing practical and theoretical instruction in music.

kŏhn-sâr-vǎh-twar′

Consolations. A cycle of six piano pieces by FRANZ LISZT, 1850, inspired by the romantic musings of the French literary critic Charles Sainte-Beuve. The characteristic epigraph of the cycle is "Notre bonheur n'est qu'un malheur plus ou moins consolé" (Our happiness is nothing but sorrow that is more or less consoled). Four pieces are in E major and two are in D♭ major, which for Liszt symbolized, respectively, the concepts of love and meditation.

console. 1. A structure or table supporting the entire apparatus of a large ORGAN: KEYBOARD, STOPS, and PEDALS. 2. A piece of furniture containing an "entertainment center," which can include a radio, phonograph, tape and/or CD player, and television.

consonance. A combination of two or more TONES, harmonious and pleasing in itself, and requiring no further progression to make it satisfactory. In common practice, consonant intervals include the perfect OCTAVE, FIFTH, and FOURTH, and the major and minor THIRDS and SIXTHS. Consonance is the opposite of DISSONANCE, the latter a combination presumably unpleasant to the ear.

Early in Western musical history only the *perfect consonances* of the octave, fifth, and fourth were considered consonant. Thirds and sixths were cast out as dissonances, and were not accepted as *imperfect consonances* until well into the 13th century.

consort (Lat. *consortium,* congregation). An old English term for an instrumental ENSEMBLE. A *whole consort* consisted of either all wind or all string instruments (e.g., RECORDERS, VIOLS), while a *broken consort* was a mixed group of wind and string instruments. Shakespeare called music played by a broken consort *broken music.*

Consort song, a vocal ensemble, usually a quartet, sometimes accompanied by a broken consort.

constructivism. An early 20th-century Russian movement in which the artwork exhibits a high degree of visible structure, based on geometric or (in music) industrial principles.

Consul, The. Opera by GIAN CARLO MENOTTI, 1950, to his own libretto, first produced in Philadelphia. This is Menotti's most dramatically powerful work, focused on the desperate effort of a couple to escape from an unidentified Fascist country. They are doomed when the Consul (who never appears onstage) of an unnamed great transoceanic nation refuses to grant their visa.

Contes d'Hoffmann, Les. See TALES OF HOFFMANN, THE.

kŏhn-tē′noo-ōh   **continuo** (It.). *See* BASSO CONTINUO. The term is often interchangeable with CEMBALO.

contra- (Lat., It., against). Prefixed to an instrument name, a larger instrument sounding an OCTAVE below the standard size. For example, the CONTRABASSOON sounds an octave lower than the standard BASSOON.

contrabassoon (Brit. double bassoon; Fr. *contre-basson;* It. *contrafagotto;* Ger. *Kontrafagott*). A lower-pitched member of the BASSOON family, sounding an OCTAVE lower than the standard instrument. Like the bassoon, the contrabassoon is bent back on itself. In its present form, established in the 19th century, the tube is 16 feet long (when laid straight).

The first references to the instrument date to the early BAROQUE. Possessed of the same nasal quality as the bassoon, the contrabassoon functioned as a bass instrument in MILITARY BANDS. It is probably for this reason that LUDWIG VAN BEETHOVEN gave the contrabassoon its most famous orchestral moment: the beginning of the military variation in the choral finale of his Symphony No. 9.

contrafactum (from Lat., *contrafacere,* counterfeit, imitate). The fitting of a new text to a preexistent melody. A technique begun in the Middle Ages, it applied more commonly to secular texts grafted to sacred melodies. In the 17th century the practice became known as a parody, not in the current sense of caricature, but as a "near song" (*para-ode*).

contralto (It.). *See* ALTO.

contrapuntal. Pertaining to the art or practice of COUNTERPOINT.

contrary motion. COUNTERPOINT wherein one part moves upward while the other moves downward. In academic terms, this is the preferred type of motion.

contratenor. COUNTERTENOR.

contredanse (Fr.; Ger. *Contratanz, Kontretanz;* It. *contradanza*). A baroque French salon dance similar to the quadrille and related to the English COUNTRY DANCE, usually in duple or compound duple meter ($\frac{6}{8}$). It is believed that

MUSICAL
INSTRUMENT

kŏhn-trăhl′tōh

kŏhn-truh-dahns′

the name is not derived from "counter-dance," but is a corrupted form of "country dance." Indeed, there are in existence collections of *contredanses anglaises,* published in France in the 17th century. LUDWIG VAN BEETHOVEN wrote several contredanses, one for the finale of his EROICA SYMPHONY.

controlled improvisation. Taking pre-existing melodies or themes and reassembling them, following a specific formal design and confined within a period of time. Modern composers such as KARLHEINZ STOCKHAUSEN, LUKAS FOSS, and EARLE BROWN have availed themselves of this manner of composition.

PEOPLE IN MUSIC

Cook, Will Marion, African-American conductor and composer; b. Washington, D.C., Jan. 27, 1869; d. N.Y., July 19, 1944. Cook entered the Oberlin (Ohio) Conservatory to study violin when he was 13, continuing his studies with Josef Joachim in Germany and at the National Conservatory in N.Y. He had a brief career as a concert violinist before devoting himself to composition for the musical theater in N.Y. He was director and composer for the two famous black vaudevillians Bert Williams and George Walker from 1900 to 1908.

Cook founded his own "syncopated" symphony orchestra in 1918, with which he toured extensively. In his later years he was active mainly as a conductor and teacher in N.Y. His best-known MUSICALS are *Clorindy, or The Origin of the Cakewalk* (1898) and *Swing Along* (1929; in collaboration with W. Vodery).

PEOPLE IN MUSIC

Cooke, Sam (born Samuel Cook), African-American balladeer; b. Chicago, Jan. 22, 1931; d. Los Angeles (shot to death), Dec. 11, 1964. Cooke began performing as a youngster. Along with his brother and two sisters, they formed a GOSPEL quartet called the Soul Children. They were popular enough that Cooke attracted the attention of the leader of an adult group, the Highway QCs, who hired him to be lead singer. He next joined the most influential gospel group of the day, the Soul Stirrers, recording and touring with them as lead singer between 1951 and 1956, when Cooke broke away from the group to pursue a mainstream career.

Cook's breakthrough came with his enormous hit *You Send Me* (1956). He followed with many other songs appealing to a wide audience, including *Wonderful World.* His light vocals, good looks, and pop arrangements aided his accession to the pop charts, which generally did not feature the recordings of African-Americans.

Cooke was also among the first African-American artists to form his own record label, producing both his own recordings and those of others beginning in 1962. However, his career was abruptly ended in a mysterious incident in the fall of 1964, when he was gunned down by the manager of a Los Angeles motel. Cooke's last hit was the Civil Rights anthem *A Change Is Gonna Come,* released immediately following his death.

cool jazz. A JAZZ style of the 1950s that developed in reaction to BEBOP. While bebop emphasized fast MELODY lines and group IMPROVISATION, cool jazz was slower and more deliberative. BRASS players in the cool style typically used MUTES and other devices to make their sound less abrasive. Arrangements were carefully worked out and drew on the techniques of classical ORCHESTRATION. A wider variety of instruments was used, again drawing from the classical family (such as baritone saxophone, flute, and French horn). Some of the more classical-oriented experiments in this style were called THIRD STREAM (reflecting a new, third approach that would bridge the gap between jazz and classical music).

Among the most famous cool jazz musicians was MILES DAVIS, who defined the style in his 1948 collaboration with arranger GIL EVANS, *Birth of the Cool.* Saxophonist GERRY MULLIGAN established a pianoless quartet with Chet Baker, as a way of avoiding the hard-driving rhythms of the bebop groups. The Modern Jazz Quartet (with pianist JOHN LEWIS and vibes player MILT JACKSON) developed a musical style that included using BAROQUE COUNTERPOINT in their arrangements. The DAVE BRUBECK Quartet showed the influence of modern composers, such as DARIUS MILHAUD, with whom Brubeck had studied.

PEOPLE IN MUSIC

Aaron Copland, c. 1945.
(Hulton-Deutsch Collection/
Corbis) ▶

Copland time line

1900	Born
1920–24	Studies with Nadia Boulanger at the American Conservatory in Fontainebleau
1925	*Music for the Theater* receives its first performance by the Boston Symphony Orchestra, Serge Koussevitzky conducting
1927	Appears as soloist with the Boston Symphony Orchestra in his Concerto for Piano and Orchestra
1928	Organizes the Copland-Sessions Concerts in N.Y.
1936	Completes *El Salón México*
1938	Completes *Billy the Kid*
1939	Writes first music appreciation book, *What to Listen For in Music*
1940	Joins faculty of the Berkshire Music Center at Tanglewood, Massachusetts

Copland, Aaron, greatly distinguished and exceptionally gifted American composer; b. N.Y., Nov. 14, 1900; d. North Tarrytown, N.Y., Dec. 2, 1990. Copland was educated at the Boys' High School in Brooklyn. He began to study piano with Victor Wittgenstein and Clarence Adler as a young child. In 1917 he took lessons in HARMONY and COUNTERPOINT with Rubin Goldmark in N.Y., and soon began to compose. His first published piece, *The Cat and the Mouse* for piano (1920), subtitled *Scherzo humoristique,* shows the influence of CLAUDE DEBUSSY.

In 1920 Copland entered the American Conservatory in Fontainebleau, near Paris, where he studied composition and orchestration with the famous teacher NADIA BOULANGER. Returning to America in 1924 he lived mostly in N.Y., where he was active as a composer, lecturer, pianist, and organizer in various musical societies.

Copland attracted the attention of the Russian conductor SERGE KOUSSEVITZKY, who was then the leader of the prestigous Boston Symphony Orchestra. Koussevitzky gave the first performance of Copland's early *Music for the Theater* in 1925. He then engaged Copland as soloist in his Concerto for Piano and Orchestra in 1927. The work produced a considerable sensation because of its JAZZ elements. Koussevitzky remained Copland's steadfast supporter throughout his career. In the meantime, Walter Damrosch conducted in N.Y. Copland's Symphony for Organ and Orchestra, with Boulanger as soloist.

Other orchestras and their conductors also performed Copland's music, which gained increasing recognition. Particularly popular were Copland's remarkable works based on folk motifs, *El Salón México* (1933–36) and the American ballets *Billy the Kid* (1938), *Rodeo* (1942), and *Appalachian Spring* (1944), the final work in collaboration with choreographer Martha Graham.

A special place is occupied by Copland's *Lincoln Portrait* for narrator and orchestra (1942), with texts arranged by the composer from speeches and letters of Abraham Lincoln. This work has had a great many performances, with the role of the narrator performed by such notables as Adlai Stevenson and Eleanor Roosevelt. Copland's patriotic FANFARE FOR THE COMMON MAN (1942) achieved tremendous popularity and continued to be played on various occasions for decades. Copland incorporated it into the score of his Third Symphony.

Copland was an important figure in the modern American musical scene, serving on the boards of many organizations that supported young composers and their work, and founding several festivals of new music. He also wrote several books introducing new musical ideas to a wide audience. As a teacher, Copland headed the composition department at the Berkshire Music Center at Tanglewood from 1940 to 1965, and from 1957 to 1965 was chair of its faculty.

About 1955 Copland developed a successful career as a conductor, leading major symphony orchestras in Europe, the U.S., South America, and Mexico. He also traveled to Russia under the auspices of the State Department. In 1982 the Aaron Copland School of Music was created at Queens College of the City University of N.Y. In 1983 he made his last appearance as a conductor in N.Y. His 85th birthday was widely celebrated. Copland attended a special concert given in his honor by ZUBIN MEHTA and the N.Y. Philharmonic, which was televised live by PBS.

As a composer, Copland's early works were modern without forsaking recognizable melody. DISSONANT harmony was used but not to the exclusion of more conventional ones. Syncopated rhythms, drawn from RAGTIME and jazz, gave his music a distinctly American flavor, as did its subject matter.

1942 Completes *Rodeo, Lincoln Portrait,* and *Fanfare for the Common Man*

1944 Completes *Appalachian Spring*

1947 N.Y. Music Critics' Circle Award for his Symphony No. 3

1950 Academy Award for his film score for *The Heiress*

1951–52 Charles Eliot Norton Professor at Harvard University

1971 Receives his tenth honorary doctorate, this one from York University in England

1982 The Aaron Copland School of Music is created at Queens College of the City University of N.Y.

1983 Last public appearance as a conductor

1985 His 85th birthday is celebrated with a special concert by Zubin Mehta and the N.Y. Philharmonic

1986 Receives the National Medal of Arts

1990 Dies

Copland was the recipient of many awards, including a Guggenheim fellowship from 1925–27, the Pulitzer Prize in music for *Appalachian Spring* in 1945, the 1950 Academy Award for the film score *The Heiress*, the 1956

Gold Medal for Music from the American Academy of Arts and Letters, the Presidential Medal of Freedom in 1964, and the National Medal of Arts in 1986. He held numerous honorary doctor's degrees awarded by many universities around the world.

When Russian composer PI-OTR ILYICH TCHAIKOVSKY heard a performance of *Coppélia* in Paris, he wrote to a friend that he felt ashamed of his own ballets.

Later in his life, in works such as his 1950 Piano Quartet and in the score of *Connotations* from 1962, Copland adopted a version of the 12-TONE TECHNIQUE of ARNOLD SCHOENBERG. However, these works did not achieve the mass popularity of his compositions from the 1930s and '40s.

Coppélia. Ballet by LÉO DELIBES, 1870, first produced in Paris. Its subtitle was *La fille aux yeux d'émail* (The girl with enamel eyes). The story is derived from a fairy tale by E. T. A. HOFFMAN. A toymaker named Coppelius creates dolls that are magically lifelike. Of them, the most entrancing is the doll Coppélia. A village youth is so struck with her beauty that he abandons his warm-fleshed human girlfriend, Swanhilda. In a fit of jealousy, Swanhilda accuses Coppélia of stealing her lover, before she realizes that Coppélia is a doll. Swanhilda marries her suitor, and Coppélia and her fellow dolls arrange a celebration.

The first Swanhilda was performed by a 16-year-old ballerina named Giuseppina Bozacchi. Tragically, she fell victim to malaria after a few performances, and even more tragically, the Prussians laid siege to Paris a few weeks after that. But *Coppélia* survived both disasters and became one of the most celebrated ballets of all time. Among separate numbers, there are many pieces drawn from European traditional dance styles, including an energetic MAZURKA, an entrancing WALTZ, an intoxicating CSÁRDÁS, and an impetuous GALOP.

copyright. The legal ownership and thus right to an individual production. It applies to musical compositions and is recognized by the laws of most nations.

The oldest performing rights society is the French Société des Auteurs, Composieurs, et Editeurs de Musique (SACEM), formed in 1851. Although Great Britain passed its first copyright act in 1709, musical works came under its protection much later. In the U.S., copyright was first based on English common law. Purely American laws were passed in 1790, then revised several times until an all-new law was passed in 1976. As new media are developed, such as the Internet and recordable CDs, copyright law has to be changed to meet these new circumstances.

Numerous lawsuits have been fought over popular American songs that were pirated because of inadequate copyright protection. A rather celebrated case is that of the song *HAPPY BIRTHDAY TO YOU,* freely used until a clerk in a Chicago music company discovered that the tune was written by two sisters, Patty and Mildred Hill, to a different set of words ("Good morning, dear teacher"). The Western Union Company, which made use of the tune for its singing birthday telegrams, had to pay a substantial sum of money for the newly discovered copyright.

Once a copyright lapses, whether by intent, accident, or legal limit, a composition enters public domain and may be performed without copyright payment.

Coq d'or, Le (The golden cockerel). Opera in three acts by NIKOLAI RIMSKY-KORSAKOV, 1909, produced after his death in Moscow. The libretto is drawn from a fairy tale by the Russian poet Alexsandr Pushkin. The story tells of a lazy czar, who employs an astrologer. The astrologer has a magical bird, the golden cockerel of the title, that warns the czar of invading armies. Meanwhile, the czar and his astrologer each seek to win the love of the exotic queen, who sings a famous COLORATURA hymn to the sun. After the jealous czar angrily murders the astrologer, the czar is pecked to death.

When the opera was originally written, everyone knew that the czar portrayed in the title role was a satirical portrait of the real Czar Nicholas II, who had just lost a war with Japan. When the czar's censors demanded changes to the script, Rimsky-Korsakov refused to submit, and the opera was not performed during his lifetime.

Corea, Chick (Armando Anthony), American JAZZ pianist and composer; b. Chelsea, Mass., June 12, 1941. Corea was raised in a musical household, where he had his first training on the piano. He first worked in Latin-jazz bands led by Mongo Santamaria and Willie Bobo in 1962 – 63. In 1964 he joined trumpeter Blue Mitchell's band, remaining with it for two years. With Mitchell, Corea had the opportunity to perform and record his own compositions for the first time. In 1966 he cut his first solo album.

Under the 1976 American law, a work of music or literature passed into the public domain 75 years after the original copyright, so that music published in 1920 would be copyright free in 1996. However, this was extended for another 25 years in 1998 when the Walt Disney Company successfully argued that it should be able to continue to exploit its copyright in the character Mickey Mouse. They were particularly concerned because the character was being illegally reproduced on the Internet.

PEOPLE IN MUSIC

In 1968 Corea joined MILES DAVIS' new JAZZ-ROCK fusion group, appearing on such seminal albums as 1969's *Bitches Brew.* In 1970 he left Davis to form the FREE JAZZ group, Circle, which lasted only a year. In 1971 he returned to jazz-rock with the successful band Return to Forever, which he formed with guitarist Al DiMeola, bassist Stanley Clarke, percussionist Airto Moreiro, and vocalist Flora Purim. The group remained together with various personnel through 1980.

Corea also continued to pursue a solo career, playing in a wide variety of styles. He also recorded with other jazz musicians, including vibes player Gary Burton. In 1985 he formed his Akoustic and Elektric Bands to pursue both sides of his musical personality: traditional BEBOP-oriented jazz and jazz-rock.

PEOPLE IN MUSIC

Corelli, Arcangelo, famous Italian violinist and composer; b. Fusignano, near Imola, Feb. 17, 1653; d. Rome, Jan. 8, 1713. Little is known of Corelli's early life, although he apparently studied violin in Bologna and also took lessons in COUNTERPOINT. About 1671 he went to Rome, where he was a violinist at the French Church in 1675. In the beginning of 1679 he played in the orchestra of the Teatro Capranica. Rome remained his chief residence to the end of his life, except for visits to Modena (1689–90) and Naples (1702).

Many unfounded stories have been associated with Corelli's biography. For example, it is not true that in 1672 he went to Paris but was driven out of France by a jealous rival, JEAN-BAPTISTE LULLY. Biographers also mention his stay at the court of the elector of Bavaria in Munich about 1680, but there is no documentary evidence. Equally unfounded is the story that while he was in Naples, a mediocre violinist, Giuseppe Valentini, won the favor of the Roman public so that Corelli returned to Rome a broken man and died shortly afterward.

Quite contrary to these fanciful legends, Corelli enjoyed respect, security, and fame. In Rome he had a powerful protector in Cardinal Benedetto Pamphili. Later he lived in the palace of Cardinal Pietro Ottoboni, conducting weekly concerts that were attended by the elite of Roman society. One of Corelli's admirers was Queen Christina of Sweden, who lived in Rome at the time. Among his pupils were Baptiste Anet, Francesco Geminiani, Pietro Locatelli, and Giovanni Somis.

Corelli was famous as a violin virtuoso and may be regarded as the founder of modern violin technique. He codified the art of proper BOWING and was among the first to use DOUBLE STOPS and CHORDS. As a composer his role in music history is great even though he wrote few works. Only six opus numbers can be definitely attributed to him. His greatest achievement was the creation of the CONCERTO GROSSO, especially the 12 concertos of op.6 (1714), which includes the *Christmas* Concerto in G Minor. GEORGE FRIDERIC HANDEL, who as a young man met Corelli in Rome, was undoubtedly influenced by Corelli's instrumental writing. Corelli was buried in the Pantheon in Rome.

Corigliano, John (Paul), American composer; b. N.Y., Feb. 16, 1938. Corigliano's father, also named John, was CONCERTMASTER of the N.Y. Philharmonic Orchestra from 1943 to 1966 and the San Antonio Symphony. The younger Corigliano studied at Columbia University with OTTO LUENING (B.A., 1959), as well as with Vittorio Giannini at the Manhattan School of Music, and privately with Paul Creston. He was subsequently employed at the radio stations WBAI and WQXR in N.Y. and as assistant director for CBS-TV from 1961 to 1972. He held a Guggenheim fellowship in 1968–69.

In 1971 Corigliano joined the faculty of the Manhattan School of Music and from 1973 taught at Lehman College. From 1987 to 1990 he was composer-in-residence of the Chicago Symphony Orchestra.

Corigliano's style of composition shows a fine capacity for lyrical expression and a strong sense of rhythm, in the tradition of BÉLA BARTÓK and SERGEI PROKOFIEV. Although he is not afraid to employ DISSONANCE in his POLYPHONIC writing, his work is always rooted in traditions of TONALITY.

cornet (Fr. *cornet à pistons;* Ger. *Kornett*). A BRASS instrument of the TRUMPET family, with a smaller CONICAL TUBE

PEOPLE IN MUSIC

MUSICAL INSTRUMENT

and larger CUPPED MOUTHPIECE than the trumpet. The result is a mellower tone and greater technical facility.

The cornet evolved from the old posthorn by the addition of three VALVES. Its range covers two octaves and three tones: It is usually tuned in B♭, so that a written C sounds a whole step lower. It is primarily found in military bands, although early JAZZ performers like LOUIS ARMSTRONG and "KING" OLIVER played it in their small groups.

cornett (It. *cornetto;* Ger. *Zink*). An early wind instrument with a CUPPED MOUTHPIECE like members of the BRASS family but with a wooden body and finger holes similar to the WOODWINDS. Some cornetts are curved to provide a more convenient placement of finger holes.

During the RENAISSANCE there were, besides the standard treble instrument, a high soprano, called *cornettino* (little cornett), and one at tenor pitch, called in Italian *cornone* (big cornett).

The bass size, added to the cornett family in the 16th century, was bent in the shape of a snake to enable the player to reach the appropriate holes. It acquired the majestic and awesome appellation "serpent" but had a melodious tone that was anything but reptilian. Disregarding the curse put on the serpent in the Book of Genesis, the instrument made regular appearances in church music. In France, it bore an explicit designation, *serpent d'église.*

The serpent underwent another change of shape in the 18th century when a section of it was bent back so as to form two adjacent tubes. In this shape it became known as the Russian bassoon.

Other varieties were the English bass horn and the OPHICLEIDE. Eventually, all these quaint instruments lapsed into disuse.

corno (It.; plural, *corni*). *See* HORN.

cornu. A tremendously impressive metal horn of ancient Rome, more than three meters in length. It was curved in the shape of the capital letter *G,* and for this reason known also as *tuba curva.* Two authentic specimens were found in the excavations in Pompeii.

MUSICAL
INSTRUMENT

MUSICAL
INSTRUMENT

The Irish playwright George Bernard Shaw began his career as a newspaper music critic. In signing his pieces, he took the fanciful name of Corno di Bassetto, the Italian for basset horn.

The cornu was used in Rome at ceremonial occasions and was revived during the French Revolution. When the noted French philosopher Voltaire was solemnly reburied in the Pantheon (he died before the Revolution), a special fanfare was played on a modernized re-creation of the cornu.

coro spezzato (It., fragmented chorus; plural, *cori spezzati*). A divided CHORUS, originating in the 16th century. These cori spezzati were used antiphonally (i.e., one group would sing and then another would respond). Sometimes the group parts would overlap. The compositional style for this music is often labeled polychoral. The technique persisted (see, for example, HECTOR BERLIOZ's *Requiem*) and continues to this day.

Coronation Concerto. Piano Concerto in D Major by WOLFGANG AMADEUS MOZART, 1788 (K. 537), premiered by him on the coronation of the Austrian emperor Joseph II in 1790.

Coronation **Mass.** 1. Mass in D Minor by FRANZ JOSEPH HAYDN, 1798, also known as the *Nelson Mass.* 2. Mass in C Major by WOLFGANG AMADEUS MOZART, 1779 (K. 317), written for the unveiling of the statue of the Virgin Mary near Salzburg.

corrente (It.). An Italian variant of the French COURANTE, marked by a faster TEMPO and less florid ORNAMENTATION.
    Corrente alla francese, the Italian equivalent of the French courante, with all of its characteristics.

kŏhr-ren′tĕh

corrido (from Sp. *correr,* run). A 20th-century Mexican topical ballad. It is usually performed in $\frac{6}{8}$ or $\frac{9}{8}$ time, with melodies consistently harmonized in THIRDS.

Corsaire, Le. Concert OVERTURE by HECTOR BERLIOZ, 1845, first performed in Paris with the composer conducting. Supposedly, the work was inspired by Byron's poem *The Corsair,* depicting the picaresque adventures of a gentleman pirate. But disconcertingly, Berlioz first entitled the work *La Tour de Nice,* then changed it to *Le Corsaire rouge,* finally abbreviating the title to *Le Corsaire*. The listener can therefore fit her impressions of the ROMANTIC score into either a tourist's trip through the Riviera or tempestuous travels on the Mediterranean.

PEOPLE IN MUSIC

Cortot, Alfred (Denis), famous French pianist; b. Nyon, Switzerland (of a French father and a Swiss mother), Sept. 26, 1877; d. Lausanne, June 15, 1962. Cortot was a pupil at the Paris Conservatory, where he won first prize for piano in 1896, the same year he made his debut in Paris. He went to Bayreuth in 1898 to study RICHARD WAGNER's works, and acted as rehearsal pianist at the festivals from 1898 to 1901.

Returning to Paris, Cortot became a major promoter of Wagner's works. In 1902 he conducted the French premiere of GOTTERDÄMMERUNG, and in the same year established the Association des Concerts A. Cortot, which he directed for two years, also to perform Wagner's works. In 1904 he became conductor of the orchestra concerts of the Société Nationale and of the Concerts Populaires at Lille, remaining in these positions until 1908. In 1905, together with Jacques Thibaud (violin) and PABLO CASALS (cello), he formed a trio that soon gained a great European reputation.

In 1919 Cortot cofounded the École Normale de Musique and became its director, also giving a summer course in piano interpretation there annually. Besides giving many lecture recitals and appearing as a guest conductor with various orchestras, he authored several books on music and piano playing.

Cosa rara, o sia Bellezza ed onestà, Una. Opera, 1786, by Vicente Martin y Soler (b. Valencia, May 2, 1754; d. St. Petersburg, Jan. 30, 1806), to a libretto by Da Ponte, first performed in Vienna. Its libretto is drawn from the history of the Ottoman Empire. The opera was probably the first to include a Viennese WALTZ. Another distinction is the use of the MANDOLIN as an accompanying instrument in a serenade. WOLFGANG AMADEUS MOZART quoted an ARIA from *Una cosa rara* in *DON GIOVANNI*.

Così fan tutte (Thus do all women). OPERA BUFFA by WOLFGANG AMADEUS MOZART, 1790, first produced in Vienna.

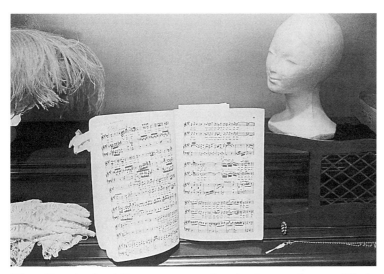

Score and props for Così fan
tutte. *(Ira Nowinski/© Corbis)*

Two disguised soldiers pursue each other's sweethearts. Their goal is to test their lover's faithfulness by trying to win their hearts.

Costello, Elvis (born Declan Patrick McManus), English rocker and songwriter; b. London, Aug. 25, 1955. Costello spent his childhood in Liverpool. His father, Ross McManus, was a popular singer and bandleader.

In 1977 Costello was signed to Stiff Records, then England's leading label for PUNK ROCK. Costello set himself apart from other punks with his complex songs that addressed both political issues (*Less Than Zero,* which attacked governmental fascism) and love gone wrong (the BALLAD *Alison*). His first albums, *My Aim Is True* (1977), *This Year's Model* (1978), and *Armed Forces* (1979), introduced his music to America, as well as his backup band, the minimal trio the Attractions.

From then on, Costello continued to be prolific, if not always consistent. He has shifted his style of repertoire, production values, and instrumentation where it suits him. Among his more interesting albums are *Get Happy* (1980), influenced by SOUL; *Almost Blue* (1981), an album of COUNTRY covers; *Imperial Bedroom* (1982), a successful concept recording; *King of America* (1986), with a varied cast of backup musicians; and 1989's *Spike*.

Costello has also attracted a wide variety of collaborators. In 1988 he collaborated with ex-BEATLE PAUL MCCART-

PEOPLE IN MUSIC

NEY on McCartney's album *Flowers in the Dirt*. In 1993 he recorded *The Juliet Letters* with the Brodsky String Quartet, a group specializing in modern classical music. In 1998 he made yet another stylistic switch to collaborate with 1960s pop composer BURT BACHARACH, wedding his usual cynical lyrics and hard-edged vocals with Bacharach's grand melodies and lush arrangements.

kōh-tē-yōhn′

GIOVANNI PIERLUIGI DA PALESTRINA composed his celebrated *Missa Papae Marcelli* (c.1555–62) as a demonstration of a possible reform of church music without abandoning all modern innovations. Exuberant music historians describe Palestrina's accomplishment as the "salvation of church music" over those who would have turned back the clock to medieval-style music.

cotillon (Fr.). An 18th- and 19th-century French dance, in $\frac{3}{4}$ time, to QUADRILLE-like music.

Council of Trent. A gathering of dignitaries of the Roman Catholic Church held in Trent from 1545 to 1563, part of which was devoted to the condemnation of the practice of using secular melodies and rhythms in sacred works. A decree was issued under the title *Abusus in sacrificio missae* (Abuse in the sacred mass). Some members of the council advocated a total elimination of POLYPHONY from the MASS and a return to PLAINCHANT, but the final verdict was to recommend that the Mass be primarily free from popular tunes.

counter. Any vocal part set to contrast in some manner with the principal part or melody, e.g., *bass counter,* a second bass part; an abbreviation for *countertenor*. Also, *counterexposition,* reentrance of a FUGUE subject; *countersubject,* a fugal theme following the subject in the same part; *countertenor clef,* the (obsolete) C clef on the second line.

counterpoint (from Lat. *punctum contra punctum*). 1. Literally, note (or point) against note (or point). The art of POLYPHONIC composition, or writing a piece with two or more melodic parts that are played at the same time.

In the middle ages the principal melodic part was called the *cantus;* added parts tended to form perfect intervals—the octave, FOURTH, and FIFTH—with the *cantus.* Among the earliest composers of counterpoint were the Parisian Notre Dame masters Leoninus and Perotinus, who flourished in the 12th and 13th centuries.

True counterpoint, as understood from a study of JOHANN SEBASTIAN BACH, belongs to the great age of the BAROQUE. The foundations of this mighty art are:

1. Several voices, above or below the basic theme, are performed at once. The individual parts create a complementary pattern when they are sounded together.

2. CONSONANT intervals are used—including the octave, fifth, major and minor THIRDS and SIXTHS—to form a harmonic fabric of extraordinary variety. Yet there is always a RESOLUTION at the end of the piece, usually a CADENCE from the DOMINANT to the TONIC chord.

3. While the individual melodic parts create variety, they tend to follow similar rhythmic patterns, to create a sense of unity.

4. DISSONANT intervals that occur in the intermingling of the voices must be resolved into consonances. However, this resolution can be delayed by the introduction of numerous passing notes or ornamentation.

5. The BASS plays a commanding role in establishing the fundamental TONALITY of the whole composition.

Double counterpoint is written so that the upper part can become the lower part, and vice versa; in *triple* and *quadruple counterpoint,* three and four parts are written so that they can be mutually exchanged.

countertenor. A very high male voice. Ideally, a countertenor sings in the CONTRALTO range while retaining a masculine tone quality. Highly praised in the middle ages, countertenors were replaced in the BAROQUE era by the CASTRATI. But when this brutal practice came to an end in the 19th century, composers resumed the use of countertenors. They remain in fashion, thanks primarily to the EARLY MUSIC movement.

country dance (It. *coranto*). A dance in $\frac{2}{4}$ or $\frac{3}{4}$ time in which partners form two opposing lines. The lines advance and retreat, with the couples also dancing down the lines and returning to their places. *See also* CONTREDANSE.

country music. A term used to describe a form of American popular music and song. Sources include Appalachian old-

JOHANN SEBASTIAN BACH's great collections, *THE WELL-TEMPERED CLAVIER* and *THE ART OF THE FUGUE,* summarize the practice of counterpoint as well as its development.

time BALLADS, fiddle tunes, BLUEGRASS, JAZZ-influenced Western SWING, and mainstream popular music.

The geographic center of modern country music is Nashville, Tennessee. Many country songs focus on love gone wrong or turned sour: men miss their women, their whiskey, or their wandering; women are left holding the bag and pouring out their hearts. Country songs also deal with topical issues, such as the problems faced by the working class, as well as spousal abuse, divorce, and even abortion.

The classic country-western instrumentation includes acoustic, electric, and bass GUITARS, pedal steel guitar, FIDDLE, and DRUMS. Other traditional and modern instruments are added as needed. Most male country singers sport cowboy hats, in homage to the Western roots of the musical form. Female country singers often sport semi-Western outfits as well, including leather boots and spangled coats.

The glittery, rhinestone-encrusted cowboy suit worn by many country stars was the special creation of the famous Nashville tailor "Nudie" Cohen. The suits earned the name "Nudie suits" in his honor.

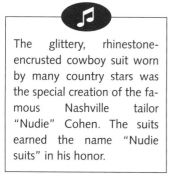

PEOPLE IN MUSIC

Couperin, François (nicknamed "le Grand" for his superiority in organ playing), the most illustrious member of a distinguished family, and one of the greatest of early French composers; b. Paris, Nov. 10, 1668; d. there, Sept. 11, 1733. Couperin was the son of Charles (b. Chaumes [baptized], Apr. 9, 1638; d. Paris, between Jan. 15 and Feb. 26, 1679) and nephew of Louis (b. Cahumes, c.1626; d. Paris, Aug. 29, 1661). He studied with his father and later was a pupil of Jacques-Denis Thomelin, organist of the king's chapel. In 1685 he became organist of St.-Gervais, which post he held until his death. On Dec. 26, 1693, after a successful competition, he succeeded Thomelin as organist of the Chapelle Royale, receiving the title of "organiste du roi." In 1701 he was appointed "claveciniste de la chambre du roi, et organiste de sa chapelle" [harpsichordist for the king's chamber and organist for his chapel] and in 1717 he received the title "ordinaire de la musique de la chambre du roi" (ordinary or director of the king's chamber music). He also was made a chevalier of the Order of Latran.

Couperin was music master to the dauphin and other members of the royal family and ranked high in the favor of Louis XIV. He composed for Louis the Concerts Royaux (Royal concerts), which, during 1714–15, were played in Sunday concerts in the royal apartments. He married Marie-

Anne Ansault (Apr. 26, 1689), by whom he had two daughters: Marie-Madeleine (1690–1742), who became organist of the Abbey of Montbuisson, and Marguerite-Antoinette (1705–78), who was a talented harpsichordist. From 1731 to 1733 she substituted for her father as harpsichordist to the king, being the first woman to hold this position. There were also two sons, Nicolas-Louis (b. July 24, 1707), who died young, and François-Laurent (b. c.1708).

Couperin's compositions may be conveniently divided into three categories: those written for the church, those written for the king, and those written for the general public. About two-thirds of his creative life was taken up with religious compositions, including complete MASSES and individual MOTETS and HYMNS.

The last third of Couperin's life was his most prolific period. He composed almost exclusively instrumental works, and in this field he achieved his greatest and most enduring distinction. In 1713, 1716, 1722, and 1730 he published the four volumes of his *Pièces de clavecin.* These totaled about 230 pieces in 27 *ordres* (SUITES), each suite consisting of a series of dances. In 1716 he published *L'Art de toucher le clavecin* (The art of playing the harpsichord), an instruction book that attained wide fame and influenced the keyboard style of Couperin's great contemporary JOHANN SEBASTIAN BACH.

Couperin also introduced the TRIO SONATA to France, his first works in this form being an imitation of ARCANGELO CORELLI. Later, in 1726, he published four sonatas, *Les Nations,* described as "sonades" or "suites de symphonies en trio," three of which are partial reworkings of earlier pieces. The third of the series, *L'Imperiale,* perhaps represents his most mature and inspired style.

Living at a time during which the rivalry between French and Italian music reached its climax, Couperin adapted the new Italian forms to his own personal, and essentially French, style. In his *Les goûts-réünis* (1724), a series of concerted pieces with strings similar in form and spirit to the *Pièces de clavecin,* he used Italian forms such as *Sicilienne* and *Ritratto dell' amore.*

Couperin's style of composition was based on the BASSO CONTINUO, the most important voices usually being the up-

In 1725 Couperin published the *Apothéose de Lully* (The apotheosis or triumph of Lully). The piece portrays an imaginary battle between the French composer JEAN-BAPTISTE LULLY and his rival, the Italian composer and violinist ARCANGELO CORELLI. The end of the piece represents their settling their argument and uniting to work together to further music.

permost, carrying the melody, and the bass. Nevertheless, his music sometimes attains considerable complexity (on occasion requiring a second harpsichordist for proper execution). His melodic invention, particularly in his use of the RONDEAU, was virtually inexhaustible, his themes swift and expressive. He was also outstanding in his ability to ornament a melody in the GALLANT style that was then popular.

couplet. 1. Two successive lines forming a pair, usually rhymed. 2. In the RONDEAU of the French BAROQUE, a contrasting EPISODE; the main section is sometimes called GRAND COUPLET.

koo-răhn´t **courante** (*courant,* Fr.; It. *coranto*). A stately and courtly old French dance in triple METER, of moderate TEMPO, with considerable melodic ornamentation. The courante became an integral part of the BAROQUE SUITE.

courtship and music. Mythology, literature, and art abound in stories of courtship and love inspired and encouraged by music making. Some examples from Greek and Roman mythology include:

> Winged cupids play the lute to speed Venus and Adonis on the road to erotic consummation.
>
> Apollo plays the lyre to win the hearts of nymphs.
>
> Orpheus, son of Apollo, enchants nymphs by his lyre, and even reclaims his wife, Eurydice, from the nether regions by singing. But when he refuses to make love to the multitudes of furiously inflamed Bacchantes, he is torn to pieces by them and his dismembered limbs sent down the river.
>
> The forest god Pan uses his vocal powers to attract the reluctant nymph Syrinx. She seeks refuge in a pond, where she is metamorphosed into a field of reeds. Frustrated, Pan collects the reeds and makes a PANPIPE out of them.

More recently, composers have used music to express their love. HECTOR BERLIOZ wrote his *Symphonie fantastique* as an offering of love to the Shakespearian actress Harriet Smithson. ROBERT SCHUMANN paid tribute to his love for Clara Wieck by inserting a brief elegy to her under the Italian form of her name, Chiara, in his piano work *CARNAVAL*.

In popular music, there are numerous stories of lovers won and lost through music. ERIC CLAPTON fell in love with his best friend's wife, Patti Harrison. He described his conflicting emotions in the famous song *Layla*. (Clapton eventually married Patti, although their marriage ended in divorce; he remained friends with GEORGE HARRISON despite stealing his wife!)

JOHN LENNON portrayed his love for his wife, Yoko Ono, in many different stages: from their marriage through their separation in the mid-1970s to their reunion and his happiness raising their child and living as a "househusband" in the late 1970s. Among his many songs dedicated to her were *O Yoko, Woman,* and *I'm Losing You.*

Coward, (Sir) **Noël,** English playwright and author of MUSICAL COMEDIES; b. Teddington, Middlesex, Dec. 16, 1899; d. Port Maria, Jamaica, Mar. 25, 1973. At the age of 11 Coward appeared on the stage, and he was associated with the theater ever after, in the varied roles of actor, playwright, songwriter, and producer. Having had no formal education in music, he dictated his songs to a secretary.

Coward's first success came with the 1923 revue *London Calling,* in which he appeared along with the singer and dancer Gertrude Lawrence. The pair performed his first hit song, *You Belong to Me.* Coward achieved his greatest success in the late 1920s and '30s, with a number of stage shows including *Bitter Sweet, Words and Music, Design and Music,* and *Tonight at 8:30.* Coward continued his streak of musical hits through the 1940s, most notably with the play *Blithe Spirit,* staged in the early months of World War II.

In the 1950s Coward became a star in America, achieving a great success with a stage show produced at Las Vegas's Desert Inn in 1955, followed by many television and nightclub appearances. In 1970 he was awarded a special Tony Award for his contributions to the theater. Three years later, a revue of his songs, *Oh! Coward,* was a hit on Broadway. Af-

PEOPLE IN MUSIC

ter seeing its premiere, Coward returned to his home in Jamaica, where he died in March 1973.

cowbell. Large metal BELL with heavy clappers worn around the neck of a cow. In the modern era scores by ANTON WEBERN and GUSTAV MAHLER have included the instrument. It is commonly found in Latin American, jazz, and other popular music.

Cowell, Henry (Dixon), remarkable, innovative American composer; b. Menlo Park, Calif., Mar. 11, 1897; d. Shady, N.Y., Dec. 10, 1965. Cowell's father, of Irish birth, was a member of a clergyman's family, and his mother was an American raised in a progressive household. As a young child Cowell studied violin in San Francisco. After the 1906 earthquake his mother took him to N.Y., but she was unable to find work there. They returned to Menlo Park, where Cowell was able to save enough money, earned from menial jobs, to buy a piano.

As a teenager Cowell began to experiment with the keyboard by striking the keys with fists and forearms. He named such chords TONE CLUSTERS and at the age of 13 composed a piece for them called *Adventures in Harmony.* Eventually Cowell organized the creation of tone clusters and created a logical notation for them. Tone clusters eventually acquired legitimacy in the works of many European and American composers. Cowell also extended the sonorities of tone clusters to instrumental combinations and applied them in several of his symphonic works.

Cowell also began experimenting in altering the sound of the piano by placing various objects on the strings. He also opened the piano's lid and played directly on its strings. He first exhibited these startling innovations on Mar. 5, 1914, at the San Francisco Musical Society, much to the shock of its members, no doubt.

In the meantime Cowell began taking lessons in composition with E. G. Strickland and Wallace Sabin at the University of California, Berkeley, and later with Frank Damrosch at the Institute of Musical Art, N.Y., and, privately, from 1914 to 1916, with Charles Seeger. After brief service in the U.S. Army in 1918, where he was employed first as a

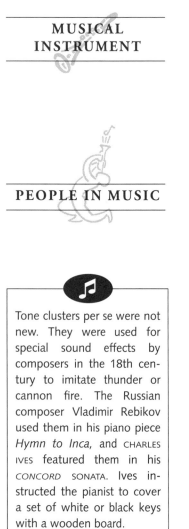

MUSICAL
INSTRUMENT

PEOPLE IN MUSIC

Tone clusters per se were not new. They were used for special sound effects by composers in the 18th century to imitate thunder or cannon fire. The Russian composer Vladimir Rebikov used them in his piano piece *Hymn to Inca*, and CHARLES IVES featured them in his *CONCORD SONATA.* Ives instructed the pianist to cover a set of white or black keys with a wooden board.

cook and later as arranger for the U.S. Army Band, Cowell began lecturing on new music, illustrated by his playing his own works on the piano. In 1928 he became the first American composer to visit communist Russia, where he attracted considerable attention. Some of his pieces were published in a Russian edition, another first for an American. Upon return to the U.S., he was appointed lecturer on music at the New School for Social Research in N.Y. In 1927 Cowell founded the *New Music Quarterly* for the publication of ultramodern music, mainly by American composers. Cowell also published in 1930 an important book, *New Musical Resources,* which is recognized as a classic guide to contemporary music.

In 1931 Cowell received a Guggenheim fellowship and went to Berlin to study ETHNOMUSICOLOGY. This was the beginning of his serious study of ethnic musical materials. He had already experimented with Indian and Chinese instruments and MODES in some of his works. In his *Ensemble for Strings* (1924) he included Indian thundersticks. This piece naturally aroused considerable curiosity.

Also in 1931 he formed a collaboration with the Russian electrical engineer LEON THEREMIN, then visiting the U.S. With Theremin's assistance, Cowell constructed an ingenious instrument that he called the Rhythmicon, which could produce 16 different rhythms played on 16 different pitches at the same time. He demonstrated the Rhythmicon at a lecture-concert in San Francisco in 1932. Cowell also composed an extensive work entitled *Rhythmicana,* but it did not receive a performance until 1971.

Cowell's career was brutally interrupted in 1936 when he was arrested in California on charges of homosexuality and solicitation. The district attorney promised a minimal sentence if Cowell pleaded guilty, so the composer did not contest the charge. The district attorney did not keep his promise, however, and Cowell was given the maximum sentence, up to 15 years. Incarcerated at the notorious San Quentin State Prison, Cowell indomitably continued to write music. Thanks to interventions in his behalf by a number of eminent musicians, he was paroled in 1940 with the Australian composer PERCY GRAINGER as a guarantor of his good conduct. Cowell obtained a full pardon in 1942 from the governor of California, Earl Warren, after it was discovered that the evidence against him was largely contrived.

In 1941 Cowell married Sidney Robertson, a noted ethnomusicologist. He then resumed his full activities as editor and instructor. He again taught at the New School in N.Y. from 1940 to 1962, as well as various other universities in California and N.Y. In 1951 Cowell was elected a member of the National Academy of Arts and Letters. In the early 1950s Cowell served as an advisor to Folkways Records, overseeing the first album releases of field recordings of different types of world music. In 1955, in collaboration with his wife, he wrote the first biography of Charles Ives. In 1956–57 he undertook a world tour with his wife through the Near East, India, and Japan, collecting traditional musical instruments and melodies.

Cradle Will Rock, The. Musical play by MARC BLITZSTEIN, 1937. The play tells the story of the founding of a steel workers' union and the difficult fight the workers have with their bosses to gain good pay and healthy working conditions.

PEOPLE IN MUSIC

Craft, Robert (Lawson), American conductor and brilliant writer on music; b. Kingston, N.Y., Oct. 20, 1923. Craft studied at the Juilliard School of Music in N.Y. (B.A., 1946) and the Berkshire Music Center in Tanglewood, Mass. He also took courses in conducting with PIERRE MONTEUX. During World War II he was in the U.S. Army Medical Corps. In 1947 he conducted the N.Y. Brass and Woodwind Ensemble. He was conductor of the Evenings-on-the-Roof and the Monday Evening Concerts in Los Angeles from 1950 to 1968.

A decisive turn in Craft's career came in 1948 when he met the great Russian composer IGOR STRAVINSKY. Stravinsky was greatly impressed by Craft's detailed knowledge of his music. Gradually Craft became Stravinsky's closest associate. Craft helped persuade Stravinsky to adopt the 12-TONE method of composition, a decision that changed the path of Stravinsky's musical career. He also collaborated with Stravinsky on six books of memoirs.

Crawford (Seeger), Ruth (Porter), remarkable American composer; b. East Liverpool, Ohio, July 3, 1901; d. Chevy Chase, Md., Nov. 18, 1953. Crawford studied music as a child. Her principal piano teacher was Heniot Levy. When still very young, she taught at the School of Musical Arts, Jacksonville, Fl. (1918–21), then gave courses at the American Conservatory in Chicago (1925–29) and at the Elmhurst College of Music in Illinois (1926–29). Meanwhile, she began composing pieces that were boldly experimental. Her work began to win recognition, and in 1930 she received a Guggenheim fellowship. This led to the composition of her most famous work, her 1931 String Quartet, which has since been recognized as a modern classic.

In the late 1920s she met the musicologist Charles Seeger, who first became her teacher and then her husband. After marrying Seeger, she adopted his interest in American FOLK SONG. She compiled several books of traditional songs, including *American Folk Songs for Children* (1948), *Animal Folk Songs for Children* (1950), and *American Folk Songs for Christmas* (1953).

Crawford tragically died of cancer in 1953. Since the mid-1970s, her works have been "rediscovered," and she is now recognized as a pioneering modern American composer.

Creation, The (*Die Schöpfung*). ORATORIO by FRANZ JOSEPH HAYDN, 1798, who conducted its first performance in Vienna. The original text was in English, compiled mainly from Genesis and John Milton's epic poem *Paradise Lost.*

The section of this work entitled *Representation of Chaos* forecasts 20th-century compositions in its use of DISSONANT harmonies and bold orchestral colors.

Création du monde, La (The creation of the world). BALLET by DARIUS MILHAUD, 1923, first performed in Paris. The music was inspired by Milhaud's 1922 visit to Harlem, where he was greatly impressed by the JAZZ bands he heard there. The score became historically important as the first example of "symphonic jazz"—combining jazz rhythms with a classical symphony orchestra—a full year before GEORGE GERSHWIN'S *RHAPSODY IN BLUE.*

creativity. Musical activity is sharply divided into two categories: creative work, that is, composition, and interpretation, that is, performance. Because the interpreter is only a servant of the composer, it is natural that performing artists are placed lower in the musical world than creative musicians. But as far as worldly success is concerned, famous interpreters gain by and large greater fame and a much greater fortune. Still, it is the composers who enter their names in gold letters on the illuminated pages of music history.

Fortunately for the cause of music, many composers are also great artists who can perform their own works. In rare instances the composer's talent as an interpreter matches his genius as a composer. FRÉDÉRIC CHOPIN, FRANZ LISZT, and NICCOLÒ PAGANINI were such complete men of music. In the 20th century perhaps the only composers who were also great performers were SERGEI RACHMANINOFF and LEONARD BERNSTEIN. Most composers can play only their own compositions, avoiding the careers of performing artists. Such were ALEXANDER SCRIABIN, CLAUDE DEBUSSY, and BÉLA BARTÓK, as interpreters of their piano works. IGOR STRAVINSKY played the piano in some of his works, but he was not a professional pianist.

Many musicians known chiefly as interpreters also compose music on the side, but this music is generally of fairly low quality. Symphonies written by professional conductors are often derisively described as *Kapellmeistermusik,* a conductor's music. Some pianists have written technical studies and minor pieces of excellent value and great popular appeal.

The creation of music combines inspiration and organization. Exactly how this process occurs is a mystery. But it is obvious that a great composer must be able to create great musical themes, and at the same time have the necessary ability to organize his or her thoughts into coherent works.

crā'doh **Credo** (Lat., I believe). The Nicene Creed, part of the ORDINARY Roman Catholic High MASS. The longest portion of the Ordinary, the Credo can be broken down into sections for compositional purposes: *Credo in unum deum* (I believe in one God); *Patrem omnipotentem* (Father almighty); *Et in unum Dominum* (and in one Lord); *Et incarnatus est* (and was incarnate); *Crucifixius* (Crucified); *Et resurrexit* (and was resurrected); *Et in Spiritum sanctum* (and in the Holy Spirit); and *Confiteor unum baptisma* (I confess one baptism).

Creedence Clearwater Revival. (Leader/guitar/vocal/songwriter: John Fogerty, b. Berkeley, Calif., May 28, 1945; guitar/piano/vocal: Tom Fogerty, b. Berkeley, Calif., Nov. 9, 1941; d. Scottsdale, Ariz., Sept. 6, 1990; bass: Stu Clark, b. Oakland, Calif., Apr. 24, 1946; drums: Doug Clifford, b. Palo Alto, Calif., Apr. 24, 1945.) Roots-revival ROCK band of the late 1960s noted for the pungent songs and vocals of John Fogerty. Growing out of a series of amateur high-school bands, the band was signed to a local California JAZZ label, Fantasy, in 1967. The group soon had major hits with Fogerty's *Proud Mary* (later covered by Ike and Tina Turner), *Born on the Bayou, Bad Moon Rising, Fortunate Son, Who'll Stop the Rain?, Run Through the Jungle,* and *Lookin' Out My Backdoor.* Most of Fogerty's songs drew on American folk themes and drew their inspiration from early rock and ROCKABILLY styles.

In early 1971 Fogerty left the group, which then struggled on for about a year before disbanding. Fogerty unsuccessfully pursued a solo career, then staged a successful comeback in the mid-1980s with a couple of hits from his album *Centerfield.* He has since made a second comeback in 1997–98 with a new album, *Blue Moon Swamp,* and a world tour.

crescendo (It., growing). A gradual increase in loudness. The abbreviation is *cresc.,* followed by hyphens to indicate the duration: cresc - - -. The word itself can also be broken up by several hyphens: cre - - scen - - do.

A crescendo may be indicated by two lines diverging at an acute angle from a point: <. Crescendo may begin from any dynamic level, including forte.

crescent (Chinese crescent, Chinese pavilion). An instrument of Turkish origin, used in military music. It has crescent-shaped brass plates hung around a staff and surmounted by a cap or pavilion. Around the plates little bells are hung, which are jingled in time with the music.

PEOPLE IN MUSIC

The effect of a gradual swelling up of sound was first cultivated in the 18th century. JOHANN STAMITZ was the orchestral conductor of a talented group of musicians in the German town of Mannheim. It was there that he developed the idea of varying the volume to emphasize different parts of a piece of music. A musician who heard the Mannheim musicians perform wrote that the power of their crescendo made the audience rise from their seats.

MUSICAL INSTRUMENT

PEOPLE IN MUSIC

Crespin, Régine, outstanding French SOPRANO, later MEZZO-SOPRANO; b. Marseilles, Feb. 23, 1927. Crespin studied pharmacology, then began taking voice lessons in Paris. She made her debut in Mulhouse in 1950 and then sang at the Paris Opéra. Crespin acquired a European reputation as one of the best Wagnerian singers. She sang Kundry at the Bayreuth Festivals (1958–60) and also appeared at La Scala in Milan and Covent Garden in London.

Crespin made her debut with the Metropolitan Opera, N.Y., in 1962, remaining there until her farewell appearance as Mme. De Croissy in FRANCES POULENC's *Dialogues of the Carmelites* in 1987. She also sang Sieglinde and Amelia in *Un ballo in maschera* and appeared as a concert singer. Her sonorous, somewhat somber voice suited dramatic parts excellently.

PEOPLE IN MUSIC

Cristofori, Bartolomeo, celebrated Italian instrument maker; b. Padua, May 4, 1655; d. Florence, Jan. 27, 1731. Cristofori is generally credited as the inventor of the first practical PIANO as opposed to the CLAVICHORD, although there are some surviving earlier transitional instruments that may have influenced his design.

Prior to making pianos, Cristofori was a leading maker of harpsichords in Padua. About 1690 he went to Florence, where he was instrument maker to Ferdinando de' Medici. On the latter's death in 1713, he was made custodian of the court collection of instruments by Cosimo III. According to an article by Maffei published in 1711, Cristofori had up to that year made three "gravecembali col piano e forte," these having, instead of the usual JACKS plucking the strings with quills, a row of little hammers striking the strings from below.

The principle of Cristofori's hammer action was adopted, in the main, by the German makers Gottfried Silbermann and the Streichers, as well as the famous English maker Broadwood and Sons (their variation of the Cristofori design was called the "English action"). Following the designation by its inventor, the new instrument was named piano-forte. A piano of Cristofori's make is in the possession of the Metropolitan Museum of Art, N.Y.

crook. A short tube, bent or straight, that can be fitted to the main tube of a HORN, TRUMPET, or CORNET to lower its fundamental PITCH. This method was widely used in the 18th and 19th centuries, but became obsolete with the invention of VALVE trumpets and horns.

cross flute. *See* TRANSVERSE FLUTE.

cross relation (Fr. *fausse relation*). The sounding of two tones in different voices that are chromatically contradictory. For example, playing a major and minor THIRD of the same TRIAD at the same time, such as playing E in the treble part and E flat in the bass in the key of C. Also called FALSE RELATION.

cross-rhythm. The simultaneous use of two or more different METERS. For example, the Spanish polymeter, placing $\frac{3}{4}$ against $\frac{6}{8}$, produces a distinctive cross-rhythm in which the strong beats of the meters alternate. They fall together only on the DOWNBEAT, the first of six.

JAZZ syncopation thrives on cross rhythm, and much world music depends on it. But European classical music tends to be dominated by the main beat or beats of the chosen meter, so that the cross-rhythm functions in a momentary or ornamental manner. JOHANNES BRAHMS was probably the most consistent of pre-20th-century composers to use the device, for example in the piano Capriccio in C♯ Minor, op.76/5.

crossover. This term evolved in mainstream popular circles to describe the phenomenon in which a recording in one style of music becomes successful with a very different audience. Typical examples are classical music recordings of performers such as VLADIMIR HOROWITZ, VAN CLIBURN, LUCIANO PAVAROTTI, ITZHAK PERLMAN, and PLACIDO DOMINGO that have soared to or near the top of the hit parade. Sometimes specific pieces become popular.

The other principal crossover situation is when a performer records in an unexpected style, such as Barbra Streisand's classical album or Mark O'Connor's Concerto for fiddle and orchestra.

MUSICAL INSTRUMENT

Michael Jackson is probably the most successful crossover artist of all time, selling 37 million copies of his *Thriller* album from 1986, and having hits on both pop and R&B charts.

MUSICAL INSTRUMENT

crotales (Fr, from Lat. *crotalum,* hand clappers). Small hollow-sphere CYMBALS of definite pitch, played with a small mallet. ANTIQUE CYMBALS. *Crotalum* (Lat., from Grk. *crotalon*), a clapper used in ancient Greek dances and choruses to punctuate stressed beats.

kroo-chē-fĕx′oos

Crucifixus (Lat.). A section of the CREDO, from the Roman Catholic High MASS.

PEOPLE IN MUSIC

Crumb, George (Henry, Jr.), distinguished and innovative American composer; b. Charleston, W. Va., Oct. 24, 1929. Crumb was raised in a musical environment: his father played the clarinet and his mother was a cellist. He began composing while in school and had some of his pieces performed by the Charleston Symphony Orchestra. He then took courses in composition at Mason College in Charleston (B.M., 1950), and later enrolled at the University of Illinois (M.M., 1952). Crumb continued his studies in composition with Ross Lee Finney at the University of Michigan (D.M.A., 1959).

In 1955, Crumb received a Fulbright fellowship for travel to Germany, where he studied with Boris Blacher at the Berlin Hochschule für Musik. He further received grants from the Rockefeller (1964), Koussevitzky (1965), and Coolidge (1970) foundations. In 1967 he held a Guggenheim fellowship and also was given the National Institute of Arts and Letters Award. In 1968 he was awarded the Pulitzer Prize in music for his *Echoes of Time and the River.* Parallel to composing, he was active as a music teacher. From 1959 to 1964 he taught at the University of Colorado at Boulder, and in 1965 he joined the music department of the University of Pennsylvania, where in 1983 he was named Annenberg Professor of the Humanities.

In his music Crumb is a universalist. Nothing in the realm of sound is out of bounds to him, no method of composition unsuited to his artistic purposes. Accordingly, his music can sing as sweetly as the proverbial nightingale, and it can be as rough, rude, and crude as a primitive man of the mountains. The vocal parts especially demand extraordinary skills to produce such sound effects as percussive tongue clicks, explosive shrieks, hissing, whistling, whispering, and sudden shouting.

Crumb also uses musical collage as a method of composition. He borrows well-known themes, such as the middle section of FRÉDÉRIC CHOPIN's *Fantaisie-Impromptu,* MAURICE RAVEL's *BOLÉRO,* or some other well-known work, to surprise or startle his listeners.

In his instrumentation Crumb is no less unconventional. Among the unusual effects in his scores is instructing the percussion player to immerse the loudly sounding GONG into a tub of water, having an ELECTRIC GUITAR played with glass rods over the frets, or having wind instrumentalists blow soundlessly through their tubes. *Spatial distribution* (spreading his vocalists and musicians around the room) also plays a role in his compositions.

Among Crumb's best work is his *Ancient Voices of Children,* which was first performed at a chamber music festival in Washington, D.C., in 1970. The text is by the Spanish poet Federico García Lorca. A female singer intones into the space under the lid of an amplified grand piano. A boy's voice responds in anguish. The accompaniment is supplied by an orchestral group and an assortment of exotic percussion instruments, such as Tibetan prayer stones, Japanese temple bells, a musical saw, and a toy piano. A remarkable group of four cycles of piano pieces, *Makrokosmos,* calls for equally unusual effects. In one, the pianist is ordered to shout at specified points of time.

Crumb's most grandiose creation is *Star-Child,* representing, in his imaginative scheme, a progression from deep despair to the exaltation of luminous joy. The score calls for a huge orchestra, which includes two children's choruses and eight percussion players performing on all kinds of utensils, such as pot lids, iron chains, and metal sheets, as well as ordinary drums. The work had its first performance under the direction of PIERRE BOULEZ with the N.Y. Philharmonic in 1977.

crumhorn (Ger. *Krummhorn,* crooked horn; Fr. *tournebout;* It. *cornamuto toto*). An obsolete DOUBLE-REED instrument, gently curved upward at the bell. Its greatest popularity was

MUSICAL
INSTRUMENT

in the late 15th, 16th, and the first half of the 17th centuries. Its sound was pure and sweet, so much so that angels in RENAISSANCE paintings were often shown playing crumhorns. However, its range was not much greater than an octave, and its dynamic range was limited.

krüth

MUSICAL
INSTRUMENT

crwth (*crouth, crouch;* Welsh, Middle Eng.; pronounced "crowd"). An ancient plucked or bowed LYRE, probably the earliest European instrument of this type. It is the national instrument of Wales. In its modern form it has a fingerboard and six (formerly three) strings. It is rectangular in shape and topped by a wooden board. The body is carved out of a single piece of wood, terminated by two parallel arms joined at the end by a crossbar, the center of which supports the fingerboard.

char'dahsh

csárdás (Hung.; misspelled *czárdás*). A stylized Hungarian folk dance in $\frac{2}{4}$ time that became popular in the first half of the 19th century. The term comes from the word *csarda*, Hungarian for a village inn.

The dance consists of two parts: a slow introduction, called *lassu*, which is danced by men only, and the csárdás proper, also called *friss* or *friszka*, a lively dance for both men and women. The csárdás became popular in Hungary toward the middle of the 19th century. Csárdás numbers are often included in ballets, with one of the best known being in COPPÉLIA by LÉO DELIBES.

Classic works in C-sharp minor include:

The first movement of LUDWIG VAN BEETHOVEN'S *MOONLIGHT SONATA*, op.27/2, which suggested to an imaginative critic the surface of a moonlit lake in Switzerland

The famous Prelude in C♯ Minor by SERGEI RACHMANINOFF (op.3/2), which solemnly recalls old Russia

ROBERT SCHUMANN'S *Études symphoniques* and PIOTR ILYICH TCHAIKOVSKY'S Nocturne in C♯ Minor (op.19/4), both pieces that inspire deep thought

C-sharp minor (Ger. *Cis moll*). This key, to judge from its use by composers, particularly in piano pieces, possesses a meditative, somewhat somber nature.

C♯ minor is rarely encountered as the principal key of a symphonic work. One outstanding exception to this rule is GUSTAV MAHLER'S Fifth Symphony, which begins with the funereal measures of doom. However, MODULATIONS are frequent in the score. SERGEI PROKOFIEV set his last symphony, the Seventh, in C♯ minor. He called the work a *Youth* Symphony, glorifying the spirit of the young Soviet generation. However, the finale is in the major tonic of the key, enharmonically notated as D♭ major.

Cuatro soles, Los (The four suns). Indigenous BALLET by CARLOS CHÁVEZ, 1930. The four suns each represent one of the four elements of heaven and earth.

Cuauhnahuac. Symphonic poem by SILVESTRE REVUELTAS, 1933, in which Mexican PERCUSSION instruments play a dominant role. Cuauhnahuac is the Indian name for Cuernavaca, a Mexican tourist resort. Revueltas described this piece as "music without tourism" and said that it represents "anti-capitalist agitation." It was first performed in Mexico City.

***Cuban* Overture.** Concert overture by GEORGE GERSHWIN, 1932, with many Cuban instruments and influences, originally entitled *Rhumba.*

Cucaracha, La (The cockroach). Famous Mexican song that became popular about the time of the 1910 Mexican revolution. La Cucaracha was the nickname of the girl in the song. The words vary, those of the modern version complaining that La Cucaracha would not go out because she had no marijuana to smoke.

Cuckoo and the Nightingale, The. Organ CONCERTO in F major by GEORGE FRIDERIC HANDEL, 1739. The nickname is suggested by falling THIRDS and TRILLS.

Cui, César (Antonovich), significant Russian composer, one of the "MIGHTY FIVE"; b. Vilnius, Jan. 18, 1835; d. Petrograd, Mar. 26, 1918. Cui was the son of a soldier in Napoleon's army who remained in Russia, married a Lithuanian noblewoman, and settled as a teacher of French in Vilnius. Cui learned musical notation by copying FRÉDÉRIC CHOPIN's MAZURKAS and various Italian OPERAS.

In 1851 Cui entered the Engineering School in St. Petersburg and, four years later, the Academy of Military Engineering. After graduation in 1857 he became a mapmaker and later an expert in fortification. He participated in the Russo-Turkish War of 1877; in 1878 he became a professor at the Engineering School and was tutor in military fortification to Czar Nicholas II.

PEOPLE IN MUSIC

In 1856 Cui met MILY BALAKIREV, who helped him master the technique of composition. In 1858 he married Malvina Bamberg, for whom he wrote a scherzo on the theme BABEG (for the letters in her name) and CC (his own initials). In 1864 he began writing music criticism in the St. Petersburg *Vedomosti* and later in other newspapers, continuing as music critic until 1900.

Cui's musical tastes were formed by his early admiration for ROBERT SCHUMANN. He opposed RICHARD WAGNER, against whom he wrote many articles. He attacked RICHARD STRAUSS and MAX REGER with even greater violence. He was a strong supporter of MIKHAIL GLINKA and the Russian national school, but was somewhat critical toward PIOTR ILYICH TCHAIKOVSKY. He published the first comprehensive book on Russian music, *Musique en Russie* (Paris, 1880).

Cui was grouped with NIKOLAI RIMSKY-KORSAKOV, MODEST MUSSORGSKY, ALEXANDER BORODIN, and MILY BALAKIREV as one of the *Moguchaya Kuchka* (Mighty Five). The adjective in his case, however, is not very appropriate, for his music lacks grandeur. He was at his best in delicate miniatures, e.g., *Orientale,* from the suite *Kaleidoscope,* op.50.

PEOPLE IN MUSIC

Cunningham, Merce, legendary American dancer and choreographer; b. Centralia, Wash., Apr. 16, 1919. With the Kronos Quartet a close contender, the Merce Cunningham Dance Company has probably been responsible for the creation of more new music than any other contemporary commissioning body. Cunningham's career from the start was closely allied to that of his lifelong friend and collaborator JOHN CAGE, who, not insignificantly, served as his company's music director from its inception in 1953 until Cage's near-dying day. Succeeding music directors were David Tudor (1992–96) and Takehisa Kosugi (from 1996). In addition to commissioning new works from many of the century's most illustrious experimental composers (Cage himself, MORTON FELDMAN, CHRISTIAN WOLFF, et al.), countless musicians and composers have participated in Cunningham's "Events," dance concerts comprised of newly coalesced snippets of existing works and in which music is created on the spot. Cage-Cunningham collaborations are distinguished by

Music and Musicians

as Portrayed in Art: From Greece to the Early 20th Century

There is a long tradition of portraying musical subjects in paintings, posters, sculpture, and even on vases and jars. In fact, the early Greeks decorated their vases with drawings of musicians performing, often as parts of rituals and ceremonies. This provides us with the only evidence of what ancient Greek music might have been like. Similarly, art throughout the ages tells a story, reflecting the importance of music in society.

"Musical Examination." A print by Roulez from 1854 based on a Greek vase painting. This print accurately recreates the typical colors, style, and design of a Greek vase painting. The second figure from the left is playing what appears to be a simple FLUTE or FIFE, made from two separate canes. These early flutes are similar to today's PENNYWHISTLES or RECORDERS, although they lack a MOUTHPIECE. Although we can't be certain, it is believed that Greek music was based on the so–called Greek MODES (or SCALES) that were carefully documented and used in MEDIEVAL music. (*Corbis/Gianni Dagli Orti*)

This print, titled "Choir of Israelite Women in Jean Racine's play, *Esther*," was made by Alex Cherry in about 1805. It recreates what a Biblical scene might have looked like. It portrays several early stringed insruments: the figure on the left is playing what appears to be a simple stringed HARP made by running strings between two sticks, set at an angle; the player on the far right holds a yoked lyre. Behind the seated figure, there is a musician playing what appears to be a SHAWM or early OBOE-like instrument. It is unknown whether such instruments really existed in Biblical times; but by the 1800s they would have been considered fairly "ancient," because they had all been replaced by more modern designs. (*Corbis/Gianni Dagli Orti*)

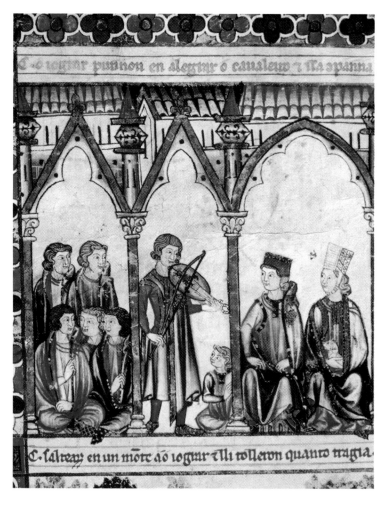

A medieval manuscript illumination showing TROUBADOURS from Alphonse Le Sage's "Las Cantigas," created in the late 13th century. This Spanish illustration shows an early VIOLIN-like instrument, played by the central figure. Unlike the modern violin, this instrument has an oval body, and the player uses a bow that is much more radically bent than a modern one would be. (*Corbis/Gianni Dagli Orti*)

The great Italian artist/inventor Leonardo da Vinci painted this panel in the early 1480s, showing an angel playing a LUTE. Lutes and HARPS were closely associated in the Renaissance with angels, because of their sweet sound that was thought to mimic the music one might hear in heaven. The lute was a recent introduction to Italy, having originated in Northern Africa and then traveled to Spain. Note the pear-shaped body of this instrument and the headstock that holds the tuning pegs that is set at a 90 degree angle to the NECK; both are typical design features of the lute. Lute music was set in a special form of MUSICAL NOTATION called TABLATURE, *(Corbis/National Gallery Collection. By kind permission, Trustees of the National Gallery, London)*

This is another manuscript illumination of musical BELLS, taken from the Velisslavoy Bible, created in the 13th century in Czechoslovakia. CHANGE-RINGING, or playing a melodies on a series of tuned bells, has been known for centuries. Sometimes a group of monks would play tunes by each handling one bell (thus playing one SCALE NOTE). This took great coordination of parts, because the notes would have to sound at their proper place (and only then) to play a MELODY. Here, a single monk using two mallets plays on a row of bells that are suspended over his head. (*Corbis/Gianni Dagli Orti*)

Music was an important part of church services from the very beginning. In order to preserve and teach musical parts, a system of MUSIC NOTATION began to be developed in the Medieval era. Very few people were taught to read music outside of the church, so these musical manuscripts were highly treasured and elaborately illustrated items, preserved in monasteries, for the education of the musical monks. This example shows some early NOTES that are square or diamond shape (indicating their TIME values). They are placed on a four–line STAFF. This manuscript was created in the 14th century and its illustration depicts a group of brothers of the fraternity of Santa Ma Carita in Venice, Italy. (*Corbis/Gianni Dagli Orti*)

This 18th century scene, showing a formal group of musicians posed in a stately drawing room, was attributed to Robert Levfrac–Tourniere, and painted around 1710. At this time, musicians were servants to the powerful princes and kings who ruled Europe. They were expected to dress appropriately to their position; FRANZ JOSEPH HAYDN, for example, could not appear in company without wearing his wig. Here, we see a number of the typical instruments of the day; on the left, the player holds a VIOL DA GAMBA, an early form of the CELLO. On the right, we see an early transverse flute; made of either ivory or a light-colored wood, it has a simple EMBOUCHURE and lacks the KEYS of a modern flute. In the center of the illustration, one musician is examining the score, while a second seated figure holds another transverse flute up, as if preparing to play. *(Corbis/National Gallery Collection. By kind permission, Trustees of the National Gallery, London)*

18th century portraits of musicians were done in a very formal style. The viewer could instantly tell that the subject was a musician, either by the fact that he was holding an instrument or, as in this painting, a small piece of music. This figure is, of course, the renowned composer JOHANN SEBASTIAN BACH, famous for his compositions for ORGAN, including intricate TOCATTAS and FUGUES. This portrait was painted by E. G. Hausmann in 1745. Bach is dressed in formal attire and wears the then-fashionable white powdered wig that was the expected uniform of a professional musician. (*Corbis/Bettman*)

In the 19th century, music escaped the church and court and entered the life of the average, middle–class person. This French print, created in 1801 by Philip de Bay, is titled "A Meeting at a Ball." Several figures are shown dancing in elaborate costumes, including a masked woman, a gallant soldier, and a dandy dressed in Moorish (or Middle Eastern) style pants with a turban–like hat. Providing the music on the far right is a cellist, who views the proceedings with a devilish grin on his face. Still, like his 18th century brethren, he wears formal clothes and a powdered wig; but this uniform would quickly disappear in the coming years when musicians became freelance performers, no longer dependent on the support of a wealthy benefactor. (*Corbis/Historical Print Archive*)

As the 19th century progressed, the music making of ordinary people—"the common folk"—became a subject of interest and study. FOLK MUSIC was recognized as an important reflection of a nation's cultural character. Images of common musicians became popular subjects for home decoration. Here we see a 19th century German plaque, made of porcelain, which was mass-produced for use as a simple decorative piece. It shows a folk musician holding a VIOLIN, dressed in full peasant clothing, including a cape and broad–brimmed hat. What a different image than the powdered–wig court musicians of a century earlier! (*Corbis/Peter Harholdt*)

Music making in the family home became popular among the middle and upper-classes in the 19th century. A well–educated young woman was expected, along with good grace and manners, to be able to play music as an entertainment for the family of dinner. Here in a print entitled "Music of the Family" created by the French artist, Grognet L. La Loup, a typical after–dinner scene is shown. At the left, a young lady sits at the PIANO entertaining a group of other young women. This print was part of a series called "Real Scenes," emphasizing the fact that this was a document of what could be commonly seen in any middle–class home in France at the time. (*Corbis/Gianni Dagli Orti*)

Music–making at home is vividly illustrated in this painting by the famous French impressionist, Edgar Degas, created around 1872. In it, he shows his father listening to a FOLK MUSICIAN who is entertaining him by playing the GUITAR. The guitar became tremendously popular in the late 19th century. Like the PIANO, it was often played by young women in family gatherings, after a meal. Traveling guitarists would go from home to home, entertaining the family in return for a meal, lodging, or tips. This musician most likely was one of the travelers who made his living by playing for customers at their homes. (*Corbis/Bettmann*)

In the late 19th and early 20th centuries, European cafes became centers for musical performances. The performers, often female, would combine several talents, such as singing, playing an instrument, juggling, dancing, and doing comic routines. Here the Parisian comedian/musician Marguerite Dufay is portrayed by the artist Louis Anquetin on a poster advertising her engagement at a local spot. The comic potential of a woman playing the ungainly brass TROMBONE was a popular part of her act, and is thus highlighted in this advertisment. (*Corbis/Historical picture*)

It is interesting to compare this early 20th century print of a dancing couple with the early 19th century print above. Here, a society couple, wearing formal evening clothes, enjoy a dance in what appears to be a lavish ballroom at a hotel. They are accompanied by two musicians playing tenor BANJOS, reflecting the influence of early JAZZ bands on society musicians. (The banjo was the rhythm instrument in jazz bands of the time). Rather than presenting dancing in a humorous or satirical way, this print emphasizes the glamor and seduction of the dance. It was created by the French artist Edweard Halouze in 1919. (*Corbis/Gianni Dagli Orti*)

◀

Merce Cunningham (right rear) watches a rehearsal. (Courtesy Henry Grossman/The John Cage Trust)

the complete independence of their constituent parts (music, sets and costumes, and choreography).

Cunning Little Vixen, The. Comic opera by LEOŠ JANÁČEK, 1924. A fairytale including human and animal actors, it tells the story of a schoolmaster and a parson who fight to gain the love of a gypsy girl. Meanwhile, the vixen of the title—a female fox—entices a group of hens to revolt against their owner. The vixen in turn is shot, and her pelt turned into a muffler for the farmer's wife.

cupped mouthpiece. The shallower, cup-shaped form of mouthpiece for BRASS wind instruments, as opposed to the deeper CONICAL MOUTHPIECE.

Cupped mouthpieces. (Courtesy Yamaha International Corporation) ▶

Curlew River. Church parable by BENJAMIN BRITTEN, 1964, first performed at the Aldeburgh Festival in England. The libretto is derived from a Japanese Noh play in which a mother searches for her son, who was taken away from her on the Curlew River. He is dead, but his grave becomes an object of pilgrimage.

Curran, Alvin, important American composer of the experimental school; b. Providence, R.I., Dec. 13, 1938. Curran studied piano and trombone in his youth, later receiving training in composition from Ron Nelson at Brown University (B.A., 1960) and from ELLIOTT CARTER and Mel Powell at Yale University (M.Mus., 1963). He went to Rome in 1965, where he founded Musica Elettronica Viva, an ensemble for the performance of live ELECTRONIC MUSIC. The ensemble later evolved to include all manner of AVANT-GARDE performance practices. His compositions range from tape works to experimental pieces using the natural environment.

cursus (Lat.). Generically, the type of prosody used at the end of a sung sentence in GREGORIAN CHANT. The type of cursus depends on the relative length of certain syllables. Some scholars maintain that a metrical cursus developed in church singing into a rhythmic cursus, in which the long syllables are sung at a higher pitch.

cut time. *See* ALLA BREVE.

cyclical forms. Forms that embrace a cycle or set of MOVEMENTS, such as the SUITE or PARTITA, SONATA, SYMPHONY, and CONCERTO.

cylindrical tube. An instrument tube that does not taper, as opposed to the CONICAL TUBE.

cymbals (It. *cinelli, piatti;* Ger. *Becken*). Orchestral PERCUSSION instrument, consisting of a pair of concave plates of brass or bronze, with broad, flat rims and holes for the straps by which they are held. It is used to make strong accents or to produce peculiar effects.

cythara. *See* KITHARA.

Czerny, Carl, composer, pianist, and influential pedagogue; b. Vienna, Feb. 20, 1791; d. there, July 15, 1857. Of Czech extraction (*czerný* means "black" in Czech), he was trained as a pianist by his stern father, whose rule of life was work without distraction. When Czerny himself became a teacher, he demanded a similar dedication from his pupils. His day began at 7:00 A.M. and included a single meal before going to bed. Czerny was fortunate in gaining LUDWIG VAN BEETHOVEN's friendship, and his only piano sonata, op.7, bears a striking resemblance to Beethoven's style. Among Czerny's own students was FRANZ LISZT.

Czerny's name is everlastingly connected with the enormous collections of piano studies that he published under such names as *School of Velocity* or *School of Finger Dexterity.* These exercises continue to inflict pianistic torture upon generations of budding pianists.

MUSICAL INSTRUMENT

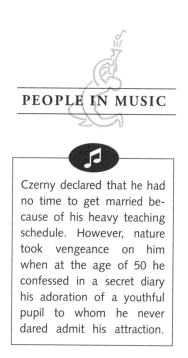

PEOPLE IN MUSIC

Czerny declared that he had no time to get married because of his heavy teaching schedule. However, nature took vengeance on him when at the age of 50 he confessed in a secret diary his adoration of a youthful pupil to whom he never dared admit his attraction.

D

In French, Spanish, Italian, and Russian terminology, D is called *Re,* derived from the first syllable of the second line of the millennian hymn *Ut queant laxis:* "**Re**sonare libris."

D (Ger. *D;* Fr. *ré;* It. *re*). 1. The second TONE and DEGREE of the C major scale. 2. In music theory, uppercase *D* designates the D-major TRIAD, lowercase *d* the d-minor triad. 3. *Da* (D.C. = DA CAPO); *Dal* (D.S. = *Dal segno,* to the sign).

D major (Ger. *D dur*). The key of classical strength and clarity. It is particularly suitable for works written for string instruments, because the TONIC (D) and the DOMINANT (A) are played on open strings on the violin, viola, and cello. CHORDS and SCALE passages can be easily and rapidly played on string instruments in this key.

The great majority of violin CONCERTOS are written in D major: those by LUDWIG VAN BEETHOVEN, JOHANNES BRAHMS, and PIOTR ILYICH TCHAIKOVSKY are the most famous examples. WOLFGANG AMADEUS MOZART set his *Prague* Symphony and the endearing *Haffner* Symphony in D major, both works expressing the joy of music making. One of the most frequently played symphonies by FRANZ JOSEPH HAYDN, written for his London concerts and catalogued as no. 104, is in D major.

When SERGEI PROKOFIEV determined to show the world that he could emulate Haydn *à la moderne,* he wrote his *Classical Symphony* in the key of D major.

D minor (Ger. *D moll*). The key of unexpressed emotion.

The greatest of all works written in D minor, LUDWIG VAN BEETHOVEN's Ninth Symphony, does not openly declare its TONALITY. Instead, the orchestra plays a series of FIFTHS, so the listener is not sure whether the work will be in a major or minor key. It is only when the tension becomes unbearable that the composer reveals the minor key signature.

Why is the D-minor triad commonly used by pianists to tune string instruments in playing chamber music? Why not

Not all D-minor works are sad or thoughtful. GUSTAV MAHLER'S Third Symphony expresses joy in the presence of nature. Its separate movements describe in musical tones the smell of flowers and the grandeur of natural beauty.

D major? The explanation may be in the neutral character of the sound of D minor, which is more suitable to the non-tempered natural pitch of the violin and cello.

da camera (It.). In the BAROQUE, secular CHAMBER MUSIC.

da capo (It., from the head). Repeat from the beginning. *Da capo al fine,* repeat from beginning to end (that is, to the word *fine* or a FERMATA); *da capo al segno,* from the beginning to the sign ([segno = sign]); *da capo al segno, poi (segue) la coda,* from the beginning to the sign, then play the CODA.

da capo aria. *See* ARIA DA CAPO.

Da Ponte, Lorenzo (born Emanuele Conegliano), famous Italian librettist; b. Ceneda, near Venice, Mar. 10, 1749; d. N.Y., Aug. 17, 1838. Although he was of a Jewish family, Da Ponte was converted to Christianity at the age of 14 and assumed the name of his patron, Lorenzo da Ponte, bishop of Ceneda. He then studied at the Ceneda Seminary and at the Portogruaro Seminary, where he taught from 1770 to 1773.

In 1774 Da Ponte obtained a post as professor of rhetoric at Treviso but was dismissed in 1776 because he refused to accept the church's teachings regarding natural law. He then went to Venice, where he led an adventurous life, but was banished from that city in 1779 for adultery.

Da Ponte subsequently lived in Austria and in Dresden; in 1782 he settled in Vienna and became official poet to the Imperial Theater. His most important professional association came in Vienna, when he met and befriended WOLFGANG AMADEUS MOZART. Da Ponte wrote the books (or LIBRETTOS) for Mozart's most famous operas, *Le nozze di Figaro,* DON GIOVANNI, and *Così fan tutte.* These are considered among the greatest operas of all time. Mozart's music and Da Ponte's text perfectly complement each other.

From 1792 to 1798 Da Ponte was in London. He traveled in Europe, then went to N.Y. in 1805. After disastrous business ventures, with intervals of teaching, he became interested in various operatic enterprises. In his last years he taught Italian at Columbia College.

PEOPLE IN MUSIC

dactyl(e) (Lat., *dactylus,* finger, in reference to the layout of the joints). A metrical FOOT with syllables arranged as one long accented syllable followed by two short unaccented ones. A rapid WALTZ without strong upbeat represents a musical equivalent of a dactyl.

Dafne. Opera by Jacopo Peri, 1597, with a text by Rinuccini. It is considered the first opera. The music is lost.

PEOPLE IN MUSIC

Dahl, Ingolf, distinguished Swedish-born American composer, conductor, pianist, and teacher; b. Hamburg (of Swedish parents), June 9, 1912; d. Frutigen, near Bern, Switzerland, Aug. 6, 1970. Dahl studied composition with Philip Jarnach at the Conservatory of Cologne between 1930 and 1932 and musicology and conducting at the University of Zurich from 1932 to 1936. He emigrated to the U.S. in 1938, settling in California and becoming a citizen in 1943.

In the U.S., Dahl became active as a conductor and composer. In 1945 he was appointed an assistant professor at the University of Southern California. He also taught at the Berkshire Music Center, Tanglewood, during the summers of 1952–55.

As a performer Dahl actively promoted the music of IGOR STRAVINSKY, who also influenced Dahl's own compositions. In his later works, such as his Sinfonietta for Concert Band (1961) and his *Aria Sinfonica* (1965), Dahl adopted ARNOLD SCHOENBERG's 12-TONE technique of composition.

PEOPLE IN MUSIC

Dale, Clamma, African-American soprano; b. Chester, Pa., July 4, 1948. Dale first studied piano, then clarinet and singing, and at 14 began to study voice at Philadelphia's Settlement Music School. She subsequently enrolled at the Juilliard School of Music in N.Y. (B.Mus., 1970; M.S., 1975). She made her debut with the N.Y. Opera as Antonia in *Les Contes d'Hoffmann* in 1975. Other roles there were Nedda, Musetta, the Countess in *Le nozze di Figaro,* Pamina, and Bess. In 1988 she sang GERSHWIN's Bess at the Theater des Westens in Berlin, and in 1989 PUCCINI's Liu at the Deutsche Oper there.

Dalibor. Opera by BEDŘICH SMETANA, 1868. It is based on a historical rebellion of Bohemian peasants led by the hero, Dalibor. He is captured, but a noblewoman who loves him attempts to free him from prison. She disguises herself as a man in an attempt to rescue him. Unlike BEETHOVEN'S *FIDE-LIO,* however, the scheme is unsuccessful. Smetana wrote three endings, all tragic.

Dallapiccola, Luigi, distinguished Italian composer and pedagogue; b. Pisino, Istria, Feb. 3, 1904; d. Florence, Feb. 19, 1975. Dallapiccola took piano lessons at an early

PEOPLE IN MUSIC

◀

Luigi Dallapiccola, 1950. (David Lees/© Corbis)

age. He went to school at the Pisino Gymnasium from 1914 to 1921, with a break in 1917–18, when his family was politically exiled in Graz, and also studied piano and harmony in nearby Trieste from 1919–21.

In 1922, Dallapiccola moved to Florence, where he studied piano and composition at the Cherubini Conservatory. He was also active in the Italian section of the ISCM from the early 1930s. From 1934 to 1967 Dallapiccola served on the faculty of the Cherubini Conservatory.

Dallapiccola visited London in 1946 and traveled on the Continent. He also taught courses in various American colleges from the early 1950s through the late 1960s. A collection of his essays was published under the title *Appunti incontri meditazioni* (1970).

As a composer, Dallapiccola has adapted the 12-TONE theory of ARNOLD SCHOENBERG to the difficult task of writing music with memorable melodies. His vocal works are particularly noteworthy. He was able to create demanding, melodic vocal parts within the strict rules of composition of modern music.

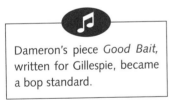

PEOPLE IN MUSIC

Dameron's piece *Good Bait,* written for Gillespie, became a bop standard.

Dameron, Tadd (Tadley Ewing), African-American JAZZ pianist, bandleader, arranger, and composer; b. Cleveland, Feb. 21, 1917; d. N.Y., Mar. 8, 1965. Dameron was inspired to follow a career as a jazz musician by his brother Caesar, a saxophone player. He subsequently played piano with the touring bands of Freddie Webster, Zack White, and Blanche Calloway.

Dameron's break came in 1939 when he joined the progressive Kansas City band the Rockets. His compositions *Dameron Stomp* and *A La Bridges* (written for band member Hank Bridges) forecast the BEBOP style. In the 1940s and 1950s Dameron moved to N.Y., where he played informally with many of the founders of bebop, including DIZZY GILLESPIE, MILES DAVIS, and CLIFFORD BROWN.

Dameron was in demand as an accomplished composer and arranger, working in Chicago and N.Y. through the 1950s and early 1960s. His career was plagued by his addiction to narcotics, however, as a result of which he served time in federal prison in Lexington, Kentucky, from 1958 to 1960. His death in 1965 was as a result of drug abuse.

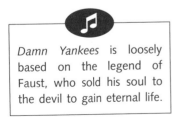

Damn Yankees is loosely based on the legend of Faust, who sold his soul to the devil to gain eternal life.

Damn Yankees. Musical by Richard Adler and Jerry Ross (the last work of the latter), 1955, based on Douglass Wallop's novel *The Year the Yankees Lost the Pennant.* With the devil's help, an aging baseball fan is transformed into a superstar who helps the lowly Washington Senators defeat the mighty N.Y. Yankees. The fan gets out of the devil's hold through a technicality. Includes *You've Got to Have Heart* and *Whatever Lola Wants.*

Damnation de Faust, La. Dramatic legend by HECTOR BERLIOZ, 1846, based on part 1 of Goethe's *Faust.* Berlioz's work was first performed in Paris.

Berlioz made many changes to the story to suit his musical adaptation. He added a sequence placed in Hungary, which includes the celebrated *Rakoczy March,* which is associated with Hungarian nationalism. He also introduced an effective choral pandemonium in which minor devils converse in a nonsense language.

Berlioz also changed the story so that the heroine, Gretchen, goes to heaven, but Faust is sent straight to hell. The reinterpretation of Goethe (found also in CHARLES GOUNOD's opera) is considered blasphemous by certain German cultural patriots. While the Berlioz work is an oratorio, there have been staged performances.

damper (Ger. *Dämpfer*). 1. A set of mechanical devices, placed over PIANO strings, that goes into operation when a key is released by the finger. The damper stops the string, thus causing the string's vibration to end.

Damper pedal, the right, or loud, piano pedal, which, when pressed, lifts the dampers from the strings.

2. The MUTE of a BRASS instrument.

dance band. An instrumental ensemble accompanying ballroom dancing and composed of SAXOPHONES, TRUMPETS, TROMBONES, and PERCUSSION.

Dance in the Place Congo, The. SYMPHONIC POEM, 1918, by Henry F. Gilbert. Place Congo is a New Orleans square where African-American slaves would meet on Sundays to dance. The borrowing of local tunes signified Gilbert's pioneering attempt to integrate classical and world musics.

Dance of the Hours. See GIOCONDA, LA.

Dancing in the Streets. A 1964 Martha and the Vandellas hit that became an anthem for 1960s inner-city youth. It was later covered by Van Halen and in a duo version by Mick Jagger and DAVID BOWIE.

Danny Boy. Sentimental text added to the *Londonderry Air* by Frederick Weatherly, 1913. This song has become associated with Irish patriotism.

Danse des morts, La. ORATORIO by ARTHUR HONEGGER, 1940, to a text by Claudel. It is based on the traditional image of the Dance of Death, including a quotation of the DIES IRAE.

Danse macabre. SYMPHONIC POEM by CAMILLE SAINT-SAËNS, 1875. It depicts a gathering of celebrating spirits on a Halloween-like evening, with ghostly violin apparitions, that comes to an end with the rooster's crow.

Danse sacrée et danse profane. A work by CLAUDE DEBUSSY, 1904, for harp and strings. The *Sacred Dance* is based on a PENTATONIC (five-note) scale, commonly heard in folk music. While it is written to a hymnlike meter, the *Profane Dance* is syncopated.

Danse sauvage. Piano piece, 1913, by Leo Ornstein. Its savagery is expressed by a series of rhythmic, DISSONANT chords. Amazingly, the piece shocked listeners when Ornstein played it in N.Y. and London on the eve of World War I, causing one bewildered English critic to describe Ornstein as "a new star in the musical sky that effectually pales the fires of SCHOENBERG and STRAVINSKY."

Dantons Tod. Opera by Gottfried von Einem, 1947, based on the life and death of a prime mover of the French revolution. The *Marseillaise* and other revolutionary songs are quoted in it.

Daphne. Bucolic tragedy by RICHARD STRAUSS, 1938. It is based on a subject found in the earliest OPERAS: the nymph, Daphne, who eludes the amorous Apollo by transforming herself into a laurel tree. In his unhappiness, he blesses the tree.

Daphnis et Chloé. Ballet by MAURICE RAVEL, 1912. It recounts the mutual love of Daphnis and Chloé, who tend sheep. It was first performed by DIAGHILEV's Ballets Russes. Ravel later drew two orchestral suites from it. The work is noted for its rich orchestral colors, meant to depict the natural beauty of farm life.

Dargomyzhsky, Alexander (Sergeievich), outstanding Russian composer; b. Troitskoye, Tula district, Feb. 14, 1813; d. St. Petersburg, Jan. 17, 1869. From 1817 Dargomyzhsky lived in St. Petersburg, where he studied piano and violin. From 1827 to 1843 he held a government position, then devoted himself exclusively to music, studying for a further eight years. As part of these studies, he visited Germany, Brussels, and Paris in 1845.

PEOPLE IN MUSIC

Dargomyzhsky then returned to Russia, producing in Moscow an OPERA, *Esmeralda* (after Victor Hugo's *Notre-Dame de Paris,* 1847), with great success. From 1845 to 1855 he published over 100 minor works. He had many works produced in St. Petersburg, including his best opera, *Rusalka* (1856) and an opera-ballet, *The Triumph of Bacchus* (1867). A posthumous opera was also produced there in 1872, *The Stone Guest* (*Kamennyi gost,* after Pushkin's eponymous poem), scored by NIKOLAI RIMSKY-KORSAKOV. He also sketched a few scenes of a fantasy-opera, *Rogdana.*

At first a follower of Italian and French opera composers, Dargomyzhsky became interested in Russia's own musical traditions. He also felt that earlier opera composers had not been realistic enough in their approach to the music and text. He applied this realistic method in treating the RECITATIVE in his opera *The Stone Guest* and in his songs (several to satirical words).

Dargomyzhsky's orchestral works, also reflecting Russian theme (*Finnish* Fantasia, *Cossack Dance, Baba-Yaga,* etc.), enjoyed wide popularity. In 1867 he was elected president of the Russian Music Society.

dark (Fr. *relâche*). In theatrical jargon, no performance.

Daughter of the Regiment, The. *See* FILLE DU RÉGIMENT, LA.

David. OPERA by DARIUS MILHAUD, 1954, commemorating the city of Jerusalem and its greatest king.

David, Hal, American lyricist, brother of MACK DAVID; b. N.Y., May 25, 1921. David studied journalism at N.Y. University following World War II. After working with a variety of composers, he made his most important partnership in 1959 with pianist BURT BACHARACH. Together they wrote a series of mid-1960s hits that defined the popular BALLAD in the rock 'n' roll age. Lyrics he wrote for Bacharach include *My Little Red Book; Love Can Break a Heart; Send Me No Flowers; What's New, Pussycat?;* and *Wives and Lovers.* They wrote the popular Broadway MUSICAL *Promises, Promises* (1968). His lyrics for *Raindrops Keep Falling on My Head* (1969) for the film *Butch Cassidy and the Sundance Kid* won an Academy Award. The David-Bacharach partnership ended in 1971.

David was less successful in later decades, although he occasionally had a hit working with various composers. From 1980 to 1986 David was president of ASCAP.

David, Mack, American lyricist and composer, brother of HAL DAVID; b. N.Y., July 5, 1912; d. Rancho Mirage, Calif., Dec. 30, 1993. David studied at Cornell University and at St. John's University Law School. Turning to writing for Broadway and for films, he collaborated with many leading JAZZ and film composers, including COUNT BASIE, BURT BACHARACH, Ernest Gold, ELMER BERNSTEIN, David Raksin, and HENRY MANCINI. Among his best-known songs are *Bibbidi, Bobbidi, Boo* (1948); *Cat Ballou* (1965); *The Hanging Tree* (1959); *It's a Mad, Mad, Mad, Mad World* (1963); and *My Own True Love* (1954).

Davidovich, Bella, esteemed Russian-born American pianist and teacher; b. Baku, July 16, 1928. Her maternal grandfather was concertmaster of the Baku opera orchestra, and her mother was a pianist. Davidovich began formal piano training when she was six, and at age nine she appeared as soloist in LUDWIG VAN BEETHOVEN's First Piano Concerto in Baku.

PEOPLE IN MUSIC

PEOPLE IN MUSIC

PEOPLE IN MUSIC

Mack David filed a spectacular lawsuit for copyright infringement of his song *Sunflower* (1948), which he claimed was plagiarized by JERRY HERMAN for the latter's sensationally popular song HELLO, DOLLY (1964). The sum paid in an out-of-court settlement was in excess of half a million dollars.

In 1939 Davidovich was sent to Moscow to pursue her studies with Konstantin Igumnov, with whom she subsequently also studied at the Moscow Conservatory from 1946 to 1948, where she completed her training with Yakov Flier during 1948–54.

In 1949 Davidovich captured joint first prize at the Chopin Competition in Warsaw, which launched her upon a highly successful career in Russia and Eastern Europe. Between 1950 and 1978 she was a soloist each season with the Leningrad Philharmonic and also taught at the Moscow Conservatory from 1962 to 1978. In 1967 she made her first appearance outside Russia, playing in Amsterdam, and in 1971 she made a tour of Italy.

Following the defection of her son, the violinist and conductor Dmitry Sitkovetsky (b. Baku, Sept. 27, 1954), to the West in 1977, Davidovich was refused permission to perform outside the Soviet Union by the government. In 1978 she emigrated to the U.S., becoming a naturalized citizen in 1984. In 1979 she made an acclaimed debut in a recital at N.Y.'s Carnegie Hall. In 1982 she joined the faculty of the Juilliard School in N.Y. but continued to pursue an international career. In 1988 she and her son returned to Russia, being the first émigrés to be invited to perform there after the Gorbachev era of reform was launched.

Davidovsky, Mario, Argentine composer; b. Buenos Aires, March 4, 1934. Davidovsky studied composition and theory with Guillermo Graetzer in Buenos Aires and also took courses with Latin American composers Teodor Fuchs, Erwin Leuchter, and Ernesto Epstein.

Davidovsky went to the U.S. in the late 1950s to continue his musical studies. He trained with MILTON BABBITT at the Berkshire Music Center, in Tanglewood, Mass., during the summer of 1958. Working with Babbitt, he was influenced to explore ELECTRONIC MUSIC and to use mathematics as a means of organizing his own works. He began working at the Columbia-Princeton Electronic Music Center in 1960, which Babbitt cofounded to enable composers to work with COMPUTERS, and became its director in 1981.

Davidovsky was awarded two Guggenheim fellowships in 1960 and 1971. He also received the Pulitzer Prize in mu-

PEOPLE IN MUSIC

sic in 1971 for his *Synchronisms No. 6* for piano and electronics. In 1982 he was elected a member of the Institute of the American Academy and Institute of Arts and Letters.

Davidsbündler-Tänze. Piano SUITE by ROBERT SCHUMANN, 1837, containing 18 pieces. The Davidsbund is an imaginary "band" that Schumann created for these works. He named it for King David of Israel, who routed the nonbelievers from his country. Similarly, these pieces are meant to drive the Philistines out of music.

Davies, Dennis Russell, American conductor; b. Toledo, Ohio, Apr. 16, 1944. Davies studied piano and conducting at the Juilliard School of Music in N.Y. (B.Mus., 1966; M.S., 1968; D.M.A., 1972), where he also taught (1968–71).

While at Juilliard, Davies cofounded, with Luciano Berio, the JUILLIARD ENSEMBLE, which he led from 1968 to 1974. This group premiered many important works by modern composers. Davies became well known as a conductor sympathetic to modern works and led various progressive groups throughout the United States during the 1970s.

Beginning in 1978, Davies worked primarily in Germany. He was Generalmusikdirektor (general director of music) at the Württemberg State Theater in Stuttgart between 1980 and 1987, then held the same position in Bonn from 1987 to 1991. In 1987 he received the Alice M. Ditson conductor's award.

Davies then returned to the U.S., where, from 1991 to 1996, he was music director of the Brooklyn Academy of Music and principal conductor of the Brooklyn Philharmonic. He also continued to hold positions in Germany.

Davies, Sir Peter Maxwell, remarkable English composer and conductor; b. Manchester, Sept. 8, 1934. Davies went to Leigh Grammar School and then to the Royal Manchester College of Music and Manchester University.

In 1957 Davies won a scholarship from the Italian government and proceeded to Rome, where he studied with Goffredo Petrassi. His orchestral work *Prolation* (named after a MEDIEVAL metrical division) received the Olivetti Prize

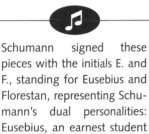

Schumann signed these pieces with the initials E. and F., standing for Eusebius and Florestan, representing Schumann's dual personalities: Eusebius, an earnest student of music, and Florestan, a romantic youth.

PEOPLE IN MUSIC

PEOPLE IN MUSIC

in 1958. It was performed at the festival of the ISCM in Rome on June 10, 1959.

Returning to England, Davies served as director of music at Cirencester Grammar School from 1959 to 1962. While teaching there, he became well known for his unusual approach to music education. Instead of emphasizing memorization and practice, he hoped to encourage creativity among his students. In 1965 he continued this interest in musical education by joining the UNESCO Conference on Music in Education and traveled around the world on a lecture tour.

In 1962 Davies went to the U.S. on a Harkness fellowship and took the opportunity to study with ROGER SESSIONS at Princeton University. Back in England, in 1967 he organized in London an ensemble called the Pierrot Players. In 1970 it was renamed the Fires of London, with the mission of presenting programs of modern works. That same year, Davies made his permanent home in the Orkney Islands, off the coast of Scotland. In 1977 he organized there the annual St. Magnus Festival, which gave its presentations at the Norse Cathedral of St. Magnus. He also staged many of his own compositions, several inspired by medieval CHANTS. Despite the remoteness of the Orkney Islands, the festival attracted worldwide attention.

In 1979 Davies was awarded an honorary doctorate of music at Edinburgh University. He was also appointed successor to Sir William Glock as director of music at Dartington Summer School and was named Composer of the Year by the Composers' Guild of Great Britain. He was commissioned to write a symphony for the Boston Symphony Orchestra on the occasion of its centennial in 1981. In 1985 he was named composer-in-residence and associate conductor of the Scottish Chamber Orchestra in Glasgow, with which he toured. In 1987 he was knighted.

In 1992 Davies was made conductor-composer for the BBC Philharmonic and associate conductor-composer for the Royal Philharmonic in London. From 1995 he served as president for the Society for the Promotion of New Music.

In his works Davies combines seemingly unrelated styles and sounds. He has an interest in medieval vocal styles but weds them to almost surrealistic plot lines and satiric depictions of modern people and events. His most arresting work in this manner is *Eight Songs for a Mad King* (1969) for male voice and instruments, a fantastic SUITE representing the development of the madness of King George III. Another is *Vesalii icones* for dancer, solo cello, and instruments, also from 1969. It is composed in 14 movements, representing 14 anatomical drawings by Andreas Vesalius and depicting Christ's Passion and Resurrection. Among his more recent works are *Resurrection*, an OPERA (1987); *Turn of the Tide* for children's chorus and orchestra (1992); *A Spell for Green Corn: The MacDonald Dances* for orchestra (1993); *The Three Kings* for soloists, chorus, and orchestra (1995); and a Piccolo Concerto (1996).

Davies is a fervent political activist. He has participated in the movement combating the spread of nuclear weapons and is a strong defender of the environment.

Davis, Anthony, African-American composer and pianist; b. Paterson, N.J., Feb. 20, 1951. Davis studied at Yale University (B.A., 1975), also working as a JAZZ pianist. He was cofounder of Advent (1973), a free jazz ensemble that included trombonist George Lewis, and then played in trumpeter Wadada Leo Smith's New Delta Ahkri band from 1974 to 1977. He also played in N.Y. with violinist Leroy Jenkins (1977–79) and with flutist James Newton, both active proponents of the Association for the Advancement of Creative Musicians (AACM).

His compositions, while strictly notated, are improvisational in tone. His OPERA *X: The Life and Times of Malcolm X* was produced in Philadelphia in 1985 and at N.Y.'s Lincoln Center four years later. Other works include *Tania* (1992), an opera inspired by the kidnapping of newspaper heiress Patty Hearst; *Lost Moon Sisters* for soprano, violin, keyboards, marimba, and vibraphone composed in 1990; and *Hemispheres,* a five-part dance work written for dancer-choreographer Molissa Fenley in 1983.

Among his many recordings are *Of Blues and Dreams* (1978), *Hidden Voices* (with J. Newton; 1979), and *Under the Double Moon* (with J. Hoggard; 1982).

Davis, Sir Colin (Rex), eminent English conductor; b. Weybridge, Sept. 25, 1927. Davis studied the clarinet at the Royal College of Music in London and played in the band of the Household Cavalry while serving in the army. He began his conducting career with the semiprofessional Chelsea Opera Group. From 1961 to 1965 Davis served as music director of the well-known London opera house Sadler's Wells.

Davis made his U.S. debut as a guest conductor with the Minneapolis Symphony Orchestra in 1960, subsequently holding positions with other leading U.S. orchestras. In 1965 he conducted at the Royal Opera at Covent Garden, succeeding SIR GEORGE SOLTI as its music director in 1971. In 1967 he made his Metropolitan Opera, N.Y., debut, conducting PETER GRIMES. From 1972 to 1983 he served as principal guest conductor of the Boston Symphony Orchestra.

Among Davis's notable achievements was the production at Covent Garden of the entire cycle of RICHARD WAGNER'S DER RING DES NIBELUNGEN in 1974–76. In 1977 he became the first British conductor to appear at the Bayreuth Festival, conducting TANNHÄUSER. He conducted the Royal Opera during its tours in South Korea and Japan in 1979 and in the U.S. in 1984. From 1983 to 1993 he was chief conductor of the Bavarian Radio Symphony Orchestra in Munich, which he led on a tour of North America in 1986. In 1986 he stepped down as music director at Covent Garden to devote himself fully to his duties in Munich and to pursue far-flung engagements as a guest conductor with the major orchestras and opera houses of the world. From 1995 he was principal conductor of the London Symphony Orchestra and from 1998 was principal guest conductor of the N.Y. Philharmonic.

Davis was made a Commander of the Order of the British Empire in 1965 and was knighted in 1980.

Davis, Miles (Dewey, III), outstanding African-American JAZZ trumpeter and bandleader; b. Alton, Ill., May 25, 1926; d. N.Y., Sept. 21, 1991. Davis learned to play trumpet while attending elementary school in East St. Louis, Ill., then continued his studies in high school, where he played in the band. Before graduation he already made professional appearances around his hometown.

PEOPLE IN MUSIC

In 1944 Davis went to N.Y. and entered the Juilliard School of Music. He also frequented jazz spots in the city. Deciding upon a full-time career as a jazz musician, he quit Juilliard in 1945 and began working with CHARLIE PARKER, COLEMAN HAWKINS, BENNY CARTER, and BILLY ECKSTINE.

Initially, Davis played in the then-popular BEBOP style, greatly influenced by trumpeter DIZZY GILLESPIE. In the late 1940s, however, Davis recorded a famous session known as *The Birth of the Cool.* In arrangements by GIL EVANS, the group introduced what would become known as COOL JAZZ, a style that was thoughtful, slower, and much less brassy than bop.

In the mid-1950s Davis continued his exploration of cool jazz, often using a MUTE in his trumpet and playing pieces at a slow tempo. His quartet featured many leading musicians, including saxophonist JOHN COLTRANE, pianist Red Garland, and Philly Joe Jones on drums.

Davis continued to perform into the 1960s, again modifying his style. In the mid-1960s he led a group that featured many of the next generation of jazz stars, including pianist HERBIE HANCOCK, bassist RON CARTER, and drummer Tony Williams. They began to experiment with more ROCK-oriented rhythms, as well as creating less structured, more improvised pieces. Then, in 1968, Davis created an entirely new band, his first in the new JAZZ-ROCK style. In a series of albums beginning with *Bitches Brew,* Davis created long, im-

Miles Daivs, c. 1963. (Hulton-Deutsch Collection/Corbis) ▶

Davis's most famous work of this period was the 1958 album *Kind of Blue.* Featuring pianist BILL EVANS, who influenced many of the compositions on it, Davis worked using MODES rather than Western SCALES, eliminating the normal harmonic base of jazz.

provised melodies set against a hard-rock rhythm section, featuring many African percussion instruments.

Davis continued to play in this style until 1975, when he retired from performing and recording, owing to increasing drug use and several illnesses. He returned to center stage with his album *The Man with the Horn* in 1981. A year later he made an extensive tour of Europe. Davis's later career was uneven, however. He tried to remain on the cutting edge by recording jazz versions of popular songs by MICHAEL JACKSON, and even collaborated with the rock star Prince. Much of his work was neither successful as jazz or rock, however, and his playing became lackluster.

Davis published his autobiography in 1989. It raised some eyebrows because of its frank use of language and his descriptions of his abusive dealings with women. Davis died in 1991 after years of battling various physical conditions.

davul (*dawūl*). Cylindrical Turkish drum with a double head, closely associated with the ZURNĀ.

MUSICAL
INSTRUMENT

Dawson, William Levi, African-American composer; b. Anniston, Ala., Sept. 26, 1898; d. Tuskegee, Ala., May 2, 1990. Dawson ran away from home at 13 to enter the Tuskegee Institute, one of the best colleges for African-American students at that time. He graduated in 1921, then studied with Carl Busch in Kansas City and at the American Conservatory in Chicago (M.A., 1927). Dawson played first trombone in the Chicago Civic Orchestra from 1926 to 1930, then conducted the Tuskegee Choir. His best-known work is the three-movement *Negro Folk Symphony* (1934). His last major work was *A Negro Song* for orchestra (1940).

PEOPLE IN MUSIC

De Franco, "Buddy" (Boniface Ferdinand Leonardo), American JAZZ clarinetist; b. Camden, N.J., Feb. 17, 1923. De Franco took up the clarinet at the age of 12. After working with many leading jazz musicians, including GENE KRUPA (1941–42), Charlie Barnet (1943-44), TOMMY DORSEY (1944-46), and COUNT BASIE (1950), he organized his own big band (1951) and quartet (1952), appearing with the latter for many years with much success. He led the

PEOPLE IN MUSIC

GLENN MILLER Orchestra from 1966 to 1974, then resumed solo touring.

deaconing (lining out). In English and American colonial churches, the deacon, or another lay singer, would read a line from a HYMN before the entire congregation sang it. In this way, church members who could not read could learn the words.

deafness. No greater misfortune can befall a musician than the loss of hearing. LUDWIG VAN BEETHOVEN gave an eloquent expression of this horror in his famous "Heiligenstadt Testament." He was willing to consult every Viennese quack who promised a cure. Some critics attributed explained the strangeness of Beethoven's last works to the composer's deafness. "Beethoven's imagination seems to have fed upon the ruins of his sensitive organs," wrote William Gardiner of London in 1837.

Among other victims of ear ailments was BEDŘICH SMETANA. Pressure on the auditory nerve made him hear a constant drone on a high E. He made use of this affliction in his First String Quartet, *From My Life*, in which he has the violin play a persistent high E. ROBERT SCHUMANN suffered from a similar disturbance technically known as tinnitus, and during his last years he heard a constant A♭. GABRIEL FAURÉ became almost totally deaf toward the end of his life, but he succeeded in hiding this condition sufficiently long to continue in his office as director of the Paris Conservatory.

Many rock stars have suffered from a persistent ringing in the ear, caused by overexposure to loud music. Pete Townshend, leader of the WHO, had to give up playing electric instruments because of this malady.

Death and the Maiden. Nickname for String Quartet No. 14 in D Minor by FRANZ SCHUBERT, 1824 (D. 810). The work contains a variation based on Schubert's song *Der Tod und das Mädchen* (Death and the maiden), which is the source of its nickname.

Death and Transfiguration (*Tod und Verklärung*). SYMPHONIC POEM by RICHARD STRAUSS, 1890, first performed in Eisenach. The music depicts the struggle of a sick man with approaching death. It is set in the key of C MINOR, the tonality of quiet horror. But the death motive is transfigured at the end into C MAJOR, as the liberated soul departs from the body.

Death in Venice. Opera by BENJAMIN BRITTEN, 1973, based on the novella of the same name by Thomas Mann. It was first performed at the Aldeburgh Festival in Great Britain.

The opera tells the story of an aging German writer, Gustav Aschenbach ("brook of ashes"), who goes to Venice in search of new meaning for his life. He encounters an adolescent Polish boy on vacation with his family. Aschenbach is inspired and moved by the boy's innocence and unsullied view of life. An epidemic of cholera breaks out in Venice, and the boy's family hurriedly leaves. After the boy's departure, Aschenbach cannot find any motivation to leave and falls victim to the dreaded disease.

Britten's opera is austere in its musical setting, with simple melodies accompanied by sparely voiced harmonies. The part of Aschenbach is set almost entirely in accompanied RECITATIVE. This lack of melody reflects Aschenbach's depression and lack of interest in life.

Death of Klinghoffer, The. Opera by JOHN ADAMS, 1991. It was inspired by the murder of a wheelchair-bound American, Leon Klinghoffer, aboard the kidnapped Italian cruise ship *Achille Lauro* in the Mediterranean in 1985. Like many modern works, the story is fragmented. Klinghoffer is not presented as a sympathetic figure.

Debussy, (Achille-) **Claude,** great modern French composer, the originator of musical IMPRESSIONISM; b. St.-Germain-en-Laye, Aug. 22, 1862; d. Paris, Mar. 25, 1918. Mme. Maute de Fleurville, the mother-in-law of the poet Paul Verlaine, trained Debussy for his audition for the Paris Conservatory. He was admitted at age 10 and studied piano and solfège, garnering many honors. He furthered his studies after graduation by studying composition and notation privately.

In 1880 Debussy's piano teacher, Antoine-François Marmontel, recommended him to Mme. Nadezhda von Meck, PIOTR ILYICH TCHAIKOVSKY's patroness. She summoned him to Interlaken, Switzerland, and they subsequently visited

The author Thomas Mann himself visited Venice in 1911 and was impressed by a vacationing Polish boy who became the model for the character in his novella. A motion picture was made of his novel, in which the character of Aschenbach was changed to that of a composer, strongly suggesting the German composer GUSTAV MAHLER (and Mahler's music is used much in the sound track). Friends of Mahler's family vigorously protested this portrayal of Mahler as an old, emotionless man. The Polish boy of the novella was found to be still living in Sweden as late as 1970 and remembered having seen Mann in Venice some 60 years before.

PEOPLE IN MUSIC

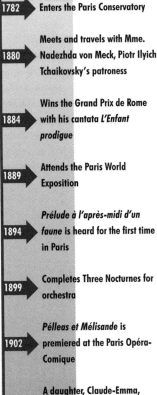

Debussy time line

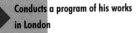

1862 ▶ Born

1782 ▶ Enters the Paris Conservatory

1880 ▶ Meets and travels with Mme. Nadezhda von Meck, Piotr Ilyich Tchaikovsky's patroness

1884 ▶ Wins the Grand Prix de Rome with his cantata *L'Enfant prodigue*

1889 ▶ Attends the Paris World Exposition

1894 ▶ *Prélude à l'après-midi d'un faune* is heard for the first time in Paris

1899 ▶ Completes Three Nocturnes for orchestra

1902 ▶ *Pélleas et Mélisande* is premiered at the Paris Opéra-Comique

1905 ▶ A daughter, Claude-Emma, a.k.a. "Chouchou," is born to Debussy and his second wife

1905 ▶ *La Mer* is completed during a sojourn in England

1906–12 ▶ Composes *Images*

1908 ▶ Conducts a program of his works in London

1913 ▶ *Jeux* is produced in Paris by Serge Diaghilev

1913–15 ▶ Completes work on the Preludes (1913) and Études (1915)

Rome, Naples, and Fiesole. During the summers of 1881 and 1882 Debussy stayed with Mme. von Meck's family in Moscow, where he became acquainted with the symphonies of Tchaikovsky. However, he failed to appreciate Tchaikovsky's music and became more interested in the Russian-flavored compositions of MODEST MUSSORGSKY.

On his return to France in 1882, Debussy became friendly with Mme. Vasnier, wife of a Paris architect and an amateur singer. That year, he made his earliest professional appearance as a composer in Paris, at a concert given by the violinist Maurice Thieberg. In 1880 he enrolled in the composition class of Guiraud at the Paris Conservatory with the ambition of winning the Grand Prix de Rome. After several tries he finally succeeded in 1884 in obtaining the Grand Prix with his cantata *L'Enfant prodigue,* written in a poetic, conservative manner reflecting the trends of French ROMANTICISM.

Debussy wrote a CHORAL work and a CANTATA while living in Rome, neither of which has survived. A second choral SUITE composed on his return to Paris, *Printemps* (1887), failed to win formal recognition. He then set to work on another cantata, *La Damoiselle élue* (1887–89), which gained immediate favor among French musicians.

In 1889 Debussy was first exposed to non-Western music. An Indonesian GAMELAN was featured that year at the Paris World Exposition. Debussy was fascinated by the intricate rhythms and the new instrumental colors achieved by these players. He also found a relationship between these oriental sounds and the verses of certain French Impressionist and Symbolist poets, including Stéphane Mallarmé, Verlaine, Charles Baudelaire, and Pierre Louÿs. These influences are reflected in Debussy's vocal works from this period, including *Cinq poèmes de Baudelaire* (1887–89), *Ariettes oubliées* (1888), *Trois mélodies* (1891), and *Fêtes galantes* (1892). He also wrote *Proses lyriques* (1892–93) to his own texts.

For the piano, Debussy composed his *Suite bergamasque* (1890–1905), which includes the famous *Clair de lune.* In 1892 he began work on his instrumental *Prélude à l'après-midi d'un faune,* based on a poem by Mallarmé. The work showcased Debussy's new approach to shifting harmonies set against a wash of instrumental color. It was first heard in Paris in 1894, at which a program book cautioned the audience that the text contained elements that might be distracting to young females!

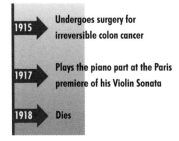

1915	Undergoes surgery for irreversible colon cancer
1917	Plays the piano part at the Paris premiere of his Violin Sonata
1918	Dies

At about this time, Debussy attended a performance of the Belgian dramatist Maurice Maeterlinck's work *Pelléas et Mélisande,* which inspired him to begin work on an OPERA on that subject, which would not be completed for nearly a decade.

Claude Debussy, 1908. (Corbis-Bettmann)

Between 1892 and 1899 Debussy also worked on *Three Nocturnes* for orchestra: *Nuages, Fêtes,* and *Sirènes.*

Debussy's love life was full of melodrama. In the late 1890s he abandoned his mistress of many years. She was so distressed that she took poison but survived this suicide attempt. Nonetheless, Debussy turned to another woman, Rosalie Texier, whom he married in 1899. This relationship was also a failure, however, and Debussy began an affair with Emma Bardac, the wife of a banker. When he informed his wife that he was in love with another, she also attempted suicide. She shot herself in the chest but missed her suffering heart. Debussy, now 42 years old, divorced Rosalie in 1905. Bardac and her husband had divorced earlier that year, and she and Debussy married in early 1908.

With his opera *Pélleas et Mélisande,* Debussy assumed a leading place among French composers. It was premiered at the Opéra-Comique in Paris in 1902. The production faced many difficulties. Maeterlinck objected to having the role of Mélisande sung by the American soprano Mary Garden. He

Debussy and Bardac had a daughter, Claude-Emma (known as "Chouchou"), born Oct. 15, 1905. She was the inspiration for Debussy's charming piano suite *Children's Corner* (the title was in English because Chouchou had an English governess). Sadly, Claude-Emma survived her father by barely a year, dying of diphtheria in 1919.

found her accent unacceptable and suggested that his mistress, Georgette Leblanc, sing the role.

The opera aroused violent controversy among French musicians and critics. The press was vicious in the extreme: "Rhythm, melody, tonality, these are three things unknown to Monsieur Debussy," wrote the leader of the Paris music critics, Arthur Pougin. Camille Bellaigue, a classmate of Debussy's at the Paris Conservatory, conceded that *Pélleas et Mélisande* "makes little noise," but, he remarked, "it is a nasty little noise."

English and American reports were no less vituperative, pejorative, and deprecatory. "Debussy disowns melody and despises harmony with all its resources," said the critic of the *Monthly Musical Record* of London. Echoing such judgments, the *Musical Courier* of N.Y. compared Debussy's "disharmony" with the sensation of "an involuntary start when the dentist touches the nerve of a sensitive tooth."

Debussy's next important work was *La Mer,* completed during a sojourn in England in 1905 and first performed in Paris. It consists of three symphonic sketches: *De l'aube à midi sur la mer* (From sunrise to noon), *Jeux de vagues* (Play of the waves), and *Dialogue du vent et de la mer* (Dialogue of wind and the sea). *La Mer* was attacked by critics with even greater displeasure than *Pélleas et Mélisande.* The American critic Louis Elson went so far as to suggest that the original title was actually *Le Mal de mer,* or seasickness.

Despite these critics, Debussy continued to work. Between 1906 and 1912 he created the remarkable three-part orchestral work *Images,* comprising *Gigues* (Jigs), *Iberia* (Iberia or Spanish sketch), and *Rondes de printemps* (Dance of springtime). In 1908 he conducted a concert of his works in London, then toured many major European and Russian capitals as a conductor through the mid-teens. Among solo piano works of the period are the 12 Preludes (2 vols., 1910, 1913) and 12 Études (2 vols., 1915). *En blanc et noir,* for two pianos, dates from 1915.

In 1913 SERGE DIAGHILEV produced Debussy's ballet *Jeux* in Paris. In 1917 Debussy played the piano part of his Violin Sonata at its premiere in Paris with the violinist Gaston Poulet. But his projected tour of the U.S. with the violinist Arthur Hartmann had to be abandoned when it was

The American writer James Gibbons Huneker exceeded all others in his negative criticism of *Pélleas et Mélisande,* attacking Debussy's physical appearance. "I met Debussy," he wrote in the N.Y. *Sun,* "and was struck by the unique ugliness of the man.... [H]e looks more like a Bohemian, a Croat, a Hun, than a Gaul." This description was followed by a suggestion that Debussy's music was fit for a procession of headhunters of Borneo, carrying home "their ghastly spoils of war."

discovered that Debussy had irreversible colon cancer. Surgery was performed in late 1915, but there was little hope of recovery.

The protracted First World War depressed Debussy. His hatred of the Germans became intense as the military threat to Paris increased. He wrote the lyrics and accompaniment to a song, *Noël des enfants* (The children's Noel), in which he begged Santa Claus not to bring presents to German children whose parents were destroying the French children's Christmas. To underline his national sentiments, he emphatically signed his last works "musicien français."

Debussy died on the evening of Mar. 25, 1918, as the great German gun "Big Bertha" made the last attempt to subdue the city of Paris by shooting shells at the city from a distance of 76 miles away.

Debussy strongly rejected the term *Impressionism* as applied to his music. Like the Impressionist poets and painters, however, Debussy created a music evocative of exotic scenes and sentimental feelings. He achieved this in music through many means. He drew on the PENTATONIC scales of Eastern music for their exotic sound quality. He also introduced harmonies in parallel FIFTHS and FOURTHS, giving his music a slightly antique feeling. His musical themes were short and rhythmic, while in instrumental treatment the role of individual solo passages is enhanced and the dynamic range made more subtle. His use of orchestral color was unparalleled, and he was a master of creating moods through shifting patterns of harmonies and textures.

Debussy was imaginative in his expression marks; here are a few examples:

Ce rhythme doit avoir la valeur sonore d'un fond de paysage triste et glacé. This rhythm must have the sound of a sad and icy landscape.

Comme un tendre et triste regret. Like a tender and sad regret.

Comme une buée irisée. Like a rainbow-colored mist.

Comme une lointaine sonnerie de cors. Like a distant sound of horns.

Comme une plainte lointaine. Like a distant plaint or lament.

Dans une brume doucement sonore. In a gently resonant mist.

début (Fr.). A first appearance by a performer or work.

Débutant, a male performer who makes his debut; *débutante,* a female performer who makes her debut.

dā-bü'

decay. The gradual falling off or extinction of a sound. *See also* ENVELOPE.

decibel (Abbrev. *db*). The minimal increment of sound energy that can be heard by the human ear, consisting of ⅒ of a bel, the arbitrary unit of sound named for Alexander Graham Bell.

The range of tolerable loudness of sound varies from 25 decibels to about 100, corresponding to the sound of a full orchestra. Rock bands reach 120 decibels. Two hundred decibels is the so-called pain threshold, potentially causing physical damage to the eardrum.

decomposition and reassembly. A modern composition technique. A MELODY can be fractured and its elements redistributed in a different configuration. VARIATIONS, tonal and atonal, can be rearranged melodically, harmonically, and rhythmically. Decomposition and reassembly can provide interesting and novel combinations of thematic materials.

dedication(s). For many centuries, composers have been in the habit of dedicating their works to the high and mighty. Usually, these dedications are earned by the financial support of the dedicatee. Sometimes a piece will be dedicated to a famous figure out of admiration, or to the first person who performed it.

In the 17th and 18th centuries, composers and musicians had a fairly low status in society. They were simply the employees of a noble court and were treated like footmen and other servants. Thus, dedications to a royal person were written in language that emphasized this master-slave relationship. When JOHANN SEBASTIAN BACH was seeking employment from the margrave of Brandenberg, he made sure to flatter his dedicatee while downplaying his own talents and worthiness:

> Since I had a couple of years ago the fortune of having been heard by Your Royal Highness at your express command and since I noticed then that Your Highness took some pleasure at my small talents which Heaven endowed me in music, and since upon taking my departure from Your Royal Highness I was given the honor of receiving from Your Highness a command to write some pieces of my own composition, I therefore according to these gracious orders took the liberty of rendering my very humble tasks to your Royal Highness by way of the present concertos, which I arranged for several instruments, beseeching Your Highness not to make judgment

of their imperfection because of the rigor of the fine and delicate taste in music that the whole world knows Your Highness to possess in the highest degree, but rather to take into benign consideration the profound respect and the most humble obeisance which I have attempted to express by this offering. For the rest, Monsiegneur, I beseech Your Royal Highness most humbly to have the goodness to continue your good graces toward me and to be persuaded that I have nothing as much to my heart as the capacity to be employed in occasions more worthy of Your Highness and in the service of Your Highness—I am, Monsiegneur, with total devotion, a very humble and very obedient servant of Your Royal Highness, Jean Sebastian Bach, Coethen, 24 March 1721.

In more recent centuries, musicians have gained greater fame and fortune, and dedications are less likely to be as fawning as this one.

Deep in the Heart of Texas. Song by Don Swander, a Californian who never went to Texas. The song became a hit in numerous western-flavored movies, beginning with *Heart of the Rio Grande* (1942), where it was sung by Gene Autry.

Deep Purple. Piano piece by Peter De Rose, 1939, based on fragments of SERGEI RACHMANINOFF's Second Piano Concerto. It was later provided with lyrics as a tear-jerking sentimental BALLAD. Babe Ruth of baseball fame had it performed for him on every birthday. When a new wave of sentimentality swept over America in 1963, the song again became a hit.

The name Deep Purple was later taken by a British heavy-metal rock group.

DeGaetani, Jan(ice), remarkable American mezzo-soprano and specialist in modern music; b. Massillon, Ohio, July 10, 1933; d. Rochester, N.Y., Sept. 15, 1989. Her father was a lawyer who encouraged her musical talents. She married the conductor Thomas DeGaetani and assumed her married name for professional appearances. The marriage was not successful, however, and they were soon divorced. She subsequently married Philip West, an oboist.

PEOPLE IN MUSIC

DeGaetani studied at the Juilliard School of Music in N.Y. with Sergius Kagan. Upon graduation she joined the Contemporary Chamber Ensemble, with which she developed a peculiar technique for performance of ultramodern vocal works. To support her musicmaking, she uncomplainingly took menial jobs, including baby-sitting and waiting on tables in restaurants. She devoted her free time to a detailed study of the solo part in ARNOLD SCHOENBERG'S *PIERROT LUNAIRE,* which became one of her finest interpretations.

DeGaetani mastered the most challenging techniques of new vocal music, including singing very small INTERVALS. She also mastered foreign languages, enabling her to perform a wide European repertoire. She became a faithful interpreter of the most demanding works by modern composers, among them PIERRE BOULEZ, GEORGE CRUMB, JACOB DRUCKMAN, PETER MAXWELL DAVIES, GYÖRGY LIGETI, ELLIOTT CARTER, and MARIO DAVIDOVSKY.

DeGaetani also developed a fine repertoire of Renaissance songs and became a unique phenomenon as a LIEDER artist. She brought an intelligence and understanding to her singing of lieder that was unparalleled by any other artist, along with her tremendous vocal technique. From 1973 she taught at the Eastman School of Music in Rochester, N.Y. With N. and R. Lloyd she published a useful textbook, *The Complete Sightsinger* (1980). DeGaetani died of irreversible leukemia.

degree. 1. One of the eight consecutive TONES in a MAJOR or MINOR DIATONIC SCALE. 2. A line or space on the STAFF. 3. A STEP.

Deidamia. Opera by GEORGE FRIDERIC HANDEL, 1741, first produced in London to an Italian LIBRETTO. The story is taken from Homer. Deidamia was a companion of the Greek warrior Achilles, who bore her a son.

Deidamia was Handel's last opera, and its complete failure made him turn toward ORATORIO. More than 200 years after its original production, it was revived in London in a successful English-language production.

PEOPLE IN MUSIC

Del Tredici, David (Walter), remarkable American composer; b. Cloverdale, Calif., Mar. 16, 1937. Del Tredici studied piano as a youngster and made his debut as a soloist with the San Francisco Symphony at age 16. He then enrolled at the University of California, Berkeley, studying composition (B.A., 1959), and earned a master's of fine arts at Princeton University in 1963, where his teachers included ROGER SESSIONS.

In 1966 Del Tredici received a Guggenheim fellowship, and in 1966–67 he was resident composer at the Marlboro Festival in Vermont. From 1966 he continued to compose and play the piano while pursuing a teaching career. He taught at Harvard, Boston College, and the City University of N.Y.

Fascinated by the creation of new literary forms and the novel language of James Joyce, Del Tredici wrote the work *I Hear an Army,* based on a Joyce poem, scored for soprano and string quartet, which was performed at Tanglewood on Aug. 12, 1964. It was an immediate success among fans of new music. Among his other settings of Joyce's work are *Night Conjure-Verse* for soprano, mezzo-soprano, woodwind septet, and string quartet, which Del Tredici conducted in San Francisco in 1966, and *Syzygy* for soprano, horn, bells, drums, and chamber orchestra, performed in N.Y. in 1968. In these works, Del Tredici used 12-TONE COMPOSITION techniques along with dense rhythmic textures, often with more than one rhythm occurring at once, as well as dramatic pauses.

But Del Tredici achieved greatest fame with a series of brilliant tone pictures based on *Alice in Wonderland* by Lewis Carroll. In a striking departure to his Joyce settings, these were written in classic harmonies with easily recognizable and lush melodies. The Alice pieces were composed between 1969 and 1981; part 1 of the final work, *Child Alice,* in 2 parts, for amplified soprano and orchestra, won the Pulitzer Prize in music. Among his later works are *Brass Symphony* for brass quintet (1992) and *Dum Dee Tweedle* for voices and orchestra (1993).

In 1984 Del Tredici was elected a member of the Institute of the American Academy and Institute of Arts and Letters. From 1988 to 1990 he was composer-in-residence of the N.Y. Philharmonic.

Delibes, (Clément-Philibert-) **Léo,** famous French composer; b. St.-Germain-du-Val, Sarthe, Feb. 21, 1836;

PEOPLE IN MUSIC

d. Paris, Jan. 16, 1891. Delibes received early musical training from his mother and an uncle, then enrolled in the Paris Conservatory in 1847. He won a *premier prix* in solfège in 1850 and also studied organ and composition.

In 1853 Delibes became organist of St. Pierre de Chaillot and accompanist at Paris's Théâtre-Lyrique. In 1856 his first work for the stage, *Deux sous de charbon,* a one-act OPERETTA, was produced at the Folies-Nouvelles. Later that year, his second work, the operette bouffe *Deux vieilles gardes,* won considerable acclaim at its premiere. Several more operettas followed, as well as his first substantial work for the stage, *Le Jardinier et son seigneur,* given at the Théâtre-Lyrique in 1863.

In 1864 Delibes became chorus master of the Paris Opéra. With the Russian choreographer Louis Minkus he collaborated on the BALLET score *La Source,* which was premiered in 1866 at the Opéra. His next ballet, *COPPÉLIA,* achieved lasting fame after its premiere at the Opéra in 1870. Another ballet, *Sylvia, ou La Nymphe de Diane* (1876), was equally successful.

Delibes then turned to OPERA. His GRAND OPERA *Jean de Nivelle* (1880), a moderate success, was followed by his triumphant masterpiece, the opera *LAKMÉ* (1883), in which he created a most effective lyric evocation of India. Its *BELL SONG* became a perennial recital favorite. In 1881 he was appointed professor of composition at the Paris Conservatory, and in 1884 he was elected a member of the Institute. His last opera, *Kassya,* was completed but not orchestrated at the time of his death. JULES MASSENET orchestrated the score, and it was premiered at the Opéra-Comique in 1893.

Delibes was a master of elegant melodies and charming harmonies. His music possessed a lyrical flow, with colorful TIMBRES. While seemingly effortless, his works were masterpieces of ROMANTIC composition.

Delius, Frederick (Fritz Theodor Albert), significant English composer of German parentage; b. Bradford, Jan. 29, 1862; d. Grez-sur-Loing, France, June 10, 1934. Delius's father was a successful wool merchant who naturally hoped to have his son follow a career in industry. He did not object to

PEOPLE IN MUSIC

his son's study of art and music, however, and Delius learned to play the piano and violin.

At the age of 22 Delius went to Solano, Fla., to work on an orange plantation owned by his father. His symphonic suite *Florida* was based on his impressions of the landscape. While living in Florida he met an American organist, Thomas F. Ward, who gave him thorough instruction in theory.

In 1885 Delius went to Danville, Va., as a teacher. A year later, he enrolled at the Leipzig Conservatory, where he took courses in harmony and counterpoint. It was there that he met the Norwegian composer EDVARD GRIEG, becoming his friend and admirer. Indeed, Grieg's music had a deep impact on his own compositions. An even more powerful influence was RICHARD WAGNER. Delius adapted Wagner's ideas of melodic motives that were developed throughout a composition as a basis of his own work.

Delius's music shares many of the same qualities as that of the other IMPRESSIONISTIC composers. He tends to compose using the full orchestral pallet, with rich harmonies moving slowly across the surface melodies. In some works he made use of English folk motifs, often in elaborate VARIATIONS.

Delius's orchestral nocturne *Paris: The Song of a Great City* is a tribute to a city in which he spent many years of his life. Much more ambitious in scope is his CHORAL work *A Mass of Life*, in which he draws on passages from the German philosopher Friederich Nietzsche's *Also sprach Zarathustra*.

Delius settled in Paris in 1888. In 1897 he moved to nearby Grez-sur-Loing, where he remained, except for a few short trips abroad. In 1903 he married the painter Jelka Rosen. His music began to win recognition in England and Germany. He became a favorite composer of the well-known conductor Sir THOMAS BEECHAM, who gave numerous performances of his music in London. But these successes came too late for Delius. An infection that he had contracted early in life eventually grew into an incurable illness accompanied by paralysis and blindness.

Still eager to compose, Delius hired a young English musician, Eric Fenby, as a secretary-companion. Fenby

Delius's most often performed pieces are his evocative symphonic sketches: *On Hearing the First Cuckoo in Spring, North Country Sketches, Brigg Fair,* and *A Song of the High Hills.*

wrote down music at the dictation of Delius, including complete orchestral scores. In 1929 Beecham organized a Delius Festival in London with six concerts, and the composer was brought from France to hear it. In the same year Delius was made Companion of Honour by King George V and given an Hon.Mus.D. by Oxford.

Delius's orchestral music is still popular today, although his other works, including a handful of operas and other vocal works, are rarely performed.

In the early 1960s the avant-garde composer Allen Kaprow composed a piece called *Piano Drop for Yoko Ono.* It consisted of pushing a grand piano out of a window, from several stories up. The resulting sound was the "piece."

demolition. Public destruction of musical instruments, usually as a means of finishing a performance.

In Stockholm a young pianist concluded his recital by igniting a dynamite charge previously hidden inside the piano, blowing it up. An exploding splinter wounded him in the leg. LA MONTE YOUNG set a violin on fire at one of his exhibits. Rock guitarists Pete Townshend and JIMI HENDRIX closed their performances with the demolition (Townshend) or setting afire (Hendrix) of their instruments.

Dempster, Stuart (Ross), American trombonist and composer; b. Berkeley, Calif., July 7, 1936. Dempster studied at San Francisco State College (B.A. in perf., 1958; M.A. in composition, 1967) and also had private trombone instruction from A. B. Moore, Orlando Giosi, and John Klock. He

PEOPLE IN MUSIC

Stuart Dempster playing the didjeridu. ▶

taught at the San Francisco Conservatory of Music from 1961 to 1966 and at California State College at Hayward from 1963 to 1966. In 1968 Dempster joined the faculty of the University of Washington in Seattle. He received a Fulbright-Hays Award as a senior scholar in Australia (1973) and a Guggenheim fellowship (1981).

Dempster's interests include non-Western instruments, and he has written many pieces for the didjeridu, a long, simple horn that is played by the Aborigines of Australia. Many of his pieces include exotic instruments or unusual instructions to the performers, including his 1982 work *Hornfinder* for trombone and audience; *JDBBBDJ* for didjeridu and audience from a year later; 1994–95's *Underground Overlays* for conch shells, chanters, and tape; and 1996's *Caprice* for unicycle-riding trombonist.

In addition to his own experimental works, Dempster has often collaborated with PAULINE OLIVEROS. He published *The Modern Trombone: A Definition of Its Idioms* (Berkeley, Calif., 1979).

Denisov, Edison, remarkable, innovative Russian composer; b. Tomsk, April 6, 1929; d. Paris, Nov. 23, 1996. Denisov was named after Thomas Alva Edison by his father, an electrical engineer. He studied mathematics at the University of Moscow, graduating in 1951, and composition at the Moscow Conservatory from 1951 to 1956. In 1959 he was appointed to the faculty of the conservatory.

PEOPLE IN MUSIC

Many of Denisov's works explore specific musical problems. Typical of these is *Crescendo e diminuendo* for harpsichord and 12 string instruments (1965), written partly in graphic notation. The titles of his pieces reveal a lyric character of subtle nuances, often marked by IMPRESSIONISTIC colors: *Aquarelle, Silhouettes, Peinture, La Vie en rouge, Signes en blanc, Nuages noires.*

Dennis Cleveland. The first-ever "talk show" OPERA, 1996, by Mikel Rouse, the second in a trilogy framed by *FAILING KANSAS* and *The End of Cinematics,* first performed in N.Y., Oct. 29, 1996. Rouse, in the title role, portrays a TV talk show host. His score draws on the absolute best of both pop and classical music worlds. The work mimics the form of the talk show, with the host moving freely among performers seated both on the stage and in the audience, all the while being under the watchful eye of television monitors. Despite its popular theme, this is a deadly serious work, inspired by John Ralston Saul's brilliant 1992 study *Voltaire's Bastards.*

Density 21.5. Work for solo FLUTE by EDGARD VARÈSE, 1936. It was commissioned by the virtuoso flute player Georges Barrère (1876–1944) to mark his acquisition of a platinum flute, and first performed by him the same year in Carnegie Hall, N.Y. The title designates the atomic weight of platinum (its specific gravity is 21.5 times as dense as water). The melodic line is angular but strangely affecting, with prominent use of the TRITONE.

Denver, John (born Henry John Deutschendorf, Jr.), popular American singer and songwriter; b. Roswell, N.M., Dec. 31, 1942; d. Monterey Bay, Calif., Oct. 12, 1997. Denver played guitar as a youngster. For a time he attended Texas Technical University in Lubbock, then made his way to N.Y. Denver joined the popular folk group the Chad Mitchell Trio, recording several albums with them. He also wrote the popular song *Leaving on a Jet Plane* in 1967, a major hit for Peter, Paul, and Mary.

In 1968 Denver launched a solo career, appearing in concerts all over the U.S. He also made television appearances and recordings. His successful songs included *Rocky Mountain High; Take Me Home, Country Roads;* and *Annie's Song,* mostly recorded in the mid-1970s. He also had a short-lived acting career, making a charming appearance as a bewildered grocery store clerk in the movie *Oh, God!* in 1977.

Denver's career slowed in the 1980s and '90s. He died when his private airplane crashed in 1997.

descant. *See* DISCANT. *Descant clef,* soprano CLEF; *descant recorder,* treble RECORDER; *descant viol,* treble VIOL.

descort (Old Fr., disorder). A 13th-century CHANSON genre, cultivated by the French TROUVÈRES.

PEOPLE IN MUSIC

Desert Song, The. OPERETTA by SIGMUND ROMBERG, 1926. A comedy of sentimental romance and mistaken identities on the plains of North Africa. Includes the title song, also called *Blue Heaven*.

Déserts. Work by EDGARD VARÈSE, 1954, for winds, percussion, and prerecorded electronic tape, first performed in Paris. It is one of the first attempts to combine live players with recorded sound.

Desmond, Paul (born Paul Emile Breitenfeld), American JAZZ alto saxophonist; b. San Francisco, Nov. 25, 1924; d. N.Y., May 30, 1977. Desmond picked up his professional name from a telephone book at random. He gained the rudiments of music from his father, who played the organ for silent movies. Desmond played the clarinet in the school orchestra, then at San Francisco State University, but eventually concentrated on the alto saxophone. He made rapid strides toward recognition and fame when he joined the DAVE BRUBECK Quartet in 1951, continuing with it until it was disbanded in 1967. He wrote some pieces for the Brubeck Quartet, including *Take Five,* an enduring jazz composition in $\frac{5}{4}$ meter, which was adopted as their signature song.

Desprez (Des Prez), **Josquin,** also known simply as Josquin, masterful Flemish composer; b. probably in Hainaut, c.1440; d. Conde-sur-Escaut, near Valenciennes, Aug. 27, 1521.

Few details of Josquin's early life are known. He may have been a boy chorister of the Collegiate Church at St.-Quentin, later becoming canon and choirmaster there. He possibly was a pupil of the early Flemish composer JOHANNES OCKEGHEM, whom he greatly admired (in 1497, he wrote *La Déploration sur la mort de Johannes Ockeghem*).

From 1459 to 1472 Josquin sang at the Milan Cathedral. By July 1474 he was at the court of Duke Galeazzo Maria Sforza, Milan, as a chorister. After the duke's assassination, he entered the service of the duke's brother, Cardinal Ascanio Sforza. From 1486 to 1494 he was a singer in the papal choir under the popes Innocent VIII and Alexander VI.

PEOPLE IN MUSIC

PEOPLE IN MUSIC

There are dozens of variations in the spelling of Josquin Desprez's name in manuscripts from the period. His epitaph reads *Jossé de Prés*. However, in the motet *Illibata Dei Virgo Nutrix*, of which the text is quite likely of Josquin's authorship, his name appears as an acrostic, thus: I, O, S, Q, V, I, N, D[es], P, R, E, Z. This seems to leave little doubt as to its correct spelling, once *I* and *V* are modernized to *J* and *U*, respectively.

Josquin was also active for various periods in Florence, where he met the famous theorist Pietro Aron, in Modena, and in Ferrara as maestro di cappella (choral director) in 1503 – 04. Later Josquin returned to Burgundy, settling in Conde-sur-Escaut in 1504, where he became provost of Notre Dame.

As a composer, Josquin was considered by contemporary musicians and theorists to be the greatest of his period. He had a strong influence on all those who came into contact with his music or with him as a teacher. Adriaan Petit Coclicus, who may have been one of Josquin's pupils, published a method in 1552 entitled *Compendium musices,* based on Josquin's teaching.

Josquin's works were sung everywhere and universally admired. In them, he achieves a complete union between word and melody. He uses COUNTERPOINT not merely as an exercise in composition but as an expressive technique, to best capture the meaning of his texts. Two contrasting styles are present in his compositions: some are intricately contrapuntal, displaying the technical ingenuity characteristic of the Netherlands style, while others, probably as a result of Italian influence, are HOMOPHONIC. He wrote numerous MOTETS, MASSES, and CHANSONS.

PEOPLE IN MUSIC

Dessau, Paul, German composer; b. Hamburg, Dec. 19, 1894; d. East Berlin, June 27, 1979. Dessau learned to play the violin at an early age and gave a concert at age 11. In 1910 he enrolled in conservatory in Berlin, where he studied violin and composition. In 1913, he worked as *répétiteur* (rehearsal pianist) at the Hamburg City Theater. In 1914 he was drafted into the German army.

After the Armistice in 1918, Dessau worked as a composer and conductor for various chamber groups in Hamburg. He then served as coach and conductor at the Cologne Opera from 1919 to 1923 and in Mainz in 1924. In 1925 he was appointed conductor at the Städtische Oper in Berlin, holding this position until 1933. When the Nazis took power, he left Germany. He lived in various European cities and also visited Palestine.

In 1939 Dessau emigrated to America, settling in Hollywood in 1944, where he composed or orchestrated 14 film scores. He returned to Berlin in 1948 and took an active part in German musical life, aligning himself with the political, social, and artistic developments in the German Democratic Republic. He became closely associated with the German playwright Bertolt Brecht and composed music for several of his plays.

Dessau's operas, choral works, songs, and instrumental music all had a strong social message. But unlike other composers with a progressive political agenda, he did not simplify his writing style.

Dett, R(obert) **Nathaniel,** distinguished African-American composer, conductor, and anthologist; b. Drummondville (now Niagara Falls), Ontario, Oct. 11, 1882; d. Battle Creek, Mich., Oct. 2, 1943. Both his parents were amateur pianists and singers. In 1893 the family moved to Niagara Falls, N.Y., where Dett studied piano with local teachers. He earned his living by playing at various clubs and hotels, then enrolled at the Oberlin (Ohio) Conservatory, where he studied piano and theory and composition, graduating in 1908. He also conducted a school choir.

PEOPLE IN MUSIC

Eventually, choral conducting became Dett's principal profession. He taught at a number of African-American colleges throughout the South from the 1910s until 1942. Concerned about his lack of technical knowledge in music, he continued to take lessons with a variety of teachers. In the summer of 1929 he went to France to study with NADIA BOULANGER. During 1931–32 he attended the Eastman School of Music in Rochester, N.Y., where he earned a master's degree.

In the meantime, Dett developed the artistic skills of the Hampton College Choir, one of the leading vocal groups of the South. It toured in Europe in 1930 with excellent success. He also periodically led his choir on the radio. In 1943 he became a musical adviser for the U.S.O., based in Battle Creek, Mich., where he died.

Dett's dominating interest was in cultivating African-American music, arranging SPIRITUALS, and publishing collections of folk songs. Some of his piano pieces became quite popular, among them the suite *Magnolia* (1912); *In the Bottoms* (1913), which contained the rousing *Juba Dance;* and *Enchantment* (1922).

Dett also wrote a number of choral pieces, mostly on biblical themes, such as his oratorios *The Chariot Jubilee* (1921) and *The Ordering of Moses* (1937). His choruses *Listen to the lambs, I'll never turn back no more,* and *Don't be weary, traveler,* became standard pieces of the choral repertoire. He published the anthologies *Religious Folk Songs of the Negro* (1926) and *The Dett Collection of Negro Spirituals* (4 vols., 1936).

Deus ex machina (Lat., God from a machine). A device developed in Greek drama and mythology as a means of ending a story, usually through a reversal in the plot. In essence, a god would come down from the heavens (or from below) to alter a situation, often at the last moment, and usually to the benefit of the main character or characters.

On stage, the gods would literally come down from the heavens by means of special "machines" (such as wires installed above the audience's sightline that could be used to lower the actors). In opera, an early example can be found in CLAUDIO MONTEVERDI's ORFEO (1607). An ironic and multiple use of the device is featured in PHILIP GLASS's *The Voyage* (1992).

Deutscher Tanz (Ger., German dance; Fr. *allemande;* It. *tedesca*). General term for late-18th- and early-19th-century couple dances in TRIPLE meter. By the 19th century the genre had branched off into the LÄNDLER (danced with arms interlaced) and the WALTZ (danced with swift turns and close embraces).

Deutsches Requiem, Ein. The German Requiem by JOHANNES BRAHMS, 1857–68, first performed in its final version in Leipzig, 1869. The title simply indicates that the text is in German, derived from Luther's translation of the Bible. Brahm's great sorrow over his mother's death in 1865 gave the long-gestating work a necessary push.

Deutschland, Deutschland über alles. The text of a nationalistic German poem written by a well-meaning German university professor at the time of the political disturbances of 1848, to the tune of FRANZ JOSEPH HAYDN's Austrian na-

One common myth in music history is that Brahms wrote the German Requiem to glorify the German soldiers who fell in the Franco-Prussian War. This is impossible, however, because the fighting occurred after the piece was written.

tional anthem, *Gott erhalte Franz den Kaiser.* The text refers to the German unification movement of the 19th century.

In later years, however, the words were misapprehended as "Germany above all" and as sung by the Nazis acquired an ominous meaning. In fact, *über alles* means "above all." After the downfall of the Nazi regime, the words *über alles* were removed from the lyrics. However, the noble tune was kept as the national anthem of West Germany.

deux (Fr.). Two. *Deux temps,* a "two-step" WALTZ.

development. The working out or elaboration of a theme by presenting it in varied melodic, harmonic, or rhythmic treatment.

Devil and Daniel Webster, The. Opera by DOUGLAS MOORE, 1939. The American statesman uses his forensic skills to free a poor artisan from a contract with the devil.

Devil and Kate, The. OPERA by ANTONÍN DVOŘÁK, 1899, first produced in Prague. Kate, a middle-aged, garrulous woman, vows to dance with the devil himself if she cannot find a partner at a country fair. The devil obligingly materializes and carries her off to hell. But Kate talks so much that the devil gets a headache and sends her back to earth.

Devil's Dream, The. Well-known American FIDDLE tune. There are many stories of fiddlers who learned a tune by leaving their violin out overnight so that the devil (or another night spirit) could play it. When the fiddler awakens, he finds himself able to play the tune as if by magic!

There are also stories of fiddle contests between the devil and an earthly fiddler. A well-known adaptation of these ancient folk tales is the country-rock hit of the 1970s *The Devil Went Down to Georgia,* by Charlie Daniels.

Devil's Trill, The. Violin Sonata in G Minor by GIUSEPPE TARTINI, composed sometime after 1744, first published posthumously, 1798. Legend has it that, while dreaming, Tartini heard the Prince of Darkness play a violin piece. When he awoke, Tartini wrote down what he could remem-

dö

The story of the devil being outwitted by the wife of a farmer is well known in European folk ballads. "The Farmer's Cursed Wife," an American folk song, ends with these words about the wife's ability to outsmart the devil:

Now we know women are superior to men,
They can go to hell and come back again!

ber and made it the basis for the last movement of this sonata.

Devin du Village, The (The village diviner). *Intermède* or comic opera, 1752, by Jean-Philippe Rousseau, first produced in Fontainebleau. In Rousseau's libretto, a village girl suspects her sweetheart of infidelity. She consults a wise friend who advises her to pretend she is in love with another. The stratagem works, and the couple is reunited.

The simple score is important historically because it breaks away from the French tradition of GRAND OPERA, with its stories based on the ancient myths, and presents theatrical music as part of common human experience.

D-flat major (Ger. *Des dur*). To judge by the music written in D♭ major, this key is descriptive of wide open spaces, capable of a great variety of expressions. The SCALE of D♭ major is marvelously pianistic, covering all five black keys, making room for two white keys at strategic positions. But this key is difficult to handle in orchestral writing, particularly in string instruments. Only one composer, NIKOLAI MIASKOVSKY, has ever written a symphony in the key of D♭ major, his 25th.

Di Capua, Eduardo, Italian composer of Neapolitan BALLADS; b. Naples, 1864; d. there, 1917. Di Capua earned his living by playing in small theaters and cafés in and around Naples, and later in cinemas, and by giving piano lessons. His most famous song was *O sole mio* (1898). Its popularity was immense and has never abated. Other celebrated songs were *Maria Mari* (1899), *Torna maggio* (1900), and *Canzona bella*.

Di Capua sold these songs to publishers outright and so did not benefit by their popularity. He died in extreme poverty.

Di Tre Re. Subtitle of ARTHUR HONEGGER's Fifth Symphony, 1951, first performed by the Boston Symphony Orchestra. The last note of each of the three movements is a D, hence the Italian title ("Of Three D's").

Some famous works in D♭ major:

FRANZ LISZT's Étude in D♭ major, in which the left hand goes over the right to maintain the requisite fullness of harmony.

CLAUDE DEBUSSY's *CLAIR DE LUNE*, delicate and subtle in its evocation of a moonlit landscape.

The celebrated principal theme of the first movement of PIOTR ILYICH TCHAIKOVSKY's Piano Concerto, nominally in the key of B♭ minor, states its theme unambiguously in D♭ major.

The 18th variation of SERGEI RACHMANINOFF's *Rhapsody on a Theme of Paganini*, in which he ingeniously inverts the principal A-minor theme.

Diabelli, Anton, Austrian composer and publisher; b. Mattsee, near Salzburg, Sept. 5, 1781; d. Vienna, Apr. 8, 1858. Diabelli was a choirboy in the monastery at Michaelbeurn and at Salzburg Cathedral. He studied for the priesthood at the Munich Latin School but continued to compose, submitting his works to MICHAEL HAYDN, who encouraged him to continue writing music.

PEOPLE IN MUSIC

After the Bavarian monasteries were closed, Diabelli embraced the career of a musician and settled in Vienna (where FRANZ JOSEPH HAYDN received him kindly). He taught piano and guitar for a living and in 1818 became a partner of Cappi, the music publisher. He assumed control of the firm in 1824 and renamed it Diabelli & Co. In 1852 he sold his firm to C. A. Spina.

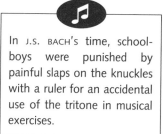

Diabelli published much of FRANZ SCHUBERT's music, but underpaid the composer and complained that Schubert wrote too much!

A facile composer, Diabelli produced an opera, *Adam in der Klemme* (Vienna, 1809), MASSES, CANTATAS, CHAMBER MUSIC, and many other lesser works, all of which have been forgotten. However, his SONATINAS are still used for beginners. His name was immortalized through LUDWIG VAN BEETHOVEN's remarkable set of 33 variations (1823, op.120), on a WALTZ theme by Diabelli.

Diabelli Variations. A set of VARIATIONS for piano by LUDWIG VAN BEETHOVEN, 1823 (op.120), based on a WALTZ by ANTON DIABELLI.

diabolus in musica (Lat., devil in music). A nickname, found in many MEDIEVAL works on music, for the TRITONE. The tritone was forbidden because it did not fit into the basic HEXACHORD of ancient music theory.

It was to be expected that an interval bearing such a satanic name would be used by composers to characterize sinister forces. Examples are many:

In J.S. BACH's time, schoolboys were punished by painful slaps on the knuckles with a ruler for an accidental use of the tritone in musical exercises.

The lowered FIFTH in the violin tune of *DANSE MACABRE* by CAMILLE SAINT-SAËNS

The LEITMOTIF of the dragon Fafner in act 2 of RICHARD WAGNER's *SIEGFRIED*

The motives of the three magical winning cards in PIOTR ILYICH TCHAIKOVSKY's OPERA *THE QUEEN OF SPADES*

The devil's motto in HOWARD HANSON's opera *Merry Mount*

The diabolus in musica is the formative interval of the diminished seventh chord, a favorite device of ROMANTIC operas suggesting mortal danger. In honor of this dramatic function, the diminished seventh chord was known in Italian opera circles as the accorde DI STUPEFAZIONE (stupefying chord). Ironically, the diabolus in musica became the cornerstone of the modern composition techniques. It is also the basic element of the WHOLE TONE SCALE used for coloristic effects in IMPRESSIONISTIC works.

Diaghilev, Sergei (Pavlovich), famous Russian impresario; b. Gruzino, Novgorod district, Mar. 31, 1872; d. Venice, Aug. 19, 1929. He was associated with progressive artistic organizations in St. Petersburg, but his main field of activity was in Western Europe. He established the Ballets Russes in

PEOPLE IN MUSIC

Diaghilev's grave. (Todd Gipstein/Corbis)

Paris in 1909. He commissioned IGOR STRAVINSKY to write the ballets *THE FIREBIRD, PETRUSHKA,* and *LE SACRE DU PRINTEMPS.* He also commissioned SERGEI PROKOFIEV, DARIUS MILHAUD, FRANCIS POULENC, GEORGES AURIC, and others of the younger generation. MAURICE RAVEL and MANUEL DE FALLA also wrote works for him. The great importance of Diaghilev's choreographic ideas lies in the complete abandonment of the classical tradition. In this respect he was the true originator of the modern dance.

Dialogues de carmélites, Les. Opera by FRANCIS POULENC, 1957. The story is based on the historical martyrdom of Carmelite nuns during the French revolution.

Diamond, David (Leo), significant and fantastically prolific American composer; b. Rochester, N.Y., July 9, 1915. Diamond's parents were of eastern European extraction, his father a cabinetmaker and his mother a dressmaker for the Yiddish theater. To make ends meet, he worked behind the soda counter at a N.Y. drugstore.

PEOPLE IN MUSIC

Diamond studied composition at the Eastman School of Music in his hometown of Rochester between 1930 and 1934. He then took courses privately with ROGER SESSIONS in N.Y. Seeking to broaden his musical horizons, he went to Paris in 1937, where he took courses with NADIA BOULANGER and became associated with many important musicians and writers of the time.

Returning to N.Y., Diamond devoted his time exclusively to composition. He received various grants and awards, and his works were featured by all the major American symphony orchestras. Some of his works, like *Rounds* for string orchestra, acquired popularity in concert performances. This score won the N.Y. Music Critics' Circle Award in 1944.

As a composer, Diamond created an original and recognizable style. The element of TONALITY, often inspired by natural folk-inspired melodies, is strong in all of his music. In his later works he adopted a modified 12-TONE method, while still maintaining his own unique voice. Diamond's strongest power lies in symphonic and chamber music, but he also shows a marked ability for vocal writing, as exemplified by his choral works.

In 1973 Diamond was appointed to the faculty of the Juilliard School in N.Y. In 1989 he was invited to the Soviet Union, where his music was performed to considerable acclaim.

diapason. (Grk.). 1. As applied to Greek music, the interval that runs "through all the tones," that is, the perfect OCTAVE. 2. In later centuries, a vocal range, used in this sense in French and Russian theory books. 3. (Fr.) Tuning fork; CONCERT PITCH. 4. The principal pipe of the ORGAN, usually eight feet long (the double diapason is a pipe 16 feet in length).

diatonic (Gr., *dia + teinein,* stretch out). Of or relating to the seven TONES of a particular MAJOR or MINOR SCALE. *Diatonic harmony* or *melody,* that employing the tones of but one scale; *diatonic instrument,* one yielding only the tones of that scale of which its fundamental tone is the key note; *diatonic interval,* one formed by two tones of the same scale; *diatonic modulation, see* MODULATION; *diatonic progression,* stepwise progression within one scale; *diatonic scale, see* SCALE.

PEOPLE IN MUSIC

Diddley, Bo (born Ellas Bates McDaniel), African-American rock 'n' roll singer and guitarist; b. Magnolia, Miss., Dec. 30, 1928. Diddley was taken to Chicago in early childhood, where he learned to play the violin and guitar.

Diddley first attracted attention in 1955 with his recordings of *Bo Diddley* and *I'm a Man.* Later that year he appeared on Ed Sullivan's television show and at N.Y.'s Carnegie Hall. His syncopated "Bo Diddley beat" influenced the first generation of rock 'n' roll musicians, including BUDDY HOLLY and ELVIS PRESLEY. In 1959 he scored great success with his recording of *Say Man.*

Diddley fell off the charts in the 1960s but continued to perform and tour through the years. In 1963 he performed in England and in 1972 at the Montreux Jazz Festival. Later tours included Europe in 1986 and Japan, two years later.

Dido and Aeneas. Opera by HENRY PURCELL, 1689, after Virgil's *Aeneid.* It deals with the love of Dido, queen of Carthage, for the Trojan hero Aeneas, and her suicide when he abandons her. It may have been first performed in a school for young gentlewomen in London. About 60 composers of many nations wrote operas on the same subject.

Dies Irae (Lat., day of wrath). Sequence of the REQUIEM MASS. It is the most famous Christian doomsday chant, describing the end of the world and imploring the Lord not to cast the repentant sinner into outer darkness. The composition of both words and melody is attributed to the 13th-century musician Thomas of Celano. A simple melody that is not easily classified as to its MODE, it is musically more repetitive than most other sequences of the mass.

In the 14th and 15th centuries the Dies Irae became an obligatory part of the requiem Mass. It was almost always sung as chant until the Council of Trent (mid-16th century), which kept it as part of the liturgy.

difference (differential) tone. *See* COMBINATION TONES, TARTINI TONES.

digital. 1. Of or pertaining to the KEYBOARD of the PIANO, ORGAN, etc. 2. Of or pertaining to recording technology in which sound is stored as numerical information, as in a compact disc. 3. Of or pertaining to COMPUTER-generated sound.

diminished interval. A perfect or minor INTERVAL lessened by a CHROMATIC SEMITONE. *Diminished chord,* one whose highest and lowest tones form a diminished interval; *diminished triad,* a root with minor third and diminished fifth; *diminished seventh chord,* a chord consisting of three conjunct minor thirds, forming the interval of the diminished seventh between the top and bottom notes, e.g., C–E♭–G♭–B♭♭.

diminution (Ger. *Verkleinerung*). A BAROQUE device whereby the theme is played twice as fast as its initial appearance, so that quarter notes become converted into eighth notes, eighth notes into sixteenth notes, etc. Often the dynamic level is also increased as well as the overall rhythmic tension. Diminution is often used as a means of giving a dramatic closing to a piece. In its formal and emotional respects, diminution performs the opposite function to that of AUGMENTATION.

The Dies Irae has been quoted in many other works as a symbol of world weariness and despair. Some famous pieces that include a reference to it are the last movement of the *Symphonie fantastique* of Hector Berlioz, the *Danse macabre* of Camille Saint-Saëns, and the *Totentanz* by Franz Liszt. The text is incorporated in the requiems of Wolfgang Amadeus Mozart, Luigi Cherubini, Giuseppe Verdi, and many others.

Dimitrj. OPERA by ANTONÍN DVOŘÁK, 1882. Its story is based on the historical life of the false czar (reigned 1603 – 06) who succeeded the Godunovs. Here he has come to believe in his own royalty, but his wife, Marina, reminds him that he is a fugitive monk. He is eventually slain by one of his followers.

Dinah. Song by Harry Akst, 1924, made famous by Ethel Waters. It later became the theme song and first name of the popular singer Fanny Rose (a.k.a. Dinah) Shore.

directional hearing. An ability common to all animals and humans to judge the direction and the relative intensity of sound, evolved from the biological necessity of anticipating approaching danger. This faculty plays an important role in stereophonic sound reproduction and also in compositions that use SPATIAL DISTRIBUTION of the performers.

dirge. A funeral song, usually for CHORUS sung A CAPPELLA. Also, an instrumental composition of a funerary nature.

"Dirge" is an English contraction of the opening of Matins of the Office of the Dead, "Dirige Domine Deus Meus in conspectu tuo viam meam."

Disappointment, or The Force of Credulity, The. BALLAD opera by Andrew Barton, composed in 1767 for the opening of a theater in Philadelphia. The performance was canceled by the censors, however, because the text contained unflattering references to important colonial officials.

The plot deals with a group of practical jokers who persuade greedy Philadelphians to dig for buried treasures on the banks of the Delaware River. The tunes were melodies popular in colonial times, including an early version of *Yankee Doodle.*

A reconstructed score, with a specially composed overture, three instrumental interludes, and BAROQUE orchestration by Samuel Adler was produced at the Library of Congress in Washington, D.C., in 1976, as part of the U.S. bicentennial celebration.

disc (disk). 1. Phonograph record. 2. COMPACT DISC. 3. Video playback record. *See also* DISC JOCKEY (DJ).

disc jockey (DJ). Radio announcer who plays records (or discs). As a "jockey," the DJ "rides" the music through commentary between the recordings and commercials. Stations sometimes encourage the development of on-air "personalities" who bring additional listeners.

During the 1950s disc jockeys selected the music to be broadcast. Because of their power, they were often the willing targets of PAYOLA (bribes) by the record companies to get their product heard. While well-publicized convictions in the 1960s relegated payola to the back rooms and in less-obvious forms, DJ personalities continued to promote their stations and themselves. However, programming is now usually determined by a station manager or market studies.

Some famous DJs have launched careers for themselves as writers, actors, and general cultural icons:

Wolfman Jack was one of the most famous and mysterious of the 1950s DJs. He operated out of several small radio stations on the Texas-Mexican border. His raspy-voiced delivery and piercing howl were his trademarks. He later appeared in the film *American Graffiti* and wrote a best-selling memoir shortly before his death in the 1990s.

Murray the K promoted rock 'n' roll shows in the 1950s and '60s. When the BEATLES came to America, he promoted himself as "The Fifth Beatle" and helped assure their success on the record charts.

Don Imus, the former NBC morning DJ, now no longer spins records at all. He has also authored books and become a political commentator.

Howard Stern developed his own, often gross, humor into an entire industry. He has authored two best-selling books and appeared in a film biography of his own life.

discant (*descant;* from Lat. *discantus,* singing apart). A term of many meanings, which have changed throughout history.

1. The first attempts at POLYPHONY (writing with two or more voices sounding at once) with contrary motion in the parts (12th century), as opposed to ORGANUM, in which parallel motion was the rule. It was applied to a contrapuntal

The Notre Dame schoolmaster Perotinus was known as an *optimus discantor* (the greatest or master discanter).

voice against the CANTUS FIRMUS, as the abbreviation of the Latin *discantus,* a translation of the Greek *diaphonia* (through sound). Discant is generally limited to a COUNTER-POINT of the first species, note against note, while organum developed eventually as a free counterpoint.

2. Used interchangeably with MOTET and, unjustifiably, with FAUXBOURDON (parallel voices in thirds and sixths).

3. Originally, the upper voice. Its use became common again in modern times to denote the highest part in a CHORAL composition.

disco. 1. DISCOTHEQUE. 2. DISCO MUSIC.

disco music (disco). A type of relentlessly rhythmic dance music that evolved from ROCK and SOUL music in the 1970s. It is characterized by a heavy accent on strong beats and the consequent weakening of the backbeat (viz. *Turn the Beat Around*). Disco music was extremely popular for a decade, then receded into the background as a substantial influence on other musics, including house and RAP.

discord (It. *discordanza*). Generically speaking, DISSONANCE. The meaning of the term, however, has changed considerably over the years. What was dissonant in the 13th century might be considered harmonious today.

discotheque (Fr., collection of recordings). A gathering place where people dance to the sounds of amplified recorded music, first evolving in the late 1950s in conjunction with the rise of rock 'n' roll. These replaced most live-music nightclubs and dance halls—because it is cheaper to hire a single DISC JOCKEY to spin records than to hire a band—and have continued with the wave of new dance music styles.

diseuse. A female reciter or narrator. Examples of compositions using a diseuse are CLAUDE DEBUSSY's *The Martyrdom of Saint Sebastian,* PAUL HINDEMITH's *Hérodiade,* and ARTHUR HONEGGER's *Jeanne d'Arc au bûcher.*

disk. 1. DISC. 2. A COMPUTER data storage device; floppy disk.

displaced tonality. Displacement of the TONIC note by an instant MODULATION a SEMITONE higher or lower. This is favored by modern composers who do not want to abandon TONALITY entirely but merely wish to make it more ambiguous or difficult to trace. Displacement works best in MAJOR keys because the major TRIAD is so easily recognized, and thus any change in the SCALE is far more obvious. Examples of this technique are found in many works of SERGEI PROKOFIEV and DMITRI SHOSTAKOVICH.

dissonance (from Lat., *dis* + *sonare*, not together + sound). A combination of two or more TONES requiring resolution. A more poetic term for dissonance is DISCORD, a disagreement of hearts (Lat., *corda,* hearts). The antonym of dissonance is CONSONANCE (sounding together), of which the synonym is *concord.*

The concept of dissonance has varied greatly through the centuries. From the standpoint of ACOUSTICS, the borderline separating dissonances from consonances is as indefinite as the line between two neighboring colors of the spectrum.

One measure of dissonance is the complexity of the division of the string or air column that is required to produce the note. For example, an OCTAVE is created by the simple division (or ratio) of ⅔₁, and is pleasing to hear. However, a MINOR SECOND is represented by the ratio ¹⁶⁄₁₅, constituting a sharper dissonance than a MAJOR SECOND, whose ratio of vibration is ⁹⁄₈. The presence of a single dissonant interval in an otherwise consonant CHORD converts it into dissonance.

Another way of looking at this is in terms of the VIBRATIONS of soundwaves. The octave sounds harmonious to the ear because two waves of the upper note correspond to a single wave of the lower note, when the crests of the waves coincide and mutually reinforce each other. When a minor second is sounded, however, the higher note produces 16 waves per time unit as against 15 waves of the lower tone. This means that only one wave out of 15 or 16 coincides with the other waves. This creates an interference that registers as a dissonance in our ears.

In traditional harmony a dissonant chord demands resolution into a consonance. The story is told that JOHANN SE-

In Greek terminology, dissonance is *diaphonia,* while consonance is *symphonia.*

383

BASTIAN BACH, who was a compulsive sleeper, was awakened in the morning by his second wife playing a dominant seventh chord on the harpsichord in the music room. Alarmed by the unresolved dissonance, Bach jumped out of bed still wearing his nightcap, rushed to the harpsichord, and resolved it into the TONIC TRIAD.

No composer before 1900 dared to leave a dissonance unresolved. FRANZ LISZT was perhaps the first to break this absolute prohibition when he used a dissonant combination of notes of the so-called GYPSY SCALE in a final cadence.

The time finally came early in the 20th century when composers accepted the art of dissonance as a legitimate idiom that no longer required the crutch of consonance to lean upon. Inevitably, the rule of consonance gave way to the dictatorship of dissonance.

It was now the turn of consonant combinations to resolve into dissonant combinations. ARNOLD SCHOENBERG went so far as to exclude all triads from his vocabulary, allowance being made only for an occasional employment of the minor sixth and minor third, while perfect octaves were totally banned.

Have the anticonsonance forces gone too far? There is a horrifying tale of a young woman whose father, a deranged biologist, fed her on a diet of poisonous herbs to test his theory that diet can be changed based on habit. When a student fell in love with her and brought her fine tropical fruit, a box of chocolates, and a plate of French pastries, she feasted on them and died, poisoned by their tasty delights. Could our modern ears become so accustomed to dissonance that traditional harmonies will sound strange to us?

dissonant chord. One containing one or more dissonant intervals.

dissonant counterpoint. A term that came into usage in the 1920s by proponents of ATONAL music. Charles Seeger published a book on composition in this style, which emphasized the equality of dissonance and consonance in all types of contrapuntal techniques.

In fugal writing, in particular, there was a strong tendency to use the TRITONE as the interval of entry for the second voice, instead of the traditional PERFECT FIFTH of TONIC-DOMINANT harmony.

Dissonant counterpoint does not exclude consonances but puts them on probation! The perfect octave is generally shunned, however, and usually replaced by a major seventh.

dissonant interval. Two TONES forming a DISSONANCE, i.e., SECONDS, SEVENTHS, and all DIMINISHED and AUGMENTED intervals.

***Dissonanzen* Quartett** (*Dissonance* quartet). The nickname for WOLFGANG AMADEUS MOZART's String Quartet in C Major, K. 465 (1785). The closest thing to harsh discord in the work occurs in the introduction to the first movement.

Distler, Hugo, important German composer; b. Nuremberg, June 24, 1908; d. Berlin, Nov. 1, 1942. Distler studied at the Leipzig Conservatory. In 1931 he became a church organist at Lübeck and joined the faculty of the conservatory there from 1933 to 1937. During this same period he also was a teacher at the School for Church Music in Spandau. From 1937 to 1940, he taught at the Stuttgart Hochschule für Musik, and then moved to Berlin. He committed suicide there during World War II.

PEOPLE IN MUSIC

Distler's early training and his connection with church music determined his style as a composer. His greatest legacy is his religious choral music, putting PAUL HINDEMITH's theories of modern composition in the service of lively and profound interpretations of texts. Among his early works are *Der Jahrkreis,* op.5 (52 motets, 1932–33), and *Choral-Passion,* op.7 (1933). His secular choral masterpiece is the three-part collection *Mörike-Chorliederbuch,* op.19 (1938–39).

Distler also wrote some organ music and a Concerto for Harpsichord and String Orchestra, op.14 (1935–36), three secular CANTATAS, and an unfinished ORATORIO, *Die Weltalter* (1942). He published a textbook on composition, *Funktionelle Harmonielehre,* in 1941.

Distratto, Il (The absentminded one). FRANZ JOSEPH HAYDN's Symphony No. 60 in C Major, 1776. The musical material was originally intended to accompany a comedy of the same title produced in Vienna.

dĭt′al

The *dital harp* was a guitar-shaped lute invented by Edward Light in 1819 with 12 to 18 strings, each equipped with a dital to raise its pitch a semitone.

Earl Scruggs, the famous BLUEGRASS BANJO player, invented Scruggs pegs in the late 1940s to accomplish the same trick on the banjo.

dital key. A key that, on pressure by the finger or thumb, raises the pitch of a GUITAR or LUTE string by a SEMITONE.

dithyramb. An ode to Dionysios (Dionysus). It was performed by a chorus accompanied by wind instruments and dancers at the Dionysian festivals in ancient Greece. Also, a song of this type.

diva (It., divine woman). A term introduced by Italian opera producers to describe a female opera singer to whom even the description *prima donna assoluta* (absolutely first lady) seems inadequate. The term was popular in the 19th century but disappeared from publicity campaigns early in the skeptical 20th century, even as it became part of the vernacular.

dē-vâr-tē-men′tōh

divertimento (It., diversion or entertainment; plur. *divertimentos, divertimenti;* Fr. *divertissement*). 1. In Italy beginning in the 17th century, a collection of music for entertainment. It often contained instrumental or vocal pieces of various genres. 2. In the latter half of the 18th century, an instrumental composition akin to the SUITE or SERENADE (also *cassation, notturno,* and *partita*). In the 20th century the genre of divertimento was revived; IGOR STRAVINSKY, BÉLA BARTÓK, and others wrote instrumental examples.

dē-vâr-tēs-măhn′

divertissement (Fr.). 1. DIVERTIMENTO. 2. An ENTR'ACTE in an OPERA, in the form of a short BALLET, etc.

Divertissement. Brilliant orchestral work by JACQUES IBERT, 1930. The work features many familiar quotations from well-known classical works, such as FELIX MENDELSSOHN'S *Wedding March* and the *Blue Danube Waltz.* It was first performed in Paris.

Divin poème, Le. Symphony No. 3 by ALEXANDER SCRIABIN, 1904, the first of his outwardly mystical pieces. Its movements are titled *Grandiose, Luttes, Voluptés,* and *Jeu divin* (divine game).

Divina commedia. Unfinished symphony by FRANZ LISZT, 1867, inspired by Dante's great epic, first performed in Dresden. Of the two movements, the best music dramatically is in the *Inferno.* The *Purgatorio* is comparatively bland. Liszt was unable to complete the planned third section, *Paradisio.*

Divine Office. *See* CANONICAL HOURS.

division. 1. A "dividing up" of a melodic series of tones into a rapid COLORATURA passage. If it is a vocal setting, the passage is to be sung in one breath (now obsolete). *To run a division,* to execute such a passage. 2. In the English BAROQUE, a free IMPROVISATION played rapidly with much ornamentation, accompanied by a given GROUND BASS. Manuals for training string, wind, and other players in this technique were common in the 17th century.

Dixie. This song, associated with the Southern cause in the American Civil War, was actually written by a Northerner, DANIEL DECATUR EMMETT of Ohio, and published a year before the Civil War in 1860.

Dixieland. Jazz style associated with early New Orleans bands of the turn of the 20th century. The term at first referred to white musicians, as is shown by the first jazz recordings, made by the all-white Original Dixieland Jazz Band (1917). Originally, a distinction was made between the relatively stiff Dixieland style and the more swinging and improvisatory New Orleans style of black musicians. When Dixieland was revived in the 1940s and '50s, however, the term was used to refer to all types of New Orleans jazz, both black and white.

Dixieland instruments are typically CORNET (trumpet, trombone), CLARINET, PIANO, BANJO (guitar), TUBA (double bass), and DRUMS. The music developed from the repertoire of the New Orleans marching bands of the turn of the century. At its best, Dixieland is characterized by group IM-PROVISATION, dotted rhythms, and SYNCOPATION, over a RAGTIME-like accompaniment.

DJ. *See* DISC JOCKEY.

Do(h) (It.). 1. The note C. 2. In sight singing, the usual syllable name for the first degree of the scale.

Do I Hear a Waltz? MUSICAL by RICHARD RODGERS and STEPHEN SONDHEIM, 1965. The plot focuses on an innocent American female tourist who thinks she hears the Viennese equivalent of bells when she meets a Venetian man-about-town. Alas, he is but a married swindler!

Do That to Me One More Time. Dance ballad-hit for the pop duo the Captain and Tennille, in 1980. Its title was changed from "Do It …" because of fear of offending some radio programmers!

Dodds, "Baby" (Warren), African-American jazz drummer, brother of JOHNNY (John M.) DODDS; b. New Orleans, Dec. 24, 1898; d. Chicago, Feb. 14, 1959. Dodds was the youngest of six children, hence his nickname. He studied drums with Dave Perkins, Walter Brundy, and Louis Cottrell, Sr., and, after performing with local jazz musicians, joined Fate Marable's riverboat band in 1918.

Dodds settled in Chicago in 1921, where he played and recorded with KING OLIVER, along with his brother, Johnny. He then worked with LOUIS ARMSTRONG and JELLY ROLL MORTON and later played with his brother in several combos.

After World War II Dodds participated in the DIXIELAND revival, playing with groups led by Bunk Johnson during 1944–45 and Art Hodes from 1946–47. In 1949–50 he suffered several strokes and thereafter made infrequent appearances until his retirement in 1957. He was the foremost drummer in the New Orleans style of his era.

Dodds, Johnny (John M.), African-American jazz clarinetist and alto saxophonist, brother of Warren BABY DODDS; b. New Orleans, Apr. 12, 1892; d. Chicago, Aug. 8, 1940. Dodds began playing clarinet when he was 17 and, al-

In the fixed-*do* method of teaching, *do* is the name for all notes bearing the letter name C, whether keynotes or not. In the movable *do* method, *do* is always the keynote, regardless of letter name.

PEOPLE IN MUSIC

PEOPLE IN MUSIC

though he had lessons with Lorenzo Tio, Jr., was mainly self-taught. After playing in KID ORY's band in New Orleans from 1912 to 1917 and again in 1919, as well as in Fate Marable's riverboat band toward the end of the 1910s, he settled in Chicago.

Dodds was a member of KING OLIVER's band and recorded in the mid-1920s with LOUIS ARMSTRONG's Hot Five and Hot Seven combos. His strong clarinet style, based on imaginative IMPROVISATION in both accompaniment and solo parts, made him a model for dozens of other musicians. He led his own band in the 1930s, then joined his brother's quartet in 1940. He was a leading exponent of the New Orleans style.

Dodecachordon (Grk., 12 modes). Famous theoretical treatise by GLAREANUS, 1547. He extended the system of AUTHENTIC and PLAGAL MODES (DORIAN, PHRYGIAN, LYDIAN, MIXOLYDIAN) from eight to 12, by adding the IONIAN and AEOLIAN modes, with their plagal derivations. It also contains important analytic descriptions of works by contemporary masters of POLYPHONY.

dodecaphonic music (Grk., *dodeca* + *phone,* 12 sound). A system of composition developed by ARNOLD SCHOENBERG as the "method of composing with 12 tones related only to one another." Schoenberg's first explicit use of his method occurs in his Serenade, op.24 (1924).

Five fundamental ideas underlie Schoenberg's method:

1. The entire work is derived from a row (Ger., *Tonreihe*) made up of the 12 different notes of the chromatic scale.

2. The tone row is used in four different forms: the original, retrograde, inversion, and retrograde inversion.

3. Although the order of the notes in the tone row is rigidly observed, the individual members of the series can be placed in any octave position. This can result in the wide distribution of the thematic ingredients over the entire vocal or instrumental range of a single part or over sections of different parts.

4. Because each of the four forms of the basic 12-TONE series can be transposed to any starting point of the chromatic scale, the total of all available forms is 48.

5. MELODY, HARMONY, and COUNTERPOINT are functions of the tone row, which may appear horizontally as melody, vertically as harmony, and diagonally as canonic counterpoint.

The 12-tone row can be arranged in six groups in two-part counterpoint, four groups in three-part counterpoint (or harmony), three groups in four-part harmony, or two groups in six-part harmony.

Passages containing 12 different notes in succession, apart from the simple chromatic scale, are found even in classical works. There were other composers and theorists who worked on this problem at about the same time as Schoenberg. Nonetheless, Schoenberg is generally recognized as the creative force and main proponent of this method.

The method of composing with 12 tones related only to one another did not remain a rigid system. Its greatest protagonists, besides Schoenberg himself, were his disciples ALBAN BERG and ANTON WEBERN. Both Berg and Webern introduced considerable innovations into 12-tone practice. Berg "broke" Schoenberg's rules by using traditional major and minor triads, as well as parallel melodic sections that violated the 12-tone rules. Webern dissected the 12-tone series into sections of six, four, or three units in a group, and related them individually to one another by inversion, retrograde, and inverted retrograde. This allowed for much more freedom in writing passages in counterpoint than Schoenberg's original rules did.

The commonly used term for dodecaphonic music in German is *Zwölftonmusik*. In American usage it was translated literally as 12-tone music. English music theorists objected to this terminology, pointing out that a tone is an acoustical phenomenon. Dodecaphony deals with the arrangement of *written* notes, and that it should be consequently called 12-note music. In Italy the method became known as *dodecafonia* or *musica dodecafonica*.

In a letter sent to Nicolas Slonimsky in 1939, the German composer and theorist ERNST KRENEK described the relationship between atonality and the method of composing with 12 tones as follows: "Atonality is a state of the musical material brought about through a general historical development. The 12-tone technique is a method of writing music within the realm of atonality. The sense of key has been destroyed by atonality. The method of composing with 12 tones was worked out in order to replace the old organization of the material by certain new devices."

Many composers of world renown embraced 12-tone theory, sometimes without making full use of the four basic forms of the tone row. The greatest conquest of Schoenberg's method was the totally unexpected conversion of IGOR STRAVINSKY. Stravinsky had been one of Schoenberg's loudest critics, opposing any predetermined method of composition. Yet he adopted the 12-tone method when he was already in his 70s.

BÉLA BARTÓK made use of a 12-tone melody in his Second Violin Concerto, but he modified its structure in the second statement of the tone row. ERNEST BLOCH, a composer for whom the modern techniques had little attraction, made use of 12-tone subjects in his *Sinfonia Breve* and in his last string quartets.

English composers who have adopted the technique of 12-tone composition with various degrees of consistency are SIR MICHAEL TIPPETT, Lennox Berkeley, Benjamin Frankel, Humphrey Searle, and Richard Rodney Bennett. WILLIAM WALTON makes use of a 12-tone subject in the fugal finale of his Second Symphony. In his expressionist OPERA *The Turn of the Screw,* BENJAMIN BRITTEN adopts a motto of alternating perfect fifths and minor thirds (or their respective inversions), aggregating to a series of 12 different notes. The Spanish composer Roberto Gerhard, who settled in England, wrote in a fairly strict dodecaphonic idiom.

In France the leader of the dodecaphonic school is René Leibowitz, who also wrote several books on the theory of 12-tone composition. Wladimir Vogel, a Russian-born composer of German parentage making his home in Switzerland, adopted Schoenberg's method in almost all of his works. The Swiss composer FRANK MARTIN extended the principles of dodecaphonic writing to include a number of further ideas.

In America Schoenberg's method found a fertile ground not only among his students but also among composers who pursued different roads. MILTON BABBITT and others extended the method into total SERIALISM. ROGER SESSIONS and DAVID DIAMOND followed Schoenberg's method with varying degrees of fidelity. AARON COPLAND used the dodecaphonic technique in some of his CHAMBER MUSIC works. In the orchestral *CONNOTATIONS* he used 12-tone composition to characterize the modern era of music.

Somewhat frivolously, Schoenberg, Berg, and Webern have been described as the Vienna Trinity, with Schoenberg the Father, Berg the Son, and Webern the Holy Spirit. Less frivolously, they have collectively been called the Second Viennese School.

WALTER PISTON interpolated a transitional 12-tone passage in his BALLET suite *The Incredible Flutist.* In his Eighth Symphony Piston adopted Schoenberg's method in all its orthodoxy after having spent decades arguing against it. SAMUEL BARBER made an excursion into the dodecaphonic field in a movement of his Piano Sonata.

Several composers have used 12-tone music specifically to describe the modern age. LEONARD BERNSTEIN inserted a 12-tone series in the score of his *AGE OF ANXIETY* to express 20th-century anxiety and despair. GIAN CARLO MENOTTI turned dodecaphony into parody in his OPERA *The Last Savage.* His primitive hero is thrust into the modern world, described by the atonal sounds of 12-tone music.

In communist Russia, dodecaphony remained officially unacceptable as a "formalistic" device. (In a speech delivered in Moscow in 1963, Nikita Khrushchev, then prime minister, observed: "They call it dodecaphony, but we call it cacophony.") Nevertheless, some blithe spirits of the young Soviet generation, among them Andrei Volkonsky, Valentin Silvestrov, and Sergei Slonimsky, wrote and published works in the 12-tone idiom.

Dodge, Charles (Malcolm), American composer and teacher; b. Ames, Iowa, June 5, 1942. Dodge initially studied composition at the University of Iowa, where he graduated with a bachelor of arts degree in 1964. He then became interested in ELECTRONIC MUSIC, studying with VLADIMIR USSACHEVSKY, one of the first composers to work with electronic sounds. He has taught computer music at Columbia, Princeton, Brooklyn College, CUNY, and Dartmouth, among other universities. He was president of the American Composers Alliance from 1971 to 1975 and the American Music Center from 1979 to 1982. In 1972 and 1975 he held Guggenheim fellowships.

Many of Dodge's works involve COMPUTER synthesis, including *Rota* for orchestra (1966), *Earth's Magnetic Field* (1970), and *Any Resemblance Is Purely Coincidental* for piano and "Caruso" voice (1980). Also remarkable is his staged setting of Samuel Beckett's radio play *Cascando* (1978). With Thomas Jerse he published *Computer Music: Synthesis, Com-*

PEOPLE IN MUSIC

position, and Performance (1985, 2d ed., 1997), a standard text on composing using computers.

Does Your Chewing Gum Lose Its Flavor (on the Bedpost Over Night)? Novelty hit (1961) for the British skiffle star Lonnie Donegan, popular among summer campers everywhere.

Dohnányi, Christoph von, eminent German conductor of Hungarian descent, b. Berlin, Sept. 8, 1929. Dohnányi began to study the piano as a child. His music training was interrupted by World War II. His father, Hans von Dohnányi, a lawyer, was executed by the Nazis for their involvement in the 1944 attempt on Hitler's life.

PEOPLE IN MUSIC

After the war, Dohnányi studied jurisprudence at the University of Munich. In 1948 he enrolled at the Hochschule für Musik in Munich, where he won the Richard Strauss Prize for composition and conducting. Making his way to the U.S., he continued his studies with his grandfather, ERNST DOHNÁNYI, at Florida State University at Tallahassee, and also attended sessions at the Berkshire Music Center at Tanglewood.

Returning to Germany, Dohnányi received a job as a coach and conductor at the Frankfurt Opera from 1952 to 1957. Progressing rapidly, he worked for several German opera companies before becoming director of the Frankfurt Opera from 1968 to 1977, and then of the Hamburg State Opera, until 1984. In 1984 Dohnányi assumed the position of music director of the Cleveland Orchestra, having been appointed music director-designate in 1982, succeeding LORIN MAAZEL. In the meantime, he had engagements as guest conductor at almost all the leading opera houses of Europe and the United States.

Both as symphony and opera conductor, Dohnányi proved himself a master technician and a versatile musician capable of interpretation of all types of music, from the BAROQUE to the AVANT-GARDE. He is regarded as a leading exponent of the works of the modern Vienna school, excelling in fine performances of the works of ARNOLD SCHOENBERG, ALBAN BERG, and ANTON WEBERN. He is married to the soprano Anja Silja.

PEOPLE IN MUSIC

Dohnányi, Ernst (Ernō) von, eminent Hungarian pianist, composer, conductor, and pedagogue, grandfather of CHRISTOPH VON DOHNÁNYI; b. Pressburg, July 27, 1877; d. N.Y., Feb. 9, 1960. Dohnányi began his studies with his father, an amateur cellist, then studied piano and theory with Karoly Forstner. In 1894 he entered the Royal Academy of Music in Budapest, where he took courses in piano and composition. In 1896 he received the Hungarian Millennium Prize, established to commemorate the thousand years of existence of Hungary, for his symphony. He graduated from the Academy of Music in 1897, then went to Berlin for additional piano studies with the noted pianist and composer Eugen d'Albert.

Dohnányi made his debut in a recital in Berlin in 1897, and in 1898 he played BEETHOVEN's Fourth Piano Concerto in London. Then followed a series of successful concerts in the U.S. Returning to Europe, he served as professor of piano at the Hochschule für Musik in Berlin from 1908 to 1915. He returned to Budapest, where he taught piano at the Royal Academy of Music. He served briefly as its director in 1919, when he was appointed chief conductor of the Budapest Philharmonic Orchestra. In 1928 he became head of the piano and composition classes at the Academy of Music, and in 1934 its director. In 1931 he assumed the post of music director of the Hungarian Radio.

As Hungary became embroiled in war and partisan politics that invaded even the arts, Dohnányi resigned his directorship in 1941, and in 1944 he also resigned his post as chief conductor of the Budapest Philharmonic. Personal tragedy also made it impossible for him to continue his work as a musician and teacher: both of his sons lost their lives to the Nazis. One, the German jurist Hans von Dohnányi, was executed for his role in the abortive attempt on Hitler's life. The other was killed in combat. Late in 1944 he moved to Austria.

In 1947–48 Dohnányi made a tour of England as a pianist. Determined to emigrate to America, he accepted the position of piano teacher at an Argentine university. In September 1949 he finally reached the U.S., where he became composer-in-residence at Florida State University in Tallahassee.

Dohnányi was a true virtuoso of the keyboard and was greatly esteemed as a teacher. His pupils included SIR GEORGE SOLTI, Géza Anda, and Bálint Vázsonyi. His music represented the final flowering of European ROMANTICISM, marked by passionate eloquence of expression while keeping within the framework of CLASSIC forms. JOHANNES BRAHMS praised his early efforts.

Dohnányi's compositions remain popular among pianists, particularly Hungarian ones, who often put his brilliant compositions on their programs. His most popular orchestral work is *Variations on a Nursery Song.* Also frequently played is his orchestral Suite in F♯ Minor.

Doktor Faust. Opera by FERRUCCIO BUSONI, 1925, left incomplete. It was performed posthumously, with an ending by Busoni's pupil Philipp Jarnach, in Dresden. The LIBRETTO is derived from the same medieval sources from which Goethe derived his Faust. Here, the title character appears as a magician and an artist. The opera features complex, ROMANTIC-style harmonies and BACH-like COUNTERPOINT.

Dolphy, Eric (Allan), African-American jazz alto saxophonist, bass clarinetist, and flutist; b. Los Angeles, June 20, 1928; d. Berlin, June 29, 1964. Dolphy took up the clarinet in early childhood, later studying music at Los Angeles City College. After working with local groups, including Chico Hamilton's quintet during 1958–59, he went to N.Y., where he performed with CHARLES MINGUS's quartet in 1959–60.

PEOPLE IN MUSIC

In 1961 Dolphy co-led a quintet with Booker Little, then worked with JOHN COLTRANE, JOHN LEWIS, and again with Mingus. He was a master at IMPROVISATION, excelling in both jazz and THIRD-STREAM genres. His repertoire included several AVANT-GARDE works, including EDGARD VARÈSE's *DENSITY 21.5.*

Dolphy left America, where he felt his avant-garde music was unappreciated, and settled in Germany in 1962. He died suddenly and unexpectedly of a circulatory system failure brought on by diabetes in 1964.

dombra. A LUTE-like Central Asian instrument, played with the finger. It differs from the Russian DOMRA by virtue of its long neck and angular body. After 1917 it was successfully introduced into Russian popular string orchestras.

dominant. The fifth TONE or STEP in the MAJOR or MINOR SCALE.

Dominant chord: 1. The dominant TRIAD. 2. The dominant chord of the seventh; *dominant section,* in a particular movement, a section written in the KEY of the dominant, lying between and contrasting with two sections in the TONIC key; *dominant triad,* a chord with the dominant as the ROOT.

PEOPLE IN MUSIC

Domingo, Placido, famous Spanish tenor; b. Madrid, Jan. 21, 1941. Domingo's parents were ZARZUELA singers. After a tour of Mexico, they settled there and gave performances with their own company. Placido joined his parents in Mexico at the age of seven and began appearing with them while still a child. He also studied piano with Manuel Barajas in Mexico City and voice with Carlo Morelli at the National Conservatory from 1955 to 1957.

Domingo made his operatic debut in the tenor role of Borsa in *RIGOLETTO* with the National Opera in Mexico City in 1959. His first major role was as Alfredo in *LA TRAVIATA* in Monterrey in 1961, the same year that he made his U.S. debut as Arturo in *LUCIA DI LAMMERMOOR* with the Dallas Civic Opera. He then was a member of the Hebrew National Opera in Tel Aviv from 1962 to 1964. He made his first appearance with the N.Y. City Opera in 1965 and, a year later, made his Metropolitan Opera debut as Turiddu in a concert performance of *CAVALLERIA RUSTICANA* at N.Y.'s Lewisohn Stadium. His formal debut on the Metropolitan stage followed in 1968, when he essayed the role of Maurice de Saxe in *ADRIANA LECOUVREUR,* establishing himself as one of its principal members. He also sang regularly at the Vienna State Opera (from 1967), Milan's La Scala (from 1969), and London's Covent Garden (from 1971).

Domingo's travels took him to all the major operatic centers of the world, and he also sang on recordings, in films, and on television. He also pursued conducting, making his formal debut with *La Traviata* at the N.Y. City

Opera in 1973. In 1984 he appeared at the Metropolitan Opera, conducting LA BOHÈME. He commissioned GIAN CARLO MENOTTI's opera *Goya* and sang the title role at its premiere in Washington, D.C., in 1986. In 1987 he had the honor of singing Otello at the 100th anniversary performances at La Scala. On New Year's Eve 1988 he appeared as a soloist with ZUBIN MEHTA and the N.Y. Philharmonic in a gala concert televised live to millions, during which he also conducted the orchestra in the overture to DIE FLEDERMAUS.

One of the best-known lyric tenors of his era, Domingo has gained international renown for his portrayals of such roles as Cavaradossi, Des Grieux, Radames, Don Carlo, Otello, Don Jose, Hoffmann, Canio, and Samson. He is a member of the "Three Tenors" with JOSÉ CARRERAS and LUCIANO PAVAROTTI.

Domino, "Fats" (Antoine, Jr.), African-American singer, pianist, and bandleader; b. New Orleans, Feb. 26, 1928. Although Domino sustained a severe hand injury as a youth, he pursued a career as a pianist. He was primarily trained on the instrument by a local performer, Harrison Verrett, who was also his brother-in-law.

Domino began appearing in local clubs after World War II, where he was heard by local producer Dave Bartholomew. Batholomew took the performer under his wing, producing, arranging, and often cowriting the singer's biggest hits of the 1950s. After a series of local hits in the early 1950s, Domino hit it big in 1955 with *Ain't That a Shame* and *Blueberry Hill.* He would score 20 hits over the remainder of the decade.

Domino continued to record through 1963, with lesser success, although he continued to create innovative music. Although he was less active in following decades, Domino continued to record and perform, and has remained a favorite on the rock revival circuit.

domra. A Russian lute, usually played with a PLECTRUM. It is very popular in Russia as an instrument of popular entertainment provided by traveling musicians (Rus. *skomorokhi*). It was replaced by the BALALAIKA in the 18th century, but 20th-century musicians revived the instrument in an effort

PEOPLE IN MUSIC

When white teen singing star Pat Boone covered Domino's hit recording of *Ain't That a Shame,* he was embarrassed to use the slang word "ain't." So his version was released as *Isn't That a Shame.* As you might expect, *Isn't That a Shame* lacked the soulfulness of Domino's original.

MUSICAL INSTRUMENT

to encourage Russian historical music. Several domra-and-balalaika orchestras were formed after 1917.

Don Carlos. Opera by GIUSEPPE VERDI, 1867, first produced in Paris. The LIBRETTO, modeled after Schiller's drama, is based on the historical relationship between King Philip II of Spain and his son Carlos, whose intended wife, Elisabeth de Valois, became his stepmother. Carlos was imprisoned in 1567 on the charge of plotting against Philip II and died (or was murdered) a year later at the age of 23.

In the opera, Don Carlos continues his clandestine trysts with his stepmother after her marriage, both appropriately disguised. They are turned in by her lady-in-waiting, Princess Eboli (who secretly loves Carlos), and the sinister Grand Inquisitor directs Philip to put his son to death. The final confrontation takes place at the tomb of Philip's father, Carlos V, where a monk dressed in the late emperor's attire (or his ghost?) emerges from behind (within?) the tomb, scaring everyone silly. Don Carlos either takes advantage of the confusion and flees, or is embraced by Carlos V and taken to a safe haven, depending on your interpretation of the opera's finale.

Don Giovanni (Don Juan). WOLFGANG AMADEUS MOZART's greatest opera, 1787. It was described by Mozart as a DRAMMA GIOCOSO (jocular drama), but the subject is not exactly merry. The LIBRETTO, in Italian, is by LORENZO DA PONTE (his second for Mozart). The alternative title was *Il dissoluto punito* (The dissolute one punished). It was first produced in Prague, a city that responded more positively to Mozart's operas than his native Vienna.

The story is based on the legend of Don Juan, the lover who was irresistible to women. Giovanni's servant Leporello, in a famous "catalogue aria," ticks off the exact number of Giovanni's conquests in various countries, culminating with *mille e tre* (1,003) seductions in Spain. He offers this information to one of Giovanni's most recent conquests.

The story centers on Don Giovanni's murder of a highly placed aristocrat, the Commendatore, and his outrageous courtship of the slain man's daughter. When a statue of the dead man is produced, it accuses Don Giovanni of wrongdoing. In an act of supreme effrontery, Giovanni challenges the statue of the slain Commendatore to have supper with him. With trombones sounding ominously in the orchestra, the statue accepts Giovanni's defiant invitation and in a deep bass voice speaks his determination to carry him to hell. The remaining protagonists gather in happy disbelief, promising to pursue their lives much as they did before meeting Giovanni.

During Mozart's lifetime, a Vienna production was announced under the title *La statua parlante* (The speaking statue). This is a reference to the work's sensational ending, where the wronged Commendatore's statue addresses Don Giovanni.

Don Juan. Symphonic poem by RICHARD STRAUSS, 1889, first performed in Weimar. This, his first important work, was written at the age of 23 and is still one of his most frequently performed compositions. The score was inspired by a poem of Lenau in which Don Juan atones for his sins by death.

Don Pasquale. Comic opera by GAETANO DONIZETTI, 1843. An elderly man, Don Pasquale, is tricked into marrying a girl whom his nephew secretly loves. However, she drives her husband to distraction. All is made right when Pasquale decides to give her over to his nephew, complete with a considerable dowry.

Don Quixote. Symphonic poem by RICHARD STRAUSS, 1898, for cello, viola, and orchestra, subtitled *Fantastic Variations on a Theme of Knightly Character.* The first performance of this quasi-SYMPHONIE CONCERTANTE took place in Cologne.

There are 10 variations depicting various adventures of the hero. The bleating of the sheep, when Don Quixote charges into the herd, is represented by a tremendously cacophonous commotion in muted brass. The cello, like Quixote, dies at the end in a downward glissando toward the tonic D. The viola portrays his trusty lieutenant Sancho Panza.

Don Rodrigo. Opera by ALBERTO GINASTERA, 1964, first produced in Buenos Aires. Don Rodrigo was the Visigoth king in Toledo, Spain, in the eighth century. The governor of Ceuta, whose daughter is raped by Rodrigo in the opening scene of the opera, avenges her honor by invading Spain and defeating Rodrigo's army. But the victim forgives Rodrigo, and he dies in her arms.

The score is written in a DODECAPHONIC (12-tone) system, while the form is built on the CLASSICAL divisions of an instrumental SUITE. Although the composer uses DISSONANCE throughout the piece, TONALITY is not totally avoided.

Donizetti, (Domenico) **Gaetano** (Maria), famed and prolific Italian composer of operas in the BEL CANTO tradition; b. Bergamo, Nov. 29, 1797; d. there, Apr. 1, 1848. Donizetti's father was from a poor family of artisans who obtained the position of caretaker in the local pawnshop. At the age of nine, Gaetano entered the Lezioni Caritatevoli di Musica, a charity institution that served as the training school for the choristers of San Maria Maggiore church. In addition to vocal training, he also studied singing and HARPSICHORD. Later he studied harmony and COUNTERPOINT with the Italian-born German opera composer J. S. Mayr. With Mayr's encouragement and assistance, Donizetti enrolled in the Liceo Filarmonico Comunale in Bologna in 1815, where he continued his studies.

Donizetti's first three operas were written quickly between 1816 and 1817 but were apparently never performed during his lifetime. Leaving the Liceo in 1817, he was determined to have an opera produced. His next work, *Enrico di Borgogna*, was performed in Venice in 1818, but it raised little interest. In 1819 he finally achieved popular success with his OPERA BUFFA, *Il Falegname di Livonia, o Pietro il grande, czar delle Russie.* Then, in 1822, his OPERA SERIA *Zoraide de Granata* proved a major success.

During the next nine years Donizetti composed 25 operas, none of which remain in the active repertoire. However, the great success of his *L'Ajo nell'imbarazzo* in 1824 brought him renown at the time. Donizetti was also employed as a musical director, at the Teatro Carolino in Palermo for a year beginning in 1825, and then at the royal theaters in Naples for a decade beginning in 1829.

Donizetti came into his own as an opera composer in the 1830s, beginning with *Anna Bolena* in 1830. The opera was an overwhelming success. Within a few years it was pro-

PEOPLE IN MUSIC

Donizetti time line

1797 ▸ Born

1815 ▸ Enters the Liceo Filarmonico Comunale in Bologna

1822 ▸ The opera seria *Zoraide de Granata* proves his first major success

1825 ▸ Musical director of the Teatro Carolino in Palermo

1829 ▸ Musical director at the royal theaters in Naples

1830 ▸ Comes into his own as an opera composer with the premiere of his *Anna Bolena*

1832 ▸ *L'elisir d'amore* is premiered

1833 ▸ *Lucrezia Borgia* is premiered

1834 ▸ Appointed professor of counterpoint and composition at the Conservatorio di San Pietro a Majella in Naples

duced in several major Italian theaters, and was also heard in London, Paris, Dresden, and other cities. His next enduring work was the charming comic opera *L'ELISIR D'AMORE* (1832).

The tragic *Lucrezia Borgia* (1833), although not entirely successful at its premiere, soon found acceptance and made the rounds of the major opera houses. In 1834 Donizetti was appointed professor of counterpoint and composition at the Conservatorio di San Pietro a Majella in Naples. After a brief stay in Paris in 1835, Donizetti returned to Italy and produced his tragic masterpiece, *LUCIA DI LAMMERMOOR* (1835).

Upon the death of Nicola Zingarelli in 1837, Donizetti was named director pro tempore of the Conservatorio in Naples. However, a year later he resigned the post when it was not made permanent. That same year, his opera *Roberto Devereux* garnered acclaim at its first performance in Naples.

After struggling with the Italian censors over the production of another opera, Donizetti decided to return to Paris. He produced three operas there in 1840: the highly successful *LA FILLE DU REGIMENT*, *Les Martyrs*, and *LA FAVORITE*. The later work made little impression at its first performance but soon became one of his most popular operas.

Donizetti spent 1841–42 in Italy, then went to Vienna. His *Linda di Chamounix* received an enthusiastic reception at its premiere there in 1842. Following its success, the emperor appointed Donizetti *maestro di cappella e di camera e compositore di corte* (master of the chapel and the chamber and composer of the court).

In 1843 Donizetti alternated between Paris and Vienna, producing three operas: his great comic masterpiece *Don Pasquale*, *Maria di Rohan*, and *Dom Sebastien*. The audience approved *Dom Sebastien* enthusiastically, but the critics were not pleased. Considering the opera to be his masterpiece, Donizetti had to wait until the 1845 Vienna premiere (performed in German) before the work was universally acclaimed.

The last opera produced in his lifetime was *Caterina Cornaro* in 1844. By this time, Donizetti had begun to age quickly. In 1845 his mental and physical condition progressively deteriorated. In 1846 he was placed in a mental clinic at Ivry, just outside Paris. In 1847 he was released into the

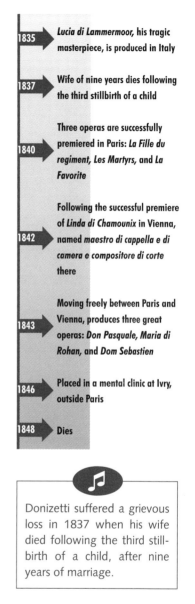

1835 *Lucia di Lammermoor*, his tragic masterpiece, is produced in Italy

1837 Wife of nine years dies following the third stillbirth of a child

1840 Three operas are successfully premiered in Paris: *La Fille du regiment*, *Les Martyrs*, and *La Favorite*

1842 Following the successful premiere of *Linda di Chamounix* in Vienna, named *maestro di cappella e di camera e compositore di corte* there

1843 Moving freely between Paris and Vienna, produces three great operas: *Don Pasquale*, *Maria di Rohan*, and *Dom Sebastien*

1846 Placed in a mental clinic at Ivry, outside Paris

1848 Dies

Donizetti suffered a grievous loss in 1837 when his wife died following the third stillbirth of a child, after nine years of marriage.

care of his nephew and was taken to his birthplace to await his end, which came a year later.

Donizetti was a prolific composer of operas whose overall number was not always equaled by his inspiration or craftsmanship. Many of his operas are hampered by the poor LIBRETTOS he was forced to use on so many occasions. Nevertheless, his genius is reflected in many of his operas. Indeed, his finest works serve as the major link in the development of Italian opera between the period of GIAOCCHINO ROSSINI and that of GIUSEPPE VERDI. Many of his operas continue to hold a place in the repertoire.

Donna del lago, La. Opera by GIAOCCHINO ROSSINI, 1819, based on Walter Scott's poem *The Lady of the Lake*. The story recounts an Arthurian legend in which the king receives his magic sword (Excalibur) from a woman (Morgan le Fay) who lives on an enchanted island (Avalon).

Don't Fence Me In. Cowboy song by COLE PORTER, 1944. It was introduced by Roy Rogers in the film *Hollywood Canteen*. It became a hit several times, as sung by Kate Smith, Bing Crosby, and the ANDREWS SISTERS.

Don't Get Around Much Anymore. Soulful song by DUKE ELLINGTON, 1942.

Don't Worry, Be Happy. An inspired hit by vocalist BOBBY MCFERRIN, 1988. The song's upbeat message, promoted with a clever video that featured comic actors Robin Williams and Bill Irwin, made it an immediate sensation.

Doors, The. (Vocal: Jim Morrison, b. Melbourne, Fla., Dec. 8, 1943; d. Paris, France, July 3, 1971; keyboards/vocal: Ray Manzarek, b. Chicago, Feb. 12, 1935; guitar: Robbie Krieger b. Los Angeles, Jan. 8, 1946; drums: John Densmore, b. Los Angeles, Dec. 1, 1945.) Psychedelic ROCK group of the 1960s led by the visionary poet Jim Morrison. Originally meeting at UCLA's film school, the band had its first success when it was performing at Los Angeles's major rock club the Whiskey-a-Go-Go.

PEOPLE IN MUSIC

Signed to Elektra Records in 1966, the Doors scored immediately with Morrison's powerful vocal on Robby Krieger's song *Light My Fire,* which was banned by some radio stations because of its lyrics. The group continued to score successes through 1968 and 1969. Their hits ranged from portraits of self-destruction (*The End, When the Music's Over*), to teenage alienation (*People Are Strange*) and sexual relationships (*Love Me Two Times; Hello, I Love You*).

The band's success was clouded by Morrison's increasingly erratic behavior. He was often hostile to the audience onstage, or too drunk or stoned to perform. In March 1969 Morrison was arrested following an appearance in Miami. The police claimed he had exposed himself onstage; others present deny the charge. Morrison spent some time on the run before the case was eventually settled.

Jim Morrison of the Doors, c. 1968. (Courtesy Elektra Records)

The band continued to issue recordings, scoring lesser hits through early 1971, when Morrison left the group to pursue his interest in writing poetry. By July of that year, however, he had died (in his bath), following years of drug and alcohol abuse. The cause of death, officially a "heart attack," may have been a heroin overdose. He was buried in Paris's Père Lachaise, the final resting place of Isadora Duncan, Gertrude Stein, Marcel Proust, and countless other artists. The rest of the Doors soldiered on as a trio through 1973.

Despite Morrison's death, the Doors have remained popular, particularly among teenagers. Director Oliver Stone made a film about the group in 1991, and in 1993 the Doors were placed in the Rock and Roll Hall of Fame.

doo-wop. A form of rock 'n' roll, popular in the mid to late 1950s, consisting of vocal groups singing in harmony. It had its beginnings with groups of four or five people singing on street corners, unaccompanied by instruments. *See* A CAPPELLA. Classic examples of this genre are the songs *Earth Angel* by the Crew Cuts (later covered by the Penguins) and *In the Still of the Nite* by the Five Satins. The term *doo-wop* comes from the nonsense syllables that were sung as part of the background vocals in most of the songs. This type of music had a brief revival in the early 1960s with such songs as *There's a Moon Out Tonight* by the Capris and *Remember Then* by the Earls. Through the following decades, doo-wop groups remained popular on tour. In the 1990s, groups like Boyz II Men revived some aspects of the traditional doo-wop sound.

dohp′pĕl

Doppel (*doppelt,* Ger.; It. *doppio*). Double, twice. *Doppelchor,* DOUBLE CHORUS; *Doppelfuge,* DOUBLE FUGUE; *Doppelgriff* (double grip); DOUBLE STOP; *Doppelgriffe,* thirds, sixths, etc. (played with one hand on the piano); *Doppelkanon, see* CANON; *Doppelkreuz,* double sharp; *Doppelschlag* (It., *gruppetto*), an ornamental figure requiring the use of the scale steps above and below the principal note, e.g., C–D–C–B–C; *Doppelt so langsam,* twice as slow; *Doppelzunge,* double- or FLUTTER-TONGUING.

PEOPLE IN MUSIC

Dorati, Antal, distinguished Hungarian-born American conductor and composer; b. Budapest, Apr. 9, 1906; d. Gerzensee, near Bern, Nov. 13, 1988. From 1920 to 1924 Dorati studied with the well-known Hungarian composers Leo Weiner and ZOLTAN KODÁLY at the Franz Liszt Academy of Music in Budapest. He spent the balance of the 1920s and '30s as a theatrical conductor, working at the Budapest Opera until 1928, and then at the Dresden State Opera from 1928 to 1929, and in Munster from 1929 to 1932. In 1933 Dorati went to France, where he conducted the Ballets Russes de Monte Carlo, which he took on a tour of Australia in 1938.

Dorati made his U.S. debut as guest conductor with the National Symphony Orchestra in Washington, D.C., in 1937. In 1940 he settled in the U.S., becoming a naturalized citizen in 1947. He began his American career as music director of the American Ballet Theatre in N.Y. from 1941 to 1944. After serving as conductor of the Dallas Symphony Orchestra from 1945 to 1949, he was music director of the Minneapolis Symphony Orchestra from 1949 to 1960.

From 1963 to 1966 Dorati was chief conductor of the BBC Symphony Orchestra in London, then of the Stockholm Philharmonic from 1966 to 1970. He was music director of the National Symphony Orchestra in Washington, D.C., for seven years beginning in 1970, and then of the Detroit Symphony Orchestra until 1981. He was also principal conductor of the Royal Philharmonic in London in the mid-1970s.

Throughout his career, Dorati made numerous guest conducting appearances in Europe and North America, earning a well-deserved reputation as an orchestra builder. His prolific recording output made him one of the best-known conductors of his time. His recordings of FRANZ JOSEPH HAYDN's symphonies and operas were particularly excellent. In 1984 he was made an honorary Knight Commander of the Order of the British Empire. In 1969 he married the Austrian pianist Ilse von Alpenheim, who often appeared as a soloist under his direction.

Dorian mode. *See* AUTHENTIC MODES.

Dorian **Toccata and Fugue** (BWV 538). A great ORGAN work by JOHANN SEBASTIAN BACH that has been mistakenly classified as being in the DORIAN MODE. In reality it is simply in the key of D MINOR. The absence of the key signature is explained by the curious fact that in Bach's time minor key signatures carried one flat fewer than is customary today; thus D minor lacked the single flat used today. All modern editions of the work supply the key signature.

Dorsey, "Georgia Tom" (Thomas Andrew), African-American pianist, BLUES singer, and GOSPEL songwriter; b. Villa Rica, Ga., 1899; d. Chicago, Jan. 23, 1993. Dorsey's father was a revivalist preacher. Tom went to Atlanta in his youth, where he first encountered blues pianists. He later took courses at the Chicago College of Composition and Ar-

PEOPLE IN MUSIC

ranging, then launched his career as a pianist, arranger, and composer, organizing his own Wildcats Jazz Band. He also made recordings with vocalist Ma Rainey and guitarist Tampa Red as "Georgia Tom."

After founding the National Convention of Gospel Choirs and Choruses (with Sallie Martin) and the Thomas A. Dorsey Gospel Songs Music Publishing Co. in 1931, Dorsey devoted himself entirely to gospel music. He wrote the gospel standard *Precious Lord, Take My Hand* in 1932 and dozens more.

Dorsey remained active up to his death as a performer and writer.

PEOPLE IN MUSIC

Dorsey brothers. Jimmy (James), popular American JAZZ clarinetist, saxophonist, and dance band leader, b. Shenandoah, Pa., Feb. 29, 1904; d. N.Y., June 12, 1957; and **Tommy** (Thomas), popular American jazz trombonist and dance band leader, b. Shenandoah, Pa., Nov. 19, 1905; d. Greenwich, Conn., Nov. 26, 1956. The Dorsey brothers led one of the most popular BIG BANDS of the 1930s, although the brothers themselves only enjoyed their success together briefly.

Both boys were raised in a musical household; their father was a music teacher. Tommy learned trumpet initially, then switched to trombone. Jimmy also started on the trumpet but switched to REED instruments when he was 11.

The brothers performed together in several local bands as teenagers before heading off to N.Y. in the mid-1920s. They worked, either together or separately, in a number of leading jazz orchestras of the day, including groups led by Jean Goldkette and PAUL WHITEMAN. They also worked in smaller group recordings, particularly with the talented trumper (LEON) BIX BEIDERBECKE.

In 1934 the brothers finally formed their own professional band. It was an immediate success, but the brothers began to argue with each other over music and personal issues. This culminated in a fight onstage in 1935, and Tommy left the band. Jimmy continued to run the band through the 1940s, scoring hits with lead singers Bob Eberly and Helen O'Connell on popular songs and BALLADS of the day. Meanwhile, Tommy took over an existing band and built it into one of the most successful units in jazz. He worked with many singers, including a young FRANK SINATRA, whom he helped groom into a star.

After World War II all the big bands suffered from changes in musical styles and the cost of staying on the road. In 1953 the brothers reunited and consolidated forces. They had their own popular television show and continued to record and perform. Both brothers suffered from heavy eating and drinking. Tommy was the first to succumb to years of abuse, dying in 1956; Jimmy outlived him only by a year.

Both were excellent and underrated musicians. Tommy developed a smooth trombone style perfectly suited to accompanying the pop ballads of his day. Jimmy was an outstanding saxophonist whose playing was influential on dozens of other musicians.

dot. In music, much more than a mere punctuation mark. When placed after a note it indicates the increase in its value by ½. A dotted quarter note equals the value of a quarter note plus an eighth note (¼ + ⅛).

In the 17th and 18th centuries, dotted notes had an indeterminate value, indicating simply that the note with a dot after it had to be prolonged. In order to avoid uncertainty, the double dot was introduced late in the 18th century, the value of the second dot being half the value of the first. Thus a quarter note with a double dot equaled seven 16th notes (¼ + ⅛ + 1⁄16).

A triple dot is very occasionally encountered. A quarter note with a triple dot equals fifteen 32nd notes (¼ + ⅛ + 1⁄16 + 1⁄32).

dotara. A plucked string instrument that usually has four strings from the Bengali region of India.

double. 1. A VARIATION. 2. Repetition of words in a song. 3. A prefix indicating a 16-foot ORGAN STOP that matches an 8-foot stop. 4. A substitute singer. 5. In CHANGE ringing, changes on five BELLS. 6. Producing a tone an OCTAVE lower, as double BASSOON, double bourdon, etc. 7. A direction to add the higher or lower octave to any TONE or tones of a melody or harmony.

Both Jimmy and Tommy Dorsey appeared in several films, including the fictionalized story of their own group, *The Fabulous Dorseys*, in 1947.

MUSICAL INSTRUMENT

double bar. The two vertical lines drawn through the STAFF at the end of a section, movement, or piece.

double bass (string bass; It. *contrabasso;* Fr. *contrebasse;* Ger. *Kontrabass*). The largest and deepest-toned instrument of the violin family, formerly with either three strings (G1–D–A being the Italian, A1–D–G the English tuning), now four strings (E1–A1–D–G). The double bass sounds an octave lower than written. *See also* VIOLIN.

double bassoon. *See* CONTRABASSOON.

double chorus. A work for two CHOIRS, or divided choir, usually in eight parts. Also, the ensemble itself.

double common meter. *See* METER.

Double Concerto for Harpsichord, Piano, and Two Chamber Orchs. Orchestral work by ELLIOTT CARTER, 1961, first performed in N.Y. Influenced by both BAROQUE forms and modern composing techniques, Carter created a work in which each instrument and each group of instruments play distinct individual roles in DISSONANT COUNTERPOINT. IGOR STRAVINSKY described it as the first true masterpiece by an American composer.

double fugue. A FUGUE with two themes (SUBJECTS) occurring simultaneously.

double note. A breve ⌢. A note twice the length of a WHOLE NOTE.

The German violinist and composer LOUIS SPOHR wrote four double string quartets.

double quartet. Work for pairs of four solo voices or instruments, as opposed to a mixed OCTET.

double reed. A type of REED used for instruments of the OBOE and BASSOON families. Two separate pieces of reed or cane are bound together. When air pressure is applied against them, the two pieces of reed vibrate against each other. The resulting sound has a distinctive nasal quality.

double stops. The technique of playing two notes simultaneously on instruments of the VIOLIN family instruments. The easiest double stops are in SIXTHS, but THIRDS and OCTAVES are also entirely playable, even in consecutive progressions.

True triple and quadruple stops are theoretically ruled out by the curved BRIDGE of the instrument. Instead, the CHORD must be broken (played as a sequence of individual notes; see, for example, the opening of LUDWIG VAN BEETHOVEN'S *KREUTZER* sonata).

Dowland, John, great English composer and famous lutenist; b. probably in London, 1563; d. there (buried), Feb. 20, 1626. In 1580 Dowland went to Paris in the service of Sir Henry Cobham. By 1584 he was back in England, where he eventually married. On July 8, 1588, he earned his Mus.B. from Christ Church, Oxford. In 1592 he played before the queen in hopes of gaining a position in her court. This was apparently unsuccessful.

Frustrated by his lack of progress at home, Dowland set out in 1594 for Germany, where he received the patronage of the duke of Braunschweig in Wolfenbüttel and the landgrave of Hesse in Kassel. He then went to Italy and visited Venice, Padua, Genoa, Ferrara, and Florence. While in Florence he played before Ferdinando I, the grand duke of Tuscany. He then made his way home, returning to England in 1595. In 1598 he was appointed lutenist to King Christian IV of Denmark, remaining in his service until 1606. He then returned to England, where he became lutenist to Lord Howard de Walden. In 1612 he became one of the lutenists to King Charles I.

Dowland was a foremost representative of the English school of lutenist-composers. He was also noted for his songs, in which he made use of unusual CHROMATIC MOTIVES. He treated the accompanying parts as separate entities, thereby obtaining harmonic effects quite advanced for his time. Most of his vocal music was published as *Bookes of Songes or Ayres of Fowre Partes with Tableture for the Lute ...* (1597, 1600, 1603); *Lachrimae, or Seven Teares Figvred in Seaven Passionate Pauans ... Set Forth for the Lute, Viols, or Violons, in Five Parts* (1604); and *A Pilgrimes Solace* (1612).

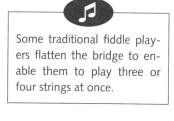

Some traditional fiddle players flatten the bridge to enable them to play three or four strings at once.

PEOPLE IN MUSIC

Dowland's son Robert Dowland (b. London, c. 1591; d. there, Nov. 28, 1641) succeeded his father as lutenist to Charles I (1626). He edited the anthologies *Varietie of Lute Lessons* (1610) and *A Musicall Banquett* (1610), which included some of his father's songs.

Down in the Valley. Folk opera by KURT WEILL, 1948. The American folk song of the same name is quoted extensively in the work. It is the tragic tale of a young man who is hanged for killing a love rival. Weill designed it as the kind of work that could be performed by AMATEUR CHORAL and theatrical groups.

downbeat (It. *battuta*). The downward stroke of the conductor's hand in beating time, marking the primary or first accent in each measure. Hence, the accent itself (strong beat, thesis).

MUSICAL
INSTRUMENT

down bow. In playing stringed instruments, the downward stroke of the BOW from nut to point. The usual sign is ⊓. Also called *downstroke*.

doxology (Grk., *doxa* + *logos,* glorious word). A HYMN of praise to God. In church services, there are three main doxologies: (1) the *greater doxology,* represented by the Gloria in excelsis in the Roman Catholic liturgy; (2) the *lesser doxology,* Gloria Patri, used at the end of the psalmody; and (3) metrical doxology as used in the Anglican liturgy. Of the last type, the most common is the metrical hymn by the 17th-century divine Thomas Kent: "Praise God, from whom all blessings flow/Praise Him all creatures here below/Praise him above ye heavenly Hosts/Praise Father, Son, and Holy Ghost."

There are also doxologies for the Jewish liturgy, including the KADDISH and the *kedusha* ("Holy, Holy, Holy/Is the Lord of Hosts …")

D'Oyly Carte, Richard. *See* CARTE, RICHARD D'OYLY.

drag. 1. A very slow dance in which the feet are dragged rather than moved on the floor.

2. A rudimentary drum stroke.

SCOTT JOPLIN wrote a "real slow drag" for his opera *Treemonisha.*

dramatic contralto. *See* ALTO.

drame lyrique (lyric drama). French designation for OPERA, especially in the 19th century. This genre may be lyric or tragic, and its designation refers only to the use of singing. The Italian term is *dramma lirico.*

dramma giocoso (It., jocular drama). An Italian term current in the 18th century for a COMIC OPERA with tragic episodes. It literally means "jocular drama." WOLFGANG AMADEUS MOZART'S *DON GIOVANNI* is described as a *dramma giocoso* in its subtitle.

dramma per musica (It., drama with music). An early term for OPERA in Italy c.1600. While the BAROQUE eventually called such works OPERA SERIA, WAGNER revived the term for his operas (*see* MUSIKDRAMA).

Dream of Gerontius, The. ORATORIO by SIR EDWARD ELGAR, 1900, based on the religious poem of Cardinal Newman. Gerontius (from Grk. *geront,* old man) is a dying man who is conducted through Purgatory by the angel of Death. The work was performed for the first time in Birmingham, and G.B. Shaw declared it a masterpiece. Its CHORAL writing is expert.

Drehleier (Ger., rotating lyre). A HURDY-GURDY, often confused with DREHORGEL.

MUSICAL
INSTRUMENT

Drehorgel (Ger., rotating organ). BARREL-ORGAN, often mistakenly called a HURDY-GURDY, with resulting confusion with the DREHLEIER.

MUSICAL
INSTRUMENT

Drei (Ger.). Three. *Dreifach,* triple; *Dreiklang,* TRIAD; *Dreivierteltakt,* a ¾ measure, ¾ time, WALTZ time.

Drei Pintos, Die. Unfinished SINGSPIEL by CARL MARIA VON WEBER. It was completed and orchestrated by GUSTAV MAHLER, 1888, using materials from Weber's other vocal works. Mahler conducted it for the first time in Leipzig. The story deals with romantic adventures in Spain in which three pintos (mottled horses) play a part.

Dreigroschenoper, Die (The threepenny opera). SINGSPIEL by KURT WEILL, 1928, first produced in Berlin. It is a modern reinterpretation of John Gay's *THE BEGGAR'S OPERA,* with a new text by Bertolt Brecht, denouncing the social hypocrisy of modern life. The score includes quasi-American FOXTROTS and RAGTIME. After a happy DEUS EX MACHINA ending, the concluding CHORUS ironically enjoins the audience to "pursue injustice, but not too much." The production was immensely successful in Germany during the era between the two world wars.

The Threepenny Opera, an English-language adaptation of the work by MARC BLITZSTEIN (1954), was equally popular. Among its many fine songs, the mocking ballad *Mack the Knife* became a perennial favorite in America. Lotte Lenya starred in both the German and American premieres.

drone. 1. In the BAGPIPE, a continuously sounding pipe of constant PITCH. A drone pipe. 2. Any sustained tone, in an inner or outer voice, creating the effect of a bagpipe, particularly on an ORGAN. *Drone bass,* a bass on the TONIC, or tonic and DOMINANT, persistent throughout a piece or section.

Druckman, Jacob (Raphael), outstanding American composer; b. Philadelphia, June 26, 1928; d. New Haven, Conn., May 24, 1996. After taking courses in solfège, harmony, and counterpoint in his native Philadelphia, Druckman studied composition with AARON COPLAND at the Berkshire Music Center in Tanglewood during the summers of 1949 and 1950. He attended Juilliard, where he worked with Peter Mennin, Vincent Persichetti, and Bernard Wagenaar, earning a bachelor's degree in 1954 and a master's two years later. A Fulbright fellowship in 1955–56 took him to Paris, where he studied with Tony Aubin at the École Normale de Musique.

Druckman began his career as a teacher at Juilliard, where he remained from 1957 to 1972. During this same period he also taught at Bard College (1961–67). He was also an associate at the Columbia-Princeton Electronic Mu-

PEOPLE IN MUSIC

sic Center (1967) and director of the ELECTRONIC MUSIC studio at Yale University (1971–72). After leaving Juilliard, Druckman taught at Brooklyn College for four years before he was named chairman of the composition department and director of the electronic music studio at Yale University in 1976, where he remained until his death.

Druckman was also a celebrated composer. From 1982 to 1986 he was composer-in-residence of the N.Y. Philharmonic. He held Guggenheim fellowships in 1957 and 1968. In 1972 he won the Pulitzer Prize in music for his *Windows* for orchestra, and in 1978 was elected a member of the Institute of the American Academy and Institute of Arts and Letters.

In his music Druckman happily combined the strict rules of composition developed during the BAROQUE period with modern techniques of DISSONANT COUNTERPOINT. At the same time, he refused to follow any doctrinaire system of composition. In his orchestrations he made much use of PERCUSSION instruments, including primitive DRUMS. Electronic sounds also had increasing importance in his works.

drum (Fr. *caisse, tambour;* It. *cassa*). In the PERCUSSION, an instrument consisting of a cylindrical, hollow body of wood or metal, over one or both ends of which a membrane of animal skin or plastic (the head) is stretched tightly by means of a hoop, to which is attached an endless cord tightened by leather braces, or by rods and screws.

Drum machine, an electronic device that performs preprogrammed rhythms and timbres.

***Drumroll* Symphony** (*Paukenwirbelsymphonie*). Nickname for FRANZ JOSEPH HAYDN's Symphony No. 102 in E♭ Major, 1795. The SYMPHONY, which opens with a roll on the TIMPANI, is the eighth of Haydn's 12 LONDON SYMPHONIES.

duda. A Slavic BAGPIPE.

duduk. A Slavic WHISTLE FLUTE.

due (It.). Two. *A due,* for two, i.e., both together again (after playing DIVISI); *a due voci,* two parts or voices; *due corde,*

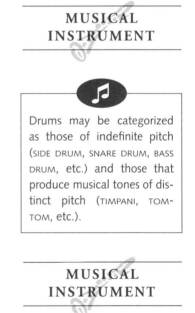

MUSICAL INSTRUMENT

Drums may be categorized as those of indefinite pitch (SIDE DRUM, SNARE DRUM, BASS DRUM, etc.) and those that produce musical tones of distinct pitch (TIMPANI, TOM-TOM, etc.).

MUSICAL INSTRUMENT

doo′ĕh

CORDA; *con due pedali,* both (damper and soft) pedals at once; *due volte,* two times, repeat.

Due Foscari, I. Opera by GIUSEPPE VERDI, 1844, based on Byron's play *The Two Foscari,* 1844. The story recounts a mortal feud between two Venetian families. The two Foscari of the title, father and son, are innocent of suspected murders, but die from mental anguish and chagrin.

Due litiganti, I. Opera by Giuseppe Sarti (1729–1802), 1782, produced in Milan. The complete title is *Fra i due litiganti il terzo gode* (Between two litigants, a third of the profits). The opera was extremely popular in its time. MOZART quotes a tune from it in act 2 of *DON GIOVANNI.*

Dueling Banjos. Originally issued in the mid-1950s as *Feudin' Banjos* by Arthur Smith (tenor BANJO) and Don Reno (five-string banjo), this instrumental was successfully revived for the film *Deliverance* by Eric Weissberg (five-string banjo) and Steve Mandell (GUITAR).

Duenna, The. *See WEDDING IN A MONASTERY, A.*

duet (It. *duetto*). 1. A composition for two voices or instruments. 2. A composition for two performers on one instrument, as the piano. 3. A composition for the organ, in two parts, each to be played on a separate manual.

Duettino, a short duet, usually with instrumental accompaniment (WOLFGANG AMADEUS MOZART's *MARRIAGE OF FIGARO* has several); *duetto da camera,* a vocal duet, usually of an amorous nature.

Dufay (Du Fay), **Guillaume,** great French composer; b. probably in or near Cambrai, c.1400; d. there, Nov. 27, 1474. Dufay was a choirboy at Cambrai Cathedral, where he came under the influence of Nicolas Malin, its *magister puerorum* (head of the choir school), and his successor, Richard Loqueville. Although there is no evidence that he formally studied with these men, he undoubtedly learned his craft while working under them and other musicians. Dufay remained in Cambrai until at least 1418, and shortly there-

PEOPLE IN MUSIC

after he entered the service of the Malatesta family in Pesaro. In 1426 he returned to Cambrai.

Dufay was in Rome as a singer in the papal choir from 1428 to 1433, during which period he built his reputation as one of the most significant musicians of his day. His MOTET *Ecclesie militantis* may have been composed for the consecration of Pope Eugene IV in 1431. He found a patron in Niccolo III, Marquis of Ferrara, in 1433, and made a visit to his court in 1437. Dufay also found a patron in Louis, Duke of Savoy. He served as MAÎTRE DE CHAPELLE for the marriage of Louis and Anne of Cyprus at the Savoy court in 1434. After a visit to Cambrai in that year, he returned to Savoy.

From 1435 to 1437, Dufay was again a singer in the papal choir, which was maintained in Florence until 1436 and then in Bologna. It was about this time that he received a degree in canon law from the University of Turin. In 1436 he was made canon of Cambrai Cathedral. After again serving the Savoy court from 1437 to 1439, he returned to Cambrai in 1440 to assume his duties as canon. In 1446 he was also made canon of Sainte-Waudru in Mons.

In 1450 Dufay returned to Italy, visiting Turin in the summer of that year. He was subsequently active in Savoy from 1451 to 1458, serving once more as *maître de chapelle* at the court from 1455 to 1456. In 1458 he returned to Cambrai, where he lived and worked in comfort for the rest of his life.

Dufay was held in the highest esteem in his lifetime by the church authorities and his fellow musicians. Compère described him as "the moon of all music, and the light of all singers." He was the foremost representative of the BURGUNDIAN SCHOOL of composition. He proved himself a master of both sacred and secular music, producing MASSES, motets, and CHANSONS of extraordinary beauty and distinction. His contributions to the development of FAUXBOURDON and the cyclic Mass are particularly noteworthy.

Dukas, Paul, famous French composer and teacher; b. Paris, Oct. 1, 1865; d. there, May 17, 1935. From 1882 to 1888 Dukas studied piano, harmony, and composition at the Paris Conservatory. He won first prize for COUNTERPOINT and

Dufay's last name is pronounced "du-fah-ee," in three syllables. We know this because this is the way he set his name to music in *Ave regina caelorum.*

PEOPLE IN MUSIC

415

FUGUE in 1886 and, two years later, the second place Prix de Rome with a CANTATA, *Velléda*.

Dukas began writing music reviews in 1892 and was music critic for several Parisian papers. In 1906 he was made a chevalier of the Légion d'Honneur, and from 1910 to 1913, and again from 1928 to 1935, he was professor of the ORCHESTRATION class at the conservatory. In 1918 he was elected CLAUDE DEBUSSY's successor as a member of the Conseil de l'Enseignement Superieur there. He also taught at the École Normale de Musique and assisted in the revising and editing of JEAN-PHILIPPE RAMEAU's complete works.

Although not a prolific composer, Dukas wrote a masterpiece of modern music in his orchestral SCHERZO *L'Apprenti sorcier* (The sorcerer's apprentice). His OPERA *Ariane et Barbe-Bleue* is one of the finest French operas in the IMPRESSIONIST style. Among his other notable works are the Symphony in C Major and the BALLET *La Péri*. Shortly before his death he destroyed several manuscripts of unfinished compositions.

Duke, Vernon. *See* DUKELSKY, VLADIMIR.

Dukelsky, Vladimir, versatile Russian-American composer of serious and popular music, the latter under the pseudonym Vernon Duke; b. Oct. 10, 1903, in the railroad station of the Russian village of Parfianovka (during his mother's trip to Pskov); d. Santa Monica, Calif., Jan. 16, 1969. Dukelsky was a pupil at the Kiev Conservatory of noted Russian composer Reinhold Glière. He left Russia in 1920 and went to Turkey, going to the U.S. shortly afterward. He later lived in Paris and London, settling in N.Y. in 1929, where he became a naturalized citizen in 1936. He was a lieutenant in the Coast Guard from 1939 to 1944. After the war he lived briefly again in Paris before returning to the U.S. to live in N.Y. and Hollywood.

Dukelsky began to compose at a very early age. He was introduced to SERGE DIAGHILEV, who commissioned him to write a BALLET, *Zephyr et Flore*, which put Dukelsky among the successful group of ballet composers. Another important meeting was with SERGE KOUSSEVITZKY, who championed his music in Paris and in Boston.

PEOPLE IN MUSIC

While living in the U.S., Dukelsky began writing popular music. Many of his songs, such as *APRIL IN PARIS*, enjoyed great popularity. At GEORGE GERSHWIN's suggestion, he adopted the name Vernon Duke for his popular works, and in 1955 he dropped his full name altogether, signing both his serious and light compositions Vernon Duke. He published the polemical book *Listen Here! A Critical Essay on Music Depreciation* in 1963.

dulcimer (from Lat. *dulcis,* sweet). 1. The *hammered dulcimer* is a predecessor of the piano. It has wire strings stretched over a soundboard or resonance box, usually in trapezoid form resembling the PSALTERY or ZITHER. The strings are struck by mallets (or hammers). The modern dulcimer has from two to three octaves' compass. It was at one time called cembalo. In Hungary it is known as the CIMBALOM. An 18th-century musician named Pantaleon Hebenstreit manufactured an instrument like a dulcimer that became known under his first name. 2. The *mountain dulcimer* is a folk instrument popular in the Appalachian Mountains in the U.S. It consists of an elongated soundbox with a fretted fingerboard and usually has three strings, which are strummed with a feather or pick. The mountain dulcimer is frequently used to accompany singers or dancers at country festivals.

dumb piano. A piano keyboard with no strings attached, used for practicing by aspiring pianists whose crowded lodgings do not permit even a joyful noise of pounding on the keys.

Dumbarton Oaks. Concerto in E♭ Major by IGOR STRAVINSKY, 1938, scored for 14 instruments. It was commissioned by a rich American music lover who lived on an estate called Dumbarton Oaks, in Germantown, a suburb of Washington, D.C. The work is written in a distinct neo-BAROQUE style typical of Stravinsky's music of the period.

dumka (Pol. *dumaç* ponder). 1. A vocal or instrumental ROMANCE, of a melancholy cast. A LAMENT or ELEGY.

MUSICAL INSTRUMENT

Electronic keyboards equipped with headsets allow contemporary pianists to practice without bothering the neighbors.

MUSICAL INSTRUMENT

Czech composers wrote the best-known examples of the dumka: ANTONÍN DVOŘÁK gave his Piano Trio op.90 (1890–91) the plural name *Dumky.* Other composers were Zdeněk Fibich, LEOŠ JANÁČEK, Josef Suk, and Jan Novák.

doomʹkäh

2. (Ukr., a little thought) Ukrainian lyric narrative BALLAD, with a meditative, sometimes melancholy character.

Dumky. Piano Trio op.90 by ANTONÍN DVOŘÁK, 1890–91, in the unusual form of six movements in the style of a DUMKA.

dummy pipes. Pipes that do not speak, displayed in the front of the ORGAN.

MUSICAL
INSTRUMENT

dump (*dompe, dumpe*). A piece, often in GROUND BASS or VARIATION form, for lute or keyboard in the 16th and 17th centuries, harmonized by alternating TONIC and DOMINANT chords.

Dunstable (Dunstaple), **John,** great English composer. b. c. 1390; d. London, Dec. 24, 1453. Almost nothing is known about Dunstable's life with any certainty. He may have been the "John Dunstaple" who was in the service of the duke of Bedford. If so, he may have accompanied his patron to France. He appears to have been well versed in astronomy and mathematics.

Dunstable's style appears to be a direct outgrowth of the English school. The Old Hall Manuscript (early 15th century) and other manuscripts reveal the existence of a highly developed musical style in England in the early 15th century, antedating the full flowering of the BURGUNDIAN SCHOOL of GUILLAUME DUFAY, GILLES BINCHOIS, and other masters.

Dunstable was the most important figure in English music in his time. His works were widely known on the Continent as well as in his homeland. Most of his known compositions are preserved in manuscripts on the Continent, although discoveries have recently been made in England. Dunstable's extant works include MASS movements, MOTETS, and secular songs.

PEOPLE IN MUSIC

Some works formerly attributed to Dunstable are now known to be by others. Other works remain doubtful. The styles of Dunstable and his contemporary Leonel Power are so close that it has not always been possible to separate their works.

doo′ōh

duo (It.). DUET. The term *duo* is loosely distinguished from DUET in this way: DUET refers to works for two pianos or for voices or instruments of different kinds, while DUO is reserved for two voices or instruments of the same kind (excepting pianos).

Also, the 12th, an ORGAN STOP. *Duodecima,* the interval of the 12th; *duodrama,* a modern type of dramatic presentation in which only two actors conduct a dialogue. It lends itself naturally to CHAMBER OPERA. The term also has been applied to 18th-century works.

Duparc (born Fouques-Duparc), (Marie-Eugène) **Henri,** notable French composer of songs; b. Paris, Jan. 21, 1848; d. Mont-de-Marsan, Feb. 12, 1933. Duparc studied in Paris with CÉSAR FRANCK, who regarded him as his most talented pupil. At the same time, he studied law. However, Duparc suffered from an early age from a psychological disease that caused him to abandon composing by the end of the 1880s. Although he lived on for many decades, he remained inactive, living in semiretirement first in southwestern France and then in Switzerland. He went blind in the 1910s and subsequently became paralyzed. He eventually died in 1933.

Duparc destroyed the manuscripts of many of his works, including the Cello Sonata and several symphonic suites. Of his instrumental works only a few manuscripts have survived, including the symphonic poems *Aux étoiles* (To the stars; 1874) and *Lénore* (1875) and a suite of five piano pieces, *Feuilles volantes* (Flying leaves; 1869). His songs, composed between 1868 and 1882 to words by Charles Baudelaire and other French poets, are distinguished by beautifully phrased melodies arranged in fluid MODAL harmonies.

duple. Double. *Duple rhythm,* rhythm of two beats to a MEASURE; *duple time, see* TIME.

duplet. A group of two equal notes to be performed in the time of three of like value in the established rhythm. It is written:

duplum (Lat.). The contrapuntal part against the CANTUS FIRMUS in ORGANUM of the ARS ANTIQUA. In ARS NOVA, the duplum was also called the *motetus* (from Fr. *mots,* words).

DuPré, Jacqueline, renowned English cellist; b. Oxford, Jan. 26, 1945; d. London, Oct. 19, 1987. DuPré entered the

PEOPLE IN MUSIC

PEOPLE IN MUSIC

London Cello School at the age of five. While still a child she began studies with her principal mentor, William Pleeth, making her first public appearance on British television when she was 12. She also studied with PABLO CASALS in Zermatt, Switzerland; Paul Tortelier at Dartington Hall and in Paris; and MSTISLAV ROSTROPOVICH in Moscow.

DuPré was awarded a gold medal upon graduation from the Guildhall School of Music in London in 1960 and the Queen's Prize. A year later, she made her formal debut in a recital at London's Wigmore Hall. In 1965 she made her North American debut at N.Y.'s Carnegie Hall as soloist in EDWARD ELGAR's Cello Concerto with ANTAL DORATI and the BBC Symphony Orchestra, which was well received by audience and critics alike.

In 1967 DuPré married the pianist and conductor DANIEL BARENBOIM in Jerusalem, with whom she subsequently performed. In 1973, however, she was diagnosed with multiple sclerosis, at which time she abandoned her career. She later gave master classes as her health permitted.

In 1976 DuPré was made an Officer of the Order of the British Empire, and in 1979 was awarded an honorary doctorate in music by the University of London. The Jacqueline DuPré Research Fund was founded to assist in the fight against multiple sclerosis.

Durey, Louis (Edmond), French composer; b. Paris, May 27, 1888; d. St. Tropez, July 3, 1979. Durey studied with Leon Saint-Requier from 1910 to 1914. The oldest member of LES SIX, he wrote the least music.

Durey's music was radically altered in 1936 when he joined the French Communist Party. During the German occupation of France, he was active in the Resistance, for which he wrote anti-Fascist songs. In 1948 he was elected vice-president of the Association Française des Musiciens Progressives. In 1950 he became the music critic of the Paris Communist newspaper *L'Humanité.* In 1961 he received the Grand Prix de la Musique Française.

Dutilleux, Henri, talented French composer; b. Angers, Jan. 22, 1916. Dutilleux studied at the Paris Conservatory, winning the first Grand Prix de Rome in 1938. He was di-

PEOPLE IN MUSIC

PEOPLE IN MUSIC

rector of singing at the Paris Opéra in 1942, and subsequently active on the Paris radio for twenty years until 1963. In 1961 he was a professor at the École Normale de Musique and in 1970 at the Paris Conservatory.

Dutilleux developed a modernistic style that incorporates many elements of IMPRESSIONISM. His CHAMBER and ORCHESTRA works have had numerous performances in France, England, and America.

Dutoit, Charles (Edouard), outstanding Swiss conductor; b. Lausanne, Oct. 7, 1936. Dutoit's father was Swiss-French, and his mother was part German, part English, and in her remote ancestry, part Brazilian. As a child, he learned to play the violin, viola, piano, and drums, and also studied conducting by watching local orchestra rehearsals. Dutoit studied theory at the Lausanne Conservatory and at the Geneva Conservatory, and also took courses in Vienna and at the Tanglewood summer music program. Returning to Switzerland, he joined the Lausanne Chamber Orchestra as a viola player.

Dutoit made his conducting debut in 1963 with the Bern Symphony Orchestra, where he was subsequently engaged as music director from 1967 to 1977. He also held other conducting positions in Switzerland and, for a time, in Mexico. In 1977 he was engaged as music director of the Montreal Symphony Orchestra. He found the work congenial, since it was centered on French culture. He greatly expanded the orchestra's repertoire, conducting HAYDN symphonies, much music of WOLFGANG AMADEUS MOZART and LUDWIG VAN BEETHOVEN, and especially French music, beginning with HECTOR BERLIOZ and including CLAUDE DEBUSSY and MAURICE RAVEL. He also promoted new Canadian music.

In 1983 Dutoit was appointed principal guest conductor of the Minnesota Orchestra in Minneapolis, and he was artistic director and principal conductor of the Philadelphia Orchestra for two summer seasons. On Dec. 21, 1987, he made his Metropolitan Opera debut in N.Y. conducting *Les Contes d'Hoffmann.* In 1990 he was named chief conductor of the Orchestre National de France in Paris.

Dutoit was married three times, his second wife being the pianist Martha Argerich.

PEOPLE IN MUSIC

dux (Lat. leader; It. *proposta;* Ger. *Vorgänger*). The SUBJECT or theme in a FUGUE, followed by the COMES. The terms became fashionable in the 16th century.

dvojnica. South Slavic double FLUTE. The right tube is for MELODY, the left is a DRONE.

Dvořák, Antonín (Leopold), famous Czech composer; b. Nelahozeves, Kralupy, Sept. 8, 1841; d. Prague, May 1, 1904. Dvořák's father ran a village inn and butcher shop and intended Antonín to learn his trade. When Dvořák showed his musical inclinations, however, his father let him study piano and violin with a local musician. He also received financial help from an uncle. Later, Dvořák went to Prague, where he studied with the director of a church music school. He also began to compose and in a short time he completed two symphonies, two operas, and some CHAMBER MUSIC.

Dvořák's first public appearance as a composer took place in Prague in 1873 with a performance of his CANTATA *The Heirs of the White Mountain* (Hymnus). A year later, BEDŘICH SMETANA conducted Dvořák's Symphony No. 3 in E♭ Major, op.10, an event that brought Dvořák much attention and fame. He then entered several of his works in a

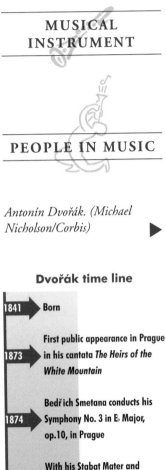

MUSICAL INSTRUMENT

PEOPLE IN MUSIC

Antonín Dvořák. (Michael Nicholson/Corbis) ▶

Dvořák time line

1841 ▶ Born

1873 ▶ First public appearance in Prague in his cantata *The Heirs of the White Mountain*

1874 ▶ Bedřich Smetana conducts his Symphony No. 3 in E♭ Major, op.10, in Prague

1880 ▶ With his Stabat Mater and Symphony No. 6 in D Major, op.60, Dvořák establishes himself as a leading Czech composer

1884 ▶ Makes the first of three visits to England, conducting his Symphony No. 7 in D Minor, op.70

1890 ▶ Conducts his works in Russia and upon his return gives the premiere in Prague of his Symphony No. 8 in G Major, op.88

Dvořák.

competition for the Austrian State Prize, adjudicated by a distinguished committee that included Johann Herbeck, Eduard Hanslick, and JOHANNES BRAHMS. He won the prize in 1875 and twice in 1877. Dvořák's Stabat Mater (Prague, 1880) and Symphony No. 6 in D Major, op.60 (Prague, Mar. 25, 1881), followed in close succession, securing for him a leading position among Czech composers.

At the invitation of the Philharmonic Society of London, Dvořák visited England in 1884 and conducted several of his works. He then was commissioned to compose a new work for the Philharmonic Society, his Symphony No. 7 in D Minor, op.70. In 1885 he returned to England to conduct the symphony's premiere, as well as *The Spectre's Bride,* which he composed for the Birmingham Festival. The following year, on his third visit to England, Dvořák conducted the premiere of his oratorio *St. Ludmila* at the Leeds Festival.

In 1890 Dvořák appeared as a conductor of his own works in Russia. That same year he conducted in Prague the first performance of his Symphony No. 8 in G Major, op.88, which became one of his most popular works. In 1891 Dvořák was appointed professor of composition at the Prague Conservatory. He then received honorary degrees from the Charles University in Prague (Ph.D.) and Cambridge University (D.Mus.). There followed his brilliant *Carnival* Overture.

In 1892 Dvořák accepted the position of director of the new National Conservatory of Music of America in N.Y. He composed his Te Deum for his first U.S. appearance as a conductor and also led a concert of his music at the 1892 World Columbian Exposition in Chicago. It was in the U.S. that he composed his most celebrated work, the Symphony No. 9 in E Minor, op.95 (*FROM THE NEW WORLD*), which received its premiere performance in late 1893 by the N.Y. Philharmonic. The melodies seemed to reflect actual African-American and Native American music, but Dvořák insisted upon their originality. Symphony No. 9 is essentially a Czech work from the old world. Nevertheless, by appearing as a proponent of the use of native themes in symphonic music, Dvořák had a significant impact on American musical nationalism.

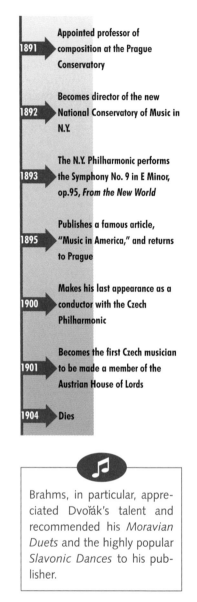

1891	Appointed professor of composition at the Prague Conservatory
1892	Becomes director of the new National Conservatory of Music in N.Y.
1893	The N.Y. Philharmonic performs the Symphony No. 9 in E Minor, op.95, *From the New World*
1895	Publishes a famous article, "Music in America," and returns to Prague
1900	Makes his last appearance as a conductor with the Czech Philharmonic
1901	Becomes the first Czech musician to be made a member of the Austrian House of Lords
1904	Dies

Brahms, in particular, appreciated Dvořák's talent and recommended his *Moravian Duets* and the highly popular *Slavonic Dances* to his publisher.

In a famous article titled "Music in America" (February 1895), Dvořák proposed that true American music could be created by drawing on the rich musical legacy found among its native peoples, particularly African-American spirituals. Some in the American musical scene welcomed the proposal, while others discounted the value of traditional American music. The controversy raged for more than two decades.

Resigning his N.Y. position in 1895, Dvořák returned home to resume his duties at the Prague Conservatory, becoming its director in 1901. During the last years of his life, he devoted much of his creative efforts to OPERA. *Rusalka* (1900) remains his best-known opera outside Czechoslovakia. He made his last appearance as a conductor in 1900, leading a concert of the Czech Philharmonic in Prague. Dvořák was made a member of the Austrian House of Lords in 1901, the first Czech musician to be so honored. Czechs celebrated his 60th birthday with special performances of his music in Prague.

Dvořák's musical style was eclectic. His earliest works reflect the influence of LUDWIG VAN BEETHOVEN and FRANZ SCHUBERT, then RICHARD WAGNER, culminating in the classicism of Brahms. After mastering his art, he proved himself to be a composer of great versatility. A diligent and meticulous craftsman, he brought to his finest works a seemingly inexhaustible melodic invention, rhythmic variety, and contrapuntal and harmonic skill. His last five symphonies, the Cello Concerto, Stabat Mater, his *Slavonic Dances,* the *Carnival* Overture, and many of his chamber works have become staples of the repertoire.

Dybbuk, The. Ballet by LEONARD BERNSTEIN, 1974. It is based on the Shlomo Ansky play depicting the exorcism of a newly bereaved Jewish bride whose body is occupied by the wandering soul of her dead bridegroom.

Dylan, Bob (born Robert Allen Zimmerman), American folksinger and songwriter; b. Duluth, Minn., May 24, 1941. Dylan was raised in rural Minnesota. He first performed in high school in a series of amateur ROCK bands, and then briefly attended college at the University of Minnesota. There he heard his first folksingers in local coffeehouses and was particularly impressed by the music of WOODY GUTHRIE, which he heard on record. He traveled to N.Y. to meet Guthrie, who was then hospitalized with Huntington's chorea.

Dylan arrived in N.Y. in late 1961 and immediately began playing in local coffeehouses. He made up many stories about his past life, portraying himself as a rootless drifter,

PEOPLE IN MUSIC

Bob Dylan, c. 1977.

impressing New Yorkers with his Midwestern drawl. He also managed to meet Guthrie, although the event was probably more meaningful to him than to the dying folksinger. He was quickly signed to Columbia Records after the *New York Times* praised one of his coffeehouse performances.

Dylan first made his mark as a topical songwriter. Such songs as *Blowin' in the Wind* and *The Times They Are A-Changin'* were hits for other folk artists, particularly PETER, PAUL AND MARY, but not for Dylan himself. He befriended JOAN BAEZ, who helped promote his songs and allowed him to share in the spotlight at her concerts during 1963–64.

When the BEATLES first arrived in America in 1964, their music was immediately embraced by the teen audience—and by many musicians who had previously performed folk music. One group of ex-folk musicians, the BYRDS, took a Dylan song called *MR. TAMBOURINE MAN* to the top of the charts. Dylan, impressed by the Beatles and by the Byrds' success with his song, began performing with a rock backup group. His decision caused two years of controversy among his audience and critics alike; some were thrilled with his new direction, others felt he had "sold out." Nonetheless, some of Dylan's greatest songs came from this period, including *Just Like a Woman, Like a Rolling Stone, Maggie's Farm,* and *Subterranean Homesick Blues.*

In 1966 Dylan broke his neck in a motorcycle accident, forcing him to interrupt his career for two years. He went into semiretirement in Woodstock, N.Y., where he worked on new material with his friends and backup group, who would soon take the name of the Band. Upon Dylan's return to recording in 1968, he had adopted yet another face, that of COUNTRY singer. In 1970 he was awarded an honorary doctorate from Princeton University, the first such honor given to a popular singer without any academic background.

Over the next three decades, Dylan has adapted many different styles. In the early 1970s he composed songs that reflected the problems in his marriage, particularly in the album *Blood on the Tracks*. In the mid-1970s he gathered a group of friends and fellow musicians to form a traveling round show he called the Rolling Thunder Revue. Then, proclaiming himself to be "born again," Dylan adopted the mantle of Christian rocker in a series of albums recorded in the late 1970s and early 1980s. His most successful album from this period was *Slow Train Coming*, which won him a Best Gospel Recording GRAMMY AWARD.

In the 1980s Dylan seemed to lose some of his focus, at least as a recording artist. He toured with both TOM PETTY and the Heartbreakers and the GRATEFUL DEAD, as well as his usual backup bands. In the late 1980s he participated in the Traveling Wilburys "super group," consisting of Petty, GEORGE HARRISON, Jeff Lynne, and ROY ORBISON.

Dylan opened the 1990s by recording two albums of traditional folk songs with just his own guitar accompaniment. Then, appearances on MTV's popular "Unplugged" program and at Woodstock II showed a new commitment to performance. In 1997 he released *Time Out of Mind*, universally hailed as his best work in years. He won a Grammy for the album.

dynamics. The degree of intensity or loudness in musical tones. Also, the notational signs used to designate these degrees (*forte, piano, crescendo, diminuendo, sforzando*, etc.).

E

E. The third note or MEDIANT of the C-major SCALE. In Italian, Spanish, French, and Russian, *mi*.

E major (Ger. *E dur*). E major has four sharps in its key signature.

To ROMANTIC composers, E major was the key of spiritual enlightenment.

E major is found in the final sections of orchestral works nominally in E MINOR, the most famous example being FELIX MENDELSSOHN's E-minor Violin Concerto.

E minor (Ger. *E moll*). The TONALITY of contemplative calm, if we are to judge by the works written in this key. It is not frequently used by the great composers of the CLASSIC period. WOLFGANG AMADEUS MOZART neglected it, as did FRANZ JOSEPH HAYDN and LUDWIG VAN BEETHOVEN. The Romantics loved it, however.

Eagles, The. (Vocal/guitar: Glenn Frey, b. Detroit, Nov. 6, 1948; drums/vocal: Don Henley, b. Gilmer, Tex., July 22, 1947; banjo/mandolin/guitar/vocal: Bernie Leadon, b. Minneapolis, July 19, 1947; bass/vocal: Randy Meisner, b. Scottsbluff, Nebr., Mar. 8, 1946; after 1974, guitar: Don Felder, b. Gainesville, Fla., Sept. 21, 1947; after 1975, guitar: Joe Walsh, b. Wichita, Kans., Nov. 20, 1947, to replace Leadon; after 1977, bass/vocal: Timothy B. Schmit, b. Sacramento, Calif., Oct. 30, 1947, to replace Meisner.) Influential country-rock band of the 1970s.

First formed as a backup group for singer Linda Ronstadt, the Eagles recorded soft country-rock in the early 1970s, scoring early hits with *Take It Easy,* a mellow, hippie-cowboy anthem, and *Desperado.* They reached their greatest

Well-known works in E major include:

ANTON BRUCKNER's grand Seventh Symphony, an ambitious and lengthy work. In composing this symphony, Bruckner's imagination was possessed by RICHARD WAGNER. He said that the second movement (*Adagio*), in the relative key of C♯ minor, forecasted Wagner's death.

Wagner's overture to *Tannhäuser*

The First Symphony of Alexander Scriabin, which ends with a choral section celebrating art

Noteworthy works in E minor include:

FELIX MENDELSSOHN's Violin Concerto.

The Fourth Symphony of JOHANNES BRAHMS, with its spacious narrative development.

PIOTR ILYICH TCHAIKOVSKY's Fifth Symphony; however, the finale, as tradition demanded, is set in the relative major.

GUSTAV MAHLER's most serene symphony, his Seventh. Even though there are lapses into the night's darkness, the finale, in unambiguous C major, reasserts the music's optimism, so unusual in Mahler's works.

The River Moldau (Vltava) in BEDŘICH SMETANA's symphonic cycle MA VLAST flows poetically in E minor. ANTONÍN DVOŘÁK's Ninth Symphony (*From The New World*) is in E minor. The nostalgic quality of this work—written during his visit to the U.S.—fits the key.

NIKOLAI RIMSKY-KORSAKOV's symphonic suite SCHEHERAZADE.

Drummer Don Henley of the Eagles. (Shelley Gazin/Corbis) ▶

The French composer MAURICE RAVEL would have probably failed a test of memory or even pitch recognition. The famous conductor ARTURO TOSCANINI sang embarrassingly off pitch when leading the orchestra. The Russian composer IGOR STRAVINSKY had an unusually poor memory even in reconstructing his own works. His ear training by any educational standards was surprisingly deficient.

success when they became a more hard-rocking outfit, focusing on social commentary (1977's *Hotel California, Life in the Fast Lane*).

In 1980 the group disbanded following internal squabbling; 14 years later, they rebanded (with the late 1970s personnel) for a hugely successful reunion tour and album. Henley went on to the greatest individual success, although Frey also had solo hits.

ear training. Music training methods used to improve the aural recognition of INTERVALS and RHYTHMS. Students who happily possess the gift of PERFECT PITCH have a tremendous advantage over others not so favored by nature. Anyone who has this natural capability can easily recognize notes, intervals, and chords and trace melodies, while others must learn this process more slowly.

Memory is another important branch of ear training, and here again, individual gifts may differ greatly. An otherwise unmusical child may possess a natural ability to remember popular tunes she hears in the street, while a virtuoso violinist or pianist may lack this ability. The ability to carry a tune is also subject to individual evaluation. Some children can pick up tunes and sing or whistle them with extraordinary accuracy, while experienced musicians may be unable to carry a tune.

Earth Angel. A 1954 DOO-WOP hit for the Crew Cuts. It was covered by the Penguins and Gloria Mann (1955) and New Edition (1986).

Easter Parade. Song by IRVING BERLIN. The melody originated in 1917, with a set of new lyrics added for the revue *As Thousands Cheers* (1933). The song served as the theme for a 1948 film.

Ebony Concerto. CONCERTO for clarinet and jazz band by IGOR STRAVINSKY, 1946. It was written for BIG BAND clarinetist Woody Herman and was first performed by him and his band in N.Y., Mar. 25, 1946.

ecclesiastical modes. The SCALES employed in MEDIEVAL MUSIC; church modes. *See also* AUTHENTIC MODES; PLAGAL MODES.

echo (It. *eco*). A subdued repetition of a strain or phrase. The natural reflection of sound in mountain landscapes was the inspiration of many composers for the use of this technique.

Canonic echo is the echoing in one voice of a melodic phrase that is first stated by another. The device is employed in many MADRIGALS. In some cases the echo repeats the last syllables of the preceding word, when it makes sense, e.g., *esempio* (example) answered by *empio* (empty). This effect is used poignantly in the last act of CLAUDIO MONTEVERDI's *ORFEO*.

The echo is also used in instrumental music. In the last movement of his *Ouvertüre nach französicher Art* (Partita in B Minor, BWV 831), JOHANN SEBASTIAN BACH makes use of it. In WOLFGANG AMADEUS MOZART's Serenade, K. 286, there is an interplay of groups of four instruments in a quadruple echo.

echoi. The Greek term for the SCALES used in BYZANTINE CHANT, paralleling closely the Gregorian system of eight MODES. Collectively they are known as *oktoechos* (eight modes). Their emergence has been traced to Syrian chant,

In Greek mythology, the nymph Echo dies of unrequited love for Narcissus. Only her voice remains as an "echo" of her being. The legend inspired several opera composers, including CHRISTOPH WILLIBALD GLUCK, in whose *Écho et Narcisse* he cleverly echoed melodic lines in different voices.

which is much older than GREGORIAN CHANT. It seems probable that both Byzantine and Gregorian chants were ultimately derived from a Syrian source.

PEOPLE IN MUSIC

Eckstine, Billy (William Clarence), also known as "Mr. B," African-American JAZZ singer and bandleader; b. Pittsburgh, July 8, 1914; d. there Mar. 8, 1993. Eckstine began singing as a teenager but was more interested in football as a possible career. After he broke his collarbone in a game, however, he decided to focus on music. In the early 1930s he moved to Chicago, where he got a job as vocalist with pianist EARL HINES's band, remaining with him until 1943.

At that time, Eckstine's manager convinced him to form his own band, which became a breeding ground for young musicians who would go on to form BEBOP, including ART BLAKEY, CHARLIE PARKER, DIZZY GILLESPIE, MILES DAVIS, Kenny Dorham, and singer Sarah Vaughan. The band lasted until 1947, when Gillespie formed his own similar unit.

Eckstine himself favored BALLADS as a singer, and his low, booming voice was particularly suited to slower numbers. He had a number of hits between 1940's *Jelly Jelly* and 1959's *Gigi,* mostly in the pop ballad style. After his band broke up, he worked as a solo act with various accompanists, and continued to record through the 1960s, '70s, and '80s.

eclecticism (from Grk., *ex + leipein,* gather). Compositional or improvisational method in which the choice of style or period is unlimited. Drawing on a wide variety of styles in composing a work.

ā-kōh-säz' **écossaise** (Fr., Scottish). Originally, a Scottish round dance in $\frac{3}{2}$ or $\frac{3}{4}$ time; later, a lively CONTREDANSE in $\frac{2}{4}$ time. The latter entered continental Europe in the early 19th century; LUDWIG VAN BEETHOVEN, FRANZ SCHUBERT, CARL MARIA VON WEBER, and FRÉDÉRIC CHOPIN composed them. While known under this and other names (*anglaise, française*), the écossaise and its relatives probably originated in English country dances. *Compare* SCHOTTISCHE.

Ecuatorial. Symphonic poem by EDGARD VARÈSE, 1934. It is scored for bass voice, brass instruments, piano, organ, percussion, and THEREMIN, to texts in Spanish from the sacred book of the Mexican priests, and was first performed in N.Y. It is one of the earliest works to employ an ELECTRONIC INSTRUMENT, the Theremin.

E-flat major (Ger. *Es dur*). Most brass instruments are pitched in either B♭ or E♭. Thus, these keys are commonly used in festive SERENADES, military MARCHES, and solemn CHORALES.

Works in E♭ major are suitable for heroic, patriotic, and religious themes. LUDWIG VAN BEETHOVEN's *EROICA* symphony cannot be imagined in any other key, nor can his *EMPEROR* concerto. One of the greatest of WOLFGANG AMADEUS MOZART symphonies, No. 39, is set in also in this key. ANTON BRUCKNER's *Romantic* Symphony, his Fourth, and GUSTAV MAHLER's grandiose Eighth Symphony, nicknamed *Symphony of a Thousand*, are in E♭.

It is not by accident that ROBERT SCHUMANN's Third Symphony is surnamed *Rhenish*, for it reflects the nature of life on the River Rhine, with its constant traffic and horns signaling the departure of stagecoaches. Beethoven's piano sonata that he named *Les Adieux* begins with an imitation of the postillion's (horn player's) signal in HORN FIFTHS.

E♭ major is peculiarly suited to the piano keyboard, because the notes of its scale are fairly evenly distributed between the white and black keys. Piano works in E♭ major number in the thousands. FRANZ LISZT set his First Piano Concerto in E♭ major, but he avoided immediately introducing the key. Rather, he teased the listener with a SYNCOPATED descent from the TONIC into the DOMINANT.

In his egocentric tone poem, *Ein Heldenleben*, Richard Strauss wrote a violin solo in E-flat major to represent himself!

When HANS VON BÜLOW was asked what his favorite key was, he replied "E♭ major, for it is the key of the *Eroica* Symphony, and it has three B's [B signifies a flat in German] for Bach, Beethoven, and Brahms." This was the origin of the famous grouping of composers as the "three B's of music."

E-flat minor (Ger. *Es moll*). This is the key of seclusion and retreat from the common elements of HARMONY. With six flats in the key signature, it lends itself to brilliant technical devices for a piano virtuoso, but it is utterly unsuitable for orchestral writing. A rare instance is NIKOLAI MIASKOVSKY's Sixth Symphony.

Egk was born Werner Mayer. Rumor had it that he took the name Egk as a self-complimentary acronym for "ein grosser [or even 'ein genialer'] Komponist" (the greatest composer). Egk himself rejected this explanation, offering instead an even more fantastic one. He claimed that "Egk" was a partial acronym of the name of his wife, ElisabethKarl, with the middle g added to make it easier to pronounce.

Egk (born Mayer), **Werner,** significant German composer; b. Auchsesheim, near Donauworth, May 17, 1901; d. Inning, near Munich, July 10, 1983. Egk studied piano with Anna Hirzel-Langenhan and composition with CARL ORFF in Munich, where he made his permanent home.

Primarily interested in theater music, he wrote several scores for a Munich puppet theater. He was also active on the radio, then wrote BALLET music to his own scenarios and a number of successful OPERAS. He was active as an opera conductor and music pedagogue. He conducted at the Berlin State Opera from 1938 to 1941, and was head of the German Union of Composers during World War II.

Unlike other composers who fled the Nazi regime, Egk enjoyed favor under the repressive government. He was commissioned to write music for the Berlin Olympiad in 1936, for which he received a Gold Medal. He also received a special commission of 10,000 marks from the Nazi Ministry of Propaganda. After the war, he stood trial for his Nazi sympathies but was cleared of any wrongdoing. From 1950 to 1953 Egk was director of the Berlin Hochschule für Musik.

As a composer Egk continued the tradition of RICHARD WAGNER and RICHARD STRAUSS, without excluding, however, modern techniques, including ATONAL writing. His rhythms were often inventive and bold. He is best known for his dramatic works.

***Egmont* Overture.** The best-known portion of LUDWIG VAN BEETHOVEN's incidental music for Goethe's drama *Egmont,* 1810, first performed in Vienna. Egmont was a historical figure, a Dutch patriot who organized resistance to the Spanish masters of the Netherlands but was killed in the process.

Egorov, Youri, talented Russian pianist; b. Kazan, May 28, 1954; d. Amsterdam, Apr. 15, 1988. Egorov was a precocious child who learned to play piano at home. At the age of 17 he won a prize at the Long-Thibaud competition in Paris, and at 20 he received third prize at the Tchaikovsky Competition in Moscow.

In 1978, Egorov made his N.Y. debut, followed by solo performances with various American orchestras. He settled in the Netherlands, where his career was cut tragically short by AIDS.

1812 **Overture.** Concert overture by PIOTR ILYICH TCHAIKOVSKY, 1882, commemorating the 70th anniversary of the defeat of Napoleon's armies in Russia. Tchaikovsky wrote it for the consecration of the Church of Christ the Savior in Moscow, and the performance was given in the open air. The score included such special effects as a contingent of church bells and even cannon shots. The warring armies are represented by warring themes, the Russians by a national HYMN and the French by their ANTHEM, the *MARSEILLAISE.* The French defeat is represented by the repetition of the *Marseillaise,* wilting away in a minor key, and a triumphant rendition of the czarist anthem *God Save the Czar.*

While Tchaikovsky found the *1812* overture "devoid of artistic value," posterity disagreed. It remains one of his most popular and often performed works.

eighth. 1. An OCTAVE. 2. An eighth note. *See* INTERVAL.

Ein (*eins;* Ger.). One. *Einfach,* simple, simply, *semplice; Eingang* or *Einleitung,* introduction; *Einklang,* UNISON, CONSONANCE; *Einlage,* interpolation, inserted piece; *Einstimmung,* MONOPHONIC.

in

Eine kleine Nachtmusik (A little night music). String SERENADE by WOLFGANG AMADEUS MOZART, 1787, in four movements, in a small-scale symphonic form. One of his most popular and greatest works.

Einem, Gottfried von, outstanding Austrian composer; b. Bern, Switzerland (where his father was attached to the Austrian embassy), Jan. 24, 1918; d. Obern, Durenbach, Austria, July 12, 1996. Einem went to Germany as a child, where he studied music. He then was OPERA coach at the Berlin State Opera. In 1938 he was arrested by the Gestapo and spent four months in prison.

PEOPLE IN MUSIC

After his release, Einem studied composition in Berlin from 1941 to 1943. In 1944 he was in Dresden, where he became resident composer and music advisor at the Dresden

State Opera. He then was active in Salzburg. In 1953 he visited the U.S. He finally settled in Vienna, where in 1965 he was appointed professor at the Hochschule für Musik.

Einem produced a number of successful short operas and BALLETS. In his music he emphasized the dramatic element by dynamic and rhythmic effects. His harmonies are terse and strident; his vocal line often borders on ATONALITY but remains singable. Einem's best-known works are operas: *Dantons Tod,* after Büchner (Salzburg, 1947); *Der Prozess,* after Kafka (Salzburg, 1953); *Der Zerrissene,* after Nestroy (Hamburg, 1964); *Der Besuch der alten Dame,* LIBRETTO by Dürrenmatt (Vienna, 1971); *Kabale und Liebe,* after Schiller (Vienna, 1976); and *Jesu Hochzeit* (Vienna, 1980), which caused a scandal for depicting Christ as having taken a wife.

Einstein on the Beach. Opera by PHILIP GLASS, in collaboration with the director Robert Wilson. It was premiered at the Avignon Festival on July 25, 1967, and subsequently performed throughout Europe. In 1976 it was presented—although not as part of the regular subscription season—at the Metropolitan Opera in N.Y., to much acclaim.

The work features Glass's typical technique of using short melodic MOTIVES that are repeated, creating a kind of hypnotic texture. The story line is fragmented, with the character of the famous mathematician and physicist Albert Einstein appearing at various times in fantastic situations.

Eisler, Hanns (Johannes), remarkable German composer of politically oriented works; b. Leipzig, July 6, 1898; d. Berlin, Sept. 6, 1962. Eisler studied music on his own while still a youth, then at the New Vienna Conservatory and later privately with ARNOLD SCHOENBERG from 1919 to 1923. He also worked for a time with Schoenberg's student ANTON WEBERN. In 1924 he won the Vienna Arts Prize.

Eisler went to Berlin in 1925 and taught at the Klindworth-Scharwenka Conservatory. In 1926 he joined the German Communist Party. After the Nazis came to power in 1933 he left Germany, making visits to the U.S. and being active in Austria, France, England, and other European countries.

Eisler settled in the U.S. and taught at the New School for Social Research, N.Y., during the 1930s and at the Uni-

PEOPLE IN MUSIC

versity of California, Los Angeles, in the 1940s. However, his communist beliefs led him to be questioned by the House Committee on Un-American Activities in 1947, whereupon he voluntarily left the U.S. In 1949 he settled in East Berlin and became a professor at the Hochschule für Musik and a member of the German Academy of the Arts.

Under Schoenberg's influence, Eisler adopted the 12-TONE method of composition for most of his symphonic works. However, he demonstrated a great capacity for writing music in an accessible style. His long association with the German dramatist Bertolt Brecht resulted in several fine scores for the theater. Eisler's songs and CHORAL works became popular in East Germany. He composed the music for its national ANTHEM, *Auferstanden aus Ruinen,* which was adopted in 1949. He never composed his projected OPERA *Johannes Faustus,* for which he wrote the LIBRETTO in 1952. Some believe the work was left uncompleted because of the resistance of government officials.

ektara (*ektār;* 1 string). An Indian LUTE. Formerly, a bamboo stick bearing a single string attached to the center of a small drum. At present, the stick is attached to a resonating gourd with a wooden bottom. The string is plucked and produces a drone.

MUSICAL INSTRUMENT

Eldridge, (David) **Roy "Little Jazz,"** outstanding African-American JAZZ trumpeter; b. Pittsburgh, Jan. 30, 1911; d. Valley Stream, N.Y., Feb. 26, 1989. In 1930 Eldridge went to N.Y., where he worked with various musicians, including Teddy Hill, and became a featured member of FLETCHER HENDERSON's orchestra during 1935–36. With his brother Joe, a saxophonist and arranger, he formed his own band in Chicago in 1936. He then took it to N.Y. in 1939, where he gained fame as a master instrumentalist of the SWING era. He played with the bands of GENE KRUPA from 1941 to 1943 and ARTIE SHAW from 1944 to 1945, and also worked with Norman Granz's touring Jazz at the Philharmonic shows from 1948.

PEOPLE IN MUSIC

From the 1950s through the early 1980s, Eldridge later worked with BENNY CARTER, JOHNNY HODGES, ELLA FITZGERALD, and COLEMAN HAWKINS, and also led his own BIG

BAND and combos. Although plagued by ill health after 1980, he made occasional appearances as a singer, drummer, and pianist.

MUSICAL INSTRUMENT

electric guitar. An electronic adaptation of the GUITAR, with a solid body, metallic strings, and miniature pickup microphones replacing natural acoustic projection. It is widely used in modern popular music.

electric organ. *See* ELECTRONIC ORGAN.

MUSICAL INSTRUMENT

electric piano. A class of KEYBOARD instruments whose sounds are produced electronically or reproduced electrically. The term applies to instruments ranging from amplified grand pianos to portable keyboards that use metal bars or COMPUTER technology to produce pianolike sounds.

electronic instruments. Musical instruments in which electricity is used to produce, modify, or alter the sound.

The earliest surviving electronic instrument, the THEREMIN, was demonstrated by its Russian inventor, Leon Theremin, in Moscow in 1920.

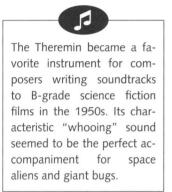

The Theremin became a favorite instrument for composers writing soundtracks to B-grade science fiction films in the 1950s. Its characteristic "whooing" sound seemed to be the perfect accompaniment for space aliens and giant bugs.

Theremin's invention was followed by a number of others. In Germany, Jörg Mager (1880–1939) constructed an ELECTRONIC ORGAN that he called the Spherophon. He later developed the more sophisticated Partiturophon and Kaleidophon. In France, MAURICE MARTENOT invented the *ondes musicales* (now called ondes Martenot, 1928), a keyboard instrument for which music is still being written. The wire-based Trautonium (1930) was developed by Friedrich Trautwein (1888–1956); PAUL HINDEMITH wrote music for it. Oscar Sala introduced some innovations into the Trautonium in an electronic organ he called the Mixturtrautonium.

The most advanced electronic instruments belong to the SYNTHESIZER group, first developed in studio settings in the 1950s and commercially available in the 1960s. These are capable of generating any desired PITCH, SCALE, RHYTHM, TONE COLOR, and degree of loudness. They are the most sophisticated of electronic instruments based on analog principles. The development of personal COMPUTERS has led to the evolution and refinement of COMPUTER MUSIC synthesis. *See also* MUSIQUE CONCRÈTE.

electronic music. A general term for compositions created by electronic means. Listed chronologically, these are the different types of electronic music that have developed over the past decades:

1920s–30s: ELECTRONIC INSTRUMENTS are first produced

1930s–40s: Composers use phonograph records or radios as "musical instruments" in compositions.

Late 1940s–50s: MUSIQUE CONCRÈTE. The invention of the tape recorder (in World War II) makes it possible for composers to create works directly on tape. Also, tape can be cut and spliced, allowing further composition.

1950s–70s: Analog synthesis, where sound and manipulation are entirely electronic. Originally, SYNTHESIZERS required a roomful of equipment; transistors allowed the invention of portable synthesizers, pioneered by ROBERT MOOG and DONALD BUCHLA.

1970s–present: LIVE ELECTRONIC MUSIC, performing or improvising music onstage using synthesizers and COMPUTERS. Electroacoustic music, in which acoustically produced sound is processed in an interactive relationship with electronic equipment.

1980s–present: Binary-controlled DIGITAL synthesis, using increasingly sophisticated and user-friendly computer equipment.

electronic organ. A powerful modern keyboard instrument activated by electronic means and capable of unlimited tone production.

MUSICAL INSTRUMENT

electronic piano. *See* ELECTRIC PIANO.

electrophones. A class of musical instruments that produce their sound by electric or electronic means. *See* ELECTRONIC INSTRUMENTS.

ā-lā-zhe′

Élégie. Popular cello solo by JULES MASSENET, 1875. Originally part of INCIDENTAL MUSIC written for the play *Les Erinnyes* in 1873, it accompanied the scene where Electra performed a ritual bath at the tomb of Agamemnon, her dead husband. It was renamed *Élégie* in 1875.

elegy (Fr. *élégie;* Ger. *Elegie*). A vocal or instrumental composition of a melancholy or nostalgic character, having no fixed form.

Elegy for Young Lovers (*Elegie für junge Liebende*). Chamber opera by HANS WERNER HENZE, 1961, with an original English LIBRETTO by W.H. Auden and Chester Kallman. It was first performed in Schwetzingen, Germany, in German translation.

The story deals with a poet living in the Swiss Alps who deliberately sends his stepson and his own mistress to the mountains during a raging snowstorm. They die as expected, and their fate gives him the needed inspiration for writing his poem, *Elegy for Young Lovers.* The poet's brutality is expressed musically by angular, ATONAL melodies and DISSONANT harmonies.

Elektra. Opera by RICHARD STRAUSS, 1909, to a LIBRETTO based on Sophocles' *Libation Bearers* by Hugo Hoffmannsthal, first produced in Dresden. In this work, Strauss reaches greatness. The classical drama, the story of a brother and sister who kill their mother to avenge her murder of their father in ancient Greece, is set to a musical score of awesome power. The vocal parts are extremely demanding. The drama is underscored by DISCORDANT harmonies.

elevator music. *See* MUZAK.

PEOPLE IN MUSIC

Elgar, (Sir) **Edward** (William), great English composer; b. Broadheath, near Worcester, June 2, 1857; d. Worcester, Feb. 23, 1934. Elgar received his earliest education from his father, who owned a music shop and was organist for the St. George's Roman Catholic Church in Worcester. He also took violin lessons from a local musician.

Sir Edward Elgar, 1919.
(Hulton-Deutsch Collection/
Corbis)

Elgar rapidly acquired the fundamentals of THEORY and served as arranger with the Worcester Glee Club, becoming its conductor at the age of 22. At the same time, he accepted a rather unusual position for a young aspiring musician with the County of Worcester Lunatic Asylum at Powick, where he was for several years in charge of the institution's concert BAND. In 1885 he succeeded his father as organist at St. George's. He married Caroline Alice Roberts in 1889 and moved to Malvern, where he stayed from 1891 to 1904. During these years he also conducted the Worcestershire Philharmonic.

In 1905 Elgar accepted the position of Peyton Professor of Music at the University of Birmingham and in 1911–12 served as conductor of the London Symphony Orchestra. He then settled in Hampstead. His beloved wife died in 1920, at which time he returned to Worcester. His composing virtually ceased after her death.

Elgar's first success was with the CONCERT OVERTURE *Froissart,* which was premiered in Worcester in 1890. Three years later, his CANTATA *The Black Knight* was produced at the Worcester Festival and was also heard in London at the Crystal Palace in 1897. The production of his cantata *Scenes from the Saga of King Olaf* in 1896 attracted considerable attention, and he gained further recognition with his *Imperial March* of 1897, composed for the Diamond Jubilee of Queen Victoria.

The first *POMP AND CIRCUM-STANCE* march became Elgar's most famous piece. Lyrics were written for it by Arthur Christopher Benson, and the piece became widely known under the title *Land of Hope and Glory*. In this form, Elgar incorporated it into his *Coronation Ode* in 1902. Its hymnlike section became a popular recession march for high school graduation exercises.

From then on, Elgar's name became familiar to the musical public. His great masterpiece, and last major vocal work, the ORATORIO *THE DREAM OF GERONTIUS,* was produced in 1900. He then began to give more and more attention to orchestral music. On June 19, 1899, Hans Richter presented the first performance of Elgar's Variations on an Original Theme (generally known as *ENIGMA VARIATIONS*) in London. Its success was followed by the production of Elgar's *Pomp and Circumstance* marches, composed between 1901 and 1930.

Elgar's two symphonies, written between 1903 and 1910, became staples in the English orchestral repertoire. His Violin Concerto, first performed by FRITZ KREISLER in 1910, won notable success. There was also a remarkable Cello Concerto, which Elgar conducted at its premiere in 1919.

The emergence of Elgar as a major composer about 1900 was all the more remarkable because he had no formal academic training. Yet he developed a masterly technique of instrumental and vocal writing. His style of composition may be described as an outgrowth of ROMANTICISM, with his harmonic techniques remaining firmly within the 19th-century tradition. The formal element is always strong, and the thematic development logical and precise.

Elgar had a melodic gift, which asserted itself in his earliest works, such as the popular *Salut d'amour.* His oratorios, particularly *The Apostles,* were the product of his fervent religious faith (he was a Roman Catholic). In his sacred works, he presented religious subjects in the more communicative style of secular drama.

Elgar was the recipient of many honors. He was knighted in 1904. He received many honorary degrees in England and the U.S. He received the Order of Merit in 1911, and was made a Knight Commander of the Royal Victorian Order in 1928 and a baronet in 1931. In 1924 he was appointed Master of the King's Musick.

Elisir d'amore, L' (The elixir of love). Opera by GAETANO DONIZETTI, 1832. It tells of an impoverished man's attempts to win the woman of his dreams by using a love potion. However, it fails to work until he inherits a fortune from his uncle. Suddenly, his beloved finds herself more attracted to him.

Ellington, "Duke" (Edward Kennedy), famous African-American pianist, bandleader, and composer; b. Washington, D.C., Apr. 29, 1899; d. N.Y., May 24, 1974. Ellington was raised in a well-to-do family in Washington, D.C. He played RAGTIME piano as a boy, then worked with various JAZZ bands in his hometown during the 1910s and early 1920s.

In 1923 Ellington went to N.Y. to work with a band led by Elmer Snowden. A year later Ellington took over the leadership of the band, which he would continue to lead for the next half-century. With the Ellington orchestra, complex arrangements were introduced, requiring both improvising skill and the ability to read scores. Eventually these scores were to take on the dimensions and scope of classical compositions while retaining an underlying jazz feeling.

◀

Duke Ellington, 1933. (Corbis-Bettmann)

In the early days, Ellington's chief collaborator in composition and arrangements was trumpeter James "Bubber" Miley (1903–32) and baritone saxophonist Harry Carney (1910–74), another arranger, who was with the band from its inception until Ellington's death. Other collaborators were BARNEY BIGARD, Otto Hardwick, and Ellington's son Mercer. From 1939 Ellington's main collaborator was pianist-composer Billy Strayhorn (1915–67). Among the many great musicians who played in the Ellington orchestra were Sonny Greer, "Tricky Saw" Nanton, Carney, Fred Guy, JOHNNY HODGES, BEN WEBSTER, Jimmy Blanton (the brilliant jazz bassist who died at age 27 in 1942), Ray Nance, Cat Anderson, Paul Gonsalves, and Jimmy Hamilton.

Ellington received many awards and honors during his life. He was the first jazz musician to receive an honorary degree from Columbia University in 1973. He was also the recipient of the Presidential Medal of Freedom. He made several European trips under the auspices of the State Department. He toured Russia in 1970 and also went to Latin America, Japan, and Australia. So highly was he esteemed in Africa that the Republic of Togo issued in 1967 a postage stamp bearing his portrait.

Ellington wrote over 1,000 compositions. Some were popular jazz instrumentals or songs, including his first major hit, 1926's *East St. Louis Toodle-Oo,* MOOD INDIGO (1930), and *Sophisticated Lady* (1932). Ellington also wrote ambitious extended works for his orchestra, including *Diminuendo and Crescendo in Blue* (1937); *Black, Brown, and Beige* (a tonal panorama of African-American history, 1943); *Liberian Suite* (1948); and *My People,* commissioned for the 100th anniversary of the Emancipation Proclamation (1963). Later in life, he turned his attention to religious themes in his *First Sacred Concert* (San Francisco, 1965) and *Second Sacred Concert* (N.Y., 1968).

Ellington's music continues to be performed and his style widely emulated in jazz today. WYNTON MARSALIS, leader of the Jazz at Lincoln Center program and orchestra, has done much to promote Ellington's arrangements and compositions.

After his death, Ellington's band was led by his son Mercer (b. Washington, D.C., March 11, 1919; d. Copenhagen, Feb. 8, 1996).

PEOPLE IN MUSIC

Elman, Mischa, remarkable Russian-born American violinist; b. Talnoy, Jan. 20, 1891; d. N.Y., Apr. 5, 1967. At the age of six, Elman was taken by his father to Odessa, where he studied violin. His progress was extraordinary, and when LEOPOLD AUER heard him play in 1902, he immediately accepted him in his class at the St. Petersburg Conservatory. In 1904 Elman made his debut in St. Petersburg with sensational acclaim. A tour of Germany was equally successful, and in 1905 he appeared in England, where he played the GLAZUNOV Violin Concerto.

In 1908 Elman made his American debut in N.Y. and was hailed as one of the greatest virtuosos of the time. He played with every important symphony orchestra in the U.S. With the Boston Symphony Orchestra alone he was a soloist at 31 concerts. In the following years he played all over the world and, with JASCHA HEIFETZ, was universally lauded as one of the greatest violinists of the day.

Elman's playing was the height of ROMANTIC interpretation. His tone was sweet but resonant. He excelled particularly in the concertos of the Romantics FELIX MENDELSSOHN and PIOTR ILYICH TCHAIKOVSKY, but he could also give impressive performances of LUDWIG VAN BEETHOVEN and WOLFGANG AMADEUS MOZART. He published several violin arrangements of CLASSIC and Romantic pieces, and also composed some short compositions for his instrument.

Élytres. Chamber ensemble work by LUKAS FOSS, 1964, first performed in Los Angeles. *Élytre* is French for the exterior wings of certain insects that protect their fragile interior. Foss uses high pitches and unpleasant string sounds to portray his insectlike theme.

embouchure (Fr.). 1. The mouthpiece of a WIND instrument. 2. The manipulation of the lips and tongue in playing a wind instrument.

ähn-boo-shür'

Emmett, Daniel Decatur, American composer of popular songs; b. Mt. Vernon, Ohio, Oct. 29, 1815; d. there, June 28, 1904. Emmett began his career as a drummer in military bands, then joined the Virginia Minstrels, singing and playing the banjo. He later was a member of Bryant's Minstrels. He wrote the lyrics and the music of *DIXIE* in 1859, first performed in N.Y. that year. Upon publication, its popularity spread, and it was adopted as a Southern fighting song during the Civil War (even though Emmett was a Northerner). His other songs, *Old Dan Tucker, The Road to Richmond, Walk Along,* etc., enjoyed great favor for some years.

PEOPLE IN MUSIC

***Emperor* Concerto.** Piano Concerto No. 5 by LUDWIG VAN BEETHOVEN, 1809 (op.73). The nickname is odd in that the work was dedicated to the Archduke Rudolph of Austria, who never became emperor.

Emperor Jones, The. OPERA by LOUIS GRUENBERG, 1933, based on Eugene O'Neill's play about a former railroad porter who briefly serves as emperor of a West Indian island.

The *Emperor's Hymn* melody was later used for the German patriotic hymn *Deutschland, Deutschland über alles.* Because of its association with the Nazis, it has taken on a sinister, negative meaning.

Emperor Quartet. FRANZ JOSEPH HAYDN's String Quartet op.76/3 (1797). The second movement is a VARIATION set based on his melody for *Gott erhalte Franz den Kaiser,* or EMPEROR'S HYMN.

Emperor's Hymn. Former national ANTHEM of the Austrian empire, 1797, also called *Gott erhalte Franz den Kaiser.* The melody was derived by FRANZ JOSEPH HAYDN from a Croatian folk song and used as the theme for the VARIATION set in his String Quartet op.76/3.

emp-find′zămr shtēl

Empfindsamer Stil (Ger.). "Sensitive" or "sentimental" style that developed in Germany in the mid-18th century. It replaced the demand for compositional unity that characterized the late German BAROQUE.

ăhn-kor′

encore (Fr., again). 1. *See* APPLAUSE. 2. A piece or performance repeated or added to the end of a scheduled program.

endless melody (*Unendliche Melodie*). A term introduced by RICHARD WAGNER to describe an uninterrupted melodic flow unhampered by sectional CADENCES. Particularly characteristic is the flow of one LEITMOTIV into another with a free interchange of voices and instrumental parts.

With the decline of the Wagnerian cult in the 20th century, the endless melody lost much of its attraction. Modern OPERAS now gravitate toward a Verdian concept of well-demarcated operatic numbers.

PEOPLE IN MUSIC

Enesco, Georges (born George Enescu), famous Romanian violinist, conductor, teacher, and composer; b. Liveni-Virnav, Aug. 19, 1881; d. Paris, May 4, 1955. Enesco began to play the piano when he was four, taking lessons with a Gypsy violinist, and began composing when he was five. On Aug. 5, 1889, just shy of his eighth birthday, he made his formal debut as a violinist in Slanic, Moldavia.

As a teenager, Enesco enrolled in the Conservatory of the Gesellschaft der Musikfreunde in Vienna (first prizes in violin and harmony, 1892; graduated, 1894). He then entered the Paris Conservatory, studying composition, theory, and performance, graduating in 1899 with the *premier prix* (first prize) for violin. At the same time he also studied cello, ORGAN, and piano, showing great talent on each.

In 1897 Enesco presented in Paris a concert of his works, which attracted the attention of Édouard Colonne, who published the youthful composer's op.1, *Poème roumain,* the next year. Enesco also launched his conducting career in Bucharest in 1898. In 1902 he first appeared as a violinist in Berlin and also organized a piano trio, and in 1904 he formed a quartet. In 1903 he conducted the premiere of his two *Romanian* Rhapsodies in Bucharest, the first of which was to become his most celebrated work.

Georges Enesco, c. 1925. (Library of Congress/Corbis)

He soon was appointed court violinist to the queen of Romania. In 1912 he established an annual prize for Romanian composers. In 1917 he founded the George Enescu symphony concerts in Iaşi.

After World War I Enesco made major tours as a violinist and conductor. He also taught violin in Paris, where his pupils included YEHUDI MENUHIN, Arthur Grumiaux, Ivry Gitlis, and Christian Ferras. He made his U.S. debut in 1923 in the triple role of conductor, violinist, and composer with the Philadelphia Orchestra in N.Y., returning in 1937 to conduct the N.Y. Philharmonic. He led that orchestra in several subsequent concerts, 14 concerts in 1938 alone, with remarkable success. He also appeared twice as a violinist and conducted two concerts at the N.Y. World's Fair in 1939. The outbreak of World War II found him in Romania, where he lived on his farm in Sinaia, near Bucharest. He visited N.Y. again in 1946 as a teacher.

In 1950, during the 60th anniversary season of his debut as a violinist, Enesco gave a farewell concert with the N.Y. Philharmonic in the multiple capacity of violinist, pianist, conductor, and composer, in a program comprising JOHANN SEBASTIAN BACH's Double Concerto (with Menuhin), a violin sonata (playing the piano part with Menuhin), and his First *Romanian* Rhapsody (conducting the orchestra). He then returned to Paris, where his last years were marked by near poverty and poor health. In July 1954 he suffered a stroke and remained an invalid for his remaining days.

Although Enesco severed relations with his communist homeland, the Romanian government paid homage to him for his varied accomplishments. His native village, a street in Bucharest, and the State Philharmonic of Bucharest were named in his honor. Periodical Enesco festivals and international performing competitions were established in Bucharest in 1958.

Enesco had an extraordinary range of musical interests. His compositions include artistic adaptations of Romanian folk strains. While his style was neo-ROMANTIC, he made occasional use of experimental devices, such as QUARTER TONES in his OPERA *Oedipe* (composed between 1921 and 1931). He possessed a fabulous memory and was able to perform many works without scores. He not only distinguished himself as a violinist and conductor but was also a fine pianist and a gifted teacher. He contributed significantly to the instrumental music of the 20th century.

Enfance du Christ, L'. Oratorio in three parts by HECTOR BERLIOZ, 1854. It traces the story of Jesus from his birth to the Holy Family's arrival in Egypt.

Enfant et les sortileges L'. Fantasy opera by MAURICE RAVEL, 1915, to a LIBRETTO by Colette, first produced in Monte Carlo. In a dream, broken dishes, mutilated toys, and torn books come to haunt the destructive boy who owns them. There is a duet of meowing cats complaining of ill treatment. When the evil boy awakens from this nightmare of destruction, he is totally reformed. The score bristles with clever sonorities and subtle rhythms.

Engel, Lehman, American composer, conductor, and writer on music; b. Jackson, Miss., Sept. 14, 1910; d. N.Y., Aug. 29, 1982. Engel began to take piano lessons with local teachers as a child, then studied at the Cincinnati College of Music from 1927 to 1929. In 1930 he went to N.Y. to take courses in composition at the Juilliard School of Music, where he remained until 1934, and also took private composition lessons with ROGER SESSIONS from 1931 to 1937. While still a student, he began to write music for BALLET and theatrical plays, and in 1934 he wrote INCIDENTAL MUSIC for Irish playwright Sean O'Casey's play *Within the Gates.*

From 1935 to 1939 Engel led the Madrigal Singers for the Works Progress Administration, a Depression-era government agency that funded the arts. Later he worked with the Mercury Theater as composer and conductor. During World War II Engel enlisted in the U.S. Navy. He conducted a military orchestra at the Great Lakes Naval Training Station and later was appointed chief composer of the Navy's film division in Washington, D.C. He wrote a great many scores for Broadway productions, which he also conducted, among them T.S. Eliot's *Murder in the Cathedral* and Tennessee Williams's *A Streetcar Named Desire.*

As a composer, Engel was happiest in the theater. He had a special knack for vivid musical illustration of the action on the stage. He conducted the first American performance of KURT WEILL's *The Threepenny Opera.* He also conducted the productions of SHOWBOAT, BRIGADOON, ANNIE GET YOUR GUN, *Fanny,* GUYS AND DOLLS, and CAROUSEL. Engel received two Tony Awards, in 1950 for conducting GIAN CARLO MENOTTI's opera THE CONSUL, and in 1953 for conducting operettas of Gilbert and Sullivan. In 1971 he received an honorary D.M. degree from the University of Cincinnati.

English horn (Fr. *cor anglais;* Ger. *englisches Horn;* It. *corno inglese*). The alto OBOE in F, transposing a FIFTH below the

PEOPLE IN MUSIC

MUSICAL INSTRUMENT

Some noteworthy appearances of the English horn in famous works:

It plays the Alpine song after the storm in GIOACCHINO ROSSINI's overture to *William Tell*.

It sounds the shepherd's pipe in the third act of RICHARD WAGNER's *Tristan und Isolde*.

It portays the mortuary messenger in JEAN SIBELIUS's symphonic poem *The Swan of Tuonela* (Tuonela is the kingdom of death in Finnish mythology).

This little poem is based on the theory of enharmonic equivalents.

B is a B is a B is a B,
And never C flat will it be.
C is a C is a C is a C,
And never B sharp will it be.
B double-flat is nonsensical
When we know it's just plain old A.
And why be unduly forensical,
Insisting that G double sharp is not A?

written note. Its range is from E below middle C to about C an octave above middle C.

It is not clear how this instrument acquired its name. It certainly did not originate in England. The French name for it may well be the corruption of *cor anglé* (angled horn), but its DOUBLE-REED mouthpiece is attached to a bent crook, rather than placed at an angle. The other distinctive element is the bulb BELL.

The sound of the English horn suggests a variety of moods, from a pastoral scene to an ominous sense of danger. It does not blend well with other instruments and thus is used mostly for solo parts. Rarely used in the CLASSIC era and only occasionally in the Romantic, it has had an increasingly important role in 20th-century orchestral music, with concertos written for virtuosos.

English Suites. Six keyboard PARTITAS by JOHANN SEBASTIAN BACH, BWV 806–11. The source for the name is unknown.

enharmonic equivalence (equivalents). Notes that sound the same in the tempered scale but are notated differently. C♯ and D♭ are enharmonically equal, as are D♯ and E♭, or E♯ and F♮.

Pianists do not have to bother about enharmonic equivalents on the EQUAL-TEMPERED keyboard. String instrument players, however, have to adjust their sharps and flats to stay within the tempered scale. String players testify that the descending augmented second, say from E to D♭, is actually larger than the minor third from E to C♯, even though the two intervals are enharmonically equivalent. Harmonic context is the final determining factor.

Enigma Variations. Remarkable set of orchestral VARIATIONS by EDWARD ELGAR, 1899, consisting of a theme and 14 variations. Each variation bears initials or nicknames of Elgar and his friends, the first being those of Lady Elgar (C.A.E.). The powerful ninth variation is entitled *Nimrod,* the name of the "mighty hunter before the Lord" in Genesis. It represents Elgar's friend A.J. Jaeger, whose surname means "hunter" in German.

But why is the theme itself described as an enigma? Elgar was asked several times to clarify the mystery, but his answers only compounded the confusion. He suggested that there might be hidden in the music a well-known classical theme, but it has never been identified. Many solutions have been offered ("Newsflash: The Enigma Solved!"), but none accepted universally.

The work was first performed under its complete title, Variations on an Original Theme, "Enigma," in London, making Elgar internationally famous. RICHARD STRAUSS considered it a masterpiece and proof that England, at last, had produced a great composer.

Enjoy Yourself (It's Later Than You Think). Black-humored song by Carl Sigman, 1948. It was revived in Woody Allen's *Everyone Says I Love You* (1997) as an ode for dancing ghosts.

Eno, Brian (Peter George St. John le Baptiste de la Salle), English composer, musician, and producer; b. Woodbridge, Suffolk, May 15, 1948. Although interested in tape recorders and recorded music at an early age, Eno received no formal music training. Instead, he studied art in school. He then became involved in AVANT-GARDE experiments, performing works by modern composers LA MONTE YOUNG and CORNELIUS CARDEW.

Eno helped found the art-rock band Roxy Music in 1971, leaving it two years later for a solo career that resulted in four modestly successful progressive-rock albums during the mid-1970s.

In 1975, while confined to bed after being struck by a London taxi, he created a new type of music he called "ambient," created rich sound textures without any recognizable melody or harmony. In additional to his ROCK-based experimental records, he has collaborated with and produced records by DAVID BOWIE, Talking Heads, and U2.

In 1979 Eno became interested in video, subsequently producing "video paintings" and "video sculptures" used as ambient music in galleries, museums, airport terminals, and private homes. His music has influenced both New Wave and New Age genres.

PEOPLE IN MUSIC

ăhn-săhn′bl

ensemble (Fr., together). Since 1600, a group of instrumental players or vocalists performing together. The term is applied to a group of players larger than a duet but smaller than a chamber orchestra.

Entertainer, The. RAGTIME work by SCOTT JOPLIN, published in 1902. It became a hit in 1973 when revived as the theme for the popular film *The Sting.* Its success spurred a revival of interest in Joplin and ragtime in general.

Entführung aus dem Serail, Die. See ABDUCTION FROM THE SERAGLIO.

ăhn-trähkt′

entr'acte (Fr., between acts). A light instrumental composition or short BALLET for performance between the acts of theater, music, and dance works.

en-trah′täh

entrata (It.; Fr. *entrée*). 1. The orchestral PRELUDE to a BALLET, following the OVERTURE. 2. Music played for the dancers' entrances in 16th- and 17th-century French ballet. 3. A division in a ballet, like a scene in a play. 4. An old dance like a POLONAISE, usually in $\frac{4}{4}$ time.

envelope. The shape of a sound's AMPLITUDE, changing over time. An important determinant of sound quality.

epanalepsis. A device, often applied to BAROQUE music, in which the opening of a melody or musical period serves as its closing.

epic opera (epic theater). In mid-20th-century German productions, a theatrical work in which the audience is made aware of the "unreality" of the production. This can be done in many ways: by characters speaking directly to the audience, exposing stagecraft such as lighting, etc., placing musicians on the stage where they can be seen, and so on.

The purpose of these techniques is usually to make sure that the audience is aware of the "message" that the playwright or composer is trying to convey, rather than becoming involved in the characters or their stories. For this reason, epic theater/opera is usually associated with political themes such as the promotion of communist or socialist ideas. The style was developed most prominently by Bertolt Brecht, who collaborated with the composers KURT WEILL, HANNS EISLER, and PAUL DESSAU.

episode (Ger. *Zwischensatz*). An intermediate or incidental section. In a FUGUE, digression from the principal SUBJECT.

ep′ĭ-sōd

Epistle sonata. An instrumental work performed in church before the reading of an Epistle from the New Testament.

epithalamium. (Grk., at the bedroom). A nuptial ode or festive wedding HYMN.

equal temperament. A precise division of the OCTAVE into 12 equal SEMITONES.

Equal temperament lies at the foundation of Western music since the mid-18th century. It enables the performer to play (or a composer to write) a tune in any KEY, but it misrepresents all basic INTERVALS except the octave itself. Accordingly, the tuning of keyboard instruments must be made deliberately off pitch for the intervals of the perfect FIFTH, the perfect FOURTH, THIRDS, and SECONDS. The deviations are small, and the musical ear easily accommodates itself to the margin of error.

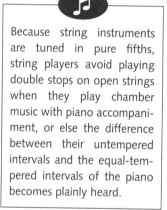

Because string instruments are tuned in pure fifths, string players avoid playing double stops on open strings when they play chamber music with piano accompaniment, or else the difference between their untempered intervals and the equal-tempered intervals of the piano becomes plainly heard.

Erdödy Quartets. Set of six STRING QUARTETS by FRANZ JOSEPH HAYDN, op.76 (1797), named after its dedicatee.

Erkel, Franz (Ferenc), distinguished Hungarian pianist, conductor, composer, and pedagogue; b. Gyula, Nov. 7, 1810; d. Budapest, June 15, 1893. Erkel studied in Pozsony in the early 1820s and then went to Koloszvar, where he began his career as a pianist. In 1834 he became conductor of the Kaschau OPERA troupe, with which he traveled to Buda a year later. He became conductor of the German Municipal Theater in Pest in 1836, where he would remain for the rest of his life.

In 1838 Erkel was made music director of the newly founded National Theater, an influential post he held until 1874. He became an important figure in the local music

PEOPLE IN MUSIC

scene, founding in 1853 the Philharmonic concerts, which he conducted until 1871. He was the first professor of piano and instrumentation at the Academy of Music, serving as its director from 1875 to 1888. In 1884 he was appointed the conductor at the Opera House. He gave his farewell performance as a pianist in 1890 and as a conductor in 1892.

Erkel was one of the most significant Hungarian musicians of his era. After successfully producing his opera *Báthory Mária* (1840), he gained lasting fame in his homeland with the opera *Hunyady László* (1844), recognized as the first truly national Hungarian work for the theater. He composed the Hungarian national ANTHEM in 1844. He later achieved extraordinary success with the opera *Bánk Bán* (1861), written in collaboration with his sons Gyula (b. Pest, July 4, 1842; d. Ujpest, Mar. 22, 1909) and Sándor (b. Pest, Jan. 2, 1846; d. Bekescsaba, Oct. 14, 1900). He also collaborated with his other sons, Elek (b. Pest, Nov. 2, 1843; d. Budapest, June 10, 1893) and László (b. Pest, Apr. 9, 1844; d. Pozsonyi, Dec. 3, 1896), who were successful musicians.

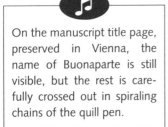

The original production of Hugo's play in Paris in 1830 helped inspire the Romantic movement in art. But Hugo himself disliked Verdi's opera.

Ernani. Opera by GIUSEPPE VERDI, 1844, based on Hugo's drama *Hernani,* first produced in Venice. The opera's story is a historical fantasy. Ernani is a banished heir of the royal house of Aragon. He loves Elvira, but she is also pursued by Silva, her elderly guardian, and the future emperor Charles V. In the end Ernani stabs himself and dies in her arms.

***Eroica* Symphony.** The Third Symphony of LUDWIG VAN BEETHOVEN, op.55, 1804. When it was published two years later, the title page bore a designation in Italian that appears cryptic: "Sinfonia eroica composta per festeggiar il sovvenire d'un grand'uomo" (Symphony Eroica composed to celebrate the memory of a great man). Who was the "grand'uomo" whose memory was celebrated by Beethoven in this "heroic symphony"? Even the least knowledgeable music lover can answer: Napoleon! Indeed, the original title was *Sinfonia grande: Buonaparte.*

Popular books on Beethoven tell us how, when he was apprised of the fact that Napoleon had proclaimed himself emperor in May 1804, Beethoven flew into a rage, tore up the dedication page, and exclaimed: "Then he is a tyrant

On the manuscript title page, preserved in Vienna, the name of Buonaparte is still visible, but the rest is carefully crossed out in spiraling chains of the quill pen.

like all conquerors!" The story is first told in the autobiography of Beethoven's student Friedrich Ries, which he apparently dictated a third of a century after the event, shortly before his own death. Beethoven's official biographer, Anton Schindler, popularized the scene in which Beethoven denounced Napoleon. How old was Schindler at the time of the *Eroica?* Born in 1795, he was only nine years old! Worse still for biographical fantasy: in a letter to his publishers dated August 1804, after Napoleon had already had himself crowned by the pope, Beethoven still referred to the symphony as "really named *Buonaparte.*" If the *Eroica* was to celebrate Napoleon's victories, why is its first movement written in $\frac{3}{4}$ time rather than in some kind of MARCH tempo? And in whose memory was written the FUNERAL MARCH that constitutes the second movement? The ensuing scherzo, also in $\frac{3}{4}$ time, reveals no possible link to the career of Napoleon. As for the finale, Beethoven used thematic materials previously applied to the finale of his BALLET score *The Creatures of Prometheus* and in his *EROICA VARIATIONS* for piano, op.35.

Eroica Variations. Piano variations in E♭ major by LUDWIG VAN BEETHOVEN, op.35, 1802. These variations are based on the so-called Prometheus theme that he had used twice previously: in the Contredanse No. 7, op.14 (c.1801), and as the finale of the BALLET *The Creatures of Prometheus,* op.43 (1801). Although this piano work was written first, after Beethoven used the same thematic material (for a third time) in his *EROICA* symphony, the piano pieces gained the title *Eroica Variations.*

Erstaufführung (Ger.). Premiere, usually a local performance.

Erwartung (Expectation). MONODRAMA by ARNOLD SCHOENBERG, 1909, first produced in Prague, 1924. The score has only one singing part, that of a woman who finds the dead body of her lover in a forest. She muses over the circumstances that led to his death, after he abandoned her for another woman. It is performed in SPRECHSTIMME (half-spoken/half-sung).

Escales (Ports of call). Orchestral SUITE by JACQUES IBERT, 1924. It portrays cities he visited during his French navy stint: Palermo, Tunis, and Valencia.

escapement (Fr. *échappement;* Ger. *Auslösung;* It. *scappamento*). The part of a piano ACTION that lets the hammer disengage from the striking mechanism and then fall away from the string while the key remains held down. Except for a few early piano designs, pianos have included escapements since the late 17th century.

Eschenbach (born Ringmann), **Christoph,** remarkably talented German pianist and conductor; b. Breslau, Feb. 20, 1940. Eschenbach's mother died in childbirth, and his father, the musicologist Heribert Ringmann, lost his life in battle soon thereafter. His grandmother died while attempting to remove him from the advancing Allied armies. Placed in a refugee camp, he was rescued by his mother's cousin, who adopted him in 1946.

Eschenbach began studying piano at age eight with his foster mother. His formal piano training commenced at the same age with Eliza Hansen in Hamburg and continued with her at the Hochschule für Musik there. He also studied piano with Hans-Otto Schmidt in Cologne and received instruction in conducting at the Hamburg Hochschule für Musik. In 1952 he won first prize in the Steinway Piano Competition. After winning second prize in the Munich International Competition in 1962, he gained wide recognition three years later by capturing first prize in the first Clara Haskil Competition in Montreux.

In 1966 Eschenbach made his London debut. Following studies with GEORGE SZELL during 1967–69, the latter invited him to make his debut as soloist in WOLFGANG AMADEUS MOZART's Piano Concerto in F Major, K. 459, with the Cleveland Orchestra in 1969. In subsequent years he made numerous tours as a pianist, appearing in major music centers. He also gave duo concerts with the pianist Justus Frantz.

In 1972 Eschenbach began to make appearances as a conductor. He made his debut as an OPERA conductor in Darmstadt with *LA TRAVIATA* in 1978. He pursued a success-

PEOPLE IN MUSIC

ful career as both a pianist and a conductor, sometimes conducting from the keyboard.

After holding positions in Germany and Zurich as a conductor, Eschenbach served as music director of the Houston Symphony Orchestra from 1988 to 1999. In 1998 he was appointed chief conductor of the North German Radio Symphony Orchestra in Hamburg. He maintains a varied repertoire as both pianist and conductor. His sympathies range from the standard literature to the cosmopolitan AVANT-GARDE.

Estampes (Fr., engravings, prints, etchings). Piano SUITE by CLAUDE DEBUSSY, 1903. It contains three picturesque movements: *Pagodes* (Pagodas), *Soirée dans Grenade* (Nights in Grenada), and *Jardins sous la pluie* (Gardens in the rain).

estampie (Fr.; It. *stampitas;* Prov. *estampida*). A MEDIEVAL instrumental composition developed by the TROUBADOURS in the 13th and 14th centuries. Primarily in TRIPLE time, the estampie is divided into several sections called *puncta* (melodic units). Different endings are provided for the repetitions of the puncta, similar to the indications of *prima volta* and *seconda volta* in the repeat sections in CLASSIC music. It is most likely that the original estampies were dances, although many also had texts.

Estro armonico, L'. Collection of 12 CONCERTOS by ANTONIO VIVALDI, 1712, for various combinations of instruments.

â′strōh ar-mō′nē-kōh

Et incarnatus. Portion of the CREDO from the Roman Catholic High MASS, often set separately in large-scale works.

ethnomusicology. This is a relatively new term, succeeding COMPARATIVE MUSICOLOGY, to describe the rigorous study of traditional musics. The primary research focus has for many years been on non-European music that would have been labeled "exotic" in previous centuries, such as that of Asia, Africa, and South America. Today, however, ethnomusicology refers broadly to any "world" music culture.

The initial focus was on recording the music of various groups and then bringing them to archives or university departments for analysis. Instruments were also gathered in order to study and categorize them. The invention of videotape allowed dance, ceremony, and other visually oriented elements to be recorded for study.

Today, there is an emphasis on understanding music from the point of view of the people who have created it. Studies of "musical communities" helps us understand the total role that music plays in society.

The real Peter the Great did hide his identity in order to study carpentry and shipbuilding in the Netherlands. However, the similarity to the opera ends there.

Étoile du Nord, L' (The north star). Opera by GIACOMO MEYERBEER, 1854. Russia's Peter the Great disguises himself in order to study carpentry abroad. He woos a village woman, marries her, and makes her his czarina.

ā-tüd′

étude (study; Fr. *étude;* It. *studio;* Ger. *Studie, Etüde*). An exercise or study. Originally, the term was applied exclusively to technical exercises. In the 19th century its meaning was enlarged to include musical works designed to show off a player's technique.

MUZIO CLEMENTI's *Gradus ad Parnassum* (Steps to Mount Parnassus, the dwelling of the Muses who inspire music), and CARL CZERNY's numerous collections of piano exercises established a higher type of étude. In their works, the étude had a true musical quality, beyond being merely a technical exercise.

Études proper, designed for improvement of technique, were called *exercises* and were usually in the form of simple melodic and rhythmic sequences, SCALES, TRILLS, ARPEGGIOS, and other technical passages. Études evolved into full-fledged compositions, often brilliant displays of instrumental technique. Études fit for public performance were called concert études, or, in French, *études de concert.*

FRÉDÉRIC CHOPIN elevated the genre to ROMANTIC grandeur in his two series of études for piano. ROBERT SCHUMANN's *ÉTUDES SYMPHONIQUES* for piano are neither études nor symphonic compositions, but VARIATIONS on a THEME. FRANZ LISZT developed a superior type of piano étude in his 12 *ÉTUDES D'EXECUTION TRANSCENDANTE.* ALEXANDER SCRIABIN followed Chopin's model in his own group of piano studies, as did CLAUDE DEBUSSY.

Violin virtuosos, above all NICCOLÒ PAGANINI, wrote brilliant études for the violin. Cellists and other instrumentalists composed études for their own instruments.

Études d'exécution transcendante (Transcendental studies). Twelve ÉTUDES by FRANZ LISZT, 1851. A very difficult series of pieces written by Liszt to display his dazzling technique at the keyboard.

Originally, Liszt let the studies speak for themselves, but he later added programmatic titles, e.g., *Feux follets* (Will o' the wisp), *Mazeppa, Wilde Jagd* (Wild hunt), and *Eroica* (in E♭ major, the key of LUDWIG VAN BEETHOVEN's *EROICA* symphony).

The entire series is dedicated to Liszt's piano teacher, CARL CZERNY, "in token of gratitude, respect, and friendship."

Études symphoniques. A cycle of piano studies by ROBERT SCHUMANN, 1837 (op.13). It was originally titled "études of an orchestral character" to emphasize the advanced POLYPHONY in the work.

Five more VARIATIONS not used by Schumann in the original edition were published posthumously and are often added to the original 12 by modern pianists.

Études-Tableaux. Cycles of CHARACTER PIECES for piano by SERGEI RACHMANINOFF, 1911 and 1917 (opp.33 and 39).

Études transcendentales. See *ÉTUDES D'EXECUTION TRANSCENDANTE.*

Eugene Onegin. Opera by PIOTR ILYICH TCHAIKOVSKY, 1879, after Alexsander Pushkin's poem, first produced in Moscow.

Two young friends, Onegin and Lensky, are visiting the summer estate of a family with two daughters, Tatiana and Olga. Fascinated by Onegin, Tatiana confesses her love to him in a passionate ARIA (in French, then the language of Russian high society). The next day he explains that he is not meant for the simple domestic happiness of marriage. At the family ball, Onegin purposely dances with Olga to annoy Lensky, her fiancé. Lensky angrily challenges him to a duel. Onegin kills him and, torn by remorse, departs on a long journey abroad.

Returning to Russia many years later, he meets Tatiana, now the wife of a retired general. He is seized with passion and begs her to go off with him. She rejects him and he leaves her forever.

The music is filled with lyric MELODY. *Eugene Onegin* is a perennial favorite in Russia and, like Tchaikovsky's QUEEN OF SPADES, is regularly heard outside its native land.

PEOPLE IN MUSIC

Euler, Leonhard, great Swiss mathematician; b. Basel, Apr. 15, 1707; d. St. Petersburg, Sept. 18, 1783. Euler was a professor of mathematics at St. Petersburg (1733) and Berlin (1741). He published several important works on music THEORY and ACOUSTICS, chief among them being the *Tentamen novae theoriae musicae* (St. Petersburg, 1739).

Euler employed ancient Greek mathematical formulas to explain CONSONANCE and DISSONANCE, modifying them to account for the modern phenomenon of EQUAL TEMPERAMENT.

Eumenides, Les. INCIDENTAL MUSIC by DARIUS MILHAUD, 1927. Written for the final part of the French playwright Paul Claudel's trilogy drawn from Aeschylus's *Orestia*.

euphonious harmony. Harmonies that contain only CONCORDS and mild DISCORDS. MAJOR SEVENTHS or MINOR SECONDS, acoustically the sharpest dissonances, are totally avoided. *See* EUPHONY.

MUSICAL INSTRUMENT

euphonium (from Grk., good-sounding). An instrument of the brass family, with a tapered body and a deep cup-shaped mouthpiece. It may have three or four VALVES.

The euphonium is considered the tenor of the TUBA family, with the range of a TROMBONE or BARITONE. It is commonly found in military bands, but rarely in classical orchestras.

euphony (Grk., good sound). Literally, any melody or melody with harmony that is pleasing to the ear. Of course, what is pleasing to one generation may be a DISCORD to the next.

Euphony is not necessarily the same thing as CONSONANCE. A succession of DISSONANCES, if they follow a natural tonal sequence, may sound entirely euphonious to the ear, while a progression of open FIFTHS or multiple OC-TAVES could register as CACOPHONY. Generally speaking, soft dissonances are tolerated better than loud consonances.

An unharmonized melody may be heard as euphonious as well. If the steps in the melody correspond to those in the major or minor SCALES, suggesting patterns based on normal harmonies, then the melody is more likely to be recognized as pleasing to the average listener. A random collection of notes is likely to strike the ear as a musical jumble.

Europe, James Reese, African-American conductor and composer; b. Mobile, Ala., Feb. 22, 1881; d. Boston, May 10, 1919. Europe studied violin and piano in childhood in Washington, D.C., then went to N.Y. There he was active as a director of MUSICAL COMEDIES.

PEOPLE IN MUSIC

Europe also founded the Clef Club (1910), a union and contracting agency for black musicians, the first of its kind. The Clef Club symphony orchestra, led by Europe, gave performances of works by black composers at Carnegie Hall in 1912–14. Europe was music director and composer for the popular dancers Irene and Vernon Castle between 1914 and 1917, and is credited with composing the first FOX-TROT for them.

Europe wrote songs for musicals and composed dances and marches for his orchestras and bands. His recordings helped popularize an early form of SYNCOPATED dance music that in many ways paved the way for the later popularity of JAZZ. His career was cut short in 1919, however, when he was stabbed to death by the drummer in his band.

Europeras 1 & 2. Opera by JOHN CAGE (composed between 1984 and 1987; premiered in Frankfurt am Main, Dec. 12, 1987). Its name is a combination of the words *Europe* and *opera* but is also a pun on "your opera." Because the opera is created by the performers each night, based loosely on a score that gives them various options, it could be said to be "their opera" as much as Cage's. The "1 & 2" of the title denotes two unequal parts—one 90 minutes in length, one 45 minutes—which are separated by a 1.5-minute looping black-and-white film of moments from both.

Europeras' cast of players includes 19 singers, 12 dancer/athletes, and a 24-piece orchestra, without the usual body of strings. Included in its percussion section is a "Truckera," a tape of 101 layered fragments of European operas.

Europeras 1 & 2 is, like all of Cage's work since the early 1950s, conceived wholly of CHANCE OPERATIONS. The orchestra can select from 64 instrumental fragments from different European operas, ranging from CHRISTOPH WILLIBALD GLUCK to GIACOMO PUCCINI. Meanwhile, the vocalists may select from various ARIAS and DUETS to perform at the same time. Lighting cues, set pieces, and costumes drawn from various performances are incorporated independently of the instrumental or vocal music

Each element—music, vocal, set, costume, lighting—is completely independent from the others, resulting in a work marked by a total absence of intended musical or dramatic relationships. In Cage's words, *Europeras 1 & 2* is a "circus of independent elements," those elements mixing in performance without suggesting or revealing any sort of order. Therefore, there is no need for a conductor in performance. Each of the soloists governs his or her prescribed actions by digital clock time displayed on video monitors. The overall effect is one of a perfectly orchestrated collage.

The synopsis is provided to the audience in 12 different program books, each one combining fragmented sentences from the synopses of the original 64 operas to create its own random "story."

Cage later produced two shorter versions in the series: *Europeras 3 & 4* (London, June 17, 1990) and *Europera 5* (Buffalo, N.Y., Apr. 18, 1991).

Euryanthe. Opera by CARL MARIA VON WEBER, 1823, first performed in Vienna. The LIBRETTO is taken from an old French legend. A good wife named Euryanthe is charged with being unfaithful to her husband by his enemies. She withstands their attacks, however, and emerges with her reputation intact. The opera failed, but its lively OVERTURE became a favorite concert piece.

eurythmics (eurhythmics). A system of musical training introduced by Émile Jaques-Dalcroze in 1910. Young children are taught to represent and experience complex rhythmic movement with their entire bodies, to the accompaniment of specially composed or improvised music.

Evans, Bill (William John), respected American JAZZ pianist and composer; b. Plainfield, N.J., Aug. 16, 1929; d. N.Y., Sept. 15, 1980. Evans attended college at Southwestern Methodist University. During the summers he played piano with local bands and had his first exposure to jazz. After serving in the army in the early 1950s, he enrolled at N.Y.'s Mannes School of Music from 1955 to 1956, and then joined clarinetist Tony Scott's band. He also made his first solo album.

In 1958 Evans joined MILES DAVIS's band. He was very influential on Davis's 1958 *Kind of Blue* album, composing many of its selections, which were based on MODAL rather than TONAL harmonies. However, he left Davis's group less than a year after joining it.

In 1959 Evans formed his first influential trio, which featured bassist Scott LaFaro and drummer Paul Motian. The group developed a decidedly COOL approach to jazz. Evans's intellectual piano playing and intricate melodies and harmonies were perfectly framed by a group that lacked any other lead instrument.

Evans's career suffered a setback in 1961 when LaFaro was killed in an automobile accident. Though he never again had as sympathetic an accompanist, he continued to record through the 1960s and early 1970s with various accompanists, and also as a soloist. He received Grammy Awards for his recordings *Conversations with Myself* (1963), *Alone* (1970), and *The Bill Evans Album* (1971).

Evans performed both original compositions and his own interpretations of the standards. Many of his works featured short melodic ideas, changing rhythms, and unusual (for jazz) harmonies derived from modern classical music. Some jazz critics and players accused him of being overly thoughtful in his approach, saying his music didn't "swing." Evans's career slowed in the 1970s due to an increasing addiction to drugs. He died of the effects of this addiction in 1980.

Evans, (Ian Ernest) **Gil**(more Green), Canadian JAZZ pianist, bandleader, and arranger; b. Toronto, May 13, 1912; d. Cuernavaca, Mexico, Mar. 20, 1988. Evans went to Calif.

PEOPLE IN MUSIC

PEOPLE IN MUSIC

in his youth. He was largely self-taught in music. After leading his own band in Stockton, Calif., from 1933 to 1938, he went to N.Y. There he worked with the innovative jazz band of CLAUDE THORNHILL in the 1940s. The group featured many unusual instruments for jazz, combining them in COUNTERPOINT to create a kind of marriage between jazz and classical music.

Another musician working with Thornhill at this time was GERRY MULLIGAN. Along with Evans, the two wrote a series of arrangements for a nine-piece band led by trumpeter MILES DAVIS. This resulted in 1948 in the recording of what was called *The Birth of the Cool.* COOL JAZZ was first popularized by this short-lived group.

Evans continued to work through the 1950s with various bands but did not achieve great success until he reunited as arranger for Miles Davis for the late 1950s albums *Miles Ahead* and *Sketches of Spain.* Davis's muted trumpet playing was perfectly accompanied by Evans's rich harmonies, and the two albums were very popular.

Evans continued to freelance through the 1960s and finally achieved his dream of having his own band in the 1970s and '80s. With this group he continued to explore new ground. He became a champion of the compositions of ROCK guitarist JIMI HENDRIX, adapting them for BIG BAND.

Evans was one of the most talented arrangers in jazz, second only to DUKE ELLINGTON for his appreciation of the individual voices that make up a band. He was able to use simple melodies to create complex but understandable arrangements. He was the last of the great big band leaders at a time when jazz was oriented increasingly toward small groups.

evensong (evening song). In the Anglican church, a daily service to be said or sung at evening. It is known as VESPERS in the Roman Catholic church.

Everly Brothers. (Vocal/guitar: Don Everly., b. Brownie, Ky., Feb. 1, 1937; vocal/guitar: Phil Everly, b. Chicago, Ill., Jan. 19, 1939.) Don appeared at the age of eight on a radio show managed by his parents in Shenandoah, Iowa. Both

PEOPLE IN MUSIC

Don and Phil then toured with their parents around the country. They moved to Nashville around 1955.

Originally, the brothers recorded (unsuccessfully) in a COUNTRY style. Don scored some success as a songwriter, but the duo failed as a recording act. Then they began playing ROCK 'N' ROLL, mixing in RHYTHM AND BLUES, pop, and country. Among their many hits were *Bye Bye Love, Wake Up Little Susie, All I Have to Do Is Dream,* and *Cathy's Clown.* Most were recorded between 1957 and 1963.

After the BEATLES arrived in America, the Everly Brothers' popularity waned. They continued to record, favoring a country-rock style, but had little success on the charts.

After performing together constantly since childhood, coupled with the pressures put on them by the music business, they split their act in 1973 and spent 10 years pursuing their own interests. In 1983 they reunited for a concert at London's Royal Albert Hall. Since their reunion, they have continued to tour through the '80s and '90s, mostly in the U.S., and also occasionally in Europe and Australia.

The Everly Brothers were among the first artists inducted into the Rock and Roll Hall of Fame in 1986.

Ewing, Maria (Louise), noted American mezzo-soprano and soprano; b. Detroit, Mar. 27, 1950. Ewing began her vocal training with Marjorie Gordon, continuing her studies with Eleanor Steber at the Cleveland Institute of Music between 1968 and 1970.

In 1973 Ewing made her professional debut at the Ravinia Festival with the Chicago Symphony Orchestra and subsequently was engaged to appear with various U.S. opera houses and orchestras. She also appeared as a recitalist. In 1976 she made her Metropolitan Opera debut in N.Y. as Cherubino and returned there to sing many other roles. In 1976 she made her first appearance at Milan's La Scala as Mélisande and in 1978 made her Glyndebourne Festival debut as Dorabella, returning there as a periodic guest.

In 1986 Ewing sang Salome in Los Angeles and appeared in THE MERRY WIDOW in Chicago in 1987. In 1988 she sang Salome at London's Covent Garden, a role she sang to enormous critical acclaim in Chicago that same year. She returned there as Tosca in 1989 and Susanna in 1991. After a dispute over artistic matters at the Metropolitan Opera in

PEOPLE IN MUSIC

1987, she refused to sing there until 1993, when she returned as Dido. She was married for a time to the noted English theater and opera producer Sir Peter Hall.

execution. 1. Style, manner of performance. 2. Technical ability.

exercise (Ger. *übung;* It. *esercizio*). A short technical study or sequence for training the fingers (or vocal organs) to overcome some special technical difficulty. Also, a short study in composition. *Compare* ÉTUDE.

exoticism. Western artists have long been interested in the "exotic" practices of other cultures. Drawing on the instruments, SCALES, and composition techniques of Eastern cultures, Western composers have attempted to add special effects to their own works. These usually have only a small relation to the source material.

The main resource of exoticism in the 18th century was Turkish music, characterized by a simple binary meter. *Alla turca* is often found in tempo indications in CLASSIC music. Turkish percussion, such as CYMBALS and bass drum, was also added to orchestral scores.

India, China, and Japan provided inspiration for French OPERA and BALLET. Russian composers were fond of exotic subjects. NIKOLAI RIMSKY-KORSAKOV'S *SCHEHERAZADE* is based on a subject of *The Arabian Nights.* The Mongolian invasion of Russia during the Middle Ages gave a historic background for stylized Tatar ballet episodes in Russian operas.

When Indonesian GAMELAN performers appeared at the Paris International Exposition in 1889, young French composers became fascinated by their music. CLAUDE DEBUSSY and MAURICE RAVEL made tasteful IMPRESSIONISTIC renditions of these exotic rhythms and melodies in their works.

Because non-Western scales do not follow traditional DIATONIC and CHROMATIC intervals, Western musicians created their own exotic tonal progressions in which the AUGMENTED SECOND often plays an important part. The ARIA of the Queen Shemaha in Rimsky-Korsakov's *LE COQ D'OR* is one example. Chinese and Japanese subjects are often expressed by using PENTATONIC melodies. Examples are found

During the 18th century, a piano was built especially to perform "Turkish" music. Bells and other percussion instruments attached to it, so the player could easily add these "exotic" effects.

in *MADAMA BUTTERFLY, THE MIKADO,* and various chinoiseries of Ravel and Debussy.

experimental music. Music that departs from the usual expectations of style, form, and genre as these have developed through history. As the term is used today, experimental music begins with ERIK SATIE and CHARLES IVES and moves through and beyond the work of JOHN CAGE (the N.Y. School), HENRY COWELL, and CORNELIUS CARDEW.

All music is experimental, and tradition merely experiment that has become accepted practice. CHROMATIC HARMONY was experimental in RICHARD WAGNER's time. Its ultimate development into ARNOLD SCHOENBERG's theory of 12-TONE music became the most important type of experimental music of the 20th century. Composing by CHANCE OPERATIONS is perhaps the most experimental method to be found.

In the second half of the 20th century, experimental music finally moved into its proper enclave, that of the laboratory, where composers and experimenters conducted their research with ELECTRONIC INSTRUMENTS and COMPUTERS.

exposition (It. *esposizione*). 1. The opening section of a SONATA-form movement, in which the principal THEMES are presented for the first time. The first theme is in the TONIC, the closing theme usually in the DOMINANT or, in many minor-key works, the RELATIVE MAJOR. 2. Sections of a FUGUE that present the SUBJECT.

expression marks. Written instructions (sign, word, or phrase) indicating the recommended type of performance.

The earliest expression marks appeared in keyboard compositions in the 16th century, and were limited to the signs for *forte* and *piano,* usually abbreviated *f* and *p.* A curious expression mark was *E,* for *echo,* found in 17th-century works. It was equivalent to *piano.*

The signs for CRESCENDO and DIMINUENDO did not achieve currency until the late 18th century. The various gradations of *forte* and *piano* were increasingly cultivated by ROMANTIC composers. The ending of the *Pathétique* Symphony by PIOTR ILYICH TCHAIKOVSKY is marked *pppppp.*

The Florentine composers who pioneered the art of opera were in the habit of using elaborate verbal descriptions such as *esclamazione spirituosa* (like a spiritual exclamation) and *quasi favallando* (as if speaking).

expressionism. A modern artistic movement, beginning in music around 1910, giving expression to the inner state of a person's mind and emotions. The term itself originated in painting.

Expressionism reflects extreme and anxious moods characteristic of modern life in a musical idiom that frequently uses ATONAL melodies and short, restless rhythms.

Expressionism stands in opposition to IMPRESSIONISM. Impressionism derives its source of inspiration from external sources such as nature, whereas expressionism draws on the inner world of the mind. Impressionism tends to be pictorial and natural, while expressionism tends to be introspective and dreamlike.

In music, the two movements are equally different. Impressionism favors rich orchestral colors, free-form structures, and lush melodies accompanied by complex harmonies. Expressionism is usually performed by a limited number of instruments, short structures, and brief statements of melodies with little harmonic accompaniment.

Impressionism developed in France, expressionism in Germany. In French impressionist poetry, the music of the words is emphasized; so French impressionist songs has flowing, euphonious melodies matched to the texts. On the other hand, the German language is noteworthy for its harsh, broken syllables, and a heavy, guttural pronunciation. This is reflected in expressionist songs that have similarly sharp, abrupt melody lines.

Some key proponents of expressionist writing are ARNOLD SCHOENBERG and ALBAN BERG.

extemporization (from It. *ex tempore,* outside of time). A spontaneous or improvised performance.

extended compass. Tones beyond the usual range of a voice or instrument.

extravaganza. An elaborate stage show with singing, dancing, and dialogue, with little concern for a coherent storyline. It is often marked by exaggerated comic turns and spectacular scenic and lighting effects.

eye music (Ger. *Augenmusik*). Using the actual appearance of a musical score to express the theme of the work.

Composers are often tempted to use the look of their scores to express the mood of a vocal or instrumental composition. Perhaps the most famous early example is the fantastic heart-shaped RONDEAU *Belle, bonne, sage* by Baude Cordier (c.1400). RENAISSANCE MADRIGAL composers may have used blackened notes to express death, night, or grief whenever such sentiments were found in the text, ignoring the fact that such blackening affected the time values of the notes.

JOHANN SEBASTIAN BACH used melodic figures that suggested the cross in his *St. Matthew Passion*. The appearance in the score of the storm scene in LUDWIG VAN BEETHOVEN's *Pastoral* Symphony actually suggests vertical rainfall in the wind instruments, swirling streams in the basses, and bolts of lightning in the brief and rapid violin passages.

There is no denying that the visual aspect of a piece of music somehow relates to how it sounds. JOHANNES BRAHMS used to say that music that looks good will sound good. Some modern composers have advanced the argument that music should not be heard at all but be regarded as a visual art. Experienced score readers claim that they can obtain greater pleasure from reading music and imagining the sound than by hearing it. As the British poet John Keats wrote, "Heard melodies are sweet, but those unheard are sweeter."

Composers of the AVANT-GARDE have adopted the patterns of eye music as points of departure for their musical inspiration. Anestis Logothetis (1921–94), a Bulgarian-born Greek composer, exhibited his scores of eye music in Vienna, bearing geometric titles such as *Cycloid, Culmination, Interpolation, Parallax,* and *Concatenation*.

The American composer GEORGE CRUMB has used eye music for expressive purposes since the mid-1960s. In his *Makrokosmos* piano cycles, scores are written in spiral, square-shaped, and other nontraditional layouts. In his CHAMBER MUSIC, instruments are indicated only when they are played and are otherwise missing, and this can give the performer a stronger sense of surprise. Crumb's eye music thus has it both ways: notation that should affect the audience's response, while informing and even surprising the performer.

Critics sometimes use the term *eye music* (usually in the German form of *Augenmusik*) to criticize works that look good on paper but are unimpressive to the ear. Yet visual symmetry usually corresponds to fine musical organization.

F

F. The fourth note, or SUBDOMINANT, of the C-major or C-minor scale. In French, Italian, Spanish, and Russian nomenclature, *fa*.

F holes. The two *f*-shaped soundholes in the belly of the violin and other string instruments.

F major (Ger. *F dur*). A key of pastoral music, descriptive of gentle landscapes and lyric, often sentimental moods. No doubt, examples can be found in which F major suggests an autumnal rather than a vernal mood, but not many.

F minor (Ger. *F moll*). A key of lyric reverie touched with melancholy.

Composers writing for string instruments or for orchestra instinctively avoid F minor because it is difficult for strings to perform. But F minor is eminently pianistic, and much ROMANTIC music is written in this key. FRÉDÉRIC CHOPIN's Second Piano Concerto is in F minor (op.21), as is FRANZ SCHUBERT's most famous *Moment musical*.

Fa. 1. In SOLMIZATION, the fourth degree of the scale. 2. Name of the tone F in Italy, France, Spain, and Russia.

faburden (Old Eng.). In the RENAISSANCE, enhancing a CHANT melody by adding parallel SIXTHS and FOURTHS below, or with the chant serving as middle voice (i.e., with parallel thirds below and parallel fourths above). The technique helped to introduce sixths and thirds as the new CONSONANCES, which were to replace consecutive open FIFTHS and fourths. Faburden is related to the GYMEL and to the FAUXBOURDON.

Well-known works in F major include:

LUDWIG VAN BEETHOVEN's *Pastoral* Symphony

Melody in F by ANTON RUBINSTEIN

JOHANNES BRAHMS's Third Symphony, his most optimistic work

The merriest two-part invention of JOHANN SEBASTIAN BACH

The Russian composer NIKOLAI MIASKOVSKY ventured to select F minor as the principal key for not just one but two symphonies: Nos. 10 and 24.

Façade. "Entertainment" by WILLIAM WALTON, 1923, for speaking voice and instruments, to poems by Edith Sitwell. The music is a tossed salad of sentimental and popular tunes and quotations from famous operas. The thing was first performed in London, when Walton was only 21 years old. A second collection of pieces originally rejected from this work were collected as *Façade II* and first performed in 1979.

Face the Music. Musical by IRVING BERLIN, 1932. The Great Depression is treated with morbid humor in this musical comedy. A crooked cop has to launder stolen money before the law gets to him. His choice of investment: a Broadway show. Includes *Let's Have Another Cup of Coffee.*

Facsimile. "Choreographic observation" by LEONARD BERNSTEIN, 1946. A blasé woman rejects one suitor after another.

fado. Popular Portuguese song and dance genre.

Failing Kansas. Opera, 1994, by Mikel Rouse. It is the first in a trilogy, followed by *DENNIS CLEVELAND* (1996) and *The End of Cinematics* (forthcoming in 2000). It is written in four large sections linked by five interludes.

Failing Kansas was inspired by Truman Capote's documentary novel *In Cold Blood,* which recounts in vivid detail a series of murders committed in the midwest. The work is scored for solo singer with a multitude of ELECTRONIC INSTRUMENTS, a virtual compendium of the possibilities of his COUNTERPOETRY technique.

Failing Kansas has been praised as the first viable music-theater work of the new, post–ROCK 'N' ROLL generation of composers known as TOTALISTS.

Fain (born Feinberg), **Sammy,** American composer of popular music; b. N.Y., June 17, 1902; d. Los Angeles, Dec. 6, 1989. Fain worked in VAUDEVILLE and as a song plugger before achieving success as a full-fledged songwriter on Broadway and in Hollywood. In collaboration with the lyricist Irving Kahal, he produced such hits as *Nobody Knows What a Red-Headed Mama Can Do; Let a Smile Be Your Umbrella on*

PEOPLE IN MUSIC

a Rainy Day; When I Take My Sugar to Tea; Dear Hearts and Gentle People; That Old Feeling; I Can Dream, Can't I; and *I'll Be Seeing You.* Later, with Paul F. Webster, he composed *Secret Love* and *Love Is a Many-Splendored Thing.*

fake book. A collection of LEAD SHEETS for standard popular and JAZZ tunes. The players use this basic information to "fake" or improvise their way through a song.

Fall River Legend. Ballet by MORTON GOULD, with choreography by Agnes de Mille, first performed in N.Y., Apr. 22, 1947. The subject is derived from the famous murder trial in Fall River, Mass., in which Lizzie Borden was accused of murdering her stepmother and her father with an ax. Borden was acquitted, but the case became part of American folklore.

Gould uses HYMNS and BALLADS of the period to lend local color to the score.

Falla (y Matheu), **Manuel** (Maria) **de,** great Spanish composer; b. Cadiz, Nov. 23, 1876; d. Alta Gracia, Cordoba province, Argentina, Nov. 14, 1946. Falla studied piano with his mother, then, after further instruction from Eloisa Galluzo, he studied harmony, counterpoint, and composition. He then went to Madrid, where he studied piano and composition at the Conservatory.

In 1902 Falla wrote several ZARZUELAS; one of them, *Los amores de la Inés,* was performed in Madrid. His opera *La vida breve* won the prize of the Real Academia de Bellas Artes in Madrid in 1905 but was not premiered until eight years later. In 1905 he also won the Ortiz y Cusso Prize for pianists.

In 1907 Falla went to Paris, where he became friendly with CLAUDE DEBUSSY, PAUL DUKAS, and MAURICE RAVEL, who aided and encouraged him. Under their influence, he adopted the principles of IMPRESSIONISM without, however, giving up his personal and national style.

Falla returned to Spain in 1914 and produced his tremendously effective BALLET *El amor brujo* a year later. It was followed by the evocative *Noches en los jardines de España* for

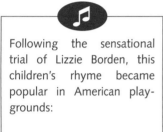

Following the sensational trial of Lizzie Borden, this children's rhyme became popular in American playgrounds:

Lizzie Borden took an ax and gave her mother 40 whacks.
When she saw what she had done she gave her father 41.

PEOPLE IN MUSIC

piano and orchestra (1916). In 1919 he made his home in Granada, where he completed work on his celebrated ballet *El sombrero de tres picos* (1919).

Falla's art was rooted in both the folk songs of Spain and the purest historical traditions of Spanish music. Until 1919 he was particularly influenced by the music of Spain's Andalusian province, particularly the traditional style of playing the guitar. Falla would often imitate effects that were created by traditional guitarists in his writing for other instruments.

Falla's later works showed a return to European classicism. In his puppet opera *El retablo de maese Pedro* (1919–22) he turned to the classical tradition of Spanish (especially Castilian) music. The keyboard style of his Harpsichord Concerto (1923–26) shows the influence of DOMENICO SCARLATTI, who lived in Spain for many years.

Falla became president of the Instituto de España in 1938. When the Spanish Civil War broke out and General Franco overcame the Loyalist government with the aid of Hitler and Mussolini, Falla left Spain and went to South America, never to return to his homeland. He went to Buenos Aires, where he conducted concerts of his music.

Falla then withdrew to the small locality of Alta Gracia, where he lived the last years of his life in seclusion, working on his large scenic CANTATA *Atlántida*. It remained unfinished at his death and was later completed by his former pupil Ernesto Halffter.

Falling in Love Again. Song by Frederick Hollander, made famous by Marlene Dietrich in the American version of the film *The Blue Angel* (1930).

falsa musica (It., false music). Medieval term for ACCIDENTALS and other alterations not justified by the rules of COUNTERPOINT.

false relation. *See* CROSS RELATION.

falsetto (It., small false one; Fr. *fausset;* Ger. *Falsett, Fidelstimme, Fistel, Fistelstimme, Kopfstimme*). The practice of voice production by using head rather than chest tones, particularly among TENORS, thus producing sounds well above the natural range.

Falsetto singing was widely practiced in the choirs at the Vatican and Italian cathedrals when the use of female or CASTRATI singers was inappropriate. Falsetto singers were also known as *alti naturali,* "natural alto singers," to distinguish them from *voci artificiali,* the "artificial voices" of the castrati. Another term for falsetto singers was *tenorini,* "little tenors."

The word *falsetto* itself is a diminutive of the Italian *falso,* because the singer, although not castrated, applies a "false" way of voice production. Falsetto voices are often used in BAROQUE operas for comic effects. The part of the Astrologer in NIKOLAI RIMSKY-KORSAKOV's *LE COQ D'OR* is cast in falsetto to indicate that he is a eunuch. Falsetto is also used in YODELING.

From the Marx Brothers film *A Night at the Opera:*
Chico: That singer has a falsetto voice.
Groucho: That's funny. I had an uncle who had a falsetto teeth!

falsobordone (It., false bass; Sp. *fabordón*). A style of chanting or reciting in root-position TRIADS, with all (usually four) parts written out. The style evolved in the latter 15th century. Eventually keyboard works and monodies with BASSO CONTINUO were composed in a similar style throughout the BAROQUE. The style was revived during the Cecilian movement (*see* CECILIANISM) of the 19th century.

Falstaff. Opera by GIUSEPPE VERDI, 1893, to a LIBRETTO by Boito. It is based on the character Falstaff, who appears in a number of Shakespeare's historical plays. He is a comic figure, a fat man, bumbling lover, and cowardly braggart.

Falstaff was Verdi's last opera and only his second comic opera. In it Verdi inaugurated a new style, approaching that of MUSIC DRAMA. It ends on a magisterial choral FUGUE with the Shakesperian words, "Il mondo e la burla" (All the world's a stage).

Falstaff. Symphonic study by EDWARD ELGAR, 1913. Elgar was fascinated by the portly figure of the Shakespearean antihero. In this work he outlined in musical images Falstaff's life from his companionship with the future King

Henry V to his fall from royal grace and pitiful death. The music is ROMANTIC, with elements of grandeur.

Fanciulla del West, La. *See* GIRL OF THE GOLDEN WEST, THE.

fancy (from It., *fantasia*). 1. A POLYPHONIC vocal composition of 16th-century England. 2. In 16th- and 17th-century England, a freely connected group of tunes or songs, written in COUNTERPOINT for the KEYBOARD or a CONSORT (group) of VIOLS. *See also* FANTASIA.

Fancy Free. Ballet by LEONARD BERNSTEIN, with choreography by Jerome Robbins, 1944. During shore leave in N.Y., three sailors chase after two women. The musical *On The Town* grew from it a few years later.

fandango (Sp.). A lively dance in TRIPLE time for two dancers, accompanied by CASTANETS or TAMBOURINE.

fanfare. A flourish of TRUMPETS or trumpetcall, traditionally based on the natural OVERTONE series.

The fanfare, whether festive or mournful, continues to serve its purely military signal function, but it has become a well-practiced musical device as well.

Fanfare for the Common Man. Fanfare by AARON COPLAND, 1943, for brass and percussion. Commissioned by Eugene Goosens for the Cincinnati Symphony Orchestra, which he conducted during World War II, it became a perennial favorite, and Copland included it in its entirety in the finale of his Third Symphony.

fantasia (It.; Fr. *fantaisie;* Ger. *Phantasie*). 1. An IMPROVISATION.

2. A POLYPHONIC instrumental piece in free imitation (17th and 18th centuries). These compositions for KEYBOARD instruments, LUTES, or VIOLS are marked by a free thematic development and many florid VARIATIONS.

3. A composition free in form and more or less fantastic in character. In the 19th century, instrumental fantasies

făhn-tăh-zē′ăh

Jean-Jacques Rousseau, in his *Dictionnaire de musique,* asserts wittily that a fantasy can never be written down because as soon as it is arranged in notes it ceases to be a fantasy.

largely abandoned their contrapuntal character and became works in SONATA form. When LUDWIG VAN BEETHOVEN described his *MOONLIGHT SONATA* as a "Sonata quasi una fantasia," he apparently intended to convey to it the character of a romantic image, but it is set in strict sonata form. FRÉDÉRIC CHOPIN's *Fantaisie-Impromptu* is organized in a symmetric TERNARY form.

    4. A POTPOURRI or paraphrase.

Fantasia contrappuntistica. Compositional tour-de-force by FERRUCCIO BUSONI, 1923, written in both one-piano and two-piano versions. Several FUGUES of JOHANN SEBASTIAN BACH are woven into an extremely complex contrapuntal fantasy.

Fantasia on a Theme by Thomas Tallis. String orchestra work by RALPH VAUGHAN WILLIAMS, 1910, one of his most popular. Thomas Tallis was one of the greatest English composers of HYMNS during the reign of Elizabeth I. Vaughan Williams set his solemn melodies in spacious modern MODAL HARMONIES.

Fantasia on Greensleeves. Work for harp and string by RALPH VAUGHAN WILLIAMS, 1934. Vaughan Williams first made use of the tune GREENSLEEVES in his opera *Sir John in Love* (1929). He then arranged it as the *Fantasia* and conducted its first performance in London.

***Fantastic* Symphony.** *See* SYMPHONIE FANTASTIQUE.

Fantasticks, The. Musical by Harvey Schmidt and Tom Jones, which premiered in 1960. Like *The Mousetrap* in London, this show survived for decades against all odds. It is a small-scale fantasy-romance in which girl meets boy, parents test love with remarkable cruelty, girl leaves boy, boy wins girl back. It is loosely based on *Romeo and Juliet.* Includes the song *Try to Remember.*

fäh-rähn-doh′läh   **farandola** (It.; Fr. *farandole*). Old Provençal and Spanish circle dance in rapid $\frac{6}{8}$ time, accompanied on pipe and TABOR.

Ironically, the most famous example (from GEORGES BIZET's *L'Arlésienne*) is in DUPLE meter.

farbenmelodie. *See* KLANGFARBENMELODIE.

farce. 1. A one-act OPERA or OPERETTA. 2. (Lat., stuff) A comic INTERMEZZO in medieval plays with music, making use of songs popular at the time, often displaying the most tasteless humor. In modern times, a farce still retains the old meaning of a frivolous comedy of manners.

farewell engagements. A means of promoting a long-dormant career by announcing a concert or series of concerts as the "final chance" to see a famous performer in action.

This flagrant means of self-promotion was pioneered by OPERA stars but has spread to others in the musical world. Long past her prime, ADELINA PATTI gave an extended series of "farewell" concerts in the U.S. The COUNTRY duo the Judds gave a year's worth of "farewell" concerts.

Farewell **Symphony** (*Abschiedssymphonie*). Symphony No. 45 by FRANZ JOSEPH HAYDN, 1772, in the unusual key of F♯ minor. The work itself is most unusual as well. Haydn instructs one player after another to leave the stage until only two violinists remain.

Haydn left no clue as to the meaning of this pantomime, but in the course of time an elaborate myth was conjured up: Haydn and his little symphony group, who were employed by the Hungarian Prince Esterházy, desired a little holiday in merry Vienna. The prince took the not-so-subtle hint from this performance and let the musicians go on a well-merited vacation.

A more plausible story is told in a book of memoirs by an obscure friend of Haydn. In this version, it was the prince who was about to dismiss his resident musicians. This saddened them all, because they enjoyed a healthy living and relatively generous salaries. Haydn arranged this little exhibition to tug at the prince's heartstrings. He succeeded, and his group remained in the service of the prince for many more contented years.

PEOPLE IN MUSIC

Farinelli (born Carlo Broschi), celebrated Italian CASTRATO soprano; b. Andria, Jan. 24, 1705; d. Bologna, July 15, 1782. Farinelli's father, Salvatore Broschi, was a musician and most likely Carlo's earliest instructor in music. He later adopted the name Farinelli to honor his benefactor, Farina.

Farinelli studied with the well-known composer NICOLA PORPORA in Naples. He made his first public appearance there in his teacher's SERENATA *Angelica e Medoro* in 1720. Subsequent appearances brought him great success, and he soon became famous as *il ragazzo* (the boy). He also sang in Rome, appearing in Porpora's opera *Eumene* at the age of 16.

Farinelli's repeated successes brought him renown throughout Italy and abroad and led to his first appearance in Vienna in 1724. He met the celebrated castrato alto Antonio Bernacchi in Bologna in 1727. In a singing contest with him, Farinelli acknowledged defeat and persuaded Bernacchi to give him lessons to achieve virtuosity in COLORATURA.

After further visits to Vienna in 1728 and 1731, Porpora called Farinelli to London to sing with the Opera of the Nobility. He made his London debut in Hasse's *Artaserse* in 1734. He remained with the company until the summer of 1736, when he went to Paris, returning to it for the 1736–37 season.

Having amassed a fortune in London, Farinelli went to Madrid in 1737. He attained unparalleled success as court singer to King Philip V. His influence on the ailing monarch and his queen was such that Farinelli was able to command considerable funds to engage famous performers for the Madrid court.

Farinelli was employed by King Philip V to sing several arias to him every evening. This was supposed to help cure the king's bad case of the blues.

When Farinelli's voice began to fail, he served as producer, decorator, and stage director. He continued to enjoy the court's favor under Philip's successor, Ferdinand VI, who made him a knight of the order of Calatrava in 1750. When Carlos III became king in 1759, however, Farinelli was dismissed. He then returned to Italy in possession of great wealth. He built a palatial villa for himself near Bologna and spent the last years of his life in contentment.

His brother Riccardo Broschi (b. Naples, c.1698; d. Madrid, 1756) was a composer who produced several operas in Naples, in which Farinelli sang.

Farley, Carole (Ann), talented American soprano; b. Le Mars, Iowa, Nov. 29, 1946. Farley studied at the Indiana University School of Music, gaining her degree in music in 1968, and on a year-long Fulbright scholarship at the Munich Hochschule für Musik. In 1969, she made her debut at the Linz Landestheater and also her U.S. debut at N.Y.'s Town Hall. Farley subsequently appeared as a soloist with major orchestras of the U.S. and Europe and with most major OPERA companies.

Farley made her Metropolitan Opera debut in N.Y. as Lulu in 1977 and continued to sing there in later seasons. In addition to her esteemed portrayal of Lulu, which she repeated over 80 times throughout the world, she also sang Poppea, Donna Anna, Violetta, MASSENET's Manon, Mimi, and various roles in RICHARD STRAUSS's operas. She married José Serebrier in 1969.

Farwell, Arthur (George), American composer and music educator; b. St. Paul, Minn., Apr. 23, 1872; d. N.Y., Jan. 20, 1952. After graduating in 1893 from the Massachusetts Institute of Technology, Farwell studied music in Boston, Berlin, and Paris. Farwell had a long and distinguished career as a music educator, teaching at Cornell University (1899–1901); at N.Y.'s Settlement Music School (1915–18), where he served as director; at the University of California, Berkeley, where he was acting head of the music department (1918–19); and at Michigan State University in East Lansing (1927–39).

In addition to his teaching, Farwell served on the editorial staff of *Musical America* (1909–14). In 1919 he founded the Santa Barbara Community Chorus, which he conducted until 1921. He also was the first holder of the composers' fellowship of the Music and Art Association of Pasadena (1921–25).

Farwell, a pioneer in new American music, tirelessly promoted national ideas in art. From 1901 to 1911 he operated the Wa-Wan Press (Newton, Mass.), publishing a periodical that printed piano and vocal music of "progressive" American composers of the period. He focused on works that drew on African-American, Indian, and cowboy melodies and instrumentation. Farwell established a second small publishing operation in 1936 to promote contemporary music.

Farewell wrote *A Letter to American Composers* (N.Y., 1903) and *Music in America* in *The Art of Music,* vol. 4 (with W. Dermot Darby; N.Y., 1915).

Fascinating Rhythm. Song by GEORGE GERSHWIN, 1924, from the MUSICAL *LADY, BE GOOD!* The song is cleverly written so that the melody and accompaniment create a rhythmic tension—the same as is described in the lyrics.

fasola. A method of teaching singing, popular in England and in colonial America, in which *fa, sol,* and *lah* are used to represent six of the seven notes of the major scale; with the addition of *mi* for the seventh step, a full scale could be sung. *See* SHAPE NOTES.

fate motive. *See* FIFTH SYMPHONY.

PEOPLE IN MUSIC

Fauré, Gabriel (-Urbain), great French composer and pedagogue; b. Pamiers, Ariège, May 12, 1845; d. Paris, Nov. 4, 1924. Fauré's father was an inspector of primary schools. Noticing his son's natural musical talents, he took him to Paris to study with the Swiss composer Louis Niedermeyer. After Niedermeyer's death in 1861, Fauré studied with CAMILLE SAINT-SAËNS, from whom he received thorough training in composition.

In 1866 Fauré went to Rennes as organist at the church of St.-Sauveur. He returned to Paris on the eve of the Franco-Prussian War in 1870 and volunteered in the light infantry. From the 1870s through the mid-1890s Fauré held several positions as a church organist and choral director.

In 1896 Fauré was appointed professor of composition at the Paris Conservatory. He was an illustrious teacher, counting among his students MAURICE RAVEL, GEORGES ENESCO, CHARLES KOECHLIN, Jean Roger-Ducasse, Florent Schmitt, and NADIA BOULANGER. In 1905 he succeeded Theodore Dubois as director of the conservatory and served until 1920.

Then, quite unexpectedly, Fauré developed ear trouble, resulting in a gradual loss of hearing. Distressed, he was eventually forced to abandon his teaching position. From 1903 to 1921 he wrote occasional music reviews in *Le Figaro* (a selection was published as *Opinions musicales,* Paris, 1930). He was elected a member of the Academie des Beaux Arts in 1909, and in 1910 was made a Commander of the Légion d'Honneur.

Fauré's stature as a composer is undiminished by the passage of time. He developed a musical style all his own. He anticipated the IMPRESSIONIST style in his use of mild DISCORDS and MODAL harmonies. In his piano works he avoided virtuosity in favor of the classical purity of the earlier French masters of the keyboard. His songs' precisely crafted melodic lines are in the finest tradition of French vocal music. His great Requiem and his *Elegié* for cello and piano have entered the general repertoire.

Faust. Grand opera by CHARLES GOUNOD, 1859, based on part 1 of Goethe's dramatic poem. It is one of the most successful operas of all times. During the first century of its spectacular career, *Faust* had more than 2,000 performances in Paris alone.

Faust sells his soul to the canny devil Mephistopheles in exchange for the elixir of youth. No sooner is the deal arranged than Faust is shown an image of the innocent weaver Marguerite. He is taken to the girl's home and tempts her anonymously with jewels, which gives her a chance to sing an ARIA with many trills and frills. With worldly advice from the cunning devil, Faust seduces her.

Marguerite's brother Valentin fights Faust in a duel but is slain. Faust runs off. Marguerite bears Faust's child but goes insane and kills her child. She is sentenced to die, but a host of angels carries her to heaven while Faust watches. He goes off with (and to) the devil.

The Germans remain so offended by Gounod's treatment of Goethe's text that, when the opera is produced in Germany, it is called *Margarete* or *Gretchen*.

***Faust* Symphony.** This work by FRANZ LISZT (1857) is the only true SYMPHONY inspired by Goethe's great epic poem *Faust*. It is subdivided into three movements, portraits of the main characters: *Faust, Gretchen,* and *Mephistopheles.* It concludes with a section sung by a male chorus along with the orchestra.

foh-boor-dŭn′

fauxbourdon (Med. Fr., false drone). A term for various compositional techniques used in the 15th century. The term and techniques seem related to the medieval English FABURDEN, which may have been its original source.

Originally, a single melodic line or CHANT was performed. Then a second part was added, either above it or below. Finally, a third part was introduced. Singing in parallel OCTAVES and FIFTHS probably came first; then THIRDS and SIXTHS were introduced, which are generally associated with the fauxbourdon style. When these parallel voices were added, the chant voice was moved to the middle or upper portion of the counterpoint. Some of the additional voices were written, others merely indicated.

The actual "fauxbourdon" or "false drone" was a bass voice, singing not the (usual) ROOT of the chord but its third. To modern ears, the fauxbourdon sound like parallel progressions of TRIADS in first INVERSION, common in later classical usage.

Eventually the technique dissolved in the more complicated COUNTERPOINT of the late RENAISSANCE and thereafter. Similar passages have appeared on occasion with the return of parallel harmony in the early 20th century, recasting the concept in modern terms (often in the hands of French composers).

Favola d'Orfeo, La. *See* ORFEO, LA FAVOLA D'.

favola per musica (It., fable with music). An early term for an OPERA LIBRETTO based on a mythological story.

Favorite, La (*La Favorita*). Opera by GAETANO DONIZETTI, 1840. The king of Castile tricks an innocent monk into wooing and winning the king's favorite mistress as a jest. When the ex-monk learns of the setup, he leaves her to rejoin the monastery. She realizes that she loves the monk and makes her way to his retreat. Realizing that he can never return her love, she dies in his arms.

Fedora. Opera by UMBERTO GIORDANO, 1898. In this grim morality tale, the Princess Fedora is a Russian woman who is about to be married to a captain of the Imperial Guards.

When he is murdered, the young bride-to-be vows to capture his escaped killer, Count Loris Ipanov. She follows him to Paris, where she intends to trick him into confessing the crime. Instead, Loris tells her that he caught her intended in the act of seducing Loris's wife and, upon being attacked, shot him in self-defense. Fedora falls in love with Loris and decides to protect him from capture. The couple flee to Switzerland, but when Loris learns of Fedora's earlier plan to turn him in, he spurns her. She commits suicide, dying in his arms.

feedback. Loud distortion in amplification equipment. It is caused when the system's output (such as the sound coming from a speaker) is picked up by the input (such as a microphone). Talented guitarists are able to control feedback and use it in their performances. JIMI HENDRIX was particularly skilled in this technique.

Feen, Die. Opera by RICHARD WAGNER, 1834, first produced posthumously in 1888. Based on Gozzi's play *La donna serpente,* it concerns the fate of two lovers, one supernatural, the other not.

Feldman, Morton, important American composer of the AVANT-GARDE; b. N.Y., Jan. 12, 1926; d. Buffalo, Sept. 3, 1987. Feldman studied piano in N.Y. and composition with the composers Max Riegger in 1941 and Stefan Wolpe in 1944.

In 1950 he met JOHN CAGE and was soon working closely with him. He was also influenced by the N.Y. school of painters who were in the process of developing what would be known as Abstract Expressionism. These two influences were clear in his early compositions, such as *Projections I–IV,* one of the first works to use GRAPHIC NOTATION.

Throughout his career Feldman would struggle over his desire to have control over the performance of his works and his desire for the performers to add their own creativity to them. He developed a series of different notation systems through the 1950s, trying to achieve the ultimate balance of control versus chance. By the late 1960s he had returned to

PEOPLE IN MUSIC

conventional notation but had found a way to get the overall effect of CHANCE OPERATIONS.

In addition to his composing, Feldman taught at SUNY, Buffalo, beginning in 1972, where he held the EDGARD VARÈSE chair in music. He won numerous awards and his pieces were widely performed. After his death of pancreatic cancer in 1987, his work has been a strong influence on young composers.

PEOPLE IN MUSIC

Feliciano, José, Puerto Rican singer, guitarist, and songwriter; b. Lares, Sept. 10, 1945. Feliciano was born blind. His family moved to N.Y. when he was five. He taught himself to play guitar and accordion, then appeared in Greenwich Village clubs, beginning in the mid-1960s. He scored his greatest success with his album *Feliciano!* in 1968 (it included his soulful version of the song *Light My Fire*). His blues rendition of *The Star-Spangled Banner* at the 1968 World Series in Detroit caused a furor, leading many radio stations to boycott him.

From the 1970s on, Feliciano has pursued three different careers. One is as a singer of popular songs in Spanish, aimed at the Latin American audience; the second is as a soul singer performing in English; and finally he has also recorded and toured as a classical guitarist. However, he has not equaled his original notoriety or success.

PEOPLE IN MUSIC

Feltsman, Vladimir, prominent Russian pianist; b. Moscow, Jan. 8, 1952. Feltsman was born into a musical family. His father, Oskar, was a composer of popular music. Vladimir began piano lessons at the age of six with his mother, then enrolled at Moscow's Central Music School, completing his training at the Moscow Conservatory.

At the age of 11 Feltsman made his debut as a soloist with the Moscow Philharmonic and later won first prize in the Prague Concertino Competition. After capturing joint first prize in the Long-Thibaud Competition in Paris in 1971, he pursued a successful career as a soloist with major Soviet and Eastern European orchestras. In 1977–78 he made particularly successful appearances in works in the ROMANTIC repertoire, his specialty, in Japan and France.

Feltsman's career was interrupted by the Soviet authorities when in 1979 he applied for a visa to emigrate to Israel with his wife. His application was denied, and he subsequently was allowed to give concerts only in remote outposts of the Soviet Union. With the support of the U.S. ambassador, he gave several private concerts at the ambassador's official residence in Moscow.

When his plight became a cause célèbre in the West, Feltsman was allowed to give his first Moscow recital in almost a decade in 1987. That year he was granted permission to emigrate. He went to the U.S., where he accepted an appointment at the State University of N.Y. at New Paltz. He gave a special concert at the White House for President Reagan, as well as his first N.Y. recital in Carnegie Hall. In 1995 he became an American citizen.

feminine ending. An old-fashioned term used to designate the unaccented syllable at the end of a line or an unemphatic type of CADENCE. In music, many ROMANTIC pieces have used such endings, with a stressed DISSONANT melodic note resolving on a weak beat.

fermata (It.; Ger. *Fermate*). The sign over ⌢, or under ⌣, a note or rest. It indicates that the performer or conductor may lengthen the note's or rest's time value. Doubling the length of the note or rest is a good approximation. Also called a HOLD.

Placed over a barline, a fermata indicates a slight pause or breath before attacking what follows. However, the overall tempo is not affected.

fâr-mah′tăh

A rest for an entire ensemble is called a *grand pause* (abbrev. G.P.).

Ferneyhough, Brian, AVANT-GARDE English composer; b. Coventry, Jan. 16, 1943. Ferneyhough studied at the Birmingham School of Music from 1961 to 1963, then took courses at the Royal Academy of Music in London from 1966 to 1967, and in Amsterdam and Basel from 1969 to 1973.

From 1971 to 1986 Ferneyhough was on the faculty at the Hochschule für Musik in Freiburg im Breisgau, and in 1976, 1978, and 1980 he lectured at the Darmstadt summer

PEOPLE IN MUSIC

courses. He also taught at the Royal Conservatory of The Hague (from 1986) and at the University of California, San Diego (from 1987).

The radical qualities of Ferneyhough's style involve unusual approaches to DISSONANT COUNTERPOINT and time structures that are totally divorced from the dance-music orientation of most European music. He is probably the least English-sounding of the prominent British composers of the latter 20th century.

PEOPLE IN MUSIC

Ferrier, Kathleen (Mary), remarkable English contralto; b. Higher Walton, Lancashire, Apr. 22, 1912; d. London, Oct. 8, 1953. Ferrier grew up in Blackburn, where she studied piano and began voice lessons. For a time she was employed as a telephone operator. In 1937 she won first prizes for piano and singing at the Carlisle Competition. She then decided on a career as a singer and subsequently studied voice.

After an engagement as a soloist in MESSIAH at Westminster Abbey in 1943, Ferrier began her professional career in earnest. BENJAMIN BRITTEN chose her to create the role of Lucretia in his *Rape of Lucretia* in 1946. She made her American debut with the N.Y. Philharmonic in 1948, singing DAS LIED VON DER ERDE, with BRUNO WALTER conducting. A year later, she made her American recital debut in N.Y.

Toward the end of her brief career, Ferrier acquired in England an almost legendary reputation for vocal excellence and impeccable taste, so that her untimely death from cancer was greatly mourned. In 1953 she was made a Commander of the Order of the British Empire. She also received the Gold Medal of the Royal Philharmonic Society.

festa teatrale (It.). A theatrical festival celebrating a royal anniversary or national victory and featuring music and dancing.

Feste Romane. *See* ROMAN FESTIVALS.

Festin de l'araignée, Le. Ballet-pantomime by ALBERT ROUSSEL, 1913, first performed in Paris. The scenario depicts the feast of a spider with a menu comprising, among other insects, a butterfly and a mayfly. In the end the bloated spider is itself devoured by a praying mantis.

festivals. A generic name for all kinds of festivities accompanied by singing, playing on instruments, and dancing.

◄

*Ladies at the Bayreuth Festival.
(Corbis-Bettmann)*

The oldest regularly produced festival was the *Eisteddfod,* a bardic gathering held in Wales. After over a century of silence, it was revived as a choral festival in 1880. England was the first nation to organize music festivals devoted to performances of classical music. The first was the Three Choirs Festival, founded in 1724, which took place in the three cathedral cities of Gloucester, Hereford, and Worcester.

The earliest festival to present the music of a single composer was the Handel Festival, organized in London at the Crystal Palace in 1857. The most grandiose opera festivals devoted to a living composer were the Bayreuth Festivals, begun by RICHARD WAGNER in 1876 with the aid of funds supplied by his devoted admirer, the young King Ludwig of Bavaria. The opening event presented the complete performance of DER RING DES NIBELUNGEN.

Music festivals in America in the 19th century tended to emphasize spectacle. For example, two festivals celebrating the end of the Civil War, held in Boston in 1869 and in 1872 under the name Peace Jubilee, advertised an orchestra of 1,000 and a chorus of 10,000! An important series of music festivals of a high professional order was initiated in Worcester, Mass., in 1858.

In the 20th century, several festivals were organized with the express purpose of promoting modern music. Of these the most ambitious were the festivals of the ISCM (International Society for Contemporary Music), founded in 1923 and held in the summer or early autumn in various countries of Europe. The Coolidge Chamber Music Festivals were established by new-music benefactor Elizabeth Sprague Coolidge, first under the name Berkshire Festival of Chamber Music in Pittsfield, Mass., in 1918, and then under the sponsorship of the Library of Congress in Washington, D.C., in 1925. In 1930 HOWARD HANSON inaugurated a series of annual festivals of American music at Rochester, N.Y. In 1940 conductor SERGE KOUSSEVITZKY and the Boston Symphony Orchestra established a series of summer concerts in Tanglewood, Mass., in programs of classical and modern music.

In 1956 Poland began an annual series of festivals of modern music under the name Warsaw Autumn. The festivals in Donaueschingen, Germany, begun in 1921 produced numerous new works, principally by German composers. The International Festival in Edinburgh, founded in 1947, presented programs of opera, SYMPHONY, and CHAMBER MUSIC. The Maggio Musicale Fiorentino (Florentine Musical May) was established in 1933, at first on a biennial, then on an annual, basis, with varied programs of opera, BALLET, and symphony concerts. The biennial Venice Festival has flourished since 1950.

In 1958 GIAN CARLO MENOTTI organized the Festival of Two Worlds in the town of Spoleto, Italy, the two worlds being Europe and America. In 1977 he opened its American counterpart in Charleston, N.C. The Israel Festival has been held in principal cities of the country since 1961, its programs emphasizing Israeli folk music and works by national composers. In 1957 the millionaire Armenian industrialist Gulbenkian founded annual festivals in Lisbon and other cities of Portugal, known as Festival Gulbenkian de Musica. The Prague Spring Festivals were inaugurated in 1946. Biennial international festivals of contemporary music have been presented in Zagreb. The annual Holland Festival, established in 1948, gives presentations of music in all genres, in Amsterdam and other Dutch cities. In 1948 BENJAMIN BRITTEN organized annual summer festivals in Aldeburgh, England. Operas, new and old, are presented during the summer months in Glyndebourne, England.

Regular festival presentations are held in virtually every European city, the most important ones being those in Berlin, Munich, Vienna, Salzburg, Stockholm, and Bergen, Norway. Festivals of the music of JEAN SIBELIUS are given in Helsinki in December, commemorating the month of his birth. In the former Soviet Union ample musical activities were maintained in Moscow, Leningrad, Kiev, Tbilisi, and other musical centers. Festivals of ethnic music, ranging from folk songs to operas and symphonies, have been given periodically in Moscow. Japan and Australia contribute to the development of festival music.

Jazz festivals held during the summer months in Newport, R.I. (later moved to N.Y.) provide special interest, as do those in Monterey, Calif. Concerts and presentations in multimedia are sporadically given by composers of the International Avant-Garde, particularly in N.Y., San Francisco, London, Cologne, and Tokyo. Festivals oriented to progressive ROCK are held annually in N.Y. City and Austin, Texas (the South by Southwest Festival).

The most famous—and perhaps best-attended—music festival of all time was the three-day 1969 Woodstock rock festival. It was immortalized on record and film.

Festschrift (Ger., festive writing; plur. *Festschriften*). A publication in honor of an esteemed musical scholar, teacher, or composer on the occasion of an advanced birthday or retirement, collecting articles by his or her students and colleagues. The custom generated in Germany, but the German term is retained for non-German publications as well, particularly in the U.S. Festschriften are usually printed on deluxe paper.

fĕst′shrĭft′

Festspiel (Ger.). German term for a stage play in which music is included. RICHARD WAGNER called *DER RING DES NIBELUNGEN* a Festspiel.

fĕst′shpēl

Fétis, François-Joseph, erudite Belgian music theorist, historian, and critic; b. Mons, Mar. 25, 1784; d. Brussels, Mar. 26, 1871. Fétis received primary instruction from his

PEOPLE IN MUSIC

father, an organist at the Mons Cathedral. He learned to play the violin, piano, and organ when very young, and at the age of nine wrote a violin concerto. As a youth he was organist to the Noble Chapter of Ste.-Waudru. In 1800 he entered the Paris Conservatory, where he studied harmony and piano. In 1803 he visited Vienna, there studying COUNTERPOINT, FUGUE, and masterworks of German music.

In 1806, Fétis began the revision of the PLAINSONG and entire ritual of the Roman Catholic Church, a vast undertaking completed, with many interruptions, after 30 years of patient research. A wealthy marriage in the same year enabled him to pursue his studies at ease for a time. The fortune was lost in 1811, however, and he retired to the Ardennes, where he occupied himself with composition and research into the theory of harmony.

In 1818 Fétis settled in Paris and in 1821 became a professor of composition at the Paris Conservatory. In 1824 his *Traité du contrepoint et de la fugue* (Treatise on counterpoint and fugue) was published and accepted as a regular manual there. In 1827 he became librarian of the conservatory, and in the same year founded his unique journal *La Revue musicale,* which he published until 1835. He also wrote articles on music for *Le National* and *Le Temps.* In 1832 he inaugurated his famous series of historical lectures and concerts.

In 1833 Fétis was called to Brussels as *maître de chapelle* to King Leopold I and director of the Brussels Conservatory. During his long tenure in the latter position, nearly 40 years, the conservatory flourished as never before. He also conducted the concerts of the Academy, which elected him a member in 1845.

Fétis was a confirmed believer in the possibility of explaining music history and theory scientifically. He was opinionated, but it cannot be denied that he was a pioneer in MUSICOLOGY. He published the first book on music appreciation, *La Musique mise è la portée de tout le monde* (Music opens the door to the world; Paris, 1830).

As early as 1806 Fétis began collecting materials for his great *Biographie universelle des musiciens et bibliographie générale de la musique* (Universal biography of musicians and general bibliography of music; 8 vols., Paris, 1835–44), a work of unprecedented scope. Entries on composers and performers whom he knew personally still remain prime sources. His *Histoire générale de la musique* (General history of music; five vols., Paris, 1869–76), which goes only as far as the 15th century, exhibits Fétis as a profound scholar but also as a writer who tends to express fixed opinions without offering convincing evidence for them.

Fétis was also a composer, although his music has been overshadowed completely by his writings. His valuable library of 7,325 volumes was acquired after his death by the Bibliothèque Royale of Brussels.

Feuermann, Emanuel, greatly gifted Austrian-born American cellist; b. Kolomea, Galicia, Nov. 22, 1902; d. N.Y., May 25, 1942. As a child he was taken to Vienna, where he first studied cello with his father. He made his recital debut in Vienna in 1913. He then went to Leipzig in 1917 to continue his studies. His progress was so great that he was appointed to the faculty of the Gürzenich Conservatory in Cologne at the age of 16. He also was first cellist in the Gürzenich Orchestra and a member of the Bram Eldering Quartet.

PEOPLE IN MUSIC

In 1929 Feuermann was appointed professor at the Hochschule für Musik in Berlin. Because he was Jewish, however, he was forced to leave Germany after the rise of the Nazis to power. He then embarked on a world tour from 1934 to 1935. He made his American debut in 1934, with the Chicago Symphony Orchestra, and then appeared as soloist with leading American orchestras. He also played chamber music with the leading classical soloists ARTUR SCHNABEL and Bronislaw Huberman, and later with ARTHUR RUBINSTEIN and JASCHA HEIFETZ.

Feuersnot (Fire famine). Opera by RICHARD STRAUSS, 1901, described by him as a *Singgedicht,* a singing poem. The LIBRETTO is based on a Flemish legend, *The Extinguished Fires of Audenarde.* A recluse tries to kiss a girl who ridicules him publicly, unaware that he possesses magical power. In revenge he creates a fire famine that extinguishes all lights in the village. The girl quickly repents, and he withdraws his ban. The opera was first produced in Dresden, with the composer conducting.

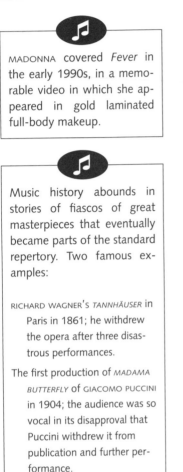

MADONNA covered *Fever* in the early 1990s, in a memorable video in which she appeared in gold laminated full-body makeup.

Music history abounds in stories of fiascos of great masterpieces that eventually became parts of the standard repertory. Two famous examples:

RICHARD WAGNER'S *TANNHÄUSER* in Paris in 1861; he withdrew the opera after three disastrous performances.

The first production of *MADAMA BUTTERFLY* of GIACOMO PUCCINI in 1904; the audience was so vocal in its disapproval that Puccini withdrew it from publication and further performance.

Fever. A 1956 Little Willie John hit with a slinky rhythm that has remained a pop favorite. It was subsequently covered by PEGGY LEE (1958), the McCoys (1965), and countless others.

fiasco (It., flask or bottle). An utter failure of a theatrical or other performance.

Fibich, Zdeněk (Zdenko) (Antonín Vaclav), important Czech composer; b. Seborie, Dec. 21, 1850; d. Prague, Oct. 15, 1900. Fibich studied piano and theory at the Leipzig Conservatory (1865–66), and composition privately through 1870. Upon his return to Prague in 1871, he became deputy conductor and chorus master at the Provisional Theater (1875–78) and director of the Russian Orthodox Church Choir (1878–81). He wrote a large amount of INCIDENTAL MUSIC and sacred music during this period, but most of it has been lost or was destroyed by the composer.

With the success of his third opera, *Nevesta mesinská* (The Bride of Messina, after Schiller, 1882–83), Fibich concentrated more on opera and the once-popular genre of MELODRAMA. The positive reception of these works led to the composition of *Hippodamie* (1888–91), a staged melodrama trilogy based on tragedies by Sophocles and Euripides, blending speech (without pitch or rhythmic specifications) with a richly orchestrated score.

In addition to other operas—*Sárka, Boure* (*The Tempest,* after Shakespeare), *Hédy* (after Byron's *Don Juan*), and *Pád Arkuna*—he also completed three SYMPHONIES, several TONE POEMS and OVERTURES (influencing both the elder SMETANA and the younger DVOŘÁK), 200 songs (in German and Czech), CHAMBER MUSIC, and a multitude of piano works.

Fibich, a fine craftsman who created memorable melodies, was a leading representative of the Czech nationalist movement in music. Yet his extensive output reveals the pronounced influence of CARL MARIA VON WEBER, ROBERT SCHUMANN, and especially RICHARD WAGNER. It was not until his last works that a Czech identity was apparent in his orchestration.

One of his most unusual works was *Nálady, dojmy a upomínky* (Moods, impressions, and reminiscences; 1892–99), a collection of 376 character pieces for piano. The secret subject matter of this work is Fibich's relationship with his mistress, piano student, and librettist Anežka Schulzová (1868–1905). Once the pieces' coded titles were deciphered in the 1920s, it became clear that they depict specific events, conversations, meetings, expressions of love, journeys, parts of Anežka's body, and her appearance in different sets of clothes. In a strange way, Fibich's collection parallels the late works of LEOŠ JANÁČEK, also inspired by a younger woman, although one who merely tolerated the composer's attentions.

Fibonacci series. A sequence of numbers in which each is the sum of the preceding pair, i.e., 1, 1, 2, 3, 5, 8, 13, 21 … Composers such as BÉLA BARTÓK have used it to predetermine the phrasing and metrical flow of some compositions. The contemporary American composer William Duckworth used this numerical sequence in the composing of his work *Time Curve* Preludes.

fiddle (from Mid. Eng., *fidel;* Lat. *vidula, vitula,* etc.). 1. A VIOLIN. 2. Any European bowed string instrument from the Middle Ages onward. It is usually applied to instruments that do not conform to standardized patterns. 3. A colloquial name for a violin, particularly one of rustic manufacture, or in reference to its use in traditional music. The fiddle is used in many European and American folk musics, and related instruments are found throughout the world. It would be undignified to call the CONCERTMASTER of a symphony or-

MUSICAL INSTRUMENT

Fiddler, c. 1890s. (Library of Congress)

chestra a fiddler, as it would be incongruous to call the leading fiddle player in a traditional folk ensemble a concertmaster.

Fiddler on the Roof. Musical by JERRY BOCK and S. Harnick, 1964, based on stories by Sholom Aleichem. It is 1905 in pogrom-ridden Czarist Russia. Tevye and his wife attempt

Topol in the 1994 production of Fiddler on the Roof. *(Robbie Jack/Corbis)* ▶

to marry off their daughters to wealthy Jews. For one, the best they can find is a tailor. The solution: emigrate to America! Includes *Matchmaker Matchmaker, Sunrise Sunset,* and *If I Were a Rich Man.*

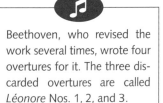

Beethoven, who revised the work several times, wrote four overtures for it. The three discarded overtures are called *Léonore* Nos. 1, 2, and 3.

Fidelio, oder Die eheliche Liebe (Conjugal love). Only OPERA of LUDWIG VAN BEETHOVEN, 1805, first produced in Vienna. It is based on Bouilly's LIBRETTO *Léonore,* the title that Beethoven wished for his opera.

Florestan is in a dungeon for his opposition to a tyrannical Spanish governor. His faithful wife Leonore enters the jail's service in a boy's attire, taking the symbolic name Fidelio (the faithful one) and surviving the jailer's daughter's crush on her. Political and marital virtue triumphs when a new governor, announced by a resonant fanfare from backstage, orders the release of Florestan and the arrest of his tormentor.

The same story was the basis of operas by Johann Simon Mayr (*L'amor coniugale,* 1805) and Ferdinando Paer (*Leonora,* 1804).

Fiedler, Arthur, highly popular American conductor; b. Boston, Dec. 17, 1894; d. Brookline, Mass., July 10, 1979. Of a musical family, he studied violin with his father, Emanuel Fiedler, a member of the Boston Symphony Orchestra. His uncle, Benny Fiedler, also played violin in the Boston Symphony Orchestra. In 1909 he was taken by his father to Berlin, where he studied violin and also had some instruction in conducting. In 1913 he formed the Fiedler Trio with two other Fiedlers.

In 1915, with the war raging in Europe, Fiedler returned to America and joined the second-violin section of the Boston Symphony Orchestra. Later he moved to the viola section, also doubling on the CELESTA when required. In 1924 he organized the Arthur Fiedler Sinfonietta, a professional ensemble of members of the Boston Symphony Orchestra.

In 1929 Fiedler started a series of free open-air summer concerts at the Esplanade on the banks of the Charles River in Boston, presenting programs of popular American music intermingled with classical numbers. The series became a feature in Boston's musical life, attracting audiences of many thousands each summer. In 1930 Fiedler was engaged as conductor of the Boston Pops, which he led for nearly half a century. Cleverly combining pieces of popular appeal with classical works and occasional modern selections, he built a large following, eventually elevating the Boston Pops to the status of a national institution.

Fiedler was a social, gregarious man. One of his favorite pastimes was riding on fire engines, and he was made honorary chief of the fire departments of several American cities. He became commercially successful and willingly accepted offers to appear in advertisements. This popularity, however, lowered his reputation in the classical music world. He had always hoped to conduct guest engagements in the regular subscription series of the Boston Symphony Orchestra, but was never able to achieve this dream (he did conduct the BSO once, when its regular conductor was ill).

PEOPLE IN MUSIC

In 1977 President Ford bestowed upon Fiedler the Medal of Freedom. As a mark of appreciation from the city of Boston, a footbridge near the Esplanade was named after him, with the first two notes of the Prelude to Richard Wagner's *Tristan und Isolde,* A and F, marking the initials of Arthur Fiedler's name, engraved on the plaque. His death was genuinely mourned by Boston.

PEOPLE IN MUSIC

Field, John, remarkable Irish pianist and composer; b. Dublin, July 26, 1782; d. Moscow, Jan. 23, 1837. Field's father was a violinist, and his grandfather an organist, who gave him his first instruction in music. At age nine he began study with well-known Italian composer Tommaso Giordani, then resident in Ireland.

A child prodigy, Field made his debut in Dublin in 1792. He went to London in 1793 and gave his first concert there that same year. He then had lessons with the famous pianist and composer MUZIO CLEMENTI and was also employed in the salesrooms of Clementi's piano company.

Field began his concert career in earnest with a notable series of successful appearances in London in 1800–1801. He then accompanied Clementi on his major tour of the Continent, beginning in 1802. After visiting Paris they proceeded to St. Petersburg in 1803. There Field settled as a performer and teacher, giving his debut performance in 1804. He made many concert tours in Russia.

Stricken with cancer of the rectum, Field returned to London in 1831 for medical treatment. He performed at a Philharmonic Society concert there the following year. Later that year he played in Paris and subsequently toured various cities in France, Belgium, Switzerland, and Italy until his health compelled him to abandon his active career. He eventually returned to Moscow, where he died.

Field's historical position as a composer is of importance, even though his music does not reveal a great original talent. He developed free FANTASIAS (improvised pieces) and piano RECITATIVE (songlike melodies), while following the basic precepts of CLASSIC music. He was also the originator of keyboard NOCTURNES, which were models for FRÉDÉRIC CHOPIN.

Fiery Angel, The. Opera by SERGEI PROKOFIEV, 1919, premiered posthumously in Venice, 1955. A mystical 16th-century girl becomes possessed by the vision of a former lover. Exorcism is begun by the Grand Inquisitor. When it fails, the unfortunate maiden is accused of intercourse with the devil and is burned at the stake.

fife (Ger. *Pfeife;* It. *piffero*). An octave TRANSVERSE FLUTE with six holes and without keys. Its compass is from d2 to d4.

fifth. 1. An INTERVAL. 2. The fifth degree of any diatonic scale (the DOMINANT).

Fifth Symphony. Whenever music lovers speak of "the Fifth Symphony," it is tacitly understood to be LUDWIG VAN BEETHOVEN's Fifth.

The piece opens with the famous "da-da-da-DAH" theme, which has been described as "fate knocking at the door." But did Beethoven really say anything like that in relation to the four portentous notes of the opening theme?

The story originated with Beethoven's biographer, Anton Schindler—but he was only 12 years old when the Fifth Symphony was written. CARL CZERNY, who was close to Beethoven, asserted that the theme was inspired by the call of the oriole or the goldfinch, two birds that Beethoven often heard during his walks in the Vienna woods.

And, again, if it were fate, would Beethoven not have orchestrated these notes with a flourish of trumpets or trombones? Yet he did not, preferring to open the symphony with two mild clarinets and strings. Furthermore, when we examine Beethoven's many sketches for the opening movement of this symphony, the "fate motive" is missing.

On the other hand, there is unmistakable evidence that Beethoven was obsessed with the rhythm of three short notes and one long note during the period when he composed the Fifth. The figure occurs, and recurs, in the Fourth Piano Concerto, the *APPASSIONATA* SONATA, and the String Quartet op.74. Remarkably, these works are closely related to C minor, the key signature of the Fifth Symphony. In each case the three short notes are eighth notes.

Prokofiev's disapproval of the church is suggested in the score by dissonant harmonies and angular melodies.

MUSICAL INSTRUMENT

Whatever the origin, the fate of the fate motive is awe-inspiring: During World War II the Allied forces broadcast the fate melody to Nazi-occupied Europe to signal "V for Victory." The letter *V* in Morse code happens to be three dots and a dash.

The second movement of the Fifth Symphony is a gentle theme with VARIATIONS. There follows a SCHERZO in triple time. The fate motive makes its appearance once more, stated persistently in the drums and, after a dynamic TRANSITION, exploding in thundering C major in the FINALE.

The first performance of the Fifth Symphony took place in Vienna in 1808. The score is dedicated to Prince von Lobkowitz (the patron of music to whom the *EROICA* SYMPHONY was assigned), and to Count Razumovsky, the Russian ambassador to Vienna.

figuration. The adorning of melodic phrases and chords by rhythmic figures, ARPEGGIOS, PASSING NOTES, TRILLS, CHANGING NOTES, etc.

La Figure humaine. CANTATA by FRANCIS POULENC, 1945, for unaccompanied DOUBLE CHORUS. The text voices the universal desire for liberty. Poulenc wrote it during the Nazi occupation of Paris. Its first performance was given in London.

figured bass. *See* BASSO CONTINUO.

Fille du regiment, La (The daughter of the regiment). Opera by GAETANO DONIZETTI, 1840, first produced in Paris.

A girl is brought up by a regiment of soldiers and serves as their army mascot. A crisis occurs when her aunt reclaims her and takes her to her castle. The soldiers lead an assault on her aunt's stronghold, and she is reinstated as the "daughter of the regiment."

film music. During the early years of motion picture production, theater owners engaged a pianist or an organist to provide appropriate music for the moving images on the screen. Romantic scenes called for sentimental salon music, while themes of sadness were enhanced by passages in a mournful minor key. Danger and tragedy were depicted by CHROMATIC runs harmonized by the DIMINISHED seventh chord. Realistic sound effects were provided behind the scene by homemade rain and thunder machines.

Musical instruments in a film studio prop room. (Hulton-Deutsch Collection/Corbis)

Most silent movie pianists were content with playing standard CLASSIC or ROMANTIC pieces, but there were also truly inspired artists who improvised music that faithfully followed the action on the screen. To aid silent movie pianists and organists, special collections of sheet music were published with a table of contents indicating subject matter: gladness, sadness, madness, married felicity, faithless duplicity, infatuation, assassination, horse races, balloon ascension, etc., all garnished by traditional folk music of many lands.

Respectable composers also showed interest in writing scores for films. One of the earliest cinema scores was composed in 1908 by CAMILLE SAINT-SAËNS for the French movie *L'Assassinat du Duc de Guise,* scored for strings, piano, and HARMONIUM. Another early film score, *Napoléon* by ARTHUR HONEGGER, was issued as an instrumental suite in 1922. ERIK SATIE'S BALLET *Relâche,* produced in 1924, featured a filmed interlude in addition to the live action on stage, which was accompanied by music. Other composers who contributed to the art of early film music were GEORGE ANTHEIL, GEORGES AURIC, AARON COPLAND, SERGEI PROKOFIEV, and DMITRI SHOSTAKOVICH. Even RICHARD STRAUSS condescended to arrange his opera *Der Rosenkavalier* for a film.

With the advent of sound in motion pictures, specially composed background music was provided on the sound track. At first it consisted of recorded compositions of a popular genre. Quite frequently producers and directors engaged a "ghost" composer to write music according to their specifications. For example, Charlie Chaplin would sing or whistle a theme and then have a professional composer orchestrate it.

From the 1930s through the 1960s, the most successful movie composers in Hollywood were Max Steiner and AL-FRED NEWMAN. They composed scores for full orchestra, which they conducted themselves. An important contribution to film music was made by ERICH WOLFGANG KORN-GOLD, a Viennese-born composer who spent many years in Hollywood. His scores have been performed separately from the films they were written to accompany. BERNARD HERR-MANN successfully combined his theatrical sense with modern composing techniques. ERNST TOCH excelled in scores for movie mysteries. DAVID RAKSIN wrote numerous remarkable scores, and his concert suites from the films *Laura* and *The Bad and the Beautiful* are sometimes performed by major symphony orchestras.

In the 1970s and '80s JOHN WILLIAMS became highly successful in providing music for films of blatant heroic content, including such science fiction hits as *Star Wars* and *Close Encounters of the Third Kind*. HENRY MANCINI specialized in theme songs calculated to appeal to the widest popular tastes. Although individual composers continue to provide entire sound tracks, many films use a selection of songs by various popular artists, hoping that at least one song will be a chart success and thereby increase business.

Composing for films usually requires precise synchronization (timing) with the changing images and actions on the screen. A technique has been developed in which a click track provides a steady beat for performers, while a sound-editing device measures the exact duration of each scene in a picture. Digital technology has refined this process further.

RICHARD WAGNER and his followers shunned the finale as a cheap musical trick. But many others continue to use it, even if only to inspire thunderous applause.

finale. In instrumental music, the last movement of a composition. In opera or ORATORIO, the finale is a summary of all major musical themes and the resolution of tangled threads of the plot. A *grand finale* is a CHORAL conclusion with the participation of all principal characters.

fine (It.). End or close. An indication either of the end of a repetition after a DA CAPO or *dal segno* or the end of a piece.

fē′něh

Fingal's Cave. CONCERT OVERTURE by FELIX MENDELSSOHN, 1832. It was inspired by his 1829 visit to the Hebrides, a group of islands off the coast of Scotland, during a concert tour. Mendelssohn was impressed by the somber dampness and mysterious surroundings of Fingal's Cave. The result was an expertly fashioned piece in the darksome key of B MINOR.

finger cymbals. Miniature CYMBALS attached to the fingers, used by belly dancers as jingles and in 20th-century revivals of RENAISSANCE ensembles.

MUSICAL INSTRUMENT

fingerboard (Fr. *touche;* Ger. *Griffbrett;* It. *tastatura*). The elongated, relatively narrow section on STRING instruments over which the strings are stretched. On the GUITAR, FRETS spaced along the fingerboard guide the player's fingers. VIOLINS and other orchestral string instruments are not fretted.

fingering (Ger. *Fingersatz*). 1. The method of applying the fingers to the KEYS, holes, STRINGS, etc., of musical instruments.

2. The marks in a score guiding the performer in placing his fingers. *English fingering* (for the piano), where notes taken by the thumb are marked ×, with 1, 2, 3, and 4 for the fingers; *German* (or *Continental*) *fingering,* notes for the thumb marked 1, and the fingers 2, 3, 4, and 5.

Finian's Rainbow. Musical by BURTON LANE and E. Y. HARBURG, 1947. The Irishman Finian settles in the southeastern U.S. and buries a gold nugget. The leprechaun who actually owns it comes to retrieve it, performing a few miracles in the process. Includes *Something Sort of Grandish* and *Old Devil Moon.*

Finlandia. Symphonic poem by JEAN SIBELIUS, 1900, written for his home country before its independence from Russia. When it was premiered, it was called *Suomi,* Finnish for "Finland."

Before the 19th century, editions of classical music, particularly for piano, rarely indicated what fingers to use and when. The task of fingering was left to editors, mostly German, of the classics published in annotated editions of the 19th century. Some established rules of standard piano fingering included not using the thumb on the black keys except in cases of dire necessity, as in F♯ major arpeggios or in Chopin's *Black Key* Étude.

Finta giardiniera, La (The dissembling gardener). OPERA BUFFA by WOLFGANG AMADEUS MOZART, 1775. A count snubs a noblewoman who loves him. She takes on the disguise of a municipal gardener in order to win his affections. After various plot twists and turns, she eventually wins his love.

Fiorello! Musical by JERRY BOCK, 1959. It tells the story of former N. Y. mayor Fiorello La Guardia, the "little flower" (1933 – 45), ending with his first election to the post. Includes *Politics and Poker.*

fē-ōh-rē-too′răh

fioritura (It., floral decoration; plur. *fioriture*). An embellishment. An ornamental turn, flourish, or phrase introduced into a melody.

It was common practice for Italian singers to embellish their arias with ARPEGGIOS, gruppetti (turns, grace notes), and TRILLS, often obscuring the main melodic line. A story is told about the great opera singer Adelina Patti, who as a young girl sang for GIOACCHINO ROSSINI one of his own ARIAS, heavily embellished. Rossini praised her singing, but then asked ironically, "But, pray, who is the composer of this aria?"

In modern times, no PRIMA DONNA would presume to go beyond the printed text of an aria except in CADENZAS. ARTURO TOSCANINI was known to explode in flowery language when a singer added as much as an unauthorized appoggiatura (grace note) to a solo.

MUSICAL INSTRUMENT

fipple flute. RENAISSANCE end-blown vertical FLUTE or RECORDER. The word is derived from *fipple,* a plug in the mouthpiece.

Fire and Rain. A 1970 hit for singer-songwriter JAMES TAYLOR that established his reputation. It tells the story of a young woman he met while residing in a mental institution. Despite his affection for her, he never expresses it nor has the chance to see her after she is released.

***Fire* Symphony** (*Feuersymphonie*). Symphony No. 59 in A Major by FRANZ JOSEPH HAYDN, 1769. Who gave this name to the work when and why is a mystery, but perhaps the music has some connection with the play *The Conflagration* that was presented at Esterház, where Haydn was employed.

Firebird, The (*L'Oiseau de feu*). IGOR STRAVINSKY's first BAL-LET, 1910. Stravinsky drew upon Russian folklore for the

◀

The Firebird, *1995 production. (Robbie Jack/Corbis)*

In 1937 Warner Brothers made a film entitled *The Firebird.* It told the story of a cunning man who uses a recording of Stravinsky's piece to seduce a woman who lives in the apartment below him. Stravinsky sued the film company for defamation of character, but the French judge could not understand why Stravinsky became so upset by it. Stravinsky was awarded the token sum of one French franc for "moral damage."

plot. The firebird gives the heroic Ivan Tsarevich a fiery feather as a reward for his letting it go free after its capture. The feather is a magic wand that helps Ivan when he himself is captured by the evil magician Kashchey. The infernal dance of the finale is bewitching in its angular rhythms.

Fireworks. Orchestral work by IGOR STRAVINSKY, 1908. It was written on the occasion of the wedding of the daughter of his revered teacher NIKOLAI RIMSKY-KORSAKOV and first performed in St. Petersburg. The score is very much in the tradition of the Russian national school, but its brilliant sparks of rhythmic fire presage the Stravinsky of the future.

Fireworks Music (or *The Musick for the Royal Fireworks*). ORCHESTRAL SUITE by GEORGE FRIDERIC HANDEL, 1749. It was written to celebrate the Peace of Aix-la-Chapelle, which ended the long war of the Austrian Succession (also known as King George's War). Peace is portrayed by a modest SICIL-IANA, followed by a fast march entitled, quite properly, *La Réjouissance* (The rejoicing), and scored for a huge orchestra.

first. 1. Of voices and instruments of the same class, the highest, as *first soprano, first violin.* 2. On the STAFF, the lowest, as *first line, first space.* 3. The *first string* of an instrument is the highest.

First Time Ever I Saw Your Face. Romantic love BALLAD by Scottish folksinger Ewan MacColl. It became a hit for soul singer Roberta Flack in 1972. The same song was updated by the group the Fugees in 1997.

Fischer-Dieskau, (Albert) **Dietrich,** celebrated German BARITONE; b. Berlin, May 28, 1925. While the surname of the family was originally Fischer, his paternal grandmother's maiden surname of Dieskau was legally added to it in 1937. His father, a teacher and headmaster, was self-taught in music, and his mother was an amateur pianist.

Dietrich began to study piano at age nine and voice at age 16. He then studied voice at the Berlin Hochschule für Musik in 1942–43. In 1943 he was drafted into the German army. He was made a prisoner of war by the Americans while serving in Italy in 1945. Upon his release in 1947 he returned to Germany and made his first professional appearance as a soloist in the BRAHMS DEUTSCHES REQUIEM.

In 1948 Fischer-Dieskau made his operatic debut in the bass role of Colas in a radio broadcast of WOLFGANG AMADEUS MOZART's *Bastien und Bastienne.* Later that year he made his stage debut as Rodrigo, Marquis of Posa, in *DON CARLOS* at the Berlin Städtische Oper, where he remained an invaluable member for 35 years. He also pursued his operatic career with appearances at leading opera houses and festivals in Europe.

It was as a LIEDER and concert artist, however, that Fischer-Dieskau became universally known. In 1955 he made his U.S. debut with the Cincinnati Symphony Orchestra. His U.S. recital debut followed at N.Y.'s Town Hall. In subsequent years he made tours all over the world to enormous critical acclaim. His finest operatic roles included Count Almaviva, Don Giovanni, Papageno, Macbeth, Falstaff, Hans Sachs, Mandryka, Mathis der Maler, and Wozzeck. He created the role of Mittenhofer in HANS WERNER HENZE's *ELEGY FOR YOUNG LOVERS* (1961) and the title role in Hugo Reimann's *Lear* (1978).

PEOPLE IN MUSIC

Fischer-Dieskau brought the lied into the modern age, with his superb recordings of virtually the entire lieder of FRANZ SCHUBERT and other important lied composers. He published anthologies of song texts and studies of the art of singing.

fish horn. Colloquial American term for the OBOE. It was common from the middle of the 19th century.

fistula (Lat., pipe). In the Middle Ages, an ORGAN pipe. *Fistula anglia,* the English flute, i.e., the RECORDER; *fistula germanica,* the German flute, i.e., TRANSVERSE FLUTE.

Fitzgerald, Ella, remarkable African-American JAZZ singer; b. Newport News, Va., Apr. 25, 1917; d. Beverly Hills, Calif., June 17, 1996. After the death of her father, Fitzgerald's mother took her to N.Y. She was discovered by drummer Chick Webb (one of Harlem's most popular musicians) in 1935 when performing at amateur night at the legendary Apollo Theater, and then joined his BIG BAND. She scored her first big hits with the band, including the update of the children's nursery rhyme A-TISKET, A-TASKET. Upon Webb's death in 1939, she became the band's leader.

In 1942 Fitzgerald became a freelance singer and subsequently worked with most major jazz musicians and groups. She was particularly adept at SCAT SINGING and improvisation. She was equally at ease in SWING and BEBOP styles, developing, over the years, a blend of musicianship, vocal ability, and interpretive insight. Her 1950s recordings of the "songbooks" of COLE PORTER, DUKE ELLINGTON, GEORGE GERSHWIN, HAROLD ARLEN, IRVING BERLIN, JEROME KERN, JOHNNY MERCER, and RODGERS and HART are a cornerstone of her legacy.

Fitzgerald achieved a popularity and respect rarely acquired by jazz singers. In 1987 she was awarded the National Medal of Arts. She continued to perform into the 1990s, until illness forced her to retire from the stage in 1994.

Five Foot Two, Eyes of Blue. Song by Ray Henderson, 1925. Used in the 1952 film *Has Anybody Seen My Gal?*

This remarkable order was issued by Vice Admiral Porter of the U.S. Naval Academy in Annapolis, dated 1867: "Midshipman Thompson (first class), who plays so abominably on a fish horn, will oblige me by going outside the limits when he wants to practice or he will find himself coming out of the little end of the horn."

PEOPLE IN MUSIC

Five Orchestral Pieces (Schoenberg). *See FÜNF ORCHESTER-STÜCKE.*

Five Pieces for Orchestra. A remarkable set of pieces by AN-TON WEBERN, 1911. They are extremely short: one comprises six measures and lasts 19 seconds, and is scored for clarinet, trumpet, trombone, mandolin, celesta, harp, drum, violin, and viola, each entering alone and thus creating a chain of sounds that may be described as a melody of timbres (*klangfarbenmelodie*). Webern at first attached descriptive titles to each of the pieces: *Urbild, Werwandlung, Rückkehr, Erinnerung, Die Seele* (Initial idea, Metamorphosis, Return, Recollection, The soul). However, he later removed them. Webern conducted their first performance in Zurich, 1926.

fixed *do(h)*. A system of SOLMIZATION based on equivalence, i.e., one in which the tone C, and all its CHROMATIC derivatives (C♯, C♭, C♯♯, C♭♭), are called *do,* D and its derivatives are called *re,* etc., no matter in what key or harmony they may appear. *Compare* MOVABLE DO(H).

fixed-tone instrument. An instrument (e.g., PIANO, OR-GAN), whose pitches cannot be modified at will while playing. Such an instrument is said to have "fixed intonation."

flag. A hook (♪) on the stem of a note: ♪ ♫ ♬

flageolet. A small FIPPLE FLUTE or RECORDER, used in the RENAISSANCE to imitate bird calls. It was used as a SO-PRANINO flute in ensembles until the 19th century. The French flageolet has a compass of two octaves and three semitones, from g1 to b3. *Flageolet tones, see* HARMONICS.

Flagstad, Kirsten (Malfrid), celebrated Norwegian SO-PRANO; b. Hamar, July 12, 1895; d. Oslo, Dec. 7, 1962. Flagstad initially studied voice with her mother and with Ellen Schytte-Jacobsen in Christiania (now Oslo), Norway, where she made her operatic debut as Nuri in Eugène d'Albert's *Tiefland* in 1913. During the next two decades she sang throughout Scandinavia.

In 1933 Flagstad sang a number of minor roles at the famous Bayreuth festival, scoring her first major success there in 1934 when she appeared as Sieglinde. She made an auspicious Metropolitan Opera debut in N.Y. in that same role in 1935, and was soon hailed as the foremost Wagnerian soprano of her time. In 1936 she made her first appearance at London's Covent Garden, as Isolde. While continuing to sing at the Metropolitan Opera, she made guest appearances at the San Francisco Opera from 1935 to 1938 and the Chicago Opera during 1937, and also gave concerts with major U.S. orchestras.

Flagstad returned to her Nazi-occupied homeland in 1941 to be with her husband, a decision that alienated many of her admirers. Nevertheless, after World War II she resumed her career with notable success at Covent Garden. In 1951 she also returned to the Metropolitan Opera, where she sang Isolde and Leonore, and again on April 1, 1952, when she made her farewell appearance in GLUCK's *ALCESTE*. She retired from the operatic stage in 1954 but continued to make recordings. From 1958 to 1960 she was director of the Norwegian Opera in Oslo. Among her other celebrated roles were Brünnhilde, Elisabeth, Elsa, and Kundry.

flamenco. Popular Andalusian art of singing and dancing, accompanied mainly by guitar and CASTANETS, which gradually developed into an important folk art form. Felipe Pedrell and MANUEL DE FALLA played crucial roles in the survival of flamenco through the special festivals they organized.

Flamenco meters and rhythms are varied and often feature more than one rhythm being stated at the same time. Scales are based on traditional PENTATONIC folk scales. The lyrics, influenced by gypsy themes, center on love, fortune, sorrow, and death.

Principal genres of flamenco singing are *cante jondo* (deep song), with many vocal embellishments, and *cante chico* (small song).

Flanagan, Tommy (Lee), African-American JAZZ pianist; b. Detroit, Mar. 16, 1930. Flanagan commenced clarinet studies at the age of six and piano training at 11, working

Flamenco singing is usually introduced by the loud exclamations "Ay! Ay!" and accompanied by vigorous heel stamping and passionate hand and arm movements. When the singing is accompanied by foot stamping, the dance is called *zapateado* (shoe dance).

PEOPLE IN MUSIC

throughout his adolescence in local jazz haunts with various older musicians, including MILT JACKSON, THAD JONES, and ELVIN JONES. In 1956 he went to N.Y., where he subsequently was pianist and music director for ELLA FITZGERALD. He also performed with Oscar Pettiford, J.J. JOHNSON, MILES DAVIS, and others. From the 1970s on, Flanagan has become known as a soloist and leader of his own small groups.

flat. The character ♭, placed before a note to indicate lowering its pitch by a SEMITONE. The double-flat, ♭♭, lowers its note by two semitones. *Flat chord,* a chord whose tones are performed simultaneously; a *solid* chord, as opposed to *broken; flat fifth,* DIMINISHED fifth.

flat pick. A triangle-shaped PLECTRUM, made of tortoiseshell or plastic, used for GUITAR and other instrumental picking in BLUEGRASS and related American music. A heavier-weight pick is used for electric string instruments.

Flatt, Lester (Raymond), American COUNTRY MUSIC singer and guitarist; b. Overton County, Tenn., June 19, 1914; d. Nashville, May 11, 1979. Flatt joined BILL MONROE's Blue Grass Boys as a singer in 1944, then formed a duo with EARL SCRUGGS, the BANJO player. They then organized their own band, the Foggy Mountain Boys, in the early 1950s and soon established themselves as leading figures in country music. Flatt became famous for his relaxed lead vocals and a special bass run on the guitar known as the "Lester Flatt G Run."

After the Flatt and Scruggs partnership came apart in 1969, Flatt played with the remaining members of the band under the name the Nashville Grass. Flatt continued to perform until his death following a heart attack in 1979. Shortly before his death, he played again for the first time with Bill Monroe and Scruggs on stage at Monroe's Bean Blossom bluegrass festival.

Fledermaus, Die (The bat). OPERETTA by JOHANN STRAUSS, JR., 1874, first performed in Vienna. The bat of the title is the costume used by one of the characters at a masked ball.

MUSICAL INSTRUMENT

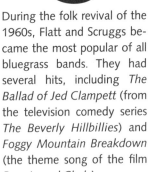

PEOPLE IN MUSIC

During the folk revival of the 1960s, Flatt and Scruggs became the most popular of all bluegrass bands. They had several hits, including *The Ballad of Jed Clampett* (from the television comedy series *The Beverly Hillbillies*) and *Foggy Mountain Breakdown* (the theme song of the film *Bonnie and Clyde*).

An Austrian baron who is sentenced to prison for a minor crime escapes the police and goes to a masked ball. His suspicious wife goes to the same ball disguised as a Hungarian countess. Not recognizing her, the baron flirts with her. A series of mistaken identities reach their climax when the baron exchanges clothes with his own lawyer and enters the jail in order to get a confession from another suspect and clear himself. A happy ending is guaranteed when all jail sentences are suspended. The guests from the masked ball join the principals to drink a toast in praise of champagne, the king of wines.

Despite the somewhat silly (and difficult to follow) plot, *Die Fledermaus* has been successful since its premiere throughout the world.

Fleisher, Leon, distinguished American pianist, conductor, and teacher; b. San Francisco, July 23, 1928, of Jewish-Russian immigrant parents. Fleisher's father was a tailor, and his mother a singing teacher. He learned the rudiments of music from his mother, then studied piano with Lev Shorr. He played in public at the age of six, then was sent to Europe for studies at Lake Como, Italy, with ARTUR SCHNABEL, with whom he also studied in N.Y.

PEOPLE IN MUSIC

At the age of 14 Fleisher appeared as soloist in FRANZ LISZT's A Major Piano Concerto with the San Francisco Symphony Orchestra, and at 16 he was soloist with the N.Y. Philharmonic. In 1952 he became the first American to win first prize at the Queen Elisabeth of Belgium International Competition in Brussels, thus launching his brilliant career. He made several European tours and gave highly successful recitals in South America. In 1961–62 he was a soloist with the San Francisco Symphony Orchestra to observe its 50th anniversary.

At the peak of his career, in 1964, Fleisher was stricken with carpal tunnel syndrome, which incapacitated his right hand. Fleisher turned to piano works written for left hand alone and also began to conduct. In 1968 he became artistic director of the Theater Chamber Players in Washington, D.C., and in 1970 he became music director of the Annapolis Symphony Orchestra as well. From 1973 to 1977 he was associate conductor of the Baltimore Symphony Orchestra, and from 1977 to 1978 its resident conductor. He appeared as a guest conductor at the Mostly Mozart Festival in N.Y. and also with the Boston Symphony, San Francisco Symphony, Cincinnati Symphony, and the Los Angeles Chamber Orchestra.

After several ineffective treatments, in 1981 Fleisher underwent surgery. It was momentarily successful, and in 1982 he made a spectacular comeback as a pianist, playing the *Symphonic Variations* by CÉSAR FRANCK with Sergiu Comissiona and the Baltimore Symphony Orchestra. He served as artistic director of the Berkshire Music Center at Tanglewood from 1986 until his resignation in 1997.

Throughout his career, Fleisher has devoted much time to teaching. He joined the faculty of the Peabody Conservatory of Music in Baltimore in 1959 and subsequently was named to the Andrew W. Mellon Chair in Piano. He was also a visiting professor at the Rubin Academy of Music in Jerusalem. Among his brilliant pupils were Andre Watts and Lorin Hollander.

MUSICAL INSTRUMENT

flexatone (It. *flessatone*). A 20th-century instrument consisting of a metal plate attached to a piece of wood. It produces a twanging, imprecisely pitched sound when the metal plate is plucked. ARNOLD SCHOENBERG used the instrument in both his Variations for Orchestra and *Moses und Aron*.

Fliegende Holländer, Der. See FLYING DUTCHMAN, THE.

flores (Lat., flowers; It. *fioretti, fiori*). In the Middle Ages, embellishments in vocal and instrumental music. The insertion of GRACE NOTES above and below the melody notes was named *florificatio*. Usually such embellishments were added to the DISCANT, but sometimes even the presumably unalterable CANTUS FIRMUS was adorned by florid ornamentation with *pulchrae ascensiones et descensiones* ("pretty ups and downs"). These were also called *licentiae* (acts of licentiousness) and *elegantiae* (elegancies).

PEOPLE IN MUSIC

Flotow, Friedrich (Adolf Ferdinand) **von,** famous German OPERA composer; b. Teutendorf, Apr. 27, 1813; d. Darmstadt, Jan. 24, 1883. Flotow was born to an old noble family, receiving his first music lessons from his mother. He also sang in the church choir.

At the age of 16 Flotow went to Paris, where he entered the conservatory to study piano and composition. After the revolution of 1830, when a new democratic government was installed in France, Flotow returned home, where he completed his first opera, *Pierre et Catherine,* set to a French LI-BRETTO. It was premiered in a German translation in 1835. Returning to Paris, he collaborated in 1838–39 with the Belgian composer Albert Grisar on two operas and with the composer Auguste Pilati on a third.

Flotow scored his first success with his romantic opera *Alessandro Stradella,* based on the legendary accounts of the life of the Italian composer. It was first performed in Hamburg in 1844 and had numerous subsequent productions in Germany. Three years later he achieved even greater success with his romantic opera *Martha, oder Der Markt zu Richmond.* It combined the German sentimental spirit with Italian lyricism and Parisian elegance. The libretto was based on a BALLET, *Lady Henriette, ou La Servante de Greenwich* (1844), for which Flotow had composed the music for act 1. The authentic Irish melody *The Last Rose of Summer* was incorporated into the opera, lending a certain nostalgic charm to the whole work.

Flotow's love of the aristocratic lifestyle made it difficult for him to remain in Paris after the revolution of 1848, when the people once again took power. He accepted the post of Intendant at the grand ducal court theater in Schwerin from 1855 to 1863, then moved to Austria. He returned to Germany in 1873, settling in Darmstadt in 1880. He died three years later.

flourish. A trumpet FANFARE or call.

Flower Drum Song. Musical by RODGERS and HAMMERSTEIN, 1958. A Chinese-American man must choose between a San Francisco nightclub performer and an innocent woman imported from the homeland. After many complications, he chooses the latter. Includes *A Hundred Million Miracles, Chop Suey,* and *I Enjoy Being a Girl.*

Flügelhorn (Ger.; Fr. *bugle;* It. *flicorno soprano*). Originally, an unvalved hunting horn in 18th-century Germany, which later became known as the BUGLE. In the early 19th century, keys were added to create the keyed bugle.

By the middle of the century, the term *flügelhorn* was applied to a similar BRASS instrument with CORNET range and VALVES. It is used more in military music and JAZZ than in classical music.

MUSICAL INSTRUMENT

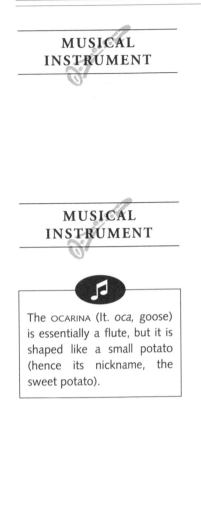

The OCARINA (It. *oca*, goose) is essentially a flute, but it is shaped like a small potato (hence its nickname, the sweet potato).

---

flute. The most ancient wind instrument, spontaneously evolved by populations in all parts of the world, from Mesopotamia to the Andes, from China to Central Africa.

Primitive flutes were all vertical pipes. They were made of baked clay or reeds with perforated holes that would change the pitch when one or several of them were covered by a finger.

Musical mythology is strewn with the appearance of the flute. When the cloven-footed god of the woods Pan pursued the nymph Syrinx, she was turned into a reed to escape him. Heartbroken, Pan made a PANPIPE out of reeds to commemorate his beloved.

In pre-Columbian South America, Indians made flutes out of bones, samples of which are still extant. There is a legend of a Peruvian Indian whose beloved died young. Distraught, he went to her place of burial, exhumed one of her legs, and fashioned a flute out of her tibia. He played wistful melodies upon it, and this intimate contact with a part of the body of his beloved gave him temporary relief from his sorrow.

The Pied Piper of Hamelin lured away the town children on their fateful journey by playing on his flute. In WOLFGANG AMADEUS MOZART's opera *THE MAGIC FLUTE*, the hero is preserved from disaster by playing a tune on a melodious flute.

In a Grimm fairy tale, a young prince is slain by his brothers in a rivalry for the throne. A shepherd finds one of his whitened bones, makes holes in it, and plays upon it. The bone flute tells the story of his murder. GUSTAV MAHLER set this tale to music in his CHORAL work *DAS KLAGENDE LIED*.

The flute is the heavenly bird of the SYMPHONY and opera. Birds of the forest speak to Siegfried in RICHARD WAG-

NER's *Ring* through the voice of the flutes. IGOR STRAVINSKY'S *FIREBIRD* is a flute, and so is the helpful bird in SERGEI PROKOFIEV'S *PETER AND THE WOLF*. It is the flute that sings the part of the nightingale in LUDWIG VAN BEETHOVEN'S *PASTORAL SYMPHONY* and in Igor Stravinsky's *Le Chant du rossignol*.

The flute is the most agile of wind instruments, capable of skipping from one note to another with the greatest of ease. It mates in perfect harmony with the human voice. When Lucia goes mad in GAETANO DONIZETTI'S opera, she sings her poignant TRILLS accompanied by a solo flute.

But with all these advantages, the flute did not become a concert instrument until the 18th century. The new flute was the TRANSVERSE (horizontal, cross) FLUTE in which the sound is produced by blowing across a side hole. Because it was first introduced in Germany, the transverse flute became known as the German flute, while the RECORDER, greatly popular in England, acquired the sobriquet of the English flute.

The transverse flute came of age when Johann Joachim Quantz, the court musician to FREDERICK THE GREAT (who, incidentally, was the finest flutist among royalty), published in 1752 his famous treatise on the art of playing the instrument.

In symphonic works flute parts are frequently used in pairs, like their fellow wind instruments the OBOES, CLARINETS, BASSOONS, HORNS, and TRUMPETS. The use of a single flute in a symphonic score, as in Beethoven's Fourth Symphony, is an exception. Concertos for flute were written by Quantz, GEORGE FRIDERIC HANDEL, and Mozart.

In the 19th century, Theobald Boehm, the great German flute manufacturer, produced a new system of fingering and rearranged the flute's KEYS. The BOEHM SYSTEM flute has a tube of cylindrical bore, with 14 holes closed by keys. It is blown through an oval orifice near the upper end. Having been made of wood for centuries, flutes began to be manufactured from alloys of silver, which permitted the flute to compete dynamically with the large Western orchestra.

Like all wind instruments, flutes are members of a family. The range of the modern flute (concert flute; Fr., *grande flute;* Ger., grosse *Flöte;* It., *flauto*) extends from middle C through three octaves (c1–c4), but it can be overblown to

Rich amateurs owned flutes made of gold. The modern French flutist Georges Barrère had a flute made of platinum, and EDGARD VARÈSE wrote a piece for him entitled *Density 21.5,* which is the density of platinum.

produce the high C♯, D, and even E♭ (e♭⁴). In modern flutes, a special key is provided to produce the low B (b).

The range of the PICCOLO is an OCTAVE higher than the regular flute, but it lacks the C and C♯ in its low register. It can blow through three octaves and its high C (c⁵) is of the same pitch as the highest note on the piano. No other instrument can rise to such stratospheric heights. Beethoven introduced the piccolo in the finale of his FIFTH SYMPHONY.

The *alto flute* in G sounds a fourth below the regular concert flute. MAURICE RAVEL's ballet *DAPHNIS ET CHLOÉ* has an important part for the alto flute, which invokes the spirit of Pan.

The BASS FLUTE is an elephantine low-voice member, with the range starting an octave below the standard flute (c). It is a long instrument and requires considerable lung power to blow and superlative lip technique to articulate. The Parisian-American composer Betsy Jolas wrote a piece for piccolo and bass flute.

There is also a monster of a flute, the *double-bass flute,* which theoretically ought to produce a sound two octaves below the concert flute. But when an American manufacturer of the double-bass flute presented a demonstration of it at a congress of flutists, he blew and blew into it without making even a wheeze.

The *flûte d'amour* may also be mentioned. In Italian it is *flauto d'amore* and in German, *Lieblichflöte.* There is no English name for it, which is just as well, since it would be ludicrous to call it a "love flute." It was introduced in the late 18th century, is pitched a minor third below the concert flute, and is more or less obsolete.

AVANT-GARDE composers, annoyed by the sweet sounds of the flute, have tried their best (or worst) to improve upon it by instructing the players to blow through the flute without producing a recognizable pitch, or to clap the keys without blowing. Double-tonguing, triple-tonguing, and FLUTTER-TONGUING are favorites in modern flute parts, as are overblown harmonics. In the last quarter of the 20th century the flute has been incorporated into ROCK and JAZZ groups, which make up for the flute's soft sound by amplifying it electronically.

flutter-tonguing (Ger. *Flatterzunge, Zungenschlag;* It. *frullato;* Fr. *coup de langue*). A special effect on wind instruments in which the player rolls the tongue as if pronouncing the liquid consonants *l* and *r.*

Fluxus. N.Y. art coalition, c.1962–78, loosely run by the architect George Macunias, that gave birth to highly original, mostly theatrical, and often humorous mixed-media stage works frequently involving novel uses of sound. Musical scores could be in the form of written instructions or graphs. Among those associated with Fluxus were LA MONTE YOUNG, YOKO ONO, Dick Higgins, Alison Knowles, Nam June Paik, Jackson Mac Low, Robert Watts, and George Brecht.

Flying Dutchman, The (*Der fliegende Holländer*). Opera by RICHARD WAGNER, 1843, first produced in Dresden. The LIBRETTO is by Wagner himself after an old legend.

The *Flying Dutchman* is a ship on which a mariner is doomed to sail until he finds a woman of absolute devotion. Stormy seas drive the ship off course to a Norwegian fjord. The voyager hears a Norwegian girl sing a ballad about the doomed ship and realizes that she could redeem him. But in her eagerness, she leaps toward the ship from a cliff and perishes. Her sacrifice is his redemption, and together they are lifted to the skies.

Foggy Day in London Town, A. Song by GEORGE GERSHWIN, 1937. It was written for the film *Damsel in Distress* and later resurrected by FRANK SINATRA.

Foley, "Red" (Clyde Julian), American country music singer; b. Blue Lick, Ky., June 17, 1910; d. Fort Wayne, Ind., Sept. 19, 1968. Foley studied briefly at Georgetown (Kentucky) College. In 1937 he formed the "Renfro Valley Barn Dance" radio program and appeared regularly at Nashville's GRAND OLE OPRY. He made popular such country music classics as *Chattanooga Shoeshine Boy, Peace in the Valley,* and *Beyond the Sunset.* In 1967 he was elected to the Country Music Hall of Fame in recognition of his promi-

PEOPLE IN MUSIC

nent place among modern country music performers. He died while on tour with the Grand Ole Opry.

folia (Sp.; It. *follia;* Eng. *folly*). A Portuguese dance that originated about 1500. It was featured in popular festivals and theatrical performances, always with singing, and accompanied by a rhythmic hand clapping and clacking of CASTANETS. In later theoretical references, the folia was usually coupled with SARABANDES and CHACONNES.

fōh-lē'äh

According to one Spanish writer of the early 17th century, the dancers behaved as if "they [had] abandoned all reason." This may explain the dance's name, though the folia has little madness in it. Rather, it is a stately rhythmic dance in TRIPLE time with a long second beat, usually in a MINOR MODE.

folk music. TRADITIONAL MUSIC, passed down through the generations by oral transmission, rather than through musical notation. Music native to a people, region, state, or country, often MODAL and with a variety of rhythmic and metric approaches. *See also* FOLK SONG.

folk song (Ger. *Volkslied*). Native song of a people, region, state, or country, passed down by oral transmission. In addition to the musical particularities of the style, there is a strong tie to language, and epic and BALLAD forms are common. *See also* FOLK MUSIC.

***Folksong* Symphony.** Symphony No. 4 by ROY HARRIS, 1940. It draws on American FOLK SONGS for its musical themes.

Follow Thru. Musical by RAY HENDERSON, 1929. It tells the story of a golf match between two women and the male golf champion who falls for one of them. Includes *Button Up Your Overcoat.*

Folsom Prison Blues. A 1968 COUNTRY hit written and performed by JOHNNY CASH in his distinctive bass voice.

Fontane di Roma, Le. *See* FOUNTAINS OF ROME, THE.

Foote, Arthur (William), distinguished American composer; b. Salem, Mass., Mar. 5, 1853; d. Boston, Apr. 8, 1937. Foote studied harmony at the New England Conservatory of Music in Boston from 1867 to 1870. He then took courses in counterpoint and fugue at Harvard College, where he received the first M.A. degree in music granted by an American university in 1875.

Foote taught piano, organ, and composition in Boston. He was organist at Boston's Church of the Disciples from 1876 to 1878 and subsequently at the First Unitarian Church until 1910. He also frequently appeared as a pianist with the Kneisel Quartet from 1890 to 1910, performing several of his own works. He was a founding member and president from 1909 to 1912 of the American Guild of Organists and taught piano at the New England Conservatory of Music from 1921 to 1937. In 1898 he was elected a member of the National Institute of Arts and Letters.

Foote's music, a product of the ROMANTIC tradition, is notable for its fine lyrical spirit. His Suite in E Major for Strings, op.63 (1907), enjoyed numerous performances and became a standard of American orchestral music. Other compositions include various orchestral, chamber, and piano and organ pieces, as well as many vocal works, including some 100 songs, 52 PART-SONGS, and 35 ANTHEMS. Foote also published several music textbooks.

For He's a Jolly Good Fellow. The English version of a satirical French tune, *Malbrouk s'en vat-en guerre* (Malbrouk has gone to war).

forlana (*furlana*, It.; Fr. *forlane*). A lively Italian dance in $\frac{6}{8}$ or $\frac{6}{4}$ time that originated in the province of Friuli. It was popular in Venice in the 18th century.

JOHANN SEBASTIAN BACH has a forlana in his C Major Orchestral Suite, BWV 1066, and MAURICE RAVEL included a forlane in his *Tombeau de Couperin*.

form. In music, a concept or organization governing the order, character, METER, and KEY of a composition. The most elementary form is BINARY, in which only two sections are presented. TERNARY form evolves from binary by the addi-

PEOPLE IN MUSIC

Some people believe that the original French song was pointed at the English duke of Marlborough, who led the British in their attacks on France.

fohr-lah′năh

tion of a middle section or by a return of the first section. In a large work, such as a SONATA or SYMPHONY, formal elements are often intermingled and are distinguished by their similarities or contrasts.

In matters of organization, musical form is parallel to that found in literature, drama, and the pictorial arts. As in a living organism that includes separate parts performing different functions, all of which are coordinated for the normal operation of the entire body, so in music form assembles all elements of a musical composition in order to produce the best possible impression of unity. This may be achieved by means of melodic SYMMETRY, alternation of melodic sections, successions of TONES within the same HARMONY, combinations of tones within a CONTRAPUNTAL framework—all driven by a rhythmic flow following a certain natural pulse of strong and weak ACCENTS.

In high developments of the formal elements, a deliberate departure from the basic form of rhythmic or melodic symmetry, harmonic unity, or contrapuntal concordance results in a new type of form that may impress a rigid musical mind as being formless. The accusation of formlessness was directed at RICHARD WAGNER'S ENDLESS MELODY, FRANZ LISZT'S SYMPHONIC POEMS, and IMPRESSIONIST compositions. In the course of time, such "formless" music becomes itself established as a classical form.

Paradoxically, even composers that profess formlessness as their aesthetic aims become inventors of superior forms based on principles of organization far removed from simple symmetry or thematic development. Thus EDGARD VARÈSE propounded the principle of ORGANIZED SOUND as the only requirement of formal composition.

formalism. A critical term used by Soviet authorities to describe modern music, particularly the compositions of the "discredited" composers DMITRI SHOSTAKOVICH and SERGEI PROKOFIEV.

In the Soviet Union, art was meant to serve the people. "Art for art's sake" was considered an elitist idea that was not acceptable in the Soviet state. Because most modern music was perceived to emphasize "form" over "content" (or meaning), Soviet authorities branded it as a product of "formalism."

Fascist governments, such as the Nazis in Germany, as well as Communists, have traditionally been opposed to modern movements in the arts, including music. Art that serves no purpose beyond its enjoyment is considered degenerate. The Nazis and Communists destroyed many works of modern art, and many artists fled those governments to avoid persecution.

formant. In ACOUSTICS, a characteristic of an instrument's construction that intensifies the relative strength (AMPLITUDE) of PARTIALS that lie within a particular FREQUENCY range. As an instrument plays through its COMPASS, different partials fall within the formant's range, accounting for the difference in TIMBRE between the instrument's high and low notes.

In singing, each vowel has its characteristic formants regardless of a singer's range.

fortepiano (It., loud-soft). A term distinguishing the late-18th-century piano from the earlier HARPSICHORD or the later grand piano. Bartolomeo Cristofori called his early-18th-century invention the *gravicembalo col piano e forte* (large CEMBALO with piano [soft] and FORTE [loud] [capabilities]).

Forza del destino, La (The force of destiny). OPERA by GIUSEPPE VERDI, 1862, first produced by an Italian opera company in St. Petersburg.

An eager lover accidentally kills the father of his beloved and flees in horror to a monastery. His intended bride follows him there dressed in a man's attire. Her brother, seeking vengeance, tracks him down, too. Failing to recognize his sister under her monastic garb, he mortally stabs her before dying himself from a wound inflicted by the now completely disoriented monk.

Despite the many plot twists and turns, this work has remained a favorite because of its excellent, melodic score.

Foss (born Fuchs), **Lukas,** brilliant German-born American pianist, conductor, and composer; b. Berlin, Aug. 15, 1922. Foss was a scion of a cultural family. His father was a professor of philosophy, and his mother a talented modern painter. He studied piano and theory with Julius Goldstein-Herford. When the dark shadow of the Nazi dominion descended upon Germany, the family moved to Paris. There Foss studied piano and flute, composition, and orchestration.

In 1937 Foss went to the U.S. and enrolled at the Curtis Institute of Music in Philadelphia, where he studied piano, composition, and conducting. He also spent several sum-

MUSICAL INSTRUMENT

PEOPLE IN MUSIC

mers studying conducting with SERGE KOUSSEVITZKY at the Berkshire Music Center. In 1939–40 he took a course in advanced composition with PAUL HINDEMITH at Yale University. He became a naturalized American citizen in 1942.

Foss's first public career was that of a concert pianist. He elicited high praise for his appearances as a soloist with the N.Y. Philharmonic and other orchestras. He made his conducting debut with the Pittsburgh Symphony Orchestra in 1939. From 1944 to 1950 he was pianist of the Boston Symphony Orchestra, then traveled to Rome on a Fulbright fellowship from 1950 to 1952. From 1953 to 1962 he taught composition at the University of California, Los Angeles, where he also established the Improvisation Chamber Ensemble to perform music of "controlled IMPROVISATION."

In 1960 Foss traveled to Russia, a trip sponsored by the U.S. State Department. From 1963 to 1970 he was music director of the Buffalo Philharmonic. During his tenure there he introduced ultramodern works, much to the annoyance of some regular subscribers. In 1971 he became principal conductor of the Brooklyn Philharmonic, a position he held until 1990. He also established the series "Meet the Moderns" there. Overlapping part of his tenure in Brooklyn, he also conducted the Jerusalem Symphony Orchestra and was music director of the Milwaukee Symphony Orchestra. Foss was elected a member of the American Academy and Institute of Arts and Letters in 1983.

As a composer, Foss has worked in many different styles, idioms, and techniques. His early compositions were marked by the spirit of ROMANTIC lyricism, following the musical language of GUSTAV MAHLER. Some other works reflected the NEOCLASSICISM of Hindemith, while still others suggested the lively rhythms and strongly accented melodies of IGOR STRAVINSKY's productions. Underlying all these various styles was an emphasis on the pulse or basic rhythmic unit, which served as the inspiration for the entire musical work.

Foss's earliest piano pieces were published when he was 15 years old. There followed an uninterrupted flow of compositions in various genres. As a virtuoso pianist, he often played the piano part in his CHAMBER MUSIC, and he conducted a number of his SYMPHONY and CHORAL works.

Among his other compositions are OPERAS, orchestral works, and chamber works, including three STRING QUARTETS.

Foster, Stephen C(ollins), famous American song composer; b. Lawrenceville, Pa., July 4, 1826; d. N.Y., Jan. 13, 1864. Foster learned to play the flute as a child but was essentially self-taught as a musician. He published his first song, *Open Thy Lattice, Love,* when he was 18. While working as a bookkeeper in Cincinnati from 1846 to 1850, he began to submit his songs to various professional performers.

PEOPLE IN MUSIC

Foster's song OLD FOLKS AT HOME (1851), sometimes known as *Swanee River,* established him as a truly American composer. It was published on Oct. 21, 1851, with the subtitle "Ethiopian Melody as sung by Christy's Minstrels." E.P. Christy, the minstrel troupe leader, was listed as the composer of the song in consideration of a small payment to Foster, whose name was not attached to it until the expiration of the copyright in 1879. About 40,000 copies of the song were sold during the year after publication, a substantial number for the time.

Foster married Jane McDowell in Pittsburgh in 1850, but the marriage proved unhappy, and he left her to live alone in N.Y. from 1853 to 1854. He settled there permanently in 1860. His last years were darkened by an addiction to alcohol, and death overtook him as a penniless patient at Bellevue Hospital. Yet his earnings were not small. He received about $15,000 during the last 15 years of his life from his songs.

Many of Foster's songs have become American standards. These include OH! SUSANNA (1848); *Sweetly She Sleeps, My Alice Fair* (1851); MASSA'S IN DE COLD GROUND (1852); MY OLD KENTUCKY HOME (1853); JEANIE WITH THE LIGHT BROWN HAIR (1854); CAMPTOWN RACES (1854); *Gentle Annie* (1856); OLD BLACK JOE (1860); and BEAUTIFUL DREAMER (1864). Other Foster works include HYMNS, piano pieces, and arrangements of popular melodies, published in an anthology, *The Social Orchestra* (N.Y., 1854).

Fountains of Rome, The (Le fontane di Roma). SYMPHONIC POEM by OTTORINO RESPIGHI, 1917, first performed in Rome. Four famous Roman fountains are portrayed in this

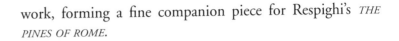

Despite its title, *Four Norwegian Moods* does not include any Norwegian folk melodies, instruments, or rhythms.

work, forming a fine companion piece for Respighi's THE PINES OF ROME.

Four Norwegian Moods. Symphonic SUITE by IGOR STRAVINSKY, 1944. He conducted its first performance in Cambridge, Mass.

Four Sacred Pieces (Verdi). *See* QUATTRO PEZZI SACRI.

Four Saints in Three Acts. Opera by VIRGIL THOMSON, 1934, first produced by the "Society of Friends and Enemies of Modern Music" in Hartford, Conn. The LIBRETTO is by Gertrude Stein, following her unusual writing style.

Thus there are really four acts and a dozen saints, some in duplicate, in the play. Her famous nonsensical line, "Pigeons on the grass, alas," is typical of the text. Thomson's score mirrors Stein's repetitive language by repeating melodic themes. He also mirrors her simplicity by emphasizing bare, simple TRIADIC harmonies. But the opera as a whole is both charming and mesmerizing.

Four Temperaments, The. *See* THEME AND VARIATIONS: THE FOUR TEMPERAMENTS.

4′33″. JOHN CAGE's landmark and notorious work, in three "silent" movements of fixed length (30″, 2′23″, and 1′40″) derived by chance means, for any instrument. It was first performed by DAVID TUDOR at the piano in Woodstock, N.Y., on Aug. 29, 1952.

While often considered a musical joke, *4′33″* is in fact a deep reflection upon both musical content and rhythmic structure. The composer carves up the time; the listener then "hears" what occurs during that time. Cage seems to be saying that almost anything can be music, if one only listens.

Four Tops, The. (Vocals: Levi Stubbs, b. L. Stubbles, Detroit, c.1938; Abdul "Duke" Fakir, b. Detroit, Dec. 26, 1935; Renaldo "Obie" Benson, b. Detroit, c.1937; Lawrence Payton, Jr., b. Detroit, c.1936.) Popular MOTOWN group of the 1960s that continued to perform with its original membership intact over four decades.

PEOPLE IN MUSIC

The group's biggest hits came in the mid-1960s, beginning with 1964's *Baby, I Need Your Lovin'*, and including *I Can't Help Myself (Sugar Pie, Honeybunch), It's the Same Old Song*, and *Reach Out*. These were all written by Motown house hitmakers Holland-Dozier-Holland, who groomed the group's sound in the studio. The Four Tops moved to ABC in the early 1970s, where they continued to enjoy hits, most notably *Ain't No Woman (Like the One I Got)*. However, they soon were relegated to the oldies circuit, where they continue to perform and record. They were inducted into the Rock and Roll Hall of Fame in 1990.

four-hand piano. Pieces written for two players at one piano. One player handles the TREBLE parts and the other the BASS. Once a popular form of AMATEUR music making, such DUETS are now uncommon outside the teaching studio.

fourth. 1. An INTERVAL. 2. The fourth degree in the DIATONIC SCALE. The SUBDOMINANT.

Fourth Symphony. 1. Work by GUSTAV MAHLER, 1901, in G major, first performed in Munich, with Mahler conducting.

This is the most ROMANTIC of Mahler's symphonies. It is in four parts, the last MOVEMENT having a SOPRANO soloist. The two principal themes of the first movement are almost overly sentimental. This quality suggested to the producers of the film *Death in Venice* (1971), after Thomas Mann's novella, to make use of the themes in the film's sound track. *See also* DEATH IN VENICE.

2. Work by PIOTR ILYICH TCHAIKOVSKY, 1878, in F minor, one of his most famous, first performed in Moscow. Its opening SYNCOPATED subject was to Tchaikovsky the call of "Fatum" (fate), although he did not apply this word as a subtitle.

fox-trot. A popular DUPLE-metered ballroom dance that originated in the 1910s, from which a variety of steps evolved. The music derives from the SYNCOPATION of RAGTIME. It was considered a JAZZ dance when European and other composers borrowed the style for their stage works and instrumental SUITES.

The fox-trot was part of a larger craze for "animal" dances, including the grizzly bear and the alligator crawl, of which only the fox-trot survived a short-lived enthusiasm.

Fra Diavolo (Brother Devil). Opera by DANIEL-FRANÇOIS-ESPRIT AUBER, 1830. It tells the story of a notorious bandit, nicknamed Fra Diavolo, who unwittingly involves a woman in a robbery. He is shot, and in his last breaths he urges her to marry her law-abiding sweetheart.

frähn-säz′

française (Fr.). A dance in TRIPLE time, resembling the COUNTRY DANCE. *See also* ÉCOSSAISE.

Francesca da Rimini. Symphonic fantasy by PIOTR ILYICH TCHAIKOVSKY, 1877, first performed in Moscow. The subject was inspired by a tragic episode in Dante's *Inferno*. It tells of two doomed lovers, Francesca and her brother-in-law lover Paolo, who die at the hands of her jealous husband. As an epigraph for this work, Tchaikovsky selected the lines "Nessun maggior dolore / Che ricordarsi del tempo felice / Nella miseria" (There is no greater sorrow than to recall happy times in the midst of misery). Tchaikovsky often repeated this phrase in his letters, applying it to his own life.

The lyric MELODY that represents Francesca is typical of Tchaikovsky's melancholy muse. His depiction of the tempestuous winds of hell, in running CHROMATICS, is very dramatic.

PEOPLE IN MUSIC

Franck, César (-Auguste-Jean-Guillaume-Hubert), great Belgian composer and organist; b. Liège, Dec. 10, 1822; d. Paris, Nov. 8, 1890. Franck studied first at the Royal Conservatory of Liège, where, at the age of nine, he won first prize for singing, and at 12 for piano. As a child prodigy he gave concerts in Belgium.

In 1835 Franck's family moved to Paris, where he studied privately with Anton Reicha, a well-known Czechoslovakian-born teacher and composer. In 1837 Franck entered the Paris Conservatory, studying piano, organ, and THEORY. In 1838 he received the first prize for piano, in 1839 a second prize for COUNTERPOINT, in 1840 a first prize for FUGUE, and in 1841 a second prize for organ.

Franck briefly returned to his home country in 1842, but a year later he was back in Paris, where he remained for the rest of his life. In 1843 he presented there a concert of his CHAMBER MUSIC. In 1846 his first major work, the ORA-TORIO *Ruth,* was given at the Paris Conservatory. In 1848, in the midst of the Paris revolution, he married, and in 1851 he became organist of the church of St.-Jean-St.-François. In 1853 he was named *maître de chapelle* (music director of the chapel school and choir) and, in 1858, organist at Ste.-Clotilde, which position he held until his death.

In 1872 Franck was appointed professor of organ at the conservatory. His organ classes became the training school for a whole generation of French composers. Among his pupils were VINCENT D'INDY, ERNEST CHAUSSON, Pierre Bréville, and a host of others, who eventually formed a school of modern French instrumental music.

Until the appearance of Franck in Paris, operatic art dominated the musical life of the entire nation. The course of instruction at the Paris Conservatory was heavily slanted toward OPERA. By his emphasis on organ music, based on the contrapuntal art of JOHANN SEBASTIAN BACH, Franck swayed the new generation of French musicians toward the ideal of ABSOLUTE MUSIC. The foundation of the famous Schola Cantorum by d'Indy and others in 1894 realized Franck's teachings. Indeed, after the death of d'Indy in 1931, several members withdrew from the Schola Cantorum and organized the École César Franck in 1938.

Franck was not a prolific composer, but his creative powers rose rather than diminished with advancing age. His only mature SYMPHONY was completed when he was 66, his remarkable Violin Sonata was written at the age of 63, and his String Quartet was composed in the last year of his life. He also composed other orchestral works and many pieces for organ and piano, as well as sacred and secular vocal works.

Franck was a classicist in his approach to composition. Clear COUNTERPOINT and full HARMONY are the distinguishing traits of his music. He was not influenced by the WAGNER-LISZT school of ROMANTIC composition, with their large forms, grand harmonies, and sweeping, CHROMATIC melodies. But Franck was not opposed to innovation when he deemed it appropriate. The use of the ENGLISH HORN in his Symphony in D Minor raised quite a few eyebrows among contemporary critics.

PEOPLE IN MUSIC

Franklin, Aretha, outstanding African-American SOUL singer; b. Memphis, Mar. 25, 1942. Her father, the Reverend C. L. Franklin, was a Baptist preacher. The family settled in Detroit, where he established a pastorate. His church became a center of gospel preaching and evangelical group singing. Aretha performed in the church choir as a youngster and toured with her father as a choir member and soloist.

At 18 Aretha went to N.Y., where she quickly attracted attention. Her singing at the Newport Jazz Festival in 1963 led to numerous important engagements. However, her early recordings did not adequately capture her style. In 1967 she signed with a new record label and began working with producer Jerry Wexler. Soon, her unique blend of GOSPEL and R&B—called soul music—was racing up the charts. She had several late 1960s and early 1970s hits, including *R-E-S-P-E-C-T* and *Natural Woman.*

Franklin continued to record and perform through the 1970s, '80s, and '90s. Her career has taken several twists and turns, although she continues to be recognized as "The Queen of Soul." In 1987 she recorded the two-disc *One Lord, One Faith, One Baptism* in her father's church, which many have recognized as a highlight of her later career.

Frau ohne Schatten, Die (The woman without a shadow). OPERA by RICHARD STRAUSS, 1919, first produced in Vienna. An empress, married to an Oriental king, is barren because

Opening page of the score of Die Frau ohne Schatten. (Ira Nowinski/Corbis) ▶

she cannot cast a shadow, a symbol of fertility. Also, her husband's life is in danger. The empress is given a tempting offer to buy a poor woman's shadow. She finally resists, not wishing to deprive the poor woman of her ability to bear a child. For this noble act she is granted the joy of a shadow so that she can become a mother after all, and her husband is saved.

Frederick II (Frederick the Great), king of Prussia; b. Berlin, Jan. 24, 1712; d. Potsdam, Aug. 17, 1786. Frederick was an enlightened patron of music, a flute player of considerable skill, and an amateur composer. He studied flute with JOHANN JOACHIM QUANTZ.

In 1740, when Frederick ascended to the throne, he established a court orchestra and an opera house, under Quantz's direction. CARL PHILIPP EMANUEL BACH was his harpsichordist until 1767. In 1747 JOHANN SEBASTIAN BACH was invited to Potsdam, the fruit of which visit was the elder Bach's *Musical Offering,* based on a theme supposedly written by the king.

In addition to composing 121 flute SONATAS and four flute CONCERTOS, Frederick contributed ARIAS to several OPERAS: *Demofoonte* by Graun (1746), *Il Re pastore* (1747; with Quantz and others), *Galatea ed Acide* (1748; with Hasse, Graun, Quantz, and Nichelmann), and *Il trionfo della fedelitá* (1753; with Hasse and others).

free canon. A CANON written with flexibility as to the rules of canonic composition.

free fugue. A FUGUE written with more or less disregard of strict rules.

free jazz. A jazz style of the 1960s and '70s, characterized by collective IMPROVISATION without reference to preset harmonic or formal structures.

free reed. A family of wind instruments. Unlike single or double reeds, free reeds each produce a specific pitch, so that a separate reed is needed to sound each note. Each free reed consists of a small metal tongue (or reed) that vibrates freely at one end; the other end is secured to a metal frame.

PEOPLE IN MUSIC

It was not unusual for royal patrons to hire composers to ghostwrite their works. It may be that many of Frederick's compositions were in fact written by others.

MUSICAL
INSTRUMENT

There are free-reed keyboard instruments such as the HARMONIUM; mouth-blown instruments such as the Chinese ZHENG, Japanese SHO, and the German HARMONICA; and bellows-driven instruments such as the ACCORDION and CONCERTINA.

Freed, Alan, American DISC JOCKEY and passionate popularizer of ROCK 'N' ROLL; b. Johnstown, Pa., Dec. 15, 1922; d. Palm Springs, Calif., Jan. 20, 1965. Freed's greatest achievement was to desegregate black music by introducing it into white-sponsored radio stations. He was also credited with originating the term *rock 'n' roll* in 1951, although it had been used long before in slang expressions among musicians.

Freed began broadcasting in Cleveland, then went to N.Y. in 1954 to take command of the radio station WINS, which became one of the most popular purveyors of rock 'n' roll. He also acted in the movie *Rock around the Clock* and produced numerous stage shows featuring black and white acts on the same bill, an innovation for the time.

Freed suffered a monumental downfall in 1963, when he pled guilty to charges of "payola," accepting bribes from commercial record companies for putting their songs on the air. On top of that, he was charged with income tax evasion. He lost his position in N.Y. and retired to California. He died soon after, a penniless and forgotten man.

Freeman, "Bud" (Lawrence), American JAZZ tenor saxophonist; b. Chicago, Apr. 13, 1906; d. there, Mar. 15, 1991. Freeman began his career in Chicago playing with the Austin High School Gang, a group of white teenagers who were enthralled with the new jazz music. Originally playing the C melody sax, Freeman switched to the tenor in 1925 and helped popularize it as the leading jazz instrument.

Freeman went to N.Y., where he worked with BIG BANDS led by Ben Pollack, RED NICHOLS, PAUL WHITEMAN, TOMMY DORSEY, and BENNY GOODMAN. He was active with various combos from 1939, including heading a long-running group at the N.Y. jazz club Eddie Condon's. He freelanced from the 1950s on, living in England in the 1970s but returning to his native Chicago in 1980. He fell ill in 1990 and died a year later.

Freischütz, Der (The Free Shooter). OPERA by CARL MARIA VON WEBER, 1821, premiered in Berlin. An ambitious sportsman, in love with a country girl, agrees to trade his soul to the devil for seven magic bullets that will guarantee a victory in a shooting competition. The last bullet must go where the devil directs. The Freischütz hits his six preliminary marks, but the last is aimed at his bride. She is saved by supernatural intervention. The marksman confesses his deal with the devil but is absolved.

Der Freischütz is regarded as the first truly ROMANTIC opera. The vivacious OVERTURE is often performed as a concert piece.

French horn (horn; Ger. *Waldhorn, Horn;* It. *corno;* Sp. *trompa;* Cz. *lesni roh*). A transposing valved BRASS instrument with a spiral CONICAL TUBE (ranging from 9 to 18 inches in length), wide and flaring BELL, and small, funnel-shaped mouthpiece. The modern French horn possesses a rich, sonorous, and mellow tone capable of great expressive power.

The source of the name "French horn" is unclear. The explanation that it is so named to prevent confusion with the ENGLISH HORN is unconvincing. It is sometimes called *Waldhorn* (forest horn) in German, and the Russians transcribed that name as *valtorna*. In its modern (19th-century) construction it is also called *valve horn* to distinguish it from the early valveless horns that could produce only a series of OVERTONES from the horn's FUNDAMENTAL. But even with VALVES enabling it to play the full CHROMATIC scale, the glory of the French horn remains in the production of its natural overtones.

The horn's range is wider than that of any other brass instrument, covering nearly four octaves, with possible extensions beyond the upper limit. Its tone production is most unusual, with its mouthpiece very small and its bell very large. In order to produce high tones, the player must adjust the lips in a precise manner. The danger of hitting a wrong

MUSICAL INSTRUMENT

The French horn descends from ancient instruments of animal horn, ivory, or wood, the valveless circular hunting horn (from the 17th century) being the closest ancestor.

note on the horn in the upper registers haunts even the greatest horn virtuosos.

One of the most difficult horn solos occurs in *Til Eulenspiegel's Merry Pranks* by RICHARD STRAUSS, in which the player reaches high into the instrument's range. The story goes that the hornist told Strauss before the first rehearsal that the passage was unplayable, to which Strauss retorted that he had gotten the idea for this part while listening to the horn player himself practice during the tuning periods.

Prior to the invention of valves and CROOKS, the natural horn yielded only the harmonics produced by its single fundamental; hence, an individual instrument's use was extremely limited. Horn parts were written in CLASSICAL-era scores in the key of the composition. From the early 18th century on, when a key change occurred, the player could insert or remove a piece of tubing, called a crook, to obtain the right fundamental. With the advent of the chromatic horn, parts came to be written and notated almost invariably in the key of F, and are still notated in an unusual manner: players transpose a fifth down in the TREBLE CLEF or a fourth up in the BASS CLEF (the latter being used only for the lowest notes).

Horn players, like all brass players, have to empty their instrument periodically to remove the condensed water vapor that accumulates in the instrument's chambers. They make use of a special key colorfully called the "spit valve." It is said that a famous violinist who was engaged to play the Horn Trio of JOHANNES BRAHMS demanded a pair of galoshes before he went onstage.

French overture. *See* OVERTURE.

French sixth. The common name for a chord containing an AUGMENTED sixth between the bottom and the top notes, other intervals from the bottom being a major third and an augmented fourth, as in A♭, C, D, and F♯. The chord resolves to either the TONIC MAJOR or MINOR TRIAD (second INVERSION) or the DOMINANT triad (root position):

F♯ resolves to	G	*or*	G	*or*	G
D	E		E♭		D
C	C		C		B
A♭	G		G		G

Freni (born Fregni), **Mirella,** noted Italian soprano; b. Modena, Feb. 27, 1935. Freni studied voice with her uncle, Dante Arcelli, making her first public appearance at the age of 11. Her accompanist was a child pianist named Leone Magiera, whom she married in 1955. She later studied voice with Ettore Campogalliani and made her operatic debut in Modena in 1955, as Micaela in CARMEN. In 1959 she sang with the Amsterdam Opera Company at the Holland Festival, then at the Glyndebourne Festival (1960), Covent Garden in London (1961), and La Scala in Milan (1962).

Freni gained acclaim as Mimi in the film version of LA BOHÈME, produced at La Scala, with HERBERT VON KARAJAN conducting, which was released in 1963. A year later, when La Scala toured Russia, she joined the company and sang Mimi at the Bolshoi Theater in Moscow. She also chose the role of Mimi for her American debut with the Metropolitan Opera in N.Y. in 1965. Freni subsequently sang with the Vienna State Opera, the Bavarian State Opera in Munich, the Teatro San Carlo in Naples, and the Rome Opera. In 1976 she traveled with the Paris Opéra during its first American tour.

In addition to Mimi, Freni sang the roles of Susanna, Zerlina, Violetta, Amelia in *Simon Boccanegra,* and Manon. She won acclaim for her vivid portrayal of Tatiana in EUGENE ONEGIN, singing this role with many major opera companies, including the Metropolitan Opera in 1989. In 1990 she appeared as Lisa in TCHAIKOVSKY's *Pique Dame* at La Scala. In 1992 she sang Alice Ford at the Metropolitan Opera, the same year also appearing as Mimi in both Barcelona and Rome. In 1994 she sang Fedora at Covent Garden, and then returned to the Metropolitan in the same role in 1997.

Freni married Nicolai Ghiaurov in 1981; she subsequently appeared frequently with him in opera performances around the world.

frequency. The rate of vibration of a string or air column, which determines the PITCH it produces. In concert tuning, the A above middle C equals 440 cycles per second (abbrev. cps, Hz).

Frequency modulation (FM) is a technique in ELECTRONIC MUSIC whereby the frequency of an electronic signal (the carrier) is affected by a second signal (the program). If the program signal has both low frequency and low AMPLITUDE, the result is VIBRATO. Raising the program's amplitude

Curiously enough, Freni's mother and the mother of the future celebrated tenor LUCIANO PAVAROTTI worked for a living in the same cigarette factory. Curiouser still, the future opera stars shared the same wet nurse!

creates GLISSANDO effects; raising the program's frequency creates complex TIMBRES called *sidebands*. Compare AMPLITUDE MODULATION.

Frère Jacques. French nursery rhyme and ROUND, first published in a *Recueil de rondes* in 1860. The melody dates to around 1775.

PEOPLE IN MUSIC

Frescobaldi, Girolamo, great Italian organist and composer; b. Ferrara (baptized), Sept. 9, 1583; d. Rome, Mar. 1, 1643. Frescobaldi studied organ initially in his hometown. By the age of 14 he was organist at the Accademia della Morte there. In early 1607 became organist of San Maria in Trastevere, then, in June, traveled to Brussels in a papal delegation.

Frescobaldi published his first work, a collection of five-part MADRIGALS, in Antwerp in 1608. Returning to Rome in the same year, he was appointed organist at St. Peter's. He retained this all-important post until his death, with the exception of the years 1628 to 1634, when he was court organist in Florence. A significant indication of Frescobaldi's importance among musicians of his time was that Johann Jakob Froberger, who was court organist in Vienna, came to Rome especially to study with him from 1637 to 1641.

Frescobaldi's place in music history is great. Particularly as a keyboard composer, he exercised a decisive influence on the style of the early BAROQUE. He enlarged the expressive resources of keyboard music so as to include daring CHROMATIC progressions and passing DISSONANCES, called *durezze* (harshnesses). In Frescobaldi's terminology *toccata di durezza* signified a work using dissonances. He used similar procedures in organ VARIATIONS on CHORALE themes (*Fiori musicali,* 1635).

Frescobaldi published 12 books of keyboard music, one book of sacred vocal music, three books of madrigals, and scattered individual pieces.

MUSICAL INSTRUMENT

fret. A narrow, raised wedge of wood, metal, or ivory crossing the FINGERBOARD of plucked string instruments, e.g., MANDOLIN, GUITAR, BANJO, LUTE, and BALALAIKA. The strings are "stopped" (pressed by the fingers), guaranteeing proper pitch. The intervals between frets are usually SEMI-TONES.

friction drum (U.K. pasteboard rattle; Ger. *Waldteufel*). A clay pot with a membrane stretched over its top through which a stick or a sturdy string is passed. The stick is rubbed with a wet finger to produce several successive tones. This type of drum is prevalent throughout the world, including England (*pasteboard rattle*), Germany (*Reibtrommel; Wald-teufel,* forest devil), and France (*cri de la belle-mère,* mother-in-law's cry).

Friedenstag, Der (The day of peace). Opera by RICHARD STRAUSS, 1938, produced in Munich. Its subject is the peace that concluded the Thirty Years' War that devastated Europe. The opera, written with the customary brilliance that distinguishes works of Strauss, ends with a CHORAL invocation to peace. Its repeated performances on the eve of Hitler's plunge into total war held special meaning to Europeans deprived of their freedom.

Friedhofer, Hugo (William), American composer of FILM MUSIC; b. San Francisco, May 3, 1901; d. Los Angeles, May 17, 1981. Friedhofer played cello in theater orchestras and also studied composition. In 1929 he went to Hollywood, where he worked as an arranger and composer for early sound films.

In 1935 Friedhofer was hired as an orchestrator for Warner Brothers. He received valuable instruction from the immigrant composers ERICH KORNGOLD and MAX STEINER, who also worked at the studio. He also studied with ARNOLD SCHOENBERG and ERNST TOCH, who were both living in Los Angeles at that time.

Friedhofer wrote his first complete film score for *The Adventures of Marco Polo* in 1938; in the following years he composed music for about 70 films. His music for *The Best Years of Our Lives* won the Academy Award in 1946. Other film scores included *Vera Cruz, Violent Saturday, The Sun Also Rises,* and *The Young Lions.*

Friedhofer was highly esteemed by the Hollywood theatrical community and by his colleagues in the film studios

MUSICAL INSTRUMENT

PEOPLE IN MUSIC

When a Hollywood producer told Friedhofer to use French horns in a film taking place in France, he agreed, shaking his head silently at the producer's literal mindedness. As a private joke, he decided to use a theme on English horn in the same film when a shot of the white cliffs of Dover came into view.

for his ability to create an appropriate musical background for the action on the screen. He was the only California native of all the famous film composers in Hollywood, the majority of whom were Germans and Austrians.

Friedman, Ignaz, famous Polish pianist; b. Podgorze, near Krakow, Feb. 14, 1882; d. Sydney, Australia, Jan. 26, 1948. Friedman studied theory in Leipzig and piano in Vienna. In 1904 he launched an extensive career as a concert pianist, subsequently giving about 2,800 concerts in Europe, America, Australia, Japan, China, and South Africa. In 1941 he settled in Sydney, Austrlia.

Friedman was renowned as an interpreter of FRÉDÉRIC CHOPIN. He prepared an annotated edition of Chopin's works in 12 volumes and edited piano compositions of ROBERT SCHUMANN and FRANZ LISZT. Friedman also wrote 100 or so pieces for piano in an effective salon manner, among them a group of *Fantasiestücke.*

Friedrich II (der Grosse). *See* FREDERICK II (FREDERICK THE GREAT).

Friml (born Frimel), (Charles) **Rudolf,** famous Bohemian-American OPERETTA composer; b. Prague, Dec. 2, 1879; d. Los Angeles, Nov. 12, 1972. Friml studied piano, theory, and composition at the Prague Conservatory. He toured Austria, England, Germany, and Russia as accompanist to JAN KUBELÍK, going with him to the U.S. in 1900 and again in 1906.

Friml remained in the U.S. after the second tour, giving numerous recitals and appearing as soloist with several orchestras (played his Piano Concerto with the N.Y. Symphony Orchestra). He also composed assiduously. He lived in N.Y. and Hollywood, composing for the stage and motion pictures. He was best known for his many successful operettas, including *The Firefly* (1912), *High Jinks* (1913), *Katinka* (1915), *Rose-Marie* (1924; very popular), and *The Vagabond King* (1925; highly successful). Friml also composed other songs and a great number of piano pieces in a light vein. In 1937 MGM made a film of *The Firefly,* the popular *Donkey Serenade* being added to the original score.

friss (friska; Hung.). The rapid second section of the Hungarian VERBUNKOS, a type of CSÁRDÁS or dance.

frog (U.K., nut; Ger. *Frosch;* Fr. *hausse;* It. *tallone*). The lower part of a BOW, nearest the player's hand, where the bow hair is tightened or loosened; also called the NUT. Playing "at the frog" produces a hard, vibratoless sound.

From the House of the Dead (*Z mrtvého domu*). OPERA by LEOŠ JANÁČEK, 1930, to his own LIBRETTO based on Fyodor Dostoyevsky's partly autobiographical novel describing his Siberian exile. It was produced posthumously in Brno.

From the New World. Symphony No. 9 in E Minor of AN-TONÍN DVOŘÁK, 1893, his most famous. It was so named because he composed it during his sojourn in the U.S. It was first performed by the N.Y. Philharmonic.

Of its four movements, the most popular is the second, marked *Largo,* which suggests an African-American SPIRI-TUAL. One of Dvořák's American pupils, William Arms Fisher, set words to the tune to create *Going Home.* The *Largo* is set in the key of D♭ major, miles away tonally from the TONIC E of the symphony.

From the New World was originally published as Dvořák's Symphony No. 5, but the discovery and introduction into the repertoire of four earlier unpublished symphonies led to its renumbering, causing great confusion among cataloguers.

From the Steeples and the Mountains. A remarkable work by CHARLES IVES, 1905, scored for church BELLS and BRASS. Ives wrote in the score: "After the brass stops, the chimes sound on until they die away. . . . From the steeples — the bells! — Then the rocks on the mountains begin to shout!" As with most works by Ives, it was not performed until decades after its composition, receiving its first public performance in 1965.

Froschquartett (Ger., "Frog" Quartet). Nickname of FRANZ JOSEPH HAYDN's String Quartet in D Major, op.50/6, 1787. The colorful nickname may be derived from the finale's UNI-SON *bariolage* effect, where two strings, one open and one

MUSICAL
INSTRUMENT

stopped, are bowed in succession to produce a quasi-TREMOLO with constantly changing tone color.

frottola (It.; plur., *frottole*). A genre of POLYPHONIC song of the Italian RENAISSANCE period, popular in northern Italy between c.1470 and 1530. The term may have been derived from the Italian *frocta,* meaning a gathering of random thoughts, or *frotta,* meaning a flock. In any case, the frottola was composed of unusual or unconnected melodies.

Many anthologies of frottole was published in the early 16th century. They are arranged in simple harmonies with SYMMETRICAL rhythms, with the potential for being accompanied on the LUTE or VIOLS. Often only the TREBLE (soprano) part was sung.

Stylistically, the frottola is related to the Spanish VILLANCICO and the Italian STRAMBOTTO. It evolved from the reading of poetry to musical accompaniment, widespread in the 15th century. The musical structure was fitted to the metrical and rhyme schemes of the poetry selected. Matching music to the texts was of little concern to the frottolists. Only when the genre evolved into the MADRIGAL did this become important.

The *Black-Key* étude of FRÉDÉRIC CHOPIN is in the key of F♯ major. ALEXANDER SCRIABIN was fond of this tonality until he abandoned key signatures altogether.

F-sharp major. A tonality that has six sharps in its key signature. It rarely appears as the principal key of a large work for orchestra, chorus, or piano. But curiously, it is favored by children of a tender age on account of its digitally convenient PENTATONIC disposition on the black keys of the piano.

The enharmonic tonality of G♭ major, with six flats in its key signature, enjoys the favor of ROMANTIC composers almost as much as its sharp alter ego.

F-sharp minor. This key, with three sharps in its signature, is characterized by a delicacy of sentiment. There are but few symphonies in the key of F♯ minor, the most notable being the *FAREWELL* SYMPHONY of FRANZ JOSEPH HAYDN. NIKOLAI MIASKOVSKY, who wrote symphonies in practically every major and minor key, assigned F♯ minor to his 21st, entitled, perhaps significantly, *Symphonie-Fantaisie.*

Two Russian piano CONCERTOS, the first by SERGEI RACHMANINOFF and the only piano concerto by ALEXANDER SCRIABIN, are in the key of F♯ minor. The romantic essence of these two concertos is unmistakenly manifested.

fugato (It., like a fugue). A passage or movement consisting of fugal imitations, but not worked out fully, as a true FUGUE.

foo-gah'tōh

fughetta (It.). A short FUGUE; a fugal EXPOSITION.

foo-get'tah

fuging (fuguing) **tune.** A type of choral PSALM or HYMN that became popular in New England in the last half of the 18th century. It is derived from the old English type of psalmody in which a hymn has a rudimentary CANONIC section before the concluding cadence.

In America the fuging tunes of WILLIAM BILLINGS became well known, and some enthusiastic musicologists describe them as the earliest native American music forms. HENRY COWELL, WILLIAM SCHUMAN, and JOHN CAGE based works on Billings's tunes.

fugue (from It., *fuga,* flight; Ger. *Fuge*). The most highly developed form of CONTRAPUNTAL IMITATION. It is based on the principle of the equality of the parts: a THEME proposed by one part is taken up successively by all participating parts, thus bringing each in turn into special prominence.

The elements essential to every fugue are:

The SUBJECT (DUX, THEME, ANTECEDENT, or leader)

The ANSWER (COMES, companion, CONSEQUENT, or follower)

The COUNTERSUBJECT (a continuation of the primary theme, which accompanies the first statement of the answer)

The STRETTO (a final development in which subject and answer are rapidly alternated)

To these are commonly added EPISODES, PEDAL POINT, and CODA.

fewg

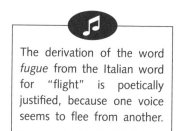

The derivation of the word *fugue* from the Italian word for "flight" is poetically justified, because one voice seems to flee from another.

With the fugue the art of POLYPHONY reached its supreme achievement. Historically, the fugue is a successor to the CANON. It is also related to the CACCIA. But the fugue is far from being a mere development of the canon. The element of imitation is common to both, but while the canon is mechanical in its structure, the fugue introduces an entirely new principle of imitation through MODULATION (a change in key) from the TONIC to the DOMINANT.

The classic fugue opens with the statement of the principal subject in a single unaccompanied voice. In the old Latin treatises on fugue, this subject is called DUX, the leader. Its imitation, or answer, in the key of the dominant, is COMES, the companion. When the comes enters in another voice, the part of the dux continues as a suitable counterpoint to the comes. This continuation of the dux is called the countersubject.

Fugues of only two voices are rare. In a fugue for three voices, the third voice enters again in the tonic imitating the dux note for note, but in another octave. In the meantime new contrapuntal material is entered in the original part of the dux. If there are four voices, the fourth voice comes in again in the dominant, imitating the comes note by note. Fugues of five or more voices alternate in the keys of the tonic and the dominant, following the form of the dux and the comes.

In a *real fugue,* the answer is an exact transposition of the subject; in a *tonal fugue,* the subject is modified in the answer in order to lead back to the original key. For example, the simple triadic phrase C–E–G, literally transposed into the dominant as G–B–D, would form an exact and therefore *real answer.* In a tonal answer, however, the third note would be altered to match (and thus emphasize) the tonic of the dux; thus, C–E–G is answered in the dominant as G–B–C. Once the tonal adjustment is made in the opening of the comes, the transposition of the original subject into the dominant key is resumed. (Not all fugal subjects can accommodate a tonal answer.)

The fugue is not the rigid form that its formidable reputation makes it out to be. The entries do not have to follow one another in mechanical succession. JOHANN SEBASTIAN

BACH, one of the creators of the art of the fugue, never followed the rules that are laid down in the textbooks.

The formal structure of the fugue often consists of three sections: EXPOSITION, episodic development, and return. The exposition presents the subject and answer in the tonic and the dominant, respectively. In the episodic development, the subject wanders far away from the initial keys. It is then broken up into fragments, appearing in a variety of keys, but usually not far from the principal key along the cycle of scales. Modulatory passages alternate with brief restatements of the subject in nontonic keys.

These phrases are tossed about in free interplay until the dominant of the principal key is once again sounded, heralding the entrance of the dux. The return is then celebrated in all solemnity, often followed by a coda or codetta, where the dux and the comes are compressed and foreshortened. With the return, a STRETTO may make its appearance, in which the theme and answer are stated in close canonic succession. If used, the pedal point is on the DOMINANT, preliminary to the conclusion on the tonic.

Many alterations may take place. The dux and comes are stood on their heads by melodic INVERSION, subjecting the harmony to the greatest stress. Unimaginable dissonances can be formed in the process, and yet in Bach the primary drive never falters.

To suggest the magnificent symmetry of the main proportions of the fugue, Ferruccio Busoni was moved in his monumental edition of Bach's *WELL-TEMPERED CLAVIER* to place an illustration showing Gothic cathedrals on the title page. This architectural style seemed to him to be a fitting complement to Bach's grand design. The fugue is indeed a cathedral of polyphony, in which the principal lines are never obscured by the gargoyles of florid ornamentation.

full. Whole, complete, all. *Full anthem,* written for CHORUS without solos; *full band,* a band or orchestra having all the customary instruments; *full choir,* draw all organ stops of the choir (great, swell); *full chord,* a chord having one or more of its original three or four tones doubled in the octave; *full orchestra,* compare *full band; full organ,* with all stops and couplers drawn; *full to fifteenth,* draw all stops but mixtures and reeds; *full score,* orchestral score in which all parts are written out and aligned vertically.

fundamental (note, tone). 1. The root note of a chord. 2. A tone consisting of a harmonic series; a generator of harmonics; a prime tone. *Fundamental bass* (Fr., basse fondamentale), the progression of harmonic roots, as proposed by

Jean-Philippe Rameau (1722); *fundamental chord, triad, see* CHORDS; *fundamental position,* any arrangement of chordal tones in which the root remains the lowest; root position.

funeral march (Ger. *Trauermarsch*). A march in slow $\frac{4}{4}$ time in a minor key, sometimes used as a part of a larger work. The most famous funeral march is the slow movement from FRÉDÉRIC CHOPIN's piano sonata in B-flat minor (1839, op.35), often played at the funerals of important persons.

Fünf Orchesterstücke. Orchestral suite by ARNOLD SCHOENBERG (1909, op.16). It introduced many new techniques, such as DISSONANT COUNTERPOINT, ATONAL MELODIES, and sequences of tone colors. It was first performed in London in 1912.

Funiculi-Funicula. One of the most popular Neapolitan songs. It was written by Luigi Denza in 1880 to celebrate the opening of the funicular railway (a cable car) leading to the crater of Mt. Vesuvius. It was commonly believed that it was a folk song and was used as such by NIKOLAI RIMSKY-KORSAKOV and RICHARD STRAUSS in their orchestra works.

funk. 1. An African-American popular music that developed in the 1960s from African POLYRHYTHMS and CALL-AND-RESPONSE textures. Funk songs often use a single chord or a few alternating, sometimes complex harmonies (VAMPING), through which clipped, SYNCOPATED lines emerge in the electric guitar and bass parts, drums and percussion, keyboards, winds (saxophones, trumpets), and vocal parts. Interjections by different instruments and voices, often repeated, is another typical element.

While many of these elements had existed in earlier popular music styles, the best funk has a highly diverse and often surprisingly thick texture that lends it a unique tension (influencing REGGAE tremendously). Some of the greatest funk performers have been JAMES BROWN, Sly and the Family Stone, Kool and the Gang, Rufus, Ohio Players, War, and Parliament/Funkadelic.

Funk has been able to blend into successive styles. It has always been associated with African-American social protest. Funk was greatly influential on 1980s HIP-HOP, which adapted funk's textures to electronic techniques, editing, and sampling, providing a background for RAP. Reggae musicians (such as BOB MARLEY and Peter Tosh) drew upon funk, although reggae rhythms quickly became overused. As a dance music, funk led quite naturally into the faster, simpler, and less politically threatening DISCO style.

Funny Face. Musical by GEORGE GERSHWIN, 1927. A woman seeks and regains her pearls from her brother with the help of her boyfriend. Includes 'S Wonderful and My One and Only.

Funny Girl. Musical by Jule Styne, 1964. It tells the biography of Fanny Brice, the Ziegfeld Follies star who rose from rags to riches and fell in love with a gangster. The show launched BARBRA STREISAND, who played the lead part. Includes Don't Rain on My Parade and People.

Funny Thing Happened on the Way to the Forum, A. Musical by STEPHEN SONDHEIM, 1962, based on the Roman farces of Plautus. A cunning slave will gain his freedom by supplying his owner with a particular beauty from the bordello next door. However, several others covet her, too, including the owner's son. Includes Comedy Tonight; Everybody Ought to Have a Maid; and Love, I Hear.

furniture music (Fr. *musique d'amueblement*). A descriptor introduced by ERIK SATIE to describe what has come to be called "background music." This type of music can be as artful as AMBIENT MUSIC or as commercial as MUZAK.

Furtwängler, (Gustav Heinrich Ernst Martin) **Wilhelm,** celebrated German conductor; b. Berlin, Jan. 25, 1886; d. Ebersteinburg, Nov. 30, 1954. His father, Adolf Furtwängler, was a noted archeologist. He grew up in Munich, where he studied piano and music privately. From 1908 to 1909, he worked as a rehearsal pianist in Munich. In 1910, he be-

As an experiment in furniture music, at a performance at a Paris art gallery, Satie placed his musicians in separate groups. He urged the public to ignore them, to speak loudly, and not to listen with attention. The performers were free to play anything they wished.

came third conductor at the Strasbourg Opera. This led to important engagements in Lubeck, Mannheim, and finally Vienna, Berlin, and Frankfurt through the mid-'20s.

A decisive turn in Furtwängler's career was his appointment in 1922 as chief conductor of the Berlin Philharmonic as successor to Arthur Nikisch. He also assumed Nikisch's post of kapellmeister of the Leipzig Gewandhaus Orchestra, which he held until 1928. In 1925 he made his American debut with the N.Y. Philharmonic, which was greeted with general acclaim, returning again in 1926 and 1927. In 1927 he was elected conductor of the Vienna Philharmonic, holding the post of artistic director until 1930, and continuing as guest conductor later on. A series of awards and honors were bestowed on him in the late '20s and early '30s in recognition of his increasingly important position in the German musical world.

In 1933, Furtwängler was appointed director of the Berlin State Opera and vice-president of the Reichsmusikkammer. Although increasingly troubled by the encroachment of the Nazi authorities on both his programs and the personnel of the Berlin Philharmonic, Furtwängler managed to maintain his independence for a while and succeeded in retaining several Jewish players in the group. In 1934, he conducted PAUL HINDEMITH's *Symphony: Mathis der Maler*. The performance was sharply berated by the Nazi propaganda minister, Joseph Goebbels, who called Hindemith a "cultural Bolshevist" and "spiritual non-Aryan" (referring to Hindemith's half-Jewish wife).

In the face of continued Nazi interference, Furtwängler decided to resign all of his posts in late 1934. However, a few months later he made an uneasy peace with the Nazi authorities and agreed to return as a conductor with the Berlin Philharmonic, giving his first concert in the spring of 1935. In 1936 he was offered a contract as permanent conductor of the N.Y. Philharmonic, but had to decline the prestigious offer after he was accused by some American musicians of being a Nazi collaborator.

In 1937, Furtwängler went to London to participate in the musical celebrations in honor of the coronation of King George VI. In 1939 he was made a Commander of the Legion of Honor by the French government. After the outbreak of World War II, he confined his activities to Germany and Austria.

Continuing to be loyal to Germany but with ambivalent feelings toward the Nazi government, Furtwängler went to Switzerland in 1945, where he remained during the last months of the war. He returned to Germany in 1946. He faced the Allied Denazification Court and was absolved from the charges of pro-Nazi activities that year. In 1947, he conducted the Berlin Philharmonic for the first time since the end of the war, leading an all-Beethoven concert to great acclaim. He also renewed his close association with the Vienna Philharmonic and the Salzburg Festival.

Furtwängler was tentatively engaged to conduct the Chicago Symphony Orchestra in 1949, but the project was canceled when public opinion proved hostile. In western Europe, however, he took both the Vienna and Berlin Philharmonic orchestras on a number of major tours and was received most enthusiastically. He also became a regular conductor with the Philharmonia Orchestra of London. In 1951 he reinaugurated the Bayreuth Festival by conducting BEETHOVEN's 9TH SYMPHONY, and in 1952 he resumed his post as chief conductor of the Berlin Philharmonic.

His last years of life were clouded by increasing deafness, so that his podium had to be wired for sound. He was to conduct the Berlin Philharmonic on its first American tour in the spring of 1955, but death intervened. HERBERT VON KARAJAN was elected his successor.

Furtwängler was a perfect embodiment of the great tradition of the German ROMANTIC school of conducting. His interpretations of the music of LUDWIG VAN BEETHOVEN, FRANZ SCHUBERT, ROBERT SCHUMANN, JOHANNES BRAHMS, ANTON BRUCKNER, and RICHARD WAGNER were models of formal purity. He never strove to achieve personal magic with the audience, and never ranked with such charismatic conductors as LEOPOLD STOKOWSKI and SERGE KOUSSEVITZKY in this respect. But to professional musicians he remained a legendary master of orchestral sound and symmetry of formal development of symphonic music.

Furtwängler was also a composer. Quite naturally, the style of his works followed the ROMANTIC tradition, although any lyrical outbursts were restrained by his severe

Did Furtwängler collaborate with the Nazis? Although freed of charges in the trials following World War II, he remains a controversial figure. A recent biography repeated charges that he was at least somewhat swept up in the Nazi turmoil.

sense of propriety. Additionally, he wrote several books on music.

fusion. *See* JAZZ-FUNK; ROCK.

futurism. A modern literary and musical movement that originated in Italy early in the 20th century. It declared a rebellion against traditional art of all kinds and preached the use of noises in musical composition.

Futurism emerged under the aegis of the Italian poet F.T. MARINETTI (1876–1942). Its musical credo was formulated by FRANCESCO BALILLA PRATELLA (1880–1955) in his *Manifesto of Futurist Musicians* (Milan, 1910) and supplemented by a *Technical Manifesto of Futurist Music* (1911). In 1913 LUIGI RUSSOLO (1885–1947) published his own Futurist manifesto (*L'arte dei rumori,* The art of noises).

In these and other works, the Italian futurists proclaimed their complete disassociation from CLASSICAL, ROMANTIC, and IMPRESSIONIST music. They announced their aim to build an entirely new music inspired by the reality of life in the new century, with the machine as the source of inspiration. And since modern machines were most conspicuous by the noise they made, Pratella and Russolo believed noise should be a key part of music-making. Russolo designed special noise instruments and subdivided them into six categories. His instruments were rudimentary and crude, with amplification obtained by megaphones, but there is no denying that the Futurists provided a prophetic vision of the electronic future of 50 years later.

It is interesting to note that most Futurist musicians and poets were also painters. Their pictures, notably those of Russolo, emphasized color rather than machinelike abstractions, and generally approximated the manner of abstract expressionism.

The Futurist music by Pratella and others emphasized the WHOLE-TONE scale (a scale consisting made up only of MAJOR SECONDS). The Futurists gave MONODY (a single melody part) preference over POLYPHONY, and steady RHYTHM to asymmetry. Although their music has not survived in performance, they opened the gates to the experimenters of the actual chronological future.

fuzztone. A distortion effect used primarily on ELECTRIC GUITAR in ROCK. The fuzztone is usually controlled by an effects box, placed at the guitarist's feet. The fuzztone activating button causes the guitar's signal to overdrive the amplifier, creating a highly controlled FEEDBACK with the desired "dirty" and powerful "fuzz" sound.

G

G. 1. The fifth (DOMINANT) degree of the C major scale. In France, Italy, Spain, and Russia, *Sol.* SOLMIZATION is the practice of singing scales beginning with Sol, the lowest note of the GUIDONIAN HAND.

2. *G., gauche* in *m.g.* (main gauche, left hand). 3. *G.* (*G.O.*), grand orgue (great organ).

G major (Ger. *G dur*). This is a favorite key of CLASSICAL and ROMANTIC composers and their public. Its TONIC, DOMINANT, and SUBDOMINANT are strongly represented on the open strings of the violin family. It suggests a cloudless landscape and warm sunshine. Not as identifiably pastoral as the key of F major, G major is wonderfully suitable for solos on the oboe or the flute, occasionally echoed by a muted horn.

G minor (Ger. *G moll*). This is a key of earnest meditation. Like G major, its TONIC and DOMINANT are represented by two open strings on every instrument of the string family. As a relative key of B-flat major, it provides for natural MODULATIONS (movements from key to key), especially for woodwind and brass instruments.

Gabrieli, Andrea, called Andrea di Cannaregio, eminent Italian organist and composer, uncle of GIOVANNI GABRIELI; b. Venice, c.1510; d. there, 1586. Gabriel studied at the church of S. Marco and was a member of its choir in 1536, then was organist at S. Geremia in Cannaregio from 1557 to 1558. He also was in Frankfurt for the coronation of Maximilian II, serving as court organist of Duke Albrecht V of Bavaria.

In 1566, Gabrieli returned to Venice and was appointed second organist at S. Marco, becoming first organist on Jan. 1, 1585, succeeding the organist and composer CLAUDIO

GUIDO D'AREZZO (c. 991–c. 1033), an Italian monk and musical educator, is famous for many important innovations in teaching music. One was the naming of the scale notes *Ut, Re, Mi, Fa, Sol, La,* establishing standard names for each degree. Another was developing the four-line music staff for notation. Finally, he pioneered the GUIDONIAN HAND, a way for choir directors to indicate the notes to be sung by assigning different scale tones to different parts of the hand.

Among the enormous number of symphonic works in G major are:

The *Oxford Symphony* and *Surprise Symphony* of Franz Joseph Haydn

Wolfgang Amadeus Mozart's entrancing *Eine kleine Nachtmusik*

Ludwig van Beethoven's Fourth Piano Concerto

Antonín Dvořák and Gustav Mahler's Fourth Symphonies

MERULO (1533–1604). He enjoyed a great reputation as an organist (his concerts with Merulo, on two organs, were popular attractions). Among his pupils was his nephew Hans Leo Hassler, who also became an organist and composer.

A prolific composer, Gabrieli wrote a large number of works, many of which were published posthumously, edited by his nephew. He was equally adept in sacred music of the greatest spirituality and in instrumental music, as well as in MADRIGALS, often of a comic nature. He was one of the first composers to mix instrumental and vocal forces in the *coro spezzato* style, in motets, masses, psalms, and sacred concertos.

Gabrieli, Giovanni, celebrated Italian organist, composer, and teacher, nephew of ANDREA GABRIELI; b. Venice, between 1554 and 1557; d. there, Aug. 12, 1612. Gabrieli lived in Munich from 1575 to 1579. In 1584 he was engaged to substitute for CLAUDIO MERULO as first organist at S. Marco in Venice, and in 1585 he was permanently appointed as second organist (his uncle meanwhile took charge of the first organ). He retained this post until his death.

As a composer, Gabrieli stands at the head of the Venetian school. He was probably the first to write vocal works with parts for instrumental groups in various combinations, partly specified, partly left to the conductor. These were used as accompaniment to the vocalists as well as interspersed instrumental sinfonie (*Sacrae symphoniae*).

Gabrieli is also important because he developed several ideas that were in the air and taught them to his pupils. These included:

Free handling of several choirs in the many-voiced vocal works

"Concerted" solo parts and duets in the few-voiced vocal works

Speech rhythm (following the natural rhythm of speech in creating a rhythmic accompaniment to the lyrics)

Trio-SONATA texture (organizing a piece following the sonata form)

Countless dances for piano are also in G major, including Ignacy Paderewski's celebrated *Minuet in G.*

One of the greatest symphonies IN G MINOR IS WOLFGANG AMADEUS MOZART's Symphony No. 40, in which the key is seldom abandoned in the lively first movement, the minuet, and the finale. Among FRANZ JOSEPH HAYDN's symphonies, *La poule* (The Hen) is in G minor.

There are any number of solo pieces for violin and other instruments in the key of G minor, including MAX BRUCH's Violin Concerto.

The key also lies well for the piano. Among notable examples are the Piano Concerto by ANTONÍN DVOŘÁK and the popular Second Piano Concerto by CAMILLE SAINT-SAËNS.

Novel dissonance treatment (introducing new and unusual harmonies)

Root progressions in fifths (harmonies based on a series of root chords harmonized in fifths)

Use of tonal and range levels for structural purposes (taking advantage of an instrument's range and tone in assigning it a specific part)

Coloristic effects (using instruments for specific purposes in the orchestration to underscore an idea expressed in the music)

Through his numerous German pupils (particularly Heinrich Schütz) and other followers, Gabrieli gave new direction to the development of music.

Gabrieli's instrumental music helped to spark the composition of German instrumental ensemble music, which reached its greatest heights in the symphonic and CHAMBER MUSIC works of the CLASSIC masters. Of interest also is the fact that one of his RICERCARI, a four-part work written in 1595, is an early example of the "FUGUE with episodes."

Gabrieli's vocal compositions include sacred CONCERTOS, sacred symphonies, and secular concerted MADRIGALS. His instrumental works include organ intonations, canzonas and SONATAS (both for ensemble with BASSO CONTINUO), TOCCATAS, FANTASIAS, MOTET and sacred symphonic intabulations, and the famous *Sonata pian e forte* (1597).

PEOPLE IN MUSIC

Gabrilowitsch, Ossip (Salomonovich), notable Russian-American pianist and conductor; b. St. Petersburg, Feb. 7, 1878; d. Detroit, Sept. 14, 1936. From 1888 to 1894, Gabrilowitsch was a pupil at the St. Petersburg Conservatory, studying piano with the famed keyboardist Anton Rubinstein and composition with a number of teachers. He graduated as winner of the Rubinstein Prize, and then spent 1894–96 in Vienna furthering his keyboard studies.

Gabrilowitsch then toured Germany, Austria, Russia, France, and England. His first American tour (debut Carnegie Hall, N.Y., 1900) was eminently successful, as were his subsequent visits between 1901 and 1916.

During the 1912–13 season, Gabrilowitsch gave in Europe a series of six historical concerts illustrating the development of the piano CONCERTO from JOHANN SEBASTIAN BACH to the present day. He repeated the entire series in several of the larger cities of the U.S. during 1914–15, meeting with enthusiastic reception. On Oct. 6, 1909, he married the contralto Clara Clemens (daughter of Mark Twain), with whom he appeared in joint recitals.

Gabrilowitsch conducted his first N.Y. concert in 1916. In 1918 he was appointed conductor of the Detroit Symphony Orchestra. From 1928 he also conducted the Philadelphia Orchestra, sharing the baton with Leopold Stokowski, while retaining his Detroit position.

gadulka. Pear-shaped Bulgarian traditional FIDDLE. Similar to the Russian GUDOK.

MUSICAL INSTRUMENT

gagaku. Orchestral music of the Japanese court and aristocracy, stately and HETEROPHONIC (multivoiced), still performed on appropriate occasions. Gagaku is the oldest extant orchestral music in the world. Instruments used include the *nyōteki* (transverse flute), *hichiriki* (shawn), *shō* (mouth organ), and *kakko* (barrel drums).

gaida. BAGPIPE found in Bulgaria, Macedonia, Poland, and Ruthenian regions.

MUSICAL INSTRUMENT

gaillard(e) (from Fr. *gai*, merry; It. *gagliarda;* Ger. *Gagliarde*). A vivacious court couple dance popular in France, Spain, and England during the late 16th and early 17th centuries.

găh-yard′

At court occasions, the gaillarde usually followed the stately pavane. The two dances are in fact related melodically, but the gaillarde transforms the symmetric BINARY (two-part) meter of the pavane into a lively TERNARY (three-part) beat. In England the gaillarde was also known under the French name *cinq pas* (five-step), named for its pattern of four strong beats ending with an extra rhythmic step.

Queen Elizabeth I reportedly practiced the gaillarde for her morning exercises.

gaita. Generic Spanish and Portuguese term for pipe. It refers to various traditional instruments, including the BAGPIPE, SHAWM, HORNPIPE, PANPIPE, FLUTE, and ACCORDION.

MUSICAL INSTRUMENT

Galanta Dances. Orchestral suite by ZOLTÁN KODÁLY, 1933. It consists of five pieces of a Gypsy character, based on folk tunes from a Hungarian town.

găh-lan-ter-ē′ehn

Galanterien (Ger.; Fr. *style élégant*). In the 18th century, the most fashionable pieces, such as theatrical compositions or dance pieces found in the Baroque SUITE (minuet, gavotte, bourrée, polonaise, air). As the ROCOCO became passé, the term was used more negatively to describe out-of-date works.

PEOPLE IN MUSIC

Galas, Diamanda (Dimitria Angeliki Elena), remarkable American AVANT-GARDE composer and vocalist of Greek extraction; b. San Diego, Aug. 29, 1955. Galas studied biochemistry, psychology, music, and experimental performance at the University of California at San Diego between 1974 and 1979. She also took private vocal lessons.

In her scientific studies, Galas and a group of medical students began investigating extreme mental states, using themselves as subjects in a series of bizarre mind-altering experiments. Her understanding of psychopathology (notably schizophrenia and psychosis) became an underlying subject in most of her work.

After some success as a jazz pianist, Galas began a vocal career, in which her remarkable precision and advanced technique attracted attention. Although she has performed such demanding works as IANNIS XENAKIS's microtonal *N'Shima* (Brooklyn Philharmonic, Jan. 15, 1981) and Vinko Globokar's *Misère* (West German Radio Orchestra, Cologne, 1980), she is best known for her theatrical performances of her own solo vocal works.

Galas has performed at a wide variety of venues ranging from the Donaueschingen Festival to the N.Y. rock club, Danceteria. Her compositions usually include live electronics and/or tape as accompaniment to her vocal improvisations. Her performances have stringent requirements for lighting and sound, and possess a shattering power.

Her brother Philip Dimitri Galas, a playwright whose works are as violent as his sister's music, died of AIDS in the late 1980s. Diamanda's increasing emotional and political involvement in this "modern plague" led to her four-part work *Masque of the Red Death* (from 1986).

Galilei, Vincenzo, celebrated Italian lutenist, composer, and music theorist, father of the great astronomer Galileo Galilei; b. S. Maria a Monte, near Florence, c.1520; d. Florence (buried), July 2, 1591. A skillful lutenist and violinist, and a student of ancient Greek theory, Galilei was a leading member of the artistic circle meeting at Count Bardi's house known as the Florentine Camerata.

Galilei attacked the earlier practice of interweaving several voices in counterpoint. He wished for a return to the classical purity that he believed was practiced in ancient Greece and Rome. His compositions for solo voice with LUTE accompaniment are early examples of MONODY (a single melody with harmonic accompaniment). This style was further developed by the founders of the OPERA IN MUSICA. He also published several tracts on music that advanced his theories, all of considerable historical interest.

Galilei placed his music in his *Fronimo* (lute transcriptions and original compositions), two books of lute intabulations (1563, 1584), two books of four- and five-voiced MADRIGALS (1574, 1587), and two-part CONTRAPUNTI (1584).

gallant style (Fr. *style galant;* Ger. *Galanter Stil*). This term was used by mid-18th-century composers to describe the more "elegant" style of composition that gradually replaced the strict and purely musical BAROQUE idiom of JOHANN SEBASTIAN BACH and GEORGE FRIDERIC HANDEL.

There is, of course, no particular gallantry in this style. The term denotes music in the salon manner, HOMOPHONIC (single-voiced) rather than POLYPHONIC (multivoiced), serving to entertain rather than to enlighten, evoking sentiment rather than thought. In this sense it is synonymous with ROCOCO.

Instrumental pieces composed in the gallant style were sometimes called *Galanterien*. In this lighter mode, dance movements are the favored forms, shortness the most striking feature. Also favored are a symmetry of phrasing, pretty melodies, and pleasing, humorous, and playful qualities.

galop (Fr.; Ger. *Galopp*). 1. A lively circle ballroom dance in syncopated $\frac{2}{4}$ time from the mid-19th century. FRANZ LISZT even wrote a *Grand Galop Chromatique*. 2. In many tradi-

PEOPLE IN MUSIC

Ironically, it was the sons of J.S. Bach, WILHELM FRIEDEMANN and CARL PHILIPP EMANUEL, who were leaders in overturning their father's more formal music. They advocated a pre-ROMANTIC style of musical affects designed to drive music toward expressing natural human emotions.

găl-lōh′

tional cultures, a group dance featuring rapid movement in imitation of horses.

Galway, James, famous Irish flute virtuoso; b. Belfast, Dec. 8, 1939. Galway's first instrument was the violin, but he soon began to study flute. At 14, he went to work in a piano shop, but a scholarship enabled him to go to London, where he continued to study flute. He also took academic courses in music at the Royal College of Music and the Guildhall School of Music and Drama. He then received a grant to go to Paris, where he studied with Gaston Crunelle at the Conservatory and privately with MARCEL MOYSE.

Galway's first professional job as a flutist was with the wind band at the Royal Shakespeare Theatre in Stratford-upon-Avon. He subsequently played with the Sadler's Wells Opera Company, Royal Opera House Orchestra, and BBC Symphony Orchestra. He then was appointed principal flutist of the London Symphony Orchestra, and later with the Royal Philharmonic. As his reputation grew, he was engaged in 1969 by Herbert von Karajan as first flutist in the Berlin Philharmonic, a post he held until 1975.

Galway then devoted himself to a career as a concert artist. In a single season, 1975–76, he appeared as a soloist with all five major London orchestras. He also toured in the U.S., Australia, Europe, and the Orient. He became successful on television, playing his 18-karat-gold flute, and has commissioned several new works for flute and orchestra.

Galway has made much of his Irish heritage, performing popular Irish folk songs and recording with the Irish folk ensemble, the Chieftains.

gahm′băh

gamba (It., knees; from Ger. *Gamben*). 1. A VIOLA DA GAMBA. 2. (U.K.). The bass VIOL.

Gambler, The. Opera by SERGEI PROKOFIEV, 1929, after a story by Fyodor Dostoyevsky, first performed not in Russia, but in Brussels. The story deals with a Russian general vacationing at a German resort. He is traveling with his very rich grandmother whose fortune he hopes to inherit. But she proceeds to gamble recklessly, and he is in despair. Fortunately, his servant manages to break the bank on his own, but this leads to further problems.

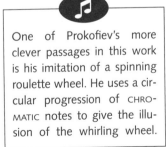

One of Prokofiev's more clever passages in this work is his imitation of a spinning roulette wheel. He uses a circular progression of CHROMATIC notes to give the illusion of the whirling wheel.

game music. Games of musical compositions in which cards, each containing a musical phrase, are put together according to special rules.

One such game, "Musikalisches Würfelspiel," was put on the market in London in 1806 and was announced as "Mozart's musical game, enclosed in an elegant box instructing in a system of easy composition by mechanical means of an unlimited number of waltzes, rondos, horn pipes, reels and minuets." Mozart had nothing to do with it, but it was still an interesting game. The players were to throw a pair of dice, and the number indicated the particular card containing a musical phrase. Because the sequence was arranged so that each card was interchangeable with other cards containing melodies in approximately the same range set in similar harmonies, there was obviously no danger of running into difficulties.

A more modern idea was suggested by the English musician William Haves in his book entitled *The Art of Composing Music by a Method Entirely New, Suited to the Meanest Capacity,* published in 1751. The author, with a rather crude satirical intent, explained the principle of the game: "Take a brush with stiff bristles (like a toothbrush), dip it into an inkwell, and, by scraping the bristles with the finger, spatter with one sweep a whole composition onto the staff paper. You have only to add stems, bar lines, slurs, etc., to make the opus ready for immediate performance. Whole and half-notes are entirely absent, but who cares for sustained tones anyway!"

This is indeed an anticipation of methods of composition used by the avant-garde some 200 years later! For example, using the imperfections found in a piece of paper, John Cage composed a work of music by transferring these marks to a grid. Composing by tossing dice, of course, is one of the most common of all modern techniques.

The most ambitious musical game of the modern era is *Strategie* by IANNIS XENAKIS, first performed at the Venice Festival in 1963. In it, two conductors lead two different orchestras in two uncoordinated works. The audience declares the winner, taking into consideration the excellence of each orchestral group, marking points on the scoreboard for most striking rhythms, best color effects, and finest instrumental solos.

Modern scores descriptive of games are numerous. ARTHUR HONEGGER wrote a symphonic movement *Rugby,* and ARTHUR BLISS composed a ballet entitled *Checkmate.* PAUL REIF selected *Philidor's Defense* as the title of a work for a chamber orchestra inspired by a chess game played in 1858. IGOR STRAVINSKY portrayed a poker game in his *Jeu de Cartes* (Card game), a "ballet in 3 deals" in which the joker is defeated by a royal flush in hearts. A more abstract score by Stravinsky, *Agon,* also portrays a competition. CLAUDE DEBUSSY's ballet score *Jeux* (Games) depicts an allegorical game of tennis.

gamelan. An Indonesian orchestra, including tuned gongs, chimes, drums, flutes, chordophones, xylophones, and small cymbals. These ensembles are most strongly associated with but not limited to the islands of Java and Bali. The ensemble

Gamelan instruments, including drums, gongs, and xylophones. (K. H. Han/Northern Illinois University) ▶

often functions as accompaniment to dance and theater performances, some lasting all night.

During its height, each royal court had its own set and style of instruments, repertoire, and performers. The end of the court system brought an end to many groups, although villages have kept the tradition alive.

The gamelan is led by the drummer, who signaled a change in parts by playing a specific pattern on the two-headed drum. Usually the melody is played by the xylophones; in Bali, the melody instruments are paired and tuned slightly off-pitch to each other, to give the sound a shimmering effect. In some ensembles, melodies are also doubled by flutes or stringed instruments. The gongs and chimes basically mark rhythmic units. There are generally two scales used, PELOG (HEPTATONIC/seven-note) and SLENDRO (PENTATONIC/five-note).

In performing the work, each player has a fairly simple part to execute. However, the parts are cleverly designed to interlock with each other in fascinating patterns. Short melodic phrases are repeated many times, at varying speeds and intensity of volume. The effect is a complicated and rich ensemble sound.

Europe heard its first gamelan at the Paris Exposition of 1889. Interest was great, and recordings circulated. But by the time Western musicologists began serious study in Indonesia, gamelan music was in decline, along with the courts. Western musicologists (and the composer COLIN MCPHEE) studied the instruments, learned, wrote down, and analyzed the music, observed the theater and dance it accompanied, recovered whatever of the older repertoire they could, and, in McPhee's case, helped reinvent a genre (*ketchak,* the monkey dance). Gamelan is one of the most thriving of world musics today, with new and historic gamelan orchestras found throughout the world.

gamut (from Grk. *gamma* + Lat. *ut;* It., Rus. *gamma;* Fr. *gamme*). 1. A scale or pitch range, derived from the Guidonian *gamma-ut,* the first note of his scale. 2. A collection of sounds available to a composer or instrument. 3. Any range of expression available to a performer.

Ganz (Ger.). 1. Whole. *Ganze Note, Ganzton,* whole note; *Ganztonleiter,* whole-tone scale. 2. Very; *Ganz langsam,* very slowly.

García Lorca, Federico, Spanish poet, playwright, and musician; b. Fuentevaqueros, June 5, 1898; d. murdered during the Spanish Civil War by Franco's Falangests, Granada, July or Aug., 1936. Although best-remembered as a playwright and poet, García Lorca was also an amateur guitarist and singer who set a number of his poems to folk melodies.

Since García Lorca's death, many of his poems have been set to music (notably by GEORGE CRUMB, Maurice Ohana, and HANS WERNER HENZE), and his plays are the basis of many operas, notably *Blood Wedding* and *Yerma.*

More importantly, he was extremely interested in the FLA-MENCO genre of CANTE JONDO, and with MANUEL DE FALLA and others encouraged its revival.

PEOPLE IN MUSIC

Gardiner, John Eliot, English conductor; b. Springhead, Dorset, April 20, 1943. Gardiner was educated at King's College, Cambridge, and while still a student there founded the Monteverdi Choir in 1964. He then went to France to study with the famous music-theory professor NADIA BOULANGER. Upon his return to England, he took postgraduate courses at King's College, London.

Gardiner made his first major conducting appearance at the Promenade Concerts in London in 1968. He made his first appearance at the Sadler's Wells Opera in 1969 conducting WOLFGANG AMADEUS MOZART's *Die Zauberflöte.* In 1973 he debuted at London's Covent Garden conducting CHRISTOPH WILLIBALD GLUCK's *Iphigénie en Tauride.* In 1977 he founded the English Baroque Soloists, which he conducted in performances utilizing original instruments of the BAROQUE era. From 1980 to 1983 he was principal conductor of the CBC Orchestra in Vancouver. He served as artistic director of the Göttingen Handel Festivals from 1981 to 1990. From 1983 to 1988 he organized the Orchestre Révolutionaire et Romantique, an orchestra devoted to performing scores on period instruments. He conducted it in LUDWIG VAN BEETHOVEN's Ninth Symphony at its U.S. debut in N.Y. in 1996.

From 1991 to 1994 Gardiner was chief conductor of the North German Radio symphony Orchestra in Hamburg. As a guest conductor, he has appeared in principal music centers of the world. In 1990 he was made a Commander of the Order of the British Empire. His repertoire is immense, ranging from the pre-Baroque to modern eras. His interpretations reflect his penchant for meticulous scholarship while maintaining stimulating performance standards.

In addition to his conducting work, Gardiner prepared performing editions of a number of scores by JEAN PHILIPPE RAMEAU and others. He is credited with the discovery (in Paris in 1971) of the manuscript of Rameau's opera *Les Boreades,* which he conducted at Aix-en-Provence in 1982.

Garfunkel, Art. *See* SIMON & GARFUNKEL

Garland, Judy (born Frances Ethel Gumm), famous American singer of popular music and actress, mother of Liza Minnelli; b. Grand Rapids, Minn., June 10, 1922; d. London, June 22, 1969. Reared in a family of vaudeville entertainers, Garland made her stage debut at the age of two and then toured with her sisters before breaking into films in 1936. She gained wide recognition for her film appearances as a teenager with Mickey Rooney.

Garland's first important role gained her a special Academy Award as well as film immortality. This was for her portrayal of Dorothy in *The Wizard of Oz* in 1939. She later adopted its *Over the Rainbow* as her theme song. She appeared in such film musicals as *For Me and My Gal* (1942), *Meet Me in St. Louis* (1944), *Easter Parade* (1948), and *In the Good Old Summertime* (1949).

While in succeeding years Garland concentrated mainly on nightclub and concert hall performances, she made several more compelling film appearances, most notably in *A Star Is Born* in 1954 and 1961's *Judgment at Nuremberg.* In spite of many successes, Garland's private life became public when a string of misfortunes, including marital difficulties, drug dependency, and suicide attempts, overwhelmed her. Her fans remained steadfastly loyal to her, despite her increasingly erratic performances. She suffered an early death at the age of 47.

PEOPLE IN MUSIC

Garner, Erroll (Louis), famous African-American jazz pianist and composer; b. Pittsburgh, June 15, 1921; d. Los Angeles, Jan. 2, 1977. Incredibly precocious, Garner played regularly over radio station KDKA in Pittsburgh at the age of seven with a group called the Candy Kids. As an adolescent he played piano on riverboats cruising the Allegheny River, and then was a featured piano player in nightclubs and restaurants. He went to N.Y. in 1944, forming his own trio in 1946. In 1948 he went to Paris, making further European tours in 1962, 1964, 1966, and 1969.

Completely self-taught, Garner composed tunes by simply singing and accompanying himself at the piano. An

PEOPLE IN MUSIC

assistant would put down the notes. He also played drums and slap-bass.

Garner's whimsical piano style especially appealed to French jazz critics, who called him "The Picasso of the Piano," and, alluding to his digital dexterity, "The Man with 40 Fingers." In 1971 the Republic of Mali issued a postage stamp in his honor.

Among his own songs, numbering some 200, the heart-tugging ballad *Misty* became greatly popular. Many others reflect similarly wistful moods, exemplified by such titles as *Dreamy, Solitaire,* and *That's My Kick.*

Gaspard de la nuit. A cycle of three piano pieces by MAU-RICE RAVEL, 1909, entitled *Ondine, Le Gibet,* and *Scarbo,* first performed in Paris. These pieces are fine examples of IMPRESSIONISTIC writing, portraying a mermaid, a gallows, and a playful sprite, respectively.

gathering note. 1. In chanting, a hold on the last syllable of the recitation. 2. In the Anglican Church, the opening note sounded on the organ, a beat before the congregation starts, to give pitch.

Gaudeamus Igitur. A German student song in Latin, suggesting that scholars enjoy life before it's too late. The song dates back to the 13th century, but the best-known use of it is heard in JOHANNES BRAHMS's *Academic Festival Overture.* The text also figures in a multivoiced episode in HECTOR BERLIOZ's *La Damnation de Faust.*

The neo-classic composers of the 20th century, including SERGEI PROKOFIEV, revived the gavotte form. It also was used as a basis for modern dance choreography by Martha Graham and others in an attempt to break away from the ROMANTIC forms of BALLET.

gavotta (It.; Fr. **gavotte**). A Baroque and Classic French dance in *alla breve* ($\frac{2}{2}$), strongly marked DUPLE time. An added upbeat of half a measure was introduced slowly but then became a common part of the form.

The gavotte's formal structure is TERNARY (three-part), the middle section being a MUSETTE, usually in the DOMINANT key. It often has a PEDAL POINT on the TONIC and the dominant in the bass, in imitation of the DRONE of a BAGPIPE.

The origin of the name *gavotte* is uncertain. It may be an old local name for the natives of the hill country in Provence.

Gay Divorce, The. Musical by Cole Porter, 1932. Mimi, an actress, goes to England to arrange a divorce from a boring husband. She hires a man to act as her lover in order to have a co-respondent for the divorce. He falls for her unexpectedly, and she gets both her divorce and a new spouse. Includes *Night and Day, You're in Love, I've Got You on My Mind,* and *I Still Love the Red, White, and Blue.*

Gay, John. *See* BALLAD OPERA and *THE BEGGAR'S OPERA*

Gayané. Ballet by ARAM KHATCHATURIAN, 1942, first performed in the city of Perm by the troupe of the Kirov Theater of Leningrad (which was evacuated to Perm during the war). Gayané is the name of an Armenian female farm worker whose husband is a traitor. She disapproves of his disloyalty. He is apprehended and suffers the supreme penalty, death, patriotically approved by Gayané.

Khatchaturian's score contains his celebrated *Sabre Dance.* There is also a nostalgic lullaby and other numbers of immediate popular appeal.

Gaye, Marvin (Pentz), gifted African-American soul singer and instrumentalist; b. Washington, D.C., April 2, 1939; d. Los Angeles, April 1, 1984. The family name was Gay, but a mute "e" was added to the end to avoid the slang connotation of the original.

Marvin sang in the choir of his father's church, and also played drums at school. In 1956 he sang with the group called the Rainbows, and then

PEOPLE IN MUSIC

◄

Marvin Gaye, c. 1964.
(Benson Collection)

he joined the Marquees, which later became the Moon-glows. In 1961 he was recruited by the MOTOWN record label in Detroit, subsequently making both solo recordings and duets with TAMMI TERRELL.

Gaye's first solo hit was *Stubborn Kind of Fellow,* released in 1962, which established his man-about-town image. In 1965, he hit the top of the charts again with the anthemic *How Sweet It Is (to Be Loved By You).* Meanwhile, he also worked as a songwriter for Motown (coauthoring the big hit *Dancing in the Streets* for Martha and the Vandellas) and played drums on numerous sessions, particularly for STEVIE WONDER.

After cutting duets with MARY WELLS and KIM WESTON, Gaye was paired with Tammi Terrell in 1967. Working with the writers/producers Ashford and Simpson, the duo scored major hits with *Ain't No Mountain High Enough* (1967) and *Ain't Nothing Like the Real Thing* (1968). Gaye also had his biggest solo hit in 1968 with *I Heard It Through the Grapevine.* Terrell collapsed in Gaye's arms during a performance in 1968. Tragically, she was diagnosed with a brain tumor, and died two years later.

Gaye's most important album was 1971's *What's Going On?*

Released despite Motown's opposition, the record reflected his concerns over civil rights and the Vietnam war. The album was an unexpected hit, and the FUNK-style arrangements that Gaye created for it influenced dozens of other artists. Oddly, he returned to his sexy leading man persona on the follow-up album, *Let's Get It On,* in 1972.

Gaye's personal troubles began to catch up with him in the mid-'70s. Increasingly addicted to cocaine, he divorced his first wife, who was the sister of the owner of Motown Records. As part of his divorce settlement, all of the income from his 1979 album, the ironically titled *Here My Dear,* went to his ex-wife. In 1980, he moved to Europe to avoid a tax investigation by the Internal Revenue Service.

Gaye finally left Motown in 1982 and re-emerged a year later with the album *Midnight Love,* including *Sexual Healing* (1983), on which he also performed almost every instrumental part. The song was an enormous hit, and unusually frank in its lyrics. Despite its success, he fell into a depression brought on by excessive cocaine use. He was tragically murdered by his father, a retired Pentecostal preacher, during an argument about money, in early 1984.

Gazza ladra, La (The Thieving Magpie). OPERA SEMISERIA by GIOACHINO ROSSINI, 1817, from a French source, produced at La Scala, Milan. A servant girl is sentenced to death by hanging on suspicion of stealing a spoon (apparently neither cruel nor unusual punishment early in the 19th century). She is saved from the gallows when the spoon is found in a magpie's nest!

Gebrauchsmusik. Utility music, or music for everyday use. This term came into use in Germany after World War I. Gebrauchsmusik should ideally be easy to perform by amateurs. Gebrauchsmusik promoted the utilization of new mechanical instruments, the radio, the phonograph, and music for the films.

gĕ-browhs′moozĭk

A variety of Gebrauchsmusik was GEMEINSCHAFTSMUSIK (community music), which cultivated choral singing. The term *Gemeinschaftsmusik* was later changed to SING- UND SPIELMUSIK, in the generic category of HAUSMUSIK (literally house music or music for the home). Probably the first work written specially for such groups by a modern composer was *Das neue Werk* by PAUL HINDEMITH. An innovation in Gebrauchsmusik is spoken rhythmic song, a variant of SPRECHSTIMME.

In opera, the LIBRETTOS were usually satirical and political, with a radical bent, especially proletarian music. From Germany, operatic Gebrauchsmusik was transplanted to America, where the mass poverty of the Depression years contributed to its popularity. Gebrauchsmusik had little success in Russia, France, or Italy, countries with a rich operatic culture, in which there was no necessity of reducing operatic productions to miniature dimensions.

Hausmusik, and Gebrauchsmusik in general, relied on the participation of the audience. Children's music is a natural product of Gebrauchsmusik, with the earliest example being Hindemith's piece for schoolchildren, *Wir bauen eine Stadt*. CARL ORFF succeeded in enlarging the academic routine by composing pieces modern in harmony, RHYTHM, and orchestration and yet demanding little professional skill to perform. Easy humor is an important part in practical Gebrauchsmusik. ERNST TOCH's *Geographic Fugue* for speaking chorus recites names of exotic places in rhythmic counterpoint. *Mikrokosmos* by BÉLA BARTÓK presents Gebrauchsmusik of considerable complexity without losing its musical innocence, and modern-minded children enjoy playing it. Nicolas Slonimsky's album of *51 Minitudes* for piano includes varieties of POLYTONAL and ATONAL music designed for the beginner.

Geisslieder (Ger. *Geissl,* scourge). Chants of the flagellants praying for the ending of the plague and other calamities during the Middle Ages. These chants became the melodic and rhythmic sources of German FOLK SONGS of the RENAISSANCE period.

gīst **Geist** (Ger.). Spirit, soul; essence. *Geistliche Musik,* sacred music.

Geister Trio, Das. *See* GHOST TRIO.

Gemeinschaftsmusik. A term used by German composers to designate communal singing or playing. Although of ancient origin, the practice was popularized as part of the program of HAUSMUSIK, in the generic category of GEBRAUCHSMUSIK.

gĕh-nĕh-rahl-pow′zŭ **Generalpause** (Ger., abbrev. G.P.). A written silence for an entire orchestra.

gĕh-nĕh-rahl-prō′bĕh **Generalprobe** (Ger.). In Europe, an open rehearsal prior to the official first night of a production.

genius. A term applied too freely to any talented musician or composer. One does not have to embrace Thomas Edison's cynical definition, "Genius is 10% inspiration and 90% perspiration," to warn critics and analysts to use the word with caution.

ROBERT SCHUMANN contributed to the use of the word *genius* when he put it in the mouth of the fictional musician

Eusebius, who exclaimed, "Hats off, a genius!", as he began to play FRÉDÉRIC CHOPIN's op.2, *Variations on a Theme from Mozart's "Don Giovanni."* Another time, as the young JOHANNES BRAHMS showed to Schumann one of his early works, Schumann noted in his diary: "Johannes Brahms was on a visit. A genius!"

When the Vienna music critic JULIUS KORNGOLD brought his ten-year-old son Erich to GUSTAV MAHLER and let him play, Mahler became greatly agitated, and kept exclaiming, "A genius! A genius!" Young ERICH KORNGOLD eventually became known as the writer of idiomatic film music in Hollywood, while his operas, which had created quite a sensation when they were first produced, were forgotten.

It is a common myth that geniuses must behave erratically, eccentrically, and unpredictably. LUDWIG VAN BEETHOVEN, HECTOR BERLIOZ, and FRANZ LISZT fit this romantic description to some extent. But Beethoven, like WOLFGANG AMADEUS MOZART before him, was a craftsman first and foremost. JOHANN SEBASTIAN BACH upsets the popular picture of a genius. To his contemporaries he appeared as an honest and earnest worker, modestly performing his functions as church composer, organist, and director of a boys' school. Brahms fit comfortably into the bourgeois framework of the Viennese middle class.

Among virtuosos who looked like geniuses was Niccolò Paganini, whose press agents spared no effort to represent him as being inspired both by God and Satan in his violin playing. The violinist GIDON KREMER virtually swept the stage in a concerto performance.

If one wishes to conjure up the romantic vision of a genius among modern composers, ALEXANDER SCRIABIN would fit the part. His appearance of a distraught visionary, his delicate physique, his inability to cope with the hard realities of life, his belief that he was called upon to unite all arts in one mystical consummation, all combined to create the impression of a genius incarnate.

The word *genius* was often applied to symphonic conductors. ARTURO TOSCANINI was not extravagant in appearance but he possessed magic as a conductor. HANS VON BÜLOW was the first to establish the outward appearance of a

Some famous geniuses who didn't look the part:

MAURICE RAVEL seemed to lack all external attributes of a great musician: he had a very poor sense of pitch, his memory was not retentive, he was a mediocre piano player, and was practically helpless as a conductor.

ARNOLD SCHOENBERG, who came close to reforming music and changing its direction, presented the very opposite to a conventional idea of genius. He was bald and lacked social graces. He also was not a good performer on any instrument and only a passable conductor of his own works.

genius of the baton: tall, erect, and imperious. The list of flamboyant conductors, in more or less chronological order, ought to include ARTHUR NIKISCH, SERGE KOUSSEVITZKY, LEOPOLD STOKOWSKI, and LEONARD BERNSTEIN. Against these, a number of masters of the baton reflect an unremarkable outward appearance.

Genoveva. Opera by ROBERT SCHUMANN, 1850. Genoveva is left under the protection of a friend of her husband's, who goes off to war. The friend immediately makes advances, which she resists. When the husband returns, the friend accuses her of unfaithfulness. At first, the husband orders her put to death, but she proves her innocence. The "friend" flees and judiciously falls off a cliff.

genre. A category of literature, painting, sculpture, and, by extension, a specific form or type of composition. Vocal music genres include opera, oratorio, cantata, or lied, while instrumental genres include symphony, sonata, concerto, or suite. The term is also applied to specific forms, such as a march, rag, or waltz. However, a genre is not the same as a historic style (Renaissance, Classic, etc.) or an idiom (orchestra, violin and piano, etc.).

Gentlemen Prefer Blondes. Musical by JULE STYNE, 1949, based on Anita Loos's novel. The satirical plot demonstrates that a textbook education may not be necessary to succeed when one is blonde, American, female, and attached to a gray-haired sugar daddy on a European journey. Includes *A Little Girl from Little Rock, Bye Bye Baby,* and *Diamonds Are a Girl's Best Friend.*

Geographic Fugue (*Fuge aus der Geographie*). A work by ERNST TOCH, 1930, for spoken chorus. It consists entirely of the rhythmic enumeration of geographical locations. The work is a good example of the spoken chorus genre.

geomusic. A relationship existing between soil and soul, between land and life.

One of the most remarkable geomusical facts is that an area of some 75,000 square miles (equivalent to about one-third of the size of Texas) and comprising such cultural centers as Bonn, Hamburg, Berlin, Prague, Leipzig, Salzburg, and Vienna, embraces the birthplaces of some of the greatest world musicians: JOHANN SEBASTIAN BACH, GEORGE FRIDERIC HANDEL, FRANZ JOSEPH HAYDN, WOLFGANG AMADEUS MOZART, LUDWIG VAN BEETHOVEN, FRANZ SCHUBERT, JOHANNES BRAHMS, ROBERT SCHUMANN, FELIX MENDELSSOHN, RICHARD WAGNER, ANTON BRUCKNER, RICHARD and JOHANN STRAUSS, BEDŘICH SMETANA, ANTONÍN DVOŘÁK, GUSTAV MAHLER, and ARNOLD SCHOENBERG.

The most accomplished violinists of the 20th century came from Poland, Ukraine, and Lithuania, among them JOSHUA HEIFETZ, MISCHA ELMAN, ISAAC STERN, and father and son OISTRAKH (DAVID and IGOR), all of them Jewish. What is the secret here? What is this peculiar affinity that exists between young Jews of Eastern Europe and the violin? The economic factor proves a dubious explanation.

The small peninsula of Italy generated the finest flowering of OPERA, a stage form that was born as an art in Florence. Florence produced through its course of three centuries such masters as CLAUDIO MONTEVERDI, GIOACCHINO ROSSINI, GIUSEPPE VERDI, and GIACOMO PUCCINI, and such great singers as ENRICO CARUSO, ADELINA PATTI, and LUCIANO PAVAROTTI. It also bore the greatest opera conductor, the uncontrollably temperamental ARTURO TOSCANINI. The most popular opera composer living in America and writing his own libretti in English is GIAN CARLO MENOTTI.

If Italy produces great tenors, Russia is the land of great basses, the grandest among them being FEODOR CHALIAPIN. The Russians did not enter the world scene as composers until the 19th century, but the names of MIKHAIL GLINKA, NIKOLAI RIMSKY-KORSAKOV, MODEST MUSSORGSKY, and PIOTR ILYICH TCHAIKOVSKY testify to the natural gift of Russia in all musical fields. And despite the political upheavals of the Communist Revolution of 1917, the Russian achievement continued to be great. IGOR STRAVINSKY, SERGEI PROKOFIEV, AND DIMITRI SHOSTAKOVICH were dominant figures in the new Russia. Russian pianists, violinists, and cellists continue to win prizes at international festivals.

France contributed to music in a less heroic, less grandiose way. The French of the modern age, CLAUDE DEBUSSY and MAURICE RAVEL among them, provided the music of sensual beauty, leaving the field of symphony and grand opera to the Germans and the Russians.

It is the task of geomusic to account for these selective pursuits within particular nations. And of course, above and behind these nations rise the totally different arts of musical North and South America, Asia, Africa, and Australia.

George M! Musical, 1968, built around the life and songs of GEORGE M. COHAN, including the songs *GIVE MY REGARDS TO BROADWAY* (from *Little Johnny Jones,* 1904), *You're a Grand Old Flag, Yankee Doodle Dandy,* and *Over There* (1917).

George White's Scandals. A series of N.Y. revues presented between 1919 and 1939. In addition to the female chorus line, songs were composed by George Gershwin (*Somebody Love Me*) and Ray Henderson (*Life Is Just a Bowl of Cherries*). It also introduced the Blackbottom dance.

Georgia on My Mind. HOAGY CARMICHAEL song, with lyrics by Stuart Gurrell, introduced by Mildred Bailey in 1930, and revived in a definitive gospel-tinged version by RAY CHARLES in 1960.

German sixth. A chord of the AUGMENTED SIXTH between the bottom and top notes. Other intervals from the bottom are a major third and doubly augmented fourth, resolving to a TONIC $\overset{6}{4}$ chord as follows (in C major):

F$^\sharp$	G
D$^\sharp$	E
C	C
A$^\flat$	G

Gershwin, George (born Jacob Gershvin), immensely gifted American songwriter and composer, brother of IRA GERSHWIN; b. N.Y., Sept. 26, 1898; d. Los Angeles, July 11, 1937. Gershwin's father was an immigrant from Russia whose original name was Gershovitz. Gershwin's extraordinary career

In the 1980s, *Georgia on My Mind* became the official state song of Georgia, and RAY CHARLES performed it on the floor of the Georgia State Senate.

PEOPLE IN MUSIC

began when he was 16. He worked playing the piano in music stores to demonstrate new popular songs.

Gershwin took piano lessons, then studied harmony as a young man. Later, when he was already a famous composer of popular music, he continued to take private lessons, studying counterpoint with the composers HENRY COWELL and WALLINGFORD RIEGGER. During the last years of his life, he applied himself with great earnestness to studying with JOSEPH SCHILLINGER in an attempt to organize his technique in a scientific manner. Some of Schillinger's methods were applied in *Porgy and Bess.* But it was his melodic talent and genius for rhythmic invention, rather than any studies, that made him a genuinely important American composer.

As far as worldly success was concerned, there was no period of struggle in Gershwin's life. One of his earliest songs, *Swanee,* written at the age of 19, became enormously popular (more than a

George Gershwin, c. 1935. (Hulton-Deutsch Collection/ Corbis)

million copies of sheet music sold, as well as some 2,250,000 phonograph records). He also took time to write a lyrical *Lullaby* for string quartet in 1920. Possessing phenomenal energy, he produced musical comedies in close succession, using fashionable jazz rhythms in original and ingenious ways.

A milestone in his career was *Rhapsody in Blue* for piano and jazz orchestra, in which he applied the jazz style to an essentially classical form. He played the solo part at a special concert conducted by PAUL WHITEMAN at Aeolian Hall in N.Y. on Feb. 12, 1924. A year later, Gershwin played the solo part of his *Piano Concerto in F,* with Walter Damrosch and the N.Y. Symphony Orchestra. While this work had a certain vogue, its popularity never equaled that of the *Rhapsody in Blue.*

Gershwin continued to explore with classical styles. He wrote a symphonic work, *An American in Paris,* which was premiered in N.Y. in 1928. Four years later, his *Rhapsody No. 2* was performed by SERGE KOUSSEVITZKY and the Boston Symphony, but was unsuccessful. There followed a *Cuban Overture,* also premiered in 1932, and *Variations for Piano and Orchestra* on his song *I Got Rhythm,* premiered in Boston in 1934 with the composer at the piano.

In the meantime, Gershwin became engaged in his most ambitious composition: *Porgy and Bess,* an American opera in a folk manner, for black singers, after the book by Dubose Heyward. It was first staged in Boston on Sept. 30, 1935, and in N.Y. on Oct. 10, 1935. Its reception by the press was not uniformly favorable, but its songs rapidly attained great popularity: *Summertime; I Got Plenty o' Nuthin'; It Ain't Neccessarily So;* and *Bess, You Is My Woman Now.* Over the decades, the work has been recognized as an American classic.

Gershwin's death from a brain tumor at the age of 38 was mourned as a great loss to American music. His songs have been rekindled in popularity through the heartfelt stylings of such performers as MAUREEN MCGOVERN and Michael Feinstein. Gershwin's musical comedies include *Our Nell* (1922); *Sweet Little Devil* (1924); *Lady, Be Good!* (1924); *Primrose* (1924); *Tip-Toes* (1925); *Oh Kay!* (1926); *Strike Up the Band* (1927); *Funny Face* (1927); *Rosalie* (1928); *Treasure Girl* (1928); *Show Girl* (1929); GIRL CRAZY (1930); *Of Thee I Sing* (1931; a political satire, the first musical to win a Pulitzer Prize); *Pardon My English* (1933); and *Let 'Em Eat Cake* (1933). Among his scores for motion pictures are *Shall We Dance, A Damsel in Distress,* and *The Goldwyn Follies* (left unfinished at his death; completed by Vernon Duke).

Gershwin, Ira (born Israel Gershvin), talented American librettist and lyricist, brother of GEORGE GERSHWIN; b. N.Y., Dec. 6, 1896; d. Beverly Hills, Cal., Aug. 17, 1983. Ira attended night classes at the College of the City of N.Y., and wrote verses and humorous pieces for the school paper. Dur-

PEOPLE IN MUSIC

ing the day, he worked as a cashier in a Turkish bath of which his father was part-owner. Ira began writing lyrics for shows in 1918, using the pseudonym ARTHUR FRANCIS. His first full-fledged show as a lyricist was the musical comedy *Be Yourself,* for which he used his own name for the first time.

Ira achieved fame when he wrote the lyrics for his brother's musical comedy, *Lady, Be Good!* (1924). He remained his brother's collaborator until George's death in 1937. The brothers George and Ira Gershwin became artistic twins, like Gilbert and Sullivan, inextricably bound in some of the greatest productions of the musical theater in America: *Strike Up the Band* (1927), *Of Thee I Sing* (1931), and the culminating product of the brotherly genius, the folk opera *Porgy and Bess* (1935).

Ira also wrote lyrics for other composers, among them VERNON DUKE (*The Ziegfeld Follies of 1936*), KURT WEILL (*Lady in the Dark,* 1941, and several motion pictures), Jerome Kern (the enormously successful song *Long Ago and Far Away* from the film *Cover Girl,* 1944), Sigmund Romberg, Arthur Schwartz, and Harold Arlen.

Gesamtkunstwerk (Ger., complete art work). It was RICHARD WAGNER who promulgated the idea that all arts are interrelated, and that ultimately they should unite into a single "art." In his music dramas, Wagner attempted to approximate the ideal of the Gesamtkunstwerk by assigning equal importance to the text, orchestra music, singing, acting, and scenic design. This operatic reform aimed at the restoration of the unity of the arts of music, literature, and painting, as was believed to have existed in ancient Greek tragedy.

gĕ-zampt-kunst′werk

Gesang der Jünglinge, Der. Cantata for boy soprano and electronically manipulated children's choir by KARLHEINZ STOCKHAUSEN, 1956. It was broadcast over five groups of loudspeakers surrounding the audience, first performed in Cologne. The text is composed of fragments from the Book of Daniel concerning Shadrach, Meshach, and Abednego and their experience in the Babylonian fiery furnace. This work was among the most successful of early electronic pieces.

Get Back. A 1969 BEATLES' hit, in a country vein, originally slated to be the title track of their last album, which eventually became *Let It Be.*

Get Together. Hippie anthem of the 1960s, written by JESSE COLIN YOUNG, and recorded by his group, the YOUNG-BLOODS.

PEOPLE IN MUSIC

Stan Getz, 1969. (Hulton-Deutsch Collection/ Corbis)

▶

Getz, Stan(ley), famous American jazz tenor saxophonist; b. Philadelphia, Feb. 2, 1927; d. Malibu, Calif., June 6, 1991.

Getz was a naturally talented player of reed instruments, playing alto saxophone as a child, but then switching to the

tenor sax as a teenager. At that time, he joined the big band led by JACK TEAGARDEN, traveling with them on the road and making his first recordings.

In 1947, Getz was invited to join WOODY HERMAN's band, which had a four-piece saxophone section known as the "Four Brothers." This put the spotlight on the young player and established his reputation. In 1949, he left Herman, and began leading several small groups on his own through the '50s.

After briefly living in Copenhagen, Getz returned to the U.S. at the end of the '50s and began a recording partnership with guitarist Charlie Byrd. Both were interested in Latin-influenced music, and introduced popular Brazilian dance forms including the SAMBA and BOSSA-NOVA into American jazz. Getz's recording of *The Girl from Ipanema*, featuring Astrud Gilberto's sexy vocal, was a major hit.

Getz was less active in the late '60s and '70s, but returned to performing in the '80s. He also was named artist-in-residence in 1984 at Stanford University. However, he began to suffer from the onset of cancer, and eventually had to stop performing. He died from the disease in 1991.

Gewandhaus (Ger., drapery shop). The building in Leipzig in which the famous Gewandhaus concerts were inaugurated in 1781. The Leipzig Gewandhaus had been a textile workshop before it was converted into a concert hall.

Ghost Trio (*Das Geister Trio*). The common German nickname for LUDWIG VAN BEETHOVEN's Piano Trio in D major, op.70, no. 1. This nickname was attached to the work for no other reason than the mysterious quality of the opening of the second movement.

Gianni Schicchi. The third of the operatic trilogy *Il Trittico,* 1918, by GIACOMO PUCCINI, from Dante's *Inferno.* The lawyer Schicchi has a daughter who loves the nephew of a wealthy man who dies at the opera's beginning. The will gives his fortune to the church, but Schicchi devises a plan by which he pretends to be the "not quite dead" old man. The greedy family comes to collect, but a disguised Schicchi dictates a will that leaves everyone but himself and the young lovers out in the cold.

Giant, The. Nickname for GUSTAV MAHLER's Fifth Symphony, in its time the longest instrumental symphony ever written.

Gibson, Sir Alexander (Drummond), distinguished Scottish conductor; b. Motherwell, Feb. 11, 1926. Gibson was educated at the University of Glasgow and the Royal College of Music in London. He also took courses at the Salzburg Mozarteum and in Siena.

Gibson made his debut as conductor at the Sadler's Wells Opera in London in 1952, then was associate conductor of the BBC Scottish Symphony Orchestra in Glasgow until 1954. From 1959 to 1984 he was principal conductor of the Scottish National Orchestra in Glasgow. In 1962 he

PEOPLE IN MUSIC

founded that city's Scottish Opera, becoming its first music director and serving until 1987. In 1977 Queen Elizabeth II knighted him for his services in behalf of the musical life of his native Scotland and Great Britain.

From 1981 to 1983 Gibson was principal guest conductor of the Houston Symphony Orchestra. In 1991 he became president of the Scottish Academy of Music and Drama in Glasgow. He is mainly renowned for his performances of the works of Romantic composers, particularly those of the English school.

Gideon, Miriam, American composer and teacher; b. Greeley, Col., Oct. 23, 1906; d. N.Y., June 18, 1996. Gideon studied piano in N.Y. and Boston, then enrolled at Boston University (B.A., 1926). She also studied composition privately with the composers Lazare Saminsky and ROGER SESSIONS.

Gideon served on the music faculty of Brooklyn College from 1944 to 1954, and in 1955 became a professor of music at the Jewish Theological Center. In 1967 she joined the faculty at the Manhattan School of Music, and then was a professor of music at the City University of N.Y. from 1971 to 1976. She was elected to the American Academy and Institute of Arts and Letters in 1975, and in 1986 was honored with a special concert in N.Y. on her 80th birthday.

Gideon's compositions, including the opera *Fortunato* (1958), *Epigrams,* suite for chamber orchestra (1941), and *Sonnets from Shakespeare* for high or low voice, trumpet, and string orchestra or quintet (1950; N.Y., April 1, 1951), are distinguished by an attractive modernism.

Gielen, Michael (Andreas), noted German conductor; b. Dresden, July 20, 1927. His father, Josef Gielen, was an opera director who settled in Buenos Aires in 1939, and his uncle was the pianist EDUARD STEUERMANN.

Gielen studied piano and composition in Buenos Aires in the '40s. From 1947 to 1950, he was on the staff of the Teatro Colón there. In 1951 he became a répétiteur (rehearsal pianist) at the Vienna State Opera, and from 1954 to 1960 was its resident conductor. Gielen has held many important conducting positions, serving as conductor of the

Royal Opera in Stockholm from 1960 to 1965, the artistic director of the Frankfurt Opera from 1977 to 1987, as well as chief conductor of its Museumgesellschaft concerts. From 1979 to 1982 he was also chief guest conductor of the BBC Symphony Orchestra in London, and from 1980 to 1986 music director of the Cincinnati Symphony Orchestra. In 1986 he became chief conductor of the South-West Radio Symphony Orchestra in Baden-Baden, and in 1987 became professor of conducting at the Salzburg Mozarteum.

Gielen has acquired a fine reputation as an interpreter of contemporary music. Among his own recent compositions are a String Quartet (1983), *Pflicht und Neigung* for 22 players (1988), *Rückblick,* trio for three cellos (1989), and *Weitblick,* sonata for solo cello (1991).

Gieseking, Walter (Wilhelm), distinguished German pianist; b. Lyons, France (of German parents), Nov. 5, 1895; d. London, Oct. 26, 1956. Gieseking studied at the Hannover Conservatory, graduating in 1916, then served in the German army during World War I. He began his concert career with extensive tours of Europe, then made his American debut in N.Y. in 1926. After that, he appeared regularly in the U.S. and Europe with orchestras and in solo recitals.

Gieseking was one of the most extraordinary pianists of his time. A superb musician capable of profound interpretations of both CLASSIC and modern scores, his dual German-French background enabled him to project with the utmost authenticity the masterpieces of both cultures. He particularly excelled in the music of WOLFGANG AMADEUS MOZART, LUDWIG VAN BEETHOVEN, FRANZ SCHUBERT, and JOHANNES BRAHMS. His playing of CLAUDE DEBUSSY and MAURICE RAVEL was also remarkable, and he was also an excellent performer of works by SERGEI PROKOFIEV and other modernists. He composed some chamber music and also made piano transcriptions of songs by RICHARD STRAUSS.

Gigi. Film musical by ALAN JAY LERNER and FREDERICK LOEWE, 1958, based on a novella by the French author Colette. A wealthy Parisian gentleman meets Gigi, a beautiful young woman who lacks the appropriate class and financial means to be a suitable match. At first, he offers to make her

PEOPLE IN MUSIC

Gieseking became the center of a political controversy when he arrived in the U.S. in 1949 for a concert tour. He was accused of cultural collaboration with the Nazi regime, and public protests forced the cancellation of his scheduled performances at Carnegie Hall. However, he was later cleared by an Allied court in Germany and was able to resume his career in America. He appeared again at a Carnegie Hall recital in 1953, and until his death continued to give numerous performances throughout the world.

his mistress, but the moral dilemma is resolved when the gentleman sees his hypocrisy and decides to marry her. Includes the title song, *Thank Heaven For Little Girls, Waltz at Maxim's, I Remember It Well, I'm Glad I'm Not Young Anymore,* and *The Night They Invented Champagne.*

zhig   **gigue** (from Old Fr. *giguer,* dance; Eng. *jig;* It. *giga*) A popular BAROQUE dance in a rapid tempo, in $\frac{6}{8}$ or $\frac{12}{8}$ meter divided into groups of three fast notes. The last movement of a Baroque SUITE was quite frequently a gigue.

The Italian *giga* tends to be in a livelier tempo than the more stately French gigue. Whether the name derives from the English or Old French is open to question; however, the term appears in English virginal music before Continental sources. *See also* JIG.

Gigues. The first of the three orchestral *Images* by CLAUDE DEBUSSY, 1913, its orchestration completed by André Caplet.

PEOPLE IN MUSIC

Gilbert, Henry F(ranklin Belknap), remarkable American composer; b. Somerville, Mass., Sept. 26, 1868; d. Cambridge, Mass., May 19, 1928. Gilbert studied at the New England Conservatory and with the violinist/composer EDUARD MOLLENHAUER. From 1889 to 1892 he was a composition pupil of the well-known composer EDWARD MACDOWELL in Boston.

Rather than do routine music work to earn his livelihood (Gilbert had previously worked as a violinist in theater orchestras), he took jobs of many descriptions, becoming, in turn, a real estate agent, a factory foreman, and a collector of butterflies in Florida, composing when opportunity afforded. In 1893, at the Chicago World's Fair, he met a Russian prince who knew NIKOLAI RIMSKY-KORSAKOV. The prince gave him many details of contemporary Russian composers whose works, as well as those of Bohemian and Scandinavian composers which were based on folk song, influenced Gilbert greatly in his later composition.

In 1894, Gilbert made his first trip abroad and stayed in Paris, subsequently returning to the U.S. When he heard of the premiere of MARC-ANTOINE CHARPENTIER's *Louise,* he became intensely interested in the work because of its popular character, and, in order to hear it, earned his passage to Paris, in 1901, by working on a cattle boat. The opera impressed him so much that he decided to devote his entire time thereafter to composition. In 1902 he became associated with ARTHUR FARWELL, whose Wa-Wan Press published Gilbert's early compositions. From 1903 he employed African-American tunes and rhythms extensively in his works.

The compositions of Gilbert's mature period (from 1915) reveal an original style, not founded on any particular native American material but infused with elements from many sources. They are an attempt at creating a "non-European" music, expressing the spirit of America and its national characteristics. His best-known works are the *Comedy Overture on Negro Themes* (1906), *The Dance in Place Congo,* symphonic poem (c.1908; revised 1916), *Indian Sketches* (1911; revised 1914), *Negro Rhapsody* (1912), *To Thee, America* for chorus and orchestra (1914), *Nocturne,* a "symphonic mood" after Walt Whitman (1925–26), and Suite for chamber orchestra (1926–27).

Gilbert, (Sir) **W**(illiam) **S**(chwenck). *See* SULLIVAN, SIR ARTHUR.

Gilels, Emil (Grigorievich), eminent Russian pianist, b. Odessa, Oct. 19, 1916; d. Moscow, Oct. 14, 1985. Gilels entered the Odessa Conservatory at the age of five, making his first public appearance at nine, followed by his formal debut at 13. After further studies, he went to Moscow for advanced studies. He won first prize at the Moscow Competition in 1933. After taking second prize at the Vienna Competition in 1936, he won first prize at the Brussels Competition in 1938, the same year that he became a professor at the Moscow Conservatory.

Following World War II, Gilels embarked upon an esteemed international career. He was the first Soviet musician to appear in the U.S. during the Cold War era, making his debut in PIOTR ILYICH TCHAIKOVSKY's First Piano Concerto with EUGENE ORMANDY and the Philadelphia Orchestra in 1955. He subsequently made 13 tours of the U.S., the last in

PEOPLE IN MUSIC

1983. A member of the Communist party from 1942, he received various honors from the Soviet government.

Gilels was one of the foremost pianists of his time, especially renowned for his performances of LUDWIG VAN BEETHOVEN, FRANZ SCHUBERT, ROBERT SCHUMANN, FRÉDÉRIC CHOPIN, FRANZ LISZT, Tchaikovsky, and JOHANNES BRAHMS.

His sister, Elizabeta (b. Odessa, Sept. 30, 1919), was a well-known violinist. She taught at the Moscow Conservatory beginning in 1967. She played duets with her husband, the violinist LEONID KOGAN. Their son, PAVEL KOGAN, was also a talented violinist.

PEOPLE IN MUSIC

Gillespie, "Dizzy" (John Birks), famous African-American jazz trumpeter and bandleader who, with CHARLIE BIRD PARKER, established the BEBOP style; b. Cheraw, S.C., Oct. 21, 1917; d. Englewood, N.J., Jan. 6, 1993. Gillespie picked up the rudiments of music from his father. At the age of 18 he went to Philadelphia, where he joined a local jazz band. In 1937, he moved to N.Y. and, two years later, became a member of CAB CALLOWAY's orchestra.

While touring with Calloway, Gillespie met saxophonist CHARLIE PARKER in 1940 in St. Louis. He encouraged Parker to come to N.Y. Meanwhile, Gillespie began jamming with other musicians, including pianist THELONIOUS MONK and Parker, at an after-hours Harlem-based club called Minton's. In this atmosphere, they began experimenting with creating new tunes based on standard jazz progressions. In 1944, Gillespie joined the BILLY ECKSTINE band, one of the breeding grounds for a new style of jazz that would be called BEBOP. In 1945 he formed his own band to continue his experiments.

In the late '40s, Gillespie and Parker co-led perhaps the most famous quintet in all of jazz history. They performed compositions by both men, many of which have become bop standards, including Gillespie's *Salt Peanuts* and *A Night in Tunisia*.

Gillespie became one of the most recognizable figures in jazz in the '50s and a spokesperson for bebop, defending it against those who thought it was more noise than music. A natural showman, he wore a small beret and horn-rimmed glasses, sported a goatee, and comically puffed up his cheeks when blowing into his horn.

Through the decades, Gillespie remained an important figure in jazz. He was one of the pioneers in wedding jazz with Cuban rhythms, working with Cuban-American musicians like drummers CHANO POZO and MACHITO. He made numerous world tours, beginnning with a 1956 State Department–sponsored tour of Africa, the Middle East, and Asia.

Remaining active leading various small ensembles, Gillespie's career was again revitalized in the mid-'70s when young trumpeter Jon Faddis became his partner and promoter. Emulating Gillespie's style, Faddis encouraged him to perform and record, and has, since Gillespie's death, helped keep his trumpet style and sound alive.

Gillespie was doubtless one of the greatest trumpeters in jazz history and practice, a true virtuoso on his instrument, extending its upper ranges and improvising long passages at breakneck speed. In 1989 he was awarded the National Medal of Arts.

gimmicks. Musical tricks are usually regarded as beneath the dignity of a composer or a performer. However, the greatest composers were known to use gimmicks that had nothing to do with music as an art.

Some highly popular works are based on a lucky arrangement of letters of the alphabet translated into musical notes. B-A-C-H (in German nomenclature, B♭-A-C-B) was used thematically by JOHANN SEBASTIAN BACH himself and many later musicians. D-S-C-H, from the German spelling of (Dmitri) SHOSTAKOVICH, yields D-E♭-C-B (where the S becomes Es, or E♭). ROBERT SCHUMANN often used this technique, most notably in *Carnaval,* based on the hometown of his first love.

ALBAN BERG used numbers to represent himself and his secret love, relating their story in the *Lyric Suite.* MARIO CASTELNUOVO-TEDESCO programmed names of his friends into notes and wrote variations and fugues for them as birthday greeting cards. The modern American composer TOM JOHNSON managed to write a whole opera based on only four notes, entitled, fittingly, *The 4-Note Opera* (1972).

Beginning in 1953, Gillespie played an unusual trumpet with its horn bent upward. He claimed this occurred after a group of comedians fell on his instrument during a party for his wife. The 45-degree angled horn became Gillespie's trademark.

ERNST BACON developed a rather curious symmetric technique in his piano works in which both hands play simultaneously or successively symmetrically positioned chords or ARPEGGIOS. For example, E♭, G, and C in the right hand would be accompanied or echoed (counting downward) by G♯, E, and B in the left, forming a perfect mirror image of one black key and two white keys. A given chord can be imitated by several symmetrical chords, provided the position of black and white keys and the intervals are in precise correspondence.

Visual elements in musical composition can aid in the greater understanding of the nature of notation. An 18th-century anonymous score exists that, when lying flat on a table, can be played in perfect harmony by two violinists sitting across from one another. Naturally, the piece is in G major, because the G major TRIAD in close and open harmony in the TREBLE CLEF does not change when the page is turned upside down. But SUBDOMINANT triads become DOMINANT ones!

Another ambitious piano piece of a more recent origin is entitled *Vice-Versa*. When it is read from page one to page eight, or upside down from page eight to page one, it comes out precisely the same. Such devices have been used with some profit for centuries.

gimping. For string instruments, the overspinning of gut strings with fine copper or silver wire. This was used in the BAROQUE period mainly on the lower strings, G on the violin, C and G on the viola and cello.

There is some argument among early music performers over how much gimping is the correct amount, as excessive gimping may create a harshly metallic sound.

Ginastera, Alberto (Evaristo), outstanding Argentine composer; b. Buenos Aires, April 11, 1916; d. Geneva, June 25, 1983. His father was of Catalan descent, and Ginastera preferred to pronounce his name with a soft "g," as in the Catalan language (the standard pronunciation, however, is with a hard "g"). His mother was of Italian origin.

Ginastera took private music lessons as a child, then entered the National Conservatory of Music in Buenos Aires,

PEOPLE IN MUSIC

where he studied composition and took piano lessons. He began to compose in his early youth, winning first prize in 1934 of the musical society El Unísono for his *Piezas infantiles* for piano. His next piece of importance was *Impresiones de la Puna* for flute and string quartet written in 1942, in which he made use of native Argentine melodies and rhythms. He discarded it, however, as immature, along with a number of other works, including the *Sinfonía Porteña,* his First Symphony (which may be identical in its musical material with *Estancia;* see below). Also withdrawn was his Second Symphony, *Sinfonía elegíaca* (1944), even though it was successfully performed.

In 1946–47, Ginastera traveled to the U.S. on a Guggenheim fellowship. Returning to Argentina, he was appointed to the faculty of his alma mater, the National Conservatory in Buenos Aires, where he taught intermittently from 1948 to 1958. He also served as dean of the faculty of musical arts and sciences at the Argentine Catholic University, and was a professor at the University of La Plata. In 1968 he left Argentina and lived mostly in Geneva, Switzerland.

From his earliest steps in composition, Ginastera had a deep attachment to the melodic and rhythmic resources of Argentine folk music. His first significant work in the Argentine national idiom was the ballet *Panambí,* composed in 1935 and performed at the Teatro Colón in Buenos Aires five years later. There followed a group of *Danzas argentinas* for piano, written in 1937. In 1938 he wrote three songs, the first, *Canción al árbol del olvido,* describing youthful love, which became popular.

In 1941 he was commissioned to write a ballet for the American Ballet Caravan, *Estancia,* inspired by the rustic scenes of the pampas. A suite from the score was performed at the Teatro Colón in 1943, and the complete work was brought out there in 1952. A series of works inspired by native scenes and written for various instrumental combinations followed, all filled with Ginastera's poetic imagination and brought to realization with excellent technical skill.

Soon, however, Ginastera began to search for new methods of musical expression, marked by modern and sometimes strikingly DISSONANT combinations of sound and

ASYMMETRICAL rhythms. Of these works, one of the most remarkable is *Cantata para América mágica,* scored for dramatic soprano and percussion instruments, to pre-Columbian texts, freely arranged by Ginastera. It was first performed in Washington, D.C., in 1961 with excellent success.

An entirely new development in Ginastera's evolution as composer came with his first opera, *Don Rodrigo,* produced at the Teatro Colón in 1964. In it he followed the general formula of ALBAN BERG's *Wozzeck,* in its use of classical instrumental forms, such as RONDO, SUITE, SCHERZO, and CANON. Drawing from the German modern tradition, he also introduced SPRECHSTIMME in this work.

In 1964 he wrote the CANTATA *Bomarzo* on a commission from the Elizabeth Sprague Coolidge Foundation in Washington, D.C. He used the same LIBRETTO for his opera *Bomarzo,* which created a sensation at its Washington, D.C., premiere in 1967 because of its portrayal of sexual violence. It was announced for performance at the Teatro Colón later that year, but was canceled at the order of the Argentine government because of its alleged immoral nature. The score uses SERIAL TECHNIQUES, not only of different scale notes, but also of different INTERVALS. His last opera, *Beatrix Cenci,* commissioned by the Opera Society of Washington, D.C., and produced there in 1971, concluded his operatic trilogy.

Among instrumental works of Ginastera's last period, the most remarkable was his Second Piano Concerto composed in 1972. It was based on the famous dissonant opening of the finale of LUDWIG VAN BEETHOVEN's Ninth Symphony. Its second movement is written for the left hand alone.

Ginastera married the pianist MERCEDES DE TORO in 1941, with whom he had a son and a daughter. They divorced in 1965 and Ginastera married the Argentine cellist AURORA NÁTOLA in 1971, for whom he wrote the Cello Sonata, which she played in N.Y. in 1979, and his Second Cello Concerto, which she played in Buenos Aires in 1981.

Gioconda, La (The Merry Girl). Opera by AMILCARE PONCHIELLI, 1876, first produced in Milan. The action takes place in 17th-century Venice. The "jocund" street singer is in trouble when her blind mother is denounced as a witch by the Inquisition. The local Inquisitor is willing to release her if the girl agrees to sleep with him. She rebukes him, whereupon he carries out his threat to have her mother put to death. La Gioconda stabs herself and dies. There are also some murky subplots centering around the Venetian palaces, involving, among other things, a cuckolded husband who tries unsuccessfully to poison his wife.

Giordano, Umberto, noted Italian composer; b. Foggia, Aug. 28, 1867; d. Milan, Nov. 12, 1948. Giordano studied music at the Naples Conservatory from 1881 to 1890. His first composition performed in public was a symphonic poem, *Delizia,* composed in 1886, which was followed by some instrumental music.

In 1888, Giordano submitted a short opera, *Marina,* for the competition established by an Italian publisher. PIETRO MASCAGNI's *Cavalleria rusticana* received first prize, but *Marina* was cited for distinction. A few more operas followed, none of which achieved great success. Then he set to work on a grand opera, *Andrea Chénier.* The 1896 premiere production of this opera at La Scala in Milan was a spectacular success, which established Giordano as one of the best composers of Italian opera of the day. The dramatic subject gave Giordano a fine opportunity to display his theatrical talent, but the score also revealed his gift for lyric expression.

Almost as successful was his next opera, *Fedora,* which premiered in 1898, but it failed to hold a place in the world repertoire after initial acclaim. A series of less-successful works followed, and it seemed that Giordano had lost his gift. However, he recaptured public attention with *Madame Sans-Gêne,* produced at a gala premiere at N.Y.'s Metropolitan Opera in 1915), conducted by Arturo Toscanini, with Geraldine Farrar singing the title role. A few more operas followed through the '20s, none as successful as his earlier work.

During his lifetime Giordano received many honors, and was elected a member of the Accademia Luigi Cherubini in Florence and of several other institutions. Although not measuring up to GIACOMO PUCCINI in musical qualities or to PIETRO MASCAGNI in dramatic skill, Giordano was a distin-

Despite its melodramatic story, *La Gioconda's* score is a particularly fine one. It includes the famous BALLET *Dance of the Hours,* as rollicking a piece of rhythmic entertainment as was ever produced by an Italian composer.

PEOPLE IN MUSIC

guished figure in the Italian opera field for some four decades.

Giorno di regno, Un (The Day of Reigning). Opera by GIUSEPPE VERDI, 1840, first performed in Milan. This is Verdi's first comic opera, and yet it was written at the most tragic period of his life, when he lost his wife and two children.

The opera tells the story of the courageous act of a Polish officer. After a threat is made on King Stanislaw's life, the officer poses as the King so the real King can travel in safety. He is rewarded by being offered a young Polish lady's hand in marriage.

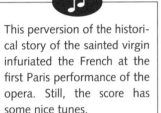

This perversion of the historical story of the sainted virgin infuriated the French at the first Paris performance of the opera. Still, the score has some nice tunes.

Giovanna d'Arco (Joan of Arc). Opera by GIUSEPPE VERDI, 1845, first performed in Milan. The actual story of Joan of Arc is ignored in this fanciful version. Here, Joan of Arc falls in love with the Dauphin, goes to battle against the English, is wounded, and dies in the arms of her royal lover, now King Charles VII.

Girl Crazy. Musical by GEORGE GERSHWIN, 1930. A rich Arizona playboy falls in love with the prim local postmistress of a sleepy backwoods town. Includes *I Got Rhythm, Embraceable You,* and *But Not for Me.*

Girl Friend, The. Musical by RICHARD RODGERS and LORENZ HART, 1926. A bicycle racer is approached by professional gamblers to fix an upcoming race. He refuses, and wins the race, thanks to the help of another racer's daughter. They fall in love. Includes the title song and *The Blue Room.*

Girl I Left Behind Me, The. This is an old song, probably of Irish origin, popular in the American colonies before the Revolution. At the time of the Civil War a new set of words was adapted to the tune, and it became known as the *American Volunteer.* It is used as the graduating class song at the military academy in West Point.

Girl of the Golden West, The (*La Fanciulla del West*). Opera by GIACOMO PUCCINI, 1910, based on Belasco's drama. It was commissioned by and produced at N.Y.'s Metropolitan Opera, with ARTURO TOSCANINI conducting and ENRICO CARUSO singing the part of the Western bad-man, Dick Johnson.

The story is a fanciful one of the old West. Dick Johnson and the sheriff are both in love with saloon-owner Minnie. When Dick seeks shelter in her quarters, she challenges the sheriff to a poker game, the stake of which is Dick's freedom. She wins by using an extra ace hidden in her petticoat. Together Dick and Minnie ride away into the sunset.

Giselle. Ballet by ADOLPHE ADAM, 1841, one of the most famous French ballets, produced in Paris, June 28, 1841. Its full title is *Giselle, ou Les Wilis.* Wilis are the spirits of young girls who die before their announced wedding. The plot concerns an encounter of a young man with his deceased fiancée.

gittern (Fr. *ghisterne, guiterne;* Lat. *ghiterna, quitarra;* Ger. *Quinterne*). Medieval plucked CHORDOPHONE, usually with a flat back, fretted neck, and single or double-COURSED gut strings. It is played with a PLECTRUM.

The gittern is depicted in artworks going back to the early 12th century. By 1400 the instrument had given way to the LUTE. The term *gittern* continued to be used through the 17th century for instruments of the guitar family. It is not to be confused with the CITTERN.

Giuditta. Opera by FRANZ LÉHAR, 1934, produced in Vienna. The subject is drawn from the apocryphal Book of Judith. Judith skillfully decapitates the sleeping Assyrian army leader and carries his severed bearded head back to her city. Finding themselves headless, the Assyrians abandon their attempt to claim the Hebrew city.

This is the only serious opera Léhar ever wrote, but musically it is much inferior to his sparkling operettas.

Giuffre, Jimmy (James Peter), American jazz clarinetist, saxophonist, and composer; b. Dallas, April 26, 1921. Giuffre studied at North Texas State Teachers College (B.Mus., 1942), then played in a U.S. Army band. He subsequently

The Girl of the Golden West's LIBRETTO has many (unintentionally) hilarious uses of American slang. The poker game also is quite comical to anyone familiar with the real rules of the game.

MUSICAL INSTRUMENT

PEOPLE IN MUSIC

joined the bands of JIMMY DORSEY, BUDDY RICH, and WOODY HERMAN. While he played flute and tenor saxophone, he was primarily known for his cool, VIBRATO-less style on the clarinet, especially in its CHALUMEAU (lower) register.

Giuffre wrote an influential score for Herman, *4 Brothers* (1947), to showcase the talented reed players in the band, including STAN GETZ. Giuffre was an important figure in AVANT-GARDE jazz of the late 1950s and '60s, especially as a promoter of FREE JAZZ. He was also active as a teacher, serving on the faculty of the New School for Social Research in N.Y. and the School of Jazz in Lenox, Massachusetts. He also published an influential text, *Jazz Phrasing and Interpretation* (N.Y., 1969). Well-known recordings of his works include *The Giuffre Clarinet* (1956), *Free Fall* (1962), and *Music for People, Birds, Butterflies and Mosquitoes* (1972).

Giulini, Carlo Maria, eminent Italian conductor; b. Barletta, May 9, 1914. Giulini began violin study as a boy. At 16, he entered the Conservatorio di Musica di Santa Cecilia

PEOPLE IN MUSIC

Carlo Maria Giulini conducting at the Hollywood Bowl, c. 1980. (Shelley Gazin/Corbis)

▶

in Rome, where he studied violin and viola, composition, and conducting. He also received instruction in conducting at the Accademia Chigiana in Siena.

Giulini then joined the Augusteo Orchestra in Rome in the viola section, under such great conductors as RICHARD

STRAUSS, BRUNO WALTER, WILLEM MENGELBERG, and WIL-
HELM FURTWÄNGLER. He was drafted into the Italian army
during World War II, but went into hiding as a convinced
anti-Fascist. After the liberation of Rome by the Allied
troops in 1944, he was engaged to conduct the Augusteo
Orchestra in a special concert celebrating the occasion. He
was then hired as assistant conductor of the RAI Orchestra
in Rome, and was made its chief conductor in 1946.

In 1950 Giulini helped to organize the RAI Orchestra in
Milan. In 1952 he conducted at La Scala as an assistant to
Victor de Sabata, and in 1954 he became principal conductor there. His performance of *La Traviata,* with MARIA
CALLAS in the title role, was particularly notable. In 1955 he
conducted *Falstaff* at the Edinburgh Festival, earning great
praise. On Nov. 3, 1955, he was a guest conductor with the
Chicago Symphony Orchestra and later served as principal
guest conductor from 1969 to 1972. During its European
tour of 1971, he was joint conductor with GEORGE SOLTI.

From 1973 to 1976, Giulini was principal conductor of
the Vienna Symphony Orchestra, and in 1975 took it on a
world tour, which included the U.S., Canada, and Japan. In
1975, he led it in at a televised concert from the United Nations. In 1978 he succeeded ZUBIN MEHTA as music director
of the Los Angeles Philharmonic, and maintained it at a
zenith of orchestral brilliance until 1984. From 1984 he
pursued a career as a guest conductor, being closely associated with the Vienna Philharmonic.

Giulini's conducting style embodied the best traditions of
the Italian school as established by ARTURO TOSCANINI. He
was above all a ROMANTIC conductor who can identify his
musical sensibilities with LUDWIG VAN BEETHOVEN, GIUSEPPE
VERDI, GUSTAV MAHLER, and PIOTR ILYICH TCHAIKOVSKY. In
works of the 20th century, he gave good interpretations of
works by CLAUDE DEBUSSY, MAURICE RAVEL, and IGOR
STRAVINSKY. The expressionist school of composers lay outside of his deeply felt musicality, and he did not actively promote the experimental school of modern music.

Guilini's behavior on the podium was free from theatrics.
He treated the orchestra as comrades-in-arms, associates in
the cause of music, rather than subordinate performers. Yet

his personal feeling for music was not disguised. Often he closed his eyes in fervent self-absorption when conducting without score the great CLASSICAL and ROMANTIC works.

Giulio Cesare in Egitto. Opera by GEORGE FRIDERIC HANDEL, 1724. The opera concentrates on Caesar's encounter with Cleopatra.

Give My Regards to Broadway. Song by GEORGE M. COHAN, from the musical *Little Johnny Jones,* 1904.

Give Peace a Chance. A 1969 peace anthem written by JOHN LENNON during the famous "Bed-In for Peace" held in Toronto with his performance-artist wife, YOKO ONO.

Glagolitic Mass. Sacred work by LEOŠ JANÁČEK, 1927, also known as the *Slavonic Mass* or *Festival Mass,* first performed in Brno. The text is in old Slavonic, common also to the Russian Orthodox Church. The use of the Slavonic vernacular by Janáček was as much of an innovation as the use of the German language by JOHANNES BRAHMS in his Requiem.

Glareanus, Henricus, also called Heinrich Glarean (born Heinrich Loris; Lat., Henricus Loritus), Swiss music theorist; b. Mollis, Glarus canton, June 1488; d. Freiburg, March 28, 1563. Glareanus studied in Bern and later in Cologne, where he was crowned poet laureate by Emperor Maximilian I in 1512, as the result of a poem he composed and sang to the Emperor. He first taught mathematics at Basel in 1514. From 1517 to 1522 he was in Paris, where he taught philosophy. He then returned to Basel, where he stayed until 1529, settling in Freiburg. There he was a professor of poetry, then of theology.

His first important work on music, *Isagoge in musicen* (Basel, 1516), dealt with SOLMIZATION, INTERVALS, MODES, and TONES. In a still more important volume, the *Dodecachordon* (Basel, 1547), Glareanus advanced the theory that there are 12 church modes, corresponding to the ancient Greek modes, instead of the commonly accepted eight. The third part of the *Dodecachordon* contains many works by 15th- and 16th-century musicians.

The song was recorded live with various participants, including LSD guru Timothy Leary and satirical singer Tommy Smothers. A heavy backbeat had to be added to the recording because the singers fell behind the beat half-way through.

PEOPLE IN MUSIC

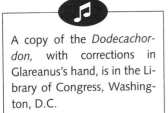

A copy of the *Dodecachordon,* with corrections in Glareanus's hand, is in the Library of Congress, Washington, D.C.

Glass, Philip, remarkable American composer; b. Baltimore, Jan. 31, 1937. Glass entered the Peabody Conservatory of Music in Baltimore as a flute student when he was eight, then took courses in piano, mathematics, and philosophy at the University of Chicago, graduating in 1956. He subsequently studied composition with Vincent Persichetti at the Juilliard School of Music in N.Y. (M.S., 1962).

Glass received a Fulbright fellowship in 1964 and went to Paris to study with NADIA BOULANGER. Also important to his future development was his meeting with RAVI SHANKAR, who introduced him to Hindu RAGAS. During a visit to Morocco, Glass absorbed the modalities of North African music, which gave him his first exposure to creating pieces by repeating short melodic ideas. When he returned to N.Y. in 1967, Glass used his knowledge of Indian modes and African melodic repetition to form a new style of composing.

Glass formed associations with modern painters and sculptors who strove to obtain maximum effects with a minimum of means. He began to practice a similar method in music, which soon acquired the name of MINIMALISM. Other Americans and some Europeans followed this practice, which was basically Eastern in its use of repeated, short melodies with minimal harmonic accompaniment. Composer/performer STEVE REICH was a close companion in Glass's early efforts.

Glass formed his own record company, Chatham Square, which recorded most of his early works. He also organized an ensemble of electrically amplified instruments, which became the chief medium of his compositions. In 1968, he presented the first concert of the Philip Glass Ensemble at Queens College in N.Y. He subsequently toured widely with it, making visits abroad as well as traveling throughout the U.S. His productions, both in America and in Europe, became extremely successful among young audiences, who were attracted to the soundscapes he created.

The high point of Glass's productions was the opera *Einstein on the Beach,* in collaboration with theater director ROBERT WILSON. Wilson's mixture of real history with imagined episodes was accompanied by Glass's slow-moving melodies accompanied by hypnotic harmonies. The opera was premiered at the Avignon Festival in the summer of

PEOPLE IN MUSIC

1976, and was subsequently performed throughout Europe. It was given in the autumn of the same year at N.Y.'s Metropolitan Opera, off the regular subscription series, where it proved something of a sensation of the season.

In Rotterdam in 1980, Glass produced his opera *Satyagraha*, a work based on Gandhi's years in South Africa. "Satyagraha" was Gandhi's slogan, composed of two Hindu words: *satya* (truth) and *agraha* (firmness). Another significant production was Glass's 1981 score for Godfrey Reggio's 1983 film *Koyaanisqatsi*, a Hopi Indian word meaning "life out of balance." The music represented the ultimate statement of the basic elements of Glass's compositional style. A series of visually arresting images, such as the blurred taillights of cars on a freeway, are accompanied by an equally hypnotic score. Likewise, Glass wrote the score for Reggio's 1988 sequel, *Powaqqatsi*, contrasting modern urban life with images of nature in the Third World.

Glass's mixed-media piece *The Photographer: Far from the Truth*, based on the life of the photographer Eadweard Muybridge, received its first performance in Amsterdam in 1983. It was followed by the exotic opera *Akhnaten*, set in ancient Egypt, which premiered in 1984.

Glass has continued to produce prolifically throughout the 1980s and '90s. He was particularly prolific in 1988, a year that saw the premiere of his opera *The Making of the Representative for Planet 8* (to a text by Doris Lessing), an opera based on Edgar Allan Poe's *The Fall of the House of Usher*, the music theater piece *1000 Airplanes on the Roof*, and *Hydrogen Jukebox*, a theater piece inspired by the poetry of Alan Ginsberg. The year 1997 saw the premiere performance of a new stage collaboration with Wilson, *Monsters of Grace*.

In addition to his theater work, Glass continues to compose more traditional works, including incidental music for plays and films. Among other well-known compositions are *Music with Changing Parts* (1972), *Music in 12 Parts* (1974), and *North Star* for two voices and instruments (1975). Some of his orchestral works include a Violin Concerto and the symphonic score *The Light* (both 1987), *The Canyon* (1988), *Itaipu* for chorus and orchestra (1989), *Lamento dell'acqua* (1990), and *Low Symphony*, after the album by

Akhnaten's text is written in ancient Egyptian and Hebrew. A narrator gives a brief introduction in English to explain the story.

David Bowie and Brian Eno (1992). His incidental music includes *The Screens,* for Jean Genet's play, composed in collaboration with Foday Musa Suso, and many film scores, including *Thin Blue Line, Amina Munda,* and *Mishima.*

glass harmonica. In its most primitive form, an instrument consisting of a set of drinking glasses partially filled with water so as to provide a complete scale. The unearthly sound is produced by rubbing the rim of the glass with a wet finger. Because of its clarity and purity, it was called the *angelic organ.*

A famous concert of "26 glasses tuned with spring water" was presented by CHRISTOPH WILLIBALD GLUCK in London in 1746. It is said that Benjamin Franklin attended and subsequently constructed a glass harmonica with mechanical attachments.

Glass harmonicas achieved a great popularity in the 18th century under the Italian name *armonica,* and even WOLFGANG AMADEUS MOZART wrote a piece for it (1791, K.356/617a). RICHARD STRAUSS used it in his opera *Frau ohne Schatten* for evocative effect, as did DANIEL LENTZ in his *Bacchus.*

Also called *glasschord* or *musical glasses.*

Glazunov, Alexander (Konstantinovich), eminent Russian composer; b. St. Petersburg, Aug. 10, 1865; d. Neuilly-sur-Seine, March 21, 1936. Of a well-to-do family (his father was a book publisher), Glazunov studied at a technical high school in St. Petersburg, and also took lessons in music. As a boy of 15, he was introduced to the famous composer NIKOLAI RIMSKY-KORSAKOV, who gave him weekly lessons in harmony, COUNTERPOINT, and ORCHESTRATION. He made rapid progress, and at the age of 16 completed his First Symphony, which was conducted by MILI BALAKIREV in St. Petersburg in 1882. So mature was this score that Glazunov was hailed by VLADIMIR STASOV, CÉSAR CUI, and others as a rightful heir to the masters of the Russian national school.

The music publisher Belaiev arranged for publication of his works, and took him to Weimar, where he met FRANZ LISZT. From that time Glazunov composed in all genres except opera. He was invited to conduct his symphonies in

PEOPLE IN MUSIC

Paris in 1889 and London in 1896–97. Returning to St. Petersburg, he conducted concerts of Russian music.

In 1899, Glazunov was engaged as an instructor in composition and orchestration at the St. Petersburg Conservatory. He resigned temporarily during the revolutionary turmoil of 1905 in protest against the dismissal of Rimsky-Korsakov by the government authorities, but returned to the staff after full freedom was granted to the Conservatory by the administration. In 1905 Glazunov was elected the Conservatory's director and retained this post until 1928, when he went to Paris. In 1929 he made several appearances as a conductor in the U.S. He was the recipient of honorary Mus.D. degrees from Cambridge and Oxford Universities in 1907.

Although Glazunov wrote no textbook on composition, his teachings left a lasting impression on Russian musicians through his many students who preserved his traditions. His music is often regarded as academic, yet his flowing, eloquent melodies place Glazunov in the ROMANTIC school. He was for a time greatly swayed by Wagnerian harmonies, but resisted this influence successfully. Actually, characteristics of Liszt's works are more pronounced in Glazunov's works.

Glazunov was one of the greatest masters of counterpoint among Russian composers, but he avoided extreme complexity. The national spirit of his music is unmistakable. In many of his descriptive works, the programmatic design is explicitly Russian (*Stenka Razin, The Kremlin,* etc.). His most popular score is the ballet *Raymonda.* The major portion of his music was written before 1906, when he completed his Eighth Symphony, after which he wrote mostly for special occasions. He also completed and orchestrated the overture to ALEXANDER BORODIN's *Prince Igor* from memory, having heard Borodin play it on the piano.

glee (from Anglo-Sax. *gléo,* entertainment). An English secular composition for three or more unaccompanied solo voices, generally for male voices and usually constructed as a series of short movements. It reached its flowering in the 18th century. Glee clubs proliferated in England, and also found enthusiastic participants in the U.S. Serious glees are written as well as merry ones.

Gli Scherzi. *See* SCHERZI, GLI.

Glinka, Mikhail (Ivanovich), great Russian composer, called "the father of Russian music" for his pioneering use of Russian folk motives; b. Novospasskoye, Smolensk district, June 1, 1804; d. Berlin, Feb. 15, 1857. A son of a fairly rich family of landowners, Glinka was educated at an exclusive school in St. Petersburg from 1817 to 1822. He also took private lessons in music, his piano teacher being a resident German musician, CARL MEYER. When the pianist JOHN FIELD was in St. Petersburg, Glinka had an opportunity to study with him, but he had only three lessons before Field departed.

PEOPLE IN MUSIC

Glinka began to compose even before acquiring adequate training in theory. As a boy he traveled in the Caucasus, then stayed for a while at his father's estate. At the age of 20 he entered the Ministry of Communications in St. Petersburg, remaining in government employ until 1828. At the same time, he constantly improved his general education by reading. He had friends among the best Russian writers of the time, including the poets Zhukovsky and Pushkin. He also took singing lessons with an Italian teacher, Belloli. In 1830 he went to Italy, continuing his studies sporadically in Milan (where he spent most of his Italian years). He also visited Naples, Rome, and Venice, meeting the famed opera composers GAETANO DONIZETTI and VINCENZO BELLINI.

Glinka loved Italian music, and his early vocal and instrumental compositions are thoroughly Italian in melodic and harmonic structure. In 1833 he went to Berlin, where he took a course in counterpoint and general composition. Thus he was nearly 30 when he completed his theoretical education. In 1834 his father died, and Glinka returned to Russia to take care of family affairs. In 1835 he was married. The marriage was unhappy, however, and he soon became separated from his wife, finally divorcing her in 1846.

Glinka's return to his native land led him to consider the composition of a truly national opera on a subject (depicting a historical episode in Russian history: the saving of the first czar of the Romanov dynasty by a simple peasant, Ivan Susanin. Glinka's opera was produced in St. Petersburg in 1836, under the title *A Life for the Czar.* The event was

A *Life for the Czar* remained in the repertoire of Russian theaters until the 1917 Revolution, when the overthrow of the Czar made it politically unacceptable. In 1939, it was revived, under the original title, *Ivan Susanin*, in Moscow, without alterations in the music, but with references to the czar eliminated from the LIBRETTO. Instead, the idea of saving the country was substituted for that of saving the czar.

hailed by the literary and artistic circles of Russia as a milestone of Russian culture, and indeed the entire development of Russian national music received its decisive creative impulse from Glinka's patriotic opera.

Glinka's next opera, *Ruslan and Ludmila*, after Pushkin's fairy tale and first produced in St. Petersburg in 1842, became extremely popular in Russia. Glinka introduced into the score many elements of oriental music: one episode contains the earliest use of the WHOLE-TONE SCALE in an opera. Both operas retain the traditional Italian form, with arias, choruses, and orchestra episodes clearly separated.

In 1844 Glinka was in Paris, where he met HECTOR BERLIOZ. He also traveled in Spain, where he collected folk songs. The fruits of his Spanish tour were two orchestral works, *Jota Aragonesa* and *Night in Madrid*. On his way back to Russia, he stayed in Warsaw for three years. The remaining years of his life were spent in St. Petersburg, Paris, and Berlin.

glis-sähn′dōh   **glissando** (*glissato, glissicando, glissicato;* from Fr. *glisser,* slide + It. suffix). A SLIDE; a rapid SCALE.

On the piano, a glissando is performed by sliding quickly over the white keys with the back of the fingernail. The thumb, or thumb and one finger, are used. Glissando on the black keys is possible, but rarely used. Piano virtuosos with fingers of steel manage to make glissando in octaves, and even in octaves with an interposed third, using the thumb, the index finger, and the little finger. The glissando effect is natural for the harp, with the hands moving toward and away from the player. It is even possible on a single string, using the pedal.

Other instruments are capable of an uninterrupted slide through a portion of their range, without a break. Trombone glissandos are possible for a limited range, as are those on timpani. The clarinet glissando, requiring a special manipulation of the keys, occurs in the opening section of George Gershwin's *Rhapsody in Blue*. Players on other wind instruments have improved techniques for sliding on their instruments. All bowed strings offer the true glissando.

Glissando is often mistakenly treated as a synonym for PORTAMENTO. While both indicate an indirect motion from one pitch to another, a true glissando should be even and consistent in its motion, i.e., neither the departure nor the arrival pitch should be unduly emphasized.

glockenspiel (Ger., bell playing; Fr. *jeu de timbres*). 1. CARIL-LON. 2. A set of steel bars struck by a hammer and producing a bell-like sound. There are two types: the first, the mallet glockenspiel, is laid out as a keyboard like the XYLOPHONE or MARIMBA and is fully chromatic; the second, the marching glockenspiel, has bars placed in a LYRE-like shape and is held upright, struck with a small hammer, with a range smaller than the 2 ½ octaves of the mallet type.

Gloria. The second main division of the Ordinary in the Roman Catholic High MASS. The separate canticles are:

Gloria in excelsis Deo (Glory to God in the Highest)

Laudamus te (We praise you)

Gratias agimus tibi (We give you thanks)

Domine Deus (Lord God)

Qui tollis peccata mundi (Who bears the sins of the world)

Qui sedes ad dexteram patris (Who sits at the right hand of the Father)

Quoniam tu solus sanctus (For you alone are holy)

Cum Sancto Spiritu (With the Holy Spirit)

Gloriana. OPERA by BENJAMIN BRITTEN, 1953, written for the coronation of Queen Elizabeth II and produced at a special gala performance in the Queen's presence in Covent Garden, London. The Gloriana of the title was Queen Elizabeth I, and the LIBRETTO tells of her romance with the Earl of Essex.

The composer used Elizabethan tunes as part of the work's melodic material. Some of the dramatic portions of the work are modeled after Elizabethan theatrical styles, particularly the MASQUE.

glŏh′ken-shpēl′

MUSICAL
INSTRUMENT

The glockenspiel is included in the score of WOLFGANG AMADEUS MOZART's opera *THE MAGIC FLUTE*, where it is listed simply as *instrumento d'acciacio* (steel instrument). In actual performance it is interchangeable with the CELESTA.

PEOPLE IN MUSIC

Gluck, Christoph Willibald, Ritter von, renowned German composer; b. Erasbach, near Weidenwang, in the Upper Palatinate, July 2, 1714; d. Vienna, Nov. 15, 1787. Gluck's father was a forester at Erasbach until his appointment as woodskeeper to Prince Lobkowitz of Eisenberg about 1729. Gluck received his elementary instruction in the village schools, where he also was taught singing and instrumental playing. Some biographers refer to his study at the Jesuit college at Komotau, but there is no documentary evidence to support this.

In 1732, Gluck went to Prague to complete his education, but it is doubtful that he took any courses at the University. He earned his living by playing violin and cello at rural dances in the area. He also sang at various churches. He met BOHUSLAV ČZERNOHORSKY, from whom Gluck likely learned the techniques of composing church music. He went to Vienna in 1736, and was chamber musician to young Prince Lobkowitz, son of the patron of Gluck's father. In 1737 he was taken to Milan by Prince Melzi. This Italian sojourn was of the greatest importance to Gluck's musical development. There he became a student of the composer G.B. SAMMARTINI and acquired a solid technique of composition in the Italian style.

After four years of study, Gluck brought out his first opera, *Artaserse.* It was produced in Milan in 1741 with such success that he was immediately commissioned to write more operas. He also contributed separate numbers to several other operas produced in Italy.

In 1745, Gluck received an invitation to go to London. On his way, he visited Paris and met the composer and organist JEAN-PHILIPPE RAMEAU. He was commissioned by the Italian Opera of London to write two operas for the Haymarket Theatre, to compete with GEORGE FRIDERIC HANDEL's opera company. The first of these works, *La Caduta dei giganti,* produced in 1746, was a tribute to the Duke of Cumberland. In the second work, a pasticcio entitled *Artamene* and produced later that year, Gluck used material from his previous operas. He also gave a demonstration concert on the GLASS HARMONICA, which was then a novelty.

Gluck left London late in 1746 when he received an engagement as conductor with a traveling Italian opera com-

The two supposed rivals, Gluck and Handel, appeared together at a public concert in London to end rumors that there was bad blood between them. One of the more widespread stories was that Handel had declared that Gluck knew no more counterpoint than his cook. (It should be added that a professional musician, Gustavus Waltz, was Handel's cook and valet at the time.)

pany. He conducted in Hamburg, Leipzig, and Dresden, and in 1747 produced a SERENATA, *Le nozze d'Ercole e d'Ebe,* to celebrate a royal wedding. It was performed at the Saxon court in Pillnitz. He then went to Vienna, where he staged his opera *Semiramide riconosciuta,* after a Metastasio LIBRETTO in 1748. In 1749, he traveled to Copenhagen, where he produced a festive opera, *La Contesa dei Numi,* on the occasion of the birth of Prince Christian.

In 1750 Gluck married Marianna Pergin, daughter of a Viennese merchant, after which, for several years, he conducted operatic performances in Vienna. As French influence increased there, he wrote several entertainments to French texts, containing spoken dialogue, in the style of OPÉRA COMIQUE. Of these, the most successful were *Le Cadi dupé* (1761) and *La Rencontre imprévue* (1764), performed also under the title *Les Pèlerins de la Mecque,* his most popular production in this genre.

Gluck's greatest work of the Vienna period was *Orfeo ed Euridice* (1762), to a libretto by Calzabigi. The part of Orfeo was sung by the famous CASTRATO Gaetano Guadagni. Gluck revised it for a Paris performance, produced in French in 1774, with Orfeo sung by a tenor. There followed another masterpiece, *Alceste* (Vienna, 1767), also to Calzabigi's text. In the preface to *Alceste,* Gluck expressed his belief that opera composers should create music that supported the storyline, and not just strive for fancy vocal effects: "I sought to reduce music to its true function, that of seconding poetry in order to strengthen the emotional expression and the impact of the dramatic situations without interrupting the action and without weakening it by superfluous ornaments."

The success of his French operas in Vienna led Gluck to try his fortunes in Paris. François du Roullet, an attaché at the French embassy in Vienna, urged him to come to the French capital. He also supplied Gluck with his first libretto for a serious French opera, an adaptation of Racine's *Iphigénie en Aulide,* which would be staged in Paris in 1774.

Gluck set out for Paris early in 1773. To draw attention to his arrival, the Paris press ran articles by du Roullet and Gluck himself, explaining in detail Gluck's ideas of dramatic music. These statements set off an intellectual battle between the followers of traditional Italian opera and Gluck's novel

French opera. Some members of the French court, who supported the Italian style of composition, hired the composer NICOLA PICCINNI to write operas to French texts, in open competition with Gluck. Charges and countercharges were hurled by the fans of each composer.

The sensational successes of the French version of Gluck's *Orfeo* and of *Alceste* were followed by the production of *Armide* in 1777, which aroused great admiration. Then followed his masterpiece, *Iphigénie en Tauride*. It was staged in 1779 and established once and for all Gluck's superiority to Piccinni, who was commissioned to write an opera on the same subject but failed to complete it in time.

Gluck's last opera, *Echo et Narcisse* (Paris, 1779), did not measure up to the excellence of his previous operas. By that time, his health had failed. He had several strokes, which resulted in partial paralysis. In the autumn of 1779 he returned to Vienna, where he lived as an invalid. His last work was a *De profundis* for chorus and orchestra, written five years before his death.

Besides his operas, Gluck wrote several ballets, of which *Don Juan* (Vienna, 1761) was the most successful. He also wrote a cycle of seven songs, seven trio sonatas, several overtures, and other works. RICHARD WAGNER made a complete revision of the score of *Iphigénie en Aulide,* which became the standard version during the 19th century. A thematic catalogue of Gluck's works was published by A. Wotquenne (Leipzig, 1904; German translation with supplement by J. Liebeskind).

Glückliche Hand, Die (The Lucky Hand). Drama with music by ARNOLD SCHOENBERG, 1913, first performed in 1924. A man beset by horrible visions meditates on his search for happiness. A chorus reassures him that his efforts are futile. This expressionist work uses Schoenberg's trademarks: SPRECHSTIMME, melodic ATONALITY, and harmonic DISSONANCE.

goat trill (Fr. *chevrotement;* Ger. *Bockstriller;* It. *caprino,* little goat). 1. A curious vocal effect produced when a singer repeats a note very fast and catches a breath after each note. It was introduced by CLAUDIO MONTEVERDI for dramatic purposes. 2. Fanciful 18th-century description of a rasping trill at the interval of a SEMITONE or less. RICHARD WAGNER also used it in *Die Meistersinger.*

God Bless America. Song by IRVING BERLIN. The composer wrote the song's chorus in 1918 with the intention of using it in a show he staged while he was in the U.S. Army. But the song was withdrawn from the production, and lay dormant until 1938, when the American soprano KATE SMITH put it on a patriotic radio program. In an atmosphere charged with the expectations of an imminent war, the song produced a profound impression. During the war it became an unofficial national anthem, and in 1955 President Eisenhower presented Berlin with a Gold Medal in appreciation of his services to the country. Berlin donated his royalties from *God Bless America* to the Boy and Girl Scouts of America.

God Bless the Child. Bluesy song credited to BILLIE HOLIDAY, who certainly popularized it through her performances and recordings in the 1940s and '50s. It was revived in 1969 by the ROCK-JAZZ band, Blood, Sweat, and Tears.

God Save the Czar. Russian Czarist anthem, 1833, composed by the director of the Imperial court chapel, ALEXIS LVOV. It was almost immediately adopted as a national anthem, with words set especially by the Russian poet Vassily Zhukovsky.

The tune, intimately associated with the Czarist regime, was banned after the Russian Revolution. Its quotation in PIOTR ILYICH TCHAIKOVSKY's *1812 Overture* was replaced by the concluding chorus from MIKHAIL GLINKA's opera *A Life for the Czar,* which itself was renamed *Ivan Susanin.*

God Save the King (*God Save the Queen*). The British national anthem, the tune of which is also used in the U.S. as *My Country, 'Tis of Thee.* It was first published in its present form in 1744, but there were earlier versions in the 17th century. Countless attempts to discover its origins have yet to succeed.

Periodically petitions have been circulated to have *God Bless America* replace THE STAR-SPANGLED BANNER as the national anthem. Indeed, the tune is much more singable, lacking the vocal-cord straining leap into the upper register that makes *The Star-Spangled Banner* so difficult to perform.

Goldberg, Johann Gottlieb, German organist, harpsichordist, and composer; b. Danzig (baptized), Mar. 14, 1727; d. Dresden, Apr. 13, 1756. As a child, Goldberg was taken to Dresden by his patron, Count Hermann Karl von Keyserling, where he is reported to have studied with WILHELM FRIEDEMANN BACH and later with Johann Sebastian Bach in 1742–43. In 1751 he became musician to Count Heinrich Brühl, a post he held until his death.

Goldberg's name is immortalized through the set of 30 variations for keyboard by the elder Bach, the so-called *GOLDBERG VARIATIONS*. This work was long believed to have been commissioned by Keyserling for Goldberg. Although this account is now doubted, it is known that Bach gave Goldberg a copy of the score.

Goldberg Variations. A famous set of variations by JOHANN SEBASTIAN BACH, 1741, for harpsichord, on an instrumental "ARIA." The 30 variations were supposedly written by Bach at the request of his pupil JOHANN GOTTLIEB GOLDBERG, purportedly as a remedy for Goldberg's employer Count Keyserling, who suffered from insomnia. The work demands considerable attention to its amazingly skillful COUNTERPOINT, so it is a wonder whether it could really put anyone to sleep. The *tour de force* of the variations is the use of a CANON at every third variation, with the interval of the canon expanding arithmetically.

Goldsmith, Jerry, American composer; b. Los Angeles, Feb. 10, 1929. Goldsmith studied piano with the Austrian-born keyboard virtuoso JAKOB GIMPEL and theory and composition with the Italian-American composer MARIO CASTELNUOVO-TEDESCO, then took music classes at Los Angeles City College. He also sat in on MIKLOS ROSZA's sessions on film music at the University of Southern California.

Goldsmith wrote music for various CBS radio and television programs throughout the 1950s. He then devoted himself mainly to writing music for films, including *A Patch of Blue* (1966), *Planet of the Apes* (1967), *Patton* (1970), *Papillon* (1973), *The Cassandra Crossing* (1976), *Islands in the Stream* (1977), *MacArthur* (1978), *Poltergeist* (1982), *Rambo* (1985), and so on. He also wrote chamber music and vocal works.

goliards. Wandering MINSTRELS, usually students or monks, who traveled through Germany during the Middle Ages. The celebrated collection *Carmina Burana* (Songs of Beuren, a Benedictine monastery where the manuscript was found) consists mainly of goliard songs.

Golitzin, Nikolai (Borisovich), Russian nobleman and patron of music; b. St. Petersburg, Dec. 19, 1794; d. Tambov district, Nov. 3, 1866. Golitzin was a talented cello player. However, his name is remembered mainly because of his connection with LUDWIG VAN BEETHOVEN, who dedicated the overture *Consecration of the House* (op.124) and the string quartets opp. 127, 130, and 132 to him. Golitzin was also responsible for the first performance of Beethoven's *Missa solemnis* (St. Petersburg Philharmonic Society, 1824).

PEOPLE IN MUSIC

Gondoliers, The, or The King of Barataria. Comic OPERA by Gilbert and Sullivan, 1889. Two Venetian boatmen are revealed to be the heirs to the Baratarian throne. They risk their noble positions by unwittingly marrying two commoners. However, the women turn out to be aristocrats after all, and everyone is happy. This is the most operatic of the Gilbert and Sullivan collaborations.

gong. A suspended circular metal plate, struck with a mallet and producing a sustained reverberation. The gong differs from the TAM-TAM in having a convex circular nub in the plate's middle. The mallet is usually struck on this nub, whose size along with that of the gong itself determines the fixed pitch of the instrument.

MUSICAL
INSTRUMENT

Good Boy. Musical by HARRY RUBY and HERBERT STOTHART, 1928. A boy from Arkansas tries to make good in N.Y., falls for a chorus girl, and loses her when he fails. Undaunted, he starts a business making dolls for adult tastes. He succeeds, and gets his girl back. Includes *I Wanna Be Loved by You.*

Good Vibrations. A 1967 No. 1 hit for the BEACH BOYS, their greatest and most ambitious recording. It features the electronic musical instrument, the THEREMIN.

PEOPLE IN MUSIC

The Goodman band performed at the Palomar Ballroom on August 21, 1935, following a long tour of the country in which their music was not well received. The enthusiastic California audience, who had heard Goodman on the radio, greeted them with loud approval. This success of the show is generally credited with launching the Swing Era.

Goodman, Benny (Benjamin David), famous American clarinetist and swing bandleader; b. Chicago, May 30, 1909; d. N.Y., June 13, 1986. Goodman acquired a taste for syncopated music as a child by listening to recordings of ragtime. He was playing professionally by the age of 12, and at 17 was working with BEN POLLACK, one of the leading Chicago jazz musicians of the period. In 1929 he went to N.Y. as a clarinetist, working in various bands. In 1934 he formed his own band, which became known nationwide from its weekly appearances on the "Let's Dance" radio program. He was among the many important musicians who were guided by the producer John Hammond.

Both as the leader of a large dance band and for his virtuoso performances in various jazz combos, Goodman was the best known and most successful musician of the swing era. Nicknamed the "King of Swing," his sidemen were among the most talented musicians of the day, including pianist TEDDY WILSON, saxophonist BENNY CARTER, drummer GENE KRUPA, vibes player LIONEL HAMPTON, and pioneering electric guitarist CHARLIE CHRISTIAN, who made most of his few recordings with Goodman.

Goodman's band continued to record and perform through the time of his death, with varying personnel. Goodman also played clarinet parts in classical works, appearing as soloist in WOLFGANG AMADEUS MOZART's Clarinet Concerto with the N.Y. Philharmonic in 1940 and recording works by AARON COPLAND, BÉLA BARTÓK, IGOR STRAVINSKY, MORTON GOULD, and LEONARD BERNSTEIN.

Goodnight Irene. Popularized by the folk/blues singer LEADBELLY, this was actually based on a popular song of the turn of the century. Leadbelly's version was different than the original, and became a folk standard. It was a No. 1 hit for the folk group the WEAVERS in 1950, shortly after Leadbelly died.

Goodnight Ladies. Song, published in 1847 as *Farewell, Ladies,* attributed to E.P. CHRISTY (1815–62). The leader of a famous blackface MINSTREL show, Christy often bought songs outright from their composers (STEPHEN FOSTER among them) and put his name on them. Therefore his authorship is doubtful.

Gordon, Dexter (Keith), prominent African-American JAZZ tenor saxophonist; b. Los Angeles, Feb. 27, 1923; d. Philadelphia, Apr. 25, 1990. Gordon studied clarinet, then took up the alto saxophone at the age of 15. He then turned to the tenor saxophone and soon began to play in a local band. He worked with LIONEL HAMPTON from 1940 to 1943 and LOUIS ARMSTRONG in 1944.

Gordon then went to N.Y., where he played in BILLY ECKSTINE's band from 1944 to 1946. After returning to Los Angeles in 1947, he appeared with WARDELL GRAY until 1952. In 1962 he moved to Copenhagen, and continued his career in Europe. He then returned to the U.S. in the late '70s, to much acclaim. He was elected a member of the Jazz Hall of Fame in 1980.

Gordon was generally acknowledged as the most influential tenor saxophonist of the bop period. He starred in the excellent 1986 film *'Round Midnight.*

PEOPLE IN MUSIC

Gordy, Berry, Jr., significant African-American record producer, creator of the Motown sound; b. Detroit, Nov. 28, 1929. Gordy trained as a featherweight boxer, then was drafted into the U.S. Army. After his discharge, he worked on the assembly line for Ford, and began writing songs. His song, *Reet Petite,* was a big hit for local singer JACKIE WILSON in 1956. Gordy continued to write and tour with the singer for two years.

In 1958, Gordy struck out on his own as a manager. A year later, he founded his first record label, Tamla. By 1960, this label was absorbed into Motown Records. Gordy co-wrote the label's first big hit, THE MIRACLES' *Shop Around,* with the group's leader, SMOKEY ROBINSON. He wrote a number of other early Motown songs, but basically turned his attention to grooming groups and running the business.

Gordy had the vision of creating a music that would appeal to teenagers of all races. He called this the "Sound of Young America." He hired a house band of musicians, composers, and producers to craft this sound. He also established a kind of finishing school for his performers, teaching them to dance, how to dress, and even how to eat and speak. The result was a Detroit-like assembly line of successful groups and single artists, including THE MIRACLES, MARY WELLS, THE

In addition to managing singers, Gordy also dabbled in prize fighting, both as a fighter and a manager.

FOUR TOPS, MARTHA AND THE VANDELLAS, THE SUPREMES (and DIANA ROSS), THE TEMPTATIONS, JR. WALKER AND THE ALL STARS, GLADYS KNIGHT AND THE PIPS, MARVIN GAYE, THE O'JAYS, STEVIE WONDER, and THE JACKSON 5.

The Motown success story was ended by the late '60s as its artists struggled for greater control of their careers. Gordy turned his attention to grooming the film career of his favorite artist, Diana Ross. Meanwhile, a few Motown stars like Stevie Wonder and Marvin Gaye continued to record for the label while creating their own unique music. Many others went to other labels in order to escape the production-line quality of Motown's recordings.

Gordy sold the Motown label to MCA in 1988. A few weeks later, he was inducted as a nonperformer into the Rock and Roll Hall of Fame.

Górecki, Henryk (Mikolaj), significant Polish composer; b. Czernica, Dec. 6, 1933. Górecki studied in the Polish town of Rybnik from 1952 to 1955, and then studied composition at the Katowice Conservatory from 1955 to 1960. While still a student there, he was honored with an all-Górecki concert, including the premieres of five of his works, in 1958.

In 1960, Górecki's *Monologhi* for soprano and three instrumental groups won first prize in the Polish Composers' Union competition. Later that year, his *Scontri* for orchestra created quite a stir at its premiere at the Warsaw Autumn Festival.

In 1961, Górecki traveled to Paris, where his First Symphony won first prize in the Second Paris Biennale. He met composer/electronic music pioneer PIERRE BOULEZ there, and KARLHEINZ STOCKHAUSEN while traveling through Cologne. Their influence was felt in his *3 Pieces in Old Style* for string orchestra, which premiered in Warsaw in 1964. The work was inspired by medieval Polish music, which would play a part in all of Górecki's vocal works, but added a modern touch by introducing "white noise" (undefined static-like sounds) to the score. In 1968, he joined the staff of the Katowice Conservatory, becoming its director in 1975.

Górecki's 1972 work, *Ad Mariem* for soprano, chorus, and orchestra was also based on medieval Polish MODES. It

PEOPLE IN MUSIC

won first prize at the International Composers' Forum a year later in Paris. During this period, Górecki was living in Berlin to study and compose.

In 1977, Górecki composed his best-known work, the Third Symphony, *Symphony of Lamentation Songs* for soprano and orchestra. This composition introduced a new spirituality into Górecki's work, which would be felt in many of his subsequent compositions. This work is divided into three parts: a Lamentation of the Holy Cross Monastery of the 15th century, the prayer of 18-year-old Helena Wanda Blazusiakowna which she inscribed on her Gestapo prison camp cell wall in Zakopane during World War II, and a folk song of the Opole region.

When Pope John Paul II made his historic trip to his homeland, Górecki composed his *Beatus Vir* for baritone, chorus, and orchestra, which was premiered in a concert attended by the Pontiff. However, Górecki's participation in this concert led the Communist government to revoke his teaching position. In support of the anti-communist solidarity movement, Górecki wrote his *Misere* for chorus in 1981, although it was not performed until six years later.

When the Polish communist government fell in 1989, Górecki was free to return to the concert stage and his work as a composer. His combination of modern techniques and traditional scales and forms has made many of his works very popular. And his unique spirituality and compassion for the suffering of his fellow man comes through strongly in his compositions. Among his later works are *Dobra Noc* (Good Night), "in memoriam Michael Vyner," for soprano, alto flute, piano, and three TAM-TAMS (London, Nov. 4, 1990), *Concerto-Cantata* for flute and orchestra (Amsterdam, Nov. 28, 1992), *Kleines Requiem für eine Polka* for piano and 13 instruments (Amsterdam, June 12, 1993), and Piece for string quartet (1993; N.Y., Jan. 20, 1994).

gospel music. 1. African-American SPIRITUALS.

Black hymnbooks were published as early as the beginning of the 19th century. Those opposed to slavery published collections of traditional spirituals in order to gain sympathy for the anti-slavery movement. The first and most famous of these books was *Slave Songs of the United States.*

Spirituals were popularized and made appropriate for the concert hall by the Fisk (University) Jubilee Singers, founded at the Nashville all-black college of the same name as a means to raise funds for its educational program. Their success in the U.S. and Europe inspired countless other groups to tour.

2. 20th-century African-American Christian song, marked by a directness of appeal or statement of belief. At its most lively, the music echoes the popular medium of the day, whether it be the blues, New Orleans, rhythm and blues (the mainstream style), DOO-WOP (in the gospel quartet), soul, or rap.

However, a mainstream style, known as gospel hymnody, can be found in the hymns of THOMAS A. DORSEY and LUCIE CAMPBELL, and, later, ROBERTA MARTIN, JAMES CLEVELAND, and ANDRAE CROUCH. The performance style followed changes in musical style, and by the 1930s, the piano (or organ) had become the primary accompaniment. The CALL-AND-RESPONSE texture of the old spiritual and the Dixieland gospel style of BESSIE JOHNSON were incorporated into the solo-and-chorus texture. SISTER ROSETTA THARPE made gospel a best-selling commodity with her recording of *Rock Me,* which was released in 1938.

In the 1950s, MAHALIA JACKSON was the "queen" of gospel music. Later generations provided singers such as CLARA WARD, MARION WILLIAMS, INEZ ANDREWS, SHIRLEY CAESAR (a "singing preacher"), and EDWIN and WALTER HAWKINS. Gospel became a vehicle for inspirational and musical improvisation with Jackson's introduction of *vamping* (a half-spoken monologue performed over the repetition of a chord progression in free time).

3. A white Protestant church hymn, traditionally sung A CAPPELLA. Although hymnody had existed in the U.S. before the American Revolution, musicologists tend to limit the definition of "white gospel music" to the popular hymns, camp-meeting spirituals, and other music associated with the revivalist movement, which began in the mid-19th century. From the beginning, this music has had a written basis, although its performance practice was freer in the camp-meeting than the hymnbooks would suggest.

LOWELL MASON and GEORGE ROOT were among the earliest composers of gospel hymns. In the next generation, ROBERT LOWRY (*Shall we gather at the river?*) and Elisha Hoffman (*Are you washed in the blood of the Lamb?*) were among the most important authors.

The last part of the 19th century was the era of the evangelists Dwight Moody, the preacher, and IRA SANKEY, the musician. They held well-attended revival meetings in the U.S. and U.K. in urban settings, and also collected hymns into several volumes.

Similar collaborations between preachers and musicians persisted into the 20th century; the preacher Billy Graham often appeared with the singers CLIFF BARROWS and GEORGE BEVERLY SHEA. In a manner reminiscent of black gospel, old-time, BLUEGRASS, and COUNTRY, musicians have used their talents in the service of gospel music.

A new form of white gospel music emerged in the 1970s which was labeled "Christian rock." Here, contemporary accompaniments of electric guitars, keyboard SYNTHESIZERS, bass, and drums, along with pop-rock melodies, were wed to Christian lyrics. One of the most successful performers in this style was AMY GRANT, although she later crossed over into secular pop.

Gothic music. This term was developed to describe the style of COUNTERPOINT of the Middle Ages that was centered in western Europe. It is also known as the school of Notre Dame POLYPHONY. It may be identified with the ARS ANTIQUA, gradually giving way to the ARS NOVA and other late medieval styles.

Gott erhalte unser Kaiser. Former national Austrian anthem, composed by FRANZ JOSEPH HAYDN, 1797.

Haydn was instructed by the Austrian court to compose a hymn melody of a solemn nature that could be used as an anthem. He succeeded triumphantly in this task.

The original text for the hymn, written by LORENZ LEOPOLD HASCHKA, began "Gott erhalte Franz den Kaiser." This hymn had a curious history: a new set of words was written by AUGUST HEINRICH HOFFMANN during a period of

Haydn also used this tune as a theme for a set of variations in his String Quartet in C major (op.76, no. 3), the *Emperor Quartet.*

revolutionary disturbances in Germany preceding the general European revolution of 1848. Its first line, "Deutschland, Deutschland über alles," later assumed the significance of German imperialism and fascism. However, in its original, it meant merely "Germany above all (in our hearts)."

Götterdämmerung (The Twilight of the Gods). The final spectacle of RICHARD WAGNER's great tetralogy *Der Ring des Nibelungen* (The Ring of the Nibelung), 1876. It was first performed at Wagner's Festival Theater in Bayreuth.

The score of Götterdämmerung. *(Ira Nowinski/Corbis)*

A magic spell cast by the Nibelungs makes the hero Siegfried forget his beloved Brünnhilde and fall for another. This magic then transforms him into the image of another Nibelung, then restores his memory and his physical shape to him before he is slain. Brünnhilde, who couldn't save his father Siegmund either (in *DIE WALKÜRE*), rides into the funeral pyre erected for Siegfried's final rites. The gods, demigods, heroes, the monstrous offspring of the sinister gnome Nibelung, and the Nordic Olympus called Valhalla all perish in the final fire. The Rhine River overflows the scene, and the Rhinemaidens regain the accursed Ring, the prize which had inspired the entire tragedy.

A complex network of LEITMOTIFS (melodic themes) attempts to guide the listener trying to trace the principal characters of the music drama. Even such a confirmed Wagnerite as GEORGE BERNARD SHAW candidly admitted his inability to penetrate the tangled web of the story!

Gottschalk, Louis Moreau, celebrated American pianist and composer; b. New Orleans, May 8, 1829; d. Tijuca, near Rio de Janeiro, Dec. 18, 1869. Gottschalk's father, an English businessman, emigrated to New Orleans. His mother was of Creole descent, the granddaughter of a governor of a Haitian province.

Gottschalk's talent for music was developed early. At the age of four, he began studying violin with FELIX MIOLAN, concertmaster of the New Orleans' opera orchestra, and piano with FRANÇOIS LETELLIER, organist at the St. Louis Cathedral. At seven he substituted for Letellier at the organ during High Mass, and the next year played violin at a benefit for Miolan. In 1841 he was sent to Paris, where he studied piano and harmony. He also later studied composition with the famous composer and teacher HECTOR BERLIOZ.

Louis Gottschalk, c. 1850.
(Corbis-Bettmann)

In 1845, Gottschalk gave a concert at Paris's Salle Pleyel, which attracted the attention of FRÉDÉRIC CHOPIN. His piano compositions of the period, including *Bamboula, Le Bananier,* and *La Savane,* were influenced by FRANZ LISZT and Chopin, but also inspired by childhood recollections of Creole and African-American dances and songs.

In 1846–47 he appeared in a series of concerts with Berlioz at the Italian Opera, and in 1850 concertized throughout France and Switzerland, playing his own compositions. In 1851 he appeared in Madrid at the invitation of the Queen and was given the Order of Isabella. During his stay there, he developed the "monster concerts," for which he wrote a symphony for ten pianos, *El sitio de Zaragosa,* later transformed into *Bunker's Hill* by replacing the Spanish tunes with American ones.

In 1853, Gottschalk returned to the U.S. and gave a highly praised concert in N.Y., followed by many concerts throughout the U.S., Cuba, and Canada over the next three years. During the winter of 1855–56, he gave 80 concerts in N.Y. alone. His compositions from this period, including *La Scintilla, The Dying Poet,* and *The Last Hope,* written to display his talents as pianist, used many novel techniques.

After playing Adolf Henselt's Piano Concerto with the N.Y. Philharmonic in 1857, he went to Cuba with the then-teenaged singer ADELINA PATTI. He then lived in the West Indies, writing works influenced by its indigenous music. In Havana, on Feb. 17, 1861, he introduced his most famous orchestral work, *La Nuit des tropiques* (The night of the tropics; Symphony No. 1). He also produced several grand "monster concerts" modeled after those of Jullien.

Although he was born in the South, Gottschalk's sympathies were with the North during the American Civil War. He had freed the slaves he inherited after his father's death in 1853. He resumed his U.S. concert career with a performance in N.Y. in 1862, and until 1865 toured the North and the West, playing (by his estimation) over a thousand concerts.

After becoming involved in a scandal with a teenage girl in San Francisco, Gottschalk was forced to flee to South America in 1865, where he appeared in concert and composed new works based on local melodies and rhythms. During a festival of his music in Rio de Janeiro in 1869, he collapsed on stage after playing the appropriately titled *Morte!!* (Death!!), dying within a month. His remains were exhumed and reburied with great ceremony in Brooklyn in 1870.

Gottschalk was a prolific composer of showy, pianistic works that enjoyed great popularity for some time even after his death. Ultimately, however, they slipped into oblivion. As a pianist he was one of the most adulated virtuosos of his era. His concerts, featuring his own compositions, empha-

Gottschalk's notebooks from this era, published after his death as *Notes of a Pianist* (Philadelphia, 1881), give a fascinating picture of life in Civil War America.

sized his incredible technique but were criticized by some as being all-show with no substance.

Two catalogs of his music have been published, although neither is definitive. Gottschalk published some of his works using the pseudonyms Steven Octaves, Oscar Litti, A.B.C., and Paul Ernest.

Gould, Glenn (Herbert), remarkable and individualistic Canadian pianist, noted for his unorthodox interpretations; b. Toronto, Sept. 25, 1932; d. there, Oct. 4, 1982. Gould's parents were musically gifted and gladly encouraged his early development. Glenn began to play piano, and even com-

PEOPLE IN MUSIC

◀

Glenn Gould. (Corbis-Bettmann)

pose, in his preteen years. At the age of ten, he entered the Royal Conservatory of Music in Toronto, where he studied piano, organ, and theory. He received his diploma as a graduate at age 13, in 1945.

Gould made his debut in Toronto in 1946. Even at this early date, Gould was developing unusual mannerisms as a performer that were to become his artistic signature: he reduced the use of the SUSTAIN PEDAL to a minimum, preferring a clear, crisp tone, and he cultivated "horizontality" in his body position, bringing his head down almost to the level of the keys.

Gould was most sympathetic to the BAROQUE and CLASSICAL composers, preferring their dense, melodic COUNTER-

POINT to the later rich harmonic writing of the ROMANTICS. For this reason, JOHANN SEBASTIAN BACH was the subject of his close study rather than FRÉDÉRIC CHOPIN. He also cultivated performances of the early keyboard composers JAN PIETERSZOON SWEELINCK, Orlando Gibbons, and others. He played works by WOLFGANG AMADEUS MOZART with emphasis on the early pianoforte techniques. However, he omitted the Romantic composers Chopin, ROBERT SCHUMANN, and FRANZ LISZT from his repertoire. Remarkably enough, Gould played the piano works of the modern Vienna school—ARNOLD SCHOENBERG, ALBAN BERG, and ANTON WEBERN—perhaps because of their classical avoidance of purely decorative harmonies.

Following Gould's U.S. debut in Washington, D.C. in 1955, he gained wide praise for his concerts. However, in 1964 he abruptly terminated his stage career and devoted himself exclusively to recording, which he regarded as a superior art. This enabled him to select the best portions of the music he played in the studio, forming a perfect performance.

While Gould was without question a supreme artist, a great part of the interest he aroused with the public at large was due to mannerisms that marked his behavior on the stage. He used a 14-inch-high chair that placed his eyes almost at the level of the keyboard; he wore informal clothing, rather than the standard concert attire of tux and tails; he had a rug put under the piano; and he kept a glass of distilled water within easy reach.

Gould was in constant fear of bodily injury. He avoided shaking hands with the conductor after playing a concerto, and actually once sued the Steinway piano company for a large sum of money when an enthusiastic representative shook his hand too vigorously. His hands were often cold, so often he wore gloves (with finger holes cut out of them) when he played.

Socially, Gould was a recluse. He found some release from his self-imposed isolation in producing several radio programs for the Canadian Broadcasting Company, including his 1967 *Solitude Trilogy* (*The Idea of North, The Latecomers,* and *The Quiet in the Land*), three hauntingly beauti-

---

Gould would also sometimes sing along while he played in a highly unmelodic voice. Although he otherwise insisted on perfection in his recordings, he strangely allowed this vocalizing to remain on his records.

ful sound documentaries devoted to the natural isolation of the Canadian Arctic, the insular life of Newfoundland, and the religious seclusion of the Mennonite sect. He also produced a radio documentary on Schoenberg. Perhaps needless to add, Gould never married. A remarkable number of books concerning his life and thought appeared throughout the 1980s and 1990s.

Gould, Morton, extraordinarily talented and versatile American composer and conductor; b. Richmond Hill, N.Y., Dec. 10, 1913; d. Orlando, Fla., Feb. 21, 1996. Gould's father was Austrian and his mother Russian, and both fostered their son's early interest in music. If the affectionate family memories are to be accepted as fact, Gould composed a piano waltz at the age of six (indeed, it was ultimately published under the title *Just 6*).

Morton Gould, c. 1960. (Corbis-Bettmann)

Gould had piano lessons with the noted teachers JOSEPH KARDOS and ABBY WHITE-SIDE. He later enrolled in the composition class of VINCENT JONES at N.Y. University where, at the age of 16, he presented a concert of his works. To support himself, he played piano in silent movies and in jazz bands, accompanied dancers, and gave demonstrations of musical skill on college circuits. In 1931–32 he served as staff pianist at Radio City Music Hall in N.Y. From 1934 to 1946 he was in charge of the series "Music for Today" on the Mutual Radio network, and in 1943 became music director of the lucrative "Chrysler Hour" on CBS Radio.

These contacts gave great impetus to Gould's bursting talent for composing singable, playable, and enjoyable light pieces. His *American Symphonette No. 1,* written in 1933, became a popular success, as did his *Chorale and Fugue in Jazz* for two pianos and orchestra from the following year. Gould then produced three more symphonettes (1935, 1938, 1941). The third in this series is the wonderful *Pavanne,* which was later published in several popular arrangements. There followed the *Latin-American Symphonette* (1940), an engaging tetrad of Latin dances (*Rhumba, Tango, Guaracha, Conga*).

Gould wrote several works that touch on American history. His *Spirituals* for strings and orchestra from 1941 is his interpretation of the religious aspect of the American people. That same year he wrote *A Lincoln Legend,* which ARTURO TOSCANINI placed on a program with the NBC Symphony. There followed the lively orchestral *Cowboy Rhapsody* in 1943. In 1945 Gould conducted a whole program of his works with the Boston Symphony Orchestra. He then turned to ballet in his *Fall River Legend,* which premiered in 1947. It was based on the story of the notorious New England old maid Lizzie Borden, who was accused of murdering her parents. Gould composed two works for the 1976 American bicentennial, *Symphony of Spirituals* and *American Ballads.*

Gould wrote the music for the Broadway show *Billion Dollar Baby* in 1945, several scores for Hollywood films, and also background music for the historical television productions *Verdun* (1963), *World War I* (1964–65), and *Holocaust* (1978).

In addition to his popular works, Gould also composed in more traditional styles. He studied BAROQUE composition techniques, and wrote several concertos, including ones for piano (1937), violin (1938), and viola (1944). He also composed a Concerto for tap dancer and orchestra in 1953.

Gould was also a conductor of excellent skills, touring Australia in 1977, Japan in 1979, Mexico in 1980, and Israel in 1981. In 1983 he received the National Arts Award. He was elected a member of the American Academy and Institute of Arts and Letters in 1986. He was president of AS-CAP from 1986 until 1994.

Gounod, Charles (François), famous French composer; b. St. Cloud, June 17, 1818; d. Paris, Oct. 18, 1893. His father, Jean François Gounod, was a painter who died when Gounod was a small child. His mother, an accomplished woman, supervised his literary, artistic, and musical education, and taught him piano.

Cover, Works of Gounod. *(Gianni Dingli Orti/Corbis)*

Gounod completed his academic studies at the Lycée St. Louis, and in 1836 entered the Paris Conservatory. In 1837 he won the second Grand Prix de Rome with his cantata *Marie Stuart et Rizzio,* and in 1839 the Grand Prix with his cantata *Fernand.* In Rome, he studied church music, particularly the works of GIOVANNI PIERLUGI DA PALESTRINA. He composed a Mass for three voices and orchestra, which was performed at the church of San Luigi dei Francesi. In 1842, during a visit to Vienna, he conducted a Requiem of his own.

Upon Gounod's return to Paris, he became choral director and organist of the Missions Etrangères. He then studied theology for two years, but decided against taking Holy Orders. Nonetheless, he was often referred to as "l'Abbé" Gounod, and some religious choruses were published in 1846 under this name.

Soon Gounod tried his hand at stage music. In 1851, his first opera, *Sapho,* was produced at the Paris Opéra, with only moderate success. He revised it much later, in 1884, but it was again unsuccessful. Two more failed operas followed. In the meantime, he conducted the choral society Orpheon from 1852 to 1860 and composed for it several choruses.

Despite its success, *Faust* was at first widely criticized for the melodramatic treatment of Goethe's poem by the librettists, and for the somewhat sentimental style of Gounod's music.

One of Gounod's most popular settings to religious words is *Ave Maria*. It was adapted to fit the melody of the first prelude of JOHANN SEBASTIAN BACH's *Well-tempered Clavier*. Its original version was *Méditation sur le premier Prélude de Piano de J.S. Bach* for violin and piano, published in 1853, with the words added six years later.

Gounod's great success came with the production of *Faust*, based on the famous work by Goethe (Théâtre-Lyrique, March 19, 1859; performed with additional recitatives and ballet at the Paris Opéra, March 3, 1869). This remained his greatest masterpiece, and indeed the most successful French opera of the 19th century. It was triumphant all over the world without any sign of diminishing effect through a century of changes in musical tastes.

Gounod's succeeding operas were only partially successful, but with the 1867 premiere of his *Roméo et Juliette*, Gounod recaptured universal acclaim.

In 1870, during the Franco-Prussian War, Gounod went to London, where he organized Gounod's Choir, and presented concerts. When Paris fell, he wrote an elegiac cantata, *Gallia*, to words from the Lamentations of Jeremiah, which he conducted in London in 1871. The work was also later performed in Paris. He wrote some incidental music for productions in Paris, without much success.

The last years of Gounod's life were devoted mainly to sacred works, of which the most important was *La Rédemption*, a trilogy, first performed at the Birmingham Festival in 1882. Another sacred trilogy, *Mors et vita*, also written for the Birmingham Festival, followed in 1885. Gounod continued to write religious works in close succession. A Requiem begun in 1893 was left unfinished, arranged by Henri Busser after Gounod's death.

Goyescas (Aspects of Goya). Originally, a piano suite by Enrique Granados, 1911, revealing his impression of the work of the great Spanish painter Goya. Granados later transformed it into an opera, which premiered at the Metropolitan Opera, N.Y., in 1916.

grace note. A vocal or instrumental ornament or embellishment not essential to the melody or harmony.

Grace notes are usually written in a smaller size than the primary melody notes. They are usually a scale degree above or below the note they accompany. If the grace note is crossed by a slant, its rhythmic value is taken from the preceding note. If it is not crossed, it becomes a long note incorporated into the following passage, usually taking half of the value of the note immediately following. The latter is typical of CLASSIC practice. Modern editors usually write these long grace notes out.

gradual. 1. In the Roman Catholic MASS, a respond (AN-TIPHON) sung between the epistle and gospel readings. 2. The main book of the Catholic liturgy containing all the principal sections of the Mass. In this sense it is a complement of the antiphonal (antiphoner, antiphonary), which contains the liturgy of the Divine Office.

Gradus ad Parnassum (Lat., steps to Parnassus, the mountain of the muses). 1. Title of the famous Latin treatise on COUNTERPOINT by Johann Joseph Fux (1660–1741), published in Vienna in 1725. It was the textbook of choice for composers and theorists for at least a century. 2. Title given by Muzio Clementi to his collection of piano studies, issued in 1817.

Graffman, Gary, outstanding American pianist; b. N.Y., Oct. 14, 1928. Graffman won a scholarship to the Curtis Institute of Music in Philadelphia when he was eight, and studied with the famed keyboard teacher ISABELLE VENGEROVA. He was only ten when he gave a piano recital at Town Hall in N.Y. After graduating from Curtis in 1946, he was a scholarship student at Columbia University for a year.

In 1946, Graffman won the first regional Rachmaninoff competition, which led to his debut with the Philadelphia Orchestra in 1947. In 1949 he was honored with the Leventritt Award. Subsequently he received a Fulbright grant to go to Europe during 1950–51. Returning to the U.S., he had lessons with VLADIMIR HOROWITZ in N.Y. and RUDOLF SERKIN in Marlboro, Vermont.

Graffman was on his way to establishing himself as a pianist of the first rank when, about 1979, he began to lose the use of his right hand through the ailment designated by doctors as carpal-tunnel syndrome. He was appointed to the faculty of the Curtis Institute of Music in 1980, and became its artistic director in 1986. On Feb. 4, 1993, he was soloist in the premiere of NED ROREM's Fourth Piano Concerto for

The word *gradual* is derived from *gradus* (step), because the chants were sung from the steps of the altar.

PEOPLE IN MUSIC

left hand and orchestra. He brought out an autobiography, *I Really Should Be Practicing* (Garden City, N.Y., 1981).

PEOPLE IN MUSIC

Grainger, (George) **Percy** (Aldridge), celebrated and eccentric Australian-born American pianist and composer; b. Melbourne, July 8, 1882; d. White Plains, N.Y., Feb. 20, 1961. Grainger received his early training from his mother, and at the age of ten appeared as pianist at several public concerts. He then had lessons with German pianist LOUIS PABST. In 1894 he went to Germany, where he studied in Frankfurt and also took a few lessons with Italian composer FERRUCCIO BUSONI.

From his youngest days, Grainger was fascinated by the ideal of the Nordic race, its physical beauty, and art. He traveled to Scandinavia and walked many kilometers through the frozen fjords. In 1901 he began his concert career in England. He then toured South Africa and Australia. In 1906 he met EDVARD GRIEG, who became enthusiastic about his talent. Grainger's performances of Grieg's Piano Concerto were famous. He later became friendly with FREDERICK DELIUS in England, whom he greatly admired, and (in Holland) with the conductor/composer JULIUS RÖNTGEN.

In 1912, Grainger made a sensational American debut, playing his own works in N.Y. He settled in the U.S. in 1914, and taught at the Chicago Musical College from 1919 to 1931 in its summer school. He also was chairman of the music department of N.Y. University in 1932–33.

A devoted son, Grainger led an intimate exchange of letters in a strange baby language with his mother. Her suicide in 1922 devastated him. But he recovered, and married the Swedish poet and artist Ella Viola Ström in 1928. The wedding was a spectacular ceremony staged at the Hollywood Bowl, at which Grainger conducted his work *To a Nordic Princess,* written for his bride.

Grainger's philosophy of life and art calls for the widest communion of peoples and opinions. Despising urban culture, he dressed in vagabond clothes, and was once refused admission to Carnegie Hall at his own concerts until he was properly identified. From composers like Grieg and Delius he gathered the conviction that music must be shaped by native melodies, steeped in ROMANTIC colors, and not be overlong in the individual forms.

Grainger's profound study of folk music underlies the melodic and rhythmic structure of his own music. He made a determined effort to recreate in art music the free flow of the songs of the people. He experimented with "gliding" intervals within the traditional scales and POLYRHYTHMIC combinations with independent strong beats in the component parts.

In a modest way, Grainger was a pioneer of electronic music. As early as 1937 he wrote a quartet for LEON THEREMIN's electronic instruments, notating pitches by zigzags and curves. His list of works, mostly for piano or small instrumental or vocal ensembles, is large, with thematic content principally derived from English and Irish tunes. Of these, *Molly on the Shore* and *Irish Tune from County Derry* are the most popular and have been arranged for various instrumental combinations.

Grainger pushed his body hard, despite suffering from various illnesses. In 1935 he founded a museum at the University of Melbourne, in which he housed all his manuscripts and his rich collection of musical souvenirs. In his last will and testament, he directed his executors to place his skeleton in a glass cage in the Grainger Museum for preservation and possible display. But the University refused to abide by his last wishes, and he was buried in an ordinary way.

Grainger introduced individual forms of notation and orchestral scoring, rejecting the common Italian designations of instruments, tempos, and dynamics. He preferred plain English descriptions, such as FIDDLE (VIOLIN), middle fiddle (VIOLA), louden lots (MOLTO CRESCENDO), soften (DIMINUENDO), short and sharp (STACCATO), and so on.

Grammy Award©. An annual series of awards dispensed by the National Academy of the Recording Arts and Sciences (NARAS) for the most successful recordings in various categories. The award itself is a miniature replica of an old-fashioned GRAMOPHONE.

gramophone (Grk., inscribed sound). 1. A trademark now commonly used in Great Britain for the PHONOGRAPH. 2. A well-known British classical music magazine.

Granados (y Campina), **Enrique,** outstanding Spanish composer; b. Lerida, July 27, 1867; d. at sea, March 24, 1916. Granados studied piano at the Barcelona Conserva-

PEOPLE IN MUSIC

tory, winning first prize on the instrument in 1883, then studied composition there with the well-known Spanish composer FELIPE PEDRELL from 1883 to 1887. In 1887, he went to Paris to study with the pianist CHARLES DE BÉRIOT.

Granados made his recital debut in Barcelona in 1890. He first supported himself by playing piano in restaurants and giving private concerts. He attracted attention as a composer with his ZARZUELA (traditional Spanish opera), *María del Carmen,* written in 1898. In 1900 he conducted a series of concerts in Barcelona, then established a music school in 1901, the Academia Granados. He wrote four operas, which were produced in Barcelona with little success.

Granados undertook the composition of a work that was to be his masterpiece, a series of piano pieces entitled *Goyescas,* completed in 1911, inspired by the paintings and etchings of Goya. Indeed, his fame rests securely on these imaginative and effective pieces, together with his brilliant *Danzas españolas,* composed between 1892 and 1900.

Later, Fernando Periquet wrote a LIBRETTO based on the scenes from Goya's paintings, and Granados used the music of his piano suite for an opera, also entitled *Goyescas.* Its premiere took place, in the presence of the composer, in 1916 at N.Y.'s Metropolitan Opera, with excellent success. The score included an orchestral *Intermezzo,* one of his most popular compositions. During his return voyage to Europe, he lost his life when the boat he was on was sunk by a German submarine in the English Channel.

Granados's music is essentially ROMANTIC, with the addition of specific Spanish rhythms and rather elaborate ORNAMENTATION.

Grand Canyon Suite. Orchestral suite by FERDE GROFÉ, 1931. It depicts five scenes of the American desert landscape, from sunrise to sunset. It was first performed in Chicago and immediately became a popular concert piece.

Grand Ole Opry. Since 1925, a weekly radio program featuring American country music. It was begun in Nashville, Tennessee, broadcast over the radio station WSM (the home station for a life-insurance company whose initials stood for "We Shield Millions"). Broadcast every Saturday night, it was originally simply known as the weekly "Barn Dance." It gained its current name in 1927.

The program's host was a Nashville newspaper reporter and radio announcer named George D. Hay. He took the nickname of "The Solemn Old Judge," and often sounded a train whistle before making his announcements. Hay supposedly came up with the program's name in an off-the-cuff remark. The program followed a national broadcast from the Metropolitan Opera in N.Y. Hay is said to have announced, "Now, you've just heard the Grand Opera. Here comes the Grand Ole Opry," and the name stuck.

Originally, the program featured local performers drawn from the Nashville area. Many of them had little or no previous professional experience, beyond playing for barn dances or participating in fiddlers' conventions. By the mid-1930s, the Opry had developed a talent and booking agency, and its musicians were primarily professionals.

The Ryman Auditorium, for many years the home of the Grand Ole Opry, *1970.* (UPI/Corbis-Bettmann)

In order to play on the program, you had to be a member, which meant that you had to agree to perform each Saturday night, the most lucrative night of the week for a musician. This meant a considerable loss of income, because the Opry paid little to its performers. Opry performers also had to give a percentage of their other performance fees to the program.

Because many leading country stars had to be in Nashville at least once a week, the town became an important center for country music. This was enhanced after World War II, when several major record labels opened Nashville offices to take advantage of the pool of local talent.

Over the decades, the Opry remained the premier country program. There were many competitors, most importantly the *National Barn Dance* out of Chicago and the *Louisiana Hayride* out of Shreveport, but none was as successful or had the stature of the *Opry.* Originally broadcast out of a small studio, it was so successful that management had to find a bigger hall that could accommodate the audience. Eventually the show settled in Nashville's Ryman Auditorium, originally built to accommodate revival meetings. This would remain the home of the program through the early 1970s.

The Opry has grown into a major business enterprise since its move just outside of Nashville to a large theme park and conference center called Opryland, U.S.A. Besides the show itself, the business includes music publishing, real estate, and other ventures.

Meanwhile, being invited to appear on the show itself remains one of the most important steps in the career of a country star.

grand opera. 1. A type of opera, usually in five acts, treating a heroic, mythological, or historical subject, richly costumed, and produced in a large opera house. It is most closely associated with 19th-century French works or works performed in Paris during the same period. 2. In English-speaking countries, any serious operatic work without spoken recitatives. 3. The principal state-supported opera company of Paris (Paris Opéra).

grand piano (Fr. *Piano à queue,* piano with a tail; Ger. *Flügel,* wing). A generic term for the horizontally strung piano, slightly smaller than the concert grand.

Grande Bande, La. *See* 24 VIOLONS DU ROY.

Grande Duchesse de Gerolstein, La. Opéra-bouffe by JACQUES OFFENBACH, 1867. The head of a mythical European

MUSICAL
INSTRUMENT

duchy adores men in uniform, but the commoner soldier she promotes to general marries a milkmaid. The downcast duchess plans a conspiracy to slay him, but another soldier who arouses her interest appears. He is also of royal blood, making the marriage even simpler. Among the other characters are the comically named General Boum and Baron de Vermont-von-bock-bier.

Grandfather's Clock. Ballad by H.C. WORK, 1876, written for a MINSTREL show. The image of the grandfather's dying and the clock's stopping simultaneously was irresistible to its audiences.

graphic notation. Symbols of notation other than those traditionally seen in musical scores. Graphic notation is used to indicate extremely precise (or intentionally imprecise) pitch or to stimulate musical behavior or actions in performance.

Ever since 1000 A.D. when GUIDO D'AREZZO drew a line to mark the arbitrary height of pitch, musical notation has been geometric in its symbolism. The horizontal coordinate of the music staff still represents the succession of melodic notes in time, and the vertical axis indicates the simultaneous use of two or more notes in a chord. Through the centuries of evolution, time values have been indicated by the color and shape of notes and stems to which they were attached.

New sounds demanded new notational symbols. HENRY COWELL, who invented TONE CLUSTERS, notated them by drawing thick vertical lines attached to a stem. Similar notation was used for similar effects by the Russian composer VLADIMIR REBIKOV. In his book *New Musical Resources,* Cowell tackled the problem of nonbinary rhythmic division and outlined a plausible system that would satisfy this need by using square, triangular, and rhomboid shapes of notes. Alois Hába, a pioneer in MICROTONAL music, devised special notation for quarter tones, third tones, and sixth tones.

But as long as the elements of pitch, duration, intervallic extension, and polyphonic simultaneity remain in force, the musical staff can accommodate these elements more or less adequately. This was true even when noises were introduced by the Italian FUTURISTS into their works. In his compositions, LUIGI RUSSOLO drew a network of curves, thick lines, and zigzags to represent each particular noise. But still the measure and the proportional lengths of duration retained their validity.

The situation changed dramatically with the introduction of ALEATORY (or chance) processes and the notion of indeterminacy of musical elements. The visual appearance of aleatory scores assumes the aspect of ideograms (or special symbols). JOHN CAGE, in particular, remodeled the old musical notation so as to give improvisatory latitude to the performer. The score of his *Variations I* suggests the track of cosmic rays in a cloud chamber, his *Cartridge Music* looks like an exploding supernova, and his *Fontana Mix* is a projection of irregular curves upon a strip of graph paper. KRZYSZTOF PENDERECKI uses various graphic symbols to designate such effects as the highest possible sound on a given instrument, or free improvisation within a certain limited range of chromatic notes or tone-clusters.

In music for mixed media, notation ceases to function *per se,* giving way to pictorial representation of the actions or psychological factors involved. Indeed, the modern Greek composer Jani Christou (1926–70) introduces the Greek letter *psi* to indicate the psychology of the musical action, with geometric symbols and masks indicating changing mental states ranging from complete passivity to panic.

The score of *Passion According to Marquis de Sade* by SYLVANO BUSSOTTI looks like a surrealistic painting with musical notes strewn across its path. The British composer CORNELIUS CARDEW drew black and white circles, triangles, and rectangles to indicate musical action. The Greek composer IANNIS XENAKIS prefers to use numbers and letters indicating the specific tape recordings to be used in his musical structures. Some composers abandon the problem of notation entirely, recording their inspirations on tape.

Grappelli (Grappelly), **Stephane,** outstanding French JAZZ violinist; b. Paris, Jan. 26, 1908; d. Paris, Dec. 1, 1997. Grappelli was trained as a classical musician, but turned to jazz in the late 1920s. Originally a pianist, he said that he abandoned the piano after hearing ART TATUM play,

PEOPLE IN MUSIC

thinking he could never equal the blind virtuoso. Instead, he turned to the violin.

Grappelli organized the Quintette du Hot Club de France with the gypsy guitarist DJANGO REINHARDT in 1934, subsequently touring widely and making recordings. The group introduced Reinhardt's lighting-fast single-note runs and Grappelli's pleasantly swinging violin. They recorded together until the Second World War, and their recordings became classics among jazz fans.

After the war, Grappelli worked in a variety of settings, mostly in his native Paris. In the 1960s, he was discovered by a new generation of jazz musicians. He made an album with Gary Burton, the young vibraphone player, that helped relaunch his career. In the '70s, he began touring with guitarist Diz Dizley, in a re-creation of the original Hot Club sound. He also began working with classical musicians, including violinist YEHUDI MENUHIN, releasing a series of very successful recordings.

Grappelli became a grand old man of jazz in the '80s and '90s. His 80th birthday was celebrated with great fanfare with a special Carnegie Hall concert. He continued to play despite suffering from increasing disability in the '90s, and in his last years had to perform from a wheelchair. He died in 1997 following an operation.

Grateful Dead, The. Original lineup: Jerry (Jerome John) Garcia (b. San Francisco, Aug. 1, 1942; d. Serenity Knolls, Marin County, Calif., Aug. 9, 1995), guitar and vocals; Ron "Pigpen" McKernan (b. San Bruno, Calif., Sept. 8, 1945; d. Corte Madera, Calif., March 8, 1973), keyboard and harmonica; Phil(ip Chapman) Lesh (b. Berkeley, Calif., March 15, 1940), bass and vocals; Bob (Robert Hall) Weir (b. San Francisco, Oct. 16, 1947), guitar and vocals; and Bill Kreutzmann (b. Palo Alto, Calif., June 7, 1946), drums. Later members included Mickey Hart (b. N.Y., c. 1950), drums; Donna Godchaux (b. San Francisco, Aug. 22, 1947), vocals; Keith Godchaux (b. San Francisco, July 19, 1948; d. Ross, Calif., July 23, 1980), keyboards; and Brent Mydland (b. Munich, Germany, 1953; d. Lafayette, Calif., July 26, 1990), keyboards; Vince Weinick (b. Phoenix, Ariz., Feb.

PEOPLE IN MUSIC

22, 1952), keyboards. Garcia (working with lyricist Robert Hunter) and Weir contributed the bulk of the songwriting, and all except Lesh, Kreutzmann, and Hart provided vocals.

Jerry Garcia was the spiritual leader of the Grateful Dead, the heart and soul of the band. He took up guitar at age 15, enlisted in the Army two years later, and then, when he was 20, moved to Palo Alto. There he met Robert Hunter, an aspiring folksinger, who would become his long-time songwriting partner. He began playing FOLK and BLUE-GRASS music and formed several short-lived groups during the mid-1960s.

Along with guitarist Bob Weir and keyboardist Ron "Pigpen" McKernan and some other local musicians, he formed Mother McCree's Uptown Jug Champions in 1964. Within a year, the group had changed its emphasis from folk and novelty music to BLUES, and also enlisted two other musicians, drummer Bill Kreutzmann and bassist Phil Lesh. They made their debut performance in July 1965 playing for Ken Kesey's famous Acid Tests, a kind of West Coast version of HAPPENINGS, featuring music, films, poetry, and large bowls of punch that were spiked with LSD.

The band took the name the Grateful Dead by 1966, and were living communally in a house in the Haight-Ashbury district of San Francisco. There they became the official band of 1967's "Summer of Love," when thousands of hippies descended on the town in search of free love and drugs. They also signed with WARNER BROS. RECORDS. Their first few albums were very experimental, appealing to the psychedelic mood of the day, but did not sell well. Nonetheless, the band appeared at the Monterey Pop, Woodstock, and Altamount festivals, the three major rock festivals of the late '60s.

The band reached their height in the studio with two albums cut in the early '70s in a COUNTRY-ROCK style: *Workingman's Dead* and *American Beauty*. Featuring short, melodic songs sung in pretty harmonies, the records had immediate appeal and gained radio play and sales for the group.

The group suffered through much of the '70s and '80s as band members succumbed to drug and alcohol addictions and the quality of the music varied. Garcia cut a solo album

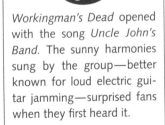

Workingman's Dead opened with the song *Uncle John's Band*. The sunny harmonies sung by the group—better known for loud electric guitar jamming—surprised fans when they first heard it.

as early as 1972, and there were periods when he toured with his own Jerry Garcia Band and undertook other outside projects.

Although they continued to record, their main income came from nearly constant touring, spending six months on the road of most years. They also nurtured an exceptionally devoted fan base through establishing a mail-order business that provided fans with up-to-the-minute information on where the band was playing. Their devoted fans, who gained the nickname Deadheads, would often travel from show to show to hear their different performances.

By the mid-'80s, Garcia's health began to fail due to years of abuse. It came to a head in July 1986, when he lapsed into a five-day, near-fatal diabetic coma. Miraculously, he recovered. The Dead's next album featured their one-and-only No. 1 pop hit single, *Touch of Grey*, seemingly vindicating Garcia's out-of-control life-style.

Garcia suffered another setback in September 1992 when he was hospitalized again suffering from diabetes, an enlarged heart, and fluid in the lungs. Swearing off cigarettes and going on a diet, he managed to recover and the group resumed touring. Then, a week after his 53rd birthday in 1995, Garcia died of a heart attack at a drug-treatment center where he had gone to once again seek treatment for drug addiction.

The group announced at the end of 1995 that they would not continue without Garcia. In 1996 they joined forces with members of the San Francisco Symphony under the command of MICHAEL TILSON THOMAS for a rare performance of JOHN CAGE's *Renga* with *Apartment House 1776*. By 1997 they were touring as the Other Ones with various other reconstituted bands of the San Francisco scene.

gravicembalo (It.). The 17th-century term for HARPSICHORD. *Gravicembalo col piano e forte*, early Italian name for PIANO; *gravicembalo con pian e forte*, CRISTOFORI's name for his piano (early 18th century).

Great Balls of Fire. A 1958 hit for piano-pounder JERRY LEE LEWIS. It introduced his GOSPEL-tinged vocals and BOOGIE-WOOGIE piano style to a broad audience. Later the

gräh-vē-chĕm-bahl′oh

**MUSICAL
INSTRUMENT**

name of a 1989 biographical film about the artist featuring actor Dennis Quaid.

Great Waltz, The. Musical derived from the music of the JOHANN STRAUSSES, Sr. and Jr., 1934. The plot embellishes upon the careers of the waltz kings, introducing a mythical Russian countess to the tale. *The Blue Danube* flows all over the score.

Greek Passion, The. Opera by BOHUSLAV MARTINŮ, 1955–59, after Kazantzakis's novel, posthumously produced in 1961. Life imitates the Passion Play in a strife-torn Greek village.

Green, Adolph. *See* COMDEN AND GREEN.

PEOPLE IN MUSIC

Green, John (Waldo), American pianist, conductor, arranger, and composer; b. N.Y., Oct. 10, 1908; d. Beverly Hills, Calif., May 15, 1989. Green studied economics at Harvard University (B.A., 1928), where he also received instruction in music theory. Later he studied piano, orchestration, and conducting.

Working as an arranger for famous dance-band leader GUY LOMBARDO, Green produced his first hit song, *Coquette*, in 1928. While working as accompanist to GERTRUDE LAWRENCE, he wrote the popular *Body and Soul* in 1930, the same year he became an arranger for Paramount Studios in Hollywood. He also made recordings with his own dance band and performed on the radio.

Green settled in Hollywood as a member of the music staff of MGM in 1942, serving as head of its music department from 1949 to 1958. He prepared award-winning adaptations of the original scores for film versions of *Easter Parade* (1948), *An American in Paris* (1951), *West Side Story* (1961), and *Oliver!* (1968), as well as the score for the film *Raintree County* (1957). He was associate conductor of the Los Angeles Philharmonic from 1959 to 1961, and also appeared as a guest conductor with several major U.S. orchestras.

Greensleeves. An old English ballad in minor MODE, dated to 1580 but probably older. It is mentioned in Shakespeare's play *The Merry Wives of Windsor,* when Falstaff says, "Let the sky thunder to the tune of 'Green Sleeves'" (V:5).

Gregorian chant. A system of liturgical PLAINCHANT in the Christian (Roman Catholic) Church. Its codification is generally attributed to POPE GREGORY I, about 600 A.D. This nonharmonized music may appear monotonous to the modern ear, but it compensates for the absence of harmony by extraordinary melorhythmic richness.

The uncertainties of the notation of Gregorian chant led to many different renderings of the same manuscripts. Disturbed by this problem, a group of learned Benedictine monks of the village of Solèsmes, France, reconciled the different versions. The result was an edition of early Gregorian chants which was published as the *Editio Vaticana* under the Pope's sponsorship.

The text of the Gregorian chant is always in Latin. The syllabic settings are entirely free, so that a syllable may be sung to a single note or to several tied notes. In such climactic passages as the singing of Alleluja, a single syllable may be sung to a group of as many as 20 notes.

What makes Gregorian chant fascinating is that singers must treat a given chant melodically and rhythmically in a variety of ways according to its position in the liturgy. In this respect, Gregorian chant has a striking resemblance to the practice of Indian RAGAS, which are sung or played differently according to the time of day. The improvisatory style of Gregorian MELISMAS is rooted in liturgical prose, as distinct from extemporized instrumental figurations of the BAROQUE school.

The historical roots of Gregorian chant are unknown. Similarities between ancient Jewish CANTILLATION in the synagogue and Gregorian chant may have a historical foundation in view of the common heritage of the Judeo-Christian tradition. Equally tenable is the theory of the Greek origin of Gregorian chant. The strongest argument of this theory lies in the modal classification of Gregorian chant and ancient Greek music. Indeed, the names of the modes in Gregorian chant are borrowed from Greece, although the actual modes are not the same in each tradition.

Great composers throughout history have made use of Gregorian melodies for their works. In such works, the generally asymmetrical melodies of Gregorian chant are made regular, and classical harmonies are added to the melodies. In these adaptations, Gregorian chant serves as raw material, as does folk music when used for similar purposes.

PEOPLE IN MUSIC

A modest practitioner of the practical art of Gregorian chant interprets its rhythmic and melodic values by way of oral tradition, so that the result sounds natural, musically satisfying, and authentic. Observation of the religious services in the old cathedrals and monasteries in Catholic Europe seems to confirm the conviction that Gregorian chant follows its own coherent rules. Most importantly, the music follows the religious text, so that words or syllables are accented according to their relative importance in the text itself, and musical phrases may be asymmetrical to fit the twists and turns of the text itself.

Gregory I (the Great); b. Rome, c.540; d. there, March 12, 604. Gregory I was Pope from 590 to his death. He is celebrated in music history as the reputed reformer of the musical ritual of the Roman Catholic Church.

It is traditionally believed that by his order, and under his supervision, a collection was made in 599 of the music used in the different churches. Then, the various offertories, ANTIPHONS, RESPONSES, and other music was revised and distributed in an arrangement which came to be known as GREGORIAN CHANT.

While for centuries the sole credit for the codification had been given to Gregory, scholars have demonstrated that some of Gregory's predecessors had begun this reform and even fixed the order of certain portions of the liturgy. The work of reform was definitely completed under some of his immediate successors.

Grieg, Edvard (Hagerup), celebrated Norwegian composer; b. Bergen, June 15, 1843; d. there, Sept. 4, 1907. The original form of the name was Greig. His great-grandfather, Alexander Greig, of Scotland, emigrated to Norway about 1765, and changed his name to Grieg.

Edvard received his first instruction in music from his mother, an amateur pianist. At the suggestion of the Norwegian violinist OLE BULL, young Grieg was sent to the Leipzig Conservatory in 1858, where he studied piano and theory. His early compositions were greatly influenced by German ROMANTICISM, particularly the works of FELIX MENDELSSOHN and ROBERT SCHUMANN.

PEOPLE IN MUSIC

In 1863 Grieg went to Copenhagen, where he met the young Norwegian composer RIKARD NORDRAAK. The two organized the Euterpe Society for the promotion of national Scandinavian music, in opposition to the German influences which were dominant at that time. The premature death of Nordraak at the age of 23 in 1866 left Grieg alone to carry on the project.

After traveling in Italy, Grieg returned to Norway, where he opened a Norwegian Academy of Music in 1867, and gave concerts of Norwegian music. He was also engaged as conductor of the Harmonic Society in Christiania (now Oslo). In 1867 he married his cousin, the singer NINA HAGERUP. At that time he had already composed his two violin sonatas and the first set of his *Lyric Pieces* for Piano, which used Norwegian motifs. On April 3, 1869, Grieg played the solo part in the world premiere of his Piano Concerto, which took place in Copenhagen. Thus, at the age of 25, he established himself as a major composer of his time.

In 1874–75, Grieg wrote incidental music to HENRIK IBSEN's *Peer Gynt.* The two orchestral suites arranged from it became extremely popular. The Norwegian government then granted Grieg an annuity of 1,600 crowns, which enabled him to devote most of his time to composition. Performances of his works were given in Germany with increasing frequency, and soon his fame spread all over Europe. On

A bird relaxes on the statue of Edvard Grieg in Bergen, Norway. (Dave Bartruff/Corbis)

May 3, 1888, he gave a concert of his works in London. He also gave recitals of his songs with his wife.

Grieg revisited England frequently, receiving honorary doctoral degrees in music from Cambridge in 1894 and, twelve years later, Oxford. Other honors were membership in the Swedish Academy in 1872 and the French Academy in 1890.

Despite his successes, Grieg spent most of his later years in his house at Troldhaugen, near Bergen, avoiding visitors and shunning public acclaim. However, he continued to compose at a steady rate. His death, of heart disease, was mourned by all Norway. He was given a state funeral and his remains were cremated, at his own request, and sealed in the side of a cliff projecting over the fjord at Troldhaugen.

Grieg's importance as a composer lies in the strongly pronounced nationalism of his music. Without resorting to literal quotation from Norwegian folk songs, he succeeded in re-creating their melodic and rhythmic flavor. In his harmony, he remained well within the bounds of tradition. The lyric expressiveness of his best works and the attractive rhythm of his dance-like pieces imparted a charm and individuality that contributed to the lasting success of his art. His unassuming personality made friends for him among his colleagues. He was admired by both JOHANNES BRAHMS and PIOTR ILYICH TCHAIKOVSKY.

The combination of lyricism and nationalism in Grieg's music led some critics to describe him as "the Chopin of the North." He excelled in miniatures, in which the perfection of form and the clarity of the musical line are remarkable.

Grieg's best-realized compositions are his lyric pieces for piano. He composed ten sets of these pieces in 34 years, between 1867 and 1901. His songs are distinguished by the same blend of Romantic and characteristically national inflections. In orchestral composition, Grieg limited himself almost exclusively to symphonic suites, and arrangements of his piano pieces. In chamber music, his three violin sonatas, a Cello Sonata, and one extant String Quartet are examples of fine instrumental writing. He also composed many song cycles and individual songs, and various works for piano.

Grieg, Nina (Hagerup), Norwegian singer; b. near Bergen, Nov. 24, 1845; d. Copenhagen, Dec. 9, 1935. Her father, Herman Hagerup, was a brother of EDVARD GRIEG's mother. Nina Hagerup studied singing with Danish vocal teacher GUSTAF HELSTED. She met Edvard Grieg in Copenhagen, and married him on June 11, 1867. Her interpretations of his songs gained much praise from critics. FREDERICK DELIUS dedicated two sets of songs to her.

PEOPLE IN MUSIC

Griffelkin. Television opera by LUKAS FOSS, 1955, with a libretto from a German fairy tale, broadcast on NBC-TV. Griffelkin is a young devil who becomes disloyal to Hell after a visit on Earth. An episode includes an entertaining out-of-key ensemble of pupils practicing their scales.

Griffes, Charles T(omlinson), outstanding American composer; b. Elmira, N.Y., Sept. 17, 1884; d. N.Y., April 8, 1920. Griffes studied piano with a local teacher, and also took organ lessons.

In 1903, he went to Berlin, where he continued his piano studies and also studied composition. To eke out his living, he gave private lessons, and also played his own compositions in public recitals. In 1907 he returned to the U.S., and took a music teacher's job at the Hackley School for Boys at Tarrytown, N.Y. At the same time he continued to study music by himself.

PEOPLE IN MUSIC

Griffes was fascinated by the new art of the French IMPRESSIONISTS, particularly their use of Oriental SCALES. He also was strongly influenced by the Russian school, particularly MODEST MUSSORGSKY and ALEXANDER SCRIABIN. A combination of natural talent and determination to acquire a high degree of craftsmanship elevated Griffes to the position of a foremost American composer in the impressionist genre. Despite changes of taste, his works retain an enduring place in American music, including orchestral, instrumental, and vocal works.

Grofé, Ferde (Ferdinand Rudolph von), American composer, pianist, and arranger; b. N.Y., March 27, 1892; d. Santa Monica, Calif., April 3, 1972. Grofé studied music

PEOPLE IN MUSIC

with Italian-born composer PIETRO FLORIDIA, and then was engaged as a viola player in the Los Angeles Philharmonic. At the same time, he worked as a pianist and conductor in theaters and cafés.

Grofé joined PAUL WHITEMAN's band in 1920 as a pianist and arranger. His scoring of GEORGE GERSHWIN's *Rhapsody in Blue* (1924) won him fame. In his own works, Grofé successfully applied jazz rhythms, interwoven with simple ballad-like tunes. His *Grand Canyon Suite* (Chicago, 1931, Whiteman conducting) became very popular. He also composed other light pieces in a modern vein.

groove. 1. An enjoyable listening experience, especially in jazz and popular music. 2. A steady rhythmic pattern associated with a particular jazz or popular style.

ground bass. An early English form of BASS accompaniment. It consists of a repeated bass phrase of four or eight measures, even notes, a distinct melodic outline, generally symmetrical in structure, which serves as the harmonic foundation of variations in the upper voices.

The technique was first used in the VIRGINAL music of the late RENAISSANCE. It became widespread during the English BAROQUE (e.g., *When I Am Laid In Earth,* Dido's farewell aria in Henry Purcell's *Dido and Aeneas*).

Some common examples of ground bass include:

One of the most common patterns in bass parts is the descending figure from the TONIC to the DOMINANT. The groups of 16 notes, descending from the tonic to the dominant in the middle section of FRÉDÉRIC CHOPIN's Polonaise in A-flat major, elaborate on this pattern.

Sometimes the bass follows an entire diatonic scale, from the tonic to the lower tonic, in even notes. The second theme in CÉSAR FRANCK's *Symphonic Variations* for piano and orchestra is an example, as is the accompaniment of SERGEI RACHMANINOFF's song *A Little Island.*

Many descending basses are set in chromatic motion, invariably in even notes. In such cases, it is the bass line that governs the melody, resulting in a changing chromatic sequence. An excellent example is the opening of EDVARD GRIEG's Ballade in G minor for piano (op.24, 1876).

Gruber, Franz Xaver, Austrian composer, great-great-grand-father of H(einz) K(arl) Gruber; b. Unterweizburg, near Hochburg, Nov. 25, 1787; d. Hallein, near Salzburg, June 7, 1863. Gruber acquired fame as the composer of the Christmas carol *Stille Nacht, Heilige Nacht.* Of a poor family, Gruber had to do manual work as a youth, but managed to study organ. By dint of perseverance he obtained, at the age of 28, his first position, as church organist and schoolmaster at Oberndorf. It was there, on Christmas Eve of 1818, that a young curate, Joseph Mohr, brought him a Christmas poem to be set to music, and Gruber wrote the celebrated song.

PEOPLE IN MUSIC

Gruber, H(einz) **K**(arl)**,** called Nali, Austrian composer, conductor, and double bass player, great-great-grandson of FRANZ XAVER GRUBER; b. Vienna, Jan. 3, 1943. Gruber studied composition, played double bass and horn, and took courses in film music at the Hochschule für Musik in Vienna from 1957 to 1963. He played principal double bass in the Niederösterreiches Tonkünstler-Orchestra in Vienna from 1961 to 1969. He was also a co-founder of an AVANT-GARDE group, MOB art & tone ART, in 1968. In 1961, Gruber joined the Vienna ensemble Die Reihe as a double bass player, and in 1969 he was engaged as double bass player in the ORF (Austrian Radio) Symphony Orchestra and also performed as an actor.

PEOPLE IN MUSIC

In his music, Gruber maintains a wide array of styles, idioms, and techniques, and he has developed a relaxed style mixing serious and humorous elements. His self-described "pan-demonium" work, *Frankenstein!!,* a multimedia affair with children's verses recited in a bizarre and mock-scary manner, became popular. It was written in 1976–77, and premiered a year later in Liverpool, England. Among his more recent works are two Violin Concertos (1977–78; 1988) Cello Concerto (1989), *Bring me the head of Amadeus,* music for the television series *Not Mozart* (BBC2-TV, London, Nov. 17, 1991), and *Gloria von Jaxtberg,* music theater (1992–93).

Gruenberg, Louis, eminent Russian-born American composer; b. near Brest Litovsk, Aug. 3, 1884; d. Los Angeles, June 9, 1964. Gruenberg was taken to N.Y. as an infant, where he studied piano as a child. He then went to Berlin, where he studied piano and composition with the FUTURIST Italian composer FERRUCCIO BUSONI.

In 1912, Gruenberg made his debut as a pianist with the Berlin Philharmonic. He then intermittently took courses at the Vienna Conservatory, where he also was a tutor. In 1919 he returned to the U.S. and devoted himself to composing. He was one of the organizers and active members of the League of Composers, a progressive group founded in 1923. He became a champion of modern music, and one of the earliest American composers to incorporate jazz rhythms within works of symphonic dimensions. From 1933 to 1936 he taught composition at the Chicago Music College. He then settled in California, where he composed several film scores.

Of Gruenberg's many operas, the most successful was *The Emperor Jones,* based on Eugene O'Neill's play (Metropolitan Opera, N.Y., 1933; awarded the David Bispham Medal). He finished four symphonies, violin, viola, and cello CONCERTOS, several CANTATAS (many influenced by African-American music), and chamber settings, including some jazz-inflected music for piano solo. He also published four volumes of SPIRITUALS.

grunge. *See* ROCK.

Gruppen. A work of spatial music by KARLHEINZ STOCKHAUSEN, 1959, first performed in Cologne. It is scored for three different chamber orchestras, with three conductors beating three different tempi.

G-sharp minor (Ger. *Gis*). This key, relative to B major and armored with five sharps in its key signature, is not often encountered as the principal key of a major work. It is best suited to short piano pieces. FRANZ LISZT's *La Campanella* for piano is in G-sharp minor.

Guarneri family, famous Italian family of violin makers. (The Italian form of the name was derived from the Latin

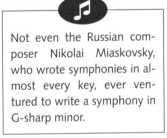

Not even the Russian composer Nikolai Miaskovsky, who wrote symphonies in almost every key, ever ventured to write a symphony in G-sharp minor.

Guarnerius; the instrument labels invariably used the Latin form.) Andrea Guarneri, head of the family (b. Cremona, c.1625; d. there, Dec. 7, 1698), was a pupil of the famous violin maker NICOLA AMATI. He lived in Amati's house from 1641 to 1646, and again from 1650 to 1654. Then, with his wife, he moved to his own house in Cremona and began making his own violins, labeling them as "alumnus" of Amati and, after 1655, "ex alumnis," often with the additional words of "sub titolo Sanctae Theresiae."

Andrea's son Pietro Giovanni, "da Mantova" (b. Cremona, Feb. 18, 1655; d. Mantua, Mar. 26, 1720), worked first at Cremona, then settled in Mantua. He also used the motto "sub titolo Sanctae Theresiae." Another son of Andrea, Giuseppe Giovanni Battista, "filius Andreae" (b. Cremona, Nov. 25, 1666; d. there, c.1740), worked in his father's shop, which he eventually inherited. In his own manufactures, he departed from his father's model and followed the models of ANTONIO STRADIVARIUS.

Giuseppe's son Pietro, "da Venezia" (b. Cremona, April 14, 1695; d. Venice, April 7, 1762), settled in Venice in 1725, and adopted some features of the Venetian masters.

Another son of Giuseppe, (Bartolomeo) Giuseppe Antonio, "Giuseppe del Gesù" (from the initials IHS often appearing on his labels; b. Cremona, Aug. 21, 1698; d. there, Oct. 17, 1744), became the most celebrated member of the family. Some of his instruments bear the label "Joseph Guarnerius Andreae Nepos Cremonae," which establishes his lineage as a grandson of Andrea. His violins are greatly prized, rivaling those of Stradivarius in the perfection of instrumental craftsmanship. He experimented with a variety of wood materials, and also made changes in the shapes of his instruments during different periods of his work.

Such great virtuoso violinists as JASCHA HEIFETZ, ISAAC STERN, HENRYK SZERYNG, Arthur Grumiaux, and NICCOLÒ PAGANINI used Giuseppe Antonio's instruments.

guasa. Venezuelan song of the CORRIDO (folk ballad) type, usually in $\frac{6}{8}$ meter.

Gubaidulina, Sofia, remarkable Russian composer of great individuality; b. Chistopol, Oct. 24, 1931. Gubaidulina was descended of a Tatar father (her grandfather was a mullah) and of a mother who had both Russian and Jewish blood (she once said that she was the place where East and West

PEOPLE IN MUSIC

met). Her sources of inspiration in composition were similarly diverse, extending from mystical Eastern elements to Catholic and Russian Orthodox conformations.

Gubaidulina studied at the Kazan Conservatory, graduating in 1954, and then enrolled at the Moscow Conservatory to study composition. From her very first essays in composition she followed different paths without following any set modern techniques. Perhaps her most astounding work is the Concerto for bassoon and low string instruments, in five movements, composed in 1975. The bassoon is accompanied by a densely voiced set of four cellos and three double basses. The solo voice struggles to make itself heard over these dominant low sounds.

Gubaidulina's music soon penetrated into the music world far beyond the Soviet frontiers, and her works were performed in Europe and the U.S. She made several voyages to the U.S. to hear performances of her works, and was a guest at the Boston Festival of Soviet Music in 1988. But it took a decisive change in official Soviet policy with the fall of the Communist government before her music was fully recognized in Russia. In 1991 she settled in Germany. Among her more recent compositions are *Jetz Immer Schnee* for chamber chorus and chamber ensemble (Amsterdam, June 12, 1993), *Und: Das Feste ist in vollem Gange,* cello concerto (1993; Las Palmas, Canary Islands, Jan. 31, 1994), *Der Seiltänzer,* violin sonata (Washington, D.C., Feb. 24, 1994), *Zeitgestalten* for orchestra (Birmingham, Nov. 29, 1994), and Flute Concerto (1994 – 95).

MUSICAL INSTRUMENT

gudok. Russian three-string instrument placed on the knees while playing. Similar to the Bulgarian GADULKA.

Guerre des Bouffons (*Querelle des Bouffons*). A famous theatrical controversy that erupted in Paris in 1752.

That year, an Italian opera company (the Bouffons) gave a performance of GIOVANNI BATTISTA PERGOLESI's *La Serva padrona*. Those who favored Italian opera over the native French work applauded it vigorously. On the other hand, the lovers of French opera, fostered by Louis XV, were angered by its great popularity. A whole series of pamphlets was written by advocates on both sides of the argument, including Jean-Jacques Rousseau's historical paper, *Lettre sur la musique française* (Letter on French music). The controversy subsided when the Bouffons left Paris in 1754.

Guido d'Arezzo (Guido Aretinus), famous Italian reformer of musical notation and vocal instruction; b. c. 991; d. after 1033. Guido received his education at the Benedictine abbey at Pomposa, near Ferrara, Italy. He left the monastery in 1025, as a result of disagreements with his fellow monks, who were envious of his superiority in vocal teaching. Guido was then summoned by Bishop Theobald of Arezzo to the cathedral school there, and it was because of this association that he became known as Guido d'Arezzo. His fame spread and reached the ears of Pope John XIX, who called him to Rome in 1028 to demonstrate his system of teaching. In his last years, he was a prior of the Camaldolite fraternity at Avellano.

Guido's fame rests on his system of SOLMIZATION, by which he established the nomenclature of the major HEXA-CHORD (six-note scale) *Ut, Re, Mi, Fa, Sol, La,* from syllables in the initial lines of the Hymn of St. John:

> *Ut queant laxis Resonare fibris*
> *Mira gestorum Famuli tuorum,*
> *Solve polluti Labii reatum,*
> *Sancte Joannes.*

No less revolutionary was Guido's introduction of the musical staff of four lines, retaining the red f-line and the yellow c-line of his predecessors, and drawing between them a black a-line, and above them a black e-line. He placed the PLAINSONG notes (which he did not invent) in regular order on these lines and in the spaces:

New black line e_____

Old yellow line c_____

New black line a_____

Old red line f_____

PEOPLE IN MUSIC

Some music historians have claimed that Guido traveled in France and spent several years at the monastery of Saint-Maur des Fossés, near Paris, while others say he traveled as far as Germany, and even to England. None of these theories are supported by any hard evidence.

Guido also added new lines above or below these, as occasion required, thus doing away with all uncertainty of pitch. Another invention credited to Guido is the so-called GUIDONIAN HAND.

Opinions differ widely as to the attribution to Guido of all these innovations. Some scholars maintain that he merely popularized already established ideas. Many believe that solmization, in particular, was introduced by a German abbot, Poncius Teutonicus, at the abbey of Saint-Maur des Fossés.

Guido's most essential treatises are *Micrologus de disciplina artis musicae* (c. 1026) and *Epistola de ignoto cantu* (c. 1028–29).

Guidonian hand (Lat. *manus guidonis;* named after GUIDO D'AREZZO, the creator of syllabic SOLMIZATION). A method of teaching a system of closely related HEXACHORDS (six-note scales).

The lowest G (the GAMUT) was represented by the upperside of the thumb of the left hand. The notes progressed scale-wise across the palm to the tip of the little finger, and continuing along the fingertips to the index finger, then descending and after another turn ending on the top of the middle finger on the E two octaves and a sixth above the initial gamut.

In the Middle Ages, the choir director indicated the points on the different joints of each finger to dictate the required notes to the singers.

Guillaume de Machaut. *See* MACHAUT, GUILLAUME DE.

Guillaume Tell. *See* WILLIAM TELL.

güiro (Cub.; Braz. *reco-reco*). A scratcher or scraper used in Latin American bands. It is made out of a long gourd with notches on its upper side. These notches are scraped with a stick. Although the güiro is usually classified as a percussion instrument, its sound production is actually caused by friction.

guitar (It. *chitarra*). The universally popular string instrument, played by plucking or strumming the strings.

The güiro is often used in modern scores, most cleverly at the end of IGOR STRAVINSKY'S *LE SACRE DU PRINTEMPS*. In MAURICE RAVEL'S *L'ENFANT ET LES SORTILÈGES*, it can replace the *rape à fromage*, a cheese grater scraped with a triangle beater.

MUSICAL
INSTRUMENT

An instrument of the LUTE family, the modern Spanish (acoustic) guitar has six strings, and a compass of three octaves and a fourth, from E to a2. The strings are tuned in perfect fourths, with the exception of the interval between the fourth and fifth strings, a major third: E, A, d, g, b, and e1. The music is written an octave higher than it sounds, in the G clef.

The fingerboard is provided with frets to indicate the position of the notes of the scale. By the very nature of the instrument, the guitar is incapable of infinitely sustained harmony, but is brilliantly adapted for arpeggiated (broken) chords.

The word *guitar* can be traced to the Greek KITHARA, but there is no similarity in the structure or sound of the two instruments. The guitar in its present form developed in Spain in the 16th century and spread all over the world.

In the 19th century in America, the classical Spanish guitar was gradually redesigned. By the early 20th century, a new type of acoustic guitar, with a larger body, steel strings, and therefore greater volume and projection, was introduced. This enabled the guitar to play with larger ensembles and to more effectively accompany a singer. A further innovation in the 1920s and '30s led to arch-top acoustic guitars, which were larger and louder still.

Toward the mid-20th century, the guitar was electrically amplified to further increase and sustain its volume. First, standard acoustic guitars were fitted with pickups, creating a loud, but hollow-sounding instrument. This was the instrument introduced by jazz musicians like CHARLIE CHRISTIAN, and it became a primary instrument of modern rock musicians.

Then in the late '40s and early '50s, a new solid-body instrument was introduced. Guitars like Leo Fender's Telecaster and Stratocaster and Gibson's Les Paul became the favorite of rock 'n' roll groups for their loud, clean sound. Soon after, the introduction of "effects"—from reverb to Wah Wah and distortion—made the electric guitar even more versatile.

Despite the popularity of more modern guitars, great acoustic guitar players like ANDRÉS SEGOVIA maintained the classical instrument and its traditions. Numerous modern composers, among them MARIO CASTELNUOVO-TEDESCO and MANUEL PONCE, wrote concertos for guitar and orchestra.

MUSICAL INSTRUMENT

guitar, acoustic. Classical or Spanish instrument, in contrast to the ELECTRIC GUITAR.

guitar, back-up. *See* RHYTHM GUITAR.

MUSICAL INSTRUMENT

guitar, bass. An electrified adaptation of the DOUBLE BASS, built and shaped like the ELECTRIC GUITAR which it is designed to match in popular music. Some electric models are made without frets, so that the performer can perform the GLISSANDOS and PORTAMENTOS possible on the acoustic instrument. These are mostly used in JAZZ-FUNK (fusion).

guitar, classical. Spanish (acoustic) guitar.

guitar, electric. *See* ELECTRIC GUITAR.

guitar, lead. In rock and other popular groups, the "first guitarist," performing on an electric guitar and responsible for melodic riffs, fills, and solos. In the original ROLLING STONES, KEITH RICHARDS generally played lead guitar while BRIAN JONES played rhythm guitar. A group may have more than one person capable of performing this role, as in the original Allman Brothers Band (DUANE ALLMAN and DICKIE BETTS).

guitar, rhythm. In rock and other popular groups, a modern term for the "second guitarist," performing on an electric guitar and providing the harmonic and rhythmic support for lead instruments or singers. In the BEATLES, JOHN LENNON generally played rhythm guitar to GEORGE HARRISON's LEAD GUITAR. Also called *back-up guitar.*

MUSICAL INSTRUMENT

guitar, Spanish. Acoustic or classical six-stringed guitar, its predecessors dating back to the 16th century, with a varying number of strings. It is made of wood, with a body modeled after the human neck and torso with a large circular soundhole. The neck is attached to a fingerboard supplied with frets. *See also* GUITARRA ESPAÑOLA.

guitarra española (Sp.). The five-string guitar of the 16th and 17th centuries.

Guntram. Opera by RICHARD STRAUSS, 1894. A medieval German duke is murdered by a minstrel named Guntram. The heiress to the throne loves him, so she forgives him for his crime. But she refuses to marry him because he does not come from her social class.

Gurre-Lieder. Secular oratorio by ARNOLD SCHOENBERG, c.1901–1911, first performed in Vienna, 1913. The work is scored for narrator, solo voices, chorus, and orchestra. The work was more or less composed by 1901, but not orchestrated until a decade later, by which time Schoenberg's style had changed radically. This earlier work shows the influence of RICHARD WAGNER in its orchestration.

The text is a German translation of poems by the Danish poet Jacobsen. The events unfold in a Danish castle in Gurre, and the songs tell of the impossible love of the King for a woman not of royal stock. The story is morbid and difficult to follow, but the music is glorious, absorbing the obscure texts much as Richard Wagner's music dramas overwhelm the obscurities of their plots.

gusle. 1. One-string FIDDLE of the South Slavic region, with a long neck and wooden resonator. 2. VIOLIN.

gusli. An ancient Russian PSALTERY, shaped in a trapezoid. The number of strings ranges from 11 to 36, strung horizontally so that the lowest pitches are furthest from the player. Early gusli types had up to seven strings, but the number was increased in the 15th century. Mikhail Glinka has a musical part for a legendary gusli player in *Ruslan and Ludmilla,* but the part is generally taken by the orchestral harp. 2. An instrument related to the Finnish KANTELE.

Guthrie, Woody (Woodrow Wilson), legendary American folksinger, guitarist, songwriter, union organizer, and writer; b. Okemah, Okla., July 14, 1912; d. N.Y., Oct. 3, 1967. Guthrie was raised on a small farm in Oklahoma. His mother suffered from the inherited disease of Huntington's chorea, and was soon separated from the family. Guthrie be-

MUSICAL
INSTRUMENT

PEOPLE IN MUSIC

Woody Guthrie, c. 1948.
(Frank Driggs Collection)

gan to play guitar by his early teen years, and by age 16 was working informally as a musician and sign painter.

The Oklahoma farming region was devastated in the early 1930s by a series of dust storms, created by the overplanting of the land. Many so-called "Okies" fled the area in search of a better life in California. Guthrie joined this migration in 1933, and soon was performing as a cowboy-styled singer on Los Angeles radio. He also became interested in radical politics, particularly the growing trade union movement, and began writing songs with a political message. In 1937 he was hired by a government agency to write a series of songs about a new dam being built in Colorado on the Columbia River, resulting in a series of songs including *Roll On, Columbia.*

In 1940, Guthrie met folksinger PETE SEEGER, who was traveling in California. Seeger invited him to N.Y., where he lived with a group of like-minded radical folksingers in a shared apartment. Guthrie went to N.Y. in 1942, and was an immediate sensation. He dressed, talked, and sang like a "real" folksinger, impressing N.Y. audiences. He published his autobiography, *Bound for Glory*, in 1943, and began writing a regular column for the union-sympathizing newspaper *The Daily Worker*.

Although Guthrie had recorded some of his early songs for RCA on an album called *Dust Bowl Ballads*, most of his recording was done for Folkways Records and other small labels. Among the songs he wrote and recorded were *So Long, It's Been Good to Know Ya; This Train Is Bound for Glory; Hard Traveling; Blowing Down This Old Dusty Road;* and *This Land Is Your Land.*

Guthrie's life and career were gradually destroyed after he was stricken with Huntington's chorea in the early 1950s. He was hospitalized by the middle of the decade, and lingered on until 1967, although he was no longer able to play or compose music. Upon his death, his cremated remains were scattered in the Atlantic Ocean.

Guthrie's son, Arlo (Davy) Guthrie (b. N.Y., July 10, 1947), followed in his father's footsteps as a socially conscious folksinger, guitarist, and songwriter. He is most famous for his talking ballad *Alice's Restaurant* (1969), which was the basis for a film in which he starred.

Guys and Dolls. Musical by FRANK LOESSER, 1950, based on stories by Damon Runyon. A playboy engages in a battle of mind and heart with a Salvation army woman, while a gambler keeps putting off marrying his nightclub dancer girlfriend. Includes the title song, *Fugue for Tinhorns* (actually a three-part CANON), *Sue Me, Take Back Your Mink, Adelaide's Lament,* and *Luck Be A Lady Tonight.*

Guys and Dolls was made into a successful movie musical in 1955 starring FRANK SINATRA, Marlon Brando, Jean Simmons, and Stubby Kaye (as Nicely-Nicely), who performs a brilliant rendition of *Sit Down, You're Rocking the Boat.*

gymel (from Lat. *gemellus,* twin). A two-part COUNTERPOINT in thirds or sixths, dating from the 5th century and common during the Middle Ages. The historical relationship of this technique to FABURDEN is not clear. It is the same as *cantus gemellus.*

Gymnopédies (from Lat., naked dances). Three piano pieces by ERIK SATIE, 1888. Their strongly anti-ROMANTIC nature and anticipation of 20th-century NEOCLASSICISM established his notoriety and represent his early style.

Gypsy. Musical by JULE STYNE and STEPHEN SONDHEIM, 1959, based on Gypsy Rose Lee's autobiography. A very romanticized version of the stripper's life, it focuses on her struggle with her mother, who gets to sing *Everything's Coming Up Roses.* It also includes *Small World, Together, Wherever We Go,* and *You'll Never Get Away From Me.*

Gypsy Baron, The (*Der Zigeunerbaron*). Operetta by JOHANN STRAUSS, 1885. The Ottomans have been forced out of Hungary. Their leader, Sandor, returns to his castle to find it ruined. His fields are occupied by Zsupan, a neighbor who is seeking a lost Turkish treasure. Sandor falls in love with Zsupan's daughter, but she is in love with her governess's son, Ottokar.

Now a band of Gypsies, led by Czipra, enters the scene. When Sandor, newly anointed as the "Gypsy baron," finds out about Arsena and Ottokar, he falls instead for the gypsy beauty Saffi. After all of this breathless action in the first act, two more acts and a war against Spain are necessary to straighten everything out happily for all (except for Zsupan, who never finds the treasure).

While the English word for the Romany seems to be a corruption of "Egyptians," Gypsies in all probability came originally out of India, where they were treated as untouchable outcasts.

Gypsy music. A nomadic people, Gypsies (properly, the Romany) lived in many countries in Europe, forming their own communities and so-called tabors or camps. They elected their "kings" in colorful rituals, but otherwise adapted themselves to the customs of their adoptive land.

In literature, painting, theatrical plays, and operas, Gypsies became stereotyped as clever and devious, possessing magical powers and practicing their arts upon superstitious men and women. They were known as fortune-tellers and thieves, seducers and international smugglers. They attracted attention by their elaborate apparel and jewelry.

With all their picturesque folkways, the Gypsies failed to develop their own art form. The so-called GYPSY SCALE, containing two augmented seconds, might more properly be called a Hungarian scale. But Gypsy music, like proverbial Gypsy love, had the ability to creep into other musical styles. In the 19th century, Gypsy music took root in the Balkans, predominately in Romania. In fact, the Gypsies call themselves "Romany," an allusion to their Romanian origin.

From the Balkans, a horde of Romanian Gypsy musicians invaded Hungary, Austria, and Russia. The most significant incursion of Gypsy music was experienced in Hungary. The national Hungarian form of *verbunkos* was directly influenced by Romanian Gypsy musicians. FRANZ LISZT avidly listened to Gypsy bands, and his *Hungarian Rhapsodies* were mainly derived from these impressions rather than from authentic Magyar folk tunes.

Another curious phenomenon of Gypsy adaptation took place in Russia, where groups of Gypsy singers, guitarists, violinists, and tambourine players, most of them from the annexed Romanian border state of Bessarabia, established themselves as popular entertainers in restaurants, cafés, circuses, and various places of amusement. "Gypsy romances," or songs, became exceedingly popular in Russia, but their words and music actually were composed by amateur Russian musicians.

Composers for more than a century have used such expressions as *alla gitana* or *alla zingarese* (in a Gypsy manner) as a definite indication of the intended style of performance. Instrumental works with Gypsy titles abound. Among the most famous are *Zigeunerweisen* (Gypsy Airs) for violin and piano by PABLO DE SARASATE and *Tzigane* for violin and orchestra by MAURICE RAVEL.

The Gypsies also play a key role in the plotlines of many famous works. The mysteries that make the plot of GIUSEPPE VERDI's *Il Trovatore* unintelligible are contrived by the Gypsies, with the famous Anvil Chorus in the second act sung by Gypsy blacksmiths. GEORGES BIZET's *Carmen* is a Gypsy who causes Don José to desert the army and join her comrades in a smuggling ring. In Michael William Balfe's *THE BOHEMIAN GIRL* (1843), the heroine is kidnapped by Gypsies as a child. Because many Gypsies came from Bohemia, the nickname Bohemians was attached to rootless artists and wandering adventurers. IGNACY PADEREWSKI's opera *Manru* glorifies the leader of a Gypsy tribe in the Carpathian mountains. GIACOMO PUCCINI's *La Bohème,* a collective noun meaning Bohemian life, might well be translated "The Gypsies."

In numerous literary romances, an aristocratic gentleman of wealth is revealed to be a Gypsy, noble of heart if not of pedigree. In JOHANN STRAUSS's famous operetta *Der Zigeunerbaron,* a young Hungarian is chosen by the Gypsies to be their leader and is elevated to the rank of a Gypsy baron. But above all, the romanticized Gypsies were passionate and often sinister lovers, such as Aleko, the Gypsy hero of Pushkin's poem *The Gypsies* and the subject for SERGEI RACHMANINOFF's opera. The title of the operetta *Zigeunerliebe* (Gypsy Love) by FRANZ LÉHAR is typical of the Gypsy image.

Gypsy scale. An informal name for the minor harmonic scale with a raised subdominant, forming two augmented seconds. This scale is also known as the HUNGARIAN SCALE.

Index

A, 1
a cappella, 1
A major, 1
A minor, 1
ABA, 1
Abbado, Claudio, 1–2
Abduction from the Seraglio, The, 2, 450
Abravanel, Maurice, 2–3
absolute music, 3
abstract music, 3
Academic Festival Overture, 3
accent, primary, 1407
accidental, 3
accompaniment, 3
accordion, 3–4
acoustics, 4–5
  amplitude, 26
  architectural, 5
  beat, 99
  combination tones, 287
  decay, 359
  decibel, 359–360
  difference tone, 287, 1811
  directional hearing, 380
  envelope, 450
  Euler, Leonhard, 458
  feedback, 481
  formant, 517
  frequency, 529–530
  fundamental, 537–538
  harmonic, 675
  harmonic series, 676
  harmonics, 676–677
  Helmholtz, Hermann von, 706
  interference beats, 780–781
  just intonation, 843–844
  node, 1225
  noise, 1225
  resonance, 1481
  resonator, 1481
  Schaeffer, Pierre, 1582–1583
  sine tone, 1669
  sonus, 1701
  sound, 1703–1704
  sum (summation) tone, 1765
  Tartini, Giuseppi, 1809–1811
  Tartini tones, 1811
  tone color, 1868–1869
  vibration(s), 1950–1951
  wavelength, 2007
  white noise, 2028
  wolf tone, 2046
act, 5
action, 5
action song, 5–6
Acuff, Roy, 6
ad libitum, 6
Adagio for Strings, 6
Adam, Adolphe, 6–7
  Giselle, 581
  If I Were King, 768
Adam de la Halle, 7, 820
Adams, John, 7–8
  Death of Klinghoffer, 355

Nixon in China, 1223
Adams, John Luther, 8–9
added seventh, 9
added sixth, 9
Adderley, "Cannonball," 9
Adeste Fideles, 9–10
Adieux, Les, 10
Adler, Kurt Herbert, 10–11
Adler, Richard, 1302
Adorno, Theodor, 11
Adriana Lecouvreur, 11
aeolian harp or lyre, 11
Aeolian mode, 58
aerophones, 12
Affects, Doctrine of, 12
A-flat major, 12
Africaine, L', 12–13
African music, 13–14
African-American music. *See also*
    blues; jazz; *specific individuals*
  gospel music, 601–603
  jug, 841
  ragtime, 1448–1449
  rhythm and blues, 1489–1490
  stomp, 1731
Afro-Pop Music, 14
Age of Anxiety, The, 14
Agnus Dei, 14
agogic, 14
Agon, 14
aguinaldo, 14
Aida, 14–15
Aida trumpet, 15
air, 1906
Air on the G String, 15
al fresco, 15
alba, 15
Albéniz, Isaac, 15–16
Alberti bass, 16
Albinoni, Tomaso, 16–17
alborada, 17
albsifono, 17
Alceste, 17
aleatory music, 17–18
Alexander Nevsky, 18
*Alexander's Feast, or The Power of
    Music,* 18
Alexander's Ragtime Band, 18
Alfvén, Hugo, 1116
alleluia, 18
allemanda (allemande), 18–19
Allison, Mose, 19
Almeida, Laurindo, 19
Aloha oe, 19
alphorn, 19
Alpine Symphony, 19
Also sprach Zarathustra, 20
alteration, 20
altered chords, 20
althorn, 20
alti naturali, 20
alto, 20
Amahl and the Night Visitors,
  20–21

amateur, 21–22
Amati, 22
ambitus, 22
Ambrosian chant, 22–23
ambulation, 23
Amen, 23
America, 23
America the Beautiful, 24
American Festival Overture, 24
American in Paris, An, 24
American Quartet, 24
Amériques, 24
Amico Fritz, L', 24
Amirkhanian, Charles, 24–25
Amor brujo, El, 25
amplifier, 25
amplitude, 26
Amplitude modulation, 26
anacrusis, 26
analysis, 26
anapest, 26
Anchors Aweigh, 26
Anderson, Laurie, 26–27
Anderson, Leroy
  Sleigh Ride, 1677
  Syncopated Clock, 1784
  Typewriter, 1913
Anderson, Marian, 27
Andrea Chénier, 27
Andrews, Julie, 28
Andrews Sisters, 28–29
Anglican chant, 29
Animals and animal music, 29–30
Anna Magdalena Book, 30
Années de pèlerinage, 30–31
Annie Get Your Gun, 31
Annie Laurie, 31
Anon, 31
answer, 31
antecedent, 31
Antheil, George, 31–32, 74–75
anthems, 32
  Chandos Anthems, 242
  national, 1206
antiphonal, 32
antiphon(e), 33, 785
antique cymbals, 33
antonality, 51
Antony and Cleopatra, 33
anvil, 33
Anvil Chorus, 33
Anything Goes, 34
Apocalyptic Symphony, 34
Apollon musagète, 34
Appalachian Spring, 34
Appassionata Sonata, 34
applause, 34–35
April in Paris, 35–36
Arab music, 36
Arabella, 36
arabesque, 37
Archduke Trio, 37
Argento, Dominick, 37–38
aria(s), 38
  Bell Song, 113

da capo, 38
  parable, 1307
Ariadne auf Naxos, 38
arietta, 38
ariette, 38
arioso, 39
Arkansas Traveler, 39
Arlen, Harold, 39–40
  Stormy Weather, 1734
  Wizard of Oz, 2041–2042
Armatrading, Joan, 40
Armide, 40–41
Armstrong, Louis, 41–42
Arne, Thomas Augustine, 42–43, 1550
arpeggio, 43
arrangement, 43, 1881
Arrau, Claudio, 43–44
ars antiqua, 44
ars musica, 45
ars nova, 45–46, 300
Art of the Fugue, The, 46
articulation, 46–47
artificial harmonics, 47
As Time Goes By, 47–48
ASCAP, 47
Ashkenazy, Vladimir, 48
Ashley, Robert, 48–49
Astaire, Fred, 49
asymmetry, 50
athematic, athematic composition, 50
A-Tisket, A-Tasket, 50
Atkins, Chet, 50–51
atonality, 1305
aubade, 52
Auber, Daniel-François-Esprit, 52, 522
Aucassin et Nicolette, 53
audiences, 53–54
  applause, 34–35
  catcalls, 235
  claque, 269
audition, 54
Auer, Leopold, 55
Aufstieg und Fall der Stadt Mahagonny, 56
augmentation, 56
augmented interval, 56
Auld Lang Syne, 56
aulos, 56–57
Auric, Georges, 57, 1060
Aus Italien, 57–58
authentic modes, 58
autoharp, 58
automatic compositon, 58
avant-garde, 58
Ave Maria, 58–59
Ax, Emanuel, 59
ayre, 59
Aznavour, Charles, 59

B, 60
B major, 60
B minor, 60

Babbit, Milton, 60–61
Babes in Arms, 61
baccheta di legno, 61–62
B-A-C-H, 62
Bach, Carl Philipp Emanuel, 62
Bach, Johann Christian, 62–63
Bach, Johann Sebastian, 63–67
 Air on the G String, 15
 Anna Magdalena Book, 30
 Art of the Fugue, 46
 B-A-C-H, 62
 Brandenburg Concertos,
  169–170
 Christmas Oratorio, 262
 Coffee Cantata, 279–280
 Dorian Toccata and Fugue, 405
 English Suites, 448
 Goldberg Variations, 596
 Italian Concerto, 791
 Well-Tempered Clavier,
  2022–2023
Bach, P.D.Q. *See* Schickele, Peter
Bach, Wilhelm Friedemann, 67
Bacharach, Burt, 67–68, 1423
Bachianas Brasileiras, 68
Badarzewska, Thekla, 1406
Baez, Joan, 68–69
bagatelle, 69
bagpipe(s), 69–70
 chanter, 244
 drone, 412
 duda, 413
 gaida, 547
 koza, 893
 pibroch, 1364
 zampogna, 2076
Baiser de la fée, Le, 70
Baker, Dame Janet, 70
Baker, Josephine, 70–71
Balakirev, Mily, 71–72, 789
balalaika, 73
Balfe, Michael William, 150
ballad opera, 73, 111–112
ballad(s), 73
 Band Played On, 76
 *On the Banks of the Wabash, Far
  Away,* 1264
 Casey Jones, 232–233
 Child, Francis, 255
 Come Home, Father, 288
 corrido, 313
 Grandfather's Clock, 619
 Greensleeves, 624–625
 plena, 1376
 *Tramp, Tramp, Tramp, or The
  Prisoner's Hope,* 1880
ballade, 73–74
ballata, 74
Ballet méchanique, 74–75
ballet(s), 74
 Agon, 14
 Amor brujo, El, 25
 Apollon musagète, 34
 Appalachian Spring, 34
 Baiser de la fée, Le, 70
 Biches, Les, 131

Billy the Kid, 135
Boléro, 154
Checkmate, 250
choreography, 261
Cinderella, 267
Coppélia, 308
Création du monde, La, 325
Cuatro soles, Los, 333
Daphnis et Chloé, 345
de cour, 74
Dybbuk, 424
entr'acte, 450
Fall River Legend, 470
Fancy Free, 473
Festin de l'araignée, Le, 484–485
Firebird, 501
Gayané, 557, 1555
Giselle, 581
Histoire du soldat, L', 725
Incredible Flutist, 776
Indes Galantes, Les, 776
Jeu de cartes, 820
Judith, 841
Matelots, Les, 1060
Nutcracker, 1243–1244
Orpheus, 1280
Parade, 1307
Péri, La, 1343
Perséphone, 1346
Petrouchka, 1351–1352
Pulcinella, 1430
Red Poppy, 1467
Relâche, 1475–1476
Rite of Spring, 1500
Rodeo, 1510
Romeo and Juliet, 1520
Seven Deadly Sins, 1640–1641
Skyscrapers, 1675
Sleeping Beauty, 1676–1677
Sombrero de tres picos, El,
  1695–1696
Swan Lake, 1771
*Theme and Variations: The Four
  Temperaments,* 1839
ballo, 75
Ballo in maschera, Un, 75
Band Played On, The, 76
banda, 77
band(s), 75–76. *See also* big band
 brass, 76
 military, 76
 string, 76
 symphonic, 76–77
 wind, 77
bandmasters, 77
 Johnson, Frank, 827
 Sousa, John Philip, 1705–1707
 Waring, Fred, 2002
 Welk, Lawrence, 2022
 Whiteman, Paul, 2028
bandola, 77
bandoneon, 77, 1364
bandoura, 77
bandurria, 77–78
banjo, 78
bar, 78–79

Barber, Samuel, 79–81
 Adagio for Strings, 6
 Antony and Cleopatra, 33
 Capricorn Concerto, 217
 Knoxville, Summer of 1915, 879
 *Medea's Meditation and Dance
  of Vengeance,* 1070
Barber of Seville, The, 79
barbershop harmony, 81
Barbirolli, Sir John, 81–83
barcarolle, 83
bard, 83, 1618
Barenboim, Daniel, 83–84
barform, 84
baritone(s), 84–85
 Fischer-Dieskau, Dietrich,
  502–503
 Hampson, Thomas, 656–657
 Heldenbariton, 704
 Milnes, Sherrill, 1122
 Prey, Hermann, 1403–1404
 Warfield, William, 2001–2002
barline, 78–79
Baroque music, 85–86. *See also
  specific composers, e.g.:* Bach,
  Johann Sebastian
 basso continuo, 93–94
 diminution, 379
 inégales, 779
 opera, 1633
 partimento, 1316
 Picardy third, 1364–1365
 sacred concerto, 1555–1556
 semiseria, 1633
 symphonia, 1776
 terraced dynamics, 1834–1835
 trio sonata, 1888–1889
Baroque organ, 86
Baroque suite, 86
barrel organ, 86, 411
barrelhouse, 86–87
Barrett, "Syd." *See* Pink Floyd
Bartered Bride, The, 87
Bartók, Béla, 87–90
 Bluebeard's Castle, 145
 Mikrokosmos, 1117–1118
Barton, Andrew, 380
baryton, 90
Basie, "Count," 90–91
bass clarinet, 92
bass drum, 92
bass flute, 92
bass guitar, 92
bass lines, 92, 94
bass(es), 91
 Chaliapin, Feodor, 240–241
 Christoff, Boris, 262–263
 Kipnis, Alexander, 867
 Nesterenko, Evgeni (Evge-
  nievich), 1211
 Pinza, Ezio, 1370–1371
 Ramey, Samuel, 1455
 Robeson, Paul, 1502–1503
bass-baritone(s), 92
 Terfel, Bryn, 1833–1834
 Treigle, Norman, 1884–1885

basse danse, 92–93
basset horn, 93
basso buffo, 93
basso continuo, 93–94, 302
basso obbligato, 94
basso ostinato, 94
basso profondo, 94
bassoon, 94
Bastien und Bastienne, 94
baton, 95
battaglia, 95
battery, 95
Battle, Kathleen, 96
Battle Cry of Freedom, The, 95
Battle Hymn of the Republic, The,
  95–96
Bax, (Sir) Arnold, 96–97
Beach, Amy Marcy Cheny (Mrs.
  H. H. A.), 97–98
Beach Boys, The, 98, 1768
beam(s), 98
Bear, The, 98–99
beat, 99
Beatles, The, 99–101
 Harrison, George, 687–688
 Lennon, John, 933–934
 McCartney, Sir Paul,
  1064–1065
 Starr, Ringo, 1717–1718
Beautiful Dreamer, 101
bebop, 102
Bechet, Sidney, 102–103
Beecham, (Sir) Thomas, 103–104
Beer, Jacob Liebmann. *See* Meyer-
  beer, Giacomo
Beethoven, Ludwig van, 104–111
 Adieux, Les, 10
 Appassionata Sonata, 34
 Archduke Trio, 37
 Choral Symphony, 259
 Diabelli Variations, 375
 Egmont Overture, 432
 Emperor Concerto, 443
 Eroica Symphony, 452–453
 Eroica Variations, 453
 Fidelio, oder Die eheliche Liebe,
  492–493
 Fifth Symphony, 495–496
 Ghost Trio, 569
 Hammerklavier Sonata, 654
 Harp Quartet, 685
 Kreutzer Sonata, 899
 Leonore Overtures, 938–939
 Ode to Joy, 1252
 Pastoral Symphony, 1320–1321
 Pathétique Sonata, 1321
 Rasoumowsky Quartets, 1458
 Turkish March, 1909
 Waldstein Sonata, 1991
Beggar's Opera, The, 111–112
beguine, 112
Beiderbecke, Bix, 112–113
bel canto, 113
bell, 113
Bell Song, 113
Bellini, Vincenzo, 113–114

Norma, 1227–1228
Puritani di Scozia, I,
  1432–1433
Sonnambula, La, 1700–1701
bells, 115–116
  campanology, 208
  carillon, 218–219
  change, 242–243
  chimes, 256
  shepherd's bell, 1648
  sonnerie, 1701
  tintinnabulum, 1858
Bells Are Ringing, 116
Benedictus, 116
Benjamin, Arthur, 801–802
Benjamin, George, 116–117
Berberian, Cathy, 117
berceuse, 118
Berg, Alban, 118–119
  Lulu, 995–996
  Lyric Suite, 1001
  Wozzeck, 2052–2053
bergerette, 119
Berio, Luciano, 119–121
Berlin, Irving, 121–122
  Alexander's Ragtime Band, 18
  Annie Get Your Gun, 31
  Call Me Madam, 205
  Face the Music, 469
  Pretty Girl is Like a Melody,
    1401
  *There's No Business Like Show
    Business,* 1840–1841
  This Is the Army, 1844
  White Christmas, 2027
  Yip, Yip, Yaphank, 2066
  Ziegfeld Follies, 2085–2086
Berlioz, Hector, 122–126
  Corsaire, Le, 313–314
  Damnation de Faust, La, 343
  Enfance du Christ, L', 446
  Harold in Italy, 682–683
  idée fixe, 767
  King Lear, 866
  Roman Carnival, 1518
  Roméo et Juliette, 1521
  Symphonie fantastique,
    1776–1778
  Troyens, Les, 1899
Bernstein, Elmer, 126
Bernstein, Leonard, 126–128
  Age of Anxiety, 14
  Candide, 209
  Dybbuk, 424
  Facsimile, 469
  Fancy Free, 473
  Jeremiah Symphony, 818
  Kaddish, 846
  On the Town, 1264
  Trouble in Tahiti, 1896
  West Side Story, 2024–2025
  Wonderful Town, 2051
Berry, Chuck, 128–129
Bethune, "Blind Tom," 129–130
B-flat major, 130
B-flat minor, 131

Biber, Heinrich, 131
Biches, Les, 131
bicinium, 131–132
Bicycle Built for Two, A, 132
big band, 132
  Basie, "Count," 90–91
  Calloway, Cab, 207
  Dorsey brothers, 406–407
  Ellington, "Duke," 441–442
  Goodman, Benny, 598
  Hampton, Lionel, "Hamp,"
    657–658
  Henderson, Fletcher, "Smack,"
    707
  Herman, Woody, 714
  James, Harry, 802
  Jones, Thad, 834
  Kaye, Sammy, 856
  Miller, Glenn, 1120–1121
  Shaw, Artie, 1646–1647
  Sun Ra, 1766–1767
  Whiteman, Paul, 2028
Bigard, "Barney," 132–133
Biggs, E. Power, 133
*Bill Bailey, Won't You Please Come
  Home?,* 133
Billings, William, 134, 253
Billy Budd, 134–135
Billy the Kid, 135
binary, 135–136
Binchois, Gilles (de), 136
Bing, Sir Rudolph, 136–137
Bingen, Hildegard von. *See*
  Hildegard Von Bingen
bitonality, 137
biwa, 137
Bizet, Georges, 138
  Carmen, 220
  Jeux d'enfants, 820
  Jolie fille de Perth, La, 830
  Pêcheurs de Perles, les, 1327
Björling, Jussi, 138–139
Blacher, Boris
  Ornamente, 1279
  *Zwischenfalle bei einer Not-
    landung,* 2092
Black Crook, The, 139
Black music. *See* African-Ameri-
  can music
Blackbirds of 1928, 139
Blades, Rubén, 139–140
Blake, Eubie, 140–141
  I'm Just Wild about Harry, 769
  Shuffle Along, 1656
Blakey, Art, 141
Bliss, Arthur
  Checkmate, 250
  Colour Symphony, 286
Bliss, Sir Arthur, 141–142
Blitzstein, Marc, 142–143
  Cradle Will Rock, 324
  Regina, 1471
Bloch, Ernest, 143–144
  Israel Symphony, 790
  Macbeth, 1005
Blow, John, 144–145

blue note, 145
Bluebeard's Castle, 145
bluegrass, 145–146, 172
blues, 146–147
  barrelhouse, 86–87
  boogie-woogie, 86–87, 155
  Broonzy, "Big Bill," 176
  Byrd, Henry Roeland, 191–192
  Charles, Ray, 245–246
  Clapton, Eric, 268–269
  Dorsey, "Georgia Tom,"
    405–406
  Handy, W. C., 665–667
  harmony, 145
  Hill, Bertha "Chippie," 720
  Hopkins, Sam "Lightnin'," 740
  Hunter, Alberta, 755–756
  Jefferson, "Blind Lemon," 816
  Johnson, Robert, 828–829
  Joplin, Janis, 836–837
  Jordan, Louis, 839–840
  King, "B. B.," 864–865
  Leadbelly, 920–921
  Lewis, Meade "Lux," 945
  Mayall, John, 1062–1063
  McGhee, Brownie, 1066
  Memphis Blues, 1084
  *Nobody Knows You When You're
    Down and Out,* 1224
  Rainey, Ma, 1450
  Raitt, Bonnie, 1450–1451
  St. Louis Blues, 1557–1558
  Smith, Bessie, 1685–1686
  Turner, "Big Joe," 1909–1910
  Washington, Dinah, 2003
  Waters, "Muddy, 2005
BMI, 147–148
boat song, 83
Boccherini, Luigi, 148
Bock, Jerry, 148–149
  Fiddler on the Roof, 492
  Fiorello!, 500
bodhran, 149
Boehm system, 149
Boethius, 149
Boeuf sur le toit, Le, 149
Bohème, La, 150
Bohemian Girl, The, 150
Böhm, Karl, 150–151
Boieldieu, François-Adrien,
  151–152
Boito, Arrigo, 1073
Bolcolm, William, 152–153
Bolden, "Buddy," 153
bolero, 153–154
Boléro (Ravel), 154
bomba, 154
bombard, 154
Bombo, 154
bones, 154
bongos, 154
boogie-woogie, 155
bop, 102
bore, 155
Borge, Victor, 155
Boris Godunov, 155–156

Borodin, Alexander, 156–157
  In the Steppes of Central Asia,
    775
  Kismet, 871–872
  Prince Igor, 1409–1410
  Vendredis, Les, 1940
bossa nova, 157
Boston, 717
bouffe, 157
bouffon, 158
Boulander, Nadia, 158–159
Boulez, Pierre, 159–160, 1041
Boult, Sir Adrain, 160–162
bourrée, 162
bow, 162
bowed instrument, 162
Bowie, David, 162–163
Bowie, Lester, 163
bowing, 163–164
Bowles, Paul, 164–165
boy (boys') choir, 165
boy soprano, 165
Boyce, William, 165
Boys from Syracuse, The, 165–166
brace, 166
Brahms, Johannes, 166–169
  Academic Festival Overture, 3
  Deutsches Requiem, Ein, 372
  Tragic Overture, 1879–1880
Branca, Glenn, 169
Brandenburg Concertos, 169–170
branle, bransle, 170
Brant, Henry, 170
brass band, 76
brass instruments, 170–171
  bell of, 113
  bore of, 155
  buccina, 183
  bugle, 184
  conical mouthpiece, 300
  conical tube, 300
  cornet, 311–312, 1892
  cornu, 312–313
  crook for, 329
  cupped mouthpiece, 336
  cylindrical tube, 337
  euphonium, 458
  fifths, horn, 742
  Flügelhorn, 510
  French horn, 527–528
  helicon, 705
  horn. *See* horn(s)
  Jagdhorn, Jägerhorn, 801
  lituus, 969
  lur, 996
  ophicleide, 1270
  post horn, 1390
  slide horn, trombone, or trum-
    pet, 1677
  tongue technique with, 1869
  transposing instruments,
    1881–1882
  triumph cornet, 1892
  trombone. *See* trombone and
    trombonists
  trompe de chasse, 1895

trumpet. *See* trumpet and
trumpeters
tuba. *See* tuba(s)
valve in, 1926–1927
wind instruments, 2039
brass music, 1909
bravura, 171
Braxton, Anthony, 171
break (jazz), 171
break (register), 171–172
breakdown, 172
Bream, Julian, 172
Brel, Jacques, 172
Brendel, Alfred, 173
Brice, Fanny, 173
Brico, Antonia, 173–174
bridge, 174
Brigadoon, 174
brindisi, 174
Britten, Benjamin, 174–176
 Billy Budd, 134–135
 Ceremony of Carols, 239
 Death in Venice, 355
 Gloriana, 591
 Illuminations, Les, 769
 Let's Make an Opera, 942
 Midsummer Night's Dream,
  1116–1117
 Noye's Fludde, 1239
 Paul Bunyan, 1322
 Peter Grimes, 1348
 Prodigal Son, 1414
 Rape of Lucretia, 1457
 Spring Symphony, 1714
 Turn of the Screw, 1909
 *Variations on a Theme by Frank
  Bridge,* 1931–1932
 War Requiem, 2001
 *Young Person's Guide to the Or-
  chestra,* 2070–2071
Broadway musicals. *See* musicals
Broonzy, "Big Bill," 176
Broschi, Carlo or Riccardo, 476
Brown, Clifford, 177
Brown, Earle, 177, 1424
Brown, James, 177–178
Brubeck, Dave, 178
Bruch, Max, 178–180, 885–886
Bruckner, Anton, 180–182
 Apocalyptic Symphony, 34
 Romantic Symphony, 1520
 Te Deum Symphony, 1822
 Zero Symphony, 2084–2085
bruitism, 182
brunette, 182
Bryars, Gavin, 182–183
buccina, 183
Buchla, Donald, 183
buffa, 184
Buffalo Springfield, 183–184
bugaku, 184
bugle, 184, 1484
Bull, John, 184–185
bull-roarer, 185
Bülow, Hans von, 185–186
Bumbry, Grace, 186–187

Burgundian school, 187–188
burlesca, 188
burlesque, 188
Burney, Charles, 188–189
Burns, Robert, 189
 Auld Lang Syne, 56
 Comin' thro the Rye, 289
Busoni, Ferruccio, 189–190
 Doktor Faust, 395
 Fantasia contrappuntistica, 474
 Indianische Fantasie, 777
Buxtehude, Dietrich, 190–191
Bye Bye Birdie, 191
Byrd, Henry Roeland, 191–192
Byrd, William, 192–193,
  1225–1226
Byrds, The, 193
Byrne, David, 193–194
Byzantine chant, 194–195, 1259
Byzantine liturgy, 886

C, 196
C major, 196
C minor, 196
cabaletta, 196
Caballé, Montserrat, 196–197
Cabaret (musical), 198
cabaret (musical form), 197–198,
  1700
Cabin in the Sky, 198
caccia, 198
Caccini, Giulio "Romano,"
  198–199, 1242
cacophony, 199
cadence, 199–201
cadenza, 201
café chantant, 201–202
Cage, John, 202–204
 Europeras 1 & 2, 459–460
 4'33," 520
 Imaginary Landscape, 770
 indeterminacy, 776
 number pieces, 1240
 Ocean, 1249
 prepared piano, 1398–1399
 Silence, 1663
 Sonatas and Interludes,
  1697–1698
 time-bracket notation, 1855
Cahn, Sammy, 204
Caissons Go Rolling Along, The,
  204–205
cakewalk, 205
California Girls, 205
call and response, 205
Call Me Madam, 205
Callas, Maria, 205–207
calliope, 207
Calloway, Cab, 207
calypso, 208
Camelot, 208
camera, 208
Camerata, 208
Campanella, La, 208
campanology, 208
Camptown Races, 208–209

canary, 209
cancan, 209
cancel, 209
canción, 209
Candide, 209
canon, 210–211, 301, 525,
  1765–1766
Canonical Hours, 211, 1949
cantabile, 211
cantata(s), 211–212
 Alexander Nevsky, 18
 *Canticum sacrum ad honorem
  Sancti Marci nominis,* 213
 Carmina Burana, 221
 Ceremony of Carols, 239
 Christmas Oratorio, 262
 Coffee Cantata, 279–280
 Figure humaine, La, 496
 Gesang der Jünglinge, Der, 567
 I Have a Dream, 763
 Klagende Lied, Das, 873
 Prairie, 1396
 sacred concerto, 1555–1556
 serenata, 1636
 Threni, 1852
canti carnascialeschi, 212–213
canticle, 213
*Canticum sacrum ad honorem
  Sancti Marci nominis,* 213
cantiga, 213
cantillation, 213–214
cantinela, 213
canto, 214
cantor, 214
cantus firmus, 214–215
canzona, 215
Capeman, The, 215
Capitan, El, 216
capo, 216
cappella, 216
capriccio, 216
Capriccio brillante, 216–217
Capriccio Espagnol, 217
Capriccio Italien, 217
Capricorn Concerto, 217
Cardew, Cornelius, 217–218,
  1621
carillon, 218–219
carioca, 219
Carlos, Wendy (Walter), 219
Carmen, 220
Carmen Jones, 220
Carmichael, Hoagy, 220–221,
  564, 1717
Carmina Burana, 221
Carnaval, 221
Carnegie Hall, 221–222
Carnival (festival), 222
Carnival (musical), 222
Carnival of the Animals, The,
  222–223
carol, 223
Carousel, 223
Carpenter, John Alden, 223–224,
  1675
Carreño, Teresa, 224–225

Carreras, José, 225
Carry Me Back to Old Virginny,
  225
Carter, Benny, 225–226
Carter, Elliott, 226–227, 408
Carter, Ron, 227–228
Carter Family, The, 227
Caruso, Enrico, 228–230
Casals, Pablo, 230–232
Casey Jones, 232–233
Cash, Johnny, 233–234, 514
cassation, 234
castanets, 234
Castelnuovo-Tedesco, Mario,
  234–235
Castor et Pollux, 235
castrato, 235, 476
catalogue, thematic, 1838–1839
catcalls, 235
catch, 235
catgut, 236
Cat's Fugue, 236
Cats (musical), 236
cats (term), 236
Caturla, Alejandro García, 236
Cavalleria rusticana, 237
Cavalli, Pier Francesco, 237–238,
  1278
cavata, 238
cavatina, 238
CD (compact disc), 290
CD-ROM, 238
Cecilianism, 238
celesta, 238
cell, 239
cellists
 Boccherini, Luigi, 148
 Casals, Pablo, 230–232
 Chung, Myung-Wha, 264
 DuPré, Jacqueline, 419–420
 Feuermann, Emanuel, 489
 Harnoncourt, Nikolaus, 682
 Lloyd Webber, Julian, 972
 Ma, Yo-Yo, 1002
 Piatigorsky, Gregor, 1363
 Rostopovich, Mstislav,
  1534–1536
cello, 239
cembalo, 239
cencerros, 239
*Cenerentola, La, o la bontà in tri-
  onfo,* 239
Ceremony of Carols, A, 239
Cesti, Antonio, 1279, 1385
cesura, 239
Chabrier, Emmanuel, 239–240
cha-cha, 240
chaconne, 240
Chaliapin, Feodor, 240–241
chalumeau, 241–242
chamber music, 242, 339
chamber opera, 242
chamber orchestra, 242
chamber symphony, 242
champagne aria, 242
chance operations, 242, 1725

Chandos Anthems, 242
change, 242–243
chanson, 243
chanson de geste, 53, 243
Chansons de Bilitis, 243
chant, 243–244
  Ambrosian, 22–23
  Anglican, 29
  Byzantine, 194–195
  Gregorian. *See* Gregorian chant
  plainchant, 1374
  Syrian, 1786
  tantric, 1806
Chant de rossignol, Le, 244
chanter, 244
chanteur, 244
chantey, 1643
Chantilly Lace, 244
chapel, 244
character piece, 244–245
charango, 245
charivari, 245
Charles, Ray, 245–246
Charleston, 246
Charpentier, Gustave, 246–247
  Julien, 842
  Louise, 985
Charpentier, Marc-Antoine, 247,
  1070
Chattanooga Choo Choo, 248
Chávez, Carlos, 248–250
  Cuatro soles, Los, 333
  Resonancias, 1481
  Xochipilli, 2062
Checker, Chubby, 250
Checkmate, 250
cheironomy, 250
cheng, 2085
Cherry, Don, 250–251
Cherubini, Luigi, 251–253, 1070
chest register, 253
Chester, 253
Chevalier, Maurice, 253–254
chiave, 254
chiesa, 254
Child, Francis, 255
Child of Our Time, A, 254
child prodigy, 254–255
Children's Corner, 256
children's songs
  action song, 5–6
  Frère Jacques, 530
  Oh! Dear, What Can the Matter Be?, 1255
  Oh Where, Oh Where Has My Little Dog Gone?, 1256
  Old MacDonald Had a Farm, 1260
  Pop! Goes the Weasel, 1387
  Row, Row, Row Your Boat, 1541
  School Days, 1599
  Sur le Pont d'Avignon, 1768
  Three Blind Mice, 1851
  Toy Symphony, 1879

Twinkle, Twinkle Little Star, 1912
chimes, 256, 1903
ch'in, 1434
Chinese blocks, 256
chocalho, 256
choir, 256
Chopin, Frédéric, 256–258
  Minute Waltz, 1129
  Raindrop Prelude, 1449–1450
  Revolutionary Etude, 1485
Chopsticks, 258–259
choral, 259
choral music, 562, 1438, 1480
  antiphon(e), 33
  boy (boys') choir, 165
  children's chorus, 255
  choir, 256
  choral, 259
  chorus, 261–262
  coro spezzato, 313
  discant, 381–382
  precentor, 1396
choral societies, 1279–1280
Choral Symphony, 259
chorale, 259–260
chord organ, 261
chord(s), 260–261. *See also* harmony
  added seventh, 9
  added sixth, 9
  altered, 20
  arpeggio, 43
  dissonant, 384
  inversion, 785–786
  Italian sixth, 791
  ninth, 1221
  pivot, 1374
  principal, 1410
  subordinate, 1760
  triad, 1885–1886
  Tristan, 1890
chordophones, 261
  harp, 683–685
  hurdy-gurdy, 756–757
  neck, 1208
  open string, 1267–1268
  v[i4]n[a4], 1960
choree, 261
choreography, 261
choreographers, 334–335
"choreographic observation," 469
chôro, 261
chorus, 261–262
Christe eleison, 262
Christian, Charlie, 262
Christmas Oratorio, 262
Christmas songs
  Jingle Bells, 821
  Rudolph the Red-Nosed Reindeer, 1549
  Silent Night, 1663
Christoff, Boris, 262–263
Christophe Colomb, 263
chromatic, 263
chromaticism, 263

Chronochromie, 263
Chung, Kyung-Wha, 264
Chung, Myung-Wha, 264
Chung, Myung-Whun, 264–265
church modes, 265, 761
church sonata, 265, 1697
Cielito lindo, 265
Cilèa, Francesco, 11, 265
Cimarosa, Domenico, 265–266,
  1061
cimbalom, 266–267
Cinderella, 267
Cinq Doigts, Les, 267
cipher, 267
circle (cycle) of fifths, 267
circular breathing, 267
circus music, 267
Circus Polka, 268
citole, 268
cittern, 268
civil rights movement, 2008
Civil War ballads, 95, 1880
Clair de lune. See Suite bergamasque
clappers, 268
Clapton, Eric, 268–269
claque, 269
clarinet and clarinet music, 92,
  269–271
  bass clarinet, 92
  basset horn, 93
  Bigard, "Barney," 132–133
  De Franco, "Buddy," 353–354
  Dodds, Johnny, 388
  Giuffre, Jimmy, 581–582
  Goodman, Benny, 598
  Herman, Woody, 714
  Shaw, Artie, 1646–1647
  Stoltzman, Richard,
    1730–1731
  zummāra, 2091
clarinet quintets, 1716
clarino, 271
Clarke, Jeremiah, 1901
Clarke, Rebecca, 271–272
Classic era, 272
classical music and forms, 272
  arabesque, 37
  aubade, 52
  bagatelle, 69
  ballade, 73–74
  battaglia, 95
  berceuse, 118
  bicinium, 131–132
  burlesca, 188
  canon, 210–211
  capriccio, 216
  cassation, 234
  chamber music, 242
  chamber opera, 242
  chamber symphony, 242
  character piece, 244–245
  comédie-ballet, 288
  concert overture, 292
  concertante, 293
  concerted music, 293

concertino, 293
concerto, 294–295
concerto for orchestra, 295
concerto grosso, 296
cyclical forms, 337
divertimento, 386
double fugue, 408
double quartet, 408
duet, 414
dumka, 417–418
dump, 418
duo, 418–419
dux, 422
elegy, 438
entrata, 450
étude, 456
falsobordone, 472
fancy, 473
fantasia, 473–474
funeral march, 538
Galanterien, 548
Hörspiel, 747
humoresque, 753
idyl, 767
impromptu, 772
incidental music, 775
In Nomine, 774
instrumental motet, 780
interlude, 781
intermezzo, 781–782
intrada, 784–785
invention, 785
nocturne, 1224–1225
nonet, 1226
notturno, 1239
novellette, 1239
octet, 1251
ordre, 1271
overture, 1283–1285
pasacaglia, 1318
pastiche, 1319–1320
pastoral, 1320
pibroch, 1364
postlude, 1391
potpourri, 1391
prelude, 1397
quatricinium, 1437
quickstep, 1439
quintet, 1439–1440
quodlibet, 1440
ranz des vaches, 1457
rêverie, 1484
rhapsody, 1486
ricercar, 1490–1491
romance, 1518
rondo, 1522
scherzo, 1585–1586
septet, 1634
serenade, 1635
serenata, 1636
sextet, 1641
sinfonia, 1669
sinfonietta, 1669
sogetto cavato, 1691–1692
solo quartet, 1693
sonata, 1696

sonata da camera, 1696–1697
sonata da chiesa, 1697
sonata form, 1697
sonata-concerto form, 1697
sonata-rondo form, 1697
sonatina, 1698
styrienne, 1760
suite, 1761–1762
symphonie concertante, 1776
symphony, 1778–1781
Tafelmusik, 1793–1794
ternary, 1834
theme and variations, 1839
tiento, 1853
toccata, 1863–1864
Todesgesang, 1866
tombeau, 1866
toye, 1879
traquenard, 1882
Trauermarsch, 1882
tricotet, 1886
trio, 1888
trio sonata, 1888–1889
Classical Symphony, 272
classicism, 272–273
clausula, 273
clavecin, 273
claves, 273
clavichord, 273–274
clavier, 274
clef(s), 274
Clementi, Muzio, 274–276, 613
Clementine, 276
Clemenza di Tito, La, 276
Cleveland, James, 276
Cliburn, Van, 276–277
Cline, Patsy, 277–278
Clock, The, 278
Clooney, Rosemary, 278–279
clusters, 1868
Cockaigne Overture, 279
Coco, 279
coda, 279
Coffee Cantata, 279–280
Cohan, George M., 280–281, 564
Cole, "Cozy," 281
Cole, Nat "King," 281–282
Coleman, Cy, 282, 1774
Coleman, Ornette, 282–283
Coleridge-Taylor, Samuel, 283–284
collage, 284
collective composition, 284
Collegium musicum, 284
colophane, 285
colophon, 285
color, 285, 1783
color hearing, 285
color organ, 1812
coloratura, 285
Colour Symphony, 286
Coltrane, John, 286–287
Columbia, the Gem of the Ocean, 287

Combattimento di Tancredi e Clorinda, Il, 287
combination tones, 287
Comden and Green, 116, 287–288
Come Home, Father, 288
comédie-ballet, 288
comedy, musical, 1192–1193
comes, 288
comic opera, 288–289, 726
dramma giocoso, 411
Ioalanthe, 787
Mikado, 1117
Pirates of Penzance, 1371
Comin' thro the Rye, 289
comma, 289
commedia dell'arte, 289, 675
commedia per music, 289
commercials, singing, 289
common time, 289–290
compact disk, 290
Company, 290
comparative musicology, 290
compass, 290
complement, 290
complin(e), 290
composers
Adam, Adolphe, 6–7
Adam de la Halle, 7
Adams, John, 7–8
Adams, John Luther, 8–9
Albéniz, Isaac, 15–16
Albinoni, Tomaso, 16–17
Amirkhanian, Charles, 24–25
Anderson, Laurie, 26–27
Antheil, George, 31–32
Argento, Dominick, 37–38
Arne, Thomas Augustine, 42–43
Ashley, Robert, 48–49
Auber, Daniel-François-Espirit, 52
Auric, Georges, 57
Babbit, Milton, 60–61
Bach, Carl Philipp Emanuel, 62
Bach, Johann Christian, 62–63
Bach, Johann Sebastian, 63–67
Bach, Wilhelm Friedemann, 67
Balakirev, Mily, 71–72
Barber, Samuel, 79–81
Bartók, Béla, 87–90
Bax, (Sir) Arnold, 96–97
Beach, Amy Marcy Cheny (Mrs. H. H. A.), 97–98
Beethoven, Ludwig van, 104–111
Bellini, Vincenzo, 113–114
Benjamin, George, 116–117
Berg, Alban, 118–119
Berio, Luciano, 119–121
Berlioz, Hector, 122–126
Bernstein, Leonard, 126–128
Biber, Heinrich, 131
Billings, William, 134
Binchois, Gilles (de), 136
Bizet, Georges, 138

Bliss, Sir Arthur, 141–142
Blitzstein, Marc, 142–143
Bloch, Ernest, 143–144
Blow, John, 144–145
Boccherini, Luigi, 148
Boieldieu, François-Adrien, 151–152
Bolcolm, William, 152–153
Borodin, Alexander, 156–157
Boulanger, Nadia, 158–159
Boulez, Pierre, 159–160
Bowles, Paul, 164–165
Boyce, William, 165
Brahams, Johannes, 166–169
Branca, Glenn, 169
Brant, Henry, 170
Britten, Benjamin, 174–176
Broadway musicals. *See* musicals
Brown, Earle, 177
Bruch, Max, 178–180
Bruckner, Anton, 180–182
Bryars, Gavin, 182–183
Buchla, Donald, 183
Bull, John, 184–185
Burns, Robert, 189
Busoni, Ferruccio, 189–190
Buxtehude, Dietrich, 190–191
Byrd, William, 192–193
Caccini, Giulio "Romano," 198–199
Cage, John, 202–204
Cardew, Cornelius, 217–218
Carlos, Wendy, 219
Carpenter, John Alden, 223–224
Carreño, Teresa, 224–225
Carter, Elliott, 226–227
Castelnuovo-Tedesco, Mario, 234–235
Caturla, Alejandro García, 236
Cavalli, Pier Francesco, 237–238
Chabrier, Emmanuel, 239–240
Charpentier, Gustave, 246–247
Charpentier, Marc-Antoine, 247
Chávez, Carlos, 248–250
Cherubini, Luigi, 251–253
Chopin, Frédéric, 256–258
Ciléa, Francesco, 265
Cimarosa, Domenico, 265–266
Clarke, Rebecca, 271–272
Clementi, Muzio, 274–276
Coleridge-Taylor, Samuel, 283–284
Cook, Will Marion, 304
Copland, Aaron, 306–308
Corelli, Arcangelo, 310–311
Corigliano, John, 311
Couperin, François, 318–320
Cowell, Henry, 322–324
Crawford (Seeger), Ruth, 325
Crumb, George, 330–331
Cui, César, 333–334
Curran, Alvin, 336

Czerny, Carl, 337
Dahl, Ingolf, 340
Dallapiccola, Luigi, 341–342
Dargomyzhsky, Alexander, 345
Davidovsky, Mario, 347–348
Davies, Sir Peter Maxwell, 348–350
Davis, Anthony, 350
Dawson, William Levi, 353
Debussy, Claude, 355–359
Del Tredici, David, 362–363
Delibes, Léo, 363–364
Delius, Frederick, 364–366
Dempster, Stuart, 366–367
Denisov, Edison, 367
Desprez, Josquin, 369–370
Dessau, Paul, 370–371
Dett, R. Nathaniel, 371–372
Di Capua, Eduardo, 374
Diabelli, Anton, 375
Diamond, David, 377
Distler, Hugo, 385
Dodge, Charles, 392–393
Dohnányi, Ernst, 394–395
Donizetti, Gaetano, 400–402
Dorati, Antal, 404–405
Dowland, John, 409–410
Druckman, Jacob, 412–413
Dufay, Guillaume, 414–415
Dukas, Paul, 415–416
Dukelsky, Vladimir, 416–417
Dunstable, John, 418
Duparc, Henri, 419
Durey, Louis, 420
Dutilleux, Henri, 420–421
Dvořák, Antonín, 422–424
Egk, Werner, 432
Einem, Gottfried von, 433–434
Eisler, Hans, 434–435
Elgar, Edward, 438–440
Ellington, "Duke," 441–442
Enesco, Georges, 444–446
Engel, Lehman, 447
Eno, Brian, 449
Erkel, Franz, 451–452
Europe, James Reese, 459
Falla, Manuel de, 470–471
Farwell, Arthur, 477–478
Fauré, Gabriel, 478–479
Feldman, Morton, 481–482
Ferneyhough, Brian, 483–484
Fibich, Zdenek, 490–491
Field, John, 494
film music. *See* film music
Flotow, Friedrich von, 508–509
Foote, Arthur, 515
Foss, Lukas, 517–519
Foster, Stephen C., 519
Franck, César, 522–523
Frederick II, 525
Frescobaldi, Girolamo, 530
Friedhofer, Hugo, 531–532
Friml, Rudolf, 532
Gabrieli, Andrea, 544–545
Gabrieli, Giovanni, 545–546
Galas, Diamanda, 548

Galilei, Vincenzo, 549
Gershwin, George, 564–566
Gideon, Miriam, 570
Gilbert, Henry F., 572–573
Ginastera, Alberto, 576–579
Giordano, Umberto, 579–580
Glass, Philip, 585–587
Glazunov, Alexander, 587–588
Glinka, Mikhail, 589–590
Gluck, Christoph Willibald, 592–594
Goldberg, Johann Gottlieb, 596
Górecki, Henryk, 600–601
Gottschalk, Louis Moreau, 605–607
Gould, Morton, 609–610
Gounod, Charles, 611–612
Grainger, Percy, 614–615
Granados, Enrique, 615–616
Greig, Edvard, 626–628
Griffes, Charles T., 629
Grofé, Ferde, 629–630
Gruber, Franz Xaver, 631
Gruber, H. K., 631
Gruenberg, Louis, 632
Gubaidulina, Sofia, 633–634
Hahn, Reynaldo, 647–648
Halévy, Fromental, 650–651
Halffter, Ernesto, 652
Handel, George Frideric, 659–665
Hanson, Howard, 668–671
Harbison, John, 673–674
Harris, Roy, 686–687
Harrison, Lou, 688–689
Hartmann, Karl Amadeus, 690–691
Haydn, Franz Joseph, 693–699
Haydn, Michael, 699–700
Heinrich, Anthony Philip, 703–704
Hensel, Fanny, 710
Henze, Hans Werner, 711
Herbert, Victor, 712–713
Hérold, Louis, 714–715
Heseltine, Philip, 716–717
Hildegard von Bingen, 719–720
Hiller, Lejaren, 720–721
Hindemith, Paul, 721–723
Hoffman, E. T. A., 727
Holliger, Heinz, 732
Holst, Gustav, 734–736
Honegger, Arthur, 737–739
Hopkinson, Francis, 740–741
Horst, Louis, 747
Hovhaness (Hovaness), Alan, 749–750
Humfrey, Pelham, 752
Humperdinck, Engelbert, 753–754
Husa, Karel, 757–758
Hüttenbrenner, Anselm, 758
Hwang, Byung-Ki, 759
Hykes, David, 759–760
Ibert, Jacques, 765

Indy, Vincent d', 777–779
Israel, Brian M., 790
Ives, Charles, 792–796
Jacquet de la Guerre, Elisabeth, 800–801
Janáček, Leoš, 802–804
Jaques-Dalcroze, Émile, 807
Jarnach, Philipp, 807–808
Jarre, Maurice, 808
jazz. See jazz
Jenks, Stephen, 817
Johansen, Gunnar, 823–824
Johnson, Frank, 827
Johnston, Ben, 829
Jullien, Louis, 842–843
Kabalevsky, Dmitri, 845–846
Kagel, Mauricio, 846–847
Kalomiris, Manolis, 847–848
Kay, Ulysses Simpson, 855–856
Khachaturian, Aram, 862
Kirchner, Leon, 868–869
Knussen, Oliver, 880
Kodály, Zoltán, 880–883
Koechlin, Charles, 883–884
Kokkonen, Joonas, 885
Korngold, Erich Wolfgang, 889–890
Krenek, Ernst, 897–898
La Barbara, Joan, 903–904
Lalo, Édouard, 906–907
Lambert, Constant, 908–909
Landini, Francesco, 910
Lasso, Orlando di, 915–917
Law, Andrew, 918–919
Leginska, Ethel, 926
Lehár, Franz, 927–928
Leigh, Mitch, 930
Lentz, Daniel, 934–936
Leoncavallo, Ruggero, 936–938
Leoninus, 938
Ligeti, György, 955–956
Lipatti, Dinu, 959–960
Liszt, Franz, 961–967
Loeffler, Charles Martin, 972–974
Loewe, Carl, 975–976
Lortzing, Albert, 982–984
Lucier, Alvin, 987–988
Luening, Otto, 990–992
Lully, Jean-Baptiste, 993–995
Lutoslawski, Witold, 998–999
MacDowell, Edward, 1005–1009
Machaut, Guillaume de, 1009–1010
Machover, Tod, 1010–1011
Maderna, Bruno, 1012–1013
Mahler, Gustav, 1018–1021
Malipiero, Gian Francesco, 1024–1025
Marais, Marin, 1031
Marschner, Heinrich, 1039–1040
Martin, Frank, 1043–1045
Martinů, Bohuslav, 1046–1047

Martirano, Salvatore, 1047–1048
Mascagni, Pietro, 1049–1050
Mason, Daniel Gregory, 1051
Mason, Lowell, 1052
Mason, William, 1053
Massenet, Jules, 1057–1058
Mayuzumi, Toshir[o4], 1063
McPhee, Colin, 1067–1068
Medtner, Nicolai, 1072–1073
Mendelssohn, Felix, 1084–1088
Mennin, Peter, 1089–1090
Menotti, Gian Carlo, 1090–1093
Messiaen, Olivier, 1100–1101
Meyerbeer, Giacomo, 1105–1108
Miaskovsky, Nikolai, 1108–1109
Miki, Minoru, 1117
Milhaud, Darius, 1118–1120
Millöcker, Carl, 1121–1122
Minkus, Léon, 1125–1126
Mitropoulus, Dimitri, 1133–1134
Nancarrow, Conlon, 1204–1205
Nazareth, Ernesto, 1207
Nicolai, Otto, 1216–1217
Nielsen, Carl, 1217–1219
Nono, Luigi, 1226–1227
North, Alex, 1230–1232
Nurock, Kirk, 1242–1243
Obrecht, Jacob, 1248
Ockeghem, Johannes, 1250–1251
Offenbach, Jacques (Jacob), 1253–1255
Ohana, Maurice, 1257
Oliveros, Pauline, 1261–1263
Orff, Carl, 1272–1273
Pachelbel, Johann, 1290–1291
Paderewski, Ignacy, 1292–1295
Paik, Nam June, 1300–1301
Paine, John Knowles, 1301
Palestrina, Giovanni Pierluigi da, 1302–1304
Panufnik, Andrzej, 1305–1306
Parker, Horatio, 1309–1311
Pärt, Arvo, 1313–1314
Partch, Harry, 1314–1315
Pasatieri, Thomas, 1317–1318
Pedrell, Felipe, 1329
Penderecki, Krzysztof, 1331–1332
Pergolesi, Giovanni Battista, 1340–1342
Peri, Jacopo, 1342–1343
Perotin, 1345–1346
Persichetti, Vincent, 1346–1348
Pettersson, Gustaf Allan, 1352–1353
Pfitzner, Hans, 1354–1355
Philidor, André Danican, 1355

Philidor, François-André Danican, 1355–1356
Piazzolla, Astor, 1364
Piccinni, Niccoló, 1365–1367
Pijper, Willem, 1368
Piston, Walter, 1371–1373
Pleyel, Ignace Joseph, 1376–1377
Ponce, Manuel, 1386
Ponchielli, Amilcare, 1386–1387
popular music. See pop(ular) music
Poulenc, Francis, 1391–1392
Pound, Ezra, 1392–1393
Pousseur, Henri, 1393–1394
Praetorius, Michael, 1395–1396
Previn, André, 1401–1403
Prokofiev, Sergei, 1418–1421
Puccini, Giacomo, 1427–1430
Purcell, Henry, 1430–1432
Quantz, Johann Joachim, 1435–1436
Rachmaninoff, Sergei, 1442–1445
Raff, Joachim, 1446
Rameau, Jean-Philippe, 1453–1455
Ravel, Maurice, 1459–1462
Read, Daniel, 1463
Reger, Max, 1469–1470
Reich, Steve, 1472–1474
Respighi, Ottorino, 1482–1483
Revueltas, Silvestre, 1485–1486
Riley, Terry, 1494–1495
Rimsky-Korsakov, Nikolai, 1495–1499
Rochberg, George, 1504–1505
Roldán, Amadeo, 1514–1515
Rorem, Ned, 1522–1524
Rosenberg, Hilding, 1525
Roslavetz, Nikolai, 1527
Rossini, Gioachino, 1529–1534
Rota, Nino, 1536–1537
Rouse, Mikel, 1538–1539
Roussel, Albert, 1540–1541
Rozsa, Miklos, 1541–1542
Rubinstein, Anton, 1542–1544
Rudhyar, Dane, 1547–1549
Ruggles, Carl, 1549–1550
Rzewski, Frederic, 1553–1554
Sachs, Hans, 1555
Sadra, I Wayan, 1556–1557
Saint-Saëns, Camille, 1558–1560
Salieri, Antonio, 1561–1562
Salonen, Esa-Pekka, 1565
Salzedo, Carlos, 1566–1567
Sankey, Ira D., 1568
Sarasate, Pablo de, 1570
Satie, Erik, 1571–1573
Scarlatti, Alessandro, 1577–1579
Scarlatti, Domenico, 1579–1581

Scelsi, Giacinto, 1581–1582
Schaeffer, Pierre, 1582–1583
Schafer, R. Murray, 1583
Schickele, Peter, 1586–1587
Schillinger, Joseph, 1588–1589
Schnittke, Alfred, 1591–1592
Schoeck, Othmar, 1592
Schoenberg, Arnold, 1592–1598
Schubert, Franz, 1599–1603
Schuller, Gunther, 1603–1605
Schuman, William, 1605–1606
Schumann, Clara Wieck, 1606–1607
Schumann, Robert, 1608–1613
Schütz, Heinrich, 1613–1615
Scriabin, Alexander, 1621–1627
Sculthorpe, Peter, 1628–1629
Sessions, Roger, 1639–1640
Shankar, Ravi, 1643
Shapey, Ralph, 1643–1645
Shifrin, Seymour, 1648–1649
Shostakovich, Dmitri, 1650–1655
Sibelius, Jean, 1656–1659
Sierra, Roberto, 1662
Six, Les, 1673–1674
Skalkottas, Nikos, 1674
Smetana, Bedřich, 1682–1685
Smith, Gregg, 1686–1687
Smyth, Ethel, 1688–1689
Soler, Antonio, 1692
Sousa, John Philip, 1705–1707
Spohr, Louis, 1709–1712
Spontini, Gasparo, 1712–1714
Steiner, Max, 1720
Steuermann, Edward, 1723–1724
Still, William Grant, 1724–1725
Stockhausen, Karlheinz, 1725–1727
Stone, Carl, 1731–1733
Strauss, Johann (I), 1736–1737
Strauss, Johann (II), 1737–1739
Strauss, Josef, 1739
Strauss, Richard, 1740–1745
Stravinsky, Igor, 1745–1752
Strouse, Charles, 1758
Subotnick, Morton, 1761
Sullivan, Arthur, 1763–1765
Suppé, Franz, 1767–1768
Sweelinck, Jan Pieterszoon, 1773–1774
Szymanowski, Karol, 1789–1791
Tailleferre, Germaine, 1794–1795
Takahashi, Yuji, 1796
Takemitsu, Tōru, 1797
Tal, Josef, 1797–1798
Tan Dun, 1802–1803
Taneyev, Sergei, 1803–1804
Tansman, Alexandre, 1806

Tartini, Giuseppi, 1809–1811
Tavener, John, 1814–1815
Tchaikovsky, Piotr Ilyich, 1816–1821
Telemann, Georg Philipp, 1824–1826
Tenney, James, 1830–1831
Theodorakis, Mikis, 1839–1840
Thomas, Ambroise, 1844–1845
Thompson, Randall, 1848–1849
Thomson, Virgil, 1850–1851
Tippett, Michael, 1859–1861
Toch, Ernst, 1864–1865
Torke, Michael, 1871–1872
Tormis, Veljo, 1873
Tower, Joan, 1878–1879
Tubin, Eduard, 1902–1903
Tudor, David, 1904–1906
Turina, Joaquín, 1908
Tye, Christopher, 1912–1913
Tyranny, Blue Gene (Robert Nathan Sheff), 1913–1914
Ullmann, Viktor, 1916–1917
Ussachevsky, Vladimir, 1920–1922
Varèse, Edgard, 1927–1930
Vaughan Williams, Ralph, 1933–1937
Verdi, Giuseppe, 1942–1947
Vicentino, Nicola, 1951–1952
Victoria, Tomás Luis de, 1953–1954
Vieuxtemps, Henri, 1955–1957
Villa-Lobos, Heitor, 1957–1959
Vitry, Philippe de, 1967–1968
Vivaldi, Antonio, 1968–1970
Wagner, Richard, 1978–1989
Wagner, Siegfried, 1977–1978
Waldteufel, Émile, 1991
Walker, George, 1991–1993
Wallen, Errollyn, 1994
Walton, Sir William, 1998–1999
Wasitodiningrat, K. R. T., 2003–2004
Waxman, Franz, 2007–2008
Weber, Carl Maria von, 2008–2013
Webern, Anton, 2013–2016
Weill, Kurt, 2016–2019
Weir, Judith, 2019–2020
Weisgall, Hugo, 2020–2021
Weiss, Silvius Leopold, 2021–2022
Werckmeister, Andreas, 2023–2024
Widor, Charles-Marie, 2031–2032
Wieniawski, Henryk, 2032–2034
Williams, John, 2036–2037
Wolf, Hugo, 2042–2046
Wolff, Christian, 2046–2047

Wolf-Ferrari, Ermanno, 2047–2048
Wolpe, Stefan, 2049–2050
Work, Henry Clay, 2052
Wuorinen, Charles, 2055–2057
Wyschnegradsky, Ivan, 2058–2059
Xenakis, Iannis, 2060–2062
Young, La Monte, 2068–2069
Ysaÿe, Eugène, 2072–2074
Yun, Isang, 2074–2075
Zandonai, Riccardo, 2076–2077
Zarlino, Gioseffo, 2080–2081
Zelter, Carl Friedrich, 2082–2083
Zemlinsky, Alexander, 2083–2084
Zimmerman, Bernd Alois, 2087
Zorn, John, 2089
Zwilich, Ellen Taaffe, 2091–2092
composition and compositional devices, 58, 291, 1267, 1839, 2024
accompaniment, 3
agogic, 14
Alberti bass, 16
ambulation, 23
answer, 31
antecedent, 31
antiphonal, 32
antiphon(e), 33
arrangement, 43
augmentation, 56
bass line, 92
basso continuo, 93–94
basso obbligato, 94
basso ostinato, 94
bitonality, 137
bruitism, 182
cadenza, 201
call and response, 205
cantus firmus, 214–215
chance operations, 242, 1725
cipher, 267
coda, 279
collective composition, 284
comes, 288
consecutive intervals, 301
consequent, 301
continuo, 302
contrafactum, 303
controlled improvisation, 304
counter, 316
counterpoint, 316–317
cross-rhythm, 329
cyclical forms, 337
decomposition and reassembly, 360
development, 373
diminution, 379
discant, 381–382
displaced tonality, 383

dissonant counterpoint, 384–385
division, 387
double, 407
drone, 412
duplum, 419
echo, 429
epanalepsis, 450
episode, 451
faburden, 468
fanfare, 473
fauxbourdon, 480
feminine ending, 483
Fibonacci series, 491
figuration, 496
fioritura, 500
flores, 508
fugato, 535
fugue, 535–537
gimmicks, 575–576
goat trill, 594–595
grace note, 612–613
ground bass, 630–631
Hauptsatz, 691
hemiola, 707
heterophony, 717
hocket, 726
horn fifths, 742
humor, 752–753
imbroglio, 770
imitation, 770–771
improvisation, 773
indeterminacy, 776
inégales, 779
instrumentation, 780
intabulation, 780
introduction, 785
invertible counterpoint, 787
isorhythm, 789
numerology, 1241–1242
obbligato, 1245
objets trouvés, 1246
omnitonality, 1263
onomatopoeia, 1266–1267
ornament, 1278
ornamentation, 1278–1279
ostinato, 1280–1281
palindrome, 1304
paraphrases and transcriptions, 1307–1308
partimento, 1316
passage, 1318–1319
passing notes or tones, 1319
pastiche, 1319–1320
pedal point, 1328
period, 1343
permutation, 1345
pes, 1348
phrase, 1358
Picardy third, 1364–1365
pivot chord, 1374
point d'orgue, 1379
polymeter, 1382–1383
polymodality, 1383
polyphony, 1383–1384
polyrhythm, 1384–1385

polytonality, 1385
proportional notation, 1424
quartal harmony, 1436
quodlibet, 1440
quotation, 1440–1441
realization, 1464
recapitulation, 1464
reduction, 1468
repercussion, 1479
repetend, 1479
reprise, 1479–1480
retardation, 1483
retrograde, 1483–1484
retrograde inversion, 1484
ripieno, 1499–1500
ritornello, 1500–1501
Rosalia sequence or modulation, 1524
rotation, 1537
rovescio, 1541
rubato, tempo, 1542
run, 1550
Schluss, 1589
Scotch snap or catch, 1620
section, 1630
sentence, 1634
sequence, 1634–1635
set, 1640
silence, 1663
slide, 1677
sogetto cavato, 1691–1692
sound effects, 1704
spatial distribution, 1707–1708
stanza, 1717
stochastic, 1725
strain, 1735
street cries, 1752–1753
stretto,-a, 1754–1755
strophic bass, 1758
structure, 1758
subject, 1760
symploche, 1782
synchrony, 1783–1784
syncopation, 1784–1785
system, 1786
texture, 1837
theme, 1839
time-bracket notation, 1855
tirata, 1861
toccato, 1864
tonal answer, 1867
tonal aura, 1867
tonality, 1867
tone clusters, 1868
transient, 1881
transition, 1881
transposition, 1882
tremolo, 1885
triadic modulation, 1886
trill, 1886–1887
Tristan chord, 1890
vagans, 1924
variable meter, 1931
variation(s), 1931
verbalization, 1941
vocalise, 1970

voice exchange, 1971
voice leading, 1971
compositional styles
absolute music/abstract music, 3
aleatory music, 17–18
ars antiqua, 44
ars nova, 45–46
athematic, athematic composition, 50
avant-garde, 58
Baroque music, 85–86
bravura, 171
Burgundian school, 187–188
a cappella, 1
Cecilianism, 238
classicism, 272–273
constructivism, 302
eclecticism, 430
Empfindsamer Stil, 444
exoticism, 464–465
experimental music, 465
expressionism, 466
eye music, 467
formalism, 516
free canon, 525
free fugue, 525
fugue, 535–537
futurism, 542
gallant style, 549
game music, 551–552
Gebrauchsmusik, 559–560
Geisslieder, 560
Gemeinschaftsmusic, 560
Gesamtkuntswerk, 567
glee, 588
Gothic music, 603
gymel, 641
hommage, 737
homophony, 737
impressionism, 772
nationalism, 1206
neoclassicism, 1210–1211
Neue Sachlichkeit, 1211–1212
new music, 1213
new romanticism, 1213
new simplicity, 1214
Notre Dame school, 1238–1239
nuove musiche, Le, 1242
open form composition, 1267
parody, 1311–1312
partita, 1316
perpetuum mobile, 1346
pluralism, 1378
pointillism, 1379–1380
polyphonic, 1383
polystylistic music, 1385
potpourri, 1391
prima prattica, 1407
primitivism, 1407
program music, 1414–1417
progressive composition, 1418
proletarian music, 1422
realism, 1463–1464
res facta, 1480

reservata, musica, 1480–1481
rococo, 1510
salon music, 1563–1564
seconda prattica, 1629–1630
serialism, 1636
socialist realism, 1690–1691
static music, 1719
strict style, 1755
Sturm und Drang, 1760
surrealism, 1769
symbolism, 1775
symphonic poem, 1776
Tafelmusik, 1793–1794
text-sound composition, 1837
through-composed, 1852
Tonmalerei, 1870
trecento, 1884
twelve-tone music, 1911–1912
Venetian school, 1940
Viennese school, 1955
compound meters, 291
computer, 291
computer music, 58, 291–292, 720–721
Comte Ory, Le, 292
concert, 292
concert overture, 292
concert pitch, 292
Concert Spirituel, 293
concertante, 293
concerted music, 293
concertina, 293
concertino, 293
concertmaster, 293
concerto, 294–295. *See also* piano concertos
for orchestra, 295
sacred, 1555–1556
triple, 1889
concerto grosso, 296
Concerto in F, 296
concord, 297
Concord Sonata, 297
concrete music, 1195
conducting, 297–299, 410
conductors
Abbado, Claudio, 1–2
Abravanel, Maurice, 2–3
Adler, Kurt Herbert, 10–11
Ashkenazy, Vladimir, 48
Barbirolli, Sir John, 81–83
Barenboim, Daniel, 83–84
Beecham, (Sir) Thomas, 103–104
Benjamin, George, 116–117
Bernstein, Leonard, 126–128
Böhm, Karl, 150–151
Boulez, Pierre, 159–160
Boult, Sir Adrain, 160–162
Brico, Antonia, 173–174
Bülow, Hans von, 185–186
Chávez, Carlos, 248–250
Chung, Myung-Whun, 264–265
Cook, Will Marion, 304
Craft, Robert, 324

Dahl, Ingolf, 340
Davies, Dennis Russell, 348
Davies, Sir Peter Maxwell, 348–350
Davis, (Sir) Colin, 350–351
Dett, R. Nathaniel, 371–372
Dohnányi, Christoph von, 393
Dohnányi, Ernst, 394–395
Dorati, Antal, 404–405
Dutoit, Charles, 421
Enesco, Georges, 444–446
Engel, Lehman, 447
Erkel, Franz, 451–452
Eschenbach, Christoph, 454–455
Europe, James Reese, 459
Fiedler, Arthur, 493–494
Fleisher, Leon, 507–508
Furtwängler, Wilhelm, 539–542
Gabrilowitsch, Ossip, 546–547
Gardiner, John Eliot, 554
Gibson, Sir Alexander, 569–570
Gielen, Michael, 570–571
Giulini, Carlo Maria, 582–584
Gould, Morton, 609–610
Hahn, Reynaldo, 647–648
Haitlink, Bernard, 649–650
Halffter, Ernesto, 652
Hanson, Howard, 668–671
Harnoncourt, Nikolaus, 682
Hoffman, E. T. A., 727
Hogwood, Christopher, 729
Järvi, Neeme, 809–810
Jullien, Louis, 842–843
Karajan, Herbert von, 849–853
Kleiber, Carlos, 874–875
Kleiber, Erich, 875–876
Klemperer, Otto, 876–878
Kontarsky, Bernhard, 887
Koopman, Ton, 887
Koussevitzky, Serge, 890–893
Kubelík, Rafael, 900–902
Lambert, Constant, 908–909
Lanner, Joseph, 913
Leinsdorf, Erich, 930–931
Leppard, Raymond, 939–940
Levine, James, 942–943
Maazel, Lorin, 1003–1005
Maderna, Bruno, 1012–1013
Malipiero, Gian Francesco, 1024–1025
Marriner, (Sir) Neville, 1037–1038
Mason, Lowell, 1052
Masur, Kurt, 1058–1059
Mauceri, John, 1062
Mehta, Mehli, 1073–1074
Mehta, Zubin, 1074–1076
Mengelberg, Willem, 1088–1089
Millöcker, Carl, 1121–1122
Mitropoulos, Dimitri, 1133–1134
Nicolai, Otto, 1216–1217

Norrington, Roger, 1229–1230
Ormandy, Eugene, 1277–1278
Ozawa, Seiji, 1286–1289
Panufnik, Andrzej, 1305–1306
Pfitzner, Hans, 1354–1355
Pollini, Maurizio, 1381–1382
Previn, André, 1401–1403
Rachmaninoff, Sergei, 1442–1445
Rattle, Simon, 1458–1459
Reiner, Fritz, 1474–1475
Rodzinski, Artur, 1513–1514
Roldán, Amadeo, 1514–1515
Rostopovich, Mstislav, 1534–1536
Rubinstein, Anton, 1542–1544
Salonen, Esa-Pekka, 1565
Sawallisch, Wolfgang, 1573–1574
Schifrin, Lalo, 1587–1588
Schoeck, Othmar, 1592
Schuller, Gunther, 1603–1605
Shapey, Ralph, 1643–1645
Slatkin, Leonard, 1675
Smith, Gregg, 1686–1687
Solti, George, 1693–1695
Spohr, Louis, 1709–1712
Stokowski, Leopold, 1727–1730
Strauss, Johann (I), 1736–1737
Strauss, Johann (II), 1737–1739
Strauss, Josef, 1739
Strauss, Richard, 1740–1745
Sullivan, Arthur, 1763–1765
Szell, George, 1786–1788
Tansman, Alexandre, 1806
Tate, Jeffrey, 1812
Tenney, James, 1830–1831
Thomas, Michael Tilson, 1845–1846
Thomas, Theodore, 1846–1848
Toscanini, Arturo, 1874–1876
Tubin, Eduard, 1902–1903
Tuckwell, Barry, 1904
Waart, Edo de, 1976–1977
Wagner, Siegfried, 1977–1978
Waldteufel, Émile, 1991
Walter, Bruno, 1996–1998
Waxman, Franz, 2007–2008
Weber, Carl Maria von, 2008–2013
Williams, John, 2036–2037
Yasser, Joseph, 2065
Ysaÿe, Eugène, 2072–2074
Zemlinksy, Alexander, 2083–2084
Zukerman, Pinchas, 2089–2090
Zukofsky, Paul, 2090–2091
conductus, 300
confinalis, 300
conga, 300
conga drum, 300

conical mouthpiece, 300
conical tube, 300
conjunct degree, 300
Connecticut Yankee, A, 300–301
Connotations, 301
consecutive intervals, 301
consequent, 301
conservatoire, 301
conservatorium, 301
conservatory, 301
Consolations, 301
console, 301–302
consonance, 302, 782–784
consort, 302
constructivism, 302
Consul, The, 302
Contes d'Hoffmann, Les, 1798–1799
continuo, 302
contra-, 303
contrabassoon, 303
contrafactum, 303
contralto(s), 20
   Anderson, Marian, 27
   Ferrier, Kathleen, 484
contrapuntal, 303
contrary motion, 303
contratenor, 317
contredanse, 303–304
controlled improvisation, 304
Cook, Will Marion, 304
Cooke, Sam, 304–305
cool jazz, 305
Copland, Aaron, 306–308
   Appalachian Spring, 34
   Billy the Kid, 135
   Connotations, 301
   Fanfare for the Common Man, 473
   Inscape, 780
   Jazz Concerto, 813
   Lincoln Portrait, 957
   Red Pony, 1466–1467
   Rodeo, 1510
   Salón México, El, 1563
   Symphony for Organ and Orchestra, 1781
   Tender Land, 1829–1830
Coppélia, 308
copyright, 47, 308–309
Coq d'or, Le, 309
Corea, Chick, 309–310
Corelli, Arcangelo, 310–311
Corigliano, John, 311
cornet, 311–312, 1892
cornett, 312
cornu, 312–313
coro spezzato, 313
Coronation Concerto, 313
Coronation Mass, 313
corrente, 313
corrido, 313, 633
Corsaire, Le, 313–314
Cortot, Alfred, 314
Cosa rara, o sia Bellezza ed onestà, Una, 314

Così fan tutte, 314–315
Costello, Elvis, 315–316
cotillion, 316
Council of Trent, 316
counter, 316
counterpoint, 316–317
   contrapuntal, 303
   contrary motion, 303
   dissonant, 384–385
   Gradus ad Parnassum, 613
   gymel, 641
   inner parts, 780
   organum, 1276–1277
   polyphony, 1383–1384
   substitution, 1761
   voice leading, 1971
   vox, 1974–1975
countertenor, 317
country dance, 317
country music, 317–318. *See also* bluegrass
   Acuff, Roy, 6
   Atkins, Chet, 50–51
   Carter Family, 227
   Cash, Johnny, 233–234
   Cline, Patsy, 277–278
   Flatt, Lester, 506
   Foley, "Red," 513–514
   Grand Ole Opry, 616–618
   Haggard, Merle, 646–647
   hillbilly, 720
   honky-tonk, 739
   Jennings, Waylon, 817–818
   Jones, George, 831
   Lynn, Loretta, 1000–1001
   Nelson, Willie, 1209–1210
   Owens, "Buck," 1285–1286
   Parton, Dolly, 1316–1317
   Pride, Charley, 1405–1406
   Rodgers, Jimmie, 1511–1512
   Scruggs, Earl, 1627–1628
   Tubb, Ernest, 1902
   Williams, Hank, 2035
   Wills, Bob, 2037–2038
   Wynette, Tammy, 2057–2058
Couperin, François, 318–320
couplet, 320
courante, 320
courtship and music, 320–321
Coward, Noel, 321–322, 1696
cowbell, 322
cowboy music, 736, 746–747
Cowell, Henry, 322–324
   Icelandic Symphony, 766
   Synchrony, 1784
Cradle Will Rock, The, 324
Craft, Robert, 324
Crawford (Seeger), Ruth, 325
Creation, The, 325
Création du monde, La, 325
creativity, 325–326
Credo, 326–327
Creedence Clearwater Revival, 327
crescendo, 327
crescent, 327

Crespin, Régine, 328
Cristofori, Bartolomeo, 328
critics, music
   Adorno, Theodor, 11
   Thomson, Virgil, 1850–1851
crook, 329
cross flute, 1882
cross relation, 329
crossover, 329
cross-rhythm, 329
crotales, 330
Crucifixus, 330
Crumb, George, 330–331
crumhorn, 331–332
crwth, 332
csárdás, 332
C-sharp minor, 332
Cuatro soles, Los, 333
Cuauhnahuac, 333
Cuban Overture, 333
Cucaracha, La, 333
Cuckoo and the Nightingale, The, 333
Cui, César, 333–334
Culver, Andrew, 1249
Cunning Little Vixen, The, 335
Cunningham, Merce, 334–335, 1249
cupped mouthpiece, 336
Curlew River, 336
Curran, Alvin, 336
cursus, 336–337
cyclical forms, 337
cylindrical tube, 337
cymbals, 33, 337, 499
cythara, 873
Czerny, Carl, 337

D, 338
D major, 338
D minor, 338–339
da camera, 339
da capo, 339
da capo, aria, 38
Da Ponte, Lorenzo, 339
dactyl(e), 340
Dafne, 340
Dahl, Ingolf, 340
D'Albert, Eugène, 796
Dalcroze, 807
Dale, Clamma, 340
Dalibor, 341
Dallapiccola, Luigi, 341–342, 1219
Dameron, Tadd, 342
Damn Yankees, 342
Damnation de Faust, La, 343
damper, 343
dance band, 343
dance forms, 1807
   allemanda, 17–18
   ballet. *See* ballet(s)
   ballet de cour, 74
   ballo, 75
   basse danse, 92–93
   beguine, 112

bergerette, 119
bolero, 153–154
bomba, 154
bossa nova, 157
bourrée, 162
branle, bransle, 170
breakdown, 172
bugaku, 184
cakewalk, 205
canary, 209
cancan, 209
carioca, 219
cha-cha, 240
chaconne, 240
Charleston, 246
choree, 261
conga, 300
contredanse, 303–304
corrente, 313
cotillion, 316
country dance, 317
courante, 320
csárdás, 332
Deutscher Tanz, 372
deux, 373
drag, 410
écossaise, 430
fado, 469
fandango, 473
farandola, 474–475
folia, 514
forlana, 515
fox-trot, 521
française, 522
friss, 533
gaillard(e), 547
galop, 549–550
gavotta, 556
gigue, 572
habanera, 645
halling, 653
hesitation tango, 717
hesitation waltz, 717
hopak, 739–740
hora lunga, 741
hornpipe, 743–744
horse trot, 747
Islamey, 789
jig, 821
jitterbug, 822
jota, 840
khorovod, 863
krakowiak, 893–894
Ländler, 910
loure, 986
malagueña, 1023
mambo, 1026
mazurka, 1064
pachanga, la, 1290
padovana, 1295
pavane, 1322–1323
polka, 1381
polonaise, 1382
quadrille, 1434
quickstep, 1439
rant, 1456

rejdowak, 1475
rigadoon, 1493
romanesca, 1518–1519
rumba, 1550
salsa, 1566
samba, 1567
sanjuanito, 1568
saraband, 1569
sardana, 1570–1571
Schottische, 1599
seguidilla, 1632
shimmy, 1649
shuffle, 1656
siciliana,-o, 1660
springar, 1714
square dance, 1716
strathspey, 1736
tambourin, 1799
tango, 1804–1805
tango-milonga, 1805
tarantella, 1808–1809
tonada, 1866
trepak, 1885
turkey trot, 1909
tyrolienne, 1914
verbunkos, 1942
volta, 1973
waltz. *See* waltz
dance halls, 1806
Dance in the Place Congo, The, 343
dance of death, 1877
Dance of the Hours. See Gioconda, La
dance parties, 727
Dancing in the Streets, 343–344
Danny Boy, 344
Danse des morts, La, 344
Danse macabre, 344
Danse sacrée et danse profane, 344
Danse sauvage, 344
Dantons Tod, 344
Daphne, 344
Daphnis et Chloé, 345
Dargomyzhsky, Alexander, 345
Rusalka, 1550–1551
Stone Guest, 1733
dark, 345
Daughter of the Regiment, The. See Fille du régiment, La
David, 346
David, Hal, 346, 1423
David, Mack, 346
Davidovich, Bella, 346–347
Davidovsky, Mario, 347–348
Davidsbündler-Tänze, 348
Davies, Dennis Russell, 348
Davies, Sir Peter Maxwell, 348–350
Davis, Anthony, 350
Davis, Miles, 351–353
Davis, Sir Colin, 350–351
davul, 353
Dawson, William Levi, 353
De Franco, "Buddy," 353–354

deaconing, 354
deafness, 354
Death and the Maiden, 354
Death and Transfiguration, 354–355
Death in Venice, 355
Death of Klinghoffer, The, 355
Debussy, Claude, 355–359
Chansons de Bilitis, 243
Children's Corner, 256
Danse sacrée et danse profane, 344
Estampes, 455
Gigues, 572
Ibéria, 764–765
Images, 770
Isle joyeuse, L', 769
Mer, La, 1096
Nocturnes, 1225
Pelléas et Mélisande, 1331
Prélude à l'après-midi d'un faune, 1397
Préludes, 1398
Six Epigraphes antiques, 1673
Suite bergamasque, 1762–1763
Syrinx, 1786
début, 359
decay, 359
decibel, 359–360
decomposition and reassembly, 360
dedication, 737
dedications, 360–361
Deep in the Heart of Texas, 361
Deep Purple, 361
DeGaetani, Jan, 361–362
degree, 362
Deidamia, 362
Del Tredici, David, 362–363
Delibes, Léo, 363–364
Bell Song, 113
Coppélia, 308
Delius, Frederick, 364–366
On Hearing the First Cuckoo in Spring, 1264
In a Summer Garden, 774
Irmelin, 789
Koanga, 880
Mass of Life, 1056
demolition, 366
Dempster, Stuart, 366–367
Denisov, Edison, 367
Dennis Cleveland, 367–368
Density 21.5, 368
Denver, John, 368
descant, 368
descort, 368
Desert Song, The, 369
Déserts, 369
Desmond, Paul, 369
Desprez, Josquin, 369–370
Dessau, Paul, 370–371
Dett, R. Nathaniel, 371–372
Deus ex machina, 372
Deutscher Tanz, 372
Deutsches Requiem, Ein, 372

Deutschland, Deutschland über alles, 372–373
deux, 373
development, 373
Devil and Daniel Webster, The, 373
Devil and Kate, The, 373
Devil's Dream, The, 373
Devil's Trill, The, 373–374
Devin du Village, The, 374
D-flat major, 374
Di Capua, Eduardo, 374, 1245
Di Tre Re, 374
Diabelli, Anton, 375
Diabelli Variations, 375
diabolus in musica, 375–376
Diaghilev, Sergi, 376–377
Dialogues de carmélites, Les, 377
Diamond, David, 377
diapason, 378
diatonic, 378
Diddley, Bo, 378
Dido and Aeneas, 378
Die Fledermaus, 506–507
Dies Irae, 379
difference (differential) tone. *See* combination tones; Tartini tones
digital, 379
diminshed interval, 379
diminution, 379
Dimitrj, 380
Dinah, 380
directional hearing, 380
dirge, 380
Disappointment, or The Force of Credulity, The, 380
disc, 380
disc jockey (DJ), 380–381
discant, 381–382
disco, 382
disco music, 382
discord, 382
discotheque, 382
diseuse, 382
disjunct, 1675
disk, 382
displaced tonality, 383
dissonance, 382, 383–384, 1398, 1769
dissonant counterpoint, 384–385
dissonant interval, 384, 782–784
Dissonanzen Quartett, 385
Distler, Hugo, 385
Distratto, Il, 385–386
dital key, 386
dithyramb, 386
diva, 386
divertimento, 386
divertissement, 386
Divertissement, 386
Divin Poème, Le, 386–387
Divina commedia, 387
Divine Office. *See* canonical hours
division, 387

Dixie, 387
Dixieland, 387–388
DJ (disc jockey), 380–381
Do I Hear a Waltz?, 388
Do That to Me One More Time,
388
Doctrine of Affects, 854
Dodds, "Baby," 388–389
Dodds, Johnny, 388
Dodecachordon, 389
dodecaphonic music, 389–392
Dodge, Charles, 392–393
Does Your Chewing Gum Lose Its
Flavor (on the Bedpost Over
Night)?, 393
Do(h), 388
Dohnányi, Christoph von, 393
Dohnányi, Ernst von, 394–395,
1931
Doktor Faust, 395
Dolphy, Eric, 395
dombra, 396
dominant, 396
Domingo, Placido, 396–397
Domino, "Fats," 397
domra, 397–398
Don Carlos, 398
Don Giovanni, 398–399
Don Juan, 399
Don Pasquale, 399
Don Quixote, 399
Don Rodrigo, 399–400
Donizetti, Gaetano, 400–402
Don Pasquale, 399
Elisir d'amore, L', 440
Favorite, La, 480
Fille du regiment, La, 496
Lucia di Lammermoor, 987
Lucrezia Borgia, 988–989
Maria Stuarda, 1034
Roberto Devereux, ossia Il Conte
di Essex, 1502
Zingara, La, 2088
Donna del lago, La, 402
Don't Fence Me In, 402
Don't Get Around Much Anymore,
402
Don't Worry, Be Happy, 402
Doors, The, 402–403
doo-wop, 404
Doppel, 404
Dorati, Antal, 404–405
Dorian Toccata and Fugue, 405
Dorsey, "Georgia Tom," 405–406
Dorsey brothers, 406–407
dot, 407
dotara, 407
double, 407
double bar, 408
double bass, 408
double bassoon, 303
double chorus, 408
Double Concerto for Harpsi-
chord, Piano, and Two
Chamber Orchestras, 408
double fugue, 408

double note, 408
double quartet, 408
double reed, 408
double stops, 409
double-bassists, 890–893
Dowland, John, 409–410
down bow, 410
Down in the Valley, 410
downbeat, 410, 1407
doxology, 410
D'Oyly Carte Opera Company,
1573
drag, 410
dramatic devices, 372
drame lyrique, 411
dramma giocoso, 411
dramma per musica, 411
Dream of Gerontius, The, 411
Drehleier, 411
Drehorgel, 411
Drei, 411
Drei Pintos, Die, 411–412
Dreigroschenoper, Die, 412
Drigo, Riccardo, 1635
drone, 412
Druckman, Jacob, 412–413
Drumroll Symphony, 413
drums and drummers, 413
bass drum, 92
Blakey, Art, 141
bongos, 154
Cole, "Cozy," 281
davul, 353
Dodds, "Baby," 388–389
huehuetl, 751
Krupa, Gene, 899
Rich, Buddy, 1491
Roach, Max, 1501
snare drum, 1689
tablā, 1792
tenor drum, 1832
timpani, 1855–1856
traps, 1882
dsaxophone and saxophone play-
ers
Dorsey, Tommy. *See* Dorsey
brothers
duda, 413
duduk, 413
due, 413–414
Due Foscari, I, 414
Due litigani, I, 414
Dueling Banjos, 414
duet, 414
Dufay, Guillaume, 414–415
Dukas, Paul, 415–416
Péri, La, 1343
Sorcerer's Apprentice, 1702
Duke, Vernon, 35–36, 198, 416
Dukelsky, Vladimir, 416–417
dulcimer, 417
dumb piano, 417
Dumbarton Oaks, 417
dumka, 417–418
Dumky, 418
dummy pipes, 418

dump, 418
Dunstable, John, 418
duo, 418–419
Duparc, Henri, 419
duple, 419
duplet, 419
duplum, 419
DuPré, Jacqueline, 419–420
Durey, Louis, 420
Dutilleux, Henri, 420–421
Dutoit, Charles, 421
dux, 422
dvojnica, 422
Dvořák, Antonín, 422–424
American Quartet, 24
Devil and Kate, 373
Dimitrj, 380
Dumky, 418
Jakobin, 801
From the New World, 533
Rusalka, 1551
Slavonic Dances, 1676
Dybbuk, The, 424
Dylan, Bob, 424–426, 1450,
1855
dynamics, 426
dynamics, terraced, 1834–1835

E, 427
E major, 427
E minor, 427
Eagles, The, 427–428
ear ailments, 1857–1858
ear training, 428, 1692
Earth Angel, 429
Easter Parade, 429
Ebony Concerto, 429
ecclesiastical modes, 429
echo, 429
echoi, 429–430
Eckstine, Billy, 430
eclecticism, 430
écossaise, 430
Ecuatorial, 430–431
editions, 1919–1920
education, music. *See* training,
music
E-flat major, 431
E-flat minor, 431
Egk, Werner, 432
Egmont Overture, 432
Egorov, Youri, 432–433
1812 Overture, 433
eighth, 433
Ein, 433
Eine kleine Nachtmusik, 433
Einem, Gottfried von, 344,
433–434
Einstein on the Beach, 434
Eisler, Hans, 434–435
ektara, 435
Eldridge, Roy "Little Jazz,"
435–436
electric guitar, 436, 481, 543
electric piano, 436
electronic amplifier, 25

electronic music, 436–437
Amplitude modulation, 26
Buchla, Donald, 183
Carlos, Wendy, 219
computer, 291
computer music, 58, 291–292,
720–721
Déserts, 369
electrophones, 437
Hymnen, 761
intermodulation, 782
live, 969
Ondes Martenot, 1265
oscillator, 1280
phase shifting, 1355
Poème électronique, 1379
ring modulator, 1499
sampler, 1567
sequencer, 1635
spectrum, 1708
synclavier, 1784
synthesizer, 1785–1786
Theremin, 1841
Theremin, Leon, 1841–1843
Trautonium, 1882
Trimpin, 1887–1888
electronic organ, 437
electronic piano, 436
electrophones, 437
Elégie, 438
elegy, 438
Elegy for Young Lovers, 438
Elektra, 438
elevator music. *See* Muzak
Elgar, Edward, 438–440
Cockaigne Overture, 279
Dream of Gerontius, 411
Enigma Variations, 448–449
Falstaff, 472–473
Pomp and Circumstance,
1385–1386
Elisir d'amore, L', 440
Ellington, "Duke," 402,
441–442, 1701
Elman, Mischa, 442–443
Élytres, 443
embouchure, 443
Emilio de'Cavalieri, 1457
Emmett, Daniel Decatur, 443
emotion, 12
Emperor Concerto, 443
Emperor Jones, The, 443
Emperor Quartet, 444
Emperor's Hymn, 444
Empfindsamer Stil, 444
encore, 444
endless melody, 444
Enesco, Georges, 444–446
Enfance du Christ, L', 446
Enfant et les sortileges, L', 446
Engel, Lehman, 447
English horn, 447–448
English Suites, 448
enharmonic equivalence (equiva-
lents), 448
Enigma Variations, 448–449

Enjoy Yourself (It's Later Than You Think), 449
Eno, Brian, 449
ensemble(s), 450
  band, 75–76
  chamber orchestra, 242
  consort, 302
  dance band, 343
  quartet, 1437
  quintet, 1439–1440
  salon orchestra, 1564–1565
  Scratch Orchestra, 1621
  steel band, 1719–1720
  string orchestra, 1756
  string quartet, 1756–1757
  theater orchestra, 1838
  wind band, 2039
Entertainer, The, 450
Entführung aus dem Serail, Die, 2, 450
entr'acte, 450
entrata, 450
envelope, 450
epanalepsis, 450
epic opera, 450–451
episode, 451
Epistle sonata, 451
epithalamium, 451
equal temperament, 451
Erdödy Quartets, 451
Erkel, Franz, 451–452
Ernani, 452
Eroica Symphony, 452–453
Eroica Variations, 453
Erstaufführung, 453
Erwartung, 453
Escales, 454
escapement, 454
Eschenbach, Christoph, 454–455
Estampes, 455
estampie, 455
Estro armonico, L', 455
Et incarnatus, 455
ethnomusicology, 455–456
Étoile du Nord, L', 456
étude, 456
Études d'execution transcendante, 456–457
Études symphoniques, 457
Études transcendentales. See Études d'execution transcendante
Études-Tableaux, 457
Eugene Onegin, 457–458
Euler, Leonhard, 458
Eumenides, Les, 458
euphonious harmony, 458
euphonium, 458
euphony, 458–459
eurhythmics, 807
Europe, James Reese, 459
Europeras 1 & 2, 459–460
Euryanthe, 460
eurythmics, 460
Evans, Bill, 461
Evans, Gil, 461–462
evensong, 462

Everly Brothers, 462–463
Ewing, Maria, 463–464
execution, 464
exercise, 464
exoticism, 464–465
experimental music, 465
exposition, 465
expression marks, 465
expressionism, 466
extemporization, 466
extended compass, 466
extravaganza(s), 466
  Black Crook, 139
  Bombo, 154
  Kismet, 871–872
eye music, 467

F, 468
F holes, 468
F major, 468
F minor, 468
Fa, 468
faburden, 468
Façade, 469
Face the Music, 469
Facsimile, 469
fado, 469
Failing Kansas, 469
Fain, Sammy, 469–470, 706
fake book, 470
Fall River Legend, 470
Falla, Manuel De, 470–471
  Amor brujo, El, 25
  Nights in the Gardens of Spain, 1220
  Retablo de Maese Pedro, El, 1483
  Sombrero de tres picos, El, 1695–1696
Falling in Love Again, 471
falsa musica, 471
false relation, 329
falsetto, 471–472
falsobordone, 472
Falstaff (Elgar), 472–473
Falstaff (Verdi), 472
Fanciulla del West, La. See Girl of the Golden West, The
fancy, 473
Fancy Free, 473
fandango, 473
fanfare, 473, 1864, 1911
Fanfare for the Common Man, 473
fantasia, 473–474
Fantasia contrappuntistica, 474
Fantasia on a Theme by Thomas Tallis, 474
Fantasia on Greensleeves, 474
Fantasticks, The, 474
farandola, 474–475
Farbenmelodie, 874
farce, 475
farewell engagements, 475
Farewell Symphony, 475
Farinelli, 476
Farley, Carole, 477

Farwell, Arthur, 477–478
Fascinating Rhythm, 478
fasola, 478
Fauré, Gabriel, 478–479
  Masques et bergamasques, 1053–1054
  Messe de requiem, 1100
Faust (Gounod), 479
Faust Symphony (Liszt), 479
fauxbourdon, 480
favola per musica, 480
Favorite, La, 480
Fedora, 480–481
feedback, 481
Feen, Die, 481
Feldman, Morton, 481–482
Feliciano, Jose, 482
Feltsman, Vladimir, 482–483
feminine ending, 483
fermata, 483
Ferneyhough, Brian, 483–484
Ferrier, Kathleen, 484
festa teatrale, 484
Feste Romane, 1518
Festin de l'araignée, Le, 484–485
festival producers, 727–728
festivals, 485–487
Festschrift, 487
Festspiel, 487
Fétis, François-Joseph, 487–489
Feuermann, Emanuel, 489
Feuersnot, 489
Fever, 490
fiasco, 490
Fibich, Zdenek, 490–491
Fibonacci series, 491
fiddle, 491–492
fiddle tunes, 373
Fiddler on the Roof, 492
Fidelio, oder Die eheliche Liebe, 492–493
Fiedler, Arthur, 493–494
Field, John, 494
Fiery Angel, The, 495
fife, 495
fifth, 495
Fifth Symphony (Beethoven), 495–496
figuration, 496
figure humaine, La, 496
figured bass. *See* basso continuo
Fille du regiment, La, 496
film music, 496–498
  Bernstein, Elmer, 126
  Goldsmith, Jerry, 596
  Green, John, 624
  Hermann, Bernard, 715–716
  Jarre, Maurice, 808
  Legrand, Michel, 926–927
  Mancini, Henry, 1027
  Newman, Alfred, 1214–1215
  Previn, André, 1401–1403
  Raksin, David, 1452–1453
  Red Pony, 1466–1467
  Rota, Nino, 1536–1537
  Rozsa, Miklos, 1541–1542

  Schifrin, Lalo, 1587–1588
  Singin' in the Rain, 1671
  Tiomkin, Dimitri, 1858
  Waxman, Franz, 2007–2008
  Williams, John, 2036–2037
  Wizard of Oz, The, 2041–2042
  Young, Victor, 2071
finale, 498
fine, 499
Fingal's Cave, 499
finger cymbals, 499
fingerboard, 499
fingering, 499
Finian's Rainbow, 499
Finlandia, 499
Finta giardiniera, La, 500
Fiorello!, 500
fioritura, 500
fipple flute, 500
Fire and Rain, 500
Fire Symphony, 500–501
Firebird, The, 501
Fireworks Music (Handel), 501
Fireworks (Stravinsky), 501
first, 502
First Time Ever I Saw Your Face, 502
Fischer-Dieskau, Dietrich, 502–503
fish horn, 503
fistula, 503
Fitzgerald, Ella, 503
Five Foot Two, Eyes of Blue, 503
Five Orchestral Pieces. See *Fünf Orchesterstücke*
fixed Do(h), 504
fixed-tone instrument, 504
flag, 504
flageolet, 504
Flagstad, Kirsten, 504–505
flamenco, 505
Flanagan, Tommy, 505–506
flat, 506
flat pick, 506
Flatt, Lester, 506
Fledermaus, Die, 506–507
Fleisher, Leon, 507–508
flexatone, 508
Fliegende Holländer, Der, 513
flores, 508
Flotow, Friedrich von, 508–509, 1042
flourish. *See* fanfare
Flower Drum Song, 509
Floyd, Carlisle, 1252–1253
Flügelhorn, 510
flute and flute music, 510–512
  albisifono, 17
  bass flute, 92
  Boehm system, 149
  Density 21.5, 368
  dvojnica, 422
  fife, 495
  fipple flute, 500
  flagolet, 504
  Galway, James, 550

Laws, Hubert, 919
membi, 1083
Night Piece, 1219
nose flute, 1233
piccolo, 1367
Quantz, Johann Joachim, 1435–1436
Rampal, Jean-Pierre, 1456
Schandeflöte, 1583–1584
shakuhachi, 1642
Stockflöte, 1725
stranka, 1735
suling, 1763
sŭpeljka, 1767
svirala, 1771
Syrinx, 1786
tibia, 1853
transverse flute, 1882
trojnice, 1893
vertical flute, 1948
flutter-tonguing, 513
Fluxus, 513
Flying Dutchman, The, 513
Foggy Day in London Town, A, 513
Foley, "Red," 513–514
folia, 514
folk music, 514, 1645–1646
folk singers
  Baez, Joan, 68–69
  Dylan, Bob, 424–426
  Guthrie, Woody, 639–641
  Ochs, Phil, 1249–1250
  Peter, Paul and Mary, 1348–1349
  Seeger, Pete, 1630–1631
folk song(s), 514
  Arkansas Traveler, 39
  Clementine, 276
  Oh, Bury Me Not on the Lone Prairie, 1255
  Old Gray Mare, 1259
  On Top of Old Smoky, 1264
  Volga Boatmen's Song, 1972
  Volkstümlich, 1972–1973
  We Shall Overcome, 2008
Folksong Symphony, 514
Follow Thru, 514
Folsom Prison Blues, 514
Fontaine di Roma, Le. See Fountains of Rome, The
Foote, Arthur, 515, 1219
For He's a Jolly Good Fellow, 515
forlana, 515
form(s), 515–516. *See also* dance forms
  binary, 135–136
  classical. *See* classical music and forms
  dance forms. *See* dance forms
  ternary, 1834
formalism, 516
formant, 517
fortepiano, 517
Forza del destino, La, 517
Foss, Lukas, 517–519

Élytres, 443
Griffelkin, 629
Prairie, 1396
Foster, Stephen C., 101, 208–209, 519, 813–814, 1773
Fountains of Rome, The, 519–520
4'33," 520
Four Norwegian Moods, 520
Four Sacred Pieces, 520
Four Saints in Three Acts, 520
Four Temperaments, The, 1839
Four Tops, The, 520–521
four-handed piano, 521
fourth, 521
Fourth Symphony, 521
fox-trot, 521
Fra Diavolo, 522
française, 522
Francesca da Rimini, 522
Franck, Cèsar, 522–523
Franklin, Aretha, 524
Frau ohne Schatten, Die, 524–525
Frederick II, 525
free canon, 525
free fugue, 525
free jazz, 525
free reed (instruments), 3–4, 77, 293, 525–526
Freed, Alan, 526
Freeman, Bud, 526–527
Freischütz, Der, 527
French horn, 527–528
French sixth, 528
Freni, Mirella, 528–529
frequency, 529–530
Frère Jacques, 530
Frescobaldi, Girolamo, 530
fret, 530–531
friction drum, 531
Friedenstag, Der, 531
Friedhofer, Hugo, 531–532
Friedman, Ignaz, 532
Friml, Rudolf, 532
  Indian Love Call, 776
  Rose-Marie, 1524–1525
  Vagabond King, 1924
friss, 533
frog, 533
From the House of the Dead, 533
From the New World, 533
From the Steeples and the Mountains, 533
Froschquartett, 533–534
frottola, 534
F-sharp major, 534
F-sharp minor, 534–535
fugato, 535
fughetta, 535
fuging tune, 535
fugue, 535–537
  answer, 31
  dux, 422
  free, 525
  fughetta, 535
  tonal answer, 1867

full, 537
fundamental, 537–538
funeral march, 538, 1882
Fünf Orchesterstücke, 504, 538
Funiculi-Funicula, 538
funk, 538–539
Funny Face, 539
Funny Girl, 539
Funny Thing Happened on the Way to the Forum, A, 539
furniture music, 539
Furtwängler, Wilhelm, 539–542
futurism, 542
fuzztone, 543

G, 544
G major, 544
G minor, 544
Gabrieli, Andrea, 544–545
Gabrieli, Giovanni, 545–546
Gabrilowitsch, Ossip, 546–547
gadulka, 547
gagaku, 547
gaida, 547
gaillard(e), 547
gaita, 547
Galanta Dances, 548
Galanterien, 548
Galas, Diamanda, 548
Galilei, Vincenzo, 549
gallant style, 549
galop, 549–550, 1882
Galway, James, 550
gamba, 550
Gambler, The, 550
game music, 551–552
gamelan, 552–553
  kulintang, 902
  pelog, 1331
  slendro, 1677
  Wasitodiningrat, K. R. T., 2003–2004
gamut, 553
Ganz, 553
García Lorca, Federico, 553–554
Gardiner, John Eliot, 554
Garland, Judy, 555
Garner, Erroll, 555–556
Gaspard de la nuit, 556
gathering note, 556
Gaudeamus Igitur, 556
Gaunt, Percy, 1889
gavotta, 556
Gay, John, 73, 111–112
Gay Divorce, The, 557
Gayané, 557, 1555
Gaye, Marvin, 557–559, 750, 763
Gazza ladra, La, 559
Gebrauchsmusik, 559–560
Geisslieder, 560
Geist, 560
Geister Trio, Das, 569
Geld, Gary, 1433
Gemeinschaftsmusic, 560
Generalpause, 560

Generalprobe, 560
genius, 560–562
Genoveva, 562
genre, 562
Gentlemen Prefer Blondes, 562
Geographical Fugue, 562
geomusic, 562–564
George M!, 564
George White's Scandals, 564
Georgia on My Mind, 564
German sixth, 564
Gershwin, George, 564–566
  American in Paris, 24
  Concerto in F, 296
  Cuban Overture, 333
  Fascinating Rhythm, 478
  Foggy Day in London Town, 513
  Funny Face, 539
  Girl Crazy, 580
  I Got Rhythm, 763
  Of Thee I Sing, 1253
  Oh, Kay!, 1256
  Porgy and Bess, 1388
  Rhapsody in Blue, 1486–1487
  Rhapsody in Rivets, 1487
  Somebody Loves Me, 1696
  Strike up the Band, 1755
  Summertime, 1766
  Swanee, 1772–1773
Gershwin, Ira, 566–567
Gesamtkunstwerk, 567
Gesang der Jünglinge, Der, 567
Get Back, 568
Get Together, 568
Getz, Stan, 568–569
Gewandhaus, 569
Ghost Trio, 569
Gianni Schicchi, 569
Giant, The, 569
Gibson, Sir Alexander, 569–570
Gideon, Miriam, 570
Gielen, Michael, 570–571
Gieseking, Walter, 571
Gigi, 571–572
gigue, 572
Gigues, 572
Gilbert, Henry F., 343, 572–573
Gilbert and Sullivan
  Gondoliers, 597
  H. M. S. Pinafore, 726
  Ioalanthe, 787
  Mikado, 1117
  Patience, 1322
  Pirates of Penzance, 1371
  Savoyards, 1573
  Yeoman of the Guard, 2065–2066
Gilels, Emil, 573–574
Gillespie, "Dizzy," 574–575
gimmicks, 575–576
gimping, 576
Ginastera, Alberto, 399–400, 576–579
Gioconda, La, 578–579
Giordano, Umberto, 27, 480–481, 579–580

Giorno di regno, Un, 580
Giovanni d'arco, 580
Girl Crazy, 580
Girl Friend, The, 580
Girl I Left Behind Me, The, 580
Girl of the Golden West, The, 580–581
Giselle, 581
gittern, 581
Giuffre, Jimmy, 581–582
Giulini, Carlo Maria, 582–584
Giulio Cesare in Egitto, 584
Give My Regards to Broadway, 584
Give Peace a Chance, 584
Glagolitic Mass, 584
Glareanus, Henricus, 389, 584
Glass, Philip, 434, 585–587
glass harmonica, 587
Glazunov, Alexander, 587–588, 1940
glee, 588
Glière, Rheinhold, 769, 1467
Glinka, Mikhail, 589–590, 848, 954, 1551
glissando, 590–591
glockenspiel, 591
Gloria, 591
Gloriana, 591
Gluck, Christoph Willibald, 592–594, 768, 788, 1271–1272
Gluck, Wilhelm Archibald, 17, 40–41
Glückliche Hand, Die, 594
goat trill, 594–595
God Bless America, 595
God Bless the Child, 595
God Save the Czar, 595
God Save the King, 595
Goldberg, Johann Gottlieb, 596
Goldberg Variations, 596
Goldsmith, Jerry, 596
goliards, 597
Golitzin, Nikolai, 597
Gondoliers, or The King of Barataria, 597
gong, 597
Good Boy, 597
Good Vibrations, 597
Goodman, Benny, 598
Goodnight Irene, 598
Goodnight Ladies, 598
Gordon, Dexter, 599
Gordy, Berry, Jr., 599–600
Górecki, Henryk, 600–601
gospel music, 601–603
  Cleveland, James, 276
  Cooke, Sam, 304–305
  Dorsey, Thomas A., 405–406
  Jackson, Mahalia, 797
  spiritual, 1708–1709
Gothic music, 603
Gott erhalte unser Kaiser, 603–604
Götterdämmerung, 604–605
Gottschalk, Louis Moreau, 605–607

Gould, Glenn, 607–609
Gould, Morton, 470, 609–610
Gounod, Charles, 611–612
  Ave Maria, 58–59
  Faust, 479
  Marche funèbre d'une marionette, 1033
  Médecin malgré lui, Le, 1070
  Roméo et Juliette, 1521
  Sapho, 1569
Goyescas, 612
grace note, 612–613
gradual, 613
Gradus ad Parnassum, 613
Graffman, Gary, 613–614
Grainger, Percy, 614–615
Grammy Award, 615
gramophone, 615
Granados, Enrique, 612, 615–616
Grand Canyon Suite, 616
Grand Ole Opry, 616–618
grand opera, 618
grand piano, 618
Grande Duchesse de Gerolstein, La, 618–619
Grandfather's Clock, 619
graphic notation, 619–620
Grappelli, Stephane, 620–621
Grateful Dead, The, 621–623
gravicembalo, 623
Great Balls of Fire, 623–624
Great Waltz, The, 624
Greek Passion, The, 624
Green, John, 624
Greensleeves, 624–625
Gregorian chant, 625–626
  cursus, 336–337
  ictus, 766
  incipit, 775
  psalm tones, 1425
  Schola cantorum, 1599
  sequence, 1634
  verse, 1948
Gregory I, 626
Grieg, Edvard, 626–628, 729, 1330, 1700
Grieg, Nina, 629
Griffelkin, 629
Griffes, Charles T., 629
Grofé, Ferde, 616, 629–630
groove, 630
ground bass, 630–631
Gruber, Franz Xaver, 631
Gruber, H. K., 631
Gruenberg, Louis, 443, 632
Gruppen, 632
G-sharp minor, 632
Guarneri family, 632–633
guasa, 633
Gubaidulina, Sofia, 633–634
gudok, 634
Guerre des Bouffons, 634–635
Guiditta, 581
Guido d'Arezzo, 635–636, 1693
Guidonian hand, 636

Guillaume de Machaut. *See* Machaut, Guillaume de
Guillaume Tell, 2034
güiro, 636
guitarra española, 639
guitars and guitar music, 636–638
  acoustic guitar, 638
  Almeida, Laurindo, 19
  bass guitar, 92, 638
  Bream, Julian, 172
  capo, 216
  charango, 245
  Christian, Charlie, 262
  classical guitar, 638
  dital key, 386
  electric guitar, 436, 481, 543
  flat pick, 506
  lead, 638
  pick, 1367
  plectrum, 1376
  Reinhardt, Django, 1475
  rhythm guitar, 638
  Romero, Angel, 1521
  Romero, Celedonio, 1521
  Romero, Celin, 1521
  Romero, Pepe, 1521
  Segovia, Andrés, 1631–1632
  tiple, 1858
  ukulele, 1916
  vihuela, 1957
  Williams, John, 2036
Guntram, 639
Gurre-Lieder, 639
gusle, 639
gusli, 639
Guthrie, Woody, 639–641
Guys and Dolls, 641
gymel, 641
Gymnopédies, 641
Gypsy, 641–642
Gypsy Baron, The, 642
Gypsy music, 642–644
Gypsy scale, 644

H, 645
H. M. S. Pinafore, or The Lass Who Loved a Sailor, 726
habanera, 645
Haffner Serenade, 645–646
Haffner Symphony, 646
Haggard, Merle, 646–647
Hahn, Reynaldo, 647–648
Hail, Columbia, 648
Hail, Hail, the Gang's All Here, 648
Hail to the Chief, 648
Hair, 648–649
Haitink, Bernard, 649–650
Halévy, Fromental, 650–651, 841
Haley, Bill, 651–652
Halffter, Ernesto, 652
Halka, 652
Halle, Adam de la. *See* Adam de la Halle
Hallelujah, 653

Hallelujah, Baby!, 653
Hallelujah Chorus, 653
Hallelujah meter, 653
halling, 653
Hamlet (Tchaikovksy), 653
Hamlet (Thomas), 653
Hamlisch, Marvin, 654
Hammerclavier, 654
Hammerklavier Sonata, 654
Hammerstein, Oscar, 654–655
Hammerstein, Oscar, II, 656, 1655. *See also* Rodgers and Hammerstein
Hammond organ, 656
Hampson, Thomas, 656–657
Hampton, Lionel, "Hamp," 657–658
Hancock, Herbie, 658
Handel, George Frideric, 659–665
  Alexander's Feast, 18
  Chandos Anthems, 242
  Cuckoo and the Nightingale, 333
  Deidamia, 362
  Fireworks Music, 501
  Giulio Cesare in Egitto, 584
  Hallelujah Chorus, 653
  Harmonious Blacksmith, 678
  Israel in Egypt, 789–790
  Jephtha, 818
  Messiah, 1101–1102
  Rinaldo, 1499
  Semele, 1633
  Utrecht Te Deum, 1923
  Water Music, 2004–2005
handle piano, 665
Handy, W. C., 665–667
  Memphis Blues, 1084
  St. Louis Blues, 1557–1558
Hanna, Roland, 667
Hanon, Charles-Louis, 667
Hans Heiling, 667–668
Hänsel und Gretel, 668
Hanson, Howard, 668–671
  Merry Mount, 1099
  Nordic Symphony, 1227
Happening, 671–672
Happy Birthday to You, 672
Happy Days Are Here Again, 672
happy ending, 672
Harawi, chant d'amour et de mort, 672
Harbach, Otto, 672–673
Harbison, John, 673–674
Harburg, E. Y. (Yip), 674–675
  Finian's Rainbow, 499
  Wizard of Oz, 2041–2042
hard bop, 675
hardingfele, 675
Harlequin, 675
harmonic, 675
harmonic series, 676
harmonica, 676
harmonicon, 676
harmonics, 676–677
Harmonie der Welt, Die, 677

Harmonious Blacksmith, The, 678
Harmoniques poètiques et re-ligieuses, 677
harmonium, 678
harmony, 678–682. *See also* chord(s)
  added seventh, 9
  added sixth, 9
  barbershop, 81
  bass line, 92
  basso continuo, 93–94
  basso obbligato, 94
  Burgundian school, 187–188
  cadence, 199–201
  change, 242–243
  chromatic, 263
  chromaticism, 263
  circle (cycle) of fifths, 267
  complement, 290
  concord, 297
  consecutive intervals, 301
  consonance, 302
  cross relation, 329
  diminished interval, 379
  discord, 382
  dissonance, 383–384
  dissonant interval, 384
  dominant, 396
  euphonious, 458
  euphony, 458–459
  French sixth, 528
  fundamental, 537–538
  German sixth, 564
  harmonic, 675
  inner parts, 780
  inversion, 785–786
  key, 859
  Neapolitan sixth, 1207–1208
  open harmony, 1267
  part, 1313
  passing notes or tones, 1319
  pedal point, 1328
  pes, 1348
  Picardy third, 1364–1365
  primary triad, 1407
  progression, 1417
  quartal, 1436
  related keys, 1476
  resolution, 1481
  substitution, 1761
  suspension, 1769
  tonal, 1867
  tonality, 1867
  triad, 1885–1886
  tritone, 375–376, 1892
  voice leading, 1971
Harnoncourt, Nikolaus, 682
Harold in Italy, 682–683
Harp Quartet, 685
harps and harpists, 11, 683–685
  Salzedo, Carlos, 1566–1567
  Zabaleta, Nicanor, 2076
harpsichord and harpsichordists, 685–686
  clavecin, 273
  gravicembalo, 623

Hogwood, Christopher, 729
  jack, 797
  Kipnis, Igor, 868
  Koopman, Ton, 887
  Landowska, Wanda, 910–912
  short octave, 1650
  virginal, 1965–1966
Harris, Roy, 514, 686–687
Harrison, George, 687–688
Harrison, Lou, 688–689
Hart, Lorenz, 690. *See also* Rodgers and Hart
Hartmann, Karl Amadeus, 690–691
Háry János, 691
hasosra, 691
Hatikva, 691
Hauptsatz, 691
Hausmusik. *See* Gebrauchs-musik
Hawaiian music, 19
Hawkins, Coleman, 692
Hawkins, Sir John, 693
Haydn, Franz Joseph, 693–699
  Bear, 98–99
  Clock, 278
  Coronation Mass, 313
  Creation, 325
  Distratto, Il, 385–386
  Drumroll Symphony, 413
  Emperor Quartet, 444
  Emperor's Hymn, 444
  Erdödy Quartets, 451
  Farewell Symphony, 475
  Fire Symphony, 500–501
  Froschquartett, 533–534
  Gott erhalte unser Kaiser, 603–604
  Hen, 707
  Impériale, L', 771
  Lark Quartet, 915
  London Symphonies, 978
  Maria Theresia, 1034
  Mass in a Time of War, 1056
  Matin, Le, 1061
  Mercury Symphony, 1098
  Midi, Le, 1114
  Military Symphony, 1120
  Nelson Mass, 1208–1209
  Ox Minuet, 1286
  Oxford Symphony, 1286
  Paris Symphonies, 1308
  Queen, The, 1438
  Quintenquartett, 1439
  Razor Quartet, 1462
  Ritterquartett, 1501
  Scherzi, Gli, 1585
  Schoolmaster, 1599
  Seasons, 1629
  Soir, Le, 1692
  Sonnenquartette, 1701
  Surprise Symphony, 1768–1769
  Tostquartette, 1876
  Vogelquartett, 1971
Haydn, Michael, 699–700
Hayes, Isaac, 700–701

head, 701
heckelphone, 701
Heifetz, Jascha, 701–703
Heinrich, Anthony Philip, 703–704
heirmos, 704
Heldenbariton, 704
Heldenleben, Ein, 704–705
Heldentenor, 705
helicon, 705
Hello, Dolly!, 705
Hellzapoppin', 706
Helmholtz, Hermann von, 706
Help, Help, the Globolinks!, 706–707
hemiola, 707
Hen, The, 707
Henderson, Fletcher, "Smack," 707
Henderson, Ray, 514, 708, 729
Hendricks, Barbara, 708–709
Hendrix, Jimi, 709
Hensel, Fanny, 710
Henze, Hans Werner, 438, 711, 843
hep, 712
Herbert, Victor, 712–713, 790–791, 1012, 1207
Herman, Jerry, 705, 713–714
Herman, Woody, 714
Hermann, Bernard, 715–716
Hérodiade, 714
Hérold, Louis, 714–715
Heseltine, Philip, 716–717
hesitation tango, 717
hesitation waltz, 717
heterophony, 717
Heure espagnole, L', 717–718
Heures séculaires et instantanées, 718
hexachord, 718
Higganbotham, J. C., 718
high fidelity, 718
high hat, 718
Hildegard von Bingen, 719–720
Hill, Bertha "Chippie," 720
hillbilly, 720
Hiller, Lejaren, 720–721
Hin und Zurück, 721
Hindemith, Paul, 721–723
  Harmonie der Welt, Die, 677
  Hin und Zurück, 721
  Long Christmas Dinner, 979
  Ludus Tonalis, 989
  Marienleben, Das, 1034–1035
  Mathis der Maler, 1060
  Neues vom Tage, 1212
  Philharmonic Concerto, 1355
  Theme and Variations: The Four Temperaments, 1839
Hindu singing, 1806
Hines, Earl "Fatha," 723–724
hip-hop, 724–725
Hippolyte et Aricie, 725
Hirt, Al, 725
Histoire du soldat, L', 725

Histoires naturelles, 725
historians, music
  Burney, Charles, 188–189
  Hawkins, Sir John, 693
Historische Symphonie, 726
Hit the Deck, 726
hocket, 726
Hodges, Johnny "Rabbit," 726–727
hoedown, 727
Hoffman, E. T. A., 727
Hoffnung, Gerard, 727–728
Hofmann, Peter, 728
Hogwood, Christopher, 729
Holberg Suite, 729
Hold Everything, 729
Holiday, Billie "Lady Day," 730–731, 1735
Holidays, 731–732
Holliger, Heinz, 732
Holly, Buddy, 732–734
Holst, Gustav, 734–736, 1374–1375
Home, Sweet Home, 736–737
Home on the Range, 736
hommage, 737
homophony, 737
Honegger, Arthur, 737–739
  Danse des morts, La, 344
  Di Tre Re, 374
  Jeanne d'Arc au bûcher, 814
  Judith, 841
  Liturgical Symphony, 969
  Pacific 231, 1292
honky-tonk, 739
hook, 739
hopak, 739–740
Hopkins, Sam "Lightnin'," 740
Hopkinson, Francis, 740–741
hora lunga, 741
horn(s), 741
  alphorn, 19
  fifths, 742
  players, 1904
  shepherd's horn, 1648
Horne, Lena, 742
Horne, Marilyn, 742–743
hornpipe, 743–744
Horowitz, Vladimir, 744–746
horse opera, 746–747
horse trot, 747
Hörspiel, 747
Horst, Louis, 747
Hot Chocolates, 747
Hot Time in the Old Town Tonight, A, 748
Hound Dog, 748
Housatonic at Stockbridge, The, 748
Houston, Whitney, 748–749
Hovhaness (Hovaness), Alan, 749–750
How Much is That Doggie in the Window?, 750
How Sweet It Is (To Be Loved By You), 750

How to Succeed in Business Without Really Trying, 750
Hubbard, Freddie, 750–751
huehuetl, 751
Huguenots, Les, 751
Humes, Helen, 752
Humfrey, Pelham, 752
humor, 752–753
humoresque, 753
humorists, musical
   Borge, Victor, 155
   Schickele, Peter, 1586–1587
Humperdinck, Engelbert, 753–754
   Hänsel und Gretel, 668
   Königskinder, 886
Hungarian Rhapsodies, 754–755
Hungarian scale, 644
Hunnenschlacht, 755
Hunter, Alberta, 755–756
Hupfeld, Herman, 756
Hupfield, Herman, 47–48
huqin, 756
hurdy-gurdy, 411, 756–757, 1276
Hurok, Sol, 757
Husa, Karel, 757–758
Hustle, The, 758
Hüttenbrenner, Anselm, 758
Hwang, Byung-Ki, 759
hydraulic organ, 759
Hykes, David, 759–760
hymn(s), 760–761
   Adeste Fideles, 9–10
   canticle, 213
   deaconing, 354
   doxology, 410
   epithalamium, 451
   fuging tune, 535
   Hallelujah meter, 653
   heirmos, 704
   Materna, 1060
   Nearer My God to Thee, 1208
   noël, 1225
   Old Hundred, 1259–1260
   Portuguese Hymn, 1390
   processional, 1414
   psalm, 1425
   recessional, 1465
   Rock of Ages, 1509
   Sankey, Ira D., 1568
   Syrian chant, 1786
   troparion, 1895
   Utrecht Te Deum, 1923
Hymnen, 761
Hyperprism, 761
hypo-, 761

I, 762
I Am Woman, 762
I Can Get It for You Wholesale, 762
(I Can't Get No) Satisfaction, 762
I Can't Give You Anything But Love, Baby, 762
I Can't Help Myself, 762

I Didn't Raise My Boy to Be a Soldier, 762
I Fall to Pieces, 763
I Got Rhythm, 763
I Got You (I Feel Good), 763
I Have a Dream, 763
I Heard It Through the Grapevine, 763
I Left My Heart in San Francisco, 763
I Married an Angel, 763
I Shot the Sheriff, 763–764
I Walk the Line, 764
I Wanna Be Loved by You, 764
I Want to Be Happy, 764
I Want to Hold Your Hand, 764
I Wonder Who's Kissing Her Now, 764
iamb, 764
Ibéria, 764–765
Ibert, Jacques, 386, 454, 765
Ice Cube, 765–766
Icelandic Symphony, 766
Ice-T, 766
ictus, 766
I'd Rather Be Right, 766–767
Ideale, Die, 767
idée fixe, 767
idiophone(s), 767, 1677, 1800
Idomeneo, Ré di Creta, 767
idyl, 767
If I Had a Hammer, 768
If I Were King, 768
Iglesias, Julio, 768
Illuminations, Les, 769
Ilya Muromets, 769
I'm Always Chasing Rainbows, 769
I'm Forever Blowing Bubbles, 769
I'm In the Mood for Love, 769
I'm Just Wild about Harry, 769
I'm Looking Over a Four-Leaf Clover, 769
I'm Walkin', 769
Images, 770
Imaginary Landscape, 770
imbroglio, 770
imitation, 770–771
imperfection, 771
Imperial Maryinsky Theater, 771
Impériale, L', 771
Impossible Dream, The, 771
Impresario, The, 772
impresario(s), 772
   Diaghilev, Sergi, 376–377
   Hammerstein, Oscar, 654–655
   Hurok, Sol, 757
Impressioni Brasiliane, 772
impressionism, 772
impromptu, 772
Imropperia, 772–773
improvisation, 773
In a Little Spanish Town, 774
In a Summer Garden, 774
In C, 774
In Memoriam, 774
In Nomine, 774

In the Steppes of Central Asia, 775
In the Still of the Nite, 775
incarnatus, Et, 775
incidental music, 775
incipit, 775
Incoronazione di Poppea, L', 776
Incredible Flutist, The, 776
Indes Galantes, Les, 776
indeterminacy, 776
Indian Love Call, 776
Indian music, 801, 862–863, 1446–1448, 1798
Indian Suite, 776
Indianische Fantasie, 777
Indonesian music. *See* gamelan
Indy, Vincent d', 777–779, 790, 1782
inégales, 779
Inextinguishable, The, 779
inner parts, 780
Inscape, 780
instrument inventors/makers
   Cristofori, Bartolomeo, 328
   Partch, Harry, 1314–1315
   Sax, Adolphe, 1574–1575
   Theremin, Leon, 1841–1843
instrumental motet, 780
instrumental technique. *See* technic (technique)
instrumentation, 780
intabulation, 780
Intégrales, 780
interference beats, 780–781
interlude, 781
intermezzo, 781–782
Intermezzo, 782
intermodulation, 782
Internationale, 782
interval(s), 782–784
   augmented interval, 56
   complement, 290
   diapason, 378
   diminshed interval, 379
   dissonant, 384
   eighth, 433
   fifth, 495
   fourth, 521
   octave, 1251
   quarter tone, 1436–1437
   sharp (adjective), 1645
   skip, 1675
   sum (summation) tone, 1765
   temperament, 1826
   tetrachord, 1835–1836
   tritone, 375–376, 1892
intonarumori, 784
intonation, 784
intrada, 784–785
introduction, 785
Introduction and Allegro, 785
introit, 785
invention, 785
inversion, 785–786
invertible counterpoint, 787
Invitation to the Dance, 787
invocation, 787

Ioalanthe, or The Peer and the Peri, 787
Ionisation, 787–788
Iphigénie en Aulide, 788
Iphigénie en Tauride, 788
Iris, 788
Irma la Douce, 788
Irmelin, 789
Islamey, 789
Isle de Merlin, L', 768
Isle joyeuse, L', 769
Isle of the Dead, The, 789
isorhythm, 789
Israel, Brian M., 790
Israel in Egypt, 789–790
Israel Symphony, 790
Istar Variations, 790
It Had to be You, 790
It Happened in Nordland, 790–791
It Was a Very Good Year, 791
Italian Concerto, 791
Italian Serenade, 791
Italian sixth, 791
Italian Symphony, 791
Italiana in Algeri, L', 791
Ite missa est, 791–792
It's De-Lovely, 792
It's Not for Me to Say, 792
It's Now or Never, 792
Itsy Bitsy Teenie Weenie Yellow Polkadot Bikini, 792
Ivan Susanin, 954
Ivanhoe, 792
Ives, Charles, 792–796
   Concord Sonata, 297
   Holidays, 731–732
   Housatonic at Stockbridge, 748
   From the Steeples and the Mountains, 533
   Three Places in New England, 1851
   Three-Page Sonata, 1852
   Unanswered Question, 1917
   Universe Symphony, 1918
Izeÿl, 796

jack, 797
Jackson, Mahalia, 797
Jackson, Michael, 797–799
Jackson, Milt, 800
Jacquet de la Guerre, Elisabeth, 800–801
Jagdhorn, Jägerhorn, 801
Jagger, Mick. *See* Rolling Stones
Jahreszeiten, Die, 1629
Jakobin, The, 801
jaltarang, 801
jam session, 801
Jamaican Rumba, 801–802
James, Harry, 802
Janáček, Leoš, 802–804
   Cunning Little Vixen, 335
   Glagolitic Mass, 584
   From the House of the Dead, 533
   Jenůfa, 818

Káta Kabanová, 853–854
Mr. Broucek's Excursion to the Moon and Mr. Broucek's Excursion into the 15th Century, 1132
Taras Bulba, 1809
Janizary music, 804–805
Jankó keyboard, 805
Japanese music, 547, 805–807
Jaques-Dalcroze, Émile, 807
Jarnach, Philipp, 807–808
Jarre, Maurice, 808
Jarreau, Al, 808–809
Jarrett, Keith, 809
Järvi, Neeme, 809–810
jazz, 810–813
Adderley, "Cannonball," 9
Allison, Mose, 19
Almeida, Laurindo, 19
Armstrong, Louis, 41–42
barrelhouse, 86–87
Basie, "Count," 90–91
bebop, 102
Bechet, Sidney, 102–103
Beiderbecke, Bix, 112–113
big band. *See* big band
Bigard, "Barney," 132–133
Blake, Eubie, 140–141
Blakey, Art, 141
blues. *See* blues
Bolden, "Buddy," 153
boogie-woogie, 155
bossa nova, 157
Bowie, Lester, 163
Braxton, Anthony, 171
break, 171
Brown, Clifford, 177
Brubeck, Dave, 178
Carmichael, Hoagy, 220–221
Carter, Benny, 225–226
Carter, Ron, 227–228
cats, 236
Charles, Ray, 245–246
Cherry, Don, 250–251
Christian, Charlie, 262
Cole, "Cozy," 281
Cole, Nat "King," 281–282
Coleman, Ornette, 282–283
Coltrane, John, 286–287
cool jazz, 305
Corea, Chick, 309–310
Dameron, Tadd, 342
dance band, 343
Davis, Anthony, 350
Davis, Miles, 351–353
De Franco, "Buddy," 353–354
Desmond, Paul, 369
Dixieland, 387–388
Dodds, "Baby," 388–389
Dodds, Johnny, 388
Dolphy, Eric, 395
Dorsey brothers, 406–407
Ebony Concerto, 429
Eckstine, Billy, 430
Eldridge, Roy "Little Jazz," 435–436

Ellington, "Duke," 441–442
Evans, Bill, 461
Evans, Gil, 461–462
fake book, 470
Fitzgerald, Ella, 503
Flanagan, Tommy, 505–506
free jazz, 525
Freeman, Bud, 526–527
funk, 538–539
Garner, Erroll, 555–556
Getz, Stan, 568–569
Gillespie, "Dizzy," 574–575
Giuffre, Jimmy, 581–582
Goodman, Benny, 598
Gordon, Dexter, 599
Grappelli, Stephane, 620–621
groove, 630
Hampton, Lionel, "Hamp," 657–658
Hancock, Herbie, 658
Handy, W. C., 665–667
Hanna, Roland, 667
hard bop, 675
harmony, 9, 145
Hawkins, Coleman, 692
Henderson, Fletcher, "Smack," 707
hep, 712
Herman, Woody, 714
Higganbotham, J. C., 718
Hines, Earl "Fatha," 723–724
Hirt, Al, 725
Hodges, Johnny "Rabbit," 726–727
Holiday, Billie "Lady Day," 730–731
Horne, Lena, 742
Hubbard, Freddie, 750–751
Humes, Helen, 752
improvisation, 773
Jackson, Milt, 800
jam session, 801
James, Harry, 802
Jarreau, Al, 808–809
Jarrett, Keith, 809
Jenkins, Leroy, 816–817
Johnson, "Bunk," 825–826
Johnson, J. J., 828
Johnson, James P., 827
Jones, Quincy, 832
Jones, Thad, 834
Jordan, Louis, 839–840
Keppard, Freddie, 857
Kirk, Roland, 869–870
Krupa, Gene, 899
Laws, Hubert, 919
Lewis, John, 944–945
lick, 951
Marsalis, Wynton, 1038–1039
McPartland, Jimmy, 1066–1067
McPartland, Marian, 1067
McRae, Carmen, 1068
McShann, Jay, 1068–1069
Mercer, Mabel, 1097–1098
Miller, Glenn, 1120–1121

Mingus, Charles, 1124
Navarro, "Fats" (Theodore), 1207
Nichols, "Red," 1216
Norvo, Red, 1232
off-beat, 1253
Oliver, "King" (Joseph), 1260–1261
Ory, "Kid," 1280
Parker, Charlie, 1308–1309
Pepper, Art, 1335
Peterson, Oscar, 1349
Powell, "Bud," 1394–1395
progressive, 1418
ragtime. *See* ragtime
Redman, Don, 1468
Reinhardt, Django, 1475
rhythm and blues, 1489–1490
rhythm section, 1490
Rich, Buddy, 1491
riff, 1493
Roach, Max, 1501
Rollins, "Sonny," 1517–1518
Russell, George, 1552
scat singing, 1581
Schuller, Gunther, 1603–1605
section, 1630
Shaw, Artie, 1646–1647
Short, Bobby, 1650
shout, 1655
sidemen, 1660
signature tune, 1663
Simone, Nina, 1667–1668
Sissle, Noble, 1672
slap-bass, 1675
Smith, Bessie, 1685–1686
Smith, Willie "the Lion," 1687–1688
standard, 1717
stomp, 1731
stop time, 1734
Strayhorn, Billy, 1752
stride piano, 1755
Sun Ra, 1766–1767
swing, 1774–1775
Tatum, Art, 1812–1813
Taylor, Cecil, 1815
Terry, Clark, 1835
Third Stream, 1844
Tormé, Mel, 1872–1873
Tristano, Lennie, 1891–1892
vamp, 1927
Vaughan, Sarah, 1933
Venuti, Joe, 1940–1941
Waits, Tom, 1990
walking bass, 1993
Waller, "Fats," 1994–1995
Washington, Dinah, 2003
Williams, "Cootie," 2034–2035
Williams, Mary Lou, 2037
Young, Lester, 2069–2070
Zorn, John, 2089
Jazz Concerto, 813
Jazz Singer, The, 813

jazz-funk, 813
Jeanie with the Light Brown Hair, 813–814
Jeanne d'Arc au bûcher, 814
Jeepers, Creepers, 814
Jefferson, "Blind Lemon," 816
Jefferson Airplane, 814–815
Jena Symphony, 816
Jenkins, Leroy, 816–817
Jenks, Stephen, 817
Jennings, Waylon, 817–818
Jenůfa, 818
Jephtha, 818
Jeremiah Symphony, 818
Jericho trumpets, 819
Jerusalem, Siegfried, 819
Jessonda, 819–820
Jeu de cartes, 820
Jeu de Robin et de Marion, 820
Jeunehomme Concerto, 820
Jeux d'eau, 820
Jeux d'enfants, 820
Jew's harp, 821
jig, 821
Jim Crack Corn (Blue Tail Fly), 821
Jim Crow, 821
Jingle Bells, 821
jingling johnny, 821–822
jitterbug, 822
Job, 822
Joel, Billy, 822–823
Johansen, Gunnar, 823–824
John, Elton, 824–825
Johnny Johnson, 825
Johnson, "Bunk," 825–826
Johnson, Edward, 826–827
Johnson, Frank, 827
Johnson, J. J., 828
Johnson, James P., 827
Johnson, Robert, 828–829
Johnston, Ben, 829
Jolie fille de Perth, La, 830
Jolson, Al, 813, 830–831
Jones, George, 831
Jones, Isham, 790
Jones, Quincy, 832
Jones, Sissieretta, 833
Jones, Spike, 833–834
Jones, Thad, 834
Jones, Tom, 474, 834–835
jongleur, 835–836
Jongleur de Notre Dame, Le, 836
Jonny spielt auf, 836
Joplin, Janis, 836–837
Joplin, Scott, 837–839
Entertainer, 450
Treemonisha, 1884
Jordan, Louis, 839–840
Josquin Desprez, 369–370
jota, 840
Jubilee, 840
jubilus, 840
Judith (Honegger), 841
Judith (Schuman), 841
Judith (Serov), 840

jug, 841
Juive, La, 841
Julien, 842
Jullien, Louis, 842–843
Jumbo, 843
Junge Lord, Der, 843
Jupiter Symphony, 843
just intonation, 843–844

Kabalevsky, Dmitri, 845–846
Kaddish, 846
Kagel, Mauricio, 846–847
Kaiserquartett, 444
Kalevala, 847
kalimba, 909
Kalomiris, Manolis, 847–848
kamānja, 848
Kamarinskaya, 848
kammer, 848
Kammersymphonie, 848
Kander, John, 848–849
kantele, 849
Karajan, Herbert von, 849–853
karatāli, 853
Kashchei, the Immortal, 853
Kát'a Kabanová, 853–854
katabasis, 854
Katerina Izmailova, 905–906
Kavafian, Ani, 854
Kavafian, Ida, 854–855
Kay, Ulysses Simpson, 855–856
kayagum, 759, 856
Kaye, Sammy, 856
kazoo, 856
Kempff, Wilhelm, 856–857
Kennedy, Nigel, 857
Keppard, Freddie, 857
Kern, Jerome, 857–858
    Roberta, 1502
    Show Boat, 1655
    Smoke Gets in Your Eyes, 1688
kettledrum, 1855–1856
key, 859
key action, 859
key harp, 859
key signature(s), 859–860
    A major, 1
    A minor, 1
    A-flat major, 12
    B major, 60
    B minor, 60
    B-flat major, 130
    B-flat minor, 131
    C major, 196
    C minor, 196
    C-sharp minor, 332
    D major, 338
    D minor, 338–339
    D-flat major, 374
    E major, 427
    E minor, 427
    E-flat major, 431
    E-flat minor, 431
    F major, 468
    F minor, 468
    F-sharp major, 534

    F-sharp minor, 534–535
    G major, 544
    G minor, 544
    G-sharp minor, 632
    sharp (adjective), 1645
    transpose, 1881
key stop, 860
keyboard music. *See also* piano
    music
    Anna Magdalena Book, 30
    Art of the Fugue, 46
    English Suites, 448
    Goldberg Variations, 596
    Well-Tempered Clavier,
    2022–2023
keyboards and keyboard instru-
    ments, 860–861
    action, 5
    calliope, 207
    celesta, 238
    cembalo, 239
    chord organ, 261
    clavecin, 273
    clavichord, 273–274
    clavier, 274
    concertina, 293
    fixed-tone instrument, 504
    fortepiano, 517
    harpsichord. *See* harpsichord
    Jankó, 805
    key action, 859
    key harp, 859
    Klavier, 874
    melodeon, 1079
    melodion, 1080
    melodium, 1080
    orchestrion, 1271
    organ. *See* organ
    pantaleon, 1305
    pedal, 1327–1328
    pedalier, 1328–1329
    piano. *See* piano
    soundboard, 1705
    spinet, 1708
    stretch, 1754
    synthesizer, 1785–1786
    temperament, 1826
    touch, 1877
    voicing, 1972
key(ed) trumpet, 860
keynote, 861
Khachaturian, Aram, 862, 1555
Khan, Ali Akbar, 862–863
Khatchaturian, Aram, 557
khorovod, 863
Khovanshchina, 863
Killing Me Softly With His Song,
    863
Kindertotenlieder, 864
King, "B. B.", 864–865
King, Ben E., 1717
King, Carole, 865–866
King, Martin Luther, 763
King and I, The, 864
King Lear, 866
King of the Road, 866

King Priam, 866
King's Henchman, The, 867
Kipnis, Alexander, 867
Kipnis, Igor, 868
Kirchner, Leon, 868–869
Kirk, Roland, 869–870
Kirkby, Emma, 870–871
Kirnberger, Johann Philipp, 871
Kismet, 871–872
Kiss, The (Hubička), 872
Kiss Me Kate, 872
Kissin, Evgeny, 872–873
kit, 873
kithara, 873
Kitt, Eartha, 873
Klagende Lied, Das, 873
Klangfarbe, 874
Klangfarbenmelodie, 874
Klavier, 874
Kleiber, Carlos, 874–875
Kleiber, Erich, 875–876
Klemperer, Otto, 876–878
Kluge, Die, 878
Knickerbocker Holiday, 878–879
Knight, Gladys, 879
Knoxville, Summer of 1915, 879
Knussen, Oliver, 880
Koanga, 880
Kodály, Zoltán, 880–883
    Galánta Dances, 548
    Háry János, 691
    Peacock Variations, 1325
    Psalmus Hungaricus, 1425
Koechlin, Charles, 883–884
Kogan, Leonid, 884–885
Kokkonen, Joonas, 885
Kol Nidrei, 885–886
Königskinder, 886
Kontakion, 886
Kontakte, 886
Kontarsky, Alfons, 886–887
Kontarsky, Aloys, 887
Kontarsky, Bernhard, 887
Konzert, 887
Koopman, Ton, 887
kora, 888–889
Korean temple blocks, 889
Korngold, Erich Wolfgang,
    889–890
koto, 890
Koussevitzky, Serge, 890–893
koza, 893
krakowiak, 893–894
Kraus, Alfredo, 894
Kreisler, Fritz, 894–896
Kremer, Gidon, 897
Krenek, Ernst, 836, 897–898
Kreutzer Sonata, 899
Krupa, Gene, 899
Kubelík, Jan, 899–900
Kubelík, Rafael, 900–902
kulintang, 902
kultrún, 902
Kunc, Božidar, 1118
kymbala, 902
Kyrie, 902

L, 903
La, 903
La, La, Lucille, 904
La Bamba, 903
La Barbara, Joan, 903–904
La Guerre, Élisabeth Jacquet de.
    See Jacquet de la Guerre,
    Élisabeth
Labèque, Katia and Marielle,
    904–905
Lacrimosa, 905
Lady, Be Good!, 905
Lady in the Dark, 905
Lady is a Tramp, The, 905
*Lady Macbeth of the Mtzensk Dis-
    trict,* 905–906
lai, 906
Lakmé, 906
Lalo, Édouard, 906–907
Lamb, Joseph Francis, 908
Lambert, Constant, 908–909
Lambert, Michel. *See* Lully, Jean-
    Baptiste
lamellaphones, 909
lament, 909
lamento, 909
Landini, Francesco, 910
Ländler, 910
Landowska, Wanda, 910–912
Lane, Burton, 912
    *On a Clear Day You Can See
    Forever,* 1263–1264
    Finian's Rainbow, 499
Langridge, Philip, 912–913
Lanner, Joseph, 913
Lanza, Mario, 913–915
Lark Ascending, The, 915
Lark Quartet, 915
Larrocha, Alicia de, 915
Lasso, Orlando di, 915–917
Last Savage, The, 917
Last Time I Saw Paris, The, 917
lauda, 917
Laudamus te, 917
launeddas, 917–918
Laura, 918
Lavignac, Albert, 918
Law, Andrew, 918–919
Laws, Hubert, 919
Le Caine, Hugh, 919–920
lead, 920
lead sheet, 920
Leadbelly, 920–921
leading, 920
Lear, 921
lectionary, 921
Led Zeppelin, 922–923
Ledbetter, Huddie, 922
ledger lines, 922
Lee, Peggy, 923–924
left-hand music, 924–925
legato, 925
legend, 925
*Legend of the Invisible City of
    Kitezh and the Maiden
    Fevronia, The,* 925

Legende von der heiligen Elisabeth, Die, 925
Leginska, Ethel, 926
Legrand, Michel, 926–927
Lehár, Franz, 927–928
 Giuditta, 581
 Merry Widow, 1099
Lehmann, Lotte, 928–929
Lehrstück, 929–930
Leigh, Mitch, 771, 930
Leinsdorf, Erich, 930–931
leitmotiv, 931–932
Leningrad Symphony, 932–933
Lennon, John, 933–934
Lentz, Daniel, 934–936
Lenya, Lotte, 936
Leoncavallo, Ruggero, 936–938
 Pagliacci, 1299–1300
 Zaza, 2082
Leoninus, 938
Leonore Overtures, 938–939
Leppard, Raymond, 939–940
Lerner, Alan Jay, 940–941
 Brigadoon, 174
 Camelot, 208
 On a Clear Day You Can See Forever, 1263–1264
 Gigi, 571–572
 Paint Your Wagon, 1301–1302
lesson, 942
Let 'Em Eat Cake, 942
Let's Make an Opera, 942
Levine, James, 942–943
Lewis, Jerry Lee, 943–944
Lewis, John, 944–945, 1844
Lewis, Meade "Lux," 945
Lhévinne, Josef, 946
Liadov, Anatoli, 1940
Liberace, 946–947
libretto and librettists, 947–951
 Da Ponte, Lorenzo, 339
 Gershwin, Ira, 566–567
 Harbach, Otto, 672–673
 Metastasio, Pietro, 1102–1103
licensing, music
 ASCAP, 47
 BMI, 147–148
lick, 951
Lidice Memorial, 951
Liebesfuss, 951–952
Liebestraum, 952
Lied, 952–953
Lied von der Erde, Das, 953
lieder
 Schubert, Franz, 1599–1603
 Schwanengesang, 1615
Lieder ohne Worte, 954
Liedertafel, 954
lieto fine, 672
Life for the Czar, A, 954
Life is Just a Bowl of Cherries, 954
ligature, 954
Ligeti, György, 955–956
Light My Fire, 956
Like A Prayer, 956
Like a Rolling Stone, 956

Like A Virgin, 956
Lin, Cho-Liang, 956–957
Lincoln Portrait, 957
Lind, Jenny, 957–958
Lindy hop, 958
linear counterpoint, 958
lining out, 354
Linus, 959
Linz Symphony, 959
Lion Sleeps Tonight, The, 959
lion's roar, 959
Lipatti, Dinu, 959–960
lira, 960
lira da braccio, 960
lira organizzata, 960
lirone, 960–961
Listen to the Mockingbird, 961
Liszt, Franz, 961–967
 Années de pèlerinage, 30–31
 Campanella, La, 208
 Consolations, 301
 Divina commedia, 387
 Études d'execution transcendante, 456–457
 Faust Symphony, 479
 Harmoniques poétiques et religieuses, 677
 Hungarian Rhapsodies, 754–755
 Hunnenschlacht, 755
 Ideale, Die, 767
 Legend of the Invisible City of Kitezh and the Maiden Fevronia, 925
 Liebestraum, 952
 Lugubre Gondole, Le, 992
 Mazeppa, 1063–1064
 Mephisto Waltz, 1095–1096
 Préludes, Les, 1398
 Prometheus, 1422
 Richard Wagner: Venezia, 1491–1492
 Sonetti del Petrarca, 1699
 Totentanz, 1877
 transcendental piano style, 1881
litany, 968
Little Drummer Boy, The, 968
Little Nemo, 2026
Little Night Music, A, 968
Little Richard. *See* Penniman, Richard
Little Russian Symphony, 968
Little Sweep, The, 942
liturgical drama, 969
 Rappresentazione di anima e di corpo, La, 1457
 rappresentazione sacra, 1458
liturgical music. *See also* Gregorian chant; oratorio
 Anglican chant, 29
 anthem, 32
 chorale, 259–260
 service, 1639
Liturgical Symphony, 969
liturgy, 969
lituus, 969

live electronic music, 969
llamada, 970
Lloyd Webber, Andrew, 236, 970–972
Lloyd Webber, Julian, 972
Loeffler, Charles Martin, 972–974
Loesser, Arthur, 974
Loesser, Frank, 974–975
 Guys and Dolls, 641
 How to Succeed in Business Without Really Trying, 750
 Praise the Lord and Pass the Ammunition, 1396
Loewe, Carl, 975–976
Loewe, Frederick, 976
 Brigadoon, 174
 Camelot, 208
 Gigi, 571–572
 Paint Your Wagon, 1301–1302
Lohengrin, 976–977
Lomax, Alan, 977–978
Lombardi alla prima Crociata, I, 978
London Bridge is Falling Down, 978
London Symphonies (Haydn), 978
London Symphony, A (Vaughan Williams), 978–979
Londonderry Aire, 979
Long Christmas Dinner, The, 979
Long Tall Sally, 979
longevity, 979–981
longhair, 981
long-playing records, 981
Look for the Silver Lining, 981
Loriod, Yvonne, 981–982
Lortzing, Albert, 982–984
Lost Chord, The, 984
Lost in the Stars, 984
Lott, Felicity, 984–985
loud pedal, 985
Louie Louie, 985
Louise, 985
Louisiana Story, 986
loure, 986
Love for Three Oranges, 986
Love Life, 986
Love Me Tender, 987
luce, 987
Lucia di Lammermoor, 987
Lucier, Alvin, 987–988
Lucio Silla, 988
Lucrezia Borgia, 988–989
ludi spirituales, 989
Ludus Tonalis, 989
Ludwig, Christa, 989–990
Luening, Otto, 990–992
Luftpause, 992
Lugubre Gondole, Le, 992
Luisa Miller, 992–993
lullaby, 118, 1510
Lullaby of Broadway, 993
Lully, Jean-Baptiste, 993–995
 comédie-ballet, 288
 Roland, 1514

Lulu, 995–996
Lupu, Radu, 996
lur, 996
Lustige Witwe, Die, 1099
lute and lutenists, 996–998
 Bream, Julian, 172
 Dowland, John, 409–410
 'ud, 1915
 Weiss, Silvius Leopold, 2021–2022
lutheal, 998
Luther, Martin, 998
Lutoslawski, Witold, 998–999
Lynn, Loretta, 1000–1001
lyre, 1001
lyric, 1001
Lyric Suite, 1001
lyrics and lyricists, 1001
 Cahn, Sammy, 204
 David, Hal, 346
 Gershwin, Ira, 566–567
 Hammerstein, Oscar, II, 656
 Harbach, Otto, 672–673
 Harburg, E. Y. (Yip), 674–675
 Hart, Lorenz, 690
 Sissle, Noble, 1672
 Sondheim, Stephen, 1698–1699

Ma, Yo-Yo, 1002
Ma Mère L'Oye, 1002
Má vlast, 1002–1003
Maazel, Lorin, 1003–1005
Macbeth (Bloch), 1005
Macbeth (Strauss), 1005
Macbeth (Verdi), 1005
MacDermot, Galt, 648–649
MacDowell, Edward, 776, 1005–1009
Machaut, Guillaume de, 1009–1010
machine music, 1010
Machover, Tod, 1010–1011
Mack the Knife, The Ballad of, 1011
Madama Butterfly, 1011–1012
Mademoiselle Modiste, 1012
Maderna, Bruno, 1012–1013
Madonna, 1013–1014
madrigal, 1014–1015
 Combattimento di Tancredi e Clorinda, Il, 287
 Madrigali guerrieri e amorosi, 1016
 napolitana, 1205
madrigal comedy (madrigal opera), 1015
Madrigali guerrieri e amorosi, 1016
Maelzel, Johannes Nepomuk, 1104–1105
maestro, 1016
Magaloff, Nikita. *See* Szigeti, Joseph
Magic Flute, The, 1016–1017, 2081

magic square, 1017–1018
Magnificat, 1018
Mahler, Gustav, 1018–1021
   Drei Pintos, Die, 411–412
   Fourth Symphony, 521
   Giant, 569
   Kindertotenlieder, 864
   Klagende Lied, Das, 873
   Lied von der Erde, Das, 953
   Ninth Symphony, 1222
   Seventh Symphony, 1641
   Summer Morning's Dream, 1766
   Symphony of a Thousand, 1782
   Tenth Symphony, 1833
   Titan Symphony, 1861
   Tragic Symphony, 1880
Maid of Orleans, The, 1021–1022
Maid of Pskov, The, 1022
Mairzy Doats, 1022
major, 1022
major-minor syndrome,
   1022–1023
Makeba, Miriam, 1023
malagueña, 1023
Malibran, María, 1023–1024
Malipiero, Gian Francesco, 774,
   1024–1025
mambo, 1026
Mame, 1026
Mamelles de Tiresias, Les, 1026
Man I Love, The, 1026
Man of La Mancha, 1026–1027
Man on the Flying Trapeze, 1027
Mancini, Henry, 1027
mandolin, 1027–1028
Manfred Symphony, 1028
mannerism, 1028–1029
Mannheim School, 1029–1030
Manning, Jane, 1030
Manon, 1030
Manon Lescaut, 1030–1031
maqäm, 1031
maracas, 1031
Marais, Marin, 1031
Marche funèbre d'une marionette,
   1033
Marche slave, 1033–1034
march(es), 1032–1033
   Semper Fidelis, 1633
   Ta-Ra-Ra-Boom-De-Re, 1809
Marching Through Georgia, 1034
Maria Stuarda, 1034
Maria Theresia, 1034
mariachi, 1034
Marienleben, Das, 1034–1035
marimba, 1035
marimbaphone, 1035
Marines' Hymn, The, 1035–1036
Marley, Bob, 763–764,
   1036–1037
Marriage of Figaro, The, 1037
Marriner, (Sir) Neville,
   1037–1038
Marsalis, Wynton, 1038–1039
Marschner, Heinrich, 667–668,
   1039–1040

Marseillaise, La, 1040–1041
Marteau sans Maître, Le, 1041
Martenot, Maurice, 1041–1042
Martha, 1042
Martin, Dean, 1043
Martin, Frank, 1043–1045
Martin, Hugh, 1893
Martin, Mary, 1045–1046
Martinů, Bohuslav, 1046–1047
   Greek Passion, 624
   Lidice Memorial, 951
Martirano, Salvatore,
   1047–1048
Marton, Eva, 1048
Mary Had a Little Lamb,
   1048–1049
Maryland, My Maryland,
   1049–1050
Masaniello, 1177
Mascagni, Pietro, 1049–1050
   Amico Fritz, L', 24
   Cavalleria rusticana, 237
   Iris, 788
   Maschere, Le, 1050–1051
Maschere, Le, 1050–1051
Mason, Daniel Gregory, 1051
Mason, Lowell, 1052
Mason, Luther Whiting,
   1052–1053
Mason, William, 1053
masque, 1053
Masques et bergamasques,
   1053–1054
mass, 1054–1056
   Agnus Dei, 14
   alleluia, 18
   Benedictus, 116
   canonical Hours, 211
   cantor, 214
   chant, 243–244
   chiesa, 254
   Christe eleison, 262
   complin(e), 290
   conductus, 300
   Coronation Mass, 313
   Council of Trent, 316
   Credo, 326–327
   Crucifixus, 330
   Dies Irae, 379
   doxology, 410
   Epistle sonata, 451
   Et incarnatus, 455
   evensong, 462
   Glagolitic Mass, 584
   Gloria, 591
   gradual, 613
   Gregory I, 626
   Improperia, 772–773
   incarnatus, Et, 775
   introit, 785
   Ite missa est, 791–792
   jubilus, 840
   Kyrie, 902
   Lacrimosa, 905
   lauda, 917
   Laudamus te, 917

   lectionary, 921
   liturgy, 969
   Magnificat, 1018
   Mass in a Time of War, 1056
   Mass of Life, 1056
   matins, 1061
   Messe de requiem, 1100
   Miserere, 1130
   Missa Papae Marcelli, 1131
   Nelson Mass, 1208–1209
   Nocturns, 1225
   Offertory, 1255
   Ordinary, 1271
   Passion, 1319
   plainchant, 1374
   Proprium, 1424–1425
   Red Mass, 1466
   requiem, 1480
   response, 1483
   responsory, 1483
   Sanctus, 1568
   Sext, 1641
   Sibilia, 1659
   Stabat Mater, 1716
   Te Deum, 1822
   tenebrae, 1830
   terce, 1833
   tonus, 1870
   tract, 1879
   trope, 1895–1896
   verse-anthem, 1948
   verset, 1948
   versicle, 1948
   Vespers, 1949
   Votive Mass, 1974
Mass in Time of War, 1056
Mass of Life, A, 1056
Massa's in the Cold Ground,
   1056–1057
Massenet, Jules, 1057–1058
   Elégie, 438
   Hérodiade, 714
   Jongleur de Notre Dame, Le, 836
   Manon, 1030
   Navarraise, La, 1207
   Sapho, 1569
   Thaïs, 1837
   Werther, 2024
Mastersinger, 1058, 1555
Masur, Kurt, 1058–1059
Matchiche, La, 1059
Matelots, Les, 1060
Materna, 1060
Mathis, Johnny, 1060–1061
Mathis der Maler, 1060
Matin, Le, 1061
matins, 1061
Matrimonio segreto, Il, 1061
Matthews, Artie, 1061–1062
Mauceri, John, 1062
Maxwell Davies, Peter. *See*
   Davies, Sir Peter Maxwell
Mayall, John, 1062–1063
Maytime, 1063
Mayuzumi, Toshirō, 1063
Mazeppa, 1063–1064

mazurka, 1064, 1932
mbira, 909
McCartney, Sir Paul, 1064–1065
McFerrin, Bobby, 1065–1066
McGhee, Brownie, 1066
McHugh, Jimmy
   Blackbirds of 1928, 139
   I Can't Give You Anything But
     Love, Baby, 762
   I'm In the Mood for Love, 769
McPartland, Jimmy, 1066–1067
McPartland, Marian, 1067
McPhee, Colin, 1067–1068
McRae, Carmen, 1068
McShann, Jay, 1068–1069
Me and Juliet, 1069
Me and My Shadow, 1069
measure, 1069
mechanical instruments, 1069
   barrel organ, 86
   handle piano, 665
   player piano, 1375–1376
Medea's Meditation and Dance of
   Vengeance, 1070
Médecin malgré lui, Le, 1070
Médée (Charpentier), 1070
Medée (Cherubini), 1070
mediant, 1070
medieval music, 1070–1071
   alti naturali, 20
   Anon, 31
   ars antiqua, 44
   ars musica, 45
   ars nova, 45–46
   bard, 83
   barform, 84
   basse danse, 92–93
   Boethius, 149
   caccia, 198
   chanson de geste, 243
   clausula, 273
   color, 285
   estampie, 455
   falsa musica, 471
   fistula, 503
   flores, 508
   Geisslieder, 560
   gittern, 581
   goliards, 597
   Gothic music, 603
   gymel, 641
   hocket, 726
   Jeu de Robin et de Marion, 820
   jongleur, 835–836
   Kalevala, 847
   pibcorn, 1364
   proportion, 1424
   quadrivium, 1434
   quodlibet, 1440
   rondeau, 1521–1522
   rotolus, 1538
   rotta, 1538
   symphonia, 1776
   tactus, 1793
   tonarium, 1867
   tonus, 1870–1871

tricotet, 1886
triplum, 1890
trope, 1895–1896
vaganti, 1924
voice exchange, 1971
vox, 1974–1975
wait, 1989–1990
meditation, 1071–1072
Medium, The, 1072
medley, 1391
Medtner, Nicolai, 1072–1073
Meeresstille und glückliche Fahrt, 1073
Meet Me in St. Louis, Louis, 1073
Mefistofele, 1073
Mehta, Mehli, 1073–1074
Mehta, Zubin, 1074–1076
Meistersinger. *See* Mastersinger
Meistersinger von Nürnberg, Die, 1076
Melba, (Dame) Nellie, 1077–1078
Melchior, Lauritz, 1078–1079
melodeon, 1079
melodic, 1079
melodic minor scale, 1079
melodion, 1080
melodium, 1080
melodrama, 1080–1081
mélodrame, 1081
melody, 1081–1083
  accidental, 3
  chromatic, 263
  chromaticism, 263
  complement, 290
  diminshed interval, 379
  inversion, 785–786
  progression, 1417
  step, 1722
  syllabic, 1775
  tonality, 1867
  tune, 1906
melograph, 1083
melopée, melopoeia, 1083
melos, 1083
membi, 1083
membranophones, 1084
Memphis Blues, The, 1084
Men and Mountains, 1084
Mendelssohn, Felix, 1084–1088
  Capriccio brillante, 216–217
  Fingal's Cave, 499
  Italian Symphony, 791
  Lieder ohne Worte, 954
  Meeresstille und glückliche Fahrt, 1073
  Midsummer Night's Dream, 1116
  Reformation Symphony, 1469
  Scotch Symphony, 1620
  Songs without Words, 1700
Mengelberg, Willem, 1088–1089
Mennin, Peter, 1089–1090
Menotti, Gian Carlo, 1090–1093
  Amahl and the Night Visitors, 20–21

Consul, 302
Help, Help, the Globolinks!, 706–707
Medium, 1072
Old Maid and the Thief, 1260
mensural notation (mensuration), 1093
  neumes, 1212
  syncopation, 1784–1785
Menuhin, (Sir) Yehudi, 1094–1095
Mephisto Waltz, 1095–1096
Mer, La, 1096
Mercer, Johnny, 814, 1096–1097
Mercer, Mabel, 1097–1098
Mercury Symphony, 1098
merengue, meringue, 1098
Merman, Ethel, 1098–1099
Merrill, Bob, 222
Merry Mount, 1099
Merry Widow, The, 1099
Merry Wives of Windsor, The, 1099–1100
Messe de requiem, 1100
Messiaen, Olivier, 1100–1101
  Chronochromie, 263
  Harawi, chant d'amour et de mort, 672
  Oiseaux exotiques, 1257
  Quartet for the End of Time, 1437
Messiah, 1101–1102
Metamorphosen, 1102
metamorphosis, 1102
Metastasio, Pietro, 1102–1103
meter(s), 1103–1104
  anapest, 26
  asymmetry, 50
  common time, 289–290
  compound, 291
  compound meters, 291
  cross-rhythm, 329
  dactyl(e), 340
  downbeat, 410
  duple, 419
  iamb, 764
  polymeter, 1382–1383
  quadruple, 1435
  quintuplets, 1440
  synchrony, 1783–1784
  syncopation, 1784–1785
  thesis, 1843
  time signature, 1854–1855
  triple time, 1890
  trochee, 1892–1893
  value, 1926
  variable, 1931
metric modulation, 1104
metronome, 1104–1105
Metz, Theodore, 748
Mexican Hayride, 1105
Mexican music, 313, 333
Meyerbeer, Giacomo, 1105–1108
  Africaine, L', 12–13

Étoile du Nord, L', 456
Huguenots, Les, 751
Prophète, Le, 1424
Robert le diable, 1501–1502
mezzo-soprano(s), 1108
  Baker, Dame Janet, 70
  Berberian, Cathy, 117
  Bumbry, Grace, 186–187
  Crespin, Régine, 328
  DeGaetani, Jan, 361–362
  Ewing, Maria, 463–464
  Horne, Marilyn, 742–743
  Malibran, María, 1023–1024
  Otter, Anne-Sophie von, 1282–1283
  Troyanos, Tatiana, 1898–1899
  Von Stade, Frederica, 1973–1974
Miaskovsky, Nikolai, 1108–1109
Michelangeli, Arturo Benedetti, 1109–1110
microtime, 1110
microtonality, 1031, 1110–1114
middle C, 1114
MIDI, 1114, 1785–1786
Midi, Le, 1114
Midler, Bette, 1114–1115
Midori, 1115–1116
Midsommarvaka, 1116
Midsummer Night's Dream, A (Britten), 1116–1117
Midsummer Night's Dream, A (Mendelssohn), 1116
Mignon, 1117
Mikado, or The Town of Titipu, 1117
Miki, Minoru, 1117
Mikrokosmos, 1117–1118
Milanov, Zinka, 1118
Milhaud, Darius, 1118–1120
  Boeuf sur le toit, Le, 149
  Christophe Colomb, 263
  Création du monde, La, 325
  David, 346
  Eumenides, Les, 458
  Scaramouche, 1577
  Suite provençale, 1763
military band, 76
military music
  Janizary music, 804–805
  reveille, 1484
  Semper paratus, 1633
  tattoo, 1812
Military Symphony, 1120
Miller, Glenn, 1120–1121
Millöcker, Carl, 1121–1122
Milnes, Sherrill, 1122
Milstein, Nathan, 1123
mimodrama, 1123
Mingus, Charles, 1124
miniature score, 1124–1125
minimalism, 1125
Minkus, Léon, 1125–1126
Minnelli, Liza, 1126
Minnesinger, 1126–1127, 1794
minor, 1127

minstrel songs
  Jim Crack Corn (Blue Tail Fly), 821
  Jim Crow, 821
  Zip Coon, 2088
minstrel(s), 1127–1128
  goliards, 597
  skomorokhis, 1675
minuet, 1129
Minute Waltz, 1129
miracle plays, 1129
Miranda, Carmen, 1129–1130
mirliton, 1130
Miroirs, 1130
Miserere, 1130
Miss Julie, 1131
Miss Liberty, 1131
Missa Papae Marcelli, 1131
Missouri Waltz, 1131
Mr. Broucek's Excursion to the Moon and Mr. Broucek's Excursion into the 15th Century, 1132
Mister President, 1132
Mr. Tambourine Man, 1132
Mrs. Robinson, 1132
Misty, 1132
Mitchell, Joni, 1132–1133
Mitridate, Re di Ponto, 1133
Mitropoulos, Dimitri, 1133–1134
mixed media, 1134–1135
  Fluxus, 513
  sound installation, 1704–1705
Mlada, 1135
M.M., 1135
modal harmony, 1135
modality, 1135
mode(s), 1135–1137
  ambitus, 22
  authentic, 58
  Byzantine chant, 194–195
  church, 265
  confinalis, 300
  Dodecachordon, 389
  ecclesiastical, 429
  hypo-, 761
  psalm tones, 1425
  tetrachord, 1835–1836
  tono, 1870
  tonus peregrinus, 1871
modern music, 1137
modernism, 1137
modinha, 1137
modulation, 1137–1139
  pivot chord, 1374
  triadic, 1886
modus, 1139
Moldau, 1140
moment musical, 1140
Momente, 1140
Mompou, Federico, 1140–1141
Mond, Der, 1141
Mondo della luna, Il, 1141
money and music, 1142–1144
Moniuszko, Stanislaw, 652, 1144

Monk, Meredith, 1144–1145
Monk, Thelonious, 1145–1146
Monkees, The, 1146–1147
monochord, 1147, 1893–1894
monodrama, 1147
monody, 1148
monophonic, 1148
monothematism and polythematism, 1148
monotone, 1148
Monroe, Bill, 1148–1149
Montemezzi, Italo, 1149
Monteux, Pierre, 1149–1150
Monteverdi, Claudio, 1150–1153
  Combattimento di Tancredi e Clorinda, Il, 287
  Incoronazione di Poppea, L', 776
  Madrigali guerrieri e amorosi, 1016
  Orfeo, L', 1272
  seconda prattica, 1629–1630
Mood Indigo, 1154
Moody Blues, The, 1154
Moog, Robert, 1154–1155
Moon River, 1155
Moonlight Sonata, 1155
Moore, Douglas, 373, 1156–1157
Moore, Gerald, 1157
Moorman, Charlotte, 1157–1158
moralities, 1158
Moran Robert, 1158–1159
morceau, 1159
moresca, 1159
Moreschi, Allesandro, 235
Morley, Thomas, 1159–1160
Morris, James, 1160–1161
Morris dance, 1160
Morrison, Van, 1161–1162
Morton, "Jelly Roll," 1162
Mose in Egitto, 1163
Moses und Aron, 1163
mosh pit, 1163
Mosolov, Alexander, 1163–1164
Most Happy Fella, The, 1164–1165
motet, 1165
  instrumental, 780
  rotolus, 1538
Mother of Us All, The, 1166
motion, 1166
motive, 1166
Mourning Becomes Electra, 1166–1167
mouth organ. *See* harmonica
mouthpiece, cupped, 336
movable Do(h), 1167, 1870
movement, 1167
Mozart, Franz Xaver Wolfgang, 1167–1168
Mozart, Leopold, 1168–1169, 1879
Mozart, Wolfgang Amadeus, 1169–1176
  Abduction from the Seraglio, 2
  Bastien und Bastienne, 94

Clemenza di Tito, La, 276
Coronation Concerto, 313
Così fan tutte, 314–315
Dissonanzen Quartett, 385
Don Giovanni, 242, 398–399
Eine kleine Nachtmusik, 433
Finta giardiniera, La, 500
Haffner Serenade, 645–646
Haffner Symphony, 646
Idomeneo, Ré di Creta, 767
Impresario, 772
Jeunehomme Concerto, 820
Jupiter Symphony, 843
Linz Symphony, 959
Lucio Silla, 988
Magic Flute, 1016–1017
Marriage of Figaro, 1037
Mitridate, Re di Ponto, 1133
Prague Symphony, 1396
Re pastore, Il, 1463
Stadler Quintet, 1716
Zaïde, 2076
Mozart i Salieri, 1176
Mozartiana, 1176
mṛidàngam, 1176–1177
Muddy Waters. *See* Waters, Muddy
Muette de Portici, Le, 1177
Mulligan, Gerry, 1177
multiphonics, 1178
Munch, Charles, 1178–1179
Munrow, David, 1179
murky bass, 1179
musette, 1179–1180
Musgrave, Thea, 1180–1181
music, 1181–1183
music(al) box, 1183–1184
Music Box Revue, The, 1184
music drama, 1184
music educators
  Jaques-Dalcroze, Émile, 807
  Kod ly, Zoltan, 880–883
  Suzuki, Shin'ichi, 1770–1771
Music for Airports, 1187
Music for Strings, Percussion, and Celesta, 1184
music hall, 1184–1185
  cabaret, 197–198
  café chantant, 201–202
  pantomime, 1305
Music in the Air, 1185
music journals, 1185–1187
Music Man, The, 1187
Music of Changes, 1187–1188
music stand, 1188
music theatre, 1188
music therapy, 1188–1190
musica, 1190–1191
Musica enchiriadis, 1191
musica ficta, 1191–1192
musica figurata, 1192
musica reservata, 1192
Musica transalpina, 1192
musical bow, 1192
musical comedy, 1192–1193
musical saw, 1193

musical(s), 1192
Annie Get Your Gun, 31
Anything Goes, 34
Babes in Arms, 61
Bells Are Ringing, 116
Blackbirds of 1928, 139
Boys from Syracuse, 165–166
Brigadoon, 174
Bye Bye Birdie, 191
Cabaret, 198
Cabin in the Sky, 198
Call Me Madam, 205
Camelot, 208
Candide, 209
Capeman, 215
Carmen Jones, 220
Carnival, 222
Carousel, 223
Cats, 236
Coco, 279
Cohan, George M., 280–281
Coleman, Cy, 282
Comden and Green, 287–288
Company, 290
Connecticut Yankee, 300–301
Coward, Noel, 321–322
Cradle Will Rock, 324
Damn Yankees, 342
Do I Hear a Waltz?, 388
Face the Music, 469
Fantasticks, 474
Fiddler on the Roof, 492
Finian's Rainbow, 499
Fiorello!, 500
Flower Drum Song, 509
Follow Thru, 514
Funny Face, 539
Funny Girl, 539
Funny Thing Happened on the Way to the Forum, 539
Gay Divorce, 557
Gentlemen Prefer Blondes, 562
George M!, 564
George White's Scandals, 564
Gigi, 571–572
Girl Crazy, 580
Girl Friend, 580
Good Boy, 597
Great Waltz, 624
Guys and Dolls, 641
Gypsy, 641–642
Hair, 648–649
Hallelujah, Baby!, 653
Hello, Dolly!, 705
Hellzapoppin', 706
Hit the Deck, 726
Hold Everything, 729
Hot Chocolates, 747
How to Succeed in Business Without Really Trying, 750
I Can Get It for You Wholesale, 762
I Married an Angel, 763
I'd Rather Be Right, 766–767
Johnny Johnson, 825
Jubilee, 840

Jumbo, 843
King and I, 864
Kiss Me Kate, 872
Knickerbocker Holiday, 878–879
La, La, Lucille, 904
Lady, Be Good!, 905
Lady in the Dark, 905
Let 'Em Eat Cake, 942
Little Night Music, 968
Lloyd Webber, Andrew, 970–972
Loesser, Frank, 974–975
Loewe, Frederick, 976
Lost in the Stars, 984
Love Life, 986
Mame, 1026
Man of La Mancha, 1026–1027
Me and Juliet, 1069
Mexican Hayride, 1105
Miss Liberty, 1131
Mister President, 1132
New Moon, 1213
Nine, 1221
No, No, Nanette, 1223
No Strings, 1223
Of Thee I Sing, 1253
Oh, Kay!, 1256
Oklahoma!, 1258–1259
On a Clear Day You Can See Forever, 1263–1264
Once Upon a Mattress, 1265
One Touch of Venus, 1265
On the Town, 1264
On Your Toes, 1264–1265
Paint Your Wagon, 1301–1302
The Pajama Game, 1302
Pal Joey, 1302
Panama Hattie, 1304
Peggy-Ann, 1330
Pins and Needles, 1370
Porter, Cole, 1388–1390
Present Arms, 1399
Previn, André, 1401–1403
Promises, Promises, 1423
Purlie, 1433
Roberta, 1502
Rodgers, Richard, 1512–1513
Schwartz, Arthur, 1615
1776, 1641
Show Boat, 1655
Shuffle Along, 1656
Silk Stockings, 1663–1664
Singin' in the Rain, 1671
Something for the Boys, 1696
Sondheim, Stephen, 1698–1699
Sound of Music, 1705
South Pacific, 1707
Strike up the Band, 1755
Sweet Charity, 1774
This Is the Army, 1844
Weill, Kurt, 2016–2019
West Side Story, 2024–2025
Willson, Meredith, 2038–2039
Wonderful Town, 2051
Yip, Yip, Yaphank, 2066

You're a Good Man, Charlie Brown, 2071
Ziegfeld Follies, 2085–2086
Zorba, 2088–2089
musicale, 1193
musicology and musicologists, 1194
comparative musicology, 290
Fétis, François-Joseph, 487–489
Glareanus, Henricus, 584
Kirnberger, Johann Philipp, 871
Lavignac, Albert, 918
Schenker, Heinrich, 1584
Schenkerian analysis, 1584–1585
Schillinger, Joseph, 1588–1589
Schoenberg, Arnold, 1592–1598
Schuller, Gunther, 1603–1605
Schweitzer, Albert, 1617–1618
Slonimsky, Nicolas, 1679–1681
Tartini, Giuseppi, 1809–1811
Taruskin, Richard, 1811–1812
musicus, 1194
Musik, 1194
musique, 1195
musique concrète, 1195
musique mesurée, 1947–1948
Mussorgsky, Modest, 1195–1198
Boris Godunov, 155–156
Khovanshchina, 863
Night on Bald Mountain, 1219
Pictures at an Exhibition, 1367
mute, 1198
Muti, Riccardo, 1198–1199
Mutter, Anne-Sophie, 1199–1200
Muzak, 539, 1200
My Blue Heaven, 1200
My Country 'Tis of Thee, 1200
My Fair Lady, 1200–1201
My Girl, 1201
My Heart Belongs to Daddy, 1201
My Heart Stood Still, 1201–1202
My Melancholy Baby, 1202
My Sweet Lord, 1202
My Way, 1202
My Wild Irish Rose, 1202
Mysterious Mountain, 1202
Mysterium, 1203
mystery plays, 1203
Mystic Chord, 1203

Nabucco, 1204
nail fiddle, 1204
naker, 1204
Nancarrow, Conlon, 1204–1205
napolitana, 1205
napura, 1205
narrator, 382, 1205
national anthems, 1206
Hatikva, 691
Internationale, 782

Star-Spangled Banner, 1718–1719
nationalism, 1206
natural, 1206
natural minor scale, 1206
naturalism, 1206
Nature Boy, 1206
Naughty Marietta, 1207
Navarraise, La, 1207
Navarro, "Fats" (Theodore), 1207
Nazareth, Ernesto, 1207
Neapolitan sixth, 1207–1208
Neapolitan songs
Funiculì-Funiculà, 538
O Sole Mio!, 1245
Santa Lucia, 1568
Nearer My God to Thee, 1208
Nebenstimme, 1208
neck, 1208
Nelson, Judith (Anne Manes), 1209
Nelson, Willie, 1209–1210
Nelson Mass, 1208–1209
neoclassicism, 1210–1211
Nesterenko, Evgeni (Evgenievich), 1211
Neue Sachlichkeit, 1211–1212
Neues vom Tage, 1212
neumes, 1212
Never on Sunday, 1212
New Age music, 1212–1213
New England Triptych, 1213
New Moon, The, 1213
new music, 1213
new romanticism, 1213
new simplicity, 1214
New World Symphony, 533
Newman, Alfred, 1214–1215
Newman, Randy, 1215–1216
Nichols, "Red," 1216
Nicolai, Otto, 1099–1100, 1216–1217
Nielsen, Carl, 779, 1217–1219
Night and Day, 1219
Night Flight, 1219
Night on Bald Mountain, A, 1219
Night Piece, A, 1219
Nightingale, The, 1219–1220
Nights in the Gardens of Spain, 1220
Nilsson, Birgit, 1220–1221
Nine, 1221
ninth chord, 1221
Ninth Symphonies, 1221
Ninth Symphony (Mahler), 1222
Nirvana, 1222
Nixon, Marni, 1223
Nixon in China, 1223
No, No, Nanette, 1223
No Strings, 1223
Nobody Knows the Trouble I've Seen, 1224
Nobody Knows You When You're Down and Out, 1224
Noces, Les, 1224
Nocturnal, 1224

nocturne, 1224–1225
Nocturnes, 1225
Nocturns, 1225
node, 1225
noël, 1225
noise, 1225
Non nobis Domine, 1225–1226
non vibrato, 1226
None, 1226
nonet, 1226
Nono, Luigi, 1226–1227
Nordic Symphony, 1227
Norfolk Rhapsody No. 1, 1227
Norma, 1227–1228
Norman, Jessye, 1228–1229
Norrington, Roger, 1229–1230
North, Alex, 1230–1232
Norvo, Red, 1232
Nose, The, 1232–1233
nose flutes, 1233
nóta, 1233
notation, 1233–1238
accidental, 3
ad libitum, 6
ars musica, 45
bar, barline, 78–79
beam, 98
bowing, 163–164
brace, 166
cancel, 209
cantabile, 211
capo, 216
cappella, 216
chiave, 254
clef, 274
colophon, 285
crescendo, 327
da capo, 339
descant, 368
Doppel, 404
dot, 407
double bar, 408
double note, 408
Drei, 411
due, 413–414
duplet, 419
dynamics, 426
expression marks, 465
fermata, 483
fine, 499
flag, 504
flat, 506
full, 537
Ganz, 553
Generalpause, 560
graphic, 619–620
Guido d'Arezzo, 635–636
Guidonian hand, 636
H, 645
head, 701
hemiola, 707
hook, 739
key signature, 859–860
neumes, 1212
note, 1238
ottava, 1282

P, 1290
pause, 1322
phrase mark, 1358
phrasing, 1359
primo(-a), 1407
proportional notation, 1424
punctus, 1430
quadruple meter or time, 1435
quintuplets, 1440
R, 1442
repeat, 1478–1479
rest, 1483
Roman numerals, 1518
rubato, tempo, 1542
score, 1619–1620
segno, 1631
segue, 1632
sextuplet, 1642
sharp, 1645
signature, key, 1663
signature, time, 1663
slur, 1681–1682
sordina, 1702–1703
space, 1707
staccato, 1716
staff, 1716
stem, 1722
tablature, 1792–1793
tacet, 1793
tempo, 1826–1828
tempo mark, 1828
tenor C., 1832
tie, 1853
time signature, 1854–1855
Ton, 1866
touche, 1878
tre, 1883
triple dot, 1889–1890
triplet, 1890
tutti, 1911
V, 1924
value, 1926
verbalization, 1941
vocal score, 1970
Zwei, 2091
note, 1238
Notre Dame school, 1238–1239
notturno, 1239
novellette, 1239
novelty, 1239
Noye's Fludde, 1239
Nozze di Figaro, Le, 1037
number, 1240
number opera, 1240
number pieces, 1240
numbers, 1240–1241
numerology, 1241–1242
Nun's fiddle. *See* Tromba Marina
nuove musiche, Le, 1242
Nurock, Kirk, 1242–1243
nursery rhymes. *See* children's songs
nut, 1243
Nutcracker, The, 1243–1244
N.W.A., 1244
nyckelharpa, 1244

o., 1245
O Sole Mio!, 1245
obbligato, 1245
Oberon, 1245–1246
Oberto, Conte di San Bonifacio, 1246
objets trouvés, 1246
oboe, 732, 1246–1247
oboe da caccia, 1247
oboe d'amore, 1248
Obrecht, Jacob, 1248
ocarina, 1248–1249
Ocean, 1249
Ocean Symphony, 1249
Ochs, Phil, 1249–1250
Ockeghem, Johannes, 1250–1251
octave, 1251
octet, 1251
ode, 1251
Ode to Billy Joe, 1252
Ode to Joy, 1252
Odhecaton, 1252
Oedipus Rex, 1252
oeuvre, 1252
Of Mice and Men, 1252–1253
Of Thee I Sing, 1253
off-beat, 1253
Offenbach, Jacques (Jacob), 1253–1255
  Grande Duchesse de Gerolstein, La, 618–619
  Orphée aux enfers, 1279
  Périchole, La, 1343
  Tales of Hoffman, 1798–1799
  Vie Parisienne, La, 1954–1955
Offertory, 1255
Officium Divinum, 1255
Oh, Bury Me Not on the Lone Prairie, 1255
Oh, How I Hate to Get Up in the Morning, 1256
Oh, Kay!, 1256
Oh, Pretty Woman, 1256
Oh, Promise Me!, 1256
Oh, Susanna, 1256
Oh, What a Beautiful Mornin', 1256
Oh! Dear, What Can the Matter Be?, 1255
Oh Where, Oh Where Has My Little Dog Gone?, 1256
Ohana, Maurice, 1257
Oiseaux exotiques, 1257
Oistrakh, David, 1257–1258
Oklahoma!, 1258–1259
oktoechos, 1259
Ol' Man River, 1259
Old Black Joe, 1259
Old Folks at Home, 1259
Old Gray Mare, The, 1259
Old Hundred, 1259–1260
Old MacDonald Had a Farm, 1260
Old Maid and the Thief, The, 1260

Olé!, 1260
oliphant, 1260
Oliver, "King" (Joseph), 1260–1261
Oliveros, Pauline, 1261–1263
ombra scene, 1263
omnitonality, 1263
On a Clear Day You Can See Forever, 1263–1264
On Hearing the First Cuckoo in Spring, 1264
On the Banks of the Wabash, Far Away, 1264
On the Good Ship Lollipop, 1264
On the Road to Mandalay, 1264
On the Sunny Side of the Street, 1264
On the Town, 1264
On Top of Old Smoky, 1264
On Your Toes, 1264–1265
Once Upon a Mattress, 1265
Ondes Martenot, 1265
One Touch of Venus, 1265
Only You, 1267
Ono, Yoko, 1265–1266
onomatopoeia, 1266–1267
oompah(-pah), 1267
open form composition, 1267
open harmony, 1267
open string, 1267–1268
opera buffa, 184, 1269
  Coffee Cantata, 279–280
  Così fan tutte, 314–315
  Grande Duchesse de Gerolstein, La, 618–619
  intermezzo, 781–782
opéra comique, 1269
opera in musica, 1269
opera seria, 1269
opera(s), 1268
  Abduction from the Seraglio, 2
  act, 5
  Adriana Lecouvreur, 11
  Africaine, L', 12–13
  Aida, 14–15
  Alceste, 17
  Amahl and the Night Visitors, 20–21
  Amico Fritz, L', 24
  Andrea Chénier, 27
  Antony and Cleopatra, 33
  applause, 34–35
  Arabella, 36
  aria, 38
  aria da capo, 38
  Ariadne auf Naxos, 38
  arietta, 38
  arioso, 39
  Armide, 40–41
  Aufstieg und Fall der Stadt Mahagonny, 56
  ballad, 73
  Ballo in maschera, Un, 75
  Barber of Seville, 79
  Bartered Bride, 87
  basso buffo, 93

Bastien und Bastienne, 94
bel canto, 113
Billy Budd, 134–135
Bing, Sir Rudolph, 136–137
Bluebeard's Castle, 145
Bohème, La, 150
Bohemian Girl, 150
Boris Godunov, 155–156
cabaletta, 196
Capitan, El, 216
Carmen, 220, 1871
Castor et Pollux, 235
Cavalleria rusticana, 237
cavata, 238
cavatina, 238
Cenerentola, La, o la bontà in trionfo, 239
Christophe Colomb, 263
Clemenza di Tito, La, 276
collective composition, 284
coloratura, 285
commedia per music, 289
Comte Ory, Le, 292
Consul, 302
Coq d'or, Le, 309
Cosa rara, o sia Bellezza ed onestà, Una, 314
Cunning Little Vixen, 335
Dafne, 340
Dalibor, 341
Dantons Tod, 344
Daphne, 344
David, 346
Death in Venice, 355
Death of Klinghoffer, 355
Deidamia, 362
Dennis Cleveland, 367–368
Devil and Daniel Webster, 373
Devil and Kate, 373
Devin du Village, 374
Dialogues de carmélites, Les, 377
Dido and Aeneas, 378
Dimitrj, 380
Disappointment, or The Force of Credulity, 380
diva, 386
divertissement, 386
Doktor Faust, 395
Don Carlos, 398
Don Giovanni, 398–399
Don Pasquale, 399
Don Rodrigo, 399–400
Donna del lago, La, 402
Down in the Valley, 410
drame lyrique, 411
dramma per musica, 411
Drei Pintos, Die, 411–412
Dreigroschenoper, Die, 412
Due Foscari, I, 414
Due litigani, I, 414
Einstein on the Beach, 434
Elegy for Young Lovers, 438
Elektra, 438
Elisir d'amore, L', 440
Emperor Jones, 443
Enfant et les sortileges, L', 446

epic, 450–451
Ernani, 452
Étoile du Nord, L', 456
Eugene Onegin, 457–458
Europeras 1 & 2, 459–460
Euryanthe, 460
Failing Kansas, 469
Falstaff, 472
farce, 475
Faust, 479
favola per musica, 480
Favorite, La, 480
Fedora, 480–481
Feen, Die, 481
Feuersnot, 489
Fidelio, oder Die eheliche Liebe, 492–493
Fiery Angel, 495
Fille du regiment, La, 496
finale, 498
Finta giardiniera, La, 500
Flying Dutchman, 513
Forza del destino, La, 517
Four Saints in Three Acts, 520
Fra Diavolo, 522
Frau ohne Schatten, Die, 524–525
Freischütz, Der, 527
Friedenstag, Der, 531
Gambler, 550
Gazza ladra, La, 559
Genoveva, 562
Gianni Schicchi, 569
Gioconda, La, 578–579
Giorno di regno, Un, 580
Giovanni d'arco, 580
Girl of the Golden West, 580–581
Giuditta, 581
Giulio Cesare in Egitto, 584
Gloriana, 591
Gondoliers, 597
Götterdämmerung, 604–605
grand, 618
Greek Passion, 624
Griffelkin, 629
Guerre des Bouffons, 634–635
Guntram, 639
Halka, 652
Hamlet, 653
Hans Heiling, 667–668
Hänsel und Gretel, 668
happy ending, 672
Harmonie der Welt, Die, 677
Háry János, 691
Heldenbariton, 704
Heldentenor, 705
Help, Help, the Globolinks!, 706–707
Hérodiade, 714
Heure espagnole, L', 717–718
Hippolyte et Aricie, 725
horse, 746–747
From the House of the Dead, 533
Huguenots, Les, 751
Idomeneo, Ré di Creta, 767

If I Were King, 768
imbroglio, 770
Imperial Maryinsky Theater, 771
Impresario, 772
Incoronazione di Poppea, L', 776
Indes Galantes, Les, 776
Intermezzo, 782
introduction, 785
invocation, 787
Iphigénie en Aulide, 788
Iphigénie en Tauride, 788
Iris, 788
Irmelin, 789
Isle de Merlin, L', 768
Italiana in Algeri, L', 791
Ivanhoe, 792
Izeÿl, 796
Jakobin, 801
Jenůfa, 818
Jessonda, 819–820
Jolie fille de Perth, La, 830
Jongleur de Notre Dame, Le, 836
Jonny spielt auf, 836
Judith (Honegger), 841
Judith (Serov), 840
Juive, La, 841
Julien, 842
Junge Lord, Der, 843
Kashchei, the Immortal, 853
Káta Kabanová, 853–854
Khovanshchina, 863
King Priam, 866
King's Henchman, 867
Kiss (Hubička), 872
Kluge, Die, 878
Koanga, 880
Königskinder, 886
Lady Macbeth of the Mtzensk District (Katerina Izmailova), 905–906
Lakmé, 906
lamento, 909
Last Savage, 917
Lear, 921
Legende von der heiligen Elisabeth, Die, 925
Let's Make an Opera, 942
Life for the Czar, 954
Lohengrin, 976–977
Lombardi alla prima Crociata, I, 978
Long Christmas Dinner, 979
Louise, 985
Love for Three Oranges, 986
Lucia di Lammermoor, 987
Lucio Silla, 988
Lucrezia Borgia, 988–989
Luisa Miller, 992–993
Lulu, 995–996
Macbeth (Bloch), 1005
Macbeth (Verdi), 1005
Madama Butterfly, 1011–1012
Mademoiselle Modiste, 1012
madrigal, 1015

Magic Flute, 1016–1017
Maid of Orleans, 1021–1022
Maid of Pskov, 1022
Mamelles de Tiresias, Les, 1026
Manon, 1030
Manon Lescaut, 1030–1031
Maria Stuarda, 1034
Marriage of Figaro, 1037
Martha, 1042
Maschere, Le, 1050–1051
Mathis der Maler, 1060
Matrimonio segreto, Il, 1061
Médecin malgré lui, Le, 1070
Medée (Charpentier), 1070
Medée (Cherubini), 1070
Medium, 1072
Mefistofélé, 1073
Meistersinger von Nürnberg, Die, 1076
Merry Mount, 1099
Merry Wives of Windsor, 1099–1100
Metastasio, Pietro, 1102–1103
Midsummer Night's Dream (Britten), 1116–1117
Mignon, 1117
Miss Julie, 1131
Mr. Broucek's Excursion to the Moon and Mr. Broucek's Excursion into the 15th Century, 1132
Mitridate, Re di Ponto, 1133
Mlada, 1135
Nabucco, 1204
Navarraise, La, 1207
Neues vom Tage, 1212
Night Flight, 1219
Nightingale, 1219–1220
Nixon in China, 1223
Norma, 1227–1228
Nose, 1232–1233
Noye's Fludde, 1239
number, 1240
Oberon, 1245–1246
Oberto, Conte di San Bonifacio, 1246
Oedipus Rex, 1252
Of Mice and Men, 1252–1253
Old Maid and the Thief, 1260
ombra scene, 1263
Orfeo, L', 1272
Orfeo ed Euridice, 1271–1272
Ormindo, 1278
Orontea, 1279
Otello, 1281–1282
Otello, ossia Il Moro di Venezia, 1282
Ox Minuet, 1286
Pagliacci, 1299–1300
parable aria, 1307
parody, 1311–1312
Parsifal, 1312–1313
Patience, 1322
Pêcheurs de Perles, les, 1327
Pelléas et Mélisande, 1331
Peter Grimes, 1348

Pomo d'oro, Il, 1385
Porgy and Bess, 1388
prima donna, 1406–1407
primo(-a), 1407
Prince Igor, 1409–1410
prologue, 1422
Prometheus, 1422
prompter, 1423
Prophète, Le, 1424
Puritani di Scozia, I, 1432–1433
Queen of Spades, 1439
Rake's Progress, 1451
Rape of Lucretia, 1457
Re pastore, Il, 1463
recitative, 1465
Regina, 1471
Renard, 1478
rescue, 1480
Retablo de Maese Pedro, El, 1483
Rheingold, Das, 1487–1488
Riders to the Sea, 1492–1493
Rienzi, 1493
Rigoletto, 1493–1494
Rinaldo, 1499
Ring des Nibelungen, Der, 1499
Robert le diable, 1501–1502
Roberto Devereux, ossia Il Conte di Essex, 1502
Roland, 1514
Roméo et Juliette (Gounod), 1521
Rosenkavalier, Der, 1525–1526
Rusalka (Dargomyzhsky), 1550–1551
Rusalka (Dvořák), 1551
Ruslan and Ludmila, 1551
Sadko, 1556
Salome, 1563
Samson et Dalila, 1567
Sapho (Gounod), 1569
Sapho (Massenet), 1569
Scala, La, 1576
scena, 1582
scene, 1582
Semiramide, 1633
semiseria, 1633
serenade, 1635
Serva Padrona, La, 1638–1639
set piece, 1640
Sicilian Vespers, 1660
Siège de Corinthe, Le, 1660–1661
Siegfried, 1661
Simon Boccanegra, 1666–1667
Singspiel, 1671–1672
Snow Maiden, 1689–1690
Sonnambula, La, 1700–1701
sortita, 1703
soubrette, 1703
spinto, 1708
Stone Guest, 1733
Street Scene, 1753
Tales of Hoffman, 1798–1799
Tancredi, 1802

Tannhäuser, 1805–1806
teatro, 1824
television, 629
Tender Land, 1829–1830
Thaïs, 1837
Tosca, 1873–1874
tragédie lyrique, 1879
Traviata, La, 1883
Treemonisha, 1884
Trouble in Tahiti, 1896
trouser role, 1896–1897
Trovatore, Il, 1897–1898
Troyens, Les, 1899
Turandot, 1907–1908
Turn of the Screw, 1909
verismo, 1947
Vestale, La, 1949
Vie Parisienne, La, 1954–1955
Voyevode (Opera), 1975
Walküre, Die, 1993–1994
War and Peace, 2000–2001
Werther, 2024
William Tell, 2034
Wozzeck, 2052–2053
Zaïde, 2076
zarzuela, 2081
Zauberharfe, Die, 2081
Zauberoper, 2081
Zaza, 2082
Zeit, 2082
Zingara, La, 2088
operetta(s), 1269–1270
Desert Song, 369
farce, 475
Fledermaus, 506–507
Gypsy Baron, 642
It Happened in Nordland, 790–791
Maytime, 1063
Merry Widow, 1099
Naughty Marietta, 1207
Orphée aux enfers, 1279
Paul Bunyan, 1322
Périchole, La, 1343
Rose-Marie, 1524–1525
Song of Norway, 1700
Student Prince (in Heidelberg), 1759
Vagabond King, 1924
Yeoman of the Guard, 2065–2066
ophicleide, 1270
opus, 1270
oratorio(s), 1270
Alexander's Feast, 18
Child of Our Time, 254
Creation, 325
Damnation de Faust, La, 343
Danse des morts, La, 344
Dream of Gerontius, 411
Enfance du Christ, L', 446
Gurre-Lieder, 639
invocation, 787
Israel in Egypt, 789–790
Jeanne d'Arc au bûcher, 814
Jephtha, 818

Legend of the Invisible City of Kitezh and the Maiden Fevronia, 925
Messiah, 1101–1102
narrator, 1205
Oedipus Rex, 1252
Psalmus Hungaricus, 1425
Seasons, 1629
Semele, 1633
tetralogy, 1836
War Requiem, 2001
Orbison, Roy, 1270–1271
orchestra, 1271
orchestral works. *See also specific types of works, e.g.:* symphony(-ies)
Adagio for Strings, 6
Air on the G String, 15
Also sprach Zarathustra, 20
American in Paris, 24
Amériques, 24
Aus Italien, 57–58
Bachianas Brasileiras, 68
Boeuf sur le toit, Le, 149
Brandenburg Concertos, 169–170
Capriccio brillante, 216–217
Capriccio Espagnol, 217
Capriccio Italien, 217
Capricorn Concerto, 217
Carnival of the Animals, 222–223
Chant de rossignol, Le, 244
Chronochromie, 263
Circus Polka, 268
Connotations, 301
Corsaire, Le, 313–314
Cuauhnahuac, 333
Dance in the Place Congo, 343
Danse macabre, 344
Death and Transfiguration, 354–355
Divertissement, 386
Don Juan, 399
Don Quixote, 399
Double Concerto for Harpsichord, Piano, and Two Chamber Orchestras, 408
Dumbarton Oaks, 417
Ebony Concerto, 429
Ecuatorial, 430–431
Eine kleine Nachtmusik, 433
Enigma Variations, 448–449
Escales, 454
Estro armonico, L', 455
Eumenides, Les, 458
Falstaff, 472–473
Fanfare for the Common Man, 473
Fantasia on a Theme by Thomas Tallis, 474
Fantasia on Greensleeves, 474
Fingal's Cave, 499
Finlandia, 499
Fireworks, 501
Fireworks Music, 501

Five Pieces for Orchestra, 504
Fountains of Rome, 519–520
Four Norwegian Moods, 520
Francesca da Rimini, 522
Fünf Orchesterstücke, 538
Galanta Dances, 548
Gigues, 572
Grand Canyon Suite, 616
Gruppen, 632
Haffner Serenade, 645–646
Hamlet, 653
Harmonious Blacksmith, 678
Heldenleben, Ein, 704–705
Holberg Suite, 729
Holidays, 731–732
Hunnenschlacht, 755
Ibéria, 764–765
Ideale, Die, 767
Images, 770
Impressioni Brasiliane, 772
Indian Suite, 776
In a Summer Garden, 774
In the Steppes of Central Asia, 775
Inscape, 780
Isle of the Dead, 789
Istar Variations, 790
Jamaican Rumba, 801–802
Job, 822
Kamarinskaya, 848
Kammersymphonie, 848
King Lear, 866
Marche funèbre d'une marionette, 1033
Marche slave, 1033–1034
Masques et bergamasques, 1053–1054
Medea's Meditation and Dance of Vengeance, 1070
Meeresstille und glückliche Fahrt, 1073
Men and Mountains, 1084
Mer, La, 1096
Metamorphosen, 1102
Midsommarvaka, 1116
Midsummer Night's Dream, 1116
New England Triptych, 1213
Night on Bald Mountain, 1219
Nights in the Gardens of Spain, 1220
Nocturnes, 1225
Norfolk Rhapsody No. 1, 1227
On Hearing the First Cuckoo in Spring, 1264
Pacific 231, 1292
Peacock Variations, 1325
Peer Gynt, 1330
Pelléas et Mélisande, 1331
Péri, La, 1343
Peter and the Wolf, 1348
Philharmonic Concerto, 1355
Pines of Rome, 1368
Pinocchio, 1370
Planets, 1374–1375
Plow that Broke the Plains, 1377

Poème de l'extase, Le, 1378
Poème satanique, 1379
Pohjola's Daughter, 1379
Pomp and Circumstance, 1385–1386
Prélude à l'après-midi d'un faune, 1397
Préludes, Les, 1398
Prométhée, 1422
Prometheus, 1422
Resonancias, 1481
Rhapsody in Blue, 1486–1487
Rhapsody in Rivets, 1487
Roman Festivals, 1518
Romeo and Juliet (Tchaikovsky), 1521
Rosamunde, 1524
Saga, En, 1557
Salón México, El, 1563
[S]árka, 1571
Scheherazade, 1584
Scherzo à la russe, 1586
Scherzo Fantastique, 1586
Scythian Suite, 1629
Serenade for String Orchestra, 1635–1636
Sérénade mélancolique, 1636
Siegfried Idyll, 1661
Slavonic Dances, 1676
Sleigh Ride, 1677
Sorcerer's Apprentice, 1702
Spring Symphony (Britten), 1714
Suite provençale, 1763
Sun-Treader, 1767
Symphony for Organ and Orchestra, 1781
Symphony in Three Movements, 1781
Symphony of Psalms, 1782
Synchrony, 1784
Syncopated Clock, 1784
Taras Bulba, 1809
Theme and Variations: The Four Temperaments, 1839
Three Places in New England, 1851
Threnody to the Victims of Hiroshima, 1852
Till Eulenspiegel's Merry Pranks, 1853
Typewriter, 1913
Valse Triste, 1926
Variations for Orchestra, 1931
Variations on a Theme by Frank Bridge, 1931–1932
Voyevode, 1975
Water Music, 2004–2005
Young Person's Guide to the Orchestra, 2070–2071
orchestration, 1271
orchestrion, 1271
Ordinary, 1271
ordre, 1271
Orfeo, L', 1272
Orfeo ed Euridice, 1271–1272

Orff, Carl, 1272–1273
Carmina Burana, 221
Kluge, Die, 878
Prometheus, 1422
organ and organists, 1273–1275
Baroque organ, 86
Biggs, E. Power, 133
Blow, John, 144–145
Boyce, William, 165
Bull, John, 184–185
Buxtehude, Dietrich, 190–191
Byrd, William, 192–193
console, 301–302
Cuckoo and the Nightingale, 333
diapason, 378
Dorian Toccata and Fugue, 405
double, 407
drone, 412
dummy pipes, 418
electronic organ, 437
Frescobaldi, Girolamo, 530
Gabrieli, Andrea, 544–545
Gabrieli, Giovanni, 545–546
Goldberg, Johann Gottlieb, 596
Hammond organ, 656
harmonium, 678
hydraulic organ, 759
Koopman, Ton, 887
Lost Chord, 984
Mason, Lowell, 1052
Pachelbel, Johann, 1290–1291
portative organ, 1388
positive organ, 1390
Praetorius, Michael, 1395–1396
rank, 1456
register, 1471
registration, 1471
slider, 1678
stop, 1733–1734
Sweelinck, Jan Pieterszoon, 1773–1774
Tavener, John, 1814–1815
Tye, Christopher, 1912–1913
Victoria, Tomás Luis de, 1953–1954
voluntary, 1973
vox, 1974–1975
Werckmeister, Andreas, 2023–2024
Werk, 2024
Widor, Charles-Marie, 2031–2032
Yasser, Joseph, 2065
organetto, 1276
organista, 1276
organistrum, 1276
organizations, musical
Camerata, 208
Collegium musicum, 284
Ratsmusiker, 1458
Singakademie, 1669
organized sound, 1276
organum, 1276–1277, 1890
Ormandy, Eugene, 1277–1278
Ormindo, 1278

ornament, 1278
ornamentation, 1278–1279
Ornamente, 1279
Ornstein, Leo, 344
Orontea, 1279
Orphée aux enfers, 1279
Orphéon, 1279–1280
Orpheus, 1280
Ory, "Kid," 1280
oscillator, 1280
ostinato, 1280–1281
Oswald, John, 1377–1378
Otello, 1281–1282
Otello, ossia Il Moro di Venezia, 1282
ottava, 1282
Otter, Anne-Sophie von, 1282–1283
oud, 1915
Over the Rainbow, 1283
Over There, 1283
overblowing, 1283
overstring, 1283
overtones, 676
overture(s), 1283–1285
    Academic Festival Overture, 3
    American Festival Overture, 24
    Cockaigne Overture, 279
    Cuban Overture, 333
    Egmont Overture, 432
    1812 Overture, 433
    Leonore Overtures, 938–939
    Roman Carnival, 1518
    Tragic Overture, 1879–1880
Owens, "Buck," 1285–1286
Ox Minuet, 1286
Oxford Symphony, 1286
Ozawa, Seiji, 1286–1289

P, 1290
pachanga, la, 1290
Pachelbel, Johann, 1290–1291
Pacific 231, 1292
Paderewski, Ignacy, 1292–1295
padovana, 1295
paean, 1295
Paganini, Niccolò (Nicoló), 1295–1298
Page, Patti, 1298
page turner, 1299
Pagliacci, 1299–1300
Paik, Nam June, 1300–1301
Paine, John Knowles, 1301
Paint Your Wagon, 1301–1302
The Pajama Game, 1302
Pal Joey, 1302
Palestrina, Giovanni Pierluigi da, 1131, 1302–1304
palindrome, 1304
Panama Hattie, 1304
pandora, 1305
panpipes, 1305
    syrinx, 1786
    zampoñas, 2076
pantaleon, 1305
pantomime, 1305

pantonality, 1305
Panufnik, Andrzej, 1305–1306
Papillons, 1306–1307
parable aria, 1307
Parade, 1307
parameter, 1307
paraphrases and transcriptions, 1307–1308
Paris Symphonies, 1308
Parker, Charlie, 1308–1309
Parker, Horatio, 1309–1311
parody, 1311–1312
Parsifal, 1312–1313
part, 1313
Pärt, Arvo, 1313–1314
partbooks, 1314
Partch, Harry, 1314–1315
particella, 1315–1316, 1964
partimento, 1316
partita, 1316
partitino, 1316
Parton, Dolly, 1316–1317
pasacaglia, 1318
Pasatieri, Thomas, 1317–1318
passage, 1318–1319
passing notes or tones, 1319
Passion, 1319
Passion music, 1319
pastiche, 1319–1320
pastoral, 1320
Pastoral Symphony, A (Vaughan Williams), 1321
Pastoral Symphony (Beethoven), 1320–1321
pastourelle, 1321
Pathétique Sonata, 1321
Pathétique Symphony, 1321–1322
Patience, or Bunthorne's Bride, 1322
patriotic music
    America, 23
    America the Beautiful, 24
    Anchors Aweigh, 26
    Battle Hymn of the Republic, 95–96
    Caissons Go Rolling Along, 204–205
    Chester, 253
    Columbia, the Gem of the Ocean, 287
    Deutschland, Deutschland über alles, 372–373
    Emperor's Hymn, 444
    God Bless America, 595
    God Save the Czar, 595
    God Save the King, 595
    Gott erhalte unser Kaiser, 603–604
    Hail, Columbia, 648
    Hail to the Chief, 648
    national anthems. *See* national anthems
    Over There, 1283
    Rákóczy March, 1451–1452
    Rule Britannia, 1550
    Stars and Stripes Forever, 1718

    Star-Spangled Banner, 1718–1719
    Tipperary, 1858–1859
    Vive la Compagnie, 1970
    Wacht am Rhein, Die, 1977
    When Johnny Comes Marching Home, 2026
    Yankee Doodle, 2065
patrons, musical
    Frederick II, 525
    Golitzin, Nikolai, 597
patter song, 1322
Paukenmesse, 1056
Paul Bunyan, 1322
pause, 1322
pavane, 1322–1323
Pavane pour une infante défunte, 1323
Pavarotti, Luciano, 1323–1325
pavillon d'amour, 1325
payola, 1325
Peacock Variations, 1325
Peanut Vendor, The, 1325
Pearl Jam, 1325–1326
Pears, Peter, 1326–1327
Pêcheurs de Perles, les, 1327
pedal, 1327–1328
pedal point, 1328
pedalier, 1328–1329
Pedrell, Felipe, 1329
Peer Gynt, 1330
Peerce, Jan, 1330
Peggy Sue, 1330
Peggy-Ann, 1330
Pelléas et Mélisande (Debussy), 1331
Pelléas et Mélisande (Schoenberg), 1331
pelog, 1331
Penderecki, Krzysztof, 1331–1332, 1852
Pennies from Heaven, 1332
Penniman, Richard (Little Richard), 1332–1334, 1911
pentachord, 1334
pentatonic scale, 1334–1335
Pepper, Art, 1335
Perahia, Murray, 1335–1336
percussion, 1336–1339
    antique cymbals, 33
    anvil, 33
    bacchetta di legno, 61–62
    Ballet mécanique, 74–75
    battery, 95
    bell, 113
    bells, 115–116
    bodhran, 149
    bones, 154
    castanets, 234
    cencerros, 239
    chinese blocks, 256
    chocalho, 256
    clappers, 268
    claves, 273
    conga drum, 300
    cowbell, 322

    crescent, 327
    crotales, 330
    cymbals, 337
    drag, 410
    drums. *See* drums and drummers
    finger cymbals, 499
    flexatone, 508
    friction drum, 531
    glockenspiel, 591
    gong, 597
    güiro, 636
    high hat, 718
    idiophone, 767
    Ionisation, 787–788
    jingling johnny, 821–822
    karatāli, 853
    Korean temple blocks, 889
    kulintang, 902
    kultrún, 902
    kymbala, 902
    maracas, 1031
    marimba, 1035
    marimbaphone, 1035
    naker, 1204
    napura, 1205
    puk, 1430
    quijada, 1439
    ratchet, 1458
    roto-toms, 1537–1538
    scabellum, 1576
    shepherd's bell, 1648
    sistrum, 1672
    slit drum, 1678–1679
    snare drum, 1689
    steel band, 1719–1720
    tabor, 1793
    taiko, 1794
    tambour militaire, 1799
    tambourin, 1799
    tambourine, 1799–1800
    tamburo scordato, 1800
    tam-tam, 1800–1801
    tenor drum, 1832
    teponaxtli, 1833
    timbales, 1853–1854
    timbrel, 1854
    timpani, 1855–1856
    tintinnabulum, 1858
    tom-tom, 1866
    triangle, 1886
    tubaphone, 1901–1902
    tubular chimes, 1903
    tupan, 1907
    Turken-Trommel, 1908
    vibraphone, 1950
    vibraslap, 1950
    washboard, 2003
    whip, 2027
    xylophone, 2062–2063
    xylorimba, 2063–2064
Perfect Day, A, 1340
perfect pitch, 1340
performance art/artists
    Anderson, Laurie, 26–27
    Happening, 671–672

Ono, Yoko, 1265–1266
total music, 1876–1877
performance(s)
  al fresco, 15
  début, 359
  demolition, 366
  farewell engagements, 475
  festivals, 485–487
  Festspiel, 487
  premiere, 1398
  Proms, 1423–1424
  recital, 1465
  season, 1629
  standing ovation, 1717
  Standing Room Only (SRO),
    1717
  swan song, 1772
  variety show, 1932
  vaudeville, 1932–1933
Pergolesi, Giovanni Battista,
  1340–1342, 1638–1639
Peri, Jacopo, 340, 1342–1343
Péri, La, 1343
Périchole, La, 1343
period, 1343
périodique, 1343–1344
Perkins, Carl, 1344
Perlman, Itzhak, 1344–1345
permutation, 1345
Perotin, 1345–1346
perpetuum mobile, 1346
Perséphone, 1346
Persichetti, Vincent, 1346–1348
pes, 1348
Peter, Paul and Mary, 1348–1349
Peter and the Wolf, 1348
Peter Grimes, 1348
Peterson, Oscar, 1349
Petri, Egon, 1349–1350
Petri, Michala, 1350–1351
Petrouchka, 1351–1352
Pettersson, Gustaf Allan,
  1352–1353
Petty, Tom, 1353–1354
Pfitzner, Hans, 1354–1355
phase shifting, 1355
Philharmonic Concerto, 1355
Philidor, André Danican, 1355
Philidor, François-André Dani-
  can, 1355–1356
Philippe de Vitry. *See* Vitry,
  Philippe De
phonograph, 1356–1358
  platter, 1375
  Victrola, 1954
phrase, 1358
phrase mark, 1358
phrasing, 1359
Piaf, Edith, 1359
pianists
  Allison, Mose, 19
  Arrau, Claudio, 43–44
  Ashkenazy, Vladimir, 48
  Ax, Emanuel, 59
  Barenboim, Daniel, 83–84
  Basie, "Count," 90–91

Benjamin, George, 116–117
Blake, Eubie, 140–141
Bolcolm, William, 152–153
Borge, Victor, 155
Brendel, Alfred, 173
Brico, Antonia, 173–174
Brubeck, Dave, 178
Bülow, Hans von, 185–186
Busoni, Ferruccio, 189–190
Carmichael, Hoagy, 220–221
Carreño, Teresa, 224–225
Charles, Ray, 245–246
Chopin, Frédéric, 256–258
Chung, Myung-Whun,
  264–265
Clementi, Muzio, 274–276
Cliburn, Van, 276–277
Cole, Nat "King," 281–282
Cortot, Alfred, 314
Czerny, Carl, 337
Dahl, Ingolf, 340
Davidovich, Bella, 346–347
Dohnányi, Ernst, 394–395
Egorov, Youri, 432–433
Erkel, Franz, 451–452
Eschenbach, Christoph,
  454–455
Evans, Bill, 461
Feltsman, Vladimir, 482–483
Field, John, 494
Flanagan, Tommy, 505–506
Fleisher, Leon, 507–508
Friedman, Ignaz, 532
Gabrilowitsch, Ossip, 546–547
Garner, Erroll, 555–556
Gieseking, Walter, 571
Gilels, Emil, 573–574
Gottschalk, Louis Moreau,
  605–607
Gould, Glenn, 607–609
Graffman, Gary, 613–614
Grainger, Percy, 614–615
Hanna, Roland, 667
Hanon, Charles-Louis, 667
Hensel, Fanny, 710
Hines, Earl "Fatha," 723–724
Horowitz, Vladimir, 744–746
Israel, Brian M., 790
Jarrett, Keith, 809
Johansen, Gunnar, 823–824
Kempff, Wilhelm, 856–857
Kipnis, Igor, 868
Kissin, Evgeny, 872–873
Kontarsky, Alfons, 886–887
Kontarsky, Aloys, 887
Kontarsky, Bernhard, 887
Labèque, Katia and Marielle,
  904–905
Landowska, Wanda, 910–912
Larrocha, Alicia de, 915
Leginska, Ethel, 926
Lhévinne, Josef, 946
Lipatti, Dinu, 959–960
Loriod, Yvonne, 981–982
Lupu, Radu, 996
Mason, William, 1053

McPartland, Marian, 1067
McShann, Jay, 1068–1069
Medtner, Nicolai, 1072–1073
Michelangeli, Arturo Benedetti,
  1109–1110
Paderewski, Ignacy, 1292–1295
Perahia, Murray, 1335–1336
Peterson, Oscar, 1349
Petri, Egon, 1349–1350
Pleyel, Ignace Joseph,
  1376–1377
Pollini, Maurizio, 1381–1382
Powell, "Bud," 1394–1395
Previn, André, 1401–1403
Rachmaninoff, Sergei,
  1442–1445
Richter, Sviatoslav, 1492
Rosenthal, Moriz, 1526–1527
Rubinstein, Anton, 1542–1544
Rubinstein, Arthur,
  1544–1546
Russell, George, 1552
Rzewski, Frederic, 1553–1554
Schnabel, Artur, 1590–1591
Schoeck, Othmar, 1592
Schumann, Clara Wieck,
  1606–1607
Serkin, Peter, 1637
Serkin, Rudolph, 1637–1638
Smith, Willie "the Lion,"
  1687–1688
Steuermann, Edward,
  1723–1724
Strayhorn, Billy, 1752
Sun Ra, 1766–1767
Takahashi, Aki, 1795–1796
Takahashi, Yuji, 1796
Tal, Josef, 1797–1798
Tan, Margaret Leng,
  1801–1802
Tansman, Alexandre, 1806
Tatum, Art, 1812–1813
Taylor, Cecil, 1815
Tenney, James, 1830–1831
Torke, Michael, 1871–1872
Tower, Joan, 1878–1879
Tristano, Lennie, 1891–1892
Tudor, David, 1904–1906
Uchida, Mitsuko, 1915
Walker, George, 1991–1993
Wallen, Errollyn, 1994
Waller, "Fats," 1994–1995
Watts, Andre, 2005–2007
Weber, Carl Maria von,
  2008–2013
Williams, Mary Lou, 2037
Wittgenstein, Paul, 2040–2041
Young, Victor, 2071
Zimerman, Krystian,
  2086–2087
piano concertos
  Concerto in F, 296
  Coronation Concerto, 313
  Emperor Concerto, 443
  Jazz Concerto, 813
  Jeunehomme Concerto, 820

piano music. *See also specific types
  of piano music, e.g.:* piano
  sonatas
Années de pèlerinage, 30–31
Campanella, La, 208
Carnaval, 221
Children's Corner, 256
Chopsticks, 258–259
Cinq Doigts, Les, 267
Consolations, 301
Danse sauvage, 344
Davidsbündler-Tänze, 348
Diabelli Variations, 375
Eroica Variations, 453
Estampes, 455
étude, 456
Études d'execution transcendante,
  456–457
Études symphoniques, 457
Études-Tableaux, 457
Fantasia contrappuntistica, 474
four-handed piano, 521
Gaspard de la nuit, 556
Ghost Trio, 569
Goyescas, 612
Gymnopédies, 641
*Harmoniques poétiques et re-
  ligieuses,* 677
Heures séculaires et instantanées,
  718
Hungarian Rhapsodies, 754–755
Invitation to the Dance, 787
Islamey, 789
Isle joyeuse, L', 769
Jeux d'eau, 820
Jeux d'enfants, 820
Ludus Tonalis, 989
Lugubre Gondole, Le, 992
Ma Mere L'Oye, 1002
Mazeppa, 1063–1064
Mephisto Waltz, 1095–1096
Mikrokosmos, 1117–1118
Minute Waltz, 1129
Miroirs, 1130
novellette, 1239
Ornamente, 1279
Papillons, 1306–1307
Pavane pour une infante défunte,
  1323
Pictures at an Exhibition, 1367
Préludes, 1398
Prière d'une vièrge, 1406
Raindrop Prelude, 1449–1450
Revolutionary Etude, 1485
Richard Wagner: Venezia,
  1491–1492
Rudepoema, 1547
Scaramouche, 1577
Six Epigraphes antiques, 1673
Sonatas and Interludes,
  1697–1698
Sonetti del Petrarca, 1699
Songs without Words, 1700
Suite bergamasque, 1762–1763
Tombeau de Couperin, Le, 1866
Träumerei, 1882

Trois morceaux en forme de poir, 1893
Trois véritables préludes flasques (pour un chien), 1893
Valse nobles et sentimentales, 1926
Vers la flamme, 1947
Vexations, 1949–1950
piano quartet, 1362
piano quintet, 1897
piano score, 1363
piano sonatas
  Adieux, Les, 10
  Appassionata Sonata, 34
  Concord Sonata, 297
  Hammerklavier Sonata, 654
  Pathétique Sonata, 1321
  Three-Page Sonata, 1852
  Waldstein Sonata, 1991
piano trios
  Archduke Trio, 37
  Dumky, 418
piano(s), 1359–1362
  Czerny, Carl, 337
  damper, 343
  dumb piano, 417
  electric piano, 436
  escapement, 454
  grand piano, 618
  handle piano, 665
  Hanon, Charles-Louis, 667
  overstring, 1283
  player piano, 1375–1376
  Pleyel, Ignace Joseph, 1376–1377
  prepared piano, 1398–1399
  soft pedal, 1691
  sordina, 1702–1703
  sostenuto pedal, 1703
  Steinway & Sons, 1720–1722
  string piano, 1756
  sustaining pedal, 1769
  Tafelklavier, 1793
  una corda, 1917
  upright, 1919
pianoforte, 654, 1363
pianola. *See* player piano
Piatigorsky, Gregor, 1363
Piazzolla, Astor, 1364
pibcorn, 1364
pibroch, 1364
Picardy third, 1364–1365
Piccinni, Niccoló, 1365–1367
piccolo, 1367
pick, 1367
Pictures at an Exhibition, 1367
piece, 1367
Pierrot Lunaire, 1367
Pijper, Willem, 1368
Pilgrim's Progress, The, 1368
Pines of Rome, The, 1368
Pink Floyd, 1368–1370
Pinocchio, 1370
Pins and Needles, 1370
Pinza, Ezio, 1370–1371
pipa, 1371

Pirates of Penzance, or The Slaves of Duty, 1371
Pistol Packin' Mama, 1371
Piston, Walter, 776, 1371–1373
pitch, 1373–1374
  alteration, 20
  concert, 292
  frequency, 529–530
  intonation, 784
  Ton, 1866
pitch class, 1374
pitch pipe, 1374
pivot chord, 1374
plainchant (plainsong), 1374
  Ambrosian chant, 22–23
  reciting note, 1465
Planets, The, 1374–1375
platter, 1375
player piano, 1375–1376
Please Mr. Postman, 1376
Please Please Me, 1376
plectrum, 1376
plena, 1376
Pleyel, Ignace Joseph, 1376–1377
Plow that Broke the Plains, The, 1377
plugging, 1377
Plunderphonic, 1377–1378
pluralism, 1378
pochette, 1378
Poème de l'extase, Le, 1378
Poème divin, Le, 1379
Poème électronique, 1379
Poème satanique, 1379
Pohjola's Daughter, 1379
point d'orgue, 1379
pointillism, 1379–1380
Police, The, 1380–1381
polka, 1381
Pollini, Maurizio, 1381–1382
polonaise, 1382
polymeter, 1382–1383
polymodality, 1383
polyphonic, 1383
polyphony, 1383–1384
  discant, 381–382
  Odhecaton, 1252
polyrhythm, 1384–1385
polystylistic music, 1385
polytonality, 1385
Pomo d'oro, Il, 1385
Pomp and Circumstance, 1385–1386
Ponce, Manuel, 1386
Ponchielli, Amilcare, 578–579, 1386–1387
Pop! Goes the Weasel, 1387
pop(ular) music, 1387–1388
  Alexander's Ragtime Band, 18
  Aloha oe, 19
  Andrews, Julie, 28
  Andrews Sisters, 28–29
  April in Paris, 35–36
  Arlen, Harold, 39–40
  Astaire, Fred, 49
  As Time Goes By, 47–48

A-Tisket, A-Tasket, 50
Aznavour, Charles, 59
Bacharach, Burt, 67–68
Baker, Josephine, 70–71
Beautiful Dreamer, 101
Berlin, Irving, 121–122
Bicycle Built for Two, 132
Bill Bailey, Won't You Please Come Home?, 133
Blades, Rubén, 139–140
Blake, Eubie, 140–141
Bock, Jerry, 148–149
Brel, Jacques, 172
Brice, Fanny, 173
California Girls, 205
Camptown Races, 208–209
Carmichael, Hoagy, 220–221
Carry Me Back to Old Virginny, 225
Chantilly Lace, 244
Chattanooga Choo Choo, 248
Chevalier, Maurice, 253–254
Cielito lindo, 265
Clooney, Rosemary, 278–279
Cole, Nat "King," 281–282
Cooke, Sam, 304–305
Cucaracha, La, 333
Dancing in the Streets, 343–344
Danny Boy, 344
David, Mack, 346
Deep in the Heart of Texas, 361
Deep Purple, 361
Denver, John, 368
Dinah, 380
Dixie, 387
Do That to Me One More Time, 388
Does Your Chewing Gum Lose Its Flavor (on the Bedpost Over Night)?, 393
Don't Fence Me In, 402
Don't Get Around Much Anymore, 402
Don't Worry, Be Happy, 402
Dueling Banjos, 414
Dukelsky, Vladimir, 416–417
Earth Angel, 429
Easter Parade, 429
Emmett, Daniel Decatur, 443
Enjoy Yourself (It's Later Than You Think), 449
Fain, Sammy, 469–470
Falling in Love Again, 471
Fascinating Rhythm, 478
Feliciano, Jose, 482
Fever, 490
Fire and Rain, 500
First Time Ever I Saw Your Face, 502
Five Foot Two, Eyes of Blue, 503
Foggy Day in London Town, 513
Folsom Prison Blues, 514
Garland, Judy, 555
Georgia on My Mind, 564
Gershwin, George, 564–566
Get Back, 568

Get Together, 568
Girl I Left Behind Me, 580
Give My Regards to Broadway, 584
Give Peace a Chance, 584
God Bless America, 595
God Bless the Child, 595
On the Good Ship Lollipop, 1264
Good Vibrations, 597
Goodnight Irene, 598
Goodnight Ladies, 598
Great Balls of Fire, 623–624
Green, John, 624
Hail, Hail, the Gang's All Here, 648
Hamlisch, Marvin, 654
Happy Birthday to You, 672
Happy Days Are Here Again, 672
Henderson, Ray, 708
Herman, Jerry, 713–714
For He's a Jolly Good Fellow, 515
Holiday, Billie "Lady Day," 730–731
Home, Sweet Home, 736–737
Horne, Lena, 742
Hot Time in the Old Town Tonight, 748
Hound Dog, 748
Houston, Whitney, 748–749
How Much is That Doggie in the Window?, 750
How Sweet It Is (To Be Loved By You), 750
Hupfeld, Herman, 756
Hustle, 758
I Am Woman, 762
(I Can't Get No) Satisfaction, 762
I Can't Give You Anything But Love, Baby, 762
I Can't Help Myself, 762
I Didn't Raise My Boy to Be a Soldier, 762
I Fall to Pieces, 763
I Got Rhythm, 763
I Got You (I Feel Good), 763
I Heard It Through the Grapevine, 763
I Left My Heart in San Francisco, 763
I Shot the Sheriff, 763–764
I Walk the Line, 764
I Wanna Be Loved by You, 764
I Want to Be Happy, 764
I Want to Hold Your Hand, 764
I Wonder Who's Kissing Her Now, 764
If I Had a Hammer, 768
Iglesias, Julio, 768
I'm Always Chasing Rainbows, 769
I'm Forever Blowing Bubbles, 769
I'm In the Mood for Love, 769

I'm Just Wild about Harry, 769
*I'm Looking Over a Four-Leaf
    Clover*, 769
I'm Walkin', 769
Impossible Dream, 771
In a Little Spanish Town, 774
Indian Love Call, 776
In the Still of the Nite, 775
Irma la Douce, 788
It Had to be You, 790
It Was a Very Good Year, 791
It's De-Lovely, 792
It's Not for Me to Say, 792
It's Now or Never, 792
*Itsy Bitsy Teenie Weenie Yellow
    Polkadot Bikini*, 792
*Jeanie with the Light Brown
    Hair*, 813–814
Jeepers, Creepers, 814
Jim Crack Corn (Blue Tail Fly),
    821
Jim Crow, 821
Jolson, Al, 830–831
Jones, Spike, 833–834
Jones, Tom, 834–835
Kander, John, 848–849
Kaye, Sammy, 856
Kern, Jerome, 857–858
Killing Me Softly With His Song,
    863
King, Carole, 865–866
King of the Road, 866
Kitt, Eartha, 873
La Bamba, 903
Lady is a Tramp, 905
Lane, Burton, 912
Last Time I Saw Paris, 917
Laura, 918
Lee, Peggy, 923–924
Legrand, Michel, 926–927
Lenya, Lotte, 936
Lerner, Alan Jay, 940–941
Liberace, 946–947
Life is Just a Bowl of Cherries,
    954
Light My Fire, 956
Like A Prayer, 956
Like a Rolling Stone, 956
Like A Virgin, 956
Lion Sleeps Tonight, 959
Listen to the Mockingbird, 961
Little Drummer Boy, 968
Long Tall Sally, 979
Look for the Silver Lining, 981
Louie Louie, 985
Love Me Tender, 987
Lullaby of Broadway, 993
Mack the Knife, Ballad of, 1011
Mairzy Doats, 1022
Makeba, Miriam, 1023
Man I Love, 1026
Man on the Flying Trapeze, 1027
Martin, Dean, 1043
Martin, Mary, 1045–1046
Mathis, Johnny, 1060–1061
McFerrin, Bobby, 1065–1066

Me and My Shadow, 1069
Meet Me in St. Louis, Louis,
    1073
Memphis Blues, 1084
Mercer, Johnny, 1096–1097
Mercer, Mabel, 1097–1098
Merman, Ethel, 1098–1099
Midler, Bette, 1114–1115
Minnelli, Liza, 1126
Miranda, Carmen, 1129–1130
Missouri Waltz, 1131
Mr. Tambourine Man, 1132
Mrs. Robinson, 1132
Misty, 1132
Mitchell, Joni, 1132–1133
Nature Boy, 1206
Near, Holly, 1208
Never on Sunday, 1212
Night and Day, 1219
Ode to Billy Joe, 1252
*Oh, How I Hate to Get Up in
    the Morning*, 1256
Oh, Pretty Woman, 1256
Oh, Promise Me!, 1256
Oh, Susanna, 1256
Oh, What a Beautiful Mornin',
    1256
Ol' Man River, 1259
Old Black Joe, 1259
Old Folks at Home, 1259
Only You, 1267
On the Sunny Side of the Street,
    1264
Over the Rainbow, 1283
Over There, 1283
Page, Patti, 1298
Peanut Vendor, 1325
Pennies from Heaven, 1332
Perfect Day, 1340
Peter, Paul and Mary,
    1348–1349
Piaf, Edith, 1359
Pistol Packin' Mama, 1371
Please Mr. Postman, 1376
Please Please Me, 1376
Porter, Cole, 1388–1390
*Praise the Lord and Pass the Am-
    munition*, 1396
Pretty Girl is Like a Melody,
    1401
*Proud Mary (Rollin' on the
    River)*, 1425
Que Sera, Sera, 1438
Rainy Day Women #12 & #35,
    1450
Respect, 1481–1482
Revolution, 1484–1485
Rise 'n' Shine, 1500
*(We're Gonna) Rock around the
    Clock*, 1509
Rodgers, Richard, 1512–1513
Rudolph the Red-Nosed Reindeer,
    1549
School Days, 1599
Schwartz, Arthur, 1615
See You Later, Alligator, 1630

Send in the Clowns, 1634
September Song, 1634
Seventy-Six Trombones, 1641
Shore, Dinah (Francis Rose),
    1649–1650
Short, Bobby, 1650
Shuffle Off to Buffalo, 1656
Sidewalks of New York, 1660
Sinatra, Frank, 1668–1669
Singin' in the Rain, 1671
(Sittin' On) The Dock of the Bay,
    1673
Sixteen Tons, 1674
Smiles, 1685
Smith, Kate, 1687
Smoke Gets in Your Eyes, 1688
Sobre las Olas, 1690
Some Day I'll Find You, 1696
Some Enchanted Evening, 1696
Somebody Loves Me, 1696
Sophisticated Lady, 1701
Stand By Me, 1717
Stand by Your Man, 1717
standard, 1717
Stardust, 1717
Stayin' Alive, 1719
Stormy Weather, 1734
Strange Fruit, 1735
Strangers in the Night, 1735
Streisand, Barbra, 1753–1754
Styne, Jule, 1760
Summertime, 1766
Sunny Boy, 1767
Surfin' Safari, 1768
Swanee, 1772–1773
Swanee River, 1773
Sweet Adeline, 1774
Sweet Rosie O'Grady, 1774
Take Me Out to the Ball Game,
    1796
Take the A Train, 1796
Taylor, James, 1815–1816
Tea for Two, 1823
Teen Angel, 1824
Teenager in Love, 1824
Ten Cents a Dance, 1829
Tennessee Waltz, 1830
Tequila, 1833
Thanks for the Memories, 1838
That Old Black Magic, 1838
That'll Be the Day, 1838
There's a Long, Long Trail, 1840
*There's No Business Like Show
    Business*, 1840–1841
*These Boots Are Made for
    Walkin'*, 1843
*Tie a Yellow Ribbon 'Round the
    Ole Oak Tree*, 1853
Times They Are A-Changin',
    1855
Tin Pan Alley, 1857
To Know Him Is to Love Him,
    1863
Tonight We Love, 1870
torch song, 1871
Tormé, Mel, 1872–1873

Trail of the Lonesome Pine, 1880
Trees, 1884
Trolley Song, 1893
Tucker, Sophie, 1903–1904
Turn, Turn, Turn, 1909
Tutti Frutti, 1911
Twist, 1912
Twist and Shout, 1912
Vallee, Rudy, 1925
Vie en Rose, La, 1954
Volare, 1972
Wake Up Little Susie,
    1990–1991
Waltzing Matilda, 2000
What's Goin' On?, 2026
When Irish Eyes Are Smiling,
    2026
*When the Red, Red Robin comes
    Bob, Bob, Bobbin' Along*, 2026
*While Strolling Through the
    Park One Day*, 2026–2027
Whispering, 2027
White Christmas, 2027
*Will You Love Me in December
    as You Do in May?*, 2034
Woody Woodpecker, 2052
Worms Crawl In, 2052
Wouldn't It Be Lovely?, 2052
Wreck of the Old 97, 2053
Wunderbar, 2053
Yes, Sir, That's My Baby, 2066
Yes, We Have No Bananas, 2066
You Ain't Heard Nothin' Yet,
    2066
*You Made Me Love You, I Didn't
    Want to Do It*, 2067
*You Must Have Been a Beautiful
    Baby*, 2067
Youmans, Vincent, 2067–2068
You're the Cream in My Coffee,
    2071
Zappa, Frank, 2077–2080
Porgy and Bess, 1388, 1766
portative organ, 1388
Porter, Cole, 1388–1390
    Anything Goes, 34
    Don't Fence Me In, 402
    Gay Divorce, 557
    It's De-Lovely, 792
    Jubilee, 840
    Kiss Me Kate, 872
    Night and Day, 1219
    Panama Hattie, 1304
    Silk Stockings, 1663–1664
    Something for the Boys, 1696
Portuguese Hymn, 1390
position, 1390
positive organ, 1390
post horn, 1390
posthumous works, 1390
postlude, 1391
postmodernism, 1137
potpourri, 1391
Poule, La, 707
Poulenc, Francis, 1391–1392
    Biches, Les, 131

Dialogues de carmélites, Les, 377
Figure humaine, La, 496
Mamelles de Tiresias, Les, 1026
Pound, Ezra, 1392–1393
Pousseur, Henri, 1393–1394
Powell, "Bud," 1394–1395
Praetorius, Michael, 1395–1396
Prague Symphony, 1396
Prairie, The, 1396
Praise the Lord and Pass the Ammunition, 1396
precentor, 1396
prelude, 1397
Prélude à l'après-midi d'un faune, 1397
Préludes, Les (Liszt), 1398
Préludes (Debussy), 1398
premiere, 1398
preparation, 1398
prepared piano, 1398–1399
Present arms, 1399
Presley, Elvis, 1399–1401
Pretty Girl is Like a Melody, A, 1401
Previn, André, 279, 1401–1403
Prey, Hermann, 1403–1404
Prez, Josquin des. *See* Desprez, Josquin
Price, Leontyne, 1404–1405
Pride, Charley, 1405–1406
Prière d'une vièrge, 1406
Příhody Lišky Bystroušky, 335
prima donna, 1406–1407
prima prattica, 1407
primary accent, 1407
primary triad, 1407
prime, 1407
primitivism, 1407
primo(-a), 1407
Primrose, William, 1408
Prince, 1408–1409
Prince Igor, 1409–1410
principal chords, 1410
printing and publishing of music, 1410–1414
 BMI, 147–148
 copyright, 308–309
 Festschrift, 487
 périodique, 1343–1344
 Verlag, 1947
processional, 1414
Prodigal Son, The, 1414
Professor Longhair. *See* Byrd, Henry Roeland
program music, 1414–1417
progression, 1417
progressive composition, 1418
progressive jazz, 1418
Prokofiev, Sergei, 1418–1421
 Alexander Nevsky, 18
 Cinderella, 267
 Classical Symphony, 272
 Fiery Angel, 495
 Gambler, 550
 Love for Three Oranges, 986
 Peter and the Wolf, 1348

Romeo and Juliet, 1520
Scythian Suite, 1629
War and Peace, 2000–2001
Youth Symphony, 2072
proletarian music, 1422
prologue, 1422
Promethée, 1422
Prometheus (Liszt), 1422
Prometheus (Orff), 1422
Promises, Promises, 1423
prompter, 1423
Proms, The, 1423–1424
Prophéte, Le, 1424
proportion, 1424
proportional notation, 1424
proprium, 1424–1425
Proud Mary (Rollin' on the River), 1425
psalm, 1425
psalm tones, 1425
psalmodicon, 1425
Psalmus Hungaricus, 1425
psalter, 1426
psaltery, 1426
pseudonymns, 1426–1427
Public Enemy, 1427
publishing, music. *See* printing and publishing of music
Puccini, Giacomo, 1427–1430
 Bohème, La, 150
 Gianni Schicchi, 569
 Girl of the Golden West, 580–581
 Madama Butterfly, 1011–1012
 Manon Lescaut, 1030–1031
 Tosca, 1873–1874
 Turandot, 1907–1908
puk, 1430
Pulcinella, 1430
pulse, 1430
punctus, 1430
punto, 1430
Purcell, Henry, 378, 1430–1432
Puritani di Scozia, I, 1432–1433
Purlie, 1433

qin, 1434
quadrille, 1434
quadrivium, 1434
quadruple meter/time, 1435
Quantz, Johann Joachim, 1435–1436
quartal harmony, 1436
quarter tone, 1436–1437
quartet, 1437
 piano, 1362
 string, 1756–1757
Quartet for the End of Time, 1437
quatricinium, 1437
Quattro pezzi sacri, 1438
Que Sera, Sera, 1438
Queen, 1438
Queen, The (Haydn), 1438
Queen of Spades, 1439
quena, 1439

Querelle des Bouffons. *See* Guerre des Bouffons
quickstep, 1439
quijada, 1439
Quintenquartett, 1439
quintet, 1439–1440
 piano, 1897
 string, 1757
quintuplets, 1440
quodlibet, 1440
quotation, 1440–1441

R, 1442
rabāb, 1442
Rachmaninoff, Sergei, 1442–1445
 Études-Tableaux, 457
 Isle of the Dead, 789
racket, 1445–1446
Raff, Joachim, 1446
raga, 1446–1448
ragtime, 1448–1449
 Entertainer, 450
 horse trot, 747
 Joplin, Scott, 837–839
 Lamb, Joseph Francis, 908
 Matthews, Artie, 1061–1062
Rag-Time, 1449
Raindrop Prelude, 1449–1450
Rainey, Ma, 1450
Rainy Day Women #12 & #35, 1450
Raitt, Bonnie, 1450–1451
Rake's Progress, The, 1451
Rákóczy March, 1451–1452
Rameau, Jean-Philippe, 1453–1455
 Castor et Pollux, 235
 Hippolyte et Aricie, 725
 Indes Galantes, Les, 776
Ramey, Samuel, 1455
Rampal, Jean-Pierre, 1456
rank, 1456
rant, 1456
ranz des vaches, 1457
rap, 1457
 hip-hop, 724–725
 Ice Cube, 765–766
 Ice-T, 766
 N.W.A., 1244
 Public Enemy, 1427
 sampler, 1567
Rape of Lucretia, The, 1457
Rappresentazione di anima e di corpo, La, 1457
rappresentazione sacra, 1458
Raskin, David, 1452–1453
Rasoumowsky Quartets, 1458
ratchet, 1458
Ratsmusiker, 1458
Rattle, Simon, 1458–1459
Ravel, Maurice, 1459–1462
 Boléro, 154
 Daphnis et Chloé, 345
 Enfant et les sortileges, L', 446
 Gaspard de la nuit, 556

Heure espagnole, L', 717–718
Histoires naturelles, 725
Introduction and Allegro, 785
Jeux d'eau, 820
Ma Mère L'Oye, 1002
Miroirs, 1130
Pavane pour une infante défunte, 1323
Shéhérazade, 1648
Tombeau de Couperin, Le, 1866
Tzigane, 1914
Valse, La, 1925–1926
Valse nobles et sentimentales, 1926
Razor Quartet, 1462
Re, 1463
Re pastore, Il, 1463
Read, Daniel, 1463
realism, 1463–1464
realization, 1464
rebec, 1464
recapitulation, 1464
recessional, 1465
recital, 1465
recitative, 1465
reciting note, 1465
record album, 1465
record player. *See* phonograph
recorded music
 compact disc, 290
 digital, 379
 disc, 380
 disk, 382
 high fidelity, 718
 phonograph, 1356–1358
 record album, 1465
 stereophonic recording, 1722
 tape recording, 1807–1808
 Victrola, 1954
recorder, 1350–1351, 1465–1466
reco-reco, 636
Red Mass, 1466
Red Pony, The, 1466–1467
Red Poppy, The, 1467
Redding, Otis, 1467–1468, 1673
Redman, Don, 1468
reduction, 1468
reed, 1468–1469
Reed, Lou, 1938, 1939
Reformation Symphony, 1469
refrain, 1469
Reger, Max, 1469–1470
reggae, 1036–1037, 1470–1471
Regina, 1471
register, 1471
registration, 1471
rehearsal, 1471–1472
Reich, Steve, 1472–1474
Reimann, Aribert, 921
Reiner, Fritz, 1474–1475
Reinhardt, Django, 1475
rejdowak, 1475
Relâche, 1475–1476
related keys, 1476
relative pitch, 1476
R.E.M., 1476–1477

remedio, 1477
Renaissance, 1477–1478
  ballata, 74
  basse danse, 92–93
  commedia dell'arte, 289, 675
  cornett, 312
  crumhorn, 331–332
  faburden, 468
  fipple flute, 500
  frottola, 534
  vagans, 1924
Renard, 1478
repeat, 1478–1479
repercussion, 1479
repetend, 1479
répétiteur,-euse, 1479
reprise, 1479–1480
repsonse, 1483
requiem(s), 1480
  Deutsches Requiem, Ein, 372
  Requiem Canticles, 1480
res facta, 1480
rescue opera, 1480
reservata, musica, 1480–1481
resolution, 1481
resonance, 1481, 2046
Resonancias, 1481
resonator, 1481
Respect, 1481–1482
Respighi, Ottorino, 1482–1483
  Fountains of Rome, 519–520
  Impressioni Brasiliane, 772
  Pines of Rome, 1368
  Roman Festivals, 1518
responsory, 1483
rest, 1483
Retablo de Maese Pedro, El, 1483
retardation, 1483
retrograde, 1483–1484
retrograde inversion, 1484
reveille, 1484
rèverie, 1484
Revolution, 1484–1485
Revolutionary Etude, 1485
revue, 1485
Revueltas, Silvestre, 333,
  1485–1486
rhapsody, 1486
Rhapsody in Blue, 1486–1487
Rhapsody in Rivets, 1487
Rheingold, Das, 1487–1488
Rhenish Symphony, 1488
rhythm, 1488–1489
  anacrusis, 26
  anapest, 26
  asymmetry, 50
  beat, 99
  binary, 135–136
  dactyl(e), 340
  imbroglio, 770
  polyrhythm, 1384–1385
  pulse, 1430
  Scotch snap or catch, 1620
  synchrony, 1783–1784
  syncopation, 1784–1785
  tattoo, 1812

rhythm and blues, 1489–1490
rhythm guitar, 638
rhythm section, 1490
ribs, 1490
ricercar, 1490–1491
Rich, Buddy, 1491
Richard Wagner: Venezia,
  1491–1492
Richter, Sviatoslav, 1492
Rider Quartet. See Ritterquartett
Riders to the Sea, 1492–1493
Rienzi, 1493
riff, 1493
rigadoon, 1493
Rigoletto, 1493–1494
Riley, Terry, 774, 1494–1495
Rimsky-Korsakov, Nikolai,
  1495–1499
  Capriccio Espagnol, 217
  Coq d'or, Le, 309
  Kashchei, the Immortal, 853
  *Legende von der heiligen Elisa-
    beth, Die,* 925
  Maid of Pskov, 1022
  Mlada, 1135
  Sadko, 1556
  Scheherazade, 1584
  Snow Maiden, 1689–1690
  Vendredis, Les, 1940
Rinaldo, 1499
Ring des Nibelungen, Der, 1499
ring modulator, 1499
ripieno, 1499–1500
*Rise and Fall of the City of Ma-
  hagonny, The,* 56
Rise 'n' Shine, 1500
Rite of Spring, The, 1500
ritornello, 1500–1501
Ritterquartett, 1501
Roach, Max, 1501
Robert le diable, 1501–1502
Roberta, 1502
*Roberto Devereux, ossia Il Conte di
  Essex,* 1502
Robeson, Paul, 1502–1503
Robinson, Smokey, 1503–1504
Rochberg, George, 1504–1505
rock, 1505–1508
  Armatrading, Joan, 40
  Beach Boys, 98
  Beatles, 99–101
  Berry, Chuck, 128–129
  Bowie, David, 162–163
  Branca, Glenn, 169
  Brown, James, 177–178
  Buffalo Springfield, 183–184
  Byrd, Henry Roeland, 191–192
  Byrds, 193
  Byrne, David, 193–194
  Checker, Chubby, 250
  Clapton, Eric, 268–269
  Costello, Elvis, 315–316
  Creedence Clearwater Revival,
    327
  Diddley, Bo, 378
  disc jockey (DJ), 380–381

disco, 382
disco music, 382
discotheque, 382
Domino, "Fats," 397
Doors, 402–403
doo-wop, 404
Dylan, Bob, 424–426
Eagles, 427–428
Eno, Brian, 449
Everly Brothers, 462–463
Four Tops, 520–521
Franklin, Aretha, 524
Freed, Alan, 526
funk, 538–539
Gaye, Marvin, 557–559
Gordy, Berry, Jr., 599–600
Grateful Dead, 621–623
Haley, Bill, 651–652
Harrison, George, 687–688
Hayes, Isaac, 700–701
Hendrix, Jimi, 709
hip-hop, 724–725
Holly, Buddy, 732–734
hook, 739
Houston, Whitney, 748–749
Jackson, Michael, 797–799
Jefferson Airplane, 814–815
Joel, Billy, 822–823
John, Elton, 824–825
Jones, Quincy, 832
Joplin, Janis, 836–837
King, Carole, 865–866
Knight, Gladys, 879
Led Zeppelin, 922–923
Lennon, John, 933–934
Lewis, Jerry Lee, 943–944
Madonna, 1013–1014
McCartney, Sir Paul,
  1064–1065
Midler, Bette, 1114–1115
Newman, Randy, 1215–1216
Nirvana, 1222
N.W.A., 1244
Ono, Yoko, 1265–1266
Orbison, Roy, 1270–1271
payola, 1325
Pearl Jam, 1325–1326
Peggy Sue, 1330
Penniman, Richard (Little
  Richard), 1332–1334
Perkis, Carl, 1344
Petty, Tom, 1353–1354
Pink Floyd, 1368–1370
plugging, 1377
Police, 1380–1381
Presley, Elvis, 1399–1401
Prince, 1408–1409
Public Enemy, 1427
Queen, 1438
Raitt, Bonnie, 1450–1451
rap, 1457
Redding, Otis, 1467–1468
R.E.M., 1476–1477
Robinson, Smokey, 1503–1504
Rolling Stones, 1515–1517
Ross, Diana, 1528–1529

sequencer, 1635
Simon, Paul, 1665–1666
soul, 1703
Springsteen, Bruce,
  1714–1715
Starr, Ringo, 1717–1718
Temptations, 1828–1829
Turner, Tina, 1910–1911
Velvet Underground,
  1933–1939
Waits, Tom, 1990
Who, 2028–2030
Wonder, Stevie, 2050–2051
Young, Neil, 2070
Zappa, Frank, 2077–2080
*(We're Gonna) Rock around the
  Clock,* 1509
rock 'n' roll, 1508–1509
Rock of Ages, 1509
Rock-a-Bye Baby, 1510
rococo, 1510
Rodeo, 1510
Rodgers, Jimmie, 1511–1512
Rodgers, Mary, 1265
Rodgers, Richard, 388, 1223,
  1512–1513
Rodgers and Hammerstein
  Carousel, 223
  Flower Drum Song, 509
  King and I, 864
  Oklahoma!, 1258–1259
  Some Enchanted Evening, 1696
  Sound of Music, 1705
  South Pacific, 1707
Rodgers and Hart
  Babes in Arms, 61
  Boys from Syracuse, 165–166
  Connecticut Yankee, 300–301
  Girl Friend, 580
  I Married an Angel, 763
  I'd Rather Be Right, 766–767
  Jumbo, 843
  Pal Joey, 1302
  Peggy-Ann, 1330
  Present Arms, 1399
  Ten Cents a Dance, 1829
  On Your Toes, 1264–1265
Rodzinski, Artur, 1513–1514
Roland, 1514
Roldán, Amadeo, 1514–1515
Rolling Stones, The, 762,
  1515–1517
Rollins, "Sonny," 1517–1518
Roman Carnival, The, 1518
Roman Festivals, 1518
Roman numerals, 1518
romance, 1518
romancero, 1518
romanesca, 1518–1519
Romantic era, 1519–1520
Romantic Symphony, 1520
Romany music. *See* Gypsy music
Romberg, Sigmund
  Desert Song, 369
  Maytime, 1063
  New Moon, 1213

Student Prince (in Heidelberg),
1759
Rome, Harold
I Can Get It for You Wholesale,
762
Pins and Needles, 1370
Romeo and Juliet (Prokofiev),
1520
Romeo and Juliet (Tchaikovsky),
1521
Roméo et Juliette (Berlioz), 1521
Roméo et Juliette (Gounod), 1521
Romero, 1521
Romero, Angel, 1521
Romero, Celedonio, 1521
Romero, Celin, 1521
Romero, Pepe, 1521
rondeau, 1521–1522
rondellus, 1522
rondo, 1522
rondo-sonata form, 1697
Rooley, Anthony. *See* Kirkby,
Emma
root, 1522
Root, George Frederick, 95
Rorem, Ned, 1131, 1522–1524
Rosalia sequence or modulation,
1524
Rosamunde, 1524
Rose-Marie, 1524–1525
Rosenberg, Hilding, 1525
Rosenkavalier, Der, 1525–1526
Rosenthal, Moriz, 1526–1527
Roslavetz, Nikolai, 1527
Ross, Diana, 1528–1529
Ross, Jerry, 1302
Rossignol, Le. See Nightingale, The
Rossini, Gioachino, 1529–1534
Barber of Seville, 79
*Cenerentola, La, o la bontà in
trionfo,* 239
Comte Ory, Le, 292
Donna del lago, La, 402
Gazza ladra, La, 559
Italiana in Algeri, L', 791
Otello, ossia Il Moro di Venezia,
1282
Semiramide, 1633
Siège de Corinthe, Le,
1660–1661
Tancredi, 1802
William Tell, 2034
Rostopovich, Mstislav,
1534–1536
rota, 1536
Rota, Nino, 1536–1537
rotation, 1537
rotolus, 1538
roto-toms, 1537–1538
rotta, 1538
round(s), 1538
Frère Jacques, 530
pes, 1348
Row, Row, Row Your Boat, 1541
roundelay, 1538
Rouse, Mikel, 1538–1539

Dennis Cleveland, 367–368
Failing Kansas, 469
Rousseau, Jean-Philippe, 374
Roussel, Albert, 484–485,
1540–1541
rovescio, 1541
Row, Row, Row Your Boat, 1541
Rozsa, Miklos, 1541–1542
rubato, tempo, 1542
Rubinstein, Anton, 1249,
1542–1544
Rubinstein, Arthur, 1544–1546
Ruby, Harry, 597
Rudepoema, 1547
Rudhyar, Dane, 1547–1549
Rudolph, Archduke of Austria.
See Beethoven, Ludwig van
Rudolph the Red-Nosed Reindeer,
1549
Ruggles, Carl, 1549–1550
Men and Mountains, 1084
Sun-Treader, 1767
Rule Britannia, 1550
rumba, 1550
run, 1550
Rusalka (Dargomyzhsky),
1550–1551
Rusalka (Dvořák), 1551
Ruslan and Ludmila, 1551
Russell, George, 1552
Russian bassoon, 1552
Russolo, Luigi, 542, 784
Rysanek, Leonie, 1552–1553
Rzewski, Frederic, 1553–1554

Sabre Dance, 1555
Sachs, Hans, 1555
sackbut, 1555
Sacre du printemps, Le, 1500
sacred concerto, 1555–1556
Sadko, 1556
Sadra, I Wayan, 1556–1557
Saga, En, 1557
Sagittarius, Henricus. *See* Schütz,
Heinrich
Sailor's Hornpipe, 1557
sainete, 1561
St. Louis Blues, 1557–1558
Saint-Saëns, Camille, 1558–1560
Carnival of the Animals,
222–223
Danse macabre, 344
Samson et Dalila, 1567
Salieri, Antonio, 1561–1562
Salome, 1563
Salomon, Johann Peter. *See*
Haydn, Franz Joseph
Salón México, El, 1563
salon music, 1563–1564
salon orchestra, 1564–1565
Salonen, Esa-Pekka, 1565
salsa, 139–140, 1566
Salzedo, Carlos, 1566–1567
samba, 1567
sampler, 1567
Samson et Dalila, 1567

sānīyī, 1568
Sanctus, 1568
sanjuanito, 1568
Sankey, Ira D., 1568
Santa Lucia, 1568
santūr, 1568–1569
Sapho (Gounod), 1569
Sapho (Massenet), 1569
saraband, 1569
sārāngī, 1570
Sarasate, Pablo de, 1570
sardana, 1570–1571
Šárka, 1571
sarōd, 862–863, 1571
sarrusophone, 1571
Sarti, Giuseppe, 414
Satie, Erik, 1571–1573
furniture music, 539
Gymnopédies, 641
Heures séculaires et instantanées,
718
Parade, 1307
Relâche, 1475–1476
Socrate, 1691
Trois morceaux en forme de poir,
1893
*Trois véritables préludes flasques
(pour un chien),* 1893
Vexations, 1949–1950
Satisfaction, 762
Savoyards, 1573
Sawallisch, Wolfgang,
1573–1574
Sax, Adolphe, 1574–1575
saxophone and saxophone play-
ers, 1575–1576
Adderley, "Cannonball," 9
Bechet, Sidney, 102–103
Braxton, Anthony, 171
Carter, Benny, 225–226
Coleman, Ornette, 282–283
Coltrane, John, 286–287
Desmond, Paul, 369
Dolphy, Eric, 395
Dorsey, Tommy, 406–407
Freeman, Bud, 526–527
Getz, Stan, 568–569
Giuffre, Jimmy, 581–582
Gordon, Dexter, 599
Hawkins, Coleman, 692
Herman, Woody, 714
Hodges, Johnny "Rabbit,"
726–727
Jordan, Louis, 839–840
Kirk, Roland, 869–870
Parker, Charlie, 1308–1309
Pepper, Art, 1335
Redman, Don, 1468
Rollins, "Sonny," 1517–1518
tenor saxophone, 1833
Young, Lester, 2069–2070
Zorn, John, 2089
scabellum, 1576
Scala, La, 1576
scale(s), 1576–1577
A, 1

B, 60
C, 196
church modes, 265
compass, 290
confinalis, 300
conjunct degree, 300
D, 338
degree, 362
diatonic, 378
Do(h), 388
dominant, 396
E, 427
ecclesiastical modes, 429
echoi, 429–430
enharmonic equivalence (equivalents), 448
equal temperament, 451
F, 468
Fa, 468
fifth, 495
fourth, 521
G, 544
Gypsy scale, 644
harmonic, 675
just intonation, 843–844
key, 859
key signature, 859–860
keynote, 861
natural minor scale, 1206
pelog, 1331
pentachord, 1334
pentatonic, 1334–1335
pitch, 1373–1374
prime, 1407
Re, 1463
solmization, 1693
submediant, 1760
subtonic, 1761
supertonic, 1767
temperament, 1826
tetrachord, 1835–1836
tonic, 1869
whole-tone scale, 2030–2031
Scaramouche, 1577
Scarlatti, Alessandro, 1577–1579
Scarlatti, Domenico, 236,
1579–1581
scat, 1581
Scelsi, Giacinto, 1581–1582
scena, 1582
scenario, 1582
scene, 1582
Schaeffer, Pierre, 1582–1583
Schafer, R. Murray, 1583
Schandeflöte, 1583–1584
Schauspieldirektor, Der, 772
Scheherazade, 1584
Schenker, Heinrich, 1584
Schenkerian analysis, 1584–1585
Scherzi, Gli, 1585
scherzo, 1585–1586
Scherzo à la russe, 1586
Scherzo Fantastique, 1586
Schickele, Peter, 1586–1587
Schifrin, Lalo, 1587–1588
Schillinger, Joseph, 1588–1589

Schluss, 1589
Schmidt, Harvey, 474
Schnabel, Artur, 1590–1591
Schnaderhüpfel, 1591
Schnittke, Alfred, 1591–1592
Schoeck, Othmar, 1592
Schoenberg, Arnold, 1592–1598
  dodecaphonic music, 389–392
  Erwartung, 453
  Fünf Orchesterstücke, 538
  Glückliche Hand, Die, 594
  Gurre-Lieder, 639
  Kammersymphonie, 848
  Klangfarbe, 874
  Klangfarbenmelodie, 874
  Nebenstimme, 1208
  pantonality, 1305
  Pelléas et Mélisande, 1331
  Pierrot Lunaire, 1367
  serialism, 1636
  Sprechstimme, 1714
  tonal aura, 1867
  Variations for Orchestra, 1931
  Verklärte Nacht, 1947
Schola cantorum, 1599
School Days, 1599
Schoolmaster, The, 1599
Schöpfung, Die, 325
Schottische, 1599
Schubert, Franz, 1599–1603
  Death and the Maiden, 354
  Rosamunde, 1524
  Schwanengesang, 1615
  Trout Quintet, 1897
  Unfinished Symphony,
    1917–1918
  Zauberharfe, Die, 2081
Schuller, Gunther, 1603–1605,
    1844
Schuman, William, 1605–1606
  American Festival Overture, 24
  Judith, 841
  New England Triptych, 1213
Schumann, Clara Wieck,
    1606–1607
Schumann, Robert, 1608–1613
  Carnaval, 221
  Davidsbündler-Tänze, 348
  Études symphoniques, 457
  Genoveva, 562
  Papillons, 1306–1307
  Rhenish Symphony, 1488
  Spring Symphony, 1714
  Träumerei, 1882
Schütz, Heinrich, 1613–1615
Schwanengesang, 1615
Schwartz, Arthur, 1615
Schwarzkopf, Elisabeth,
    1615–1617
Schweitzer, Albert, 1617–1618
scoop, 1618
scop, 1618
scordatura, 1618–1619
score(s), 1619–1620
  particella, 1315–1316
  partitino, 1316

piano, 1363
scoring, 780, 1271
Scotch Bagpipe Melody, 1620
Scotch snap or catch, 1620
Scotch Symphony, 1620
Scotto, Renata, 1620–1621
Scratch Orchestra, 1621
Scriabin, Alexander, 1621–1627
  Divin Poème, Le, 386–387
  Poème de l'extase, Le, 1378
  Poème divin, Le, 1379
  Poème satanique, 1379
  Prométhée, 1422
  tasierta per luce, 1812
  Vers la flamme, 1947
Scruggs, Earl, 1627–1628
Sculthorpe, Peter, 1628–1629
Scythian Suite, 1629
Sea Symphony, A, 1629
season, 1629
Seasons, The, 1629
second, 1629
seconda prattica, 1629–1630
section, 1630
secular music, 1630
See You Later, Alligator, 1630
Seeger, Pete, 1630–1631, 1909
Seeger, Ruth Crawford, 325
segno, 1631
Segovia, Andrés, 1631–1632
segue, 1632
seguidilla, 1632
Seitensatz, 1633
Semele, 1633
Semiramide, 1633
semiseria, 1633
Semper Fidelis, 1633
Semper paratus, 1633
Send in the Clowns, 1634
sentence, 1634
September Song, 1634
septet, 1634
sequence (Gregorian chant), 1634
sequence (melodic), 1634–1635
sequencer, 1635
serenade, 1635
Sérénade d'Arlequin, 1635
Serenade for String Orchestra,
    1635–1636
Sérénade mélancolique, 1636
serenata, 1636
serialism, 1636, 1882
Serkin, Peter, 1637
Serkin, Rudolph, 1637–1638
Serov, Alexander, 840
serpent, 1638
Serva Padrona, La, 1638–1639
service, 1639
Sessions, Roger, 1639–1640
set, 1640
set piece, 1640
1776, 1641
Seven Deadly Sins, The,
    1640–1641
seventh, 1641
Seventh Symphony (Mahler), 1641

Seventy-Six Trombones, 1641
Sext, 1641
sextet, 1641
sextuplet, 1642
shading, 1642
shakuhachi, 1642
shamisen, 1642
Shankar, Ravi, 1643
Shannāi, 1568
shanty, 1643
Shapey, Ralph, 1643–1645
Sharp, Cecil (James), 1645–1646
sharp (adjective), 1645
sharp (noun), 1645
Shave and a Haircut, 1646
Shaw, Artie, 1646–1647
shawm, 1647
Shéhérazade, 1648
sheng, 1648
shepherd's bell, 1648
shepherd's horn, 1648
Shifrin, Seymour, 1648–1649
shift, 1649
shimmy, 1649
shō, 1649
shofar, 1649
Shore, Dinah (Francis Rose),
    1649–1650
Short, Bobby, 1650
short octave, 1650
Shostakovich, Dmitri,
    1650–1655
  Leningrad Symphony, 932–933
  Nose, 1232–1233
shout, 1655
Show Boat, 1655
shuffle, 1656
Shuffle Along, 1656
Shuffle Off to Buffalo, 1656
Sibelius, Jean, 1656–1659
  Finlandia, 499
  Pohjola's Daughter, 1379
  Saga, En, 1557
  Valse Triste, 1926
Sibila, 1659
Sicilian Vespers, The, 1660
siciliana,-o, 1660
side drum, 1689
sidemen, 1660
Sidewalks of New York, The, 1660
Siège de Corinthe, Le, 1660–1661
Siegfried, 1661
Siegfried Idyll, 1661
Siegmeister, Elie, 763
Sierra, Roberto, 1662
sight reading, 1662–1663
signature
  key, 1663
  time, 1663
signature tune, 1663
silence, 1663
Silence, 1663
Silent Night, 1663
Silk Stockings, 1663–1664
Sills, Beverly, 1664–1665
Simon, Paul, 215, 1665–1666

Simon Boccanegra, 1666–1667
Simone, Nina, 1667–1668
Sinatra, Frank, 1668–1669
  It Was a Very Good Year, 791
  Strangers in the Night, 1735
sine tone, 1669
sinfonia, 1669
sinfonia concertante, 1669
sinfonietta, 1669
Singakademie, 1669
Singin' in the Rain, 1671
singing, 1669–1671. *See also*
    choral music
  alti naturali, 20
  alto, 20
  baritone, 84–85
  bass, 91
  bass-baritone, 92
  basso profondo, 94
  bel canto, 113
  boy soprano, 165
  break (register), 171–172
  cappella, 216
  castrato, 235
  chest register, 253
  countertenor, 317
  extended compass, 466
  falsetto, 471–472
  mezzo-soprano, 1108
  scoop, 1618
  soprano, 1702
  Sprechstimme, 1714
  tenor, 1831–1832
  tessitura, 1835
  thrush, 1852
  vibrato, 1951
  voice production, 1972
  yodel, 2066
single reed, 1671
Singspiel, 1671–1672
  Drei Pintos, Die, 411–412
  Dreigroschenoper, Die, 412
Sissle, Noble, 1672
  I'm Just Wild about Harry, 769
  Shuffle Along, 1656
sistrum, 1672
sitar, 1643, 1672
(Sittin' On) The Dock of the Bay,
    1673
Six, Les, 1673–1674
Six Epigraphes antiques, 1673
Sixteen Tons, 1674
Skalkottas, Nikos, 1674
skiffle, 1675
skip, 1675
skomorokhis, 1675
Skriabin, Alexander. *See* Scriabin,
    Alexander
Skyscrapers, 1675
slap-bass, 1675
Slatkin, Leonard, 1675–1676
Slavonic Dances, 1675
Sleeping Beauty, 1676–1677
Sleigh Ride, 1677
sleighbells, 1677
slendro, 1677

slide, 1677
slide horn/trombone/trumpet, 1677
slider, 1678
slit drum, 1678–1679
Slonimsky, Nicolas, 1679–1681
slur, 1681–1682
Smetana, Bedřich, 1682–1685
  Bartered Bride, 87
  Dalibor, 341
  Kiss (Hubička), 872
  Má vlast, 1002–1003
  Šárka, 1571
  Smiles, 1685
Smith, Bessie, 1685–1686
Smith, Gregg, 1686–1687
Smith, Kate, 1687
Smith, Willie "the Lion," 1687–1688
Smoke Gets in Your Eyes, 1688
Smyth, Ethel, 1688–1689
snare drum, 1689
Snow Maiden, The, 1689–1690
Sobre las Olas, 1690
socialist realism, 1690–1691
Socrate, 1691
soft pedal, 1691
sogetto cavato, 1691–1692
Soir, Le, 1692
Soler, Antonio, 1692
Soler, Vicente Martin y, 314
sol-fa, 1692
solfège, 1692
  fixed Do(h), 504
  movable Do(h), 1167
  sight reading, 1662–1663
  syllable name, 1775
solmization, 1693
  fixed Do(h), 504
  Guido d'Arezzo, 635–636
  hexachord, 718
  movable Do(h), 1167
  sol-fa, 1692
  syllable name, 1775
solo, 1693
solo quartet, 1693
Solti, George, 1693–1695
Sombrero de tres picos, El, 1695–1696
Some Day I'll Find You, 1696
Some Enchanted Evening, 1696
Somebody Loves Me, 1696
Something for the Boys, 1696
son, 1696
sonata, 1696. See also piano sonatas; violin sonatas
sonata da camera, 1696–1697
sonata da chiesa, 1697
sonata form, 1633, 1697
sonata-concerto form, 1697
sonata-rondo form, 1697
Sonatas and Interludes, 1697–1698
sonatina, 1698
Sondheim, Stephen, 1698–1699
  Company, 290

Do I Hear a Waltz?, 388
Funny Thing Happened on the Way to the Forum, 539
Gypsy, 641–642
Send in the Clowns, 1634
West Side Story, 2024–2025
Sonetti del Petrarca, 1699
song cycles
  Chansons de Bilitis, 243
  Harawi, chant d'amour et de mort, 672
  Histoires naturelles, 725
  Illuminations, Les, 769
  Kindertotenlieder, 864
  Marienleben, Das, 1034–1035
  Shéhérazade, 1648
song form, 1700
Song of Norway, 1700
song(s), 1699. See also ballad(s)
  ABA form, 1
  aguinaldo, 14
  alba, 15
  alborada, 17
  aria, 38
  aria da capo, 38
  arietta, 38
  ariette, 38
  arioso, 39
  ayre, 59
  ballads. See ballad(s)
  ballata, 74
  barcarolle, 83
  bergerette, 119
  bossa nova, 157
  brindisi, 174
  brunette, 182
  caccia, 198
  canción, 209
  cantata, 211–212
  canti carnascialeschi, 212–213
  cantiga, 213
  cantilena, 213
  canzona, 215
  catch, 235
  chanson, 243
  charivari, 245
  conductus, 300
  descort, 368
  dirge, 380
  dithyramb, 386
  double chorus, 408
  double quartet, 408
  duet, 414
  dumka, 417–418
  elegy, 438
  falsobordone, 472
  fancy, 473
  flamenco, 505
  folk. See folk song(s)
  frottola, 534
  hymns. See hymn(s)
  lai, 906
  lament, 909
  legend, 925
  Lied, 952–953
  madrigal, 1014–1015

nóta, 1233
oratorio, 1270
paean, 1295
pastourelle, 1321
patter song, 1322
plena, 1376
punto, 1430
refrain, 1469
remedio, 1477
ritornello, 1500–1501
romance, 1518
romancero, 1518
rondeau, 1521–1522
rondellus, 1522
rota, 1536
round, 1538
roundelay, 1538
Schnaderhüpfel, 1591
serenade, 1635
son, 1696
Spinnenlied, 1708
stanza, 1717
strain, 1735
strambotto, 1735
strophe, 1758
styrienne, 1760
Tagelied, 1794
threnody, 1852
tonadilla, 1866–1867
tricinium, 1886
vers mesuré, 1947–1948
verse-anthem, 1948
vidalita, 1954
villancico, 1959
villanella, 1959
villotta, 1959–1960
virelai, 1965
vocalise, 1970
Volkstümlich, 1972–1973
zamacueca, 2076
song-and-dance man, 1699
Songs without Words, 1700
songspiel, 1700
Sonnambula, La, 1700–1701
Sonnenquartette, 1701
sonnerie, 1701
sonority, 1701
sonus, 1701
Sophisticated Lady, 1701
sopila, 1701
sopranino, 1701
soprano string, 1702
soprano(s), 1702
  Battle, Kathleen, 96
  Caballé, Montserrat, 196–197
  Callas, Maria, 205–207
  Crespin, Régine, 328
  Dale, Clamma, 340
  Ewing, Maria, 463–464
  Farinelli, 476
  Farley, Carole, 477
  Flagstad, Kirsten, 504–505
  Freni, Mirella, 528–529
  Hendricks, Barbara, 708–709
  Jones, Sissieretta, 833
  Kirkby, Emma, 870–871

Lehmann, Lotte, 928–929
Lind, Jenny, 957–958
Lott, Felicity, 984–985
Ludwig, Christa, 989–990
Manning, Jane, 1030
Marton, Eva, 1048
Melba, (Dame) Nellie, 1077–1078
Milanov, Zinka, 1118
Nelson, Judith (Anne Manes), 1209
Nilsson, Birgit, 1220–1221
Nixon, Marni, 1223
Norman, Jessye, 1228–1229
Price, Leontyne, 1404–1405
prima donna, 1406–1407
Rysanek, Leonie, 1552–1553
Schwarzkopf, Elisabeth, 1615–1617
Scotto, Renata, 1620–1621
Sills, Beverly, 1664–1665
Stratas, Teresa, 1735–1736
Studer, Cheryl, 1759–1760
Sutherland, Joan, 1769–1770
Te Kanawa, Kiri, 1822–1823
Tebaldi, Renata, 1824
Tetrazzini, Luisa (Luigia), 1836–1837
Upshaw, Dawn, 1919
Sorcerer's Apprentice, The, 1702
sordina, 1702–1703
sortita, 1703
sostenuto pedal, 1703
soubrette, 1703
soul, 1703
sound, 1703–1704
sound effects, 1704, 1852–1853
sound hole, 1704
sound installation, 1704–1705
Sound of Music, The, 1705
soundboard, 1705
soundtracks. See film music
Sousa, John Philip, 1705–1707
  Capitan, El, 216
  Semper Fidelis, 1633
  Stars and Stripes Forever, 1718
sousaphone, 1707
South Pacific, 1707
space, 1707
spatial distribution, 1707–1708
spectrum, 1708
Spiel, 1708
spinet, 1708
Spinnenlied, 1708
spinto, 1708
spiritual(s), 1708–1709
  Nobody Knows the Trouble I've Seen, 1224
  Swing Low, Sweet Chariot, 1775
  When the Saints Go Marching In, 2026
Spohr, Louis, 819–820, 1709–1712
Spohr, Maurice, 726
Spontini, Gaspare, 1712–1714, 1949

Sprechstimme, 1367, 1714
Spring Symphony (Britten), 1714
Spring Symphony (Schumann), 1714
springar, 1714
Springsteen, Bruce, 1714–1715
square dance, 1716, 1908
Stabat Mater, 1716
staccato, 1716
Stade, Frederica von. *See* von Stade, Frederica
Stadler Quintet, 1716
staff, 1716
stalls, 1716
Stand By Me, 1717
Stand by Your Man, 1717
standard, 1717
standing ovation, 1717
Standing Room Only (SRO), 1717
stanza, 1717
Stardust, 1717
Starr, Ringo, 1717–1718
Stars and Stripes Forever, 1718
Star-Spangled Banner, The, 1718–1719
static music, 1719
Stayin' Alive, 1719
steel band, 1719–1720
Stein, Gertrude, 520
Steiner, Max, 1720
Steinway & Sons, 1720–1722
stem, 1722
step, 1722
stereophonic, 1722
Stern, Isaac, 1722–1723
Steuermann, Edward, 1723–1724
Still, William Grant, 1724–1725
stochastic, 1725
Stockflöte, 1725
Stockhausen, Karlheinz, 1725–1727
  Gesang der Jünglinge, Der, 567
  Gruppen, 632
  Hymnen, 761
  Kontakte, 886
  Zeitmasse, 2082
Stokowski, Leopold, 1727–1730
Stoltzman, Richard, 1730–1731
stomp, 1731
Stomp, 1731
Stone, Carl, 1731–1733
Stone Guest, The, 1733
stop (organ), 1733–1734
stop (strings), 1734
stop time, 1734
storage media. *See* recorded music
Stormy Weather, 1734
Stothart, Herbert, 597
Stradivari, Antonio, 1734–1735
strain, 1735
strambotto, 1735
Strange Fruit, 1735
Strangers in the Night, 1735
stranka, 1735
Stratas, Teresa, 1735–1736

strathspey, 1736
Strauss, Eduard, 1739–1740
Strauss, Johann, I, 1736–1737
Strauss, Johann, II, 1737–1739
  Fledermaus, 506–507
  Gypsy Baron, 642
  Wein, Weib, und Gesang, 2019
Strauss, Josef, 1739
Strauss, Richard, 1740–1745
  Alpine Symphony, 19
  Also sprach Zarathustra, 20
  Arabella, 36
  Ariadne auf Naxos, 38
  Aus Italien, 57–58
  Daphne, 344
  Death and Transfiguration, 354–355
  Don Juan, 399
  Don Quixote, 399
  Elektra, 438
  Feuersnot, 489
  Frau ohne Schatten, Die, 524–525
  Friedenstag, Der, 531
  Guntram, 639
  Heldenleben, Ein, 704–705
  Intermezzo, 782
  Macbeth, 1005
  Metamorphosen, 1102
  Rosenkavalier, Der, 1525–1526
  Salome, 1563
  Till Eulenspiegel's Merry Pranks, 1853
Stravinsky, Igor, 1745–1752
  Agon, 14
  Apollon musagète, 34
  Baiser de la fée, Le, 70
  Canticum sacrum ad honorem Sancti Marci nominis, 213
  Chant de rossignol, Le, 244
  Cinq Doigts, Les, 267
  Circus Polka, 268
  Dumbarton Oaks, 417
  Ebony Concerto, 429
  Firebird, 501
  Fireworks, 501
  Four Norwegian Moods, 520
  Histoire du soldat, L', 725
  Jeu de cartes, 820
  Nightingale, 1219–1220
  Noces, Les, 1224
  Oedipus Rex, 1252
  Orpheus, 1280
  Perséphone, 1346
  Petrouchka, 1351–1352
  Pulcinella, 1430
  Rag-Time, 1449
  Rake's Progress, 1451
  Renard, 1478
  Requiem Canticles, 1480
  Rite of Spring, 1500
  Scherzo à la russe, 1586
  Scherzo Fantastique, 1586
  Symphony in Three Movements, 1781
  Symphony of Psalms, 1782

Threni, 1852
Strayhorn, Billy, 1752, 1796
street cries, 1752–1753
Street Scene, 1753
Streisand, Barbra, 1753–1754
stretch, 1754
stretto(-a), 1754–1755
strict style, 1755
stride piano, 1755
Strike up the Band, 1755
string, 1755
string band, 76
string orchestra, 1756
string piano, 1756
string quartet(s), 1756–1757
  American Quartet, 24
  Death and the Maiden, 354
  Dissonanzen Quartett, 385
  Emperor Quartet, 444
  Erdödy Quartets, 451
  Froschquartett, 533–534
  Harp Quartet, 685
  Italian Serenade, 791
  Lark Quartet, 915
  Lyric Suite, 1001
  Quintenquartett, 1439
  Rasoumowsky Quartets, 1458
  Razor Quartet, 1462
  Ritterquartett, 1501
  Scherzi, Gli, 1585
  Sonnenquartette, 1701
  Tostquartette, 1876
  Vendredis, Les, 1940
  Vogelquartett, 1971
string quintet, 1757
string trio, 1758
string(ed) instruments, 1755–1756
  artificial harmonics, 47
  autoharp, 58
  balalaika, 73
  bandola, 77
  bandoura, 77
  bandurria, 77–78
  banjo, 78
  baryton, 90
  biwa, 137
  bow, 162
  bowed instrument, 162
  bowing, 163–164
  bridge, 174
  catgut, 236
  chordophones, 261
  cimbalom, 266–267
  citole, 268
  cittern, 268
  colophane, 285
  crwth, 332
  ditol key, 386
  dombra, 396
  domra, 397–398
  dotara, 407
  double bass, 408
  double stops, 409
  down bow, 410
  Drehleier, 411

dulcimer, 417
ektara, 435
F holes, 468
fiddle, 491–492
fingerboard, 499
fret, 530–531
frog, 533
gadulka, 547
gamba, 550
gimping, 576
gittern, 581
gudok, 634
guitar. *See* guitars and guitar music
gusle, 639
gusli, 639
hardingfele, 675
harp. *See* harps and harpists
huqin, 756
hurdy-gurdy, 756–757
kamānja, 848
kantele, 849
kayagum, 856
key stop, 860
kit, 873
kithara, 873
kora, 888–889
koto, 890
lira, 960
lira da braccio, 960
lirone, 960–961
lute, 996–998
lyre, 1001
mandolin, 1027–1028
neck, 1208
nut, 1243
nyckelharpa, 1244
pandora, 1305
pipa, 1371
pochette, 1378
position, 1390
psalmodicon, 1425
psaltery, 1426
qin, 1434
rabāb, 1442
rebec, 1464
ribs, 1490
rotta, 1538
santūr, 1568–1569
sārāngī, 1570
sarōd, 1571
scordatura, 1618–1619
shamisen, 1642
shift, 1649
sitar, 1672
soprano string, 1702
sordina, 1702–1703
sound hole, 1704
stop, 1734
string, 1755
sympathetic strings, 1775–1776
tambura, 1800
tanbūr, 1802
tar, 1808
tenor violin, 1833

theorbo, 1840
touche, 1878
tromba marina, 1893–1894
'ud, 1915
ukulele, 1916
vibrato, 1951
vihuela, 1957
vīnā, 1960
viol, 1960
viola, 1961
viola bastarda, 1961
viola da braccio, 1961
viola da gamba, 1961–1962
viola d'amore, 1962
viola poposa, 1962
violetta, 1962
violin. *See* violin and violin music
violin piccolo, 1964
violincello, 1965
violone, 1965
wolf tone, 2046
zheng, 2085
zither, 2088
strophe, 1758
strophic bass, 1758
Strouse, Charles, 191, 1758
structure, 1758
strumento, 1759
Student Prince (in Heidelberg), The, 1759
Studer, Cheryl, 1759–1760
Sturm und Drang, 1760
styles, compositional. *See* compositional styles
Styne, Jule, 1760
  Bells Are Ringing, 116
  Funny Girl, 539
  Gentlemen Prefer Blondes, 562
  Gypsy, 641–642
  Hallelujah, Baby!, 653
styrienne, 1760
subject, 1760
submediant, 1760
subordinate chords, 1760
Subotnick, Morton, 1761
substitution, 1761
subtonic, 1761
suite, 1761–1762
Suite bergamasque, 1762–1763
Suite provençale, 1763
suling, 1763
Sullivan, Arthur, 1763–1765. *See also* Gilbert and Sullivan
  Ivanhoe, 792
  Lost Chord, 984
sum (summation) tone, 1765
Sumer is icumen in, 1765–1766
Summer Morning's Dream, 1766
Summertime, 1766
Sun Ra, 1766–1767
Sunny Boy, 1767
Sun-Treader, 1767
šupeljka, 1767
supertonic, 1767
Suppé, Franz, 1767–1768

Sur le Pont d'Avignon, 1768
Surfin' Safari, 1768
Surprise Symphony, 1768–1769
surrealism, 1769
suspension, 1769
sustaining pedal, 1769
Sutherland, Joan, 1769–1770
Suzuki, Shin'ichi, 1770–1771
Suzuki method, 1771
svirala, 1771
Swan Lake, 1771
swan song, 1772
Swanee, 1772–1773
Swanee River, 1773
Sweelinck, Jan Pieterszoon, 1773–1774
Sweet Adeline, 1774
Sweet Charity, 1774
Sweet Rosie O'Grady, 1774
swing, 1774–1775
Swing Low, Sweet Chariot, 1775
syllabic melody, 1775
syllable name, 1775
symbolism, 1775
sympathetic strings, 1775–1776
symphonia, 1776
symphonic, 1776
symphonic band, 76–77
symphonic poem, 1776
symphonie concertante, 1776
Symphony of Psalms, 1782
symphony(-ies), 1778–1781
  Age of Anxiety, 14
  Alpine Symphony, 19
  Apocalyptic Symphony, 34
  Bear, 98–99
  Choral Symphony, 259
  Classical Symphony, 272
  Clock, 278
  Colour Symphony, 286
  Di Tre Re, 374
  Distratto, Il, 385–386
  Divin Poème, Le, 386–387
  Divina commedia, 387
  Drumroll Symphony, 413
  Eroica Symphony, 452–453
  Farewell Symphony, 475
  Faust Symphony, 479
  Fifth Symphony, 495–496
  Fire Symphony, 500–501
  Folksong Symphony, 514
  Fourth Symphony, 521
  Giant, 569
  Haffner Symphony, 646
  Harold in Italy, 682–683
  Hen, 707
  Historische Symphonie, 726
  Icelandic Symphony, 766
  Ilya Muromets, 769
  Impériale, L', 771
  Inextinguishable, 779
  Israel Symphony, 790
  Italian Symphony, 791
  Jena Symphony, 816
  Jeremiah Symphony, 818
  Jupiter Symphony, 843

  Kaddish, 846
  Leningrad Symphony, 932–933
  Lied von der Erde, Das, 953
  Linz Symphony, 959
  Little Russian Symphony, 968
  Liturgical Symphony, 969
  London Symphonies, 978
  London Symphony, 978–979
  Má vlast, 1002–1003
  Macbeth (Strauss), 1005
  Manfred Symphony, 1028
  Maria Theresia, 1034
  Matin, Le, 1061
  In Memoriam, 774
  Mercury Symphony, 1098
  Midi, Le, 1114
  Military Symphony, 1120
  From the New World, 533
  Ninth Symphonies, 1221
  Nordic Symphony, 1227
  Ocean Symphony, 1249
  Oxford Symphony, 1286
  Paris Symphonies, 1308
  Pastoral Symphony (Beethoven), 1320–1321
  Pastoral Symphony (Vaughan Williams), 1321
  Pathétique Symphony (Tchaikovsky), 1321–1322
  Poème divin, Le, 1379
  Prague Symphony, 1396
  Queen, The, 1438
  Reformation Symphony, 1469
  Rhenish Symphony, 1488
  Romantic Symphony, 1520
  Roméo et Juliette (Berlioz), 1521
  Schoolmaster, 1599
  Scotch Symphony, 1620
  Sea Symphony, 1629
  Seventh Symphony, 1641
  Soir, Le, 1692
  Spring Symphony (Schumann), 1714
  Summer Morning's Dream, 1766
  Surprise Symphony, 1768–1769
  Symphonie fantastique, 1776–1778
  Symphony for Organ and Orchestra, 1781
  Symphony in Three Movements, 1781
  Symphony of a Thousand, 1782
  Symphony on a French Mountain Theme, 1782
  Te Deum Symphony, 1822
  Tenth Symphony, 1833
  Third Symphony, 1844
  Titan Symphony, 1861
  Tragic Symphony, 1880
  Unfinished Symphony, 1917–1918
  Universe Symphony, 1918
  Valse, La, 1925–1926
  Winter Dreams, 2040
  Youth Symphony, 2072
  Zero Symphony, 2084–2085

symploche, 1782
synaesthesia, 1783
synchrony, 1783–1784
Synchrony, 1784
synclavier, 1784
Syncopated Clock, The, 1784
syncopation, 1784–1785
synthesizer, 1785–1786
Syrian chant, 1786
syrinx, 1786
Syrinx, 1786
system, 1786
Szell, George, 1786–1788
Szeryng, Henryk, 1788
Szigeti, Joseph, 1788–1789
Szymanowski, Karol, 1789–1791

tablā, 1792
tablature, 1792–1793
tableau, 1793
tabor, 1793
tacet, 1793
tactus, 1793
Tafelklavier, 1793
Tafelmusik, 1793–1794
Tagelied, 1794
taiko, 1794
tailgate, 1794
Tailleferre, Germaine, 1794–1795
Takahashi, Aki, 1795–1796
Takahashi, Yuji, 1796
Take Me Out to the Ball Game, 1796
Take the A Train, 1796
Takemitsu, Tōru, 1797
Tal, Josef, 1797–1798
tala, 1798
Tales of Hoffman, The, 1798–1799
Talking Heads, 193–194
tambour militaire, 1799
tambourin, 1799
tambourine, 1799–1800
tambura, 1800
tamburo di legno, 1800
tamburo scordato, 1800
tam-tam, 1800–1801
Tan, Margaret Leng, 1801–1802
Tan Dun, 1802–1803
tanbūr, 1802
Tancredi, 1802
Taneyev, Sergei, 1803–1804
tango, 1804–1805
tango-milonga, 1805
Tannhäuser, 1805–1806
Tansman, Alexandre, 1806
tantric chants, 1806
Tanzhalle, 1806
tap dance, 1807
tape recording, 1807–1808
tar, 1808
tarantella, 1808–1809
Ta-Ra-Ra-Boom-De-Re, 1809
Taras Bulba, 1809
tárogató, 1809

Tartini, Giuseppe, 373–374, 1809–1811
Tartini tones, 1811
Taruskin, Richard, 1811–1812
tasierta per luce, 1812
Tate, Jeffrey, 1812
tattoo, 1812
Tatum, Art, 1812–1813
Taubner, Richard, 1813–1814
Tavener, John, 1814–1815
Taylor, Cecil, 1815
Taylor, Deems, 867
Taylor, James, 1815–1816
Tchaikovsky, Piotr Ilyich, 1816–1821
　Capriccio Italien, 217
　1812 Overture, 433
　Eugene Onegin, 457–458
　Francesca da Rimini, 522
　Hamlet, 653
　Little Russian Symphony, 968
　Maid of Orleans, 1021–1022
　Manfred Symphony, 1028
　Marche slave, 1033–1034
　Nutcracker, 1243–1244
　Pathétique Symphony, 1321–1322
　Queen of Spades, 1439
　Romeo and Juliet, 1521
　Serenade for String Orchestra, 1635–1636
　Sérénade mélancolique, 1636
　Sleeping Beauty, 1676–1677
　Swan Lake, 1771
　Symphonie pathétique, 1778
　Third Symphony, 1844
　Variations on a Rococo Theme, 1931
　Voyevode (opera), 1975
　Voyevode (symphonic ballad), 1975
　Winter Dreams, 2040
Te Deum, 1822
Te Deum Symphony, 1822
Te Kanawa, Kiri, 1822–1823
Tea for Two, 1823
teatro, 1824
Tebaldi, Renata, 1824
technic (technique), 1824
　articulation, 46–47
　artificial harmonics, 47
　break (register), 171–172
　circular breathing, 267
　fingering, 499
　glissando, 590–591
　virtuosity, 1966–1967
Teen Angel, 1824
Teenager in Love, 1824
Telemann, Georg Philipp, 1824–1826
temperament, 1826
　comma, 289
　interference beats, 780–781
temple blocks, 256
tempo, 1826–1828
tempo mark, 1828

Temptations, The, 1828–1829
Ten Cents a Dance, 1829
Tender Land, The, 1829–1830
tenebrae, 1830
Tennessee Waltz, 1830
Tenney, James, 1830–1831
tenor drum, 1832
tenor saxophone, 1833
tenor violin, 1833
tenor(s), 1831–1832
　Björling, Jussi, 138–139
　Carreras, José, 225
　Caruso, Enrico, 228–230
　Domingo, Placido, 396–397
　Heldentenor, 705
　Hofmann, Peter, 728
　Jerusalem, Siegfried, 819
　Johnson, Edward, 826–827
　Kraus, Alfredo, 894
　Langridge, Philip, 912–913
　Lanza, Mario, 913–915
　Melchior, Lauritz, 1078–1079
　Pavarotti, Luciano, 1323–1325
　Pears, Peter, 1326–1327
　Peerce, Jan, 1330
　Taubner, Richard, 1813–1814
　Tucker, Richard, 1903
　Vickers, Jon, 1952
　Wunderlich, Fritz, 2055
Tenth Symphony (Mahler), 1833
teponaxtli, 1833
Tequila, 1833
terce, 1833
Terfel, Bryn, 1833–1834
ternary, 1834
terraced dynamics, 1834–1835
Terry, Clark, 1835
terzo suono, 1835
tessitura, 1835
tetrachord, 1835–1836
tetralogy, 1836
Tetrazzini, Luisa (Luigia), 1836–1837
text-sound composition, 1837
texture, 1837
Thaïs, 1837
Thanks for the Memories, 1838
That Old Black Magic, 1838
That'll Be the Day, 1838
theater, musical. *See* musical(s)
theater orchestra, 1838
theater set, 1838
theatrical festivals, 484
thematic catalogue, 1838–1839
thematic composition, 1839
theme, 1839
theme and variations, 1839
Theme and Variations: The Four Temperaments, 1839
Theodorakis, Mikis, 1839–1840
theorbo, 1840
theory, 1840
Theremin, 1841
Theremin, Leon, 1841–1843
There's a Long, Long Trail, 1840

There's No Business Like Show Business, 1840–1841
These Boots Are Made for Walkin', 1843
thesis, 1843
Thibaud, Jacques, 1843
Third Stream, 1844
Third Symphony (Tchaikovsky), 1844
This Is the Army, 1844
Thomas, Ambroise, 1844–1845
　Hamlet, 653
　Mignon, 1117
Thomas, Michael Tilson, 1845–1846
Thomas, Theodore, 1846–1848
Thompson, Randall, 1848–1849
Thomson, Virgil, 1850–1851
　Four Saints in Three Acts, 520
　Louisiana Story, 986
　Plow that Broke the Plains, 1377
Three Blind Mice, 1851
Three Places in New England, 1851
Three-Page Sonata, 1852
Threepenny Opera, The, 412
three-step, 1852
Threni, 1852
threnody, 1852
thrush, 1852
thunder machine, 1852–1853
tibia, 1853
tie, 1853
Tie a Yellow Ribbon 'Round the Ole Oak Tree, 1853
tiento, 1853
tierce de Picardy. *See* Picardy third
Till Eulenspiegel's Merry Pranks, 1853
timbales, 1853–1854
timbre, 1854
timbrel, 1854
time, 1854
　common, 289–290
　microtime, 1110
　quadruple, 1435
　triple, 1890
time signature, 1854–1855
time-bracket notation, 1855
Times They Are A-Changin', The, 1855
timpani, 1855–1856
tin ear, 1857
Tin Pan Alley, 1857
tin whistle, 1857
tinnitus, 1857–1858
tintinnabulum, 1858
Tiomkin, Dimitri, 1858
típico, 1858
tiple, 1858
Tipperary, 1858–1859
Tippett, Michael, 1859–1861

　Child of Our Time, 254
　King Priam, 866
tirata, 1861
Titan Symphony, 1861
titles, 1861–1863
To Anacreon in Heaven, 1863
To Know Him Is to Love Him, 1863
toccata, 1863–1864
toccato, 1864
Toch, Ernst, 1864–1865
　Geographical Fugue, 562
　Pinocchio, 1370
Tod und Verklärung, 354–355
Todesgesang, 1866
tombeau, 1866
Tombeau de Couperin, Le, 1866
tom-tom, 1866
Ton, 1866
tonada, 1866
tonadilla, 1866–1867
tonal, 1867
tonal answer, 1867
tonal aura, 1867
tonality, 1867
tonarium, 1867
tone, 1868
tone clusters, 1868
tone color, 874, 1868–1869
tone row, 1869
tongue, 1869
tonguing, 1869
tonic, 1869
tonic sol-fa, 1870
Tonight We Love, 1870
Tonmalerei, 1870
tono, 1870
tonus, 1870–1871
tonus peregrinus, 1871
torch song, 1871
Toreador Song, 1871
Torke, Michael, 1871–1872
Tormé, Mel, 1872–1873
Tormis, Veljo, 1873
Tosca, 1873–1874
Toscanini, Arturo, 1874–1876
Tostquartette, 1876
total music, 1876–1877
Totentanz (form), 1877
Totentanz (Liszt), 1877
touch, 1877
touche, 1878
Tower, Joan, 1878–1879
tower music, 1909
Townshend, Pete. *See* Who, The
Toy Symphony, 1879
toye, 1879
tract, 1879
tragédie lyrique, 1879
Tragic Overture, 1879–1880
Tragic Symphony, 1880
Trail of the Lonesome Pine, The, 1880
training, music
　ear training, 428
　eurythmics, 460

exercise, 464
fasola, 478
relative pitch, 1476
sight reading, 1662–1663
Suzuki method, 1771
technic, technique, 1824
theory, 1840
tonic sol-fa, 1870
Tramp, Tramp, Tramp, or The Prisoner's Hope, 1880
Trampler, Walter, 1880–1881
transcendental, 1881
transcription, 1881
Transfigured Night, 1947
transient, 1881
transition, 1881
transpose, 1881
transposing instruments, 1881–1882
transposition, 1882
transverse flute, 1882
traps, 1882
traquenard, 1882
Trauermarsch, 1882
Träumerei, 1882
Trautonium, 1882
Traviata, La, 1883
tre, 1883
treble, 1883
trecento, 1884
Treemonisha, 1884
Trees, 1884
Treigle, Norman, 1884–1885
tremolo, 1885
trepak, 1885
triad, 1407, 1885–1886
triadic modulation, 1886
triangle, 1886
trichord, 1886
tricinium, 1886
tricotet, 1886
trill, 1886–1887
Trimpin, 1887–1888
trio, 1888
trio sonata, 1888–1889
Trip to Chinatown, A, 1889
triple concerto, 1889
triple dot, 1889–1890
triple time, 1890
triplet, 1890
triplum, 1890
Tristan chord, 1890
Tristan und Isolde, 1890–1891
Tristano, Lennie, 1891–1892
tritone, 375–376, 1892
triumph cornet, 1892
trochee, 1892–1893
Trois morceaux en forme de poir, 1893
Trois véritables préludes flasques (pour un chien), 1893
trojnice, 1893
Trolley Song, The, 1893
tromba marina, 1893–1894
trombone and trombonists, 1894–1895

Dempster, Stuart, 366–367
Dorsey, Jimmy. *See* Dorsey brothers
Higganbotham, J. C., 718
Johnson, J. J., 828
Miller, Glenn, 1120–1121
Ory, "Kid," 1280
sackbut, 1555
slide horn, 1677
tailgate, 1794
trompe de chasse, 1895
troparion, 1895
trope, 1895–1896
troubadour, 1896
Trouble in Tahiti, 1896
trouser role, 1896–1897
Trout Quintet, 1897
trouvére, 7, 1897
Trovatore, Il, 1897–1898
Troyanos, Tatiana, 1898–1899
Troyens, Les, 1899
trumpet and trumpeters, 1899
Aida trumpet, 15
Armstrong, Louis, 41–42
Beiderbecke, Bix, 112–113
Bolden, "Buddy," 153
Bowie, Lester, 163
Brown, Clifford, 177
Cherry, Don, 250–251
clarino, 271
Eldridge, Roy "Little Jazz," 435–436
fanfare, 473
Gillespie, "Dizzy," 574–575
hasosra, 691
Hirt, Al, 725
Hubbard, Freddie, 750–751
James, Harry, 802
Jericho trumpets, 819
Johnson, "Bunk," 825–826
Keppard, Freddie, 857
key(ed) trumpet, 860
Marsalis, Wynton, 1038–1039
McPartland, Jimmy, 1066–1067
Navarro, "Fats" (Theodore), 1207
Nichols, "Red," 1216
oliphant, 1260
Oliver, "King" (Joseph), 1260–1261
shofar, 1649
sonnerie, 1701
Terry, Clark, 1835
wa-wa, 2007
Williams, "Cootie," 2034–2035
yurupari, 2075
Trumpet Voluntary, 1901
tuba(s), 1901
Hoffnung, Gerard, 727–728
sousaphone, 1707
Wagner tuba, 1978
tubaphone, 1901–1902
Tubb, Ernest, 1902
Tubin, Eduard, 1902–1903

tubular chimes, 1903
Tucker, Richard, 1903
Tucker, Sophie, 1903–1904
Tuckwell, Barry, 1904
Tudor, David, 1249, 1904–1906
tune, 1906
tuning, 1906–1907
tuning fork, 1907
tupan, 1907
Turandot, 1907–1908
Turina, Joaquín, 1908
Turken-Trommel, 1908
Turkey in the Straw, 1908
turkey trot, 1909
Turkish March, 1909
Turkish music, 804–805
Turm-musik, 1909
Turn, Turn, Turn, 1909
Turn of the Screw, The, 1909
Turner, "Big Joe" (Joseph Vernon), 1909–1910
Turner, Tina, 1910–1911
Tusch, 1911
tutti, 1911
Tutti Frutti, 1911
twelve-tone music, 1911–1912
atonality, 51
dodecaphonic music, 389–392
hexachord, 718
rotation, 1537
set, 1640
tone row, 1869
trichord, 1886
24 Violins of the King, 1960
Twilight of the Gods. See Götterdämmerung
Twinkle, Twinkle Little Star, 1912
Twist, The, 1912
Twist and Shout, 1912
Two Guitars, 1912
Tye, Christopher, 1912–1913
tympani. *See* timpani
Typewriter, The, 1913
Tyranny, Blue Gene (Robert Nathan Sheff), 1913–1914
tyrolienne, 1914
Tzigane, 1914

Uchida, Mitsuko, 1915
'ud, 1915
ukulele, 1916
Ullmann, Viktor, 1916–1917
una corda, 1917
Unanswered Question, The, 1917
Unfinished Symphony, 1917–1918
unison, 1918
Universe Symphony, 1918
unvocal, 1918
upbeat, 1918
upright piano, 1919
Upshaw, Dawn, 1919
Urtext, 1919–1920
Ussachevsky, Vladimir, 1920–1922

Ut, 1922–1923
Utrecht Te Deum, 1923

V, 1924
Vagabond King, The, 1924
vagans, 1924
vaganti, 1924
Valkyries, The. See Walküre, Die
Vallee, Rudy, 1925
Valse, La, 1925–1926
Valse nobles et sentimentales, 1926
Valse Triste, 1926
value, 1926
valve, 1926–1927
vamp, 1927
Varése, Edgar, 1927–1930
Amériques, 24
Density 21.5, 368
Déserts, 369
Ecuatorial, 430–431
Hyperprism, 761
Intégrales, 780
Ionisation, 787–788
Nocturnal, 1224
Poème électronique, 1379
variable meter, 1931
variation(s), 1931
Variations for Orchestra, 1931
Variations on a Nursery Song, 1931
Variations on a Rococo Theme, 1931
Variations on a Theme by Frank Bridge, 1931–1932
variety show, 1932
Varsoviana, 1932
vaudeville, 1932–1933
song-and-dance man, 1699
songspiel, 1700
Vaughan, Sarah, 1933
Vaughan Williams, Ralph, 1933–1937
Fantasia on a Theme by Thomas Tallis, 474
Fantasia on Greensleeves, 474
Job, 822
Lark Ascending, 915
London Symphony, 978–979
Norfolk Rhapsody No. 1, 1227
Pastoral Symphony, 1321
Pilgrim's Progress, 1368
Riders to the Sea, 1492–1493
Sea Symphony, 1629
Velvet Underground, 1938–1939
Vendredis, Les, 1924
Venetian school, 1940
Venuti, Joe, 1940–1941
verbalization, 1941
verbunkos, 1942
Verdi, Giuseppe, 1942–1947
Aida, 14–15
Anvil Chorus, 33
Ballo in maschera, Un, 75
Don Carlos, 398
Due Foscari, I, 414
Ernani, 452

Falstaff, 472
Forza del destino, La, 517
Giorno di regno, Un, 580
Giovanni d'arco, 580
Lombardi alla prima Crociata, I, 978
Luisa Miller, 992–993
Macbeth, 1005
Nabucco, 1204
Oberto, Conte di San Bonifacio, 1246
Otello, 1281–1282
Quattro pezzi sacri, 1438
Rigoletto, 1493–1494
Sicilian Vespers, 1660
Simon Boccanegra, 1666–1667
Traviata, La, 1883
Trovatore, Il, 1897–1898
verismo, 1206, 1947
Verklärte Nacht, 1947
Verlag, 1947
Vers la flamme, 1947
vers mesuré, 1947–1948
verse, 1948
verse-anthem, 1948
verset, 1948
versicle, 1948
vertical flute, 1948
Vespers, 1949
Vespri Siciliani, I, 1660
Vestale, La, 1949
Vexations, 1949–1950
vibraphone and vibraphonists, 1950
 Hampton, Lionel, "Hamp," 657–658
 Jackson, Milt, 800
 Norvo, Red, 1232
vibraslap, 1950
vibration(s), 1950–1951
vibrato, 1951
Vickers, Jon, 1952
Victoria, Tom s Luis de, 1953–1954
Victrola, 1954
vidalita, 1954
Vie en Rose, La, 1954
Vie Parisienne, La, 1954–1955
Viennese school, 1955
Vieuxtemps, Henri, 1955–1957
vihuela, 1957
Villa-Lobos, Heitor, 1957–1959
 Bachianas Brasileiras, 68
 chôro, 261
 Rudepoema, 1547
villancico, 1959
villanella, 1959
villotta, 1959–1960
vīnā, 1960
Vincentino, Nicola, 1951–1952
Vingt-quartre Violons du Roi, 1960
viol, 1960
viola and violists, 1961
 Primrose, William, 1408
 Trampler, Walter, 1880–1881

Zukerman, Pinchas, 2089–2090
viola bastarda, 1961
viola da braccio, 1961
viola da gamba, 1031, 1961–1962
viola d'amore, 1962
viola poposa, 1962
violetta, 1962
violin and violin music, 1962–1964
 Albinoni, Tomaso, 16–17
 Amati, 22
 Auer, Leopold, 55
 Biber, Heinrich, 131
 Chung, Kyung-Wha, 264
 concertmaster, 293
 Corelli, Arcangelo, 310–311
 Elman, Mischa, 442–443
 Enesco, Georges, 444–446
 Grappelli, Stephane, 620–621
 Guarneri family, 632–633
 Heifetz, Jascha, 701–703
 Heinrich, Anthony Philip, 703–704
 Kavafian, Ani, 854
 Kavafian, Ida, 854–855
 Kennedy, Nigel, 857
 Kogan, Leonid, 884–885
 Kreisler, Fritz, 894–896
 Kremer, Gidon, 897
 Kubelík, Jan, 899–900
 Lanner, Joseph, 913
 Lin, Cho-Liang, 956–957
 Mehta, Mehli, 1073–1074
 Menuhin, (Sir) Yehudi, 1094–1095
 Midori, 1115–1116
 Milstein, Nathan, 1123
 Minkus, Léon, 1125–1126
 Oistrakh, David, 1257–1258
 Paganini, Niccolò (Nicoló), 1295–1298
 Perlman, Itzhak, 1344–1345
 Roldán, Amadeo, 1514–1515
 Sarasate, Pablo de, 1570
 Spohr, Louis, 1709–1712
 Stern, Isaac, 1722–1723
 Szeryng, Henryk, 1788
 Szigeti, Joseph, 1788–1789
 Tartini, Giuseppi, 1809–1811
 tenor violin, 1833
 Thibaud, Jacques, 1843
 Venuti, Joe, 1940–1941
 Vieuxtemps, Henri, 1955–1957
 Wieniawski, Henryk, 2032–2034
 Ysaÿe, Eugène, 2072–2074
 Zukerman, Pinchas, 2089–2090
 Zukofsky, Paul, 2090–2091
violin family, 1964
violin piccolo, 1964
violin sonatas
 Devil's Trill, 373–374
 Kreutzer Sonata, 899

violincello, 1965
violin-conductor score, 1964
violone, 1965
virelai, 1965
virginal, 1965–1966
virtuosity, 1966–1967
Vitry, Philippe de, 1967–1968
Vivaldi, Antonio, 455, 1968–1970
Vive la Compagnie, 1970
vocal, 1970
vocal music. *See* singing
vocal score, 1970
vocalise, 1970
vocalization, 1971
Vogelquartett, 1971
voice, 1971. *See also* singing
voice exchange, 1971
voice leading, 1971
voice production, 1972
voicing, 1972
Volare, 1972
Volga Boatmen's Song, 1972
Volkstümlich, 1972–1973
volta, 1973
voluntary, 1973
von Stade, Frederica, 1973–1974
Vortrag, 1974
Votive Mass, 1974
vox, 1974–1975
Voyevode, The (opera), 1975
Voyevode, The (symphonic ballad), 1975

Waart, Edo de, 1976–1977
Wacht am Rhein, Die, 1977
Wagner, Cosima, 1977. *See also* Wagner, Richard
Wagner, Richard, 1978–1989
 endless melody, 444
 Feen, Die, 481
 Flying Dutchman, 513
 Gesamtkunstwerk, 567
 Götterdämmerung, 604–605
 Lohengrin, 976–977
 Meistersinger von Nürnberg, Die, 1076
 Parsifal, 1312–1313
 Rheingold, Das, 1487–1488
 Rienzi, 1493
 Ring des Nibelungen, Der, 1499
 Siegfried, 1661
 Tannhäuser, 1805–1806
 Tristan und Isolde, 1890–1891
 Walküre, Die, 1993–1994
 Zukunftmusik, 2091
Wagner, Siegfried, 1977–1978
Wagner tuba, 1978
wait, 1989–1990
Waits, Tom, 1990
Wake Up Little Susie, 1990–1991
Waldstein Sonata, 1991
Waldteufel, Émile, 1991
Walker, George, 1991–1993
walking bass, 1993

Walküre, Die, 1993–1994
Wallen, Errollyn, 1994
Waller, "Fats," 747, 1994–1995
Walpurgis Night, 1995–1996
Walter, Bruno, 1996–1998
Walton, Sir William, 469, 1998–1999
waltz(es), 1999–2000
 three-step, 1852
 trochee, 1892–1893
Wein, Weib, und Gesang, 2019
Waltzing Matilda, 2000
War and Peace, 2000–2001
War of the Buffoons. *See* Guerre des Bouffons
War Requiem, 2001
Ward, Samuel Augustus, 1060
Warfield, William, 2001–2002
Waring, Fred, 2002
Warren, Harry, 814, 1656
washboard, 2003
Washington, Dinah, 2003
Wasitodiningrat, K. R. T., 2003–2004
Water Music, 2004–2005
Waters, "Muddy," 2005
Watts, Andre, 2005–2007
wavelength, 2007
wa-wa, 2007
Waxman, Franz, 2007–2008
We Shall Overcome, 2008
Webber, Andrew Lloyd. *See* Lloyd Webber, Andrew
Webber, Julian Lloyd. *See* Lloyd Webber, Julian
Weber, Carl Maria von, 2008–2013
 Drei Pintos, Die, 411–412
 Euryanthe, 460
 Freischütz, Der, 527
 Invitation to the Dance, 787
 Oberon, 1245–1246
Webern, Anton, 2013–2016
 Five Pieces for Orchestra, 504
 Klangfarbe, 874
Weill, Kurt, 2016–2019
 Aufstieg und Fall der Stadt Mahagonny, 56
 Down in the Valley, 410
 Dreigroschenoper, Die, 412
 Johnny Johnson, 825
 Knickerbocker Holiday, 878–879
 Love Life, 986
 One Touch of Venus, 1265
 September Song, 1634
 Seven Deadly Sins, 1640–1641
 songspiel, 1700
 Street Scene, 1753
Wein, Weib, und Gesang, 2019
Weir, Judith, 2019–2020
Weisgall, Hugo, 2020–2021
Weiss, Silvius Leopold, 2021–2022
Welk, Lawrence, 2022
Well-Tempered Clavier, The, 2022–2023

Werckmeister, Andreas, 2023–2024
Werk, 2024
Werther, 2024
West Side Story, 2024–2025
Westminster Chimes, 2025–2026
What's Goin' On?, 2026
When Irish Eyes Are Smiling, 2026
When Johnny Comes Marching Home, 2026
When the Red, Red Robin comes Bob, Bob, Bobbin' Along, 2026
When the Saints Go Marching In, 2026
Whiffenpoof Song, The, 2026
While Strolling Through the Park One Day, 2026–2027
whip, 2027
Whispering, 2027
whistle, 1857, 2027
White Christmas, 2027
white noise, 2028
Whiteman, Paul, 2028
Who, The, 2028–2030
whole-tone scale, 2030–2031
Widor, Charles-Marie, 2031–2032
Wieck, Clara Josephine. *See* Schumann, Clara Wieck
Wieniawski, Henryk, 2032–2034
Wilhelm, Carl, 1977
Will You Love Me in December as You Do in May?, 2034
William Tell, 2034
Williams, "Cootie," 2034–2035
Williams, Hank, 2035
Williams, John (composer/conductor), 2036–2037
Williams, John (guitarist), 2036
Williams, Mary Lou, 2037
Williams, Ralph Vaughan. *See* Vaughan Williams, Ralph
Wills, Bob, 2037–2038
Willson, Meredith, 1641, 2038–2039
wind band, 77, 2039
wind instruments, 2039. *See also* brass instruments; woodwinds
  bagpipe(s), 69–70
  harmonica, 676
  vibrato, 1951
wind machine, 2040
Winter Dreams, 2040
Witt, Friedrich, 816
Wittgenstein, Paul, 2040–2041
Wizard of Oz, The, 2041–2042

Wohltemperierte Clavier, Das. See Well-Tempered Clavier, The
Wolf, Hugo, 791, 2042–2046
wolf tone, 2046
Wolff, Christian, 2046–2047
Wolf-Ferrari, Ermanno, 2047–2048
Wolpe, Stefan, 2049–2050
Wonder, Stevie, 2050–2051
Wonderful Town, 2051
woodblocks, 256
woodwinds, 2051–2052
  althorn, 20
  aulos, 56–57
  bassoon, 94
  bombard, 154
  bore, 155
  chalumeau, 241–242
  clarinet. *See* clarinet and clarinet music
  conical tube, 300
  contrabassoon, 303
  cornett, 312
  crumhorn, 331–332
  cylindrical tube, 337
  double reed, 408
  embouchure, 443
  English horn, 447–448
  fish horn, 503
  fistula, 503
  flageolet, 504
  flute. *See* flute and flute music
  flutter-tonguing, 513
  free reed, 525–526
  heckelphone, 701
  launeddas, 917–918
  nose flutes, 1233
  oboe, 1246–1247
  oboe da caccia, 1247
  oboe d'amore, 1248
  ocarina, 1248–1249
  overblowing, 1283
  panpipes, 1305
  pavillon d'amour, 1325
  pibcorn, 1364
  quena, 1439
  racket, 1445–1446
  recorder, 1465–1466
  reed, 1468–1469
  Russian bassoon, 1552
  sānāyī, 1568
  sarrusophone, 1571
  saxophone. *See* saxophone and saxophone players
  serpent, 1638
  shawm, 1647
  sheng, 1648
  shō, 1649

single reed, 1671
sopila, 1701
Stockflöte, 1725
syrinx, 1786
tárogató, 1809
tin whistle, 1857
tongue, 1869
tonguing, 1869
transposing instruments, 1881–1882
vertical flute, 1948
whistle, 2027
wind instruments, 2039
zurnā, 2091
Woody Woodpecker, 2052
Work, Henry Clay, 288, 2052
Worms Crawl In, The, 2052
Wouldn't It Be Loverly?, 2052
Wozzeck, 2052–2053
Wreck of the Old 97, The, 2053
Wunderbar, 2053
Wunderkind, 2053–2054
Wunderlich, Fritz, 2055
Wuorinen, Charles, 2055–2057
Wynette, Tammy, 2057–2058
Wyschnegradsky, Ivan, 2058–2059

Xenakis, Iannis, 1725, 2060–2062
Xochipilli, 2062
xylophone, 2062–2063
xylorimba, 2063–2064

Yale University, 2026
Yankee Doodle, 2065
Yasser, Joseph, 2065
Yeoman of the Guard, or The Merryman and His Maid, The, 2065–2066
Yes, Sir, That's My Baby, 2066
Yes, We Have No Bananas, 2066
Yeston, Maury, 1221
Yip, Yip, Yaphank, 2066
yodel, 2066
You Ain't Heard Nothin' Yet, 2066
You Made Me Love You, I Didn't Want to Do It, 2067
You Must Have Been a Beautiful Baby, 2067
Youmans, Vincent, 2067–2068
  Hit the Deck, 726
  I Want to Be Happy, 764
  No, No, Nanette, 1223
Young, La Monte, 2068–2069
Young, Lester, 2069–2070
Young, Neil, 2070
Young, Victor, 2071

Young Person's Guide to the Orchestra, The, 2070–2071
You're a Good Man, Charlie Brown, 2071
You're the Cream in My Coffee, 2071
Youth Symphony, 2072
Yo-Yo Ma. *See* Ma, Yo-Yo
Ysaÿe, Eugène, 2072–2074
Yun, Isang, 2074–2075
yurupari, 2075

Z mrtveho domu, 533
Zabaleta, Nicanor, 2076
Zaïde, 2076
zamacueca, 2076
zampogna, 2076
zampoñas, 2076
Zandonai, Riccardo, 2076–2077
Zappa, Frank, 2077–2080
Zarlino, Gioseffo, 2080–2081
zarzuela, 2081
  sainete, 1561
  tonadilla, 1866–1867
Zauberflöte, Die. See Magic Flute, The
Zauberoper, 2081
Zaza, 2082
Zeit, 2082
Zeitmasse, 2082
Zelter, Carl Friedrich, 2082–2083
Zemlinksy, Alexander, 2083–2084
Zero Symphony, 2084–2085
zheng, 2085
Ziegfeld Follies, 2085–2086
Zigeunerbaron, Der, 642
Zimmerman, Krystian, 2086–2087
Zimmerman, Bernd Alois, 2087
Zingara, La, 2088
Zip Coon, 2088
zither, 2088
  psalmodicon, 1425
  zheng, 2085
zopf, 2088
Zorba, 2088–2089
Zorn, John, 2089
Zukerman, Pinchas, 2089–2090
Zukofsky, Paul, 2090–2091
Zukunftmusik, 2091
zummāra, 2091
zurnā, 2091
Zwei, 2091
Zwilich, Ellen Taaffe, 2091–2092
Zwischenfalle bei einer Notlandung, 2092